Race in America

Race in America

Matthew Desmond
Harvard University

Mustafa Emirbayer
University of Wisconsin-Madison

W. W. NORTON & COMPANY, INC.
New York • London

W. W. Norton & Company has been independent since its founding in 1923, when William Warder Norton and Mary D. Herter Norton first published lectures delivered at the People's Institute, the adult education division of New York City's Cooper Union. The firm soon expanded its program beyond the Institute, publishing books by celebrated academics from America and abroad. By mid-century, the two major pillars of Norton's publishing program—trade books and college texts—were firmly established. In the 1950s, the Norton family transferred control of the company to its employees, and today—with a staff of four hundred and a comparable number of trade, college, and professional titles published each year—W. W. Norton & Company stands as the largest and oldest publishing house owned wholly by its employees.

Previous edition published under the title *Racial Domination, Racial Progress: The Sociology of Race in America*

Editor: Karl Bakeman
Project Editor: Diane Cipollone
Editorial Assistant: Mary Williams
Managing Editor, College: Marian Johnson
Managing Editor, College Digital Media: Kim Yi
Production Manager: Vanessa Nuttry
Media Editor: Eileen Connell
Media Project Editor: Danielle Belfiore
Media Editorial Assistant: Grace Tuttle
Marketing Manager, Sociology: Julia Hall
Design Director: Rubina Yeh
Designer: Anna Reich
Photo Editor: Trish Marx
Permissions Manager: Megan Jackson
Composition: Graphic World
Manufacturing: Quad Graphics-Taunton

Permission to use copyrighted material is included on p. A85.

Library of Congress Cataloging-in-Publication Data

Desmond, Matthew, author.
  [Racial domination, racial progress]
  Race in America / Matthew Desmond, Harvard University, Mustafa Emirbayer, University of Wisconsin-Madison. — [2015 edition].
     pages cm
  Previous edition published under title: Racial domination, racial progress. New York : McGraw-Hill Higher Education, 2010.
  Includes bibliographical references and index.
  ISBN 978-0-393-93765-7 (pbk. : alk. paper) 1. United States--Race relations. 2. Race. I. Emirbayer, Mustafa, author. II. Title.
  E184.A1D36 2015
  305.800973--dc23
                                          2015033574

W. W. Norton & Company, Inc., 500 Fifth Avenue, New York, NY 10110-0017
W. W. Norton & Company Ltd., Castle House, 75/76 Wells Street, London W1T 3QT
wwnorton.com

1 2 3 4 5 6 7 8 9 0

For Tessa

CONTENTS

PREFACE

More than a generation after the Civil Rights Movement, we continue to be tongue-tied when it comes to race and, as a result, are constrained from fully understanding our society and fellow citizens.

Old ways of thinking about race and ethnicity no longer seem to apply in a society that has moved well beyond the struggles of the 1950s and 1960s, a society that now confronts problems of racial division in some ways far more complex and ambiguous than those of straightforward segregation or bigotry, persistent as those tendencies may still be in the present day. What is needed is a new way of thinking about race for a society itself quite new. This book addresses that pressing need. It is our hope that *Race in America* will provide a more effective language with which to think and talk about—and effectively to address—the problem of racial inequality and injustice in today's society. (An earlier version of this work, which now is significantly updated and revised, was published under the title *Racial Domination, Racial Progress: The Sociology of Race in America*.)

Race in America breaks with current textbooks in several ways. We rely on innovative advances in modern social thought, advances taking place not only in sociology but also in philosophy, anthropology, political science, economics, history, and literary and art criticism—not to mention exciting developments in such literatures as whiteness studies, critical race theory, and cultural studies. We fuse this social thought with music, literature, poetry, and popular culture. In this book you can find the sociology of Pierre Bourdieu alongside spoken-word poetry; American pragmatist philosophy followed by country music lyrics; ideas from the likes of W. E. B. Du Bois, Toni Morrison, Alejandro Portes, Ella Baker, Edward Said, and Ruth Frankenberg (to list but a few)—applied to modern society. *Race in America* is steeped in up-to-date social-scientific research on race and ethnicity, as well as in examples from contemporary life, including youth culture. We have taken seriously American sociologist C. Wright Mills's famous dictum that "data is everywhere" and have drawn on social science to illuminate racial dynamics in all areas of social life.

Race in America confronts some of today's most controversial and misunderstood issues, including immigration, affirmative action, racial segregation, interracial relationships, political representation, racialized poverty and affluence, educational inequality, incarceration, terrorism, cultural appropriation, civil society, religion, marriage and divorce, and racial identity formation. Throughout, it treats racial inequality not as some "hot topic" issue to be debated in loose, unsystematic fashion but as a complex sociological phenomenon properly understood only through critical socioanalysis that arrives at conclusions after sifting carefully through the best available evidence.

Race in America is uncompromisingly intersectional. It refuses artificially to separate the sociology of race and ethnicity from those of class and gender. It highlights how racial division overlaps other forms of division based on economic standing and gender (as well as religion, nationality, and sexuality), and it does so because these bases of inequality are inextricably bound together.

This book's organization is nothing like that of previous-generation textbooks on race and ethnicity. Instead of proceeding, chapter by chapter, from one racial group to the next—which only naturalizes racial divisions and renders the sociology of race and ethnicity nothing more than a collection of isolated snapshots of different groups—it pursues the analysis of racial dynamics into many of the different areas or fields of life of our society. Examining how race is a matter not of separate entities but of *systems of social relations*, it unpacks how race works in the political, economic, residential, legal, educational, aesthetic, associational, and intimate fields of social life. In each of these fields, it analyzes how white privilege is institutionalized and naturalized, such that it becomes invisible even to itself.

At bottom, this book is about the workings of race and ethnicity in contemporary America. It offers you a comprehensive overview of the causal mechanisms or processes whereby racial divisions are established, reproduced, and in some cases transformed. In doing so, it necessarily engages in a serious and sustained way with history. Here, historical processes are not relegated to a single introductory chapter but inform the entire work.

Race in America does not reduce one of today's most sociologically complicated, emotionally charged, and politically frustrating topics to a collection of bold-faced terms and facts you memorize for the midterm. Rather, this non-textbook textbook seeks to connect with you, its readers, in a way that combines disciplined reasoning with a sense of engagement and passion, conveying sophisticated ideas in a clear and compelling fashion. Accordingly, the book works just as well in lower-division courses as it does in more advanced settings. Conventional textbooks on race and ethnicity stimulate a type of reading that can only be called *contemplative*, a reading that devotes academic interest to social problems without ever being touched by them or resonating deeply with them. By contrast, we seek to stimulate *generative* readings, which simultaneously engage the world you find intimately familiar and yet also effect a sharp rupture with that world, defamiliarizing the familiar and helping you to arrive at a deeper sociological understanding of your world, offering solutions and strategies so that we all can work toward racial justice.

We seek to offer you, in short, a way of thinking about race that you can apply to your everyday lives. More, we hope to cultivate in you a sociological imagination, one that rejects easy explanations and that takes into account social and historical forces that operate on an expansive scale. We are living in an age in which racial inequality and discrimination persists. But we also are living in an age when racism has come under serious and sustained attack. We are living in an age when multicultural coalitions have formed and all people, regardless of race, have taken stands against racial intolerance. And many of the most powerful and important antiracist movements have been led by young people. Considerable progress has been made, but considerable work also remains unfinished.

It is commonplace for students in a course on the sociology of race and ethnicity to think the course really is for someone else. A course such as this one, however, is meant for everyone.

We all have something to learn in this class—and we all have something to teach. This book is not just about "them" but about you. It seeks to educate—and unsettle—the righteous along with the disengaged, those who have long discussed matters of racism as well as those who are just now joining the conversation.

Let us begin a conversation, then. This conversation might make you feel uncomfortable, since topics as important and as personal as race are difficult to discuss. You might feel a bit unsteady and awkward, clumsy even. You might feel exposed and vulnerable. Your words might trip and stumble at times, and you might say things you later regret. Take courage in the fact that many of your classmates (and perhaps even your professors) feel the same way. And know, too, that we *have* to have this conversation, lest we allow racial inequality and injustice to poison the promising vitality of American society.

ACKNOWLEDGEMENTS

We relied on a number of scholars who read chapters of the manuscript and offered helpful suggestions: Clifford Brown, University of New Hampshire; Sarah Bruch, University of Iowa; Mindelyn Buford, Northeastern University; David Embrick, Loyola University Chicago; Meredith Greif, Johns Hopkins University; Aaron Gullickson, University of Oregon; Jennifer Jones, University of Notre Dame; Tiffany Joseph, Stony Brook University; David Leonard, Washington State University; Ana Liberato, University of Kentucky; Nancy Lopez, University of New Mexico; Jillian Powers, Brandeis University; Jacob Rugh, Brigham Young University; Kathryn Tillman, Florida State University; Milton Vickerman, University of Virginia.

We'd like to thank everyone at Norton involved in publishing *Race in America*. In particular, we owe a large debt of gratitude to our editor, Karl Bakeman, for his vision and superb guidance. We'd also like to thank editorial assistant Mary Williams, project editor Diane Cipollone, and production manager Vanessa Nuttry, who handled every stage of the manuscript and worked together to produce this book. We would also like to thank Norton's sales and marketing team, especially Julia Hall, the sociology marketing manager, and the social science sales specialists Jonathan Mason, Roy McClymont, and Julie Sindel. They have been enthusiastic advocates for the book throughout its development. Finally, we must thank our photo editors, Trish Marx and Julie Tesser, for providing such powerful visual images as well as Eileen Connell and the rest of the digital media team responsible for all the innovative video and electronic resources that accompany *Race in America*.

RESOURCES FOR STUDENTS AND INSTRUCTORS

InQuizitive

inquizitive.wwnorton.com

Paul Dean, Ohio Wesleyan

Norton's formative, adaptive learning platform personalizes quiz questions and facilitates students' understanding of important learning goals from the text in an engaging, game-like environment. The software is easy to use and can be accessed on a wide range of mobile devices, including tablets and smartphones.

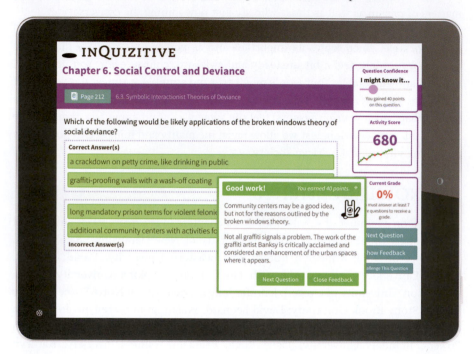

Sociology in Practice: Thinking About Race and Ethnicity DVD

Offering more than four hours of video clips from documentaries by independent filmmakers that explore the topic of race and ethnicity from various perspectives, this two-disc DVD is ideal for initiating classroom discussion and encouraging students to apply sociological concepts to real world issues.

Norton Coursepack

wwnorton.com/coursepacks

The free Norton Coursepack offers a variety of activities for self-assessment and review, including an optional ebook, 34 independent documentary film clips, integrated InQuizitive activities, chapter outlines and learning goals, key term flashcards and matching quizzes, "Theory to Practice" activities found at the end of each chapter of the book, and gradable quizzes on select clips from the *Sociology in Practice: Race and Ethnicity* DVD.

Norton Ebook

The ebook for *Race in America* provides students and instructors an enhanced reading experience at a fraction of the cost of a print textbook.

Test Bank

The Test Bank conforms to Bloom's taxonomy and includes 40 to 50 multiple-choice and 5 to 10 essay questions per chapter. Every question is tagged with difficulty level and metadata that places it in the context of the chapter, making it easy for instructors to construct meaningful and diagnostic tests.

Lecture and Art Slides

All of the art from the book is available for classroom use. These visually engaging PowerPoint slides feature concept check questions and discussion questions as well as lecture outlines.

Matthew Desmond is an associate professor of sociology and social science at Harvard University and co-director of the Justice and Poverty Project. A former member of the Harvard Society of Fellows, Desmond is the author of the award-winning book, *On the Fireline,* and editor of a collection of studies on severe deprivation in America. His work has been supported by the MacArthur, Ford, Russell Sage, and National Science Foundations, and his writing has appeared in the *New York Times* and the *Chicago Tribune.*

Mustafa Emirbayer is a professor of sociology at University of Wisconsin-Madison. He has published widely on sociological theory, the sociology of race and ethnicity, comparative-historical analysis, and cultural sociology. He is editor of *Sociological Theory,* a past chair of the Social Theory section of the American Sociological Association, and past winner of the Lewis A. Coser Award for Theoretical Agenda-Setting in Sociology.

Together, they are the authors of *The Racial Order,* a companion to this volume.

Race in America

1

Race in the Twenty-First Century

MAIN POINTS

- Explain why one should avoid the individualistic fallacy, the legalistic fallacy, the tokenistic fallacy, the ahistorical fallacy, and the fixed fallacy, when thinking about racism.

- Distinguish between institutional racism and interpersonal racism and understand how these types of racism often interpenetrate and inform one another.

- Understand how racism intersects with other forms of social division— those based on gender, class, sexuality, religion, nationhood, and ability.

- Understand what is meant by symbolic violence and explain its significance for the perpetuation of racial inequality.

- Learn why race is a symbolic category and understand why there is no biological foundation for race.

- Understand how whiteness is racial domination normalized, which produces and reproduces many privileges for white people.

- Recognize how race and ethnicity are overlapping symbolic categories and explain why they cannot be collapsed into one category.

A CANCER

As we enter a promising new millennium, we continue to be confronted with a problem as old as America itself. That problem is the problem of the color line. It is the problem of racism, of inequality and privilege, of the suffering and oppression of some groups of people at the hands of another.

Some have argued that in these modern times there is no problem at all. A growing number of commentators, from political leaders to radio talk-show hosts, have suggested that race no longer matters.[1] They have boasted that we have, a mere forty years after the Civil Rights Movement, "reached the promised land" that Martin Luther King, Jr., so eloquently described in one of the most famous speeches of the last century: the "I Have a Dream" speech, delivered on August 28, 1963. We have *arrived*, they say, at true racial democracy. We are living in a so-called color-blind society, in which people are judged, in King's words, "not by the color of their skin but by the content of their character." Does such an optimistic idea truly reflect the state of America today?

In some respects, we have good reason to be optimistic. Thanks to the brave activists of the Civil Rights Movement, the United States no longer upholds legally enforced residential, educational, and economic segregation. Most of us will not experience grotesque acts of racial violence that many people of color experienced fifty years ago. A number of social institutions, moreover, have been thoroughly integrated, most notably the American military. The black middle class and the Hispanic middle class have grown; American Indian nations have developed effective economic development strategies based on the principle of tribal sovereignty; Asian Americans have made impressive inroads into positions

Anti-Muslim graffiti defaces a Shi'ite mosque at the Islamic Center of America in Dearborn, Michigan.

of influence in politics, science, business, and the arts. There are other encouraging trends as well—in religion, sports, the mass media, voluntary associations, and other significant areas in American life. In politics, one need only say the name "Barack Obama." And in the social and cultural order, Americans are beginning to appreciate the inherent value and dignity of all persons, regardless of origins or skin color. This is especially true of the youth, who in terms of their racial and ethnic attitudes probably are the most open-minded and tolerant generation in U.S. history. And today, many corporations, universities, organizations, and congregations consider racial and ethnic diversity an asset to be fostered and sought after, not a problem to be avoided. To say that nothing has gotten better certainly would be inaccurate.

But has racism been completely vanquished? Let's take a glance at race relations in the United States to find out.

- The FBI tallied 6,933 incidents of hate crime that took place in 2013 alone. That's 19 hate crimes a day. (This number is underestimated, because it accounts only for those crimes *reported* to the FBI by participating law enforcement agencies.) These offenses included intimidation, destruction of property and vandalism, assault, burglary, murder, and rape. Race-based hate crimes accounted for almost half the total number of offenses, and religion-based crimes accounted for 17 percent. Sixty-six percent of the race-based hate crimes were committed against black people.[2]

- America is unmatched among developed democracies for the depths of its poverty. In 2014, almost 50 million Americans lived below the poverty line. That's more people than the entire population of Spain. With poverty rates of around 26 percent, Native Americans and African Americans were the poorest racial groups in the nation. Twenty-two percent of Hispanic Americans lived in poverty. Only 11 percent of Asian Americans and white Americans lived under similarly harsh economic conditions.[3] Since 1940, the unemployment rate of African Americans has been nearly twice that of whites. And over half of the Native Americans living on some reservations are unemployed. Despite these vast inequalities, 50 percent of whites recently surveyed believe that the average African American and the average white person are equally well off.[4]

- Today, nearly 7 million people are serving time in prison, being held in jails, awaiting trail, or under probation or parole supervision. Almost 6 million Americans either are in prison or have been locked up at some point in their lives; this amounts to one in thirty-seven Americans. The United States has the highest incarceration rate in the world. Severe racial inequalities are at work within the criminal justice system. African Americans are eight times more likely to be incarcerated than whites. Among black men born in the late 1960s who did not earn a high school diploma, 60 percent had prison records by the time they reached the age of thirty-five. Sociologists and criminologists have demonstrated that racial inequalities in the justice system are largely accounted for by examining how racial exclusion has resulted in high concentrations of poor African Americans and Latinos living in inner-city areas that offer little to no opportunity for economic advancement or survival.[5]

Given these facts—facts that barely scratch the surface of the problem—can we confidently conclude that race does not matter today? Would such logic be acceptable when considering other types of problems? Consider, for example, cancer. What if a group of citizens suddenly declared that cancer is not a problem anymore? "We solved cancer years ago," they might say. Surely upon hearing such a bold proclamation we would examine the facts, which overwhelmingly would dispute the claim. We would point to the 10 million Americans with a history of cancer as well as the 1 million Americans expected to be victims of cancer this year. We would identify the symptoms of cancer manifest in fever, fatigue, pain, sores, bleeding, lumps, and so forth. We would consult doctors and epidemiologists who have documented case after case of abnormal cell growth and tumor development. In short, we would disavow the claim that "cancer was cured long ago" simply by pointing to the plethora of signs, symptoms, and effects of cancer obvious in everyday life.

The same logic applies to social diseases. Earlier in this section we listed some symptoms of racism, evidence that race, indeed, is a fundamental part of everyday life. Race penetrates all aspects of our lives—our history, our collective memory, our schools, our jobs, our streets. It structures the inner workings of our hospitals, our prisons, our bastions of political power, and our economy. We witness its effects on our art, our entertainment, and our churches, mosques, and synagogues. Our intimate relationships—the relationships we have with family, friends, lovers, leaders, role models, heroes, enemies, teachers, landlords, and supervisors—are influenced by relations of race. Race is even there in the basic ways we understand ourselves; it informs our inner thoughts and, indeed, our very identities as people. Life in America—and, indeed, life around the globe—is a life saturated with the reality of race.

This reality of race, like many other social realities, has grown adept at shape-shifting. Unlike cancer, which looks the same as it did 100 years ago, the racism of our generation looks different from the racism our parents witnessed, which, of course, looked different from the racism their parents witnessed. Racism is mercurial, ever changing. Twenty-first-century patterns of racial stigmatization, exclusion, and repression—as well as promises of racial reconciliation and multicultural coalitions—do not immediately resemble those of the twentieth century. Although racial violence still occurs in America today, there are fewer victims than there were in the previous generation. And although many high schools, universities, neighborhoods, job sites, nursing homes, country clubs, restaurants, and parks remain segregated along lines of race, this racial segregation no longer is enforced by law.

Today's racism is not always obvious. It can be slippery, elusive to observation and analysis. Like a recessive tumor, twenty-first-century racism has disguised itself, calling itself by other names and cloaking itself behind seemingly "race-neutral" laws, policies, practices, and language. But it is still with us, influencing our relationships, our institutions, and our world. And it will not simply fade out of existence if we turn a blind eye toward it. A tumor will destroy a body regardless of whether its bearer recognizes it or not.

We should also keep in mind that present-day society is directed by the past. History structures the workings of today in innumerable ways, some of which are so deeply familiar to us that we fail to notice them. In the words of Émile Durkheim, a French sociologist and one of the founding fathers of the discipline, "in each one of us, in differing degrees, is contained the person we were yesterday. . . . The present is necessarily insignificant when compared with the long period of the past because of which we have emerged in the form we have today."[6] If the world we occupy is shaped by the struggles of yesterday, then we cannot divide past racism from present racism in a hard-and-fast manner.

What is more, racial inequalities, as well as racial privileges, accumulate over generations. In other words, our standing in today's world largely is dictated by the ways in which our parents, grandparents, and great-grandparents were treated during their own lifetimes. If our parents *suffered* from systematic social exclusion and discrimination based on their race, then many aspects of our lives—our economic and educational opportunities, for example—will be disadvantaged. In the same way, if our parents *benefited* from the very race-based methods of social exclusion and discrimination that caused the parents of some of our peers to suffer, then we will enjoy a certain degree of privilege in today's society. The accruing afflictions or affluence of our mothers and fathers are visited upon us, sons and daughters.

Racism persists as the cancer of American life. Pervasive, corrosive, dehumanizing, and deadly, modern-day racism infects the health of our society. It is our responsibility, then, as students of society, and as future citizens of our communities, to understand the realities of racism. As citizens of a world that grows more racially diverse every year, we must understand how race and racism work. And we must develop tools to analyze this social creation that is responsible for so many cleavages and inequalities in our world today. This book aims to do just that. It seeks to explain the inner logic of race and racism and to describe the nature of race relations in the present day. In addition, it hopes to provide you with a way of understanding race that is informed by historical sensitivity, critical thought, sociological analysis, and a global imagination.

AMERICAN RACISM IN THE TWENTY-FIRST CENTURY

How, then, should we begin to wrap our minds around race in America in the twenty-first century? Consider this chapter a necessary prelude to a conversation, a conceptual cornerstone on which everything else rests. Many debates about race involve people heatedly talking past one another. If conversations about affirmative action or immigration leave us frustrated, it often is because we have very different understandings not necessarily about these specific policies, but about the nature of race itself. What are the realities of American racism and multiculturalism today? How should we think about enduring problems and recent progress? How should we conceptualize racism alongside other forms of privilege and disadvantage, such as those based on religious identity, class background, sexuality, or gender? And what is "race," in the first place? This section begins to address some of these questions. Before we articulate what we believe race to be, however, perhaps the best way to start is by offering some suggestions as to how *not* to think about race.

Five Fallacies about Racism

There are many misconceptions about the character of racism. Americans are deeply divided over its legacies and inner workings, and much of this division is a result of the fact that many Americans understand racism in limited or misguided ways.[7] We have identified five fallacies about racism—logical mistakes, factual or logical errors in reasoning—that are recurrent in many public debates, fallacies one should avoid when thinking about racism.[8]

1. Individualistic Fallacy. Here, racism is assumed to belong to the realm of ideas and attitudes. Racism is only the collection of nasty thoughts a "racist individual" has about another group: "Mexicans are lazy"; "Blacks are criminals"; "A black person driving a nice car is a criminal"; "Native Americans are lazy drunkards." It is a matter of personal "prejudices" (defined by social psychologist Gordon Allport as "antipathies based upon faulty and inflexible generalizations") and of "stereotypes" ("exaggerated beliefs associated with a [racial] category").[9] Someone operating with this fallacy thinks of racism as one thinks of a crime and, therefore, divides the world into two types of people: those guilty of the crime of racism ("racists") and those innocent of the crime ("nonracists").[10] Crucial to this misconceived notion of racism is intentionality. "Did I intentionally act racist? Did I cross the street because I was scared of the Hispanic man walking toward me, or did I cross for no apparent reason?" Upon answering "No" to the question of intentionality, one assumes they can classify their actions as "nonracist," despite the character of those actions, and go about their business as innocent. In a society with signs of racial injustice everywhere, virtually everyone can say they are not racist.

This conception of racism simply won't do, for it fails to account for the racism woven into the very fabric of our schools, political institutions, labor markets, and neighborhoods. Conflating racism with prejudice ignores the more systematic and structural forms of racism; it looks for racism within individuals and not institutions.[11] Labeling someone a "racist" shifts our attention from the social surroundings that enforce racial inequalities to the individual with biases. It also lets the accuser off the hook—"He is a racist; I am not"—and treats racism as aberrant and strange, whereas American racism is quite normal.

Furthermore, intentionality is in no way a prerequisite for racism. Racism often is habitual, unintentional, commonplace, polite, implicit, and well meaning.[12] Thus, not only is racism located in our intentional thoughts and actions; it also thrives in our dispositions and habits, as well as in the social institutions in which we are all embedded.

2. Legalistic Fallacy. This fallacy conflates *de jure* legal progress with *de facto* racial progress. "De jure" and "de facto" are Latin expressions meaning, respectively, "based on the law" and "based in fact." Thus, one who operates under the legalistic fallacy assumes that abolishing racist laws (racism in principle) automatically leads to the abolition of racism in everyday life (racism in practice).

This fallacy begins to crumble after a few moments of critical reflection. After all, we would not make the same mistake when it comes to other criminalized acts: laws against theft do not mean that one's car never will be stolen. By way of tangible illustration, consider *Brown v. Board of Education*, the landmark 1954 case that abolished de jure segregation in schools, making it illegal to enforce racially segregated classrooms. Did that lead to the abolition of de facto segregation? Absolutely not. Fifty years later, schools still are drastically segregated and drastically unequal.[13] In fact, some social scientists have documented a nationwide movement of educational resegregation, which has left today's schools even more segregated than those of 1954.[14]

3. Tokenistic Fallacy. One who is guilty of the tokenistic fallacy assumes that the presence of people of color in influential positions is evidence of the complete eradication of racial obstacles. This logic runs something like this: "Many people of color, such as Barack Obama, Condoleezza Rice, Colin Powell, Carol Moseley Braun, and Alberto Gonzales, have held high-ranking political posts; therefore, racism does not exist in the political arena. Many people of color, such as Bill Cosby, Oprah Winfrey, Jennifer Lopez, and Lucy Liu, are celebrities and multimillionaires; therefore, there is no racial inequality when it comes to income and wealth distribution. Poor people of color (not society) are to blame for their own poverty."

Although it is true that many people of color have made significant inroads to seats of political and economic power over the course of the last fifty years, a disproportionate number remain disadvantaged in these arenas.[15] We cannot, in good conscience, ignore the millions of African Americans living in poverty and, instead, point to Oprah's millions as evidence of economic inequality. Instead, we must explore how Oprah's financial success can coexist with the economic deprivation of millions of black women. We need to explore, in historian Thomas Holt's words, how the "simultaneous idealization of Colin Powell [or, for that matter, Barack Obama] and demonization of blacks as a whole . . . is replicated in much of our everyday world."[16]

Besides, throughout the history of America, a handful of nonwhite individuals have excelled financially and politically in the teeth of rampant racial domination. The first black congressperson was not elected after the Civil Rights Movement, but in 1870! Joseph Rainey, a former slave, served in the House of Representatives for four terms. Madame C. J. Walker is accredited as being the first black millionaire. Born in 1867, she made her fortune inventing hair and beauty products. Few people would feel comfortable pointing

South Park comments on the Tokenistic Fallacy by naming the black character "Token Black."

to Rainey's or Walker's success as evidence that late-nineteenth-century America was a time of racial harmony and equity. Such tokenistic logic would not be accurate then, and it is not accurate now.

4. Ahistorical Fallacy. This fallacy renders history impotent. Thinking hindered by the ahistorical fallacy makes a bold claim: most U.S. history—namely, the extended period of time during which this country did not extend basic rights to people of color (let alone classify them as fully human)—is inconsequential today. Legacies of slavery and colonialism, the eradication of millions of Native Americans, forced segregation, clandestine sterilizations and harmful science experiments, mass disenfranchisement, race-based exploitation, racist propaganda distributed by the state caricaturing Asians, blacks, and Hispanics, racially motivated abuses of all kinds (sexual, murderous, and dehumanizing)—all of this, purport those operating under the ahistorical fallacy, does not matter for those living in the here-and-now. This idea is so delusional that it is hard to take seriously. Today's society is directed, constructed, and molded by the past.[17] All that is socially constructed is historically constructed, and since race, as we shall see, is a social construction, it, too, is a historical construction.

A "soft version" of the ahistorical fallacy might admit that events in the "recent past"—such as the time since the Civil Rights Movement or the attacks on September 11, 2001—matter, but things in the "distant past"—such as slavery or the colonization of Mexico—have little consequence. But this idea is no less fallacious than the "hard version," since many events in America's "distant past"— especially the enslavement and murder of millions of Africans—are the *most* consequential in shaping present-day society. In this vein, consider the question French historian Marc Bloch poses: "But who would dare to say that the understanding of the Protestant or Catholic Reformation, several centuries removed, is not *far more important* for a proper grasp of the world today than a great many other movements of thought or feeling, which are certainly more recent, yet more ephemeral?"[18] (Additionally, any historian would remind us that, since America is just over 200 years old, *all* American history is "recent history.")

5. Fixed Fallacy. Those who assume that racism is fixed, that it is immutable, constant across time and space, partake in the fixed fallacy. Since they take racism to be something that does not develop in any way, those who understand racism through the fixed fallacy often are led to ask such questions as "Has racism increased or decreased in the past decades?" And because practitioners of the fixed fallacy usually take as their standard definition of racism only the most heinous forms of racism—racial violence, for example—they confidently conclude that, indeed, things have gotten better.

It is important to trace the career of American racism and to analyze, for example, how racial attitudes or measures of racial inclusion and exclusion have changed over time. Many social scientists have developed sophisticated techniques for doing so.[19] But the question "Have things gotten better or worse?" is legitimate *only* after we account for the morphing attributes of racism. We cannot quantify racism in the same way we can quantify, say, birthrates. The nature of "birthrate" does not fluctuate over time; thus, it makes sense to ask, "Are there more or less births now than there were fifty years ago?" without bothering to analyze if and how a birthrate is different today than it was in previous historical moments.

American racism assumes different forms in different historical moments. Although race relations today are informed by those of the past, we cannot hold to the belief that twenty-first-century racism takes on the exact same form as twentieth-century racism. And we certainly cannot conclude that there is "little or no racism" today because it does not resemble the racism of the 1950s. (Modern-day Christianity looks very different, in nearly every conceivable way, than the Christianity of the early church. But this does not mean that there is "little or no Christianity" today.) So, before we ask, "Have things gotten better or worse?" we should ponder the essence of racism today and how it differs from racism experienced by those living in our parents' or grandparents' generation. We should ask, further, to quote Holt once more, "What enables racism to reproduce itself after the historical conditions that initially gave it life have disappeared?"[20]

Racial Domination

We have spent a significant amount of time talking about what racial domination or racism is not. We have yet to spell out what it is. Racial domination is the arrangement of racial life in such a way that its ordinary, everyday workings serve to benefit certain racial groups (in our society, predominantly whites) at the expense of others (in our society, predominantly nonwhites). The dominants of a racial order are those who occupy a place in it such that the regular operation of that racial order works in their favor. The dominated are those who occupy a position in it such that its regular operation works against them.

Far from always involving overt coercion or violence, as in the days of slavery, racial domination is a matter of how institutions ordinarily operate, how interpersonal exchanges (within and across racial divides) typically unfold, and even how individuals (whites and nonwhites alike) unthinkingly come to see themselves and their place in the racial order.

We can delineate two specific manifestations of racial domination: institutional racism and interpersonal racism. *Institutional racism* is systematic white domination of people of color, embedded and operating in corporations, universities, legal systems, political bodies, cultural life, and other social collectives. The word "domination" reminds us that institutional racism is a type of power that encompasses the *symbolic power* to classify one group of people as "normal" and other groups of people as "abnormal," the *political power* to withhold basic rights from people of color and marshal the full power of the state to enforce segregation and inequality, the *social power* to deny people of color full inclusion or membership in associational life, and *economic power* that privileges whites in terms of job placement, advancement, and wealth and property accumulation.

Informed by centuries of racial domination, institutional racism withholds from people of color opportunities, privileges, and rights that many whites enjoy. Examples of institutional racism include the tendency of schools and universities to support curricula that highlight the accomplishments of European Americans, ignoring the accomplishments of non-European Americans; the disproportionate numbers of white people in high-ranking political, economic, and military posts and the ongoing exclusion of people of color from such posts; and the prevalence of law enforcement practices that target people of color, especially African Americans and Arab Americans, as criminals or terrorists. In all three of these examples, racial domination is carried out at the institutional level, sometimes despite the motives or attitudes of the people working in those institutions. Because institutional racism operates outside the scope of individual intent, many people do not recognize institutional racism as racism when they experience it.

Below the level of institutions, yet informed by the workings of those institutions, we find *interpersonal racism*. This is racial domination manifest in everyday interactions and practices. Interpersonal racism can be *overt*, as in old-fashioned bigotry (old-fashioned but not outmoded, as the examples at the start of this chapter indicate). In such instances, people act out their prejudices, giving direct expression to their negative attitudes and guided by their demeaning stereotypes of others. However, most of the time, interpersonal racism is quite *covert*: it is found in the habitual, commonsensical, and ordinary practices of our lives. This is part of the reason why our racial problems are so challenging: they extend far beyond the confines of straightforward, conscious bigotry. Our racist attitudes, as Lillian Smith remarked

With *Mimic*, a staged photograph, Canadian-born artist Jeff Wall re-created an incident he had once witnessed when a white man mocked an Asian man with this small but deeply powerful gesture.

in *Killers of the Dream*, easily "slip from the conscious mind deep into the muscles."[21] Since we are disposed to a world structured by racial domination, we develop racialized dispositions—some conscious, many more unconscious and bodily—that guide our thoughts and behaviors.

We may talk slowly to an Asian woman at the farmer's market, unconsciously assuming that she speaks poor English. We may inform a Mexican woman at a corporate party that someone has spilled his punch, unconsciously assuming that she is a janitor. We may unknowingly scoot to the other side of the elevator when a large Puerto Rican man steps in, or unthinkingly eye a group of black teenagers wandering the aisles of the store at which we work, or ask to change seats if an Arab American man sits down next to us on an airplane. Many miniature actions such as these have little to do with one's intentional thoughts; they are orchestrated by one's practical sense, one's habitual know-how, and informed by institutional racism.

"Can people of color be racist?" This question is a popular one in the public imagination, and the answer depends on what we mean by racism. Institutional racism is the product of years of white supremacy, and it is designed to produce far-reaching benefits for white people. Institutional racism carries on despite our personal attitudes. Thus, there is no such thing as "black institutional racism" or "reverse institutional racism," since there is no centuries-old socially ingrained and normalized system of domination designed by people of color that denies whites full participation in the rights, privileges, and seats of power of our society.[22] Interpersonal racism, on the other hand, takes place on the ground level and has to do with attitudes and habitual actions. It is certainly true that members of all racial groups can harbor negative attitudes toward members of other groups. An African American may hold ill feelings toward Jews or Koreans. An Asian American may be suspicious of white people. And such prejudiced perceptions often are rampant *within* racial groups as well, as when a Cuban American feels superior to a Mexican American, a Japanese American feels uncomfortable around Chinese Americans, or dark-skinned African Americans profess to being "more authentically black" than light-skinned African Americans. Indeed, some nonwhite groups have a deep, conflict-ridden history with other nonwhite groups. One thinks here of the Black-Korean conflict, the so-called Black-Brown divide, bitter relations among Latino subgroups, and animus among various American Indian Nations.

People of color, then, can take part in overt and covert forms of interpersonal racism. That said, we must realize that interpersonal racism targeting dominated groups and interpersonal racism targeting the dominant group do not pack the same punch. Two young men, one black, the other white, bump into each other on the street. The black man calls the white man a "honky." In response, the white man calls the black man a "boy." Both racial slurs *are* racial slurs and should be labeled as such, and both reinforce racial divisions. However, unlike "honky," "boy" connects to the larger system of institutional racial domination. The word derives its meaning (and power) from slavery, when enslaved African men were stripped of their masculine honor and treated like children. "Boy" (and many other epithets aimed at blacks) invokes such times—times when torturing, whipping, and raping enslaved blacks were not illegal acts. Epithets toward white people, including "honky," have no such equivalent. ("Honky" comes from derogatory terms aimed at Bohemian, Hungarian, and Polish immigrants who worked in the Chicago meat-packing plants.) "Boy" also reminds the black man how things stand today: if the confrontation escalates and the police are called, the black man knows that the police officers will probably be white and that he might be harassed or looked on as a threat; if the two men meet in court, the black man knows that the lawyers, judge, and jurors will possibly be mostly (if not all) white; and if the two men are sentenced, the African American man knows, as do many criminologists, that he will get the harsher sentence.[23] "Boy" brings the full weight of institutional racism—systematic, historical, and mighty—down on the African-American man. "Honky," even if delivered with venomous spite, is powerless by comparison.

Moreover, sociologists have shown that, unlike white people, people of color are confronted with interpersonal racism on a regular basis, sometimes daily. For people of color, there is a cumulative character to an individual's racial experiences. These experiences do not take place in isolation. Humiliating or degrading acts always are informed by similar acts that individuals have experienced in the past. To paraphrase sociologist Joe Feagin, the interpersonal events that take place on the street and in other public settings are not simply rare and isolated events; rather, they are recurring events shaped by social and historical forces of racial domination.[24]

Institutional and interpersonal racism are not altogether distinct phenomena, however useful it may be to distinguish them analytically. When Stokely Carmichael and Charles Hamilton first brought the concepts into race studies in their 1967 classic, *Black Power*, they acknowledged that "institutional racism relies on the active and pervasive operation of anti-black attitudes and practices"; that is, they affirmed that those who "would and do perpetuate institutionally racist policies"— and who would do so "deliberately"—are driven as much by racism as are the perpetrators of interpersonal acts of insult and humiliation.[25] For instance, the judge who sentences a person of color to a prison term longer than a white person would receive enacts institutional racism yet also engages (in an indirect and mediated way) in an interpersonal interaction. Likewise, cemetery owners who put out a sign forbidding the consumption of food on their premises also interact, after a fashion, with visiting family members of color, whose ritual practices they specifically are targeting—some nonwhite groups consider bringing food to a cemetery a long-standing cultural practice—even as these authorities lay down their impersonal organizational rules in the isolation of their executive offices. Carmichael and Hamilton easily could have made the inverse point as well, namely, that every act of interpersonal racism also carries with it the force of institutional racism. Not only do institutions shape the perpetrator through past practices of socialization, but institutions also authorize her or his racist actions in the present. Institutional and interpersonal racism interpenetrate and support one another: whenever one comes to light, the other's shadow can be found alongside it. Their common root is a social psychology of racial animus, dispositions and habits of thought, perception, feeling, and action that lead one to denigrate the racial Other, whether in face-to-face interaction or in more regularized practices that establish the rules and policies of an institution. This especially is important to note in light of the tendency to invoke institutional racism in ways that absolve racial dominants of their culpability. As originally conceived, it may have been useful for finding ways to talk about the historical legacy of racial inequality. Yet it also allows personal responsibility to be neutralized. After all, someone did lay down those prison sentences; someone did write up those cemetery rules.

A neutral dress code or something more?

Symbolic Violence

Elaborating on the nature of "unconscious racism," law professor Charles Lawrence has observed, "Americans share a common historical and cultural heritage in which racism has played and still plays a dominant role. Because of this shared experience, we also inevitably share many ideas, attitudes, and beliefs that attach significance to an individual's race and induce negative feelings and opinions about nonwhites. *To the extent that this cultural belief system has influenced all of us, we are all racists.* At the same time, most of us are unaware of our racism. We do not recognize the ways in which our cultural experience has influenced our beliefs about race or the occasions upon which those beliefs affect our actions. In other words, a large part of the behavior that produces racial discrimination is influenced by unconscious racial motivation."[26] Take note of the italicized sentence. Why didn't Lawrence write, "To the extent that this cultural belief system has influenced all of us, *all white people are racists*?" The answer is that such a statement would be inaccurate.

Racism surrounds us. To borrow an analogy developed by Beverly Tatum, racial domination is like polluted air. On some days, the pollution is weighty and visible, while on other days, it is virtually invisible—"but always, day in and day out, we are breathing it in."[27] Because racism infuses all of social life, nonwhites and whites alike develop thoughts and practices molded by racism; nonwhites and whites alike develop stereotypes about other racial groups.

In fact, people of color may internalize prejudice aimed at their own racial group, unintentionally contributing to the reproduction of racial domination. Psychologists have labeled this phenomenon "internalized oppression" or "internalized

THE BOONDOCKS   BY AARON McGRUDER

"It is the peculiar triumph of society—and its loss—that it is able to convince those people to whom it has given inferior status of the reality of this decree."—James Baldwin

racism." Following the work of Pierre Bourdieu, we label it "symbolic violence": "violence which is exercised upon a social agent with his or her complicity."[28] In the case of racial domination, symbolic violence refers to the process of people of color unknowingly accepting and supporting the terms of their own domination.[29] "So we learned the dance that cripples the human spirit," laments Lillian Smith, "step by step by step, we who were white and we who were colored, day by day, hour by hour, year by year until the movements were reflexes and made for the rest of our life without thinking."[30]

The pervasiveness of symbolic violence presents a challenge to all students of color who might read this textbook—or any other work on race in America—and feel they have little to gain from it, as if the study of race merely were a way of enlightening their peers who are white. Regrettably, symbolic violence operates everywhere. It can be found among whites, to be sure, who perhaps out of racial guilt repudiate their own whiteness by engaging in misguided attempts, say, to "act black" by altering their outward patterns of dress, bodily mannerisms, or way of speaking in ways that conform to blackness as they envision it (often, however, without also repudiating their own white privilege). We shall have more to say about this in Chapter 10. However, symbolic violence also and most often is found among nonwhites who learn from an early age that nonwhiteness is devalued.

A good example of symbolic violence is the nearly worldwide acceptance of European standards of beauty. The false aesthetic separation between "white beauty"—epitomized by long, straight, blond hair, blue eyes, and pale skin—and "black ugliness"—epitomized by short, curly, black hair, brown eyes, and dark brown skin—grew out of slavery. Features associated with the African American phenotype were demonized. Since the "Black Is Beautiful" movement of the 1960s, many African American women have resisted such standards, taking pride in their curly hair and their ebony-colored skin. Nevertheless, many others have internalized white standards of beauty, using costly and painful methods to straighten and dye their hair and, less frequently, to lighten their skin. In fact, Madame C. J. Walker, the first black millionaire mentioned earlier, made her fortune developing a product to straighten black women's hair! Today, many black women, to borrow a philosopher's line, have been "poisoned by the stereotype others have of them."[31]

Madame C. J. Walker, known as the first African-American millionaire, made her fortune developing a product to straighten black women's hair.

Symbolic violence operates by virtue of the fact that the dominated perceive and respond to the structures and processes that dominate them through modes of thought (indeed, also of feeling) that are themselves the products of domination. The racial "order of things" seems to them natural, self-evident, and even legitimate. Such an insight neither grants everything to structural forces somehow detached from human volition nor blames the hapless victim. "The only way to understand this particular form of domination is to move beyond the forced choice between constraint (by forces) and consent (to reasons), between mechanical coercion and voluntary, free, deliberate, even calculated submission."[32] This in turn has an important practical implication. What is required is a radical transformation of the social conditions that produce embodied habits, dispositions, tastes, and lifestyles that lead people to become actively complicit in their own domination. The only way to bring about change that does not entail merely replacing one modality of racial domination with another is to address specifically and to undo the mechanisms of dehistoricization and universalization—"always and everywhere it has been this way"—whereby arbitrary workings of power are enabled to continue.

Audre Lorde said, "There is no such thing as a single-issue struggle, because we do not live single-issue lives."

Intersectionality

Racial domination does not operate inside a vacuum, cordoned off from other modes of domination. On the contrary, it *intersects* with other forms of domination—those based on gender, class, sexuality, religion, nationhood, ability, and so forth. Social scientists have evoked the term "intersectionality" to explain the overlapping systems of advantages and disadvantages that affect people differently positioned in society.

The notion that there is a monolithic "Asian experience," "African American experience," or "white experience"—experiences somehow detached from other pieces of one's identity—is nothing but a chimera, an illusion. Researchers have labeled such a notion "*racial essentialism*," for such a way of thinking boils down vastly different human experiences into a single "master category": race.[33] When we fail to account for these different experiences, we create silences in our narratives of the social world and fail to explain how overlapping systems of advantages and disadvantages affect individuals' opportunity structures, lifestyles, and social hardships. When we speak only of "Hispanic people," for instance, we overlook how Latinas (Hispanic women) confront not only racism but sexism in their day-to-day lives. We also overlook how poor Hispanic families must struggle against poverty and worker exploitation, whereas more well-off Hispanic families may not be confronted by such obstacles. And we overlook how Hispanics with disabilities and those whose faith would not be considered mainstream are disadvantaged in ways that able-bodied Hispanics and those who practice mainstream religion are not. Finally, we overlook the ways in which gay Hispanics face ridicule, discrimination, and violence that heterosexual Hispanics do not, as well as the fact that Cubans, Puerto Ricans, Mexicans, and Dominicans—all of whom would be classified as Hispanic—have very different cultures and experience life in the United States in very different ways.

The idea of intersectionality implies that we cannot understand the lives of poor white single mothers or gay black men by examining only one dimension of their lives—class, gender, race, or sexuality; no, we must explore their lives in their full complexity, examining how these various dimensions come together and structure their existence. When we speak of racial domination, then, we always must bear in mind the ways in which it interacts with masculine domination (or sexism), heterosexual domination (or homophobia), class domination (poverty), religious persecution, disadvantages brought on by disabilities, and so forth.[34]

In addition, we should not assume that one kind of oppression is more important than another or that being advantaged in one dimension of life somehow cancels out other dimensions that often result in disadvantage. Although it is true that poor whites experience many of the same hardships as poor blacks, it is not true that poverty somehow de-whitens poor whites. In other words, although they are in a similarly precarious economic position as poor blacks, poor whites still experience race-based privileges, while poor blacks are oppressed not only by poverty but also by racism. In a similar vein, well-off people of color cannot "buy" their way out of racism. Despite their economic privilege, middle- and upper-class nonwhites experience institutional and interpersonal racism on a regular basis.[35]

As is suggested by some of our previous examples, people of color, too, can enjoy important societal advantages, whether by dint of economic standing or being straight as opposed to gay or personal attractiveness (beauty capital or erotic capital, as in the expression "pretty-girl privilege") or any number of other considerations. This is yet another reason why critical thinking is crucial not only for whites in our society but for nonwhites as well.

But how, exactly, should we conceptualize these intersectional modes of domination? Many scholars have grappled with this question, and we do so here, if only in the most provisional way.[36] The notion of intersectionality is perhaps as old as the social problems of racial, masculine, and class domination, but in recent memory it has been popularized by activists who criticized the feminist and civil rights movements for ignoring the unique struggles of women of color. The term itself is credited to critical race scholar Kimberlé Crenshaw, who imagined society as divided every which way by multiple forms of inequality.[37] In Crenshaw's view, society resembles an intricate system of crisscrossing roads, each representing a different social identity (e.g., race, gender, class, religion, age). Your unique social position (or structural location) is identified by listing all the attributes of your social identity and then pinpointing the nexus (or intersection) at which all those attributes converge. This conception of intersectionality has been the dominant one for many years, leading scholars to understand overlapping modes of oppression as a kind of "matrix of domination."[38]

Recently, however, scholars have criticized this way of thinking about intersectionality, claiming it reproduces, in minimized form, the very essentialist reasoning it sought to dismantle.[39] For example, those who have concentrated on the ways "class intersects with race" largely have bifurcated racial groups (especially African Americans) into two classes—the middle class and the poor (or "the underclass")—attributing to each certain social characteristics, principles, and practices. Thus, instead of Black Culture, we now have two distinct black cultures; instead of the Black Community, we think in terms of two subcommunities. When scholars divide racial groups into a set number of classes, genders, sexualities, and so forth, the end result is not a critique of essentialism, but a new, softer kind of essentialism. At best, an approach that represents society as a hierarchy of culturally discrete boxes encourages us to conceptualize oppression through a simple additive model (one often hears of a "double jeopardy" or "triple oppression"). At worst, it replaces larger homogenizing rubrics ("Hispanic") with smaller ones ("Hispanic women") and offers little conceptual refuge from essentializing tendencies.

A better metaphor for intersecting modes of oppression might be not crisscrossing roads, but a web of relations within which struggles over opportunities, power, and privileges take place.[40] One implication of this new theoretical development is the realization that racial domination is deeply implicated in the perpetuation of other forms of domination—and vice versa. Systems of domination, in other words, are mutually reinforcing: to flourish, each system relies on the logic and ramifications of others. Dissecting the details of this process—uncovering, for example, precisely how racial domination supports and is supported by masculine domination—is crucial for developing effective strategies to combat all kinds of social suffering. The result of intersectional thinking, in other words, should not only be a picture of your complex identity, however important that may be; it should also entail a thorough understanding of the ways in which intertwined modes of domination rely on one another for survival.

A BIOLOGICAL REALITY?

Up to this point, we have spoken of race only in social or cultural terms. We have said nothing about biological or natural differences. Race, after all, is about biological markers—skin color, hair texture, eyes, and cheekbones, for example. Is race a biological concept? Can modern science, using the most sophisticated techniques possible—including genetic testing—identify natural differences separating racial groups? Modern scientists have answered these questions with a resounding "No."

To fully understand this point, a quick biology lesson is in order. Biologists call the building blocks of life, of our bodies, the *genome*. The genome (a combination of the words "gene" and "chromosome") of an organism is the collection of that organism's entire hereditary information, encoded in deoxyribonucleic acid, or DNA. DNA is made up of *genes*, or single units of hereditary information, and is responsible for the organism's biological development. So, how genetically different are we?

We share 99.9 percent of the same genes with other human beings. If you examined the DNA makeup of a Chinese golfer, an entrepreneur from the White Mountain Apache Nation, a Swedish politician, an African American surgeon, a Mexican geologist, and an Iranian sculptor, they would all be indistinguishable when it comes to racial differences. As a species, humans have dramatically low levels of genetic variation. In fact, there is more genetic variation within a single tribe of chimpanzees native to West Africa than there is within the entire human species. Regarding race, there is much more genetic variation—8.6 times more variation, to be precise—*within* traditionally defined racial groups than *between* them. Why? Evolutionary biologist Joseph Graves, Jr., provides the answer: "Because there is 8.6 times more genetic variation between any given individual on the planet and another individual than there is between the populations they belong to. In other words, the variability that makes one African-American person different from another is greater than the variability between African Americans and Swedes or Tibetans or Amazonian tribes."[41]

Race does not exist on the genetic level. Scientists cannot "see race" by examining humans' DNA strands. This finding is nothing new. In *Man's Most Dangerous Myth: The Fallacy of Race*, a book published in 1942, physical anthropologist Ashley Montagu demonstrated that race is not a biologically sound concept. And long before Montagu wrote his book, Charles Darwin, the founder of modern-day biology, proclaimed that race has no biological grounding.[42]

"Obvious" Physical Differences

Nevertheless, many people still assume that racial differences are dictated by nature. One might question, "Even if genetic comparisons disclose no race-based differences among groups, don't obvious physical differences prove the natural existence of race?"

This is a fair question, but it assumes that there are such things as "obvious physical differences." People do have different skin tones, to be sure, but those tones do not fit "naturally" into the limited racial categories operating in America today. Physical traits vary enormously among people classified as racially similar. Consider the category of "white," which could include Spaniards, Russians, Italians, Afrikaners, Scots, Persians, Norwegians, Greeks, and Tajiks, not to mention thousands of people with mixed heritage. There is a vast amount of variation when it comes to "obvious physical differences"—average height, hair and eye color, and skeletal structure—between these groups.

Or consider the category "black." Aboriginal Australians, Ethiopians, Sri Lankans of India, and Trinidadians all have a dark skin tone; however, they have very different facial structures and hair types. In fact, when scientists have focused exclusively on the populations of sub-Saharan Africa, they have discovered that

Korean-born artist Nikki Lee, who specializes in blending into different American subcultures, adopts the look of a young Hispanic woman in this photograph, smudging racial lines often assumed to be obvious and fixed.

there is more genetic and physical variation within all the populations of sub-Saharan Africa than there is among any other populations on the globe. This means that, biologically, it is likely that a woman from the Congo would have more in common with a woman from Germany than she would with a woman from Botswana. Nevertheless, if all three women moved to the United States, the woman from the Congo and the woman from Botswana would be classified as belonging to the same race, "black," while the woman from Germany would be labeled "white."[43]

If we examine how race has been defined throughout the history of the United States—a task we will take up in detail in Chapter 2—we see that "obvious physical differences" supposedly separating one race from another have been anything but "obvious." Many people who "look" white with minuscule amounts of African ancestry have been classified as black.[44] And if we think about it, the skin tone of many light-skinned blacks resembles that of Hispanics; the skin tone of many dark-skinned whites resembles that of light-skinned Native Americans; and the color of many Asian people's skin looks like the color of many Italians' skin.

Moreover, in some parts of the world, "obvious physical differences" matter very little when it comes to partitioning people. In India, what divides people is not skin color but one's position in the caste system. A *caste system* is a social and symbolic hierarchical system of classification and separation that organizes people into rigid groups characterized by inner-group marriage, heredity, lifestyle, and occupation. Indian Hindus caught up in the caste system are grouped along a continuum ranging from those who enjoy high status and rights to those deemed "untouchable" and denied many social rights. Physical differences do not demarcate different caste groups. As the well-known American sociologist Oliver Cromwell Cox once put it, "when we refer to groups such as Chamars, Bayas, Telis, Doms, Brahmans, Kayasthas, or Jolahas [all of which are names of distinct castes], no sense of physical distinction need be aroused. We see rather only East Indians."[45]

There is nothing naturally obvious about race; moreover, this kind of thinking can lead to dangerous consequences. In biomedical research, for example, dozens of doctors falsely have assumed that a dying patient is more likely to find an organ donor among those of the same race, among those who "look" the same as the patient. This false assumption has proved deadly: it has resulted in many clinical errors and lost lives.[46]

We must resist, therefore, accepting as given the existence of obvious physical differences that demarcate the races. British social scientist Michael Banton was correct in observing that we "do not perceive racial differences . . . [but] phenotypical differences of colour, hair form, underlying bone structure and so on."[47]

But we can go further still, acknowledging that the processes of racialization actually can create difference where previously no phenotypical or biological difference existed. A recent and alarming example is found within genetics. Uncritically accepting racial boundaries as legitimate demarcations of distinct populations, scientists have claimed to document different distributions of genetic sequences across racial groups. This has led some to advance claims about the genetic foundations of racial variation. However, as sociologist Troy Duster has stressed, "finding a higher frequency of some alleles [a form of a gene] in one population versus another is a guaranteed outcome of modern technology, even for two randomly chosen populations."[48]

Athletic Ability and IQ

Even though race has no genetic existence and even though obvious physical differences become quite unobvious upon closer inspection, some people still hold fast to the idea that certain races are naturally different from others. To justify this position, they usually point to two areas where ostensible differences between racial groups appear manifest: athletic ability and IQ rankings. Let us take up each of these in turn.

Athletic Ability. "Black people are better at basketball." "Dominicans naturally excel at baseball." "Asians are excellent dancers." "White men can't jump!" Blanket statements such as these permeate popular discourse and are sometimes marshaled as evidence of biological differences between races.

Over the decades, some have claimed that African Americans are innately superior athletes. Evidence for this claim, some say, is found in the fact that African Americans seem to dominate the NBA and many Olympic games, including track and field. Sportscasters have referred to black athletes as "thoroughbreds" and "superathletes," and professional athletes themselves, black and white, have offered generalizations about athletic superiority supposedly based in racial genes.[49] Statements such as these are not supported by any scientific evidence. Claims of inherent racial ability—including myths about "fast-twitch" and "slow-twitch" muscles—are disconfirmed by modern biology.[50]

In the 1920s and 1930s, basketball was thought of as a "Jews' game." The top players in college and professional leagues were Jewish, and Jewish players were thought to have the biological edge, "being endowed by nature with superior balance, greater speed, and sharper eyes—not to mention, in the words of one sportswriter, a 'scheming mind' and 'flashy trickiness.'"[51] (These last two descriptive phrases come from the stereotype of Jews as "crafty.") Soon, however, Jews disappeared from the game, and many black players rose to prominence. What happened? Did nature suddenly change its mind, deciding to strip Jews of their so-called innate skills and bestow such biological gifts on blacks? Certainly not. A better explanation is a sociological one. The changing racial composition of basketball corresponded to the changing racial composition of inner cities. Traditionally, basketball has been a game for the inner-city poor: courts can be found in most urban playgrounds, and all one needs is a ball and a pair of

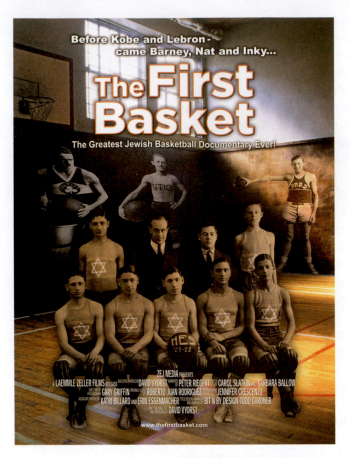

Before Kobe and Lebron –
came Barney, Nat and Inky...

The First Basket

The Greatest Jewish Basketball Documentary Ever!

ZEJ MEDIA PRESENTS

A LAEMMLE ZELLER FILMS RELEASE EXECUTIVE PRODUCER DAVID VYORST NARRATED BY PETER RIEGERT EDITED BY CAROL SLATKIN AND BARBARA BALLOW
DIRECTOR OF PHOTOGRAPHY GARY GRIFFIN ORIGINAL SCORE ROBERTO JUAN RODRIGUEZ PRODUCTION MANAGER JENNIFER CRESCENZO
ASSOCIATE PRODUCER KATRI BILLARD AND ERIN ESSENMACHER TITLE DESIGN, GRAPHICS AND ANIMATION BIT N BY DESIGN TODD GARDNER
WRITTEN, DIRECTED AND PRODUCED BY DAVID VYORST

www.thefirstbasket.com

In the 1920s and 1930s, the top college and professional basketball players were Jewish.

sneakers. Jews dominated basketball in the early twentieth century because ghettos in northern cities were teeming with Jewish immigrants. By midcentury, the nature of the inner city was undergoing a sea change, as many blacks were migrating northward from the rural South. Basketball offered these newly migrated black youth the same thing it had offered Jewish youth decades before: an accessible and inexpensive recreational activity.[52]

Turning our attention to the present day, sociologists have shown that many talented white high school athletes, many of whom come from high-income backgrounds, come to see sports as a waste of time, as "pissing in the wind," whereas numerous talented black high school athletes, many of whom come from low-income backgrounds, see sports as their one and only shot at upward mobility and social status. Accordingly, many young white athletes, no matter how talented, intentionally drop out of the "sports game" early, since they have been socialized into the conviction that pursuing an athletic career is not a wise choice to make. A sports career may seem like "small potatoes" to white youth, whereas the one-in-a-million shot at a career in the pros might seem like the "only potatoes" to black youth whose opportunities are severely limited.[53] Thus, the racial composition of professional sports rosters is more a reflection of decisions young people make—decisions guided by structures and histories of racial inequality—than it is of biological superiority. Of course, there are a handful of "exceptions to the rule," black players, such as Grant Hill or Ken Griffey, Jr., who came from prosperous backgrounds. But we should bear in mind that exceptions do not prove the rule—especially if that rule is biological.

Are blacks naturally superior athletes? The question has been answered by biology—the only evidence that counts for this kind of question—and the answer is no. The racial composition of several professional sports teams can be explained only through historical and sociological analysis. Now, let's ask another question: Why do we care so much? Why do we continue to come back to this age-old question? Why do we desire so much to know if blacks are innately superior athletes?

Do we care so much because blacks are perhaps "obviously" better at, say, track and field than everyone else? This cannot be the case. At the 2008 Summer Olympic Games, gold medals in track and field events were awarded to athletes from Portugal, Panama, Russia, Jamaica, Great Britain, Romania, Italy, Kenya, Ethiopia, the

United States, and Bahrain. Maybe we care so much because blacks are "obviously" better at jumping? This doesn't seem to wash out either, for it would be easy to argue the opposite, that whites are actually better at jumping. For "proof," consider volleyball. The skills involved in basketball and those of volleyball are nearly identical: talented players must exhibit highly attuned hand-eye coordination, superior jumping ability, and quick reflexes. Yet volleyball leagues continue to be dominated by white athletes. And those who claim that "white people can't jump" must have overlooked Andrey Silnov, the Russian Olympian who won the gold medal in men's high jump at the 2008 Summer Games, and Tia Hellebaut, the Belgian who won the gold medal in women's high jump.

Thus, white people are naturally superior at jumping. "Our evidence does not prove this," you might say. "You cannot make sweeping generalizations about all white people based on the spectacular performance of a few." We agree! But why, then, is it socially acceptable to make such sweeping generalizations about black people based on the spectacular performance of a few? Why, upon observing the play of LeBron James, Kevin Durant, Brittney Griner, or Maya Moore—or even the entire NBA and WNBA rosters—do we feel justified in making far-reaching statements about *all* African Americans? After all, we don't subject white people to the same false logic. After watching Alexander Ovechkin, Sidney Crosby, or Jaromir Jagr perform their magic on the ice rink, do we conclude that *all* white people are good at hockey? Rugby and football require the same types of players: tough, fast, hard hitting, and team oriented. If this is the case, then why have people pointed to black NFL players and declared that blacks are better athletes when they could just as easily have pointed to the scores of white rugby players and made the same proclamation for white people?

Questions such as these urge us to reevaluate how we form conclusions about African Americans, and other people of color, based on one-sided and casually collected observations, while we tend not to form such conclusions about white people. If we *question* the question about natural differences in athletic prowess, we soon discover that it only serves to perpetuate stereotypes about nonwhites and whites alike and makes into something real "natural differences" that simply do not exist.

More important, perhaps, when it comes to sports, notions of racial superiority and inferiority are not innocent ideas. The idea that blacks are better athletes rarely exists in isolation. It is often connected to another idea. Inherent athletic superiority is usually thought to be negatively correlated with inherent intellectual superiority. When two things are negatively correlated, this means that as the one thing increases, the other decreases. Here is the real danger in making claims about race-based athletic ability: those claims insinuate that groups that are good at sports are bad at thinking. This brings us to the next assumption about biological differences between races: inequalities in IQ levels.

Intellectual Ability. Another stereotype that rests on assumptions of biological differences is that certain races of people are naturally more intelligent than others. "Asians are better at math." "Whites excel in the humanities." Statements such as these can be heard on many college campuses around the country.

IQ testing is a mechanism through which racial hierarchies are reinforced. IQ stands for intelligence quotient. First developed in 1905 by French psychologist Alfred Binet, who developed the device in order to locate children with special needs, IQ is a measure of general intelligence computed by multiplying the ratio of one's "mental age" and one's chronological age by a number representing average intelligence, in this case, 100. Binet fervently rejected the interpretation that IQ was dictated by heredity. That interpretation came to prominence in America at the conclusion of World War I. The idea resurfaced in 1969 when educational psychologist Arthur Jensen published an article, now generally viewed as infamously misleading, that emphasized innate differences in IQ levels between whites and blacks. And, most recently, in 1994, Americans witnessed yet another resurgence of ideas of inherent intellectual inequalities with the publication of Richard Herrnstein and Charles Murray's *The Bell Curve*, a book 845 pages from bow to stern that claimed, among other things, that whites have higher IQs than blacks; that, for the most part, these differences are genetic; and that these intractable differences can explain all kinds of social ills and inequalities.[54]

Immediately after publication, *The Bell Curve* became a target of criticism from intellectuals belonging to several disciplines. Biologists rallied against the idea that IQ could be measured as a single number extracted from a person's head and placed in a linear ranking. They also criticized the notion that IQ was genetically based and therefore immutable. IQ is much better understood as a panoply of capabilities used creatively to adapt to complex problems; it cannot be reduced to a unitary, unwavering, and quantifiable thing. Statisticians, for their part, discovered that Herrnstein and Murray displayed their findings in a manner that obscured their analyses and hid results that contradicted their central claims regarding racial differences in intelligence levels. For example, a statistic demonstrating the strength of many of their findings was excluded from the text because most of the findings on which their arguments actually rested were embarrassingly weak. Finally, social scientists pointed to countless studies that demonstrate that IQ differences cease to matter once social and historical factors are taken into consideration. These studies show that assumed natural differences do not exist at the aggregate group level and that they do nothing to explain inequality in America. What does explain such inequality are social conditions, historical contexts, and state policies. Today, the overall scientific consensus is that *The Bell Curve* is a deeply flawed work (at best) or racist propaganda masquerading as science (at worst).[55]

Arguments that suppose that social and economic differences between races are the result of immutable, inherited, and inborn distinctions are grouped under the rubric "biological determinism." As the preceding two sections have shown, biological deterministic arguments that attempt to separate races according to innate, genetic properties do not hold water. Biological determinism is nothing new. On the contrary, and as we will see in Chapter 2, this train of thought has been around since the invention of race. But despite being an outdated mode of thinking and despite being proven wrong, biological determinism refuses to go away. Why is this?

American biologist and historian of science Stephen Jay Gould provides an insightful answer. Writing specifically about IQ, Gould argues that "resurgences of biological determinism correlate with episodes of political retrenchment, particularly with campaigns for reduced government spending on social programs, or at times of fear among ruling elites, when disadvantaged groups sow serious social unrest or even threaten to usurp power. What argument against social change could be more chillingly effective than the claim that established orders, with some groups on top and others at the bottom, exist as an accurate reflection of the innate and unchangeable intellectual capacities of people so ranked?"[56]

When American psychologists first used the IQ test to rank the intellectual capacities of races, America had just emerged from World War I and was involved in an energetic campaign to develop a foreign policy based on principles of isolationism, patriotism, and "national purity." When Arthur Jensen revisited biological deterministic arguments in 1969, America's racial tensions and political unrest were boiling over: Martin Luther King, Jr., had been assassinated a year earlier, the Black Power Movement was gaining steam, and thousands of people were protesting the Vietnam War. And with what social change did the publication of *The Bell Curve* coincide? In the mid-1990s American social policies underwent a drastic transformation. Social services were slashed and welfare spending was rolled back and reorganized, ushering in "the age of austerity," and more and more, the poor were viewed not as troubled citizens in need of help, but as perverse problems in need of discipline.[57] Thus, in times when the social status quo has been met with a severe challenge—either by subordinated groups who lash out at the snares of their subordination or by dominant groups who look to ratchet up their own power by further exploiting the powerless—biological determinism often is to be found, reassuring people that social inequalities are really natural inequalities.

But biological determinism is bad science. More importantly, biological determinism has been used to justify injustices and to naturalize inequalities. Gould knew well the pitfalls of such thinking: "Few tragedies can be more extensive than the stunting of life, few injustices deeper than the denial of an opportunity to strive or even to hope, by a limit imposed from without, but falsely identified as lying within."[58]

WHITENESS

As should be clear from the preceding examples, the United States, since its inception, has been a nation that placed supreme value on whiteness. During its early stages, American democracy—which prided itself on liberty and valued freedom from oppression—did not cover nonwhite people. On the contrary, America was built on the backs of Native Americans, millions of whom were killed and uprooted, and on the backs of African Americans, kidnapped, enslaved, and forced to toil for their white owners. The original section of the U.S. Capitol building, which still stands today in Washington, D.C., and houses a predominantly white Congress, was erected by black slaves. It also was slaves who, in 1860, placed the statue *Freedom* atop the Capitol Dome—a statue of a helmeted Native American woman.[59]

"Whiteness" is a term we do not use much. Perhaps this is because many people have the tendency to assume that race is about people of color. But race is a fundamentally relational concept: we cannot understand the meaning of Hispanic, Asian, Native American, or black without simultaneously understanding the meaning of white. But white is not "just another" racial category; it is the *dominant* category, that with which all other categories are compared and contrasted. Whiteness, then, is *racial domination normalized*. This normalization produces and reproduces many cultural, political, economic, and social advantages and privileges for white people and withholds such advantages and privileges from nonwhite people.

The Race That Need Not Speak Its Name

Think, for a moment, about who you are. What qualities are most salient to your identity? Perhaps think about three characteristics that best describe your makeup.

Chances are that if you are white, you probably did not list your race as one of the characteristics most important to you. You might have listed your ethnicity—Irish, Italian, Jewish—religion, gender, sexual orientation, or political affiliation. On the other hand, if you are not white, there is a good chance that you listed your race as an important characteristic. You might have identified as a "Black woman Christian" or as an "Asian American gay man."[60]

What explains this difference? Why are white people more unlikely than people of color to identify themselves in racial terms? Sociologists have shown that many white people have a hard time coming to terms with their whiteness. In fact, many white people seem to believe they do not belong to a racial group. They see themselves, simply, as "normal."[61] And herein lies the power of whiteness. By refusing to speak its own name, whiteness presents itself as normality.

In our popular culture, history books, and political discussions, whiteness is treated as the standard. For instance, if you are wandering the aisles of your local bookstore searching for titles by Ralph Ellison, Toni Morrison, or Richard Wright—three of America's most accomplished novelists—you probably will not find what you are looking for in the "Literature" section. Ellison, Morrison, and Wright are most likely to be found in the "African American" section. There, too, you will find historical treatises on slavery, segregation, and the Civil Rights Movement. Novelist Leslie Marmon Silko and Pulitzer Prize–winning poet N. Scott Momaday are probably shelved in the "Native American" section; there, too, you will find historical books on the creation of reservations and tribal culture. In the "Literature" section, you will find shelves full of white authors: Jack Kerouac, Jane Austen, Herman Melville, and so forth. And in the "History" section, you will find book after book about white people: this one about Benjamin Franklin; that one about the Dust Bowl of the 1930s. Why, then, are not these sections respectively labeled "White Literature" and "White History"?

Consider some other examples of how whiteness is held up as the status quo:

- We often hear of "black churches." Seldom do we hear churches described (or describing themselves) as "white churches," even though their congregations are primarily white. These are simply "churches."

- Certain television shows, like *Empire* or *Black-ish*, are considered "African-American television." Popular shows such as *Girls* or *Game of Thrones* are made up of majority- or all-white casts, but those shows are not called "white television."

- Many African American artists are said to produce "black music"; many African American comedians are said to write "black jokes." But when is the last time you heard pop, rock, or country songs sung by white artists described as "white music"? Are the jokes written by Jim Gaffigan, Jon Stewart, or Larry the Cable Guy called "white jokes"?

- There are "black ghettos," "Mexican barrios," "Chinatown," and "Native American reservations," but gated suburban communities, many of which are nearly all white, are simply referred to as "gated communities" or "suburbs."

- "Asian culture" might be located in a piece of artwork or a type of fashion. The "Hispanic influence" might be pointed out in architecture or cuisine. Someone might be said to have "black style." But "white culture," "white influence," and "white style" are seldom-uttered phrases.

- Many colleges and universities across the United States are majority-white campuses, but while these institutions are simply called "colleges and universities," majority-black campuses are called "historically black colleges." Similarly, college courses that focus on Anglo-European history, literature, music, art, or architecture are not called "white studies," but many courses are listed under "African American studies," "Chicano studies," or "Asian American studies."

"Joe, these people say they want flesh-colored Band-Aids."

These examples demonstrate how whiteness surrounds us though it often goes unnamed. Whiteness positions itself against blackness, indigenousness, Asian-ness, Hispanic-ness, and Arab-ness; in so doing, it fades into the background by highlighting the differences of nonwhites. This is what we mean when we say that whiteness is racial domination normalized.

White Privilege

If whiteness is normal, then nonwhiteness is abnormal. Owing to centuries of racial domination, whiteness is infused with an essence of the positive, and this essence can exist only through its negation: an essence of the negative that marks nonwhiteness.[62] Look up "white" in any dictionary, and you will learn that the term means "the absence of color," as well as "free from spot or blemish," "innocent," "not intended to cause harm" (as in a "white lie"), "favorable," and "fortunate." According to the most recent version of *The Merriam-Webster Dictionary*, "white" also can mean "marked by upright fairness," as in "That's mighty white of you." Under the antonyms for "white," we find "black." Upon looking up "black," we see that it means "very dark color" as well as "dirty," "soiled," "wicked," "indicative of condemnation,"

"Satanic" (as in "black magic"), "calamitous," "marked by the occurrence of disaster," "sullen," and "grotesque" (as in "black humor").

Although whiteness permeates all areas of society—we breathe it in every day—it seems weightless to many of us. Like fish in the ocean, who fail to feel the weight of the water, whites tend to take their whiteness for granted. Conversely, for many who are not white, whiteness is very much a visible reality. As one sociologist has put it, "whiteness, as a set of normative cultural practices, is visible most clearly to those it definitively excludes and those to whom it does violence. Those who are securely housed within its borders usually do not examine it."[63]

Though they may not notice it, many white people benefit from belonging to the dominant race. White privilege is the collection of unearned cultural, political, economic, and social advantages and privileges possessed by people of Anglo-European descent or by those who pass as such. One need not look far to find substantive evidence of it. At the cultural level, white privilege marks the reactions even of those reading this book. "I am so tired of hearing all of this," some might say. "I am so tired of opening up this book—or walking into this classroom—and hearing continually about racism!" Most of the time, white students are the ones who voice this complaint, a complaint that itself is a product of white privilege. (For this reason, they are not to blame for it! One must conceive of white privilege as so deeply ingrained as to be almost automatic; hence the importance of thoughtful, critical self-reflection, which this work, in a constructive and problem-solving spirit, aims to stimulate.) Nonwhites, whose own livelihood depends on overcoming racial domination, do not have much of a choice in the matter; their weariness comes not from discussions of racial domination, but from the thing itself.

Yet another way in which white privilege manifests itself is through the discomfort many whites feel simply at being spoken of as "whites" or as "white people." "I am an individual," they reply. "I am a human being. Why are you racially categorizing me?" Sometimes the very description "white people" feels to them like an accusation or a hostile gesture, as if a racial rebuke—"You white people are all racists!"—were soon to follow. And sometimes whites' awkwardness at being described this way shifts into aggression: "You must not like us! Perhaps you yourself are anti-white! Perhaps you yourself are the racist!" Again, nonwhites do not have the privilege of denying or repudiating their own designation as racialized beings.

White privilege also is evident in the tendency of many whites to deny that certain circumstances or events are "racial" to begin with. The maddening thing about race is that it often is impossible to know with complete certainty whether something is really "about race." You are treated rudely at a restaurant. Is it because you are Mexican American or because you are a woman or because the server is having a bad day—or all three? You get pulled over by the police. Is it because you are a young black man or because you were speeding—or both? Because it often is impossible to say, smart and good-natured people often heatedly disagree about whether certain interactions really were about race. And maybe what is most revealing about those disagreements is not who is right or who is wrong but what about our own experiences makes us think one way or another. Because many white people often go about their lives without feeling the weight of race on

Because many white people often go about their lives without feeling the weight of race on their shoulders, they sometimes are more reluctant to see how race might color a situation.

their shoulders, they sometimes are more reluctant to see how race might color a situation. Similarly, because many nonwhite people have had multiple experiences guided by their minority status, they may be more likely to suggest that, yes, you were treated rudely or pulled over because of the color of your skin. Our experiences give us a frame through which we see the world, and that frame can tell us a lot about the way we have been uniquely privileged or disadvantaged. There is nothing wrong with thinking that something really is or is not about race, but we need to be thoughtful about why we think the way we do—and we need to wonder, too, if our understanding of the world jibes with general social patterns and with history. We all "play race cards." But some of us do not recognize our card as "raced," and that is a privilege associated with the lightness of whiteness.

It is important to recognize that however significant these aspects of white privilege may be, its benefits by no means are limited to the ability to engage in cultural denial. Social scientists also have amassed a substantial amount of evidence that whites, strictly because of their whiteness, reap considerable advantages of a more material kind—for instance, when buying and selling a house, choosing a neighborhood in which to live, getting a job and moving up the corporate ladder, securing a first-class education, and seeking medical care. That whites accumulate more property and earn more income than members of minority populations, that they possess immeasurably more political power, and that they enjoy greater access to the country's cultural, social, medical, legal, and economic resources are well-documented, and indisputable, historical and sociological facts.[64]

Consider the links between race, neighborhoods, and safety. Even after adjusting for income and occupation, whites are far less likely to be exposed to toxic chemicals and pollutants than are Latinos or African Americans. One reason for this is that white neighborhoods are far less likely to house institutions of pollution, such as garbage dumps, trash incinerators, and chemical plants. (In Houston, Texas, 100 percent of the city's garbage dumps are located in black neighborhoods!) We can also see white privilege at work within the criminal justice system. Although most drug addicts are white, African Americans are four times more likely to be arrested on drug charges than whites. In the federal prison system, whites enjoy sentences that are, on average, 20 percent shorter than those given African Americans guilty of the exact same crime.[65] We will explore in detail how white privilege pervades other realms of social life throughout this book.

Peggy McIntosh understands white privilege as "an invisible package of unearned assets which I can count on cashing in each day, but about which I was 'meant' to remain oblivious. White privilege is like an invisible weightless knapsack of special provisions, assurances, tools, maps, guides, codebooks, passports, visas, clothing, compass, emergency kit, and blank checks."[66] McIntosh, a white woman, goes on to provide a list of "special circumstances and conditions" attached to her own skin-color privilege.

This list demonstrates many ways in which white people benefit from their skin privilege. And, in turn, if white people benefit from their skin privilege, people of color are disadvantaged by it. Whites have accumulated many opportunities as a result of racial domination, but people of color have suffered from disaccumulation. If we talk about "black poverty," then we must also talk about white affluence; if we speak of "Hispanic unemployment," then we must also keep in mind white employment; and if we ponder public policies for people of color, then we must also critically examine the public policies that directly benefit white people. In all cases, one group's privilege results in other groups' disadvantage.[67] It is precisely for this reason that, when asked by a reporter his views on America's "Negro problem," African American novelist Richard Wright replied, "There isn't any Negro problem; there is only a white problem."[68]

White Antiracists

Some white people are fully aware of how the current system of racial domination benefits them and work to uphold such a system; they intentionally invest in their whiteness. Many others, who do not recognize their privilege, unknowingly support a system of racial domination that disadvantages people of color, unintentionally investing in their whiteness. Important here is the ideal of color-blindness. While some confuse physical differences with obvious racial differences, as we discussed earlier, others err in the opposite direction by claiming to ignore all racial markers. "I don't see color at all," they declare. "I'm color-blind!" Such avowals usually are well intentioned—indeed, many of us have been taught, since childhood, to "ignore race"—but, upon closer inspection, we realize that color-blindness is an illogical proposition, for it requires the simultaneous recognition and nonrecognition of racial markers (such as skin color). As law professor Neil Gotanda has pointed out, color-blindness "is self-contradictory, because it is impossible not to think about a subject without having first thought about it at least a little. . . . To be racially color-blind . . . is to ignore what one has already noticed. The medically color-blind individual never perceives color in the first place; the racially color-blind individual perceives race and then ignores it."[69]

Color-blindness would be the ideal response to a society unaffected by racial domination.[70] But, sadly, ours is not such a society. Accordingly, color-blindness is not only a self-contradictory code—"At once I see and fail to see your blackness"—but also a fundamentally wrong response to racial injustice, one that "fosters the systematic denial of racial subordination and the psychological repression of an individual's recognition of that subordination, thereby allowing it to continue."[71] The opposite of color-blindness is not a kind of racial exaggeration, where all you notice about a person is her or his race. Nor is it a demobilizing sense of racial guilt, where you wallow in the stereotypes you harbor. Learning about racial domination and about whiteness and white privilege can lead many whites in particular to think their reaction ought to be "I am guilty! I am the bearer of racial sins!" But nothing could be further from the truth—or further from our own intentions in writing this textbook. Racial guilt is a faulty emotion for two reasons. First, it rests on an erroneous premise, namely, that responsibility for racial injustice is a collective matter that can be passed on across generations and, indeed, through one's blood. There is no such thing as collective guilt. Each person is responsible—and culpable—for his or her own actions, not for anyone else's. Second, racial guilt is problematic because it is a destructive, not a constructive, emotion. It does not stimulate forward-looking, problem-solving modes of reflection and action. It does not lead in a positive direction.

If racial exaggeration and racial guilt are not the answer, then what is? The opposite of color-blindness is simple honesty: honesty about our modes of perception and racialized ways of thinking, as well as about the true nature of our world, a world rife with racial inequality. Noticing race means observing a long history of misery, exploitation, and inequality; recognizing systems of social meanings that have affixed themselves to different skin pigments; and perhaps confronting stereotypes and misunderstandings we hold deep inside. At bottom, it means shifting from a nonracist stance ("I don't have a racist bone in my body!") to a proactively antiracist one.

Some whites recognize their own white privilege and disavow—in some cases, actively struggle against—the racial structures from which they draw their privilege. In fact, they leverage their very advantages in the fight to dismantle racial domination. As one sociologist has aptly said with white antiracists in mind, "We do not choose our parents, but we do choose our politics."[72] Throughout the history of the United States, some whites have fought racism. Charles Sumner was one such person. Sumner served in the U.S. Senate in the mid-nineteenth century and was recognized widely as a powerful orator and a radical abolitionist. Advocating a civil rights bill that sought to ensure equal treatment for African Americans after the fall of slavery, Sumner once addressed the Senate with these stirring words: "There is beauty in art, in literature, in science, and in every triumph of intelligence, all of which I covet for my country; but there is a higher beauty still—in relieving the poor, in elevating the downtrodden, and being a succor to the oppressed. There is true grandeur in an example of justice, making the rights of all the same as our own, and beating down prejudice, like Satan, under our feet." The civil rights bill did not succeed, but Sumner doggedly pursued his mission. On his deathbed, surrounded by friends and fellow politicians, Sumner repeated an urgent message three times over: "You must take care of the civil rights bill—my bill, the civil rights bill—don't let it fail!"[73]

There was also Bill Moore, a white postman working in Baltimore during the Civil Rights Movement. When the governor of Mississippi, Ross Barnett, refused to desegregate the University of Mississippi, Moore staged a one-man march from

William Lewis Moore staging a lone protest against racial segregation.

Chattanooga, Tennessee, to Jackson, Mississippi. Playing up his identity as a letter carrier, Moore sought to "deliver a letter" arguing for integration to Governor Barrett. Wearing two placards on his back and chest—one reading "Equal Rights for All: Mississippi or Bust," the other, in reference to segregated diners, reading, "Black and White: Eat at Joe's"—Moore began his march on April 21, 1963.[74]

He was murdered three days later. Found dead and abandoned next to a northern Alabama highway, Moore had been shot twice in the head and once in the neck at point-blank range. He was thirty-three and a father of three. Likewise, Charles Sumner paid dearly for threatening white supremacy. In 1856, two days after delivering a speech that criticized proslavery groups in Kansas, Sumner was beaten unconscious by Preston Brooks, a congressman from South Carolina. Brooks approached Sumner as he worked at his desk in the nearly empty Senate chamber and smashed his thick wooden cane over Sumner's head. Brooks continued to assault Sumner until his cane broke. Sumner suffered massive head trauma and would not return to the Senate for three years.

The sacrifices made by Sumner and Moore should not overshadow the sacrifices borne by hundreds of nonwhite women and men who fought against slavery, segregation, and other racist structures. For every white person beaten or killed for fighting against racism, there are hundreds of people of color who suffered equally. We speak here of the passion of Charles Sumner and Bill Moore only to illustrate that throughout the history of the United States, white people have aligned with people of color to struggle against racial domination.

RACE IS A SOCIAL REALITY

James Baldwin, the great American novelist, poet, and social critic, once observed, "Color is not a human or personal reality; it is a political reality."[75] Baldwin was correct: race, as we have just seen, is not a biological reality. It is a political reality, or what we might call a social construction. *Race is a symbolic category, based on phenotype or ancestry and constructed according to specific social and historical contexts, that is misrecognized as a natural category.* This definition deserves to be unpacked.

Symbolic Category
A symbolic category belongs to the realm of ideas, meaning-making, and language, as opposed to the realm of nature and biology. It is something that is actively

created and re-created by human beings rather than pregiven. (By "pregiven," we mean something that objectively exists and has simply to be assigned a name.) Symbolic categories mark differences between grouped people or things. In so doing, they actually bring those people or things into existence.[76] (Emphatically, this does not mean that refusing to recognize racial groups created in the course of centuries of oppression, colonialism, and scientific manipulation will somehow lead those races—and racial inequality—magically to disappear.)

For example, the term "Native American" is a symbolic category that encompasses all peoples indigenous to America. But the term "Native American" did not exist before non–Native Americans, Europeans, came to the Americas. Choctaws, Crows, Iroquois, Hopis, Dakotas, Yakimas, Utes, and dozens of other people belonging to indigenous tribes existed. "Native American" is a category that subsumes all these tribes under one *homogenizing heading*. ("Homogenizing" means "combining different things under the same category.") Thus, the term "Native American" flattens out the immensely different histories, languages, traditional beliefs, and rich cultural practices of various indigenous tribes. The term transforms the multitude of indigenous people into one single category of people. Similarly, people have traveled from one geographical territory to the next since the beginning of humanity; however, it was not until national borders were erected and strictly enforced that such people became known through the symbolic categories of "immigrants" or "refugees."

The same is true of other racial categories. In naming different races, racial categories create different races. In the United States, the current racial taxonomy, or race-based classification system, delineates five major groups: Native American and Alaskan Natives, Asians and Pacific Islanders, Africans Americans (or blacks), Hispanics (or Latinos), and Caucasians (or whites). This taxonomy is imposed by nearly all the institutions in the United States—from political institutions like the U.S. Bureau of the Census, which asks citizens to check one or more boxes next to racial categories, to educational institutions like universities, which carry out surveys to obtain the racial composition of their schools.

The racial taxonomies that powerful institutions impose sometimes conflict with other racial taxonomies, including those embraced by people in their everyday lives.[77] An institution, such as the university, might assign you a racial or ethnic label that may not align with the racial or ethnic label you have assigned yourself.[78] This certainly happens to multiracial people, for whom "checking a single box" simply does not accurately reflect their full sense of who they are. In the 2000 Census, biracial citizens who checked white as well as another, nonwhite category were categorized as belonging only to the nonwhite group, an outcome that certainly conflicted with their own self-identity.[79]

Now, if racial categories create different races, then would eradicating those categories—refusing to recognize racial groups that were created through centuries of oppression, colonialism, political discourse, and scientific manipulation—result in those races (and racial inequality) magically disappearing? Of course not. The process of racial misrecognition is found at both the structural and individual levels and, most important, is a historical process. It follows, then, that the practice of refusing to recognize the misrecognition, as with France's aversion to acknowledging racial categories or the prematurely celebratory declaration of a "color-blind" or "race free" America, is an ineffective and wrongheaded response to a world itself not color-blind. In many cases, the refusal to recognize race, social construction though it is, only exacerbates racial inequalities by rendering anti-racist programs impossible.

Phenotype or Ancestry

Race, then, is a symbolic category. It is also based on phenotype or ancestry. A person's phenotype is her or his physical appearance and constitution, including skeletal structure, height, hair texture, eye color, and skin tone. A person's ancestry is her or his family lineage, which often includes tribal, regional, or national affiliations. The symbolic category of race organizes people into bounded groupings based on their phenotype, ancestry, or both. It is difficult to say which matters more, phenotype or ancestry, in determining racial membership in the United States. In some settings, ancestry trumps phenotype; in others, the opposite is the case.

Recent immigrants often are pigeonholed into one of the dominant racial categories because of their phenotype; however, many resist this classification based on their ancestry. Upon arriving in the United States, many first-generation West Indian immigrants, quite familiar with racism against African Americans, actively resist the label "black." Despite their efforts, many are considered African American because of their dark skin (that is, they "look" black to the American eye). The children of West African immigrants, many of whom are disconnected from their parents' ancestries, more readily accept the label "black."[80] Moreover, many individuals with mixed heritage often are treated as though they belong to only one "race." For instance, many people think superstar golfer Tiger Woods is African American because of his darker skin tone. Woods, however, does not identify as African American, since he is part white, part black, part American Indian, part Thai, and part Chinese. In fact, as a child, Woods called himself a "Cabalinasian," a term he invented to reflect his multiracial roots.[81]

Tiger Woods constructs his racial identity through his ancestry, regardless of the assumptions people make about him based on his phenotype. Some people, however, rely on their phenotype to form a racial identity, though they often are grouped in another racial category based on their ancestry. Susie Guillory Phipps, a blond-haired, blue-eyed woman who always considered herself "white," discovered, upon glancing at her birth certificate while applying for a passport, that her native state, Louisiana, considered her "black." How could this be? The reason was that Louisiana grouped people into racial categories according to the "one thirty-second rule," a rule that stated that anyone who was one thirty-second black—regardless of what he or she looked like—was legally "black." In 1982, Susie Guillory Phipps sued Louisiana for the right to be white. She lost. The state genealogist discovered that Phipps was the great-great-great-great-grandchild of a white Alabama plantation owner and his black mistress and, therefore (although all of Phipps's other ancestors were white), "black." (This outlandish law finally was erased from the books in 1983.) In this case, Phipps's ancestry was more important in determining her race, as identified by the state, than was her phenotype.[82]

Social and Historical Contexts

Race is such a fundamental part of American life that we tend to think of it as a natural boundary, one that has existed in the same form throughout history and across all other societies. But this is not true. Racial taxonomies are bound to their specific social and historical contexts.

The racial categories that exist in America are nonexistent in other parts of the globe. In South Africa, racial groups are organized around three dominant categories: white, black, and "coloured." The coloured category was designed during apartheid—South Africa's system of legalized segregation, now abolished—to include all "mixed-race" people. In Brazil, five racial categories are employed in the official census: *blanco* (white), *pardo* (brown), *preto* (black), *amarelo* (Asian), and *indígena* (indigenous). However, in everyday usage, many Brazilians identify themselves and one another through several other racial terms—including *moreno* (another type of brown), *moreno claro* (light brown), *negro* (another type of black), and *claro* (light)—which have much more to do with the tint of one's skin than with one's ancestry. Before racial language was outlawed by the Communist regime, Chinese racial taxonomies were based first and foremost on blood purity, then on hair, then odor, then brain mass, then finally, and of least importance, skin color, which, according to the taxonomy, was divided into no fewer than ten shades ("pure Chinese" identified by "pure yellow"). And in Japan, members of a group called the Burakamin are considered "unclean" and are thought to constitute a separate race, although it is impossible to distinguish someone with Burakamin ancestry from the rest of the Japanese population.[83]

Cross-national comparisons, then, reveal that systems of racial classification vary greatly from one country to the next. (The same cannot be said of systems of natural classification.) Racial categories, therefore, are *place-specific*, bound to certain geographical and social contexts.

Racial categories also are *time-specific*, changing between different historical time periods. Historians have found that in times of antiquity, the historical period before the Middle Ages, the main social division for Greeks and Romans was not between people of different skin color, or even between men and women. During that time, the key social division was between masters and slaves. To us, a master and slave of antiquity would look nearly identical, sharing similar skin color, hair color, and body build; however, to the Greeks and Romans of those days, masters and slaves almost were different species.[84] And although most Americans of European ancestry today would be considered white, their admittance into the "white race" was much less certain only 100 years ago, when ethnic distinctions among European immigrant groups—Poles, Germans, Italians, Russian Jews—were much more pronounced and consequential than they are today.[85] That is why many social scientists have asserted that we must grapple with "the historical specificity of race in the modern world" in order to gain an accurate understanding of racial phenomena.[86]

Misrecognized as Natural

The last part of the definition we have been unpacking has to do with a process of naturalization. This word signifies a metamorphosis of sorts, where something created by humans is mistaken as something dictated by nature. Racial categories

not always race

are naturalized when these symbolic groupings, the products of specific historical contexts, are wrongly conceived of as natural and unchangeable. We misrecognize race as natural when we begin to think that racial cleavages and inequalities can be explained by pointing to attributes somehow inherent in the race itself (as if they were biological) instead of understanding how social powers, economic forces, political institutions, and cultural practices have resulted in these divisions.

Naturalized categories are powerful, for they are the categories through which we understand the world around us. Such categories divide the world along otherwise arbitrary lines and make us believe there is nothing at all arbitrary about such a division. They convince us that otherwise illegitimate boundaries erected between groups of people actually are legitimate. What is more, when categories become naturalized, alternative ways of viewing the world begin to appear more and more impossible. Why, we might ask, should we have only five main racial groups? Why don't we have ninety-five? Why should we divide people according to their skin color? Why is ancestry so important? Why not base our racial categories on regions—north, south, east, and west? You might find these suggestive questions silly, and, indeed, they are. But they are no sillier than the idea that people should be sorted into different racial groups according to skin color or blood composition. To twist French sociologist Pierre Bourdieu's phrase, we might say, "When it comes to race, one never doubts enough."[87]

The system of racial classification at work in America today is not the only system imaginable, nor is it the only system that has existed in the life of the United States. Race is far from fixed; rather, its forms have shifted and fluctuated over time, depending on the social, economic, political, and cultural pressures of the day.[88] Indeed, a multiracial movement today is challenging America's dominant racial categories (which remained relatively stable during the latter half of the twentieth century), as people of mixed-race heritage refuse to accept as given the state's racial classification system.[89]

Research by sociologists Aliya Saperstein of Stanford University and Andrew Penner of the University of California at Irvine shows just how fluid a person's race can be—even over the span of his or her lifetime. In a series of papers, Saperstein and Penner draw on longitudinal survey data that followed 12,000 Americans since they were teenagers.[90] Each time they interviewed somebody, the survey interviewers had to identify the race of the person. Over the survey's timespan of nineteen years, one in five persons "changed races"—that is, people were identified by interviewers as having one racial identity at one point in time but years later were categorized differently. What explains these changes? The authors observe that "all else being equal, including how they had been racially classified before, respondents who were unemployed, had children outside of marriage, or lived in the inner city were less likely to be classified as white and more likely to be classified as black. . . . These changes line up in ways that reflect widespread racial stereotypes. Interviewers became likelier to see someone as black the more the respondents' situations fit the stereotype of black people—and vice-versa for white people. The studies we have conducted show that while race shapes our life experiences, our life experiences also shape our race."[91] The researchers even found, after analyzing thousands of death certificates, that people who died of cirrhosis of the liver from excessive drinking were more likely to be recorded as American Indian on their death certificates and homicide victims were more likely to be recorded as African American, even after controlling for how the deceased had been racially classified while alive.[92]

Race is not natural in the slightest respect. In fact, we can regard race as a *well-founded fiction*. It is a fiction because it has no natural bearing, but it is well founded since most people in society provide race with a real existence and have come to see the world through its lens. Racial taxonomies often lead us to conclude that we are inherently different from one another, that nature dictates the separation of people. In truth, only society can be blamed for that. Race is social through and through.

This section opened with a quotation from James Baldwin, and it is fitting that it close with one as well: "For the sake of one's children, in order to minimize the bill that they must pay, one must be careful not to take refuge in any delusion—and the value placed on the color of the skin is always and everywhere and forever a delusion. I know that what I am asking is impossible. But in our time, as in every time, the impossible is the least that one can demand—and one is, after all, emboldened by the spectacle of human history in general, and American Negro history in particular, for it testifies to nothing less than the perpetual achievement of the impossible."[93]

ETHNICITY AND NATIONALITY

The categories of ethnicity and nationality are intrinsically bound up with race. Ethnicity refers to a shared lifestyle informed by cultural, historical, religious, and/or national affiliations. Nationality is equated with citizenship—membership in a specific politically delineated territory controlled by a government.[94] Like race, both ethnicity and nationality are symbolic categories.

Race, ethnicity, and nationality are overlapping symbolic categories that influence how we see the world around us, how we view ourselves, and how we divide "us" from "them." The categories are mutually reinforcing: each category educates, upholds, and is informed by the others. That is why these three categories cannot be understood in isolation from one another.[95] For example, if one identifies as ethnically Norwegian, which, for that person, might include a shared lifestyle comprising Norwegian history and folklore, language, cultural rituals and festivals, and food (such as meatcakes, lamb and cabbage stew, potato dumplings, cod, and lutefisk), that person may also reference a nationality, based in the country of Norway, as well as a racial group, white, since nearly all people of Norwegian descent would be classified as white by American standards. Here, ethnicity is informed by nationality (either past or present) and signifies race.

Importantly, ethnicity, at least in the definition provided at the beginning of this section, only makes sense in a U.S.-specific context. In the early twentieth century, it was invented by American social thinkers to make sense of the new immigration from southern and eastern Europe. How were the new European immigrants to be classified in relation to whites and nonwhites? How was their difference from the Anglo-Saxon norm to be signified without lumping them into the same "racially Other" category as blacks or American Indians? No other country deployed the concept in quite this way, as an answer to this precise analytic challenge. To export the race-ethnicity-nationality complex to other social or historical settings would be deeply U.S.-centric and misleading. But in the American context at least, it often is useful to deploy this complex when studying the intricate dynamics of societal classification.

In the United States, ethnicity often carves out distinctions and identities within racial groups. Ten people can be considered Asian American according to our modern racial taxonomy; however, those people might have parents or grandparents who emigrated to the United States from ten different countries, including Thailand, Vietnam, Cambodia, Singapore, China, South Korea, North Korea, Japan, Indonesia, and Laos. They might speak different languages, uphold different traditions, worship different deities, enjoy very different kinds of food, and go through diverse experiences. What is more, many Asian countries have histories of conflict with each other (such as China and Japan, and North and South Korea). As such, we cannot assume that a Chinese American and a Japanese American have similar lifestyles or see the world through a shared vision simply because both are classified as "Asian" under American racial rubrics. Therefore, just as race, ethnicity, and nationality cannot be separated from one another, neither can all three categories be collapsed into one.

Although ethnic affiliations often are informed by national affiliations, ethnicity can also transcend national borders. Jewish ethnic affiliation encompasses a wide array of people who vary in terms of nationality (from those living in the United States and Canada to those living in Israel, Eastern Europe, Argentina, or Mexico), political commitments (from the far Right to the far Left), languages (from English to Hebrew to Polish), and religious beliefs and practices (from Eastern Orthodox to Hasidic to atheist). Despite these differences—which cut across national and religious boundaries—many Jews see themselves as bound together in a group, sharing a common history, culture, and ethnic identity.

Ethnicity is a very fluid, layered, and situational construct. One might feel very American when voting, very Irish when celebrating St. Patrick's Day, very Catholic when attending Easter mass, very "New Yorker" when riding the subway, and very northern when visiting a relative in South Carolina. Race, too, can be performed to varying degrees.[96] One might act "very black" when celebrating Kwanzaa with relatives but may repress her blackness while in a business meeting with white colleagues. As we explain in more detail in Chapter 10, race and ethnicity are both marked and made. We may create, reproduce, accept, or actively resist systems of racial classification; we may choose to accentuate our ethnicity or racial identity. But in many cases, our choices, our racial or ethnic performances, will have little impact on how we are labeled by others. A person born to Chinese parents but adopted, at infancy, by a Jamaican-American couple might identify as ethnically Jamaican. She might enjoy Jamaican cuisine, read Jamaican literature, listen to Jamaican music, and study Jamaican history. However, although her adopted parents may be classified as racially black, she would be classified as Asian, her race decided for her.[97]

The degree to which an individual can slip and slide through multiple ethnic identities—this point is crucial—depends on the degree to which those identities are stigmatized. White Americans typically enjoy a high degree of fluidity and freedom when self-identifying ethnically. They can choose to give equal weight to all aspects of their ethnicity or to highlight certain parts while deemphasizing others. The same person could identify as either "half-Italian, quarter-Polish, quarter-Swiss," or "Polish and Italian," or just "Italian," for instance. Many people of color do not enjoy the same degree of choice. Someone whose father is Arab American and whose mother is Dutch American could not so easily get away with ethnically identifying only as "Dutch."

In some instances, nonwhites may perform ethnicity in order to resist certain racial classifications (as when African migrants teach their children to speak with an accent so they might avoid being identified as African Americans); in other instances, they might, in an opposite way, attempt to cleanse themselves of all ethnic markers (be they linguistic, religious, or cultural in nature) to avoid becoming victims of discrimination or stigmatization. Either way, their efforts may prove futile, since those belonging to dominated racial groups have considerably less ethnic agency than those belonging to the dominant (and hence normalized) racial group. (This is why some scholars have observed that, in its popular usage, the term "Hispanic" is deployed much more often as a racial, not ethnic, classification, while Hispanic subcategories, such as "Mexican" or "Cuban," are treated as ethnic markers.)[98] In fact, many (white) Americans tend to focus on ethnic differences within the white race while treating blacks, Latinos, and Asian Americans as if they had no ethnicity and minimizing cultural or historical differences between (for black Americans) Haitians, Jamaicans, Ethiopians, Trinidadians, Angolans, or Nigerians, or between (for Latinos) Puerto Ricans, Cubans, Mexicans, Peruvians, or Dominicans, or between (for Asians) Laotians, Indonesians, Cambodians, Vietnamese, Chinese, and Japanese people.[99]

One reason why race and ethnicity are relatively decoupled for white Americans but bound tightly together for nonwhite Americans is found in the history of the nation's immigration policies and practices. Until the late nineteenth century, immigration to America was deregulated and encouraged (with the exception of Chinese exclusion laws). However, at the turn of the century, native-born white Americans, who blamed immigrants for the rise of urban slums, crime, and class conflict, began calling for immigration restrictions. Popular and political support for restrictions swelled and resulted, after World War I, in the development of a strict immigration policy, culminating in the Johnson-Reed Act of 1924.

America's new immigration law, complete with national quotas and racial restrictions on citizenship,

America's Immigration Act of 1921 imposed national quotas and racial restrictions on citizenship.

would fundamentally realign the country's racial taxonomy. "The national origins system classified Europeans as nationalities and assigned quotas in a hierarchy of desirability," writes historian Mae Ngai in *Impossible Subjects: Illegal Aliens and the Making of Modern America*, "but at the same time the law deemed all Europeans to be part of a white race, distinct from those considered to be not white. Euro-American identities turned both on ethnicity—that is, a nationality-based cultural identity that is defined as capable of transformation and assimilation—and on a racial identity defined by whiteness."[100]

Nonwhites, however, either were denied entry into the United States (as was the case for Asian migrants) or were associated with illegal immigration through harsh border-control policies (as was the case for Mexicans). Indeed, the immigration laws of the 1920s applied the newly formed concept of "national origin" only to European nations; those classified as members of the "colored races" were conceived as bereft of a country of origin. The result, Ngai observes, was that "unlike Euro Americans, whose ethnic and racial identities became uncoupled during the 1920s, Asians' and Mexicans' ethnic and racial identities remain conjoined."[101]

The history of America's immigration policy underscores the intimate connection between race, ethnicity, citizenship, and national origin. Racial categories often are defined and changed by national lawmakers, as citizenship has been extended or retracted depending on one's racial ascription. The U.S. justice system has decided dozens of cases in ways that have solidified certain racial classifications in the law. During the nineteenth and twentieth centuries, legal cases handed down rulings that officially recognized Japanese, Chinese, Burmese, Filipinos, Koreans, Native Americans, and mixed-race individuals as "not white." In 1897, a Texas federal court ruled that Mexicans were legally "white." And Arabs and Indian Americans (individuals who emigrated from India or who are of Indian descent) have been classified as "white" at some points in time and "not white" at other points.

For instance, Indian Americans were deemed white by law in the case of *U.S. v. Dolla* in 1910. Abdullah Dolla emigrated from Calcutta to New York City. A businessman, he worked in Georgia selling Indian merchandise. While applying for citizenship, Dolla argued that he was white because he was accepted as such by fellow Georgia citizens. He was found to be white and granted citizenship, and this ruling set a precedent, legally classifying Indian Americans as white. However, that ruling was challenged thirteen years later in *U.S. v. Bhagat Singh Thind*. Bhagat Singh Thind was an immigrant from Punjab, India, who paid his way through the University of California—Berkeley by spending his summers working for a lumber mill in Oregon. When World War I broke out, he joined the U.S. Army and was honorably discharged in 1918. Nevertheless, Thind was denied citizenship because the court found him (and therefore other Indian Americans) "not white."

The United States often has been thought of as a country of immigrants, a country that asks for "your tired, your poor, your huddled masses yearning to breathe free," as inscribed in Emma Lazarus's famous poem, "The New Colossus," and displayed on a plaque at the Statue of Liberty. Yet, for over 150 years, the United States denied citizenship—and all the rights that came with it—to thousands of hopeful immigrants because they were not white. As law professor Ian Haney López has observed in his book *White by Law,* "in its first words on the subject of citizenship, Congress in 1790 restricted naturalization to 'white persons.' Though the requirements for naturalization changed frequently thereafter, this racial prerequisite to citizenship endured for over a century and a half, remaining in force until 1952. From the earliest years of this country until just a generation ago, being a 'white person' was a condition for acquiring citizenship."[102]

Citizenship is accompanied by many social privileges, such as the right to vote when one is so inclined, the right to own property when one has the means, the right to legal protection when one is victimized, the right to receive medical treatment when one is sick, and the right to receive an education when one is young. Because they could not obtain citizenship, many nonwhites lacked access to these basic privileges.

Blacks were granted the right to naturalize (meaning, in this context, admittance to citizenship) in 1870. However, that right was denied other nonwhites until the 1940s, when Congress began granting it in piecemeal fashion. In 1952, Congress passed the Immigration and Nationality Act, which reorganized U.S. naturalization law and forbade denying citizenship on the basis of race. While the Immigration and Nationality Act abolished race-based restrictions on citizenship, it did retain a quota system that limited the number of people who could immigrate to America from certain countries.

Briefly examining how the legal definitions of white and nonwhite have changed over the years demonstrates the unstable and fluid nature of racial categories. It also shows how our legal system helps to construct race. Legal cases that determined people's race in order to determine their eligibility for U.S. citizenship—what were known as prerequisite cases—had poisonous symbolic consequences. Deemed worthy of citizenship, white people were understood as upstanding, law abiding, moral, and intelligent. Conversely, nonwhite people, from whom citizenship was withheld, were thought of as base, criminal, untrustworthy, and of lesser intelligence. For most of American history, courts determined race, and race determined nationality; thus, nationality can be understood only within the context of U.S. racial and ethnic conflict.[103]

Today, many foreign-born residents still face great barriers when applying for U.S. citizenship. Compare U.S. naturalization rates with those of Canada. Around the time the Immigration and Nationality Act was signed into law, Canadian and U.S. naturalization rates were identical: approximately 80 percent of foreign-born residents were granted citizenship in each country, and both countries opened their doors to immigrants from Asia, the Caribbean, and Latin America. However, since that time, U.S. naturalization rates have declined rapidly, while Canadian rates have experienced little change. In 1980, only 50 percent of foreign-born residents were naturalized in the United States, while 70 percent were naturalized in Canada. In 1990, U.S. naturalization rates fell to 40 percent, while Canadian rates remained the same. And in 2000, Canadian rates climbed to 75 percent, while U.S. rates remained around 40 percent. Over the past three decades, Canada has awarded most of its foreign-born population citizenship, while the United States has not naturalized the majority of its foreign-born population.[104]

THINKING LIKE A SOCIOLOGIST

Understanding race in the complex world in which we all live does not simply mean memorizing certain terms, statistics, and historical events. It means breaking with commonsense comprehensions of the world, apprehending society with a sophisticated mindset that takes into account economic, political, cultural, and social forces that operate on a national and global scale. It means approaching the world skeptically and critically, rejecting overly simplified explanations, and evaluating and reevaluating the nature of things with a new outlook. It means, in a phrase, cultivating a sociological imagination.

American sociologist C. Wright Mills coined the term "sociological imagination" in 1959.[105] By this, he meant one's ability to understand everyday life not through personal circumstances, but through the broader historical forces that structure and direct it. The sociological imagination allows its possessor to discover larger forces at work in the smallest of social scenarios—in one's home life, one's romantic adventures, even in one's innermost thoughts; thus, it unearths "the social at the heart of the individual, the impersonal beneath the intimate, the universal buried deep within the most particular."[106] As a result, individuals who think with the sociological imagination can perceive how their choices, and the choices of others, are constrained and enabled by social structures and processes. Once this is accomplished, they can transform personal problems into public issues.

Perhaps the single most dangerous threat to developing a sociological imagination is our failure to put aside our self-centeredness. It is a perplexing and powerful truth that to fully understand ourselves we must get over ourselves. In particular, conversations about race too often are encumbered by proverbial and petty debates over terminology. Countless conversations about race remain on a superficial level because someone focuses on a *word* rather than on the *thing*. Thus, some indigenous people prefer the term "Native American"; some prefer "American Indian"; and some say they belong to a "tribe," others to a "nation." Some people of European descent prefer the term "white"; others say "European American" or "Caucasian." Some people of African descent refer to themselves as "black"; others prefer "African American"; still others use variants such as "Afro-American" or "Black American." Some Hispanic Americans prefer "Latino/a" to "Hispanic," "Mexican American," or "Chicano/a"; others feel differently. Some are offended at the use of "Americans" (as opposed to "North Americans") to refer to all people living in the United States. Some say "minorities," others "people of color," "nonwhites," or "underrepresented groups." Some hyphenate terms; others do not. Some capitalize "Black" and "White"; others do not. Some place the word "race" inside quotation marks; others do not. You probably have opinions about many or all of these choices. Some have very strong opinions backed by thoughtful justifications. But it's not about you.

In truth, there is no right or wrong racial label. Indeed, ten Hispanic Americans might offer ten different racial labels for themselves. If there is no superior racial terminology—and we aren't speaking here of hateful epithets, which should never be used—it is because the foundation on which this terminology rests, race, is nothing more than a well-founded fiction. Arguing with each other about racial terminology breeds a spirit of uncertainty and fear, a spirit that forces mouths—and minds—to close. If so many people stutter nervously when talking about race, it is because they do not want to say the wrong thing and have someone pounce irritably on a phrase they used, declaring, "That term offends me!" Let us choose wisely the battles in which we engage. There are times to grow outraged and to make our outrage known. But rather than waste our energy on racial labels and on what offends us, let us instead channel our outrage to bigger problems. Let us grow outraged at racial domination, white supremacy, and rampant inequality. If we grow offended at a racial term, let us evaluate the system that created it, picking a fight with the system, not with the word itself —or with the one who uttered it. Changing words, after all, doesn't amount to much. W. E. B. Du Bois knew well this fact. Writing in 1928 to a young reader who objected to Du Bois's use of the term "Negro," a common term for African Americans at the time, Du Bois advised, "Do not . . . make the all too common error of mistaking names for things. Names are only conventional signs for identifying things. Things are the reality that counts. If a thing is despised, either because of ignorance or because it is despicable, you will not alter matters by changing its name. . . . It is not the name—it's the Thing that counts. Come on, Kid, let's go get the Thing!"[107]

Pursuing the thing, we use many different racial labels throughout this book and encourage you not to get hung up on any one of them. It is true, of course, that words—labels—do help to create the very things they "identify" or describe. Words do matter in social life. But to become heavily, one-sidedly, invested in words is self-defeating. In your conversations, we encourage you to think beyond yourselves and to reach through the words to a deeper engagement with the thing itself: the complex system of racial domination.

How best, then, to move forward? How to make sense of this complex system? Our approach in this book will not be to proceed, chapter by chapter, from one racial group to the next—which only would naturalize very unnatural racial divisions, emphasize our differences at the expense of our many similarities, and render the sociology of race and ethnicity nothing more than a collection of isolated snapshots of different groups. Instead, the core chapters of this work will pursue the analysis of racial domination into many of the different areas or fields of life of our society. Examining how race is a matter not of separate entities but of *systems of social relations*, we shall unpack how race works in the political, economic, residential, legal, educational, aesthetic, associational, and intimate fields of social life. In each chapter, we will think about race with an outlook large and long. *Large*, because we are aware of the ways structural processes condition our everyday actions. And *long*, because we bear in mind how history helps to determine modern life. We shall plumb some of the deep connections that make up society: connections between individual and institution, past and present, the powerful and the powerless.

In the following chapters, we also will pay attention to the ways different fields of life are connected to one another. Although we have divided the eight core chapters into separate fields of life, in reality each field influences the others. If we want to understand the ghetto, for example, we simultaneously should bring to mind the suburbs because these two institutions were formed in relation to one another. We also should think about the ghetto's relationship to the economic field (joblessness), the political field (disenfranchisement), the legal field (the war on drugs), and the educational field (school violence). Further, we must analyze how cultural producers like movie executives churn out exaggerated images of the inner city. And how can we fully understand the ghetto without viewing it historically, grasping it in relation to slavery, Reconstruction, and legally enforced segregation?

As you can see, the ghetto, like all other aspects of race, cannot be analyzed in isolation. It must be apprehended in its full complexity, as a creation of intersecting fields of life. Race is a complex social phenomenon and so deserves an equally complex mode of thinking. The task is big, and intimidating—like eating an elephant. And how do we do that? One bite at a time.

But before we even launch into this venture, we must pause and consider one other large question: How did the racial categories we take for granted today come into being? How did our racial classification system emerge and take shape? How was our racial common sense crystallized? It is to this set of issues that we turn in Chapter 2.

THE BIG PICTURE
Chapter 1: Race in the Twenty-First Century

MAIN POINTS	KEY TERMS	FROM THEORY TO PRACTICE

Keep an eye out for one or more of the five fallacies about racism. Analyze a conversation, newspaper article, movie, play, everyday interaction, or any other object or event with respect to the five fallacies. Did you spot a fallacy? If so, which one? Or, did the people you observed avoid all the fallacies, and, if so, how did they pull it off? In either case, use the object you analyze to reflect on how you might avoid the fallacies when thinking about racial domination.

Explain why one should avoid the individualistic fallacy, the legalistic fallacy, the tokenistic fallacy, the ahistorical fallacy, and the fixed fallacy, when thinking about racism.

- five fallacies about racism, page 7

Distinguish between institutional racism and interpersonal racism and understand how these types of racism often interpenetrate and inform one another.

- institutional racism, page 10
- interpersonal racism, page 11

Think about all the aspects of your identity, other than your race and ethnicity, such as your gender, religion, nationality. What part of your identity is most salient to you? Explore, in a reflexive fashion, why this is, paying close attention to how your multiple identities intersect with one another. What does intersectionality mean to you? Can you think of ways in which you do not identify with some members of your race (or ethnicity, gender, religion, etc.) because of another aspect of your identity? For example, perhaps many members of your racial group fail to tolerate your religious preference, or maybe, some members of your gender just do not understand your sexual orientation.

Understand how racism intersects with other forms of social division—those based on gender, class, sexuality, religion, nationhood, and ability.

- intersectionality, page 16

Understand what is meant by symbolic violence and explain its significance for the perpetuation of racial inequality.

Learn why race is a symbolic category and understand why there is no biological foundation for race.

- race as a social reality, page 32

How do you identify racially and ethnically? How did you learn to identify in such a way? Critically evaluate how your racial composition might advantage or disadvantage you in your daily life.

Understand how whiteness is racial domination normalized, which produces and reproduces many privileges for white people.

- whiteness, page 25

While watching television, reading the newspaper, attending classes, taking in a sporting event, attending religious services, keep an eye out for whiteness. How does whiteness influence the classes you attend or your social circles? Identify examples of whiteness in the movies you watch and the music you listen to. Can you pinpoint some of the ways in which whiteness goes unnoticed?

Recognize how race and ethnicity are overlapping symbolic categories and explain why they cannot be collapsed into one category.

- ethnicity, page 37

London, Published by James Reynolds, 174 Strand May 3, 1850.

2

The Invention of Race

MAIN POINTS

- Explain how the modern concept of "race" emerged amid the revolutionary transformations of modernity—the rise of capitalism, nationalism, science, and colonialism—as a new way of viewing and ordering the world.

- Recognize how the concepts of American whiteness and blackness emerged with the African slave trade.

- Understand how the growth of the U.S. economy and the institutionalization of black slavery between 1660 and 1860 are inextricably linked.

- Learn how the annexation of land from Mexico and Native American tribes led to widespread poverty, cultural devastation, and the loss of rights and citizenship.

- Explain how new racial discourses devised by philosophers, writers, and scientists rose to prominence and helped form classification systems riveted in white supremacy.

- Examine how immigration patterns in the late nineteenth and early twentieth centuries led to the creation of new racial categories and redefinitions of whiteness.

You do not come into this world African or European or Asian; rather, this world comes into you. You are not born with a race in the same way you are born with fingers and eyes and hair. Fingers and eyes and hair are natural creations, whereas race is a social fabrication, a symbolic category misrecognized as natural. And if it is misrecognized as such so frequently, it is because we fail to examine race as a historical product, one that, in the larger scheme of things, is quite new.

White, African, Hispanic, Asian, American Indian—it wasn't always this way. Before the sixteenth century, race as we know it today did not exist. During antiquity and the Middle Ages, prejudices were formed and wars were waged against "other" people. But those "other" people were not categorized or understood as people of other races. Instead of the color line, the primary social division in those times was that between the "civilized" and the "uncivilized." Since religion greatly influenced this division, at least in the Middle Ages, we might say that the world at that time was divided between "sophisticated Christians" and "barbarous heathens."[1] The racial categories so familiar to us began to calcify only around the beginning of the nineteenth century, a mere 200 years ago.

The boundaries separating West from East and white from black are not divisions that always have been and always will be.[2] Fully grasping race in America today means examining it as a historical invention. The project of exploring the history of race is, at the same time, one of uncovering the reasons behind our everyday actions. We cannot stand outside history and watch far-off lands and peoples of old with detached bemusement. Far-off lands, peoples of old—we have inherited them. They are part of us.

This chapter aims to uncover how race as we now know it came to be. We must start by traveling backward in time some 600 years to a world without race. This world soon would find itself turned inside out. A "New World" would be discovered and, in it, a "new people." At the same time, a new economic system—capitalism—would arise, as would a new political arrangement: nations. Science and rationality, too, would flourish. Amid such revolutionary transformations, race would emerge as a new way of viewing and ordering the world.

MODERNITY RISING

More than any others, two European countries would give birth to the system of racial classification we know today: England and Spain. Before the European discovery of the Americas, England, like all of northern Europe, was virtually shut off from the rest of the world.[3] There was, however, one piece of land the English coveted since the middle of the twelfth century: Ireland. Over and over, England invaded Ireland, labeling the Irish "rude, beastly, ignorant, cruel and unruly infidels."[4] The Irish were regarded as nothing short of "savages" in the English mind, and this mindset—that the Irish were in need of correction (if not enslavement)—would greatly influence how the English would come to view America's indigenous peoples. In fact, the cruel saying that circulated in North America during the nineteenth century—"The only good Indian is a dead Indian"—first circulated in England as "The only good Irishman is a dead Irishman."[5]

While England was fighting for control of Ireland, Catholic Spain was contemplating what to do about the Jews and Muslims who populated the Iberian Peninsula—a stretch of land that Spain had wrested from the Moors, Muslims who had inhabited the region. Under Moorish control, the peninsula had developed into a fairly pluralistic society, one marked by religious and cultural tolerance and frequent intermarriage.[6] But Ferdinand and Isabella, Spain's king and queen, sought homogeneity. Their subjects had to be of one religion and one culture. The crown offered Jews and Muslims three choices: leave, convert, or die. Many, especially the rich, converted to Catholicism to escape persecution. The newly converted, or *conversos*, soon began gaining economic standing, and some even began acquiring influence in the church. But church leaders soon began questioning the sincerity of the *conversos*. Were these people Christians by day but Jews by night? Thus, in 1478, the Spanish Inquisition began in earnest. Family ancestries were interrogated for "religious contamination," and many Spaniards began to purchase certificates of ancestral purity, issued by the Catholic Church, to affirm their religious wholesomeness. Soon enough, interest in religious purity morphed into an obsession with blood purity.[7]

In fifteenth-century Spain, a new kind of identity was being fashioned, one based not on religion, family, or tribe, but on national affiliation. Newly formed nations were beginning to create a "people," an "imagined community," bound together inside artificially created political borders.[8] Political leaders initiated new ways to tie together the population they governed. Spain did so through religious repression; other nations would do so through racial repression. In fact, race soon would come to guide the emergence and development of many modern states, and these states would, in turn, serve as key actors in the development and maturation of modern systems of racial classification.[9]

As Europe's political landscape was undergoing massive reorganization, so, too, was its economic system. The medieval workshop was transformed into the capitalist factory. Products were manufactured ever more quickly and cheaply. And products began to be developed not to meet needs, but to make profits. Economic markets began to swell, money gained in importance, and an entrepreneurial spirit captured ambitious hearts.

Since new trading routes and economic partnerships were being sought to satisfy Europe's growing capitalist enterprise, expeditions began to set off for new corners of the globe ("new" by European standards, of course). The so-called Age of Discovery commenced as Spanish and Portuguese explorers traveled south to Africa and east to Indochina. Travelers' accounts began to trickle back to Europe, narratives in the tradition of *The Travels of Marco Polo*, composed in the thirteenth century. These narratives preferred fantasy and legend to fact. One German text of the period asserted, "In Libya many are born without heads and have a mouth and eyes. . . . In the land of Ethiopia many people walk bent down like cattle, and many live four hundred years."[10] Such tall tales gave rise to fantasies about non-Europeans in general and people of the Orient in particular. As a result, Europe, a region once divided by internal strife and warfare, a landmass with no obvious geographic claim to the status of "continent," began to congeal around a shared identity. A new and powerful division entered the world, one separating "the West" from "the Rest."[11]

This also was the age of great intellectual revolutions in science, economics, political theory, philosophy, religion, and art. In 1492, Leonardo da Vinci, the Italian artist/inventor/mathematician, was forty and enjoying widespread fame; Niccolò Machiavelli, the influential Italian philosopher and author of *The Prince*, was twenty-three; and Thomas More, the English cleric and humanist scholar who coined the term "utopia," was twenty-nine. Copernicus, who would forever change the face of science with his finding that the Earth rotated around the sun, not vice versa, was concluding his adolescent years, while the monk who would spark the Protestant Reformation, Martin Luther, was a child of eight.[12]

Christopher Columbus was forty-one. A ruddy, red-headed sailor, Columbus, with the support of Queen Isabella of Spain, set sail in August in search of a western trade route to the riches of China and the East Indies. Approximately one month later, he stumbled on an island in what are now the Bahamas. Columbus named the island San Salvador. The island's original inhabitants called it Guanahan. He then sailed to the second-largest island in the Antilles, an island that today is shared by Haiti and the Dominican Republic. The island's indigenous people, the Taíno, called their homeland Haití and Quizqueia, among other things. Columbus would christen it La Española, or Hispaniola, meaning "the Spanish island." Columbus sailed back to Spain with several kidnapped Taínos, captives whom he would present to the Spanish royal court and, afterward, train as translators.[13] Although figures vary widely, it is estimated that at that time, the Americas were populated by 50 million to 100 million indigenous people.[14]

The old world was passing away, and to replace it, a new modernity was rising. A new worldview would be needed for a world itself quite new. And race would soon emerge as an important element in that worldview.

Amerigo Vespucci (1454–1512) landing in America, engraved by Theodor Galle (1571–1633). Vespucci was a friend and companion of Christopher Columbus and gave his name to the American continent.

COLONIZATION OF THE AMERICAS

News of Columbus's voyage spread throughout Europe, sparking a rush of expeditions to the Americas. In short order, much of the "New World" would come under Spanish colonial rule, followed by English colonization of parts of North America. (The French and Dutch colonized still other parts of North America, but the histories of Spanish and English colonization are most relevant to the story of the emergence of race in the United States.) Colonialism occurs when a foreign power invades a territory and establishes enduring systems of exploitation and domination over that territory's indigenous populations. Through military acts, supported by technological superiority and executed through violence and deception, the foreign power appropriates the resources and lands of the conquered territories for its own enrichment. In doing so, it destroys indigenous ways of life, including tribal sovereignty, cultural and religious beliefs, kinship systems, and local economies.[15]

The Spanish Conquest

The Spaniards were the first to colonize the Americas. Hungry for gold and silver, eager to claim the land for the Spanish Crown, and compelled to convert unbelievers to Catholicism, Spanish explorers descended on modern-day Cuba, Hispaniola, and the east coast of Mexico.[16] One of the most famous explorers was Hernán Cortés. In 1519, Cortés led a band of *conquistadores*, mercenary soldiers licensed by the Spanish Crown to capture the lands and riches of the "New World" as well as the souls of its inhabitants. In search of a city that, rumor had it, was overflowing with wealth, Cortés resolutely marched inland. He and the conquistadores soon arrived at the capital of what today we call the Aztec empire (its inhabitants most likely referred to themselves by several different names): Tenochtitlán (present-day Mexico City).

Diego Rivera's mural of the Spanish Conquest depicts Spanish cruelties to Native Americans.

Tenochtitlán was an engineering marvel—a city constructed in the middle of a lake, accessible only through a complex system of causeways—and booming with a population of 250,000 inhabitants. When Cortés discovered Tenochtitlán, London was a city of 50,000 and Seville, the largest city in Spain, was home to only 40,000.[17] Bernal Díaz del Castillo, a conquistador alongside Cortés, describes the stunning city: "With such wonderful sights to gaze on we did not know what to say, or if this was real that we saw before our eyes. On the land side there were great cities, and on the lake many more. The lake was crowded with canoes. . . . We saw cues and shrines in these cities that looked like gleaming white towers and castles: a marvelous sight. . . . Some of our soldiers who had been in many parts of the world, in Constantinople, in Rome, and all over Italy, said that they had never seen a market so well laid out, so large, so orderly, and so full of people."[18]

The ruler of the Aztec empire, Motecuhzoma (also known as Xocoyotzin or, in its Anglicized form, Montezuma), welcomed Cortés and his men, hosting them in Tenochtitlán. But Cortés and his followers soon laid siege to Tenochtitlán, killing Motecuhzoma and thousands of Aztecs.[19] To the Spaniards went the spoils of war. Aztec land was given to the conquistadores by the Spanish Crown. The conquistadores captured gold, silver, gems, animals, textiles, and artwork. And Aztec women were baptized and presented by Cortés to his captains as wives. Spaniards, indigenous men and women, and Africans (brought en masse to the Caribbean and Latin America through the Atlantic slave trade) married each other and raised children. The Spanish crown even encouraged intermarriage between conquistadores and indigenous women, a practice they thought would help stabilize the region.[20] The territories soon were populated by children of mixed heritage. Systems of racial classification began to take shape, but miscegenation (intermarriage and sexual intercourse between people with different skin tones) resulted in the categories becoming blurry and numerous.[21]

After the fall of the Aztec empire, the Spaniards quickly colonized the lands it had encompassed, ushering in an era of brutality and exploitation. Aztecs and other indigenous peoples of the region were forced to work as farmers, miners, builders, and servants on land that once was theirs.[22] But the Spanish oppression of indigenous peoples did not go without reproach. Among the most outspoken critics of

Tenochtitlán (as portrayed above by Diego Rivera) was a city of 250,000, constructed in the middle of a lake and accessible only through a complex system of causeways.

Spanish colonialism was Bartolomé de Las Casas, a Spanish bishop. "From the very beginning," he wrote, "Spanish policy towards the New World has been characterized by blindness of the most pernicious kind: even while the various ordinances and decrees governing the treatment of the native peoples have continued to maintain that conversion and the saving of souls has first priority, this is belied by what has actually been happening on the ground."[23]

Along with other clergymen, Las Casas would rally the church to protect native populations and to outlaw indigenous slavery (which took place under a different guise, a system of trusteeship and forced labor known as the *encomienda* system). Finally, in 1542, Spain handed down a set of reforms known as *Leyes Nuevas*, or the "New Laws," which were designed to curb the exploitation of indigenous peoples and outlaw their enslavement. The New Laws, however, never took hold, as Spanish colonizers refused to loosen their grip. In fact, messengers who delivered the New Laws to the colonies were shunned, beaten, and, in the case of modern-day Peru, even killed.

The New Laws said nothing about the abolition of African slavery in the colonies. In fact, Las Casas and other "protectors of the Indians" often "called for the sparing of Indian lives, especially in the mines, by importing many more African slaves." The result was the "slow but almost universal replacement of Indian slaves with black Africans." As would occur in the United States, slavery would transform from a multiracial institution, which placed in bondage a wide variety of racialized groups, to one that reserved the shackle primarily for Africans.[24]

The English Conquest

The English began colonizing North America a full century after the Spaniards. The first permanent British colony was founded in Jamestown in 1607. And unlike the Spaniards, the English were not keen on intermarrying with Native Americans. In fact, English settlers developed statutes to distance themselves from the indigenous populations and frowned on sexual relations with the Native Americans.[25] Nor were the English very interested in "converting the lost." What mattered to them were not the natives' souls so much as their land.

When settling the eastern coast of North America, the English created something that had never before existed in that part of the world: "the Indian." This was accomplished in two steps. First, all the indigenous peoples—who practiced different systems of government, employed different economies, spoke different languages, and observed different religious traditions—were lumped together under a single rubric: Indian. Tribes that had fought one another for decades and even centuries, tribes different in every conceivable way, were suddenly the same thing through English eyes.[26] If the first step entailed *homogenization*, the second step involved a process of *polarization*. The category "Indian" was split into two: the good and the bad. On the one hand, the Indian was seen as unadulterated humanity: simple, innocent, peaceful. Here is the "noble savage"—childlike yet pure, primitive yet one with nature. (Fundamental to this image of the Indian was the misconception that indigenous populations lived without organized government, the marker of "civilization" to the European. Such a picture hardly could have been more distorted. In fact, it was from the Iroquois that some of America's core democratic values, such as a devotion to individual rights, federalism, and participatory politics, were adopted by our Founding Fathers.)[27] On the other hand, the Indian was depicted as a brute, a monster. Here, then, is the "ignoble savage"—wicked and fearsome.[28] In these two contradictory guises, the "Indian" thus came into this world, a European invention.

As the English began to thrive in North America, the land's indigenous populations began to die off at alarming rates. The Europeans had brought to the "New World" Old World diseases—such as smallpox, measles, the bubonic plague, cholera, typhoid, diphtheria, and malaria—to which Native Americans had little immunity.[29] Death swept across the native population, rendering some tribes extinct. Just in the English-colonized regions alone, between 1630 and 1730, European-introduced diseases killed off nearly 80 percent of the indigenous population of New England, including 98 percent of the Western Abenaki, who inhabited the lands that are now New Hampshire and Vermont. In five deadly years, between 1615 and 1620, 90 percent of the indigenous population of Massachusetts died of the plague.[30] Millions of Native Americans perished, resulting in "the greatest human catastrophe in history, far exceeding even the disaster of the Black Death in medieval Europe."[31]

Disease spread quickly across the Native American population not only because indigenous peoples had little to no inborn resistance to such biological threats but also because of large-scale changes brought about by English colonization. The English introduced domesticated animals, which spread disease. The relocation and concentration of indigenous communities made it more likely that infected individuals would come into contact with other members of the population. Many Native Americans' diets were flipped upside-down, as their normal means of sustenance, such

FIGURE 2.1 **AMERICAN INDIAN AND NON-INDIAN POPULATIONS, 1492–1980**

American Indian Population Decline and Recovery in the United States, 1492–1980

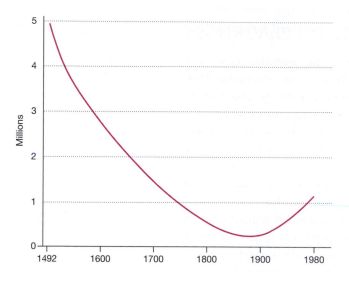

Non-Indian Population Growth in the United States, 1492–1980

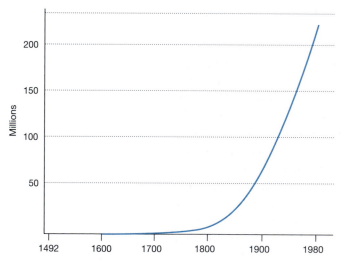

After the English settled on North America, the American Indian population plummeted, while the non-Indian population soared.

as traditional crops and (in the Great Plains) the buffalo, were eradicated.[32] More heinously, historians have documented a handful of cases in which British soldiers intentionally infected Native Americans. In 1763, the commander-in-chief of the British army, Sir Jeffrey Amherst, facing an indigenous uprising, sought ways to introduce smallpox to the dissonant rebels. One of his officers came up with the plan: "I will try to inoculate the bastards with some blankets that may fall into their hands, and take care not to get the disease myself." Pleased with the plan, Amherst penned the following reply: "You will do well to inoculate the Indians by means of blankets, as well as every other method that can serve to extirpate this execrable race." That year, a smallpox epidemic broke loose, spreading rapidly through the Ohio Valley.[33]

Many Native Americans who escaped disease would succumb instead to warfare. The first major outbreak of organized violence against Native Americans occurred in 1622. After English settlers murdered a respected leader, natives attacked Chesapeake Colony, leaving nearly 350 settlers dead. The English retaliated with vengeance, killing entire tribes and enslaving others. Some of their methods were deceitful. On one occasion, the English lured some 250 Native Americans to a meeting where a peace treaty would be signed. During the signing ceremony, English settlers poisoned their guests' share of the liquor, used in a ceremonial toast, killing 200. The remaining fifty were butchered by hand.

The events of 1622 unleashed a flood of violence against North America's indigenous population, a flood that only added to the military atrocities already being carried out by Spaniards. Historians call this violence the Indian Wars. They usually point to the 1540 Spanish subjugation of the Zuni and Pueblo (who occupied lands in modern-day Arizona and New Mexico) as the starting point of the wars. The end would not come until 350 years later, at a massacre called Wounded Knee.

America's indigenous population eventually was brought under the heel of European colonization. As a result, at the beginning of the twentieth century, the entire indigenous population of Canada, the United States, and Greenland combined numbered only 375,000.[34] From 1600 to 1900, over 90 percent of America's indigenous peoples died as a direct result of European colonization, mostly from disease. Never before has our world witnessed such massive loss of human life. Noting this, historian Francis Jennings wrote, "The American land was more like a widow than a virgin. Europeans did not find a wilderness here; rather, however involuntarily, they made one."[35]

THE INVENTION OF WHITENESS AND BLACKNESS

Encouraged by the swiftly advancing global capitalist economy, powerful English settlers sought to extract the riches of the "New World." But they could not do it alone. An "exploitable people" was needed to exploit the resources of America, to cultivate the tobacco and corn fields, to mine for precious stones, to trap animals whose pelts could be shipped back to Europe. To meet this need, indentured servants began pouring into North America by the shiploads. Indentured servants were laborers who were bound to an employer for a fixed amount of time, after which they were freed.

Many indentured servants had bartered their passage to America in exchange for years of labor. Others were ex-prisoners who had been released from English jails. Still others were impoverished English men, women, and children, kidnapped from the streets of London and Liverpool. Some were Native Americans, stolen from their tribal homelands; some were Africans brought to America by the slave trade, which began in the mid-fifteenth century; and hundreds were the "savage Irish," conquered in war and sold through the "Irish slave trade" into bondage.[36] By the 1620s, a plantation system, comprising dozens of large settlements organized around agricultural production for profit and reliant on coerced labor, had been set up. In such settlements, servants lived in separate and substandard housing and often were whipped or maimed if they failed to please their masters.[37]

As colonization pushed forward, the demand for servants increased and the conditions under which servants toiled grew ever harsher. Indentured servants were stripped naked and sold at auctions, and many were worked to the bone, dying before they were able to earn their freedom. *Indentured servitude* in America steadily evolved into *slavery*. Workers became bound to their masters, not for a set period of time, but for life.[38] Suffering through abysmal working conditions, some servants openly rebelled against the system. In 1676, an uprising called Bacon's Rebellion broke out in Jamestown. Bonded laborers of African, English, and Irish descent rose up against wealthy plantation owners, as well as against the colonial government that supported worker exploitation. The rebellion was no small matter: it was supported by most settlers, the majority of whom were poor, and until put down by armed soldiers from England, it threatened the very existence of the system of involuntary servitude on which the plantation owners relied.

If enslaved whites struggled hand in hand with enslaved blacks during Bacon's Rebellion, it was because they *imagined themselves as slaves*. But in the decades following the rebellion, the majority of free Americans began to view white servants as people who could be assimilated into American citizenry and black servants as slaves for life. In the years leading up to the American Revolution, "freedom" took on a whole new meaning for poor whites. The American military offered freedom in exchange for service to white indentured servants, who took up arms by the droves. As the War of Independence unfolded, they began to see themselves as slaves no

"An army of blacks, natives, whites, mulattoes—freedmen, slaves and indentured— . . . waged war against local gentry led by members of that very class. When that 'people's war' lost its hopes to the hangman, the work it had done . . . spawned a thicket of new laws authorizing chaos in defense of order. By eliminating manumission, gatherings, travel and bearing arms for black people only; by granting license to any white to kill any black for any reason; by compensating owners for a slave's maiming or death, they separated and protected all whites from others forever."—Toni Morrison, *A Mercy*

longer. They were "freemen"—nonslaves and non-black—who no longer would reach across the color line when struggling against labor exploitation.[39]

As poor whites gained their freedom, enslaved blacks descended into a state of permanent chattel slavery. Africans were treated as any other piece of property, bought and sold at owners' discretion. While the Constitution secured whites' freedom, granting them access to "life, liberty, and the pursuit of happiness," it legalized black slavery. Revolutionary thinkers, even the most radical of the bunch, such as Benjamin Franklin and Thomas Paine, understood black slavery to be a "necessary evil," a compromise that would secure (white) American freedom.[40] Stunned at this hypocrisy, David Cooper, a leading writer of the revolutionary period, observed that "our rulers have appointed days for humiliation, and offering up of prayer to our common Father to deliver us from *our* oppressors, when sights and groans are piercing his holy ears from oppressions which we commit a thousandfold more grievous."[41] Indeed, freedom came into the world on the scarred backs of slaves. As one sociologist has argued, "Before slavery people simply could not have conceived of the thing we call freedom."[42]

Black slavery provided wealthy planters a new and powerful system of labor exploitation.[43] But why weren't Native Americans permanently enslaved? For one thing, their numbers already were decreasing rapidly. Second, Native Americans, who were familiar with the land, easily could escape their captors and find refuge in surrounding tribes. And third, Native Americans were relied on as guides and trappers in the fur trade, a lucrative business that lasted up to the eighteenth century.[44] What about the "savage Irish"—could they be permanently enslaved? Not likely. Primarily pastoralists—who tended to animals on open pastures—the Irish knew little about farming and agriculture. And, upon escaping, an Irish slave could blend in with the English population.[45] The enslaved African, in contrast, could not blend in with the white population, nor was she or he accustomed to the American landscape. Kidnapped and transported to a strange land, Africans had little refuge other than that provided by their masters. They also were immune to Old World diseases and were used to a tropical climate similar to the one found in the American South. Finally, many Africans were farmers. Africans soon came to be seen as "the perfect slaves"—but it was *not* strictly because of their blackness that they were viewed as such.

As white servants were winning their freedom, not only from their old masters but also from the British, blacks were losing theirs. Twins birthed from the same womb, that of slavery, whiteness and blackness entered the world as new creations whose very essences were defined by and through each other. The white race began to be formed "out of a heterogeneous and motley collection of Europeans *who had never before perceived that they had anything in common*."[46] Blacks, too, who beforehand had belonged to hundreds of different tribal and ethnic groups, were at once brought together under a single racial category and brought low, into bondage, through the might of European domination. America, and all the world with it, awoke to a new era, not one separating Christian from heathen, or gentleman from barbarian, but a world separating people of different "races."

AFRICANS ENSLAVED

Black slavery would become institutionalized—meaning it would be incorporated into American society as a formalized establishment—through a series of social and legal changes that took place between 1660 and 1860. Rights began to be stripped from Africans specifically and nonwhites in general. When Virginia introduced laws in the early 1660s that defined Africans as lifelong servants, it became the first colony to legalize chattel slavery.

The Atlantic Slave Trade

Africans were brought to America through the Atlantic slave trade (see Figure 2.2). The Atlantic slave trade had been in operation since the mid-fifteenth century, and several countries, including Portugal, Spain, England, France, the Netherlands, and America, participated in the trade. Africans participated in the slave trade as well, kidnapping men, women, and children from various tribes and selling them into bondage for European goods, such as cloth, weapons, tobacco, and liquor. Kidnapped slaves were shackled together and marched, under the sting of the whip and the barrel of the gun, to the African west coast, where they were imprisoned until being sold to European captains and loaded onto ships.[47]

Why did Africans sell fellow Africans into slavery? This popular question assumes there was such a thing as "Africa" and "Africans" during the slave trade, whereas, in fact, the notion of "Africa" as a continent inhabited by people who, to varying degrees, understand one another as "Africans" came about only in modern times. Before the slave trade, many African communities were disconnected from one another. Although Europeans and Africans were not equal players in the Atlantic slave trade, Africans did play an active role in it, and they did so for the same reasons as Europeans: money. Many African societies that participated in the slave trade did get rich, at least for a short while. In the long run, however, the slave trade underdeveloped Africa as a whole, depleting its population (especially of young men), directing its attention away from more productive economic activities, and, most destructively, constructing Africans as an inferior people and Africa as an exploitable land in the minds of Europeans.[48]

The voyage from the west coast of Africa to America, across the broad waters of the Atlantic, was called the Middle Passage. It typically lasted two to three months, but depending on the characteristics of the vessel and the weather, it could take

FIGURE 2.2 **THE AFRICAN SLAVE TRADE 1501–1867**

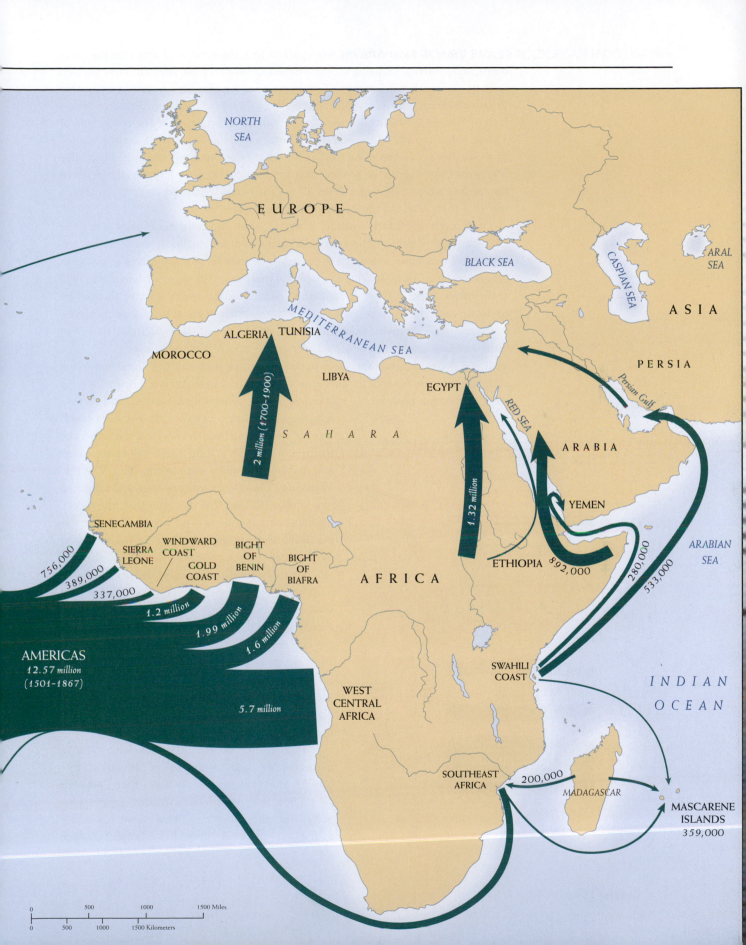

NORTH
SEA

EUROPE

BLACK SEA

CASPIAN
SEA

ARAL
SEA

ASIA

MEDITERRANEAN SEA

ALGERIA   TUNISIA

MOROCCO

LIBYA

EGYPT

PERSIA

Persian Gulf

RED SEA

SAHARA

2 million (1700–1900)

1.32 million

ARABIA

YEMEN

SENEGAMBIA

SIERRA
LEONE

WINDWARD
COAST

GOLD
COAST

BIGHT
OF
BENIN

BIGHT
OF
BIAFRA

ETHIOPIA

892,000

280,000

533,000

ARABIAN
SEA

756,000

389,000

337,000

AFRICA

1.2 million

1.99 million

4.6 million

AMERICAS
12.57 million
(1501–1867)

SWAHILI
COAST

INDIAN

OCEAN

5.7 million

WEST
CENTRAL
AFRICA

SOUTHEAST
AFRICA

200,000

MADAGASCAR

MASCARENE
ISLANDS
359,000

0   500   1000   1500 Miles

0   500   1000   1500 Kilometers

several times as long. Africans were packed into the bowels of ships by the hundreds, sometimes after being stripped naked. On some ships, Africans were shelved next to one another in spaces seldom larger than a coffin. One historian notes that British and French traders "would hold their captives in a space five feet, three inches high by four feet, four inches wide."[49] A firsthand description of the conditions of a slave ship from the late seventeenth century reads as follows: "If anyone wanted to sleep, they lay on top of each other. To satisfy their natural needs, they had bilge places over the edge of the sea but, as many feared to lose their place, they relieved themselves where they were, above all the men cruelly pushed together, in such a way that their heat and the smell became intolerable."[50]

Overcrowding left little room for food and water, and many slaves died of malnutrition and dehydration. Others perished from dysentery, smallpox, and other disease. While some captains attempted to preserve the lives of as many slaves as possible, others were tyrannical, abusing and raping slaves during the voyage. Many slaves died at the hands of the ship's crew. Still others committed suicide by starving themselves to death. Eager to preserve their cargo, some shipmen took to force-feeding slaves. A scissor-like instrument would be forced into the lips of the recalcitrant slave, and his or her jaws would then be forced open by the turn of a thumbscrew.[51]

It was not uncommon for slaves to rise up against their captors. Some historians estimate that one of eight to ten voyages experienced insurrection.[52] Few rebellions were successful, however, as mutinying slaves, unorganized, starved, and powerless, were put down brutally. After a slave revolt was squelched on a Danish ship sailing in 1709, the insurrection leader's right hand was chopped off and displayed to every slave on the ship. The following day, his left hand was severed and exhibited in a similar fashion. The day after that, the rebel's head was cut off and his torso was hoisted onto the mainsail, where it hung for two days. Those who participated in the rebellion were flogged, their wounds rubbed with salt, ashes, and pepper.[53]

Fifteen to thirty percent of slaves died aboard slave ships. In 1717, only 98 slaves out of 594 survived the voyage on a ship named *George*. In 1805, the citizens of Charleston refused to eat any fish, since so many dead bodies were thrown into the harbor from the decks of slave ships.[54] Despite such massive loss of life, a profit still could be made even if 45 percent of the slaves died during the voyage.[55]

The enormity of the Atlantic slave trade is immeasurable and a matter of historical debate.[56] Most historians believe that between 10 million and 15 million Africans were transported to the Americas. This figure is likely a fraction of total lives lost, however, since

Plans for the French slave ship *Vigilante*.

it does not include those who died on slave ships, on forced marches in Africa, in villages in defiance of would-be captors, or in cages on the west coast of Africa. Of 100 people captured in Africa, 64 would arrive at the coast alive, 57 would live through coastal imprisonment to be packed onto ships, 48 would survive the journey to be placed on the auction block, and only 28 of the original 100 would survive the first few years of slave labor. In other words, for each enslaved African bent over in the plantation fields, there were three others who perished en route.[57]

The Rise of the Cotton Kingdom

From 1640 to 1700, slaves made up 61 percent of all transatlantic migrants who arrived in the Americas. In the following fifty years, that percentage increased to 75 percent.[58] The Atlantic slave trade gained momentum during the eighteenth century, but most slaves were transported to the British West Indies and Cuba to work in the sugar plantations. Relative to the slave labor force of the Caribbean, that of North America grew slowly during this time period; in fact, in 1700, Africans in the British Caribbean outnumbered those in the North American colonies by a ratio of six to one. The majority of slaves in North America worked in the areas of small-scale farming, domestic service, and craft manufacturing, though by midcentury tobacco, indigo, and rice began to be produced in the Southern plantations, a shift that increased the demand for slave labor.[59]

It was only at the start of the nineteenth century, a few years after Eli Whitney invented the cotton gin (1793), that the dynamics of slavery in North America transformed dramatically. The cotton gin—a simple enough contraption made of a wooden box, a set of hooks that pulled cotton through a wire mesh, and a crank— deseeded cotton with speed and efficiency. By hand, one could clean a pound of cotton in a day. Using the gin, one could clean fifty pounds of cotton in a day. Suddenly, the production of cotton was made simple, the price of cotton fell, and cotton plantations emerged. Cotton quickly surpassed tobacco as America's leading cash crop. In 1790, America produced 140,000 pounds of cotton. By 1800, it would be producing 35 million pounds. Cotton became king—with black slaves doing its bidding. As the demand for cotton increased in Europe, North American slavery was reinvigorated.

As the slave population began to grow, Southern and Northern politicians began to debate how slaves should be counted for the purposes of appointing members to Congress. Delegates from abolitionist states argued that slaves should not be counted among the population for purposes of political representation, since slaves could not vote. Delegates from slaveholding states took the opposite position, arguing that slaves should be counted among the population.

From sunup to sundown, six days a week, slaves, including children and pregnant women, were forced to work in the fields.

A decision was reached in 1787, known as the Three-Fifths Compromise, in which it was decided that a slave would be counted as three-fifths of a person. This policy inflated the political power of Southern states, which enjoyed disproportionate representation in relation to voting citizens, but not to the degree slaveholding states originally had desired. The Three-Fifths Compromise remained in effect until 1865.

By then, there were close to 4 million slaves in America.[60] Maximization of productivity was the goal, and plantation owners had this down to a science. Every slave was utilized, including pregnant women who often were forced to work in the fields until the final week before giving birth—and then forced to return only two weeks thereafter. On average, slaves worked "sunup to sundown," for six days a week. The cotton flowed, making plantation owners, on the eve of the Civil War, some of the richest men in the world.[61]

Of course, most white people were not plantation owners. In fact, most were poor—too poor to purchase large pieces of land, let alone slaves. Of the 2 million slaveholders living in the South in the mid-nineteenth century, the vast majority owned a very small number of slaves, while an elite group of planters owned virtual slave armies. But at the height of slavery, over 5 million whites in the South did not own slaves.[62] Poor whites fared poorly during slavery, since free labor naturally pulled down the price of all labor.

Landless and poverty-stricken white families resembled enslaved blacks, but they tended to identify with wealthy white plantation owners with whom they shared only skin color. They were poor, but they were free—and in their minds they could someday, by a stroke of luck perhaps, come to own slaves themselves. They worked as the planters' overseers, patrolled the planters' fields with their "cats of nine tails" (that is, whipping devices made of thongs of braided cord), and served as the planters' police force, chasing down runaway slaves. To quote a keen observation made by W. E. B. Du Bois, "It must be remembered that the white group of laborers, while they received a low wage, were compensated in part by a sort of public and psychological wage. They were given public deference and titles of courtesy because they were white. They were admitted freely with all classes of white people to public functions, public parks, and the best schools. . . . Their vote selected public officials, and while this had small effect upon the economic situation, it had great effect upon their personal treatment and the deference shown them."[63]

Plantation owners strove to convince poor whites to overlook how they were exploited by the slave economy. They did so by convincing poor white families to take pride in their whiteness. As Pem Davidson Buck puts it in *Worked to the Bone*, to thwart the formation of interracial coalitions between poor whites and enslaved blacks, white elites had to "teach Whites the value of whiteness."[64]

The Horrors of Slavery

Black slaves came to be regulated under a set of laws called slave codes. The codes denied blacks citizenship and governed even the most intimate spheres of their lives. Slaves were not allowed to own or carry arms, trade goods, possess land, leave their master's property without permission, or venture out at night. They were forbidden to socialize with free blacks, and a marriage between two slaves went unrecognized as an official union. Since slaves could not marry, slave families did not exist in the eyes of the law. Children were snatched from the arms of their mothers;

wives were torn from the embrace of their husbands. Black families were scattered.

It was illegal for a slave to testify in court against a white person, and a slave who argued with or struck a white person was punished severely. In Washington, D.C., for instance, slaves who hit white persons would have their ears cut off. In some states, even free blacks could not lay a hand on whites, even in self-defense. In Virginia, free blacks who defended themselves against the assaults of whites received thirty lashes. During this time, the rights of free blacks were eroded alongside those of enslaved blacks. By 1723, the right to vote was withheld from all blacks residing in the Southern colonies, free or not.[65]

Laws also were put in place that broadened the scope of slavery to include children of mixed heritage, thereby expanding the very definition of blackness. Sexual unions, many of which were rapes, between free white men and enslaved black women produced biracial children. If a child grew in the womb of a slave woman as a result of such a union, that child would bear the "condition of the mother," becoming not the white man's son or daughter but a slave—one who increased the value of the master's estate.[66]

This foreshadowed a peculiar trend in the career of American blackness. Since its inception, blackness always had been defined through the

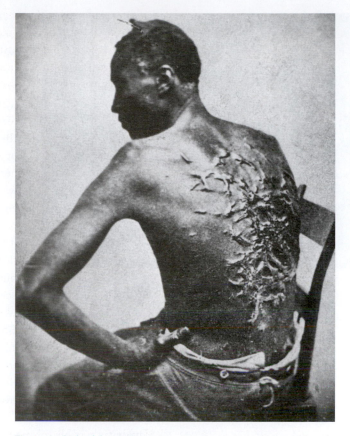

The back of a Louisiana cotton plantation slave who had been whipped by his owner.

"one-drop rule," which renders "black" anyone with any amount, no matter how minuscule, of African blood. More than a social convention, this rule was given legal existence through several statutes enacted during and after the time of slavery. For instance, in 1896 the U.S. Supreme Court, in *Plessy v. Ferguson*, a case to which we will return later in this chapter, ruled that Homer Plessy, a light-skinned man who was one-eighth black, was "black" and therefore not entitled to rights reserved for whites. Blackness, then, was regarded as a mark, a blemish, whereas whiteness, by implication, was constructed as the essence of racial purity. In its ideal form, whiteness was unpolluted by Africa.[67]

Slaves were denied access even to the most basic education. Some states made it illegal to teach a slave to read or write. Others forbade slaves from practicing religious worship and expression. Slaves were denied access to their African roots. They were forbidden to speak in their native tongue and were forced to dress in the style of their captors. Their names were changed, sometimes to insulting nicknames, such as Monkey or Villain. Slaves were given "marks of servitude." Their ears were cropped, and they were tattooed and branded (sometimes with the same iron used to brand an owner's cattle) on the breast or forehead. Runaways were marked with clear identifiers, such as the letter "R" branded on their cheek.[68]

"Soon she will learn to tremble when she hears her master's footfall."—Harriet Jacobs

Under the slave codes, white masters lived in a world typified by the absence of restraints. The whip was the master's favorite weapon of correction. In the Southern colonies, thirty-nine lashes often were given to offending slaves, the same prescription stipulated in Roman law. Though it was illegal for masters to murder a slave, they committed no crime if they accidentally killed a slave while punishing him or her.[69] Elizabeth Keckley, a slave separated from her parents at a young age, recalls a time when she was flogged, for no apparent reason, at the age of eighteen. Keckley tells us she was stripped naked and bound. "Then he picked up a rawhide, and began to ply it freely over my shoulders. With steady hand and practiced eye he would raise the instrument of torture, nerve himself for a blow, and with fearful force the rawhide descended upon the quivering flesh. It cut the skin, raised welts, and the warm blood trickled down my back. Oh God! I can feel the torture now—the terrible, excruciating agony of those moments."[70] Much thought and creativity was devoted to the question of how best to torture slaves. Slaves thought to be indolent were placed in stocks and pillars and displayed in the town square; slaves thought to be high-spirited were mutilated or castrated; slaves thought to be ill-mannered were forced to wear iron masks and collars.[71]

Slavery "is terrible for men; but it is far more terrible for women," wrote Harriet Jacobs.[72] Since slave children increased a master's wealth, slave women often were forced to copulate with whomsoever the master chose. Planters often prided themselves on owning a good "breeding woman." In large part, slavery rested on the control of black women's bodies.[73] "Here," writes Dorothy Roberts, "lies one of slavery's most odious features: it forced its victims to perpetuate the very institution that subjugated them by bearing children who were born the property of their masters."[74]

Slave women also lived in constant fear of rape. In her slave narrative, *Incidents in the Life of a Slave Girl*, published in 1861, Harriet Jacobs describes her "trials of girlhood": "But I now entered my fifteenth year—a sad epoch in the life of a slave girl. My master began to whisper foul words in my ear. . . . Soon she [the slave girl] will learn to tremble when she hears her master's footfall. She will be compelled to realize that she is no longer a child. If God has bestowed beauty upon her, it will prove her greatest curse. . . . I cannot tell you how much I suffered in the presence of these wrongs, nor how I am still pained by the retrospect. My master met me at every turn, reminding me that I belonged to him, and swearing by heaven and earth that he would compel me to submit to him."[75] The rape of a slave woman was not recognized as a crime.[76] White masters used rape as a technique of terror, one that degraded both black women and men, since the latter could not keep their sisters, mothers, and wives safe from violation.[77]

Gradually, enslaved Africans were reduced to "socially dead persons," and blackness became associated with inferiority.[78] Out of slaves' social death grew

American prosperity. While blacks lost their freedom, honor, and lives, the United States' economy grew exponentially, becoming what it is today: the most powerful economic force in the world.

Resistance, Great and Small

Slaves fought back. Sometimes their methods of resistance were quiet and subtle. Slaves sang of the fall of slavery, as well as of an afterlife in which there would be no more tears. Jokes were made at whites' expense. Poems were penned that rejoiced in the deaths of masters.[79] In addition, if whites thought of blacks as unintelligent and lazy, some blacks often acted as such to affront their masters. Tools were left out in the rain; plows were mishandled; shovels and hoes were sabotaged; livestock "escaped." Slaves misunderstood instructions; got lost on the way to town; oversalted the dinner; made the coffee scalding hot. Everyday forms of resistance, whispered "nos" amid the roar of racial tyranny, demonstrate that slaves did not believe of themselves what the whites told them to believe. They found ways to retain their honor.[80]

Sometimes, slaves' resistance was not so subtle. Slaves took up arms against their masters, burning buildings and crop fields and engaging whites in bloody warfare. When news of the Haitian Revolution—an enormously successful slave revolt that overthrew French colonialism and emancipated the entire Haitian slave population—reached America at the beginning of the nineteenth century, it inspired many American slaves to risk their lives to break the chains of tyranny. One of the most significant revolts occurred in 1831, when a man by the name of Nat Turner, a slave and fiery preacher, led some sixty slaves in open revolution. Turner and his followers marched defiantly from farm to farm throughout Virginia, fighting and killing whites and recruiting other slaves. The rebellion eventually would be put down, and Turner hanged, but not before it had left almost sixty whites dead in its path.[81] Of slave revolutionaries, American historian Herbert Aptheker would observe, "They were firebells in the night; cries from the heart; expressions of human need and aspiration in the face of the deepest testing. They manifest that victimization does not simply make victims; it also produces heroes."[82]

Flight was yet another form of resistance. Slaves could run north to freedom, and to help them do so, there was a network of secret routes on land and water, safe-holds, and allies to fugitive slaves—collectively known as the Underground Railroad. The Underground Railroad helped thousands reach freedom in large part because of its brave and brilliant leaders. There was William Still, a black man called "the father of the Underground Railroad," who hid over sixty fugitive slaves in his home. There was Harriet Tubman, too, an ex-slave who would return to the South time and again to guide hundreds of slaves to freedom without losing a single one along the way. Tubman was so effective that whites offered a $10,000 reward for her capture. And there was William Garrett, a white Quaker, who, though arrested and fined to such a degree that he nearly met financial ruin, thought that freeing slaves was his Christian duty.[83]

Whites and blacks worked side by side in the Underground Railroad, and indeed, since the beginning days of American slavery, whites and blacks, together, called for its abolition, thus earning the name abolitionists. The abolitionist movement was strong in the North, which is in part why all the Northern states had abolished slavery by 1804. In the years leading up to the Civil War, the abolitionist movement gained

FIGURE 2.3 GENERALIZED ROUTES OF SLAVES SEEKING FREEDOM

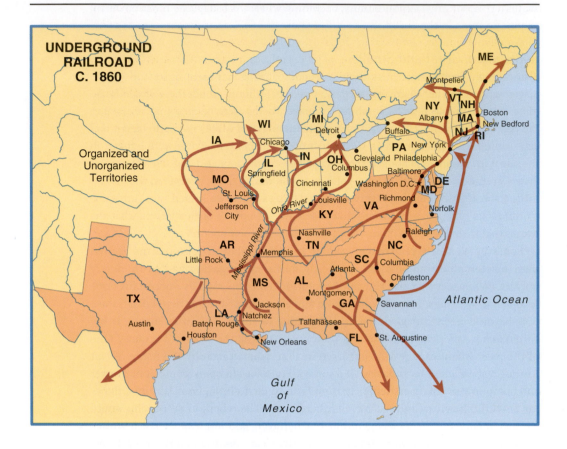

steam, and slavery was decried from all corners of the country. From Massachusetts, it was criticized by William Lloyd Garrison, a white journalist and founder of the first abolitionist newspaper called *The Liberator*, who would write, "I accuse the land of my nativity of insulting the majesty of Heaven with the grossest mockery that was ever exhibited to man." From Kansas, it was challenged by John Brown, a white man who organized several armed insurrections in the name of black liberation and who eventually was found guilty of treason against (white) America and executed. From South Carolina, it would be called "despotic," "sinful," and a "violation of the natural order of things" by Sarah and Angelina Grimké, sisters ostracized by their white family for arguing that "the white man should take his foot off the Negro's neck."[84]

Most powerfully, slavery was condemned from the mouths of former slaves. Frederick Douglass was one of them. Douglass taught himself to read and write while a child in bondage. He later escaped slavery at the age of nineteen and went on to become one of the most influential African Americans of his day. A skilled writer and an orator of the highest caliber, Douglass launched many pointed assaults on the institution of slavery, including a famous address given on July 5, 1852, in Rochester, New York. Addressing an audience of influential white politicians, Douglass boomed, "This Fourth [of] July is *yours*, not *mine*. *You* may rejoice, *I* must mourn. . . . Fellow citizens; above your national, tumultuous joy, I hear the mournful wail of millions!

whose chains, heavy and grievous yesterday, are, to-day, rendered more intolerable by the jubilee shouts that reach them. . . . What, to the American slave, is your Fourth of July? I answer: a day that reveals to him, more than all other days in the year, the gross injustice and cruelty to which he is the constant victim."[85]

Whereas Douglass's voice was commanding and elegant, that of another black abolitionist spoke with weather-worn wisdom and without sentiment. Sojourner Truth has been described as "an unsmiling sibyl, weighted with the woe of the world."[86] This tall, slender grandmother cast a powerful shadow over both the abolitionist and women's rights movements (at this time, women, most of them white, were fighting for the right to vote). Disappointed with the suffrage movement for overlooking the plight of black women, and highlighting the intimate ties between racism and sexism, Truth once addressed a white audience gathered for a women's rights convention with these stirring words: "Dat man ober dar say dat woman needs to be helped into carriages, and lifted over ditches, and to have the best place eberywhar. Nobody eber helps me into carriages, or ober mud-puddles, or gives me any best place. And ar'n't I a woman? Look at me, look at my arm! I have plowed and planted and gathered into barns, and no man could head me—and ar'n't I a woman? I could work as much and eat as much as a man (when I could get it), and bear de lash as well—and ar'n't I a woman? I have borne thirteen chillen, and seen 'em mos' all sold off into slavery, and when I cried out with a mother's grief, none but Jesus heard—and ar'n't I a woman?"[87]

From Emancipation to Jim Crow

Sojourner Truth gave this address in 1851. Ten years later, on a still April morning, fifty confederate cannons opened fire on Fort Sumter, marking the beginning of the Civil War. In 1863, President Abraham Lincoln issued the Emancipation Proclamation, an executive order that manumitted all slaves in the Confederacy. In 1865, the Confederate Army would be defeated by the Union, and more slaves would be freed. At the end of that year, the Thirteenth Amendment was ratified, permanently abolishing slavery in the United States. The first section of the Amendment reads, "Neither slavery nor involuntary servitude . . . shall exist within the United States, or any place subject to their jurisdiction." As the cannon smoke cleared, all black men and women stood legally free upon American soil.

But, in reality, what leg did they have to stand on? Here were millions of blacks who, for 250 years, had endured kidnapping, torture, and rape; who had been denied education, property, and wealth; who, surrounded by powerful whites who ground their teeth at emancipation, had no place to turn, least of all to their families, who had been scattered throughout the country. Recognizing the slaves' poverty and eager to punish the rebellious South, William Sherman, a general in the Union Army, issued a decree in January 1865 that allotted forty acres of land to recently freed heads of households as well as to slaves who had fought in the Union Army. This policy came to be known as Forty Acres and a Mule (the beast would be used to pull a plow) and was the nation's first—and only—attempt at offering reparations for slavery.[88]

It is estimated that some 40,000 freed slaves saw Sherman's policy fulfilled. However, later that year, President Andrew Johnson, Lincoln's successor, overturned Sherman's order, returning the property to former Confederates who swore an oath to the Union. The promise of Forty Acres and a Mule was never fulfilled, leaving the freed slave in a state of utter destitution. Du Bois's words ring true here: "To emancipate four million laborers whose labor had been owned, and separate them from the land upon which they had worked for nearly two and a half centuries, was an operation such as no modern country had for a moment attempted or contemplated. The German and English and French serf, the Italian and Russian serf, were, on emancipation, given definite rights in the land. Only the American Negro slave was emancipated without such rights and in the end this spelled for him the continuation of slavery."[89]

The period from 1865 to 1877 is known as Reconstruction, a time when the nation put itself back together, reincorporating the Southern states and reinventing American citizenry, white and black alike. Immediately after the fall of slavery, Southern states began implementing "black codes," variants of the slave codes that restricted the rights of newly freed blacks. Many blacks would be forced back onto the plantation fields, as black codes severely limited other employment opportunities. At the national level, however, freed blacks were winning rights. The ratification of the Fourteenth Amendment came in 1868 and extended citizenship rights to blacks. "All persons born or naturalized in the United States," it read, " . . . are citizens of the United States. . . . No State shall make or enforce any law which shall abridge the privileges or immunities of citizens of the United States; nor shall any State deprive any person of life, liberty, or property, without due process of law." The ratification of the Fifteenth Amendment, the last of the three great amendments of Reconstruction, came two years later and gave black men—but not other nonwhites or women—the right to vote: "The right of citizens of the United States to vote shall not be denied or abridged by the United States or by any State on account of race, color, or previous condition of servitude."

Some black men went to the polls, and some even were elected to public office. But white supremacy would not yield so easily. By and large, blacks were neither treated as American citizens nor respected as voters. After the Civil War, whites lashed out at freed blacks, first through sporadic, unorganized hostility, then through organized terror, especially through the founding of the Ku Klux Klan (the Klan, or KKK) in 1865.[90]

Dressed as ghosts of dead Confederate soldiers, the Klan terrorized blacks and other nonwhite persons, as well as Jews and Catholics. Klansmen whipped, tarred, raped, and murdered their victims. Their violence was an explicit attempt to uphold white supremacy and to bar blacks from any political or economic advancement. If a black man voted, he risked his life in doing so. Some ballot boxes even were patrolled by armed white men. And behind everything—behind the Constitution and

Rubin Stacy was a homeless farmer who had knocked on Marion Jones's door to ask for food. When she saw his face, she was frightened, slammed the door, and made a complaint against him to the police. The KKK intercepted his transport between jails and lynched him on July 19, 1935.

all its new amendments, behind all the changes of Reconstruction— lurked the threat of the lynch mob. Thousands of blacks were lynched during Reconstruction and on up through the mid-twentieth century. Far from being erratic acts of mob aggression, lynchings commonly were preplanned events, bloody rituals that drew large crowds of onlookers. Often the victim would be tortured, his limbs severed, his flesh impaled with hot irons, and his body strung up a tree or burnt alive. Many victims accused of raping white women—indeed, the "rape complex" was the warrant most often marshaled for lynching—would be castrated. Victims would be mutilated after their death, parts of their bodies sold to spectators as macabre souvenirs. Often, whites would dance and sing around the corpse, carrying on in a festive spirit.[91] It was of lynchings that jazz great Billie Holiday sang in her famous 1939 recording of "Strange Fruit": "Southern trees bear a strange fruit / Blood on the leaves and blood at the root / Black body swinging in the Southern breeze / Strange fruit hanging from the poplar trees."[92]

As Reconstruction came to a close, the era of Jim Crow segregation began in earnest. The name derives from a song called "Jump Jim Crow" (1828), by Thomas "Daddy" Rice, a white man who popularized minstrel shows. (Minstrelsy was a form of popular entertainment in which performers using makeup known as blackface invoked racist stereotypes and caricatures to portray black people in a degrading light.) By the late 1830s, the term "Jim Crow" had become associated with strict racial segregation reinforced under the terms of law. Nearly all aspects of everyday life were governed by Jim Crow laws, as whites and blacks were forced to use separate water fountains, parks, and bathrooms. It was illegal for blacks to attend white schools, to sit in railroad cars designated for white patrons, or to use white libraries. These laws were supported with the full weight of the Supreme Court in *Plessy v. Ferguson* (1896), the case mentioned earlier, which ruled that racial segregation was constitutional, since black and white facilities were "separate but equal." Of course, they were anything but, as facilities designated for blacks usually were in far worse shape that those allotted to whites. Jim Crow would command American life—in the South through formal law, in the North through custom—from the late nineteenth century until the 1960s.[93]

If we have devoted a considerable amount of attention to slavery and its aftermath, it is because, more than any other institution, slavery has dictated the career of race in America. American slavery emerged to meet the needs of colonial exploitation and capitalist expansion. Before slavery, what we now know to be whiteness and blackness did not exist. After slavery, whiteness and blackness were understood as durable and everlasting features of nature. Capitalist colonization encouraged the rise of slavery, and slavery shaped the very contours of racism.[94]

MANIFEST DESTINY

Conquering Mexico and the Invention of the Mexican American

Let us back up and cast our gaze farther southward. While the U.S. cotton kingdom reigned supreme during the beginnings of the nineteenth century, wars were raging throughout the lands colonized by the Spaniards. Inspired by the successful American Revolution, many people oppressed by Spanish colonization, some of whom even fought with Washington's rebels, were fighting for their independence. "America," thought the Latin American patriots, "can identify with our struggle. It

John Gast's Painting *American Progress* depicts "Manifest Destiny."

fought and won its freedom from European monarchs, and it will support us." But U.S. politicians, eager to expand westward, thought of Latin America as land that later could be exploited rather than as a country bravely wrestling for democracy. In fact, President James Monroe, when signing the Adams-Onís Treaty of 1819, a treaty that gave the United States lands that now are Florida, promised the Spanish Crown that he would withhold support from the rebels. The United States did not extend its hand as Latin American rebels fought for independence.[95]

And fight they did. The Mexican War of Independence began in September 1810, when a parish priest, Padre Miguel Hidalgo, sounded the church bells and led an insurrection of indigenous peasants and miners against Spanish colonialism. The bloody conflict lasted eleven years, claiming over 600,000 lives: over 10 percent of the country's population. (By contrast, only 25,000 died fighting for American independence.) Finally, in 1821, Mexico rested, having established itself as an independent nation whose borders included modern-day Texas, Arizona, New Mexico, California, Nevada, Utah, and Colorado.[96]

A year later, President Monroe, surprisingly, recognized Mexican independence, announcing that the Americas were "henceforth not to be considered as subjects for future colonization by any European powers." Monroe's declaration was praised by Mexican leaders. "America for the Americans!" became the slogan that emerged from the Monroe Doctrine. That Latin America should not belong to Europe, few Americans disputed. However, many began asking, "Should Latin America belong to the Latin Americans?" Many North Americans did not believe so, and a new slogan soon emerged: "Manifest Destiny!" In other words, "The western frontier, all of North America and the lands of Mexico—yes, this is God's will—is ours for the taking!"

In 1845, the United States forced Mexico to relinquish the lands that now are Texas, the end result of an uprising started by white settlers who had illegally emigrated to Mexico.[97] With the annexation of Texas, the battle cry "Manifest Destiny!" grew ever louder. Consider one declaration, that of a politician named William Wharton, reflecting the public sentiment of many white Americans: "The justice and benevolence of God will forbid that . . . Texas should again become a howling wilderness trod only by savages, or . . . benighted by the ignorance and superstition, the anarchy and rapine of Mexican misrule. The Anglo-American race are destined to be forever the proprietors of this land of promise and fulfillment. Their laws will govern it, their learning will enlighten it, their enterprise will improve it. . . . The wilderness of Texas has been redeemed by Anglo-American blood and enterprise."[98]

A year after annexing Texas, the United States declared war on Mexico. The Mexican-American War was fought between 1846 and 1848. Over 100,000 U.S. troops descended on Mexican soil. Mexico, a country of only twenty-five years and still reeling from its costly war of independence, stood little chance, especially considering that most of the fighting done on the borderlands was carried out by untrained civilians.

General Ulysses S. Grant, the most important Union general of the Civil War and eighteenth president of the United States, would call the Mexican-American War "one of the most unjust ever waged by a stronger against a weaker nation."[99] Mexico was defeated in 1848, and, through the Treaty of Guadalupe Hidalgo, the United States acquired the land that today is New Mexico, California, Utah, Nevada, parts of Arizona, and disputed areas of Texas.

But why did the United States stop there? Why did this superior military power show restraint instead of claiming all of Mexico? The answer lies in the ways white Americans viewed the people of Mexico.[100] Recall that the Mexicans were a people of mixed heritage, a people birthed from the unions of Spaniards, Africans, and Native Americans. Not surprisingly, white Americans understood Mexicans to be inferior. Thus, when U.S. troops marched on Mexico City, America's leaders had a decision to make: Should they lay claim to the entirety of Mexico, and thus absorb millions of "inferior" Mexicans into their borders, or should they capture only a portion of Mexico, the portion populated with the least numbers of Mexicans? So as not to threaten America's white majority, political leaders chose the latter option.[101]

The Treaty of Guadalupe Hidalgo promised citizenship rights to Mexicans in ceded lands; however, that promise was never fulfilled. The United States continued to refuse complete citizenship rights to nonwhites. In the eyes of American law, Mexican identity was determined by blood quantum. Those with one-half or more of Mexican blood were classified as Mexican. Those classified as such were then brought under the governance of race-based law, which denied them privileges. Mexicans were not allowed to vote. And under the Homestead Act of 1862, many Mexicans were dispossessed of their land, which Congress promised to citizens of the United States or immigrants eligible for naturalization (read: white settlers).[102] As a result, "Mexican Americans of the Southwest became a foreign minority in the land of their birth."[103] As the United States grew rich off gold and silver acquired through the Mexican-American War, as well as off the cattle- and sheep-ranching industries booming throughout the Southwest, Mexicans, denied rights, descended into poverty. With the construction of the political border separating the United States from Mexico came the construction of a racial border, one separating whites from Mexicans, Mexicans from "Indians," and Mexicans from Africans. This also was an economic border, separating landowners from landless, and a psychological border, separating "superior" from "inferior."[104]

Citizenship rights finally would be extended to Mexicans born in the United States in 1898. Mexicans who immigrated to the United States, however, could not apply to become citizens. Until 1940, that right was reserved only for "free white immigrants." With African Americans, Mexicans within American borders

FIGURE 2.4 **LAND MEXICO CEDED TO THE UNITED STATES AFTER THE TREATY OF GUADALUPE**

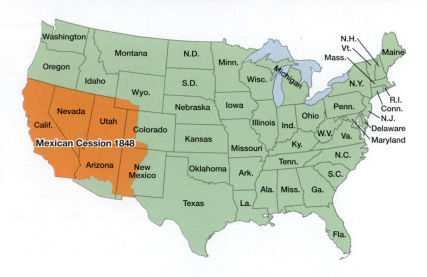

FIGURE 2.5 EUROCENTRIC AND NATIVE AMERICAN VIEWS OF EXPANSIONISM

were subjected to Jim Crow segregation. In the Southwest, Mexican students would attend segregated, rundown schools until legal segregation was outlawed in the middle of the twentieth century.[105]

"The Indian Problem"

Shouts of "Manifest Destiny" were not only directed at Mexico. They echoed across Indian Country as well. Before the nineteenth century, American business relied on Native American labor to carry on the fur trade. By 1800, the fur trade had bottomed out, and what mattered to America's swelling capitalist economy was not Native Americans' labor but Native America itself, the land. The question as to what would be done with tribes and their valuable land came to be known as "the Indian problem."

Broadly speaking, two strategies for acquiring tribal land, for solving "the Indian problem," were put forth: assimilation and removal. *Assimilation* required the dashing out of indigenous ways of life. Native Americans would be taught to treat the land the "American" way—that is, to parcel up the land into homesteads "owned" by individuals (not by tribal communities), to develop that land for profit (not for sustenance), and to abandon vast hunting grounds. *Removal* simply meant that tribes would be kicked off their land at gunpoint. Assimilation proved costly and time consuming. Removal, then, would solve "the Indian problem."[106]

A series of laws passed between 1830 and 1890 created what was called Indian Territory, or land allotted by the U.S. government for tribal use. The Indian Removal Act of 1830, signed into law by President Andrew Jackson, permitted the forcible removal of Native Americans occupying fertile lands east of the Mississippi River. Native Americans were pushed west into "the Great American Desert," as it was then known, "which white men would never covet since it was thought fit mainly for horned toads and rattlesnakes."[107] Over the next fourteen years, over 70,000 Native Americans were driven from their homes and marched west of the Mississippi. A particularly violent removal took place in 1838, when the U.S. military rounded up approximately 17,000 Cherokees from Georgia, Tennessee, North Carolina, and Alabama as well as an unknown number of their black slaves. (Some Native Americans, especially those belonging to the Five "Civilized Tribes"—the Cherokee, Chickasaw, Choctaw, Creek, and Seminole—owned African slaves.) Corralled into camps with only the possessions they could carry, the Cherokees and their slaves were transported to Oklahoma and the western edge of Arkansas, a 1,200-mile journey. They traveled by foot, on horse, and by wagon, forever leaving behind the land of their ancestors. Along the way, nearly 4,000 Cherokees and an unaccounted-for number of black slaves died, which is why the Cherokees refer to this ordeal as *nunna dual Isunui*: "The Trail where we Cried," or the Trail of Tears.[108] "People feel bad when they leave Old Nation," observed one Cherokee exile. "Women cry and make sad wails. Children cry and many men cry, and all look sad when friends die, but they say nothing and just put heads down and keep on going towards West."[109]

The Indian Intercourse Act of 1834 further delineated the boundaries of Indian Territory and ordered several tribes to relocate themselves within these boundaries. Those who refused could be put to death. Nomadic tribes were imprisoned within the confines of land set forth by Congress. By the mid-1800s, the reservation system we know today began to crystallize. And in 1887, the two strategies to solve "the Indian problem," assimilation and removal, were brought together under the Indian Allotment Act. The act dissolved tribal landholding by allotting certain pieces of land to *individual* Indians residing on reservations: heads of households were allotted 160 acres, single individuals a smaller parcel. "The General Allotment Act of 1887 marks the acme of U.S. political control over Native Americans. . . . Indians were to be incorporated *as individuals* into both the economic and political structures of the larger society. It was the ultimate form of control: the end of the tribe itself as a political and social entity."[110]

The Indian Allotment Act was the brainchild of Northern abolitionists who sought to humanize Native Americans by giving them that which, by the standards of Anglo-American culture, made one fully human: land and property. But indigenous

FIGURE 2.6 REMOVAL OF THE SOUTHEASTERN TRIBES

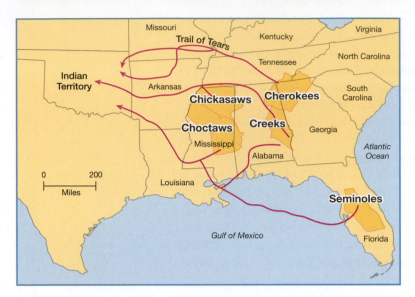

The Indian Removal Act of 1830 drove over 70,000 Native Americans from their homes on the fertile land east of the Mississippi over 14 years.

farming declined under the act, since many of the most fertile parcels of tribal land were claimed by whites. Nor did the allotted land remain in Indian hands for long. Between 1887 and 1934, 90 million acres passed into white hands. The Allotment Act, after all, did not allot Native Americans any additional land. Rather, it dispossessed tribes of land already in their possession. The allotment of 160 acres per Indian household actually freed a surplus of tribal land for white settlers. (It was as if you owned a large mansion and then, one day, the government knocked on your door and declared it was giving you a bedroom and bathroom to live in. The rest of your mansion was up for grabs.) Additionally, a significant amount of Native American land was sold or leased to non-Indians, since Native Americans were accused of failing to develop the land "up to white standards." In the end, the Allotment Act dispossessed Indians of more than 60 percent of their remaining landholdings.[111] Author Vine Deloria has observed, "Often when discussing treaty rights with whites, Indians find themselves told that 'We gave you the land and you haven't done anything with it.' . . . [But] never did the United States give any tribe any land at all. Rather, the Indian tribe gave the United States land in consideration for having Indian title to the remaining land confirmed."[112]

Native Americans resisted in large numbers. One form of resistance melded anguished cries for help with indigenous spirituality. In 1889, a Paiute spiritual leader named Wovoka claimed to have experienced a powerful vision during a solar eclipse. The walls of heaven were opened before him, revealing God and the Paiute, living in paradise. Wovoka urged his people to live in peace with the whites, since their rewards would come in the afterlife. He also developed a dance that would uplift the Paiute, the Ghost Dance. News of the Ghost Dance spread throughout the West, and tribes incorporated it into their traditional belief systems. While Wovoka was, by and large, a pacifist, other tribes interpreted Wovoka's prophesies as foretelling the destruction of the whites. The Lakotas, in particular, believed that the Ghost Dance would usher in a new era, one marked by the return of the buffalo and the fall of the whites.

Reservation agents and white settlers soon grew fearful of the Ghost Dance movement. As tensions mounted, U.S. troops were mobilized to suppress the dance. These tensions finally exploded on a cold December morning in 1890. Troops were ordered to disarm the Lakotas, and as they did so, a shot was fired, sparking a massive shoot-out that felled twenty-five troopers and over 150 Lakotas, a third of whom were women and children. This bloody event, known as the Wounded Knee Massacre, marked the gruesome finale to the 350-year-old Indian Wars.[113]

The nineteenth century witnessed the virtual destruction of tribal sovereignty, massive loss of Native American life, and near-total dispossession of tribal land. At the beginning of the nineteenth century, much of the land that now makes up the continental United States had still been in tribal hands. By the end of the century, nearly all that land was controlled by whites. For the American Indian, therefore, white colonialism in the Americas brought a threefold infliction: an infliction of the body, in the form of disease and bullet wounds; an infliction of the spirit, in the form of cultural reeducation, religious suppression, and Anglo-American assimilation; and an infliction of the land, in the form of the eradication of tribal property.

IMMIGRATION FROM ASIA AND EUROPE

During the mid-nineteenth century, immigrants flocked to America by the millions. The 1830s witnessed a swell of German immigrants, while the 1830s and 1840s saw over 2.5 million Irish move to America, more than a million of them between 1845 and 1849, the years of the Irish Potato Famine. Approximately 200,000 German Jews also immigrated to the United States, and the California gold rush of the late 1840s drew many immigrants from Asia. Between 1850 and 1882, the Chinese population in the United States would grow to 100,000.[114] We can now understand why, in 1855, American poet Walt Whitman penned the following words: "Here is not merely a nation but a teeming nation of nations."[115]

The Invention of the Asian American

Recall that, during the so-called Age of Discovery, Europeans were defining themselves as a collective group against the "strange" peoples of the East, peoples described in travelers' tales as fearsome and otherworldly. Thus, people from China, Japan, and other Asian countries, as well as those from the Middle East, came to the United States already "othered."[116]

The term "Asian" is a European invention, a kind of racial shorthand that subsumes under a single homogenizing category the peoples of China, Japan, Korea, India, Nepal, Bangladesh, Burma, Hawaii, the Pacific Islands, and all of Southeast Asia, including the Philippians, Cambodia, Vietnam, Indonesia, Thailand, Laos, Malaysia, and Singapore—peoples with immensely different and sometimes conflicting cultures, languages, and histories. These peoples of Asia had intermingled and traded with Europeans practically since the beginning of humanity; some even manned slave ships, while others came to the North American colonies as indentured servants. European contact with native Hawaiians is thought to have begun when Captain James Cook, a British sailor, landed on the islands in 1778. Because of its fertile climate, Hawaii soon was overrun by American and European planters eager to develop sugar plantations. Many Hawaiians died from warfare and disease as a result of European contact. It has been estimated that Hawaii's population numbered between 200,000 and 800,000 when James Cook discovered the islands. Only 100 years later, the population had plummeted to less than 48,000. Hawaii's sovereignty, chipped away throughout the nineteenth century, finally was dissolved in 1893 when the American military overthrew the Hawaiian monarchy and annexed the islands.[117]

Chinese laborers were imported to work the sugar fields of Hawaii. Around the same time, gold was discovered in California, and Chinese laborers migrated to the West

Coast to work for mining companies. The influx of Chinese laborers sparked a powerful anti-Chinese movement. Starting in 1850, all foreign miners in California were forced to pay an extra tax, one that fell most heavily on Chinese workers. Chinese also were prevented from testifying against white people in court, and, since Jim Crow segregation was enforced, Chinese children also were forced to attend separate schools.[118]

Chinese people were distorted in the popular press as parasitic, soulless, and criminal. A newspaper announcing an "Anti-Chinese Meeting" in 1877 declared that "the Chinese as a class are a detriment and a curse to our country. . . . They have supplanted white labor and taken the bread out of the mouths of the white men and their families."[119] Chinese laborers, furthermore, were the victims of mob violence. In 1871, a white mob lynched, shot, and torched twenty-one Chinese immigrants in Los Angeles; in 1880, Denver's Chinatown was burnt to the ground, a laundryman beaten to death; in 1885, white workers killed twenty-eight Chinese men employed by the Union Pacific Railroad. Just as many poor whites during black slavery and Reconstruction blamed their poverty on African Americans, white workers during the nineteenth century saw Chinese immigrants as thieves who took "the bread out of the mouths of the white men and their families." The real culprit—an economic system that flourished by keeping labor cheap and pitting white worker against nonwhite worker—often escaped reproach.[120]

At the same time that American capitalists were encouraging the migration of an expendable labor force from Asia, American lawmakers were regulating Asian immigration and denying Asian immigrants the right to naturalize. In 1875, the Page Law, intended to bar Chinese prostitutes from the United States, had the effect of barring virtually all Chinese women from American shores. Chinese men were needed to dig for gold and hammer railroad spikes, but Chinese women could bear children who, under the Fourteenth Amendment, would become American citizens. It was not long

Chinese laborers were often victims of mob violence and vandalism.

(the Chinese Exclusion Act of 1882) before *all* Chinese immigrants, men and women, were forbidden entry into the United States. Peoples of west, south, and Southeast Asia suffered the same fate under the Immigration Act of 1917, as did nearly all Asian groups under the Immigration Act of 1924.[121] And, of course, the task of defining citizenship eligibility led courts to construct Asians as a nonwhite group. From 1878 to 1941, Hawaiians and Chinese, Burmese, Japanese, Filipino, and Korean immigrants were deemed "not white," while the whiteness of Indian Americans, as we learned in the last chapter, was a matter of great debate and legal uncertainty.[122]

Immigrants from the Old World

America at the end of the nineteenth century was shaped not only by immigrants from Asia but also—and especially—by immigrants from Europe. "About 1882, the character of our immigration changed in a very remarkable manner. Immigration from Northern Europe dropped off rather abruptly, and in its place immigration from Southern, Central, and Eastern Europe set in and soon developed into a great stream."[123] Between 1886 and 1935, some 13 million immigrants from countries such as Austria, Hungary, Italy, and Russia flocked to America, 70 percent of them between 1901 and 1915. How were these "new immigrants," as they were called, accepted? One observer in 1909 echoed a widely shared sentiment of the period: "These southern and eastern Europeans are a very different type from the north European who preceded them. Illiterate, docile, lacking in self-reliance and initiative and not possessing Anglo-Teutonic conceptions of law, order and government, their coming has served to dilute tremendously our national stock, and to corrupt our civic life."[124]

Jews, Poles, Slavs, Hungarians, Ukrainians, Armenians, Greeks, and Italians generally were not welcomed by native-born white Americans. In some circles, new immigrants were framed as members of "inferior races," "lesser breeds," "scoundrels," and "thieves," who had contributed considerably less to civilization than the upstanding people of the "English race."[125]

New immigrants did not face the extreme levels of racial hatred and brutality that blacks, Asians, American Indians, and Mexicans had to endure. But neither were they fully accepted into the (white) American mainstream. On the one hand, they enjoyed a fair amount of white privilege.[126] On the other, new immigrants were not looked on as the racial equals of northern Europeans or native-born Anglo-Saxons. New European immigrants, then, were caught between exclusion and inclusion. These "in-between people," to use the

The film *The Godfather, Part II* shows 11-year-old Vito Corleone (Oreste Baldini) gazing at the Statue of Liberty as his boat from Italy pulls into Ellis Island. This scene would be familiar to the thousands of immigrants to America during the mid-nineteenth century.

TABLE 2.1 IMMIGRATION FROM SOUTH, CENTRAL, AND EASTERN EUROPE, 1820-1919

Decade	All South, Central[c] and Eastern Europe	Italy	Greece	Eastern Europe Jews
1820–1829	3,343	430	17	7,500[a]
1830–1839	5,758	2,225	49	
1840–1849	4,275	1,476	17	
1850–1859	20,063	8,110	25	40,000
1860–1869	26,522	10,238	n.a.	200,000
1870–1879	172,655	46,296	209	300,000
1880–1889	836,265	267,660	1,807	
1890–1899	1,753,916	603,761	12,732	1,500,000[b]
1900–1909	5,822,355	1,930,475	145,402	
1910–1919	3,937,395	1,229,916	198,108	
1920–1924	1,114,730	460,644	52,144	

Sources: Carpenter, 1927, pp. 324-325; Rischin, 1962, p. 20; Willcox, 1929, p. 393.
[a]Between 1800 and 1869
[b]Between 1900 and 1914
[c]Persons born in Germany are not included

label developed by the eminent historian John Higham, struggled to find their place in America, battling poverty, ridicule, and sometimes violence along the way.[127] The swelling waves of immigrants from southern, eastern, and central Europe resulted in a kind of fracturing of American whiteness. Ethnic hierarchies were established within the white race, with landowning, native-born Anglo-Saxons occupying the highest positions and impoverished new immigrants demoted to the status of "low-ranking members of the whiteness club."[128]

By the 1920s and 1930s, however, white ethnic hierarchies began to fade. How did the new immigrants— "dark whites," as they sometimes were called—become just "white?" Social scientists have offered four complementary answers to this question. The first has to do with the development of "ethnicity" as a concept. Around the beginning of the twentieth century, "race" and "ethnicity" were used interchangeably and in a loose fashion; there was no sharp distinction between the two. This began to change as scholars and policymakers began assigning the term "ethnic" to new immigrants from Europe, while "race" was used to differentiate blacks, Mexicans, American Indians, or Asians from the white population. This implied that the distance between new immigrants and native-born whites was the result of *social and cultural differences*, which could be addressed with enough time and education, while the distance separating blacks, Mexicans, American Indians, and Asians from white Americans was *natural and fixed*. In the words of one commentator writing in 1932, the "white immigrant [is] patently handicapped by foreign language and tradition," while the "Negro . . . is . . . more of a biological problem."[129]

There was a second way in which new immigrants pulled themselves more fully into the white race. When impoverished newcomers from Italy, Hungary, and other European lands arrived in America in search of work, they found themselves in competition with blacks, who had gained emancipation less than half a century earlier. Many new immigrants worked and lived side by side with blacks. Soon enough, however, the new immigrants began to sense that they could gain an advantage over black workers by tapping into white employers' racial prejudices. The rise of unions in the early decades of the twentieth century provided new immigrants an opportunity to mobilize as "whites." Nonwhite groups had little opportunity to retaliate, and by asserting their right to employment on the basis of their whiteness (instead of, say, their "Italianness"), new immigrants avoided a nativist backlash by native-born white Americans.[130]

New immigrants quickly learned to use America's racial divisions to their advantage. A third way new immigrants became white, then, was by lashing out against nonwhites, chiefly blacks. New immigrants led antiblack propaganda campaigns and terrorized the black community through mob violence.[131] To transform themselves from "lying Italians" or "pitiful Greeks" into "entitled whites," new immigrants learned the ropes of racial contempt. In the elegant words of Toni Morrison, "Whatever the lived experience of immigrants with African Americans—pleasant, beneficial or bruising—the rhetorical experience renders blacks as non-citizens, already discredited outlaws. . . . The move into mainstream America always means buying into the notion of American blacks as the real aliens. Whatever the ethnicity or nationality of the immigrant, his nemesis is understood to be African American."[132]

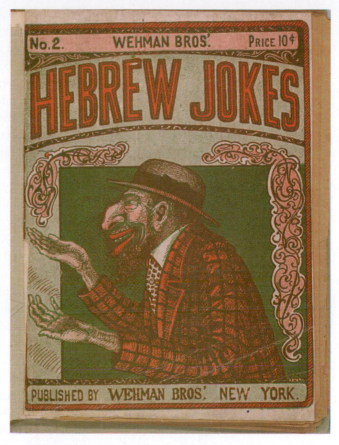

Ethnic hierarchies were established within the white race, with landowning, native-born Anglo-Saxons occupying the highest positions and impoverished new immigrants demoted to the status of "low-ranking members of the whiteness club."

All these transformative changes took place within the framework of Jim Crow segregation, the fourth mechanism by which new immigrants became more fully white. Racial segregation, accompanied by white-on-nonwhite violence, solidified a culture of whiteness throughout the United States. Because new immigrants by and large were not subjected to the same painful processes of segregation as nonwhites, they could take advantage of the benefits of whiteness, from restaurants and restrooms to neighborhoods and schools.[133] To escape racial persecution, new immigrants joined the persecutors, thereby broadening the definition of whiteness and further strengthening the might of white supremacy.

RACIAL DISCOURSES OF MODERNITY

If the "Middle Ages regarded skin color with mild curiosity," as Du Bois has observed, then the modern age defined itself on this very thing.[134] Between the European discovery of America and the early twentieth century, new *racial discourses*—collections of ideas about race developed by secular authorities such as philosophers, writers, and scientists—rose to prominence and helped to form classification systems riveted in white supremacy.[135]

Philosophers such as Hobbes, Locke, Voltaire, Montesquieu, and Hume justified slavery and racism in their writings.[136] "I am apt to suspect the negroes," wrote Hume, ". . . to be naturally inferior to the whites."[137] Let us consider here the great eighteenth-century philosopher Immanuel Kant, a supreme source of philosophic inspiration for modern Western ideals of autonomy, rights, and justice. Kant spoke inspiringly of a "Kingdom of Ends" in which all are treated with equal respect, holding up for special admiration "the friend of humanity who treats all persons—'that is, the whole race'—with equality, whatever their status" (or, one would hope, their skin color).[138] Yet this paragon of modern liberalism also was a founder of modern racism, "the founder of the first theory of race worthy of the name."[139] As has been suggested in a recent revisionist study, "Kant's lectures and writings on anthropology and physical geography (usually ignored by philosophers) provide a detailed account of a racialized human nature classified into four categories—white Europeans, yellow Asians, black Africans, red Amerindians—who are related to one another in a hierarchy of superiors and inferiors."[140] It is by no means clear that nonwhites merit in this account the same moral status of personhood as white Europeans. Perhaps "when Kant talks about the importance of treating all persons with respect," philosopher Charles Mills has suggested, "when he outlines the responsibilities of the state, when he maps his inspiring cosmopolitan vision, he is not making race-neutral and racially-inclusive pronouncements; *he is really talking about the white population.*"[141] Modern philosophic liberalism and modern racism thus grew up together—a historical fact that challenges deep-seated views about the nature and development of Western thought.

Literary authors, too, contributed to the elaboration of racial discourses, culminating in the late nineteenth century with Rudyard Kipling, a British poet and supporter of his country's colonial conquests, whose famous work "The White Man's Burden" (1899) began with the lines, "Your new-caught, sullen peoples / Half-devil and half-child." As Morrison has observed of poets and novelists in the United States, but in words that apply as well to literary figures across the modern West, "Living in a nation of people who *decided* that their world view would combine agendas for individual freedom *and* mechanisms for devastating racial oppression presents a singular landscape. . . . How do embedded [racial] assumptions . . . work in the literary enterprise that hopes and sometimes claims to be 'humanistic'?"[142]

However, of all the secular authorities, the group that proved most influential in solidifying racial taxonomies were the natural historians, precursors to modern-day biologists and physical anthropologists. The natural historians were interested in classifying plants, animals, and so-called people groups. It was through their endeavors that, in 1624, the term "race" was first used—by François Bernier, a French physician—to label and separate human bodies.[143] Others followed suit. For example, in 1775, a German medical researcher named Johann Blumenbach published a typology of humanity that divided humans into five groups that correspond to different geographical areas—Caucasians, Mongolians, Ethiopians, Americans, and Malays—and held that Caucasians exemplified the standards of "pure beauty" in human form.[144] Blumenbach and other European scientists did not gather "data" to support their typologies by

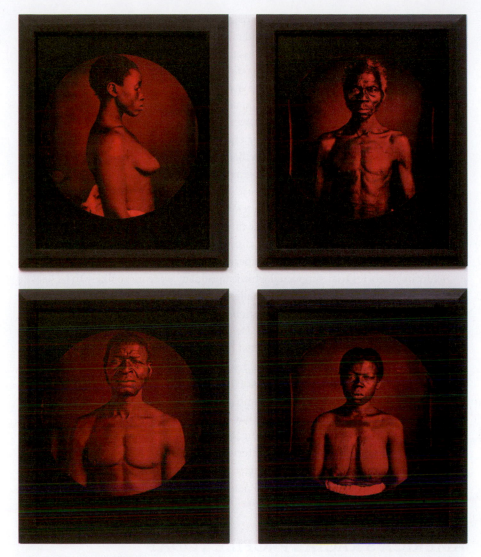

Racism did not naturally flow from systems of racial classification; rather, systems of racial classification flowed from racism.

traveling the world. Instead, they relied on the accounts of European planters, travelers, missionaries, and soldiers—accounts that often were highly fallacious.

Typologies such as those proposed by Blumenbach presented distinct racial groups as fixed and immutable. They also attached behavioral traits to physical characteristics, claiming, for example, that Europeans were naturally ingenious while Africans were naturally lazy. Most harmfully, racial classifications justified racial inequality by suggesting that such inequality was a natural ordering of the world.[145]

Soon enough, a theory was developed suggesting that all human behavior was hereditary. The person most often associated with this idea is Francis Galton, a wealthy cousin of Charles Darwin. Galton believed that levels of intelligence and creativity, diligence and determination, moral fortitude and uprightness all were linked to heredity. To squeeze the best possible traits out of the human line, Galton suggested that marriage be regulated and child rearing modulated, according to the genetic giftedness of parents.[146] Eager to set this plan in motion, he coined the term "eugenics" to refer to a program that would ensure genetic purity. To its founder, eugenics was "the science of improving stock, which is by no means confined to questions of judicious mating but which, especially in the case of man, takes cognizance of all influences that tend in however remote a degree to give to the more suitable races or strains of blood a better chance of prevailing speedily over the less suitable than they otherwise would have had."[147]

With eugenics, science became a program; that is, "solutions" were advanced for the "natural inferiority of the lower races." An especially cruel solution was forced sterilization. From the end of the nineteenth century to *the 1970s*, thousands of Native Americans and African Americans, as well as people deemed mentally retarded or criminal, underwent surgical procedures against their will, sometimes without their knowing, that resulted in permanent infertility.[148]

Scientific theories that supported white supremacy were more likely to be backed by the power elite than theories that challenged the status quo. But a good number of scientists did criticize racist pseudoscience and eugenics when it was out of fashion to do so. For example, in *Man's Most Dangerous Myth*, Ashley Montagu chastised eugenicists, writing, "Our troubles, it must be repeated, emanate not from biological defectives but from social defectives; and social defectives are produced by society, not by genes. Obviously, it is social, not biological, therapy that is indicated."[149] Nevertheless, the doctrine of eugenics spread throughout the world.

Science authoritatively legitimated that which had been developing throughout Europe's colonial conquests and America's enslavement of Africans: the notion that nonwhite people were naturally inferior to the white race.[150] More pointedly, these social classifications masquerading as scientific truth made the horrors done to nonwhite people easier to swallow. Racism did not naturally flow from systems of racial classification; rather, systems of racial classification flowed from racism.[151]

AMERICA'S RACIAL PROFILE TODAY

By the middle of the twentieth century, the racial categories so familiar to us today were firmly established. Although the second half of the twentieth century would bring great changes in the realm of race, including the rise of the Civil Rights Movement and the fall of Jim Crow, the racial categories that emerged in America over the course of the previous 300 years would remain, for the most part, unchallenged. Americans, white and nonwhite alike, would understand themselves as raced and accept the dominant racial classification system even if they refused to accept the terms of racial inequality. That is why this chapter, one concerned with the genesis and historical development of racial categories, has not ventured too deeply into the mid- and late twentieth century. We take up that task in the chapters ahead.

Before moving on to that task, however, let us take up one final issue. Having examined both the genesis and historical development of racial categories, on the one hand, and the historical transformation of American society itself, on the other,

FIGURE 2.7 **FOREIGN-BORN POPULATION AND PERCENTAGE OF TOTAL POPULATION, UNITED STATES, 1850–2010**

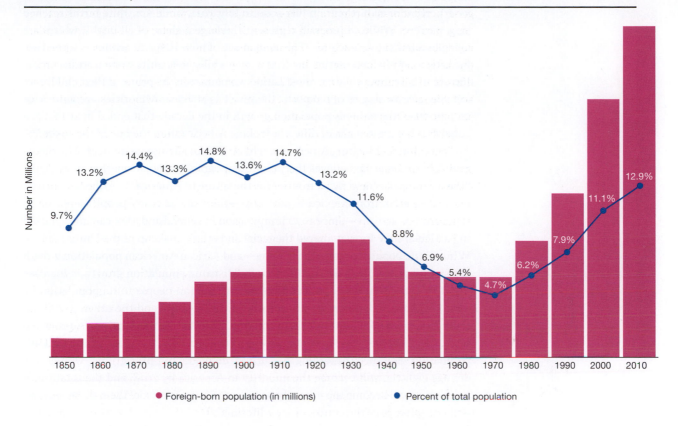

- ● Foreign-born population (in millions)
- ● Percent of total population

what can we say about what American society looks like today, in terms of the racial categories we have inherited?

As of 2012, whites made up 63 percent of the population, Hispanics made up 17 percent, and blacks made up 13 percent. Asians made up 5 percent, and Native Americans and Native Hawaiians made up 1 percent. Roughly 13 percent of the U.S. population were born in another country. And for one in five Americans, a language other than English was spoken at home.[152]

Certain nonwhite populations are represented in significant numbers in some areas of the country but not in others. Hispanics make up 38 percent of Californians and Texans but only 12 percent of all people who live in the state of Washington and 1 percent of those living in Maine. Likewise, blacks are numerous in the Deep South—constituting around one-third of the population in Louisiana, Mississippi, and Georgia—but make up less than 2 percent of the population in Wyoming, Montana, and North Dakota.[153]

Whites constitute a considerable majority of America's population today, but things may look different in the future. In many metropolitan areas, such as Houston, Los Angeles, New York, and Miami, whites are numerically outnumbered, as they are in some states. In California, for example, the white population dropped from two-thirds to less than half between 1980 and 2000.[154]

Recently, for the first time since the founding of the United States, white babies did not make up the majority of U.S. births. Non-Hispanic whites accounted for 49.6 percent of all births from July 2010 to July 2011, while nonwhite births reached 50.4 percent. While whites still represent the largest share of all births, whites are aging in relation to nonwhites. The median age of non-Hispanic whites is forty-two; for Latinos, it is twenty-seven. In other words, while most white women are becoming too old to have more children, most Latino women are in the prime of their childbearing years. According to one report, "the result is striking: Minorities accounted for 92 percent of the nation's population growth in the decade that ended in 2010, . . . a surge that has created a very different looking America from the one of the 1950s."[155]

"Very different looking America" might be a bit of an understatement. The historian Albert Camarillo believes that recent demographic transformations may signal "the dawning of a 'new' racial frontier for the future of America."[156] Although current net immigration from Mexico is now zero—there are as many people deported as there are new arrivals—since 1970 immigration in general and Mexican immigration in particular have forever altered the racial and ethnic makeup of the United States. While white population growth is falling—and African American population growth is remaining steady—Asian and especially Hispanic population growth is increasing. The United States is projected to add 117 million people to its population by 2050; of those, 67 million are projected to be immigrants and the other 50 million their U.S.-born children and grandchildren. The Latino population is projected to triple in size between now and 2050 and will account for most of the nation's population growth.[157] According to current demographic projections, whites under age eighteen will become the minority in America by 2018, and the total white population will become the minority by 2043.[158] For most of you, then, these changes will take place over the course of your lifetime.

FIGURE 2.8 **U.S. RACE-ETHNIC COMPOSITION, 1970–2050**

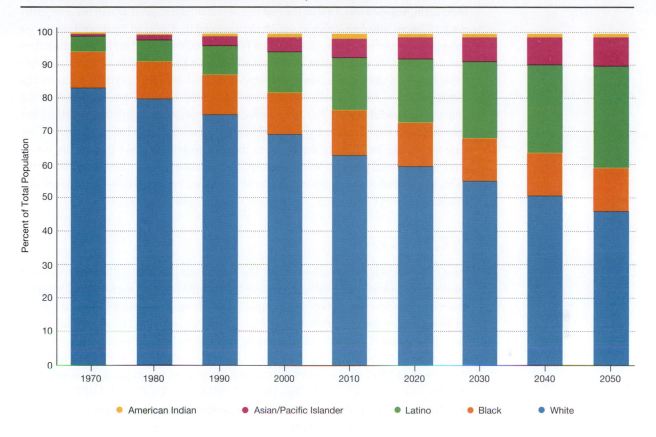

As the United States grows more diverse, racial markers themselves seem to be growing more porous and fluid. A racial taxonomy comprising five major groups now seems more inadequate than ever. Today, one in forty people claim multiracial heritage—that is, to belong to two or more racial groups—but that ratio jumps to one in twenty for people under the age of eighteen. By some projections, as many as one in five Americans will identify as multiracial by 2050. After asking multiethnic readers to contribute nicknames that describe their mixed heritage, a California newspaper compiled a list of terms. A half-Canadian, half-Mexican reader referred to himself as "Canexican"; a half-Pakistani, half-Mexican as "Mexistani"; a half-Scottish, half-Mexican as "McRiguez."[159]

Asians and Latinos have the highest proportion of people identifying as biracial or multiracial. Because whites far outnumber other groups, most of those who claim multiracial identity report being white plus something else. Blacks have the lowest proportion of people who claim multiracial identity.[160] This is not necessarily because there actually are fewer multiracial people of African ancestry, but because in the eyes of many, blackness remains a totalizing racial category. To many Americans, black and nonblack alike, one cannot be "black and Asian" or "black and white." All such people are simply black.[161] Although the son of a black father and a white mother, Barack Obama is usually not referred to as the "first biracial president" but "the first black president."

If multiracial identification is on the rise today, it is not only because of immigration from Latin America and Asia or the rise in interracial marriage. It is also because many people—especially young people—wish to transcend the limits of rigid racial categories and place themselves in two, three, or four histories, cultures, and heritages, rather than just one. The U.S. government, by finally allowing in 2000 citizens to check multiple racial boxes on the Census, has encouraged or at least officially permitted multiracial identification. If America is becoming more and more the multiracial nation, it is not only because racial populations have moved across national borders (immigration) but also because racial borders have moved across populations (reclassification).[162] If we look far enough back in our family trees, most of us will discover that we are mixed ethnically or racially. And if we think about how racial categories have changed over the years, many of us who would not consider ourselves multiracial today—we who are, say, Russian Jews or of Italian and Irish descent—might have in an earlier era.

WE, THE PAST

Race as we know it did not always exist. The Indian was invented within the context of European colonization, as indigenous peoples of the Americas were lumped together under one rubric to be uprooted and exploited. Whiteness and blackness were invented as antipodes within the context of English, and later American, slavery. Blackness became associated with bondage, inferiority, and social death; whiteness with freedom, superiority, and life. The Mexican was invented within the context of the colonization of Mexico. At the end of the nineteenth century, the Asian was invented as a response to immigration from the Far East. Whiteness expanded during the early years of the twentieth century as new immigrants from southern, central, and eastern Europe transformed themselves from "lesser whites" to, simply, "whites." All the while, white supremacy was legitimated by racial discourses in philosophy, literature, and science. By the middle of the twentieth century, the racial categories so familiar to us today were firmly established. Although the second half of the twentieth century would bring great changes in the realm of race, including the rise of the Civil Rights Movement and the fall of Jim Crow, the racial categories that emerged in America over the course of the previous 300 years would remain, for the most part, unchallenged.

This chapter reviewed the specific social and historical contexts by which race entered the world. To think of race as a biological entity, as something that never has and never will change, is to forget the history of race. But if we remember our history, we come to the conclusion that race is neither an innocent nor an obvious part of humanity, but a European invention, forged in the context of colonization and slavery.

Moreover, a thorough understanding of the past enhances a thorough understanding of ourselves. We do not exist in a vacuum, magically undisturbed by historical and social forces. Rather, we are the products of history. The contours of our society—our current institutions, our schools, our neighborhoods, and our prisons—have been designed by the hands of history, as have our social sufferings and inequalities. When we look each other in the eye, we must look *past* the person standing before us, comprehending that person as someone who has been historically and socially constituted. That person does not lack in freedom but *is* partly conditioned by the actions of those who came before. We inheritors of history should bear this in mind as we turn our attention now to unpacking how race works in society's different fields of life.

THE BIG PICTURE

Chapter 2: The Invention of Race

MAIN POINTS

Explain how the modern concept of "race" emerged amid the revolutionary transformations of modernity—the rise of capitalism, nationalism, science, and colonialism—as a new way of viewing and ordering the world.

Recognize how the concepts of American whiteness and blackness emerged with the African slave trade.

Understand how the growth of the U.S. economy and the institutionalization of black slavery between 1660 and 1860 are inextricably linked.

Learn how the annexation of land from Mexico and Native American tribes led to widespread poverty, cultural devastation, and the loss of rights and citizenship.

Explain how new racial discourses devised by philosophers, writers, and scientists rose to prominence and helped form classification systems riveted in white supremacy.

Examine how immigration patterns in the late nineteenth and early twentieth centuries led to the creation of new racial categories and redefinitions of whiteness.

KEY TERMS

- colonialism, page 50

- alavery, page 57

- Manifest Destiny, page 69

- eugenics, page 82
- Multiethnic heritage, page 85

- immigration, page 75

FROM THEORY TO PRACTICE

Identify three ways in which present-day society mirrors seventeenth-, eighteenth-, or nineteenth-century America. Look for parallels in the realm of culture (recycled ideas, stereotypes, fears), politics (similar issues, agendas, practices) and everyday life (job market, romantic relationships, recurrent social problems).

How have the people with whom you identify been systematically privileged or disadvantaged racially over the course of American history? How do you think your own life is privileged or disadvantaged because of this? In other words, how is your own social position shaped by historical forces?

How does the history reviewed in this chapter compare to the history of early America that you learned elsewhere? Meditate on the reasons for such similarities and differences.

Of the history reviewed in this chapter, which parts do you feel often are forgotten by people in your life? Why do you think that is? What do you think would change if this history was remembered?

3 Politics

MAIN POINTS

- Examine the strategies and tactics used by the African American Civil Rights Movement, the American Indian movement, and the Chicano movement to push for racial justice and the end of discrimination and segregation.

- Describe the backlash to the Civil Rights Movement from whites and explain how it led to the creation of the so-called Southern Strategy.

- Explain why nonwhites are underrepresented in the American electorate and how American politics continues to be racially polarized.

- Evaluate the role of race in voting patterns and voter turnout.

- Discuss how political campaigns have shifted from class-based appeals to race-based appeals.

She was the daughter of black sharecroppers, a woman who had worked a Mississippi plantation all her life. At the age of six, she started picking cotton. Because her family needed her in the fields, she received only six years of formal schooling. But when Fannie Lou Hamer took the front seat at the 1962 Democratic Convention Credentials Committee hearing, she arrested the country's attention. After explaining to the committee the widespread disenfranchisement of southern blacks and recounting a brutal beating she and other women had been given by police officers for trying to order food at a segregated restaurant, Mrs. Hamer concluded, "All of this on account we want to register, to become first-class citizens.... I question America. Is this America, the land of the free and the home of the brave, where we have to sleep with our telephones off the hooks because our lives be threatened daily because we want to live as decent human beings? In America?"[1] The question cuts to the quick of the matter: the drastic disconnection between the lofty ideals of American democracy and American democracy in practice, the simultaneous inclusion of "the people" in the high halls of governance and the exclusion of "certain people" from full citizenship. It is the contradiction of penning "We hold these truths to be self-evident: That all men are created equal" while sponsoring a system of slavery and colonialism. It is criticizing the Nazi Holocaust while, fearing espionage, imprisoning thousands of Japanese American citizens in internment camps.

Things have changed since Fannie Lou Hamer questioned America. The Civil Rights Movement arose in response to racial terrorism and segregation. We begin this chapter by exploring how the Civil Rights Movement changed the face of American politics. We then turn to the present day, examining how race works in the political field, focusing on partisanship and representation,

Fannie Lou Hamer speaks before the credentials committee of the Democratic national convention in Atlantic City, August 22, 1964.

voting, and elections. Although the United States no longer legally supports racial segregation, race continues to play a defining role in American politics.

THE CIVIL RIGHTS MOVEMENT

One hundred years after the Emancipation Proclamation, freedom had not come to African Americans. In the southern states, Jim Crow laws institutionalized social practices that attempted to deny blacks their humanity. If a black woman went shopping, she was forbidden to try on her new dress, since store owners thought white shoppers would not want clothes worn by blacks. If a black father sought food

FIGURE 3.1 **THE STATE OF LOUISIANA LITERACY TEST**

The State of Louisiana

Literacy Test (This test is to be given to anyone who cannot prove a fifth grade education.)

Do what you are told to do in each statement, nothing more, nothing less. Be careful as one wrong answer denotes failure of test. You have 10 mintutes to complete the test.

1. Draw a line around the number or letter of this sentence.

2. Draw a line under the last word in this line.

3. Cross out the longest word in this line.

4. Draw a line around the shortest word in this line.

5. Circle the first, first letter of the alphabet in this line.

6. In the space below draw three circles, one inside (engulfed by) the other.

7. Above the letter X make a small cross.

8. Draw a line through the letter below that comes earliest in the alphabet.

    Z V S B D M K I T P H C

9. Draw a line through the two letters below that come last in the alphabet.
    Z V B D M K T P H S Y C

10. In the first circle below write the last letter of the first word beginning with "L".

11. Cross out the number necessary, when making the number below one million.

    10000000000

12. Draw a line from circle 2 to circle 5 that will pass below circle 2 and above circle 4.

13. In the line below cross out each number that is more than 20 but less 30.

    31 16 48 29 53 47 22 37 98 26 20 25

14. Draw a line under the first letter after "h" and draw a line through the second letter after "J".

    a b c d e f g h i k l m n o p q

15. In the space below, write the word "noise" backwards and place a dot over what would be its second letter should it have been written forward.

16. Draw a triangle with a blackened circle that overlaps only its left corner.

17. Look at the line of numbers below, and place on the blank, the number that should come next.

    2 4 8 16 ____

18. Look at the line of numbers below, and place on the blank, the number that should come next.

    3 6 9 ____ 15

19. Draw in the space below, a square with a triangle in it, and within that same triangle draw a circle with a black dot in it.

for his family, he would have to enter the restaurant through the back door, out of sight. Separate schools were anything but equal. For example, consider Yazoo City, Mississippi, which in the late 1950s dedicated $245 per white child for educational expenses and only $3 per black child.[2]

Unable to obtain jobs elsewhere, blacks were forced back onto southern plantations through a new system of (informal) slavery called sharecropping. White planters gave blacks a small piece of land on which to grow crops and live (often in squalid shacks). In return, blacks gave white planters a portion of their crop. Often, planters left black sharecroppers only with enough crops on which to survive, not enough to profit. Sharecroppers were kept in dirt-floor poverty through a system of unending debt.

---

20. Spell backwards, forwards.

21. Print the word vote upside down, but in the correct order.

22. Place a cross over the tenth letter in this line, a line under the first space in this sentence, and circle around the last the in the second line of this sentence.

23. Draw a figure that is square in shape. Divide it in half by drawing a straight line from its northeast corner to its southwest corner, and then divide it once more by drawing a broken line from the middle of its western side to the middle of its eastern side.

24. Print a word that looks the same whether it is printed frontwards or backwards.

25. Write down on the line provided, what you read in the triangle below.

Paris
in the
the spring

26. In the third square below, write the second letter of the fourth word.

27. Write right from the left to the right as you see it spelled here.

28. Divide a vertical line in two equal parts by bisecting it with a curved horizontal line that is only straight at its spot bisecting of the vertical.

29. Write every other word in this first line and print every third word in same line. (original type smaller and first line ended at comma) but capitalize the fifth word that you write.

30. Draw five circles that one common inter-locking part.

At the time, whites also withheld from blacks the most basic right of American citizenship: the vote. Although black men won the right to vote with the ratification of the Fifteenth Amendment in 1870 and women won suffrage rights in 1920, black women and men remained disenfranchised. When blacks in the old Confederacy went to the courthouse to register, for example, they were told that they had to own property or that they needed to be accompanied by a white person who could vouch for their character. Some were forced to take complicated literacy tests requiring them to copy down and explain portions of the state's Constitution. Many blacks were illiterate—recall that slaves often were forbidden from learning how to read— and failed the tests. Many poor whites were illiterate as well, but they were exempted from literary tests by "grandfather clauses." These clauses, often amendments to southern state constitutions, extended the right to vote to those whose relatives were enfranchised before the end of the Civil War and the ensuing passage of the Fifteenth Amendment: that is, whites only. In the South, in short, most blacks were not registered to vote. For example, in 1960 fewer than 2 percent of Mississippi's black adults were registered.[3]

Black disenfranchisement was safeguarded not only in law but also by white terrorism. Between 1930 and 1950, thirty-three blacks (that we know of) were lynched in Mississippi. There was Henry Bedford, a seventy-two-year-old tenant farmer beaten to death for apparently speaking disrespectfully to a white man. There was J. B. Grant, a seventeen-year-old shot over 100 times by a lynch mob and hung on a railroad trestle (for what, we do not know). There were Charlie Lang and Ernest Green, both fourteen, tortured, castrated, and murdered for allegedly raping a young white girl. It later would be discovered that the boys and the white girl, all childhood friends, simply were playing together.[4]

Then there was Emmett Till, a fourteen-year-old from Chicago who had traveled to Mississippi to visit relatives. Till, making good on a dare, whistled at a white woman in a country store on August 24, 1955. He would be dead two days later. White men broke into his relative's home, kidnapped Emmett, beat him, cut off his testicles, shot him, and tossed him into the Tallahatchie River. Till's aggrieved mother allowed photographers to take pictures of her son's mutilated body so that others might see what had been done. The grisly image was displayed in magazines and television broadcasts around the United States, exposing millions to the racial violence ravaging the South.

It has been said that Emmett Till's murder galvanized and energized many Americans, black and white, to participate in the Civil Rights Movement, that collection of organizations and people who carried out political acts aimed at abolishing racial segregation, nonwhite disenfranchisement, and economic exploitation. The movement drew inspiration from what historians have called the "black organizing tradition," which runs from

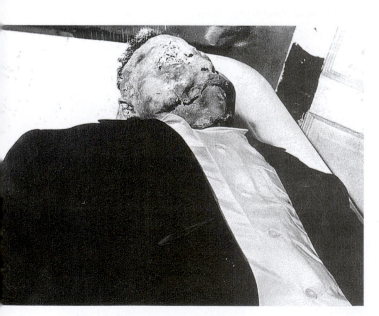

Chicago native Emmett Till was brutally murdered in Mississippi after an encounter with a white woman.

slave revolts (large and small) through Reconstruction and the tumultuous 1960s.[5] During the 1950s and 1960s, a fire first ignited by revolting slaves, tended by every-day black people struggling against racism during Reconstruction, and rekindled by those who refused to lower their eyes when met with Jim Crow's icy stare roared up in combusting waves. In the words of civil rights veteran Fred Shuttlesworth, it was "a fire you [could not] put out!"[6] "We know through painful experience," wrote Martin Luther King, Jr., from a Birmingham jail cell, "that freedom is never volun-tarily given by the oppressor; it must be demanded by the oppressed."[7] During the Civil Rights Movement, blacks demanded their freedom.

The NAACP

The National Association for the Advancement of Colored People (NAACP) was the dominant black protest organization that preceded the modern Civil Rights Movement. Founded in 1909 by black and white intellectuals, the NAACP did battle with racial domination primarily in the courts. Soon after its founding, the NAACP won several Supreme Court cases that dismantled legal barriers preventing blacks from voting. The organization also launched education programs targeting white America. Working with the assumption that white racism was rooted in ignorance, the NAACP produced press releases, speeches, pamphlets, and a magazine (*The Crisis*), depicting nonwhite people as realistic, reasonable, and intelligent. In direct opposition to the mainstream press, the NAACP supported works that celebrated the accomplishments of nonwhite scholars and artists.[8]

As the NAACP grew stronger, incorporating more members and winning more court battles, so did its opposition. At midcentury, precisely the time when the NAACP began fighting for the integration of public schools, whites launched a co-ordinated attack that eventually would bring the organization to its knees. In 1956, most southern state legislatures demanded that the NAACP release its membership lists. "The intention was clear. If the NAACP yielded to this pressure and revealed its members' addresses, the members would suffer economic reprisals, violence, and other forms of repression. It was clear that the organization could be destroyed by exposing its members."[9] The NAACP refused to capitulate and, as a result, was banned in southern states. And cruel acts of terror were visited on NAACP leaders, such as Medgar Evers, Mississippi's first NAACP field secretary who was fatally shot in the back on the steps of his home.

But the weakening of the NAACP seemed to strengthen a new kind of political protest, one that involved not just intellectuals and lawyers but ordinary folk: sharecroppers, teachers, students, and even children. This new movement was based in the South, and it brought the fight not only to the courtroom but also to the street. Civil rights organizing began shifting from a model based on legal action to one based on direct action and from a bureaucratic organization to community-based groups.[10]

SCLC and Church-Driven Direct Action

Although blacks had engaged in direct action since the slave revolts, this form of political protest was revisited and reinvented in earnest after World War II. Black veterans who fought Hitler's armies returned home only to ask, "How can my country criticize racism abroad but not at home? Why is it that America right-ly defends Jews from Nazi violence but fails to defend blacks from the KKK?" Many black soldiers, among them Medgar Evers, returned to their communi-ties determined to stand up against racial injustice. They found support in the Double-V Campaign—"Victory at Home; Victory Abroad"—that was launched by the *Pittsburgh Courier*, a black newspaper.

Along with military veterans, black preachers and their congregants played a vital role in steering and energizing the Civil Rights Movement. More than any other in-stitution, the black church would serve as the institutional hub of the movement. The church was relatively isolated from the white power structure, and it housed a mass base of blacks, who under its roof could voice their problems and needs in a safe space. Because the black church was financially independent, preachers did not have to worry about losing their jobs if they caused a stir. Thus, the black church would produce some of the most outspoken critics of white domination. For example, there was Reverend T. J. Jemison, who led a boycott against segregated buses in Baton Rouge years before the better-known Montgomery bus boycott; there was Birmingham's Reverend Fred Shuttlesworth, who, having been whipped and beaten with chains for trying to enroll his children in an all-white public school and having his house bombed one Christmas Eve, was fond of quoting Jesus's injunction that "one must lose his life to find it"; and there was a young preacher from Atlanta, the son and grandson of preachers, bearing the name of a revolutionary who had come before him: Martin Luther King, Jr.[11]

One of the first major demonstrations of the Civil Rights Movement was the Montgomery Bus Boycott, which began a few days after December 1, 1955, when Rosa Parks, in defiance of Alabama segregation laws, refused to relinquish her bus seat to a white man.[12] Parks was bailed out of jail by E. D. Nixon, who, along with members of the Women's Political Council and the black clergy, had worked with Parks to organize the boycott. (In fact, the Women's Political Council had first conceived of the boycott and had been planning it for months. In popular historical accounts, the faces of the Civil Rights Movement typically belong to men, but women provided committed leadership as well as thankless labor throughout the struggle.)[13] It soon was decided that a new organization must be formed to support the boycott; hence, the Montgomery Im-provement Association (MIA) was born. Nixon was nominated as head of the MIA but declined, keenly observing that a minister, who had his fingers on the pulse of and was greatly respected in the black community, would be better suited for the job. Nixon volunteered King, who had just arrived in Montgomery months earlier and whose oratorical skills Nixon greatly admired. King accepted.

Hundreds of Montgomery's blacks supported the boycott, refusing to ride on the segregated buses.

The Reverend Martin Luther King, Jr., shown speaking to an over-flow crowd at a mass meeting at the Holt Street Baptist Church, led the mass Montgomery bus boycott.

The MIA organized carpools, funded primarily by black churches, to transport women and men to and from work. As the boycott spread, whites flocked to organizations determined to maintain the racial status quo, organizations such as the White Citizens' Counsel and the KKK. Some reacted with violence, firebombing black ministers' churches and houses. Nevertheless, the boycott persisted for more than a year.

By all standards, the Montgomery Bus Boycott was successful. For one, it helped to bring about a Supreme Court ruling, handed down on November 15, 1956, outlawing racial segregation on buses. What is more, the boycott trained hundreds of black activists in nonviolent resistance, a form of weaponless warfare inspired by Jesus and Gandhi, that encouraged people not only to resist striking back when struck but also to focus their energy on systematic racism, embedded in social institutions, rather than on individual people with racist beliefs. When news of the boycott was broadcast around the country, it inspired other blacks to join the movement for racial equality through public protest. The boycott also organized black clergy as a political force. The MIA soon would give way to a larger and more powerful organization—the Southern Christian Leadership Conference (SCLC)—which was founded in 1957.[14]

The SCLC would serve as the key organization of the civil rights struggle. It would organize many mass demonstrations, marches, boycotts, and rallies. Under the encouragement of Ella Baker, it also would help to run Citizenship Schools: mini-courses often held in the backs of stores and the basements of churches, teaching blacks to read so they could pass literacy tests. Miss Baker, as she was called, believed deeply in the goals of the SCLC but was critical of the style of charismatic (masculine) leadership that soon emerged within the organization. She once stated, "I have always felt it was a handicap for oppressed people to depend so largely on a leader. . . . Such people get so involved with playing the game of being important that they exhaust themselves and their time and they don't do the work of actually organizing people."[15] King was a powerful leader, it is true; but far greater was the power of the people. (Malcolm X was another powerful leader of the black liberation struggle. He is discussed in Chapter 9, as are the Black Panthers.)

SNCC and Youth-Driven Direct Action

Miss Baker also was instrumental in the formation of the Student Nonviolent Coordinating Committee, or SNCC (pronounced "snick"). Students had proven themselves a powerful force in the movement, and Miss Baker suggested they could benefit from collective coordination based on local leadership. Hence, just as SCLC was formed out of preexisting networks made of black clergy engaged in political action, SNCC (founded in 1960) incorporated into one organization hundreds of politically mobilized young people, many of whom were college students.

Students and young people had been involved in the modern Civil Rights Movement since its inception. Among the first major demonstrations invented and orchestrated by students were "sit-ins." On February 1, 1960, four black freshmen at Greensboro's North Carolina Agricultural and Technical College took seats at a "whites-only" lunch counter at the local Woolworth department store. They were not served, though they repeatedly asked for a menu and remained on their stools until closing time. Word got out, and the following day, twenty-four students took seats at the counter. By the end of the week, there were more students who wanted to sit-in than there were seats to hold them.

The Greensboro events sparked a national movement. Hundreds of high school and college students staged sit-ins all around the South. The sit-ins captured the nation's attention and, in so doing, exposed the absurdity of Jim Crow laws. Here were American citizens, money in hand, simply asking for a cup of coffee or a turkey sandwich but being denied. Many were jailed and beaten for doing so. But the sit-ins persisted, and Jim Crow finally buckled. By the summer of 1960, many cities had desegregated their lunch counters. The sit-ins also reinvigorated the Civil Rights Movement by demonstrating the power of student-led demonstrations and by drawing many white and nonwhite college students into the fray.[16]

Another key event initiated by young people was the Freedom Rides of 1961. The Supreme Court had just outlawed racial segregation in interstate bus terminals, and a small group of activists, made up of white and black members of a group called the Congress of Racial Equality (CORE), decided to test the new

Lunch Counter sit-ins were major demonstrations that helped highlight the absurdity of the Jim Crow laws.

ruling. The group chartered two buses and its members rode, white and black side by side, from Washington, D.C., to New Orleans. They got as far as Birmingham, the city King called "the country's chief symbol of racial intolerance," where the activists were beaten so severely by a white mob that the Freedom Rides were put on hold.[17] Members of Nashville's SNCC chapter stepped in, offering replacement riders and encouraging the rides to continue. If the white mob was successful in stopping the Freedom Rides, it was argued, then violence would be seen as an effective weapon against the movement. The buses rolled out of Birmingham and made it to Montgomery, where white and black riders were pulled from the buses and beaten again. As these violent scenes made front-page news, President John F. Kennedy sent federal marshals to protect the riders, who eventually would make it as far as Jackson, Mississippi. Freedom Rides would continue throughout the summer of 1961, further calling national attention to the plight of blacks in the South.

Activists were greeted with beatings and violence in the Freedom Rides of 1961.

The public demonstrations persisted, and President Kennedy finally proposed the Civil Rights Act in a speech delivered in June 1963. "One hundred years of delay have passed since President Lincoln freed the slaves," said Kennedy, "yet their heirs, their grandsons, are not fully free. They are not yet freed from the bonds of injustice. . . . Now the time has come for this Nation to fulfill its promise. . . . I am, therefore, asking the Congress to enact legislation giving all Americans the right to be served in facilities which are open to the public—hotels, restaurants, theaters, retail stores, and similar establishments. This seems to me to be an elementary right. Its denial is an arbitrary indignity that no American in 1963 should have to endure, but many do."[18] Five months after sending his bill to Congress, Kennedy was assassinated. His successor, Lyndon B. Johnson, pushed the bill through Congress and—after a fifty-four-day filibuster led by eighteen senators from southern states—the Senate as well. The Civil Rights Act of 1964 outlawed discrimination on the basis of race, religion, sex, or national origin in hotels, theaters, transportation, restaurants, and the workplace. It also ended legal segregation in schools, the workplace, and public accommodations like parks and swimming pools and created the Equal Employment Opportunity Commission to investigate discrimination complaints against employers. The Civil Rights Act of 1964 was the most important piece of antidiscrimination legislation to date.

Freedom Summer

The Civil Rights Movement is known for its large-scale demonstrations. But from the movement there emerged another kind of protest tradition, one based in local organizing, long-term investment in community leaders, and very specific practical goals.[19] Miss Baker called the latter kind of tradition "spadework," referring to the nitty-gritty, tiresome, and unglamorous labor of chipping away at the

"Ordinary people who learn to believe in themselves are capable of extraordinary acts, or better, of acts that seem extraordinary to us precisely because we have such an impoverished sense of the capabilities of ordinary people."—Charles Payne

white power structure day by day and door to door. Recognizing the importance of this kind of work, SNCC in 1961 deployed to the South a collection of grassroots organizers determined to bring the vote to disenfranchised blacks living in rural poverty.

The situation was bleak. In several Mississippi counties, only one or two blacks out of a thousand were registered. In others the electorate was 100 percent white.[20] The SNCC workers knew they needed some help, so in the summer of 1964, 1,000 volunteers, most of them white college students, were trained in nonviolent tactics and sent to Mississippi in a massive project known as Freedom Summer. The volunteers lived with black families and worked toward two important goals. The first was increasing voter registration, a task that entailed building relationships with residents of the community and urging them to register. The second was bringing quality education to Mississippi's poorest areas through the establishment of Freedom Schools. These schools sought to teach black children not only reading, writing, and arithmetic but also self-worth, critical thinking, and leadership.[21]

Freedom Summer was highly successful by many measures. Many blacks registered to vote, and the Freedom Schools attracted between 3,000 and 3,500 students, three times the number for which volunteers originally had hoped.[22] However, these victories came at a cost. Just ten days into Freedom Summer, three volunteers, all in their early twenties—James Chaney, Michael Schwerner, and Andrew Goodman—were murdered. The two white men, Goodman and Schwerner, had been shot, while Chaney, the black volunteer, was tortured before being shot three times. By the end of Freedom Summer, another volunteer had been killed, four critically wounded, eighty beaten, and one thousand arrested; thirty-seven churches had been bombed; and thirty homes had been burned.[23]

The volunteers of Freedom Summer came face to face with the violence and hatred that had victimized Mississippi's black population for years. This was quickly realized when law enforcement officials, searching for the bodies of Chaney, Schwerner, and Goodman, dragged the Pearl River and discovered eight other bodies of murdered black men. One of the men had been decapitated. Reflecting on this macabre discovery, one volunteer wrote, "Negroes disappear down here every week and are never heard about. Things are really much better for rabbits here. There is a closed season on rabbits when they may not be killed. Negroes are killed all year round. So are rabbits. The difference is that arrests are made for killing rabbits out of season."[24]

It is worth underscoring that it was mostly young people who risked their lives during Freedom Summer and who made up the backbone of the Civil Rights Movement. Were these young people an especially courageous and extraordinary lot? "There are heroes and, emphatically, heroines enough in this history," answers

Whites terrorized black families throughout the South, many committing acts of violence that went unpunished.

historian Charles Payne. "Yielding to the temptation to focus on their courage, however, may miss the point . . . that ordinary people who learn to believe in themselves are capable of extraordinary acts, or better, of acts that seem extraordinary to us precisely because we have such an impoverished sense of the capabilities of ordinary people. If we are surprised at what these people accomplished, our surprise may be a commentary on the angle of vision from which we view them. That same angle of vision may make it difficult to see that of the gifts they brought to the making of the movement, courage may have been the least."[25]

The Selma-to-Montgomery March

Although SNCC and SCLC had their differences, the two organizations often worked together. This was the case with the Freedom Rides and sit-ins, both supported by SCLC, and it was the case with the famous Selma-to-Montgomery March. The white power structure was firmly entrenched in Alabama, where four black girls were murdered when whites bombed the Sixteenth Street Baptist Church in Birmingham (a city that had grown so used to such attacks that it was nicknamed "Bombingham"), where police chief Eugene "Bull" Connor ordered firefighters to aim their water cannons at the legs of demonstrating black children, as the cannons were known to break legs, and where in Lowndes County—the stretch of land that activists would traverse during the Selma-to-Montgomery March—not a single black voter was registered. Local residents, determined to secure for blacks the right to vote, decided to stage a massive demonstration, a fifty-four-mile trek from Selma to the steps of Alabama's capitol building.

On March 7, 1965, hundreds of activists lined up in pairs and began the march, but they never made it out of Selma. Sheriff's deputies and state troopers, using billy clubs and tear gas, attacked the peaceful marchers, forcing them to retreat. So many demonstrators were injured that the black hospital overflowed with victims, and churches had to be turned into ad hoc hospitals. Because of this, the event is remembered as Bloody Sunday.

Immediately, SCLC leaders began organizing another march. King issued a press release, calling all American citizens who supported the Civil Rights Movement to join him in Selma, and hundreds responded to the call. At the end of the month, thousands of marchers of diverse races set off again. Amid white hecklers who lined stretches of the highway waving Confederate flags and yelling racial slurs, the demonstrators traveled fifty-four miles over the course of four days. On being asked about her weariness, one elderly woman marcher reflected, "My feets is tired, but my soul is at rest."[26] At the conclusion of the march, a crowd 25,000 strong gathered at the capitol building. King stood at the top of the steps and boomed to the swelling crowd, in one of his most famous speeches, "Yes, we are on the move and no wave of racism can stop us. . . . The burning of our churches will not deter us. The bombing of our homes will not dissuade us. We are on the move now. The beating and killing of our clergymen and young people will not divert us. We are on the move now. The wanton release of their known murderers would not discourage us. We are on the move now. Like an idea whose time has come, not even the marching of mighty armies can halt us. We are moving to the land of freedom. . . . I come to say to you this afternoon, however difficult the moment, however frustrating the hour, it will not be long, because 'truth crushed to earth will rise again.' How long? Not long, because 'no lie can live forever.'"[27]

Roughly five months later, President Johnson signed into law the Voting Rights Act of 1965—one of the most significant victories of the Civil Rights Movement.

Tear gas fumes fill the air as state troopers break up a demonstration march in Selma, Alabama on what will come to be known as Bloody Sunday, March 7, 1965.

FIGURE 3.2 VOTING GAP 1965 VS. 2004

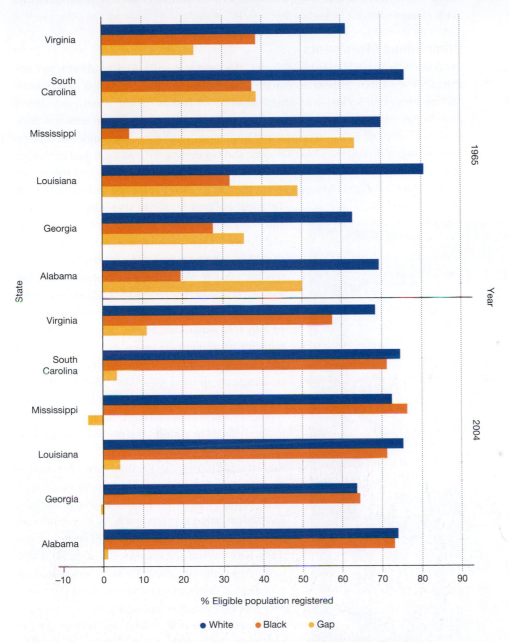

Between 1965 and 2004 the gap between white and black voters has shrunk significantly.

The act prohibited voter discrimination, outlawed literacy tests, and gave the federal government power to oversee voter registration. As a result, for the first time in their lives—a full century after the fall of slavery—blacks were able to participate in American democracy. The results speak for themselves: whereas only 5 percent of black Mississippians were registered voters in 1964, 24 percent were registered in

1968, a 380 percent increase.[28] Today, major southern cities—even Birmingham and Selma—have had black mayors, and southern states can boast of having the most black elected officials in the nation.

Other Ethnic Movements

In addition to these legislative victories, the predominantly African American Civil Rights Movement inspired other marginalized groups to engage in similar tactics while fighting for deeper inclusion in American society.[29] Just as African American political protest was rooted in the black organizing tradition, American Indian activism drew on a long legacy of Indian rebellion and resistance, symbolized by important figures, such as Geronimo and the Ghost Dancers, and key events, such as the defeat of Custer. However, American Indian activism was reenergized during the 1950s and 1960s, not only by the Civil Rights Movement but also by its direct response to federal "Indian Termination" policies aimed at eroding tribal sovereignty and reservations. Between the postwar years and the mid-1960s, federal recognition was terminated for over 100 tribes. When federal recognition was removed from a tribe, so too were federal aid and protection of that tribe's land. Many lawmakers felt it was best if Native Americans were assimilated fully into American society, and the Indian Termination resulted in the loss of native landholdings and the exacerbation of Native American poverty.[30]

American Indians organized together against Indian Termination as well as the failure of government organizations (such as the Bureau of Indian Affairs) to address the needs of indigenous people and the economic hardships in Native America. Tribes in the Pacific Northwest staged "fish-ins" in tribe-owned rivers and lakes that were being overrun by local and state officials. Pan-Indian organizations such as the American Indian movement (founded in 1968) were formed, along with Indian newspapers. Between 1969 and 1978, American Indian activists participated in acts of civil disobedience that involved over seventy property seizures, including, in 1972, a week-long takeover of the Bureau of Indian Affairs headquarters. Like the black organizing struggle, many of these actions and demonstrations were organized and led by young people, especially Native American college students.[31]

One of the most important demonstrations, one that drew the country's attention to the plight of American Indians and would spur on further activism, was the occupation of Alcatraz

The occupation of Alcatraz by American Indians in 1969 drew 10,000 to 15,000 Indians during a 19-month period, demanding the federal government release the island to Indians. They argued that the land was rightly theirs according to an 1868 treaty.

Island (in San Francisco Bay) in November 1969. The protesters—including Wilma Mankiller, later to become the first woman chief of the Cherokee Nation—wanted the federal government to release the island to Indians for the explicit development of Indian education. Indeed, the island belonged to them anyway, they argued, according to an 1868 treaty stating that all abandoned federal land would be given back to Native peoples from whom it had been taken. Federal marshals eventually removed the protesters, but not until June 1971—nineteen months after the occupation began. Although the protesters' formal demands went unmet, the Alcatraz standoff, and similar demonstrations, did raise people's awareness of the struggles of indigenous Americans and resulted in an American Indian cultural revival—manifest in the National Museum of the American Indian, dozens of university-sponsored American Indian Studies programs, and efforts aimed at preserving indigenous culture, religion, and language.[32]

Mexican American—led movements emerged alongside those led by African Americans and Native Americans. One of the most powerful protest movements addressed the pressing problems of migrant farm workers, who included not only large numbers of Latinos but also many Filipinos. César Chávez, a migrant worker from southern Arizona, emerged as an outspoken critic of migrant worker exploitation. Chávez organized workers, leading fasts, strikes, demonstrations, and nationwide boycotts to win contracts for poor migrant workers who picked crops under oppressive conditions. Chávez later cofounded the United Farm Workers of America (UFW), a labor union dedicated to "provide farm workers and other working people with the inspiration and tools to share in society's bounty."

One of the most important events of the protest movement on behalf of farm workers was the Delano grape strike, which began in 1965 and lasted five years until the UFW finally succeeded in gaining better wages as well as national attention to the grape-pickers' cause. Chavez led the farmworkers on a historic 300-mile march from Delano, a small city in central California where grape-pickers first had walked off the farms, to the state capitol in Sacramento. This strike featured nonviolent resistance, echoing the African American Civil Rights Movement, as well as boycotts, through which grapes belonging to targeted farms and corporations were prevented from being transported and sold. Other strikes and boycotts on behalf of farmworkers would occur well

"What really counts is labor: the human beings who torture their bodies, sacrifice their youth, and numb their spirits to produce this great agricultural wealth—a wealth so vast that it feeds all of America and much of the world. And yet the men, women, and children who are the flesh and blood of this production often do not have enough to feed themselves."— César Chávez

into the 1970s. Through these efforts, the UFW won many rights for migrant farm workers, including union contracts that secured fair working conditions such as rest periods, access to clean water, and pension plans.[33]

As with the black liberation struggle, this battle against oppressive labor conditions on farmlands dotting the U.S.-Mexican border was bloody. Protesters were fired, beaten, and killed. After Rufino Contreras, a twenty-seven-year-old farm worker protesting dreadful work conditions of lettuce pickers, was shot and killed in February 1979, Chávez, standing on top of a flatbed truck, delivered his eulogy to thousands of fellow farm workers: "What is the worth of a farm worker? Rufino, his father, and brother together gave the company twenty years of their labor. They were faithful workers who helped build up the wealth of their boss, helped build up the wealth of his ranch. What was their reward for their service and their sacrifice? When they petitioned for a more just share of what they themselves produced, when they spoke out against the injustice they endured, the company answered them with bullets; the company sent hired guns to quiet Rufino Contreras."[34] Chávez continued, exhibiting keen sociological insight: "Capitol and labor together produce the fruit of the land. But what really counts is labor: the human beings who torture their bodies, sacrifice their youth, and numb their spirits to produce this great agricultural wealth—a wealth so vast that it feeds all of America and much of the world. And yet the men, women, and children who are the flesh and blood of this production often do not have enough to feed themselves."[35]

Arab Americans—people who immigrated (or whose relatives once immigrated) to the United States from Arabic-speaking regions of the Middle East—also would organize during the 1960s.[36] People of Arab descent had immigrated in large numbers since the 1870s and had been met with bigotry. They often were depicted in the popular press as violent and malicious, conniving and wicked.[37]

Although bound together by a common language, cultural practices, and lifestyles, many Arab Americans did not view themselves as such until the 1960s. During that time, the Middle East was undergoing major transitions owing to the creation of the Israeli state and the Six-Day War of 1967, a brief yet consequential conflict between Israel and Egypt, Jordan, Iraq, and Syria. Many Arabs felt that America's unwavering support of Israel was unfair and generated anti-Arab sentiment in the United States. Arabs reacted by mobilizing politically, combating stereotypes and urging U.S. politicians to seek more balanced solutions to Middle Eastern conflicts. Lebanese, Iraqis, Syrians, and others of Middle Eastern heritage began viewing one another as a people with similar interests and struggles. They began referring to themselves as "Arabs."[38] Thus, the very term "Arab American" came about because people of Middle Eastern descent decided to mobilize around this pan-ethnic rubric.

Asian Americans, too, organized during this time, speaking out against economic exploitation and racial segregation. Some of their most vibrant and effective demonstrations took place in California. Within San Francisco's Chinatown, for example, political organizations were formed and peaceful demonstrations were carried out to protest city officials' neglect of their Chinese citizens. And college campuses across the Golden State erupted with Asian American activism.[39]

Asian American student activists played a key role in forming the Third World Liberation Front, a multiracial organization founded on the campuses of the University of California—Berkeley and San Francisco State College. The Third World Liberation Front challenged these campuses' Eurocentric curricula, which they claimed ignored or distorted the histories and cultures of people of color. Seeking a "relevant education," as one of its posters declared, the Third World Liberation Front went on strike between 1968 and 1969. Student protesters formed picket lines, blocked campus entrances, disrupted classes, and marched on the president's office with a list of demands, including additional support for underrepresented students, the hiring of faculty of color, and support to help nonwhite students use their education to better their communities. Some protesters were beaten and arrested by police officers. In the end, however, the university capitulated to many of their demands.[40]

BACKLASH

The Civil Rights Movement stopped short of fulfilling all of its goals. Neither the Civil Rights Act nor the Voting Rights Act fixed everything. Many employers forced to take down their "Blacks Need Not Apply" signs simply continued their discriminatory practices more covertly. Recognizing this, civil rights activists sought to change not only the law but the very structures of society that perpetuate poverty and racial division.[41] Here, however, the movement fell short and eventually was put down. Why did the Civil Rights Movement stop? The answer lies in the white backlash that mounted in direct response to the movement, a backlash fueled by conservatives and liberals alike.

The political right gained a new identity—and a new constituency—through its reaction to the Civil Rights Movement. When George Wallace, Democratic governor of Alabama, stood in 1963 on the steps of the University of Alabama to block the entrance of two black students to the all-white university, he taught politicians two strategic lessons. The first was that politicians who opposed racial justice could garner great support from white voters. After receiving over 100,000 telegrams and letters commending him for his stand against racial integration, Wallace exclaimed, "The whole United States is Southern!"[42] Indeed, Wallace never lost an election in Alabama after 1963, and although he was unable to win the presidency, he made a shockingly strong showing, winning 12.5 percent of the vote in 1968 while running on a third-party ticket. That means that in the 1968 election one out of every eight Americans voted for a man whose most famous line was "Segregation now! Segregation tomorrow! Segregation forever!"

The second lesson can be stated as an injunction: "Promote white supremacy, but never do so explicitly." When Wallace took his stand on the university steps, he claimed to do so not because he opposed racial integration (although he had said as much a few months earlier in his inaugural address), but because he opposed "illegal usurpation of power by the Central Government." By cloaking a race-specific issue (segregation) in race-neutral language (states' rights), Wallace was able to win support from white Americans willing to endorse policies promoting racial inequality but unwilling to get behind an overtly racist politician. As one

A National guardsman confronts Governor Wallace in front of the University of Alabama. Wallace claimed he took this stance because he opposed "illegal usurpation of power by the Central Government."

Alabama senator said of Wallace: "He can use all the other issues—law and order, running your own schools, protecting property rights—and never mention race. But people will know he's telling them: 'A nigger's trying to get your job, trying to move into your neighborhood.'"[43]

Other politicians would follow suit, using coded language to defend the white status quo. Richard Nixon appealed subtly to racial stereotypes and fears, vowing to confront problems (like crime and moral failure) that many white Americans wrongly assumed were nonwhite problems. In 1969, Nixon's chief of staff, H. R. Haldeman, penned the following words in his diary: "President emphasized that you have to face the fact that the whole [welfare] problem is really the blacks. The key is to devise a system that recognizes this, while not appearing to."[44] Additionally, one of Nixon's top aides, Kevin Phillips, author of *The Emerging Republican Majority*, convinced Republicans to work on expanding black voting rights in the South, "not as a moral issue, but because such a stratagem would hasten the departure of southern whites into the Republican Party."[45]

The strategy worked, helping to polarize the electorate around racial politics and to recruit masses of southern whites, who had been loyal Democrats since Reconstruction, into the Republican Party. Nixon's approach came to be known as the Southern Strategy. While rarely explicitly talking about race, Nixon spoke frequently of "states' rights," which was broadly understood as an indictment against federally imposed civil rights legislation, such as measures to desegregate schools or to extend voting rights to minority citizens. The traditionally Democratic South already had begun to shift toward the Republican Party after the passage of the Civil Rights Act, and Nixon pushed forward that momentum. Lyndon Johnson recognized the political consequences of passing major civil rights legislation for the Democratic Party. While still vice president, Johnson told Kennedy, "I know these risks are great, and we might lose the South [in the 1964 national election] . . . but if [the president] goes down there and looks them in the eye and states the moral issue and the Christian issue, and he does it face to face, these southerners will at least respect his courage."[46]

Ronald Reagan used racially coded language as well. While governor of California, he opposed the Civil Rights Act of 1964 as well as the Voting Rights Act of 1965, calling the latter "humiliating" to southerners. In 1980, he opened his campaign for the presidency with a speech in Philadelphia, Mississippi, the small town where Goodman, Chaney, and Schwerner had been murdered. As one journalist observed, "It was at that sore spot on the racial map that Reagan revived talk about states' rights and curbing the power of the federal government."[47]

By opposing racial equality while never admitting to doing so, the political Right staged a successful counterrevolution against the Civil Rights Movement—but not without help from the Left. White liberals who supported the Civil Rights Movement were faced with a fact many found unsettling: guaranteeing nonwhites freedom from discrimination and disenfranchisement meant little if those laws were not accompanied by programs that attempted to compensate victimized groups for years of unfair treatment. "Freedom is not enough," announced President Lyndon Johnson. "You do not take a person who, for years, has been hobbled by chains and liberate him, bring him up to the starting line of a race and then say, 'you are free to compete with all the others,' and still justly believe that you have been completely fair. . . . We seek not just freedom but opportunity—not just legal equity but human ability—not just equality as a right and a theory but equality as a fact and as a result."[48] Past wrongs had to be redressed through reparatory action—a reality many liberals did not want to face.

White liberal politicians feared that compensatory programs, such as affirmative action, would fracture the Democratic Party, allowing Republicans to gain power. For that reason, they began arguing that much progress had been made with respect to racial equality and that it was time to support a broader liberal agenda, one that focused not on the wounds inflicted by racism, but on general social uplift. Thus, liberals mirrored Republicans in refusing to confront racism head on.

Democrats mirrored Republicans in another way as well: they sought to account for problems ravaging many nonwhite communities, not by examining the historical career of racial oppression or by investigating systematic forms of discrimination, but by blaming the failures on nonwhites themselves.[49] As Daniel Patrick Moynihan wrote in *The Negro Family*, a controversial report that located blame in the individual, not the system that created the individual, "at the center of the tangle of pathology is the weakness of the family structure. Once or twice removed, it will be found to be the principal source of most of the aberrant, inadequate, or antisocial behavior that did not establish, but now serves to perpetuate, the cycle of poverty and deprivation."[50] Left-wing politicians invoked the language of racial equality but refused to support bold programs that had a fighting shot at achieving that goal. Instead, they maintained that real change would come about only through universal policies—"a rising tide lifts all boats," as President Kennedy once said—and advised nonwhites to stop fighting for systematic change and to start fixing their families.[51]

Thus, in the mid-1960s, most white liberals joined their conservative counterparts in "a retreat from racial justice in American thought and policy."[52] Was this retreat from racial justice itself an outwardly visible movement? Was it a predominantly organized, explicit, and hate-filled campaign? Just as most whites were not (and are not) antiracists, neither were they, in the main, members of hate groups such as the KKK. The majority of whites sat in the middle between these two camps, apparently members of no social movement. However, this appearance itself is a product of whiteness's invisibility, for, as we have seen throughout this chapter, when whites' racial interests are threatened, they can act as a social movement that need not speak its name. When faced with legislation that promotes racial equality, most whites came together to oppose such measures, thereby acting as a solidified political force that usually dissipated once the threat was eliminated. A white man might not belong to any political organization, but when state representatives begin considering using tax money to offer reparations for slavery, he might join other whites in writing letters to his congressperson, signing petitions, and attending demonstrations against reparations. In doing so, this man participates as a member of a mass-based social movement, one without a name or structure but able effectively to mobilize, nonetheless, to uphold the status quo. Once state representatives drop the reparations idea, this man can go back to his daily life, never knowing all the other people like him who joined together to block the legislation.

PARTISANSHIP AND REPRESENTATION

How do things stand now? Two generations removed from the Civil Rights Movement, are people of color full citizens in American society, represented fairly, elected proportionately, and treated justly? In the remaining sections of this chapter, we address how race works in the present-day political field.

Partisanship and Racial Polarization

The American electorate is racially polarized: the majority of whites tilt toward the GOP, while the majority of nonwhites support the Democratic Party. Since the partisan realignment in the 1970s, most white voters have supported the Republican Party. (In turn, the Republican Party has promoted white candidates: "Among state-level elected Republican officials nationwide," reports Ian Haney-López, "98 percent are white. Notwithstanding some prominent minority faces pushed to the fore to suggest otherwise, this is a party of white persons.")[53] At the national level, too, in the last eight presidential elections, the majority of whites voted Republican. Since 1960, in ten out of eleven elections, most whites have backed the GOP ticket.[54] As one analyst put it, "if the electorate were entirely white, the GOP would always win the presidency."[55]

Most nonwhites, on the other hand, remain loyal Democrats. In all the national elections that took place between 2000 and 2012, most nonwhite voters cast their ballots for Democratic candidates. In 2012, nearly nine in ten Republican and Republican-leaning registered voters were white, and around one in ten were nonwhite. By contrast, six in ten Democrat or Democrat-leaning registered voters were white, and four in ten were nonwhite.[56]

Since the presidential election of 1936, African Americans have proven a mainstay of the Democratic Party. Although Republicans enjoyed an increase in support after September 11, 2001, most African Americans did not take part in this shift. Black loyalty to the Democratic Party remains virtually unaffected by socioeconomic standing. That is, poor, middle-class, and wealthy blacks alike pledge their support in equal numbers to the Democrats.[57]

Most Hispanics also vote Democratic. Although upper-class Hispanics—unlike their lower-income counterparts—are more likely to register as Republicans, they do so in far lower numbers than whites with similar incomes. While Puerto Rican Americans and Mexican Americans usually vote blue, most Cuban Americans, who since the 1970s generally have felt that Democrats cut Fidel Castro too much slack, stand by the Republican Party.[58]

The election of Barack Obama as the first African American president of the United States was heralded by Republicans and Democrats as a proud moment for America, especially in light of its history of racial inequality. Some even granted that Obama's election was evidence of the United States entering a "postracial" era. But Obama was elected (like all other Democratic presidents since Lyndon B. Johnson) with a *minority* of the white vote.

Obama secured 53 percent of all votes, but only 43 percent of the white vote. He beat the Republican nominee, Arizona senator John McCain, by a large, seven-point margin, but McCain beat Obama among white voters by an even larger twelve-point margin.[59] Since Johnson's election, in fact, the Democratic nominee for president on average has garnered only 39 percent of the white vote.[60]

In 2008, black voters voted for Obama in overwhelming numbers (95 percent).[61] Latinos voted for Obama over McCain by a margin of 67 percent to 31 percent.[62] Overall, in the 2008 presidential election, white voters accounted for no less than 90 percent of the Republicans' support, while nonwhites accounted for only 8 percent. Obama drew only 62 percent of his total support from whites, nonwhites contributing nearly all the rest: 23 percent black, 10 percent Hispanic, 2 percent Asian.[63] Again, during the 2012 election, most whites (59 percent) voted for the Republican nominee, Mitt Romney, while most nonwhites voted to reelect Obama. Ninety-three percent of blacks, 71 percent of Hispanics, and 73 percent of Asians voted for Obama in that election.[64]

Although Obama's election victories should be seen as markers of racial progress, they also indicate that the United States has not fully ridded itself of racial animus. Recent research by economist Seth Stephens-Davidowitz offers convincing evidence that racial prejudice cost Obama votes. Because most Americans would deny any prejudice in a survey, Stephens-Davidowitz compared Google searches to voting patterns. Specifically, he ranked states and media markets based on the proportion of their searches that included the word "nigger(s)." (This word is included in roughly the same number of searches as is "migraine," "Lakers," and "Daily Show.") Next, Stephens-Davidowitz "predicted how many votes Mr. Obama should have received based on how many votes [white Democratic nominee] John Kerry received in 2004 plus the average gain achieved by other 2008 Democratic Congressional candidates. The results were striking: The higher the racially charged search rate in an area, the worse Mr. Obama did. . . . Add up the totals throughout the country, and racial animus cost Mr. Obama three to five percentage points of the popular vote."[65] Stephens-Davidowitz also noted that Obama gained some votes because of his race—for example, he gained roughly one percentage point owing to increased turnout

FIGURE 3.3 ELECTORAL SHIFTS IN 2011

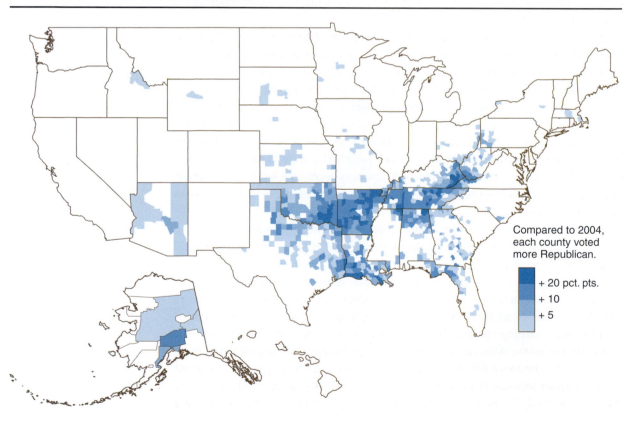

Compared to 2004, each county voted more Republican.

+ 20 pct. pts.
+ 10
+ 5

among black voters—but gains in this direction were comparatively minor. The bottom line of this study is that were Obama white, he would have won more votes. "Racial prejudice gave John McCain the equivalent of a home-state advantage nationally."[66]

With roughly one in four votes cast by nonwhite citizens, the 2008 presidential election was, to that point, the most racially and ethnically diverse in American history.[67] African Americans made up 12 percent of all voters, Hispanics 7 percent, and Asians 2.5 percent. Although the majority of votes still are cast by white Americans, the white vote makes up a smaller share of the electorate each year.[68] As the proportion of Americans who are nonwhite continues to grow, politicians of all persuasions have made attempts to capture a bigger percentage of the African American or Hispanic vote. (Roughly 60,000 new Latinos become eligible to vote every month!)[69] After losing the 2012 presidential election, the Republican National Committee issued a 100-page report about what went wrong. Much of the report addressed demographic shifts that seem to be working against Republicans. "We are not a policy committee," the report read, "but among the steps Republicans take in the Hispanic community and beyond, we must embrace and champion comprehensive immigration reform. If we do not, our party's appeal will continue to shrink to its core constituencies only." But winning the Hispanic vote likely will take a lot more than immigration reform. Just one in ten Republican voters in 2012 were not white, and Latinos increasingly identify with the Democratic Party, which most feel has more concern for Latino issues.[70]

It has been estimated that the number of Hispanic voters grows by some 3 percent a year, as compared to only 0.5 percent for white voters and 1 percent for black voters.[71] This growth, moreover, compounds over time, increasingly imperiling Republican prospects in several states with large Hispanic populations, including California, New Mexico, Nevada, Florida, and Colorado; in the more distant future, Arizona and Texas—long considered "safe" Republican strongholds—also may become battleground states. (Ninety percent of the growth in Texas's electorate comes from new Latino—along with black and Asian— voters.[72] And in Arizona, the voting-age Hispanic population nearly has doubled in the past ten years and now constitutes nearly 20 percent of Arizona residents of voting age.[73])

Is demography destiny? Perhaps—but complicating the story are at least three factors. First, Latinos historically turn out to vote in smaller proportions than do other groups, including whites, perhaps out of fears of reprisal (this holds true even for legal immigrants), distrust of government, or subpar registration drives in their communities; yet another factor might be the relatively young age of eligible Latino voters, since youth come out to the polls in smaller proportions than do older voters. Whatever the reason(s), low voter participation means less impact on elections. Second, political parties can change their appeals over time. In the future, the Republican Party might well succeed in broadening its racial and ethnic base and in coming to be seen by Latinos and other nonwhites as more sympathetic to their concerns. Demographic projections are wrong to assume a static or unchanging set of political actors. And finally, there is the question of the possible future whitening of currently nonwhite groups. If racial and ethnic boundaries are symbolic in nature and there is no such thing as a static or unchanging racial or ethnic group, and if in fact whiteness itself expanded during the nineteenth and twentieth centuries to incorporate groups (such as the Irish and Italians) whose whiteness originally was in question, the same social process may well occur again, this time with lighter-skinned Latinos as well as Asians. "In 2045 whites may account for 7 percent *more* of the population than they do today, depending on how white Latinos are counted. . . . If . . . a segment of the Hispanic population identifies and is seen as white," in other words, "the next few decades may witness a surge in the country's white population. . . . Significant numbers of Hispanics already consider themselves white, and this pattern bids likely to continue."[74] What implications such a development might hold for American politics is a wide-open question.

Political Representation

Barack Obama's election notwithstanding, very few nonwhites are elected at the national, state, and local levels. Over the entire span of U.S. history, 1,895 people have been elected to the Senate, of which only 19 (or 1 percent) were nonwhite. From 1966 to 2007, only one Native American has been elected to the Senate, along with four Hispanics, four Asian Americans, and three African Americans. Between 1966 and 2002, of the 316 people who served as state governors, 307 were white, 4 were Asian American, 4 were Hispanic, and 1 was African American. Since the passage of the Voting Rights Act, 97 percent of these two high-ranking political positions have been held by whites.[75] The 112th Congress that served from 2011 to 2013 was made up of 438 delegates, of whom 361 were white (82 percent), 44 were black (10 percent), 25 were Hispanic (8 percent), 7 were Asian, and 1 was Native American. That same legislative session, the 100-person Senate was made up of 96 whites, two Hispanics, two Asian Americans, no African Americans, and no Native Americans. (Recall that whites make up 63 percent of the population, Hispanics make up 17 percent, African Americans 13 percent, Asians 5 percent, and Native Americans and Native Hawaiians 1 percent.)

Just as the Civil Rights Act did not wipe out de facto racial discrimination in employment opportunities (we speak more about this in Chapter 4), the Voting Rights Act did not automatically kick open the gates of political power. The unbalanced representation of people of color in high political positions should concern us because researchers have found that white elected officials often do not work to meet the needs of their nonwhite constituencies as well as their nonwhite counterparts. Compared to white Democrats, for example, nonwhite Democrats are more likely to represent the interests of their nonwhite constituents, to draft policy that matters to many nonwhites, and to sponsor bills and make speeches about racial justice.[76] In one study, political scientist David Canon demonstrated that white members of Congress elected from districts with sizable black populations were far less knowledgeable of and attentive to the needs of their black constituents than were black legislators elected from similar districts. Does this mean that black elected officials only care about "black issues?" Canon found the opposite to be true. Although white legislators often do a poor job of representing black interests, black legislators often are proficient at representing the needs of their white constituencies.[77]

Put simply, many nonwhite politicians who are familiar with the unique hardships experienced by many nonwhite Americans, whose close friends and family members are nonwhite, and who have experienced American racism firsthand seem able to marshal their political influence on behalf of nonwhite voters much more effectively than their white counterparts belonging to the same party. Many nonwhite voters are fully aware of this fact. In one survey, about two-thirds of blacks polled stated they believe black politicians are better at representing their needs than white politicians.[78] Perhaps now we can understand why, once Senator Barack Obama, whose father is Kenyan and whose mother is white, tossed his hat into the presidential race leading up to the 2008 election, many African Americans began asking, "Is he black enough?"

Here, we must be wary of committing the tokenistic fallacy, mistakenly assuming that, say, all Latinos holding political positions care about the needs of Latino citizens or even are aware of those needs. Many prominent nonwhite politicians refuse to lobby for policies that promote racial justice or equality. In fact, some have ascended to high political posts precisely because they will not shake up the racial status quo. Thus in 1991, when Clarence Thomas, an African American, was nominated to the Supreme Court by George H. W. Bush, major civil rights organizations, such as the NAACP and the Urban League, protested because Thomas opposed many policies designed to promote racial equality. Obviously, one's race does not guarantee one's political convictions. When it comes to nonwhite political leadership, we can distinguish between *superficial* and *substantive* representation. Superficial representation speaks to the process of appointing to political positions nonwhites disconnected from the needs and problems of most nonwhite citizens. Substantive representation involves a correspondence between the goals of nonwhite representatives and those of nonwhite citizens. Superficial representation cares only about diversity in skin color, not diversity in political conviction. Substantive representation is not satisfied until both these requirements are met; it requires not only that political representatives be drawn from nonwhite communities but also that they be committed to working on behalf of those communities.[79]

Gerrymandering

We cannot conclude our discussion of political representation without unpacking the complicated system of political maneuverings known as *gerrymandering*. The word was coined around the beginning of the nineteenth century when American statesman Elbridge Gerry created an irregularly shaped political district to secure his reelection. Many thought Gerry's district resembled a salamander. Hence: Gerry + salamander = gerrymander.[80] Gerrymandering is a set of processes by which elected politicians redraw and manipulate the borders of political districts to secure political advantage.

Here is how it works: Pretend you are a Republican elected to Congress. To secure an easy reelection, one with the least amount of competition possible, you gather sympathetic state legislators and begin thinking of ways to redraw your state's congressional districts. Further pretend that your state is made up of four electoral districts, each of which has an equal number of white and black voters. Because you know that most of the white voters in your state will vote Republican, you pack as many black voters as you can into one district. Republicans will lose that district because most blacks support the Democratic ticket. But you are confident your party will pick up the remaining three because your redistricting plans have successfully diluted the black vote, spreading it thinly over the three redrawn districts and thus severely limiting blacks' ability to vote as a group (what is known as bloc voting). If you are successful, you will have created a political arrangement where many black votes are somewhat wasted. They are wasted in the majority-black district, where their candidate of choice easily wins by receiving an overwhelming amount of support, and they are wasted in the majority white districts, where the white, Republican-leaning majority easily outnumbers them.

All parties seek to secure advantage through gerrymandering. In fact, those seeking to increase the political representation of minority groups historically have favored "majority-minority districts," which purposefully are created to promote minority bloc voting. Arizona's second congressional district was redrawn to ensure that the Navajo Nation and the Hopi Tribe—two tribes that have an antagonistic history—are represented by different congresspersons. That way, Hopi concerns are not overlooked by a representative pandering to the Navajo majority. Because the Hopi reservation is enveloped by the larger Navajo reservation, the oddly shaped district surrounds the Hopi reservation before snaking west, following a chain of rivers for hundreds of miles, before broadening out to cover the northwest area of the state. Similarly, Illinois's fourth congressional district was designed to join two Hispanic areas separated geographically. Thus, the district surrounds one neighborhood before making its way west, narrowly following Interstate Highway 294, then circling back east to surround the other Hispanic area.

Because it is very difficult for nonwhite politicians to get elected in majority white districts, some have argued that drawing districts in which nonwhites can wield significant influence over the election helps to secure nonwhite representation. Others, however, have pointed out that this form of packing the vote concentrates nonwhite influence in single districts and can diminish Democratic power writ large.[81]

In the early 1990s, the Supreme Court set down rulings in *Shaw v. Reno* (1993) and *Miller v. Johnson* (1995) that deemed race-based gerrymandering unconstitutional. In both cases, plaintiffs took issue with newly created black-majority districts

FIGURE 3.4 ILLINOIS'S FOURTH CONGRESSIONAL DISTRICT

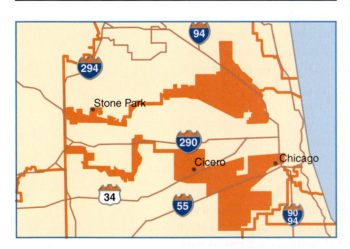

The orange shaded areas represent the irregular borders of Illinois's fourth Congressional District, one of the more infamous examples of gerrymandering.

redrawn in North Carolina and Georgia, respectively. The Court did not outlaw the practice of gerrymandering, just gerrymandering based on race. Writing for the majority, Justice Sandra Day O'Connor argued, "Racial classifications of any sort pose the risk of lasting harm to our society. They reinforce the belief, held by too many for too much of our history, that individuals should be judged by the color of their skin. . . . Racial gerrymandering, even for remedial purposes, may balkanize us into competing racial fractions."[82]

Yet if we consider the Court's decision, we can witness how whiteness works in the highest echelons of political power. By outlawing "race-based" gerrymandering while allowing for "political" gerrymandering, the Court failed to recognize white majority districts *as white districts*. Whiteness thus was rendered invisible, while "race" came to mean "not white." As some social scientists have put it, "Whites who insist on color-blind redistricting are really demanding an electoral system that acknowledges *their* majority status. Their objection is to districts where they are not the majority, where they might have to relinquish the privileges of their racial status."[83]

Although race-based gerrymandering is illegal, it continues. In recent years, gerrymandering has been employed most extensively by the Republican Party seeking to preserve political power in states and districts that fast are becoming majority-minority. Consider Texas. Between 2000 and 2010, Texas grew by 4.3 million people. Hispanics accounted for two-thirds of this growth and African Americans accounted for 11 percent. Accordingly, Texas gained four congressional seats but—owing to racial gerrymandering—did not extend much political power to its growing population of nonwhite citizens. To quote one report, "According to a lawsuit filed by a host of civil rights groups, 'even though Whites' share of the [Texas] population declined from 52 percent to 45 percent [between 2000 and 2010], they remain the majority in 70 percent of Congressional Districts.' . . . [For example,] in the Dallas—Fort Worth area, the Hispanic population increased by 440,898, the African-American population grew by 152,825[,] and the white population fell by 156,742. Yet white Republicans, a minority in the metropolis, control four of five Congressional seats. . . . In fact, whites are the minority in the state's five largest counties but control twelve of nineteen Congressional districts."[84] A federal court ruled that Texas's redistricting was "enacted with discriminatory purpose" and stood in violation of the Voting Rights Act. The issue continues to be litigated.

Nationwide, gerrymandering has proven to be a highly successful strategy for the Republican Party. In the 2012 election, one observer notes, "through gerrymandered districts, the Republicans won control of the House by a 234 to 201 margin, yet the Democrats cumulatively received 1.4 million more votes."[85]

What is at stake here is whether the votes of minority citizens matter as much as white votes, whether the demands of nonwhite citizens effectively can influence the course of this country, and whether their lives demand the attention of the political leaders of our democracy or are muted by the white majority. Alexis de Tocqueville worried about this. The author of *Democracy in America* observed that our political system often is steered by majority interests that overrun minority rights and concerns, a problem he called the *tyranny of the majority*.

"What is a majority," he asked, "in its collective capacity, if not an individual with opinions, and usually with interests, contrary to those of another individual, called the minority? Now, if you admit that a man [or a woman] vested with omnipotence can abuse it against his adversaries, why not admit the same concerning a majority? . . . My greatest complaint against the democratic government as organized in the United States is not, as many Europeans make out, its weakness but rather its irresistible strength."[86]

VOTING

Race plays a deciding role in determining voter turnout and political preferences. Repeatedly, studies have shown that both nonwhites and whites will vote in larger numbers if the ticket is racially mixed than during elections when all candidates are of the same race. If, say, a Hispanic woman is running for city council, Hispanic voters, figuring that this candidate will better represent their interests, will do their best to see that she is elected. That logic is fairly straightforward, but it is not immediately clear why white voters will turn out in larger-than-usual numbers when the ticket is mixed. Not only this, but white voters are much more politically mobilized in communities that are racially integrated. For decades, social scientists have documented that as the size of the nonwhite population increases, so too does white voter turnout.[87] What might explain this trend?

The answer begins to materialize once we examine how white citizens in racially mixed areas tend to vote. As the nonwhite population increases, so, too, do white voter turnout *and* whites' levels of racial intolerance. Political scientists have explained this relationship through the *threat hypothesis*. This theory holds that compared to whites who live in racially homogeneous areas, whites who live near nonwhites are more likely to develop racist attitudes and to oppose policies designed to combat racial inequality or promote multiculturalism.[88] For example, whites who live in areas that have experienced substantial growth in the Hispanic population are much more likely to oppose bilingual education, even after controlling for a host of important factors (like income and age).[89]

The Effects of Racial Attitudes on Voting Behavior

Once we examine how policy and candidate preferences vary across racial groups, we are immediately struck by obvious and substantial differences. Although no racial group should be treated as a unified mass—there is great variation among Asians, whites, Arab Americans, and other racial groups along all lines, political and otherwise—it nonetheless is true that racial groups, to varying degrees, exhibit a coherent set of political persuasions. In the post–Civil Rights Era, class-based voting has decreased, whereas race-based voting has increased. All else equal, working-class and middle-class citizens do not vote very differently from one another, but white and nonwhite citizens exhibit strikingly different voting patterns.[90]

With respect to race-specific policies—involving, say, civil rights, equal economic opportunity, or affirmative action—whites and nonwhites, in aggregate, hold drastically different stances. Consistently, whites disapprove of such policies. Consider these statistics from the National Election Study: 90 percent of blacks polled thought "the government should ensure fair treatment of blacks," whereas only 46 percent of whites felt the same way. Fifty percent of whites thought that securing fair treatment for blacks "was not the government's business," while only 7 percent of blacks felt the same way. Over 74 percent of blacks and 18 percent of whites believed that "federal spending on programs that assist blacks should be increased." By contrast, 20 percent of whites and 3 percent of blacks thought it should be decreased. When it came to affirmative action, 50 percent of blacks strongly favored policies promoting employment hiring and promotional preferences, but only 5 percent of whites did.[91]

Are these differences strictly race based, or can they be explained by other factors? That is, what is more important in determining voters' opinions about racial politics, one's racial attitudes or one's education, political party, religion, or something else? Several studies have demonstrated that racial attitudes are the single most important factor when it comes to explaining opinions about public policies designed to promote racial equality. For white Americans, racial attitudes—measured by one's opinions about continuing discrimination, positive or negative emotions toward nonwhites, and stereotypes of nonwhites—are more important than political ideology, party identification, educational level, and demographic variables (e.g., sex and age) in predicting one's evaluation of race-specific policies and political candidates.[92] In another study, Martin Gilens evaluated whites' views of welfare. Since the Reagan years, welfare has emerged as a program that many associate with poor black women (even though most welfare recipients are white). Do many whites oppose welfare because of their dislike of blacks or for other reasons dissociated from race? Gilens provided strong evidence that whites' perception of blacks as "lazy" has a more powerful effect on their evaluations of welfare policy than anything else, including their political party, financial interests, or beliefs about American individualism.[93]

The Tea Party—a conservative movement that rose to prominence after the 2008 presidential election and is associated with a strong belief in small government and spending reduction—has since its inception faced charges of racism and intolerance. At Tea Party rallies, some people have carried signs depicting President Obama as a monkey or tribal African or plainly stating "Save White America!" Tea Party supporters bristle at these accusations, saying that every movement has its fringe elements, but recent research has linked Tea Party support to racial resentment. One survey found that 73 percent of Tea Party supporters agreed with the statement that "if blacks would only try harder, they could be just as well off as whites," compared to 33 percent of people who disapproved of the Tea Party. Another survey found that Tea Party supporters were more likely to believe that the Obama administration favors blacks over whites.[94]

Recent research conducted by social psychologists suggest that racial attitudes may play a role in Tea Party support even if they are not explicitly recognized. In a study conducted by Robb Willer of Stanford University, 356 participants were asked to identify and express their political views while being shown a picture of President Barack Obama. Half of the participants were shown a picture of Obama in

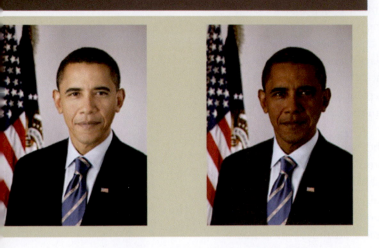

OBAMA PRIME

Social Psychologist Rob Willer's photos of Obama with artificially lightened and darkened skin.

which his skin was artificially lightened; the other half were shown a picture in which his skin was artificially darkened. Professor Willer found that white participants who were shown the darkened picture of Obama were significantly more likely to report supporting the Tea Party. By contrast, fewer nonwhite participants expressed support for the Tea Party after seeing the darkened Obama picture.[95]

Principle-Implementation Gap

Since the Civil Rights Movement, opinion polls have shown that most white Americans consistently have accepted the *principle* of racial inclusion while rejecting many of the *policy measures* designed to carry this out. For instance, between 1963 and 1986, white attitudes in favor of school integration increased by 30 percent, but white support for federal programs intending to do just that declined by 9 percent.[96] The same is true across a wide range of issues. Whites disapprove of discrimination in housing and racial segregation but also disapprove of federal programs aimed at combating these problems, and most whites disapprove of racialized poverty but tend not to support race-based antipoverty programs. Social scientists have referred to this disconnect as the *principle-implementation gap*.[97]

The principle-implementation gap can be explained by examining whites' ideas about race. According to a recent poll, 34 percent of whites believe that racial inequalities are caused by systematic discrimination, but 52 percent believe that they are brought about because nonwhites "lack motivation." Informed by ideas that emerged from the white backlash following the Civil Rights Movement, most whites today explain racial disparities by pointing to individual failings. Surveys show that many believe if nonwhites want full inclusion into American society, all they need to do is to work hard.[98] In fact, whites committed to the norm of individualism—the idea that social problems and achievements can be explained solely by examining individual-level characteristics like talent, drive, and intelligence—are highly likely to reject policies aimed at uplifting disadvantaged racial groups.[99]

The view that racial inequalities occur because nonwhites don't work hard enough ignores the history of racial domination in America, present-day discrimination, and institutional racism. If the majority of white Americans hold this view, then they fundamentally misunderstand how race works in American society. "But we are all entitled to our own opinion about this," one might reply. You may be entitled to your own opinion on how racial inequalities are best addressed, but questions about the causes of racial inequalities are satisfied exclusively by historical and social-scientific evidence. You very well might be of the opinion that individual failings, and individual failings alone, account for racial inequalities, just as you might be of the opinion that the sun revolves around the Earth.

Voter Intimidation and Felon Disenfranchisement

Today, almost a half-century after the passage of the Voting Rights Act of 1965, many people of color still face modern-day voter intimidation, which mirrors, in a softer and shrewder form, techniques deployed by southern whites during the mid-twentieth century. Here are some examples:

- In 2010, a Tea Party group, True the Vote—which uses its own software programs to comb voter registration records in largely minority precincts "for the slightest misspelling or address error," which it might use "to challenge voters at the polls" and reduce turnout—targeted the Houston congressional district represented by Sheila Jackson Lee, an African American Democrat. "After poring over the records for five months, True the Vote came up with a list of 500 names it considered suspicious and challenged them with election authorities. Officials put these voters on 'suspense,' requiring additional proof of address, but in most cases voters simply had changed addresses. That did not stop the group from sending dozens of white 'poll watchers' to precincts in the district during the 2010 elections, deliberately creating friction with black voters."[100]

- Less than a month before the 2008 presidential election, a supporter of the Republican ticket displayed in several of Philadelphia's black neighborhoods fliers "warning that people with outstanding warrants or unpaid parking tickets could be arrested if they show up at the polls on election day."

- In 2006, a congressional campaign worker for California's Orange County Republican Party circulated a letter, written in Spanish, to roughly 14,000 Hispanics threatening them with arrest if they voted. "You are advised that if your residence in this country is illegal or you are an immigrant," the letter warned, "voting in a federal election is a crime that could result in jail time." (It goes without saying that naturalized immigrants older than eighteen have voting rights.)

- Also in 2006, Native American voters attempting to participate in South Dakota's primary were asked to show a valid photo ID at the polling place—a mandate not required by either federal or state law. Those who did not have such an ID were not given a ballot.[101]

Moreover, since 2001 nearly 1,000 voter ID bills have been introduced in forty-six states, twenty-four of which passed major pieces of legislation tightening identification requirements.[102] Ostensibly, voter ID requirements are designed to combat in-person voter fraud. But most experts agree that in-person voter fraud is virtually nonexistent. A nationwide analysis of reported fraud cases found a total of *ten* credible voter impersonations between 2000 and 2012. That means, in a nation of 146 million registered voters, there is one case of in-person voter fraud for every 15 million prospective voters.[103] UFO sightings are 3,615 times more common than voter impersonation.[104]

Minority citizens disproportionately lack photo identification. According to one study, 25 percent of African American and 16 percent of Hispanic voting-age citizens have no current government-issued photo identification, compared with only

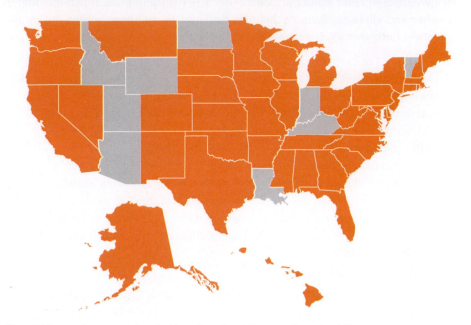

Since 2011, over forty states (orange) have introduced laws restrictry the ability to vote.

8 percent of voting-age white citizens.[105] Accordingly, some have argued that the real purpose of voter ID laws is to discourage minorities and low-income people—who overwhelmingly vote for Democratic candidates—from voting. Although many supporters of voter ID laws would never admit to this claim, this is not universally the case. When Tea Party activist Ken Emanuelson was asked, "What can Republicans do to get black people to vote?," he responded, "I'm going to be real honest with you, the Republican Party doesn't want black people to vote if they're going to vote nine-to-one for Democrats."[106]

In June 2013, a divided Supreme Court rendered inoperable a key part of the Voting Rights Act, Section 5, which requires nine states with a history of minority disenfranchisement—Alabama, Alaska, Arizona, Georgia, Louisiana, Mississippi, South Carolina, Texas, and Virginia—as well as dozens of counties and municipalities in other states to seek federal approval if they wish to change their election laws. Without this requirement—called "preclearance"—the Voting Rights Act was deprived of much of its enforcement capability. Within hours of the ruling, Texas announced it would begin enforcing a voter ID requirement, blocked the year before by a federal court that found it discriminatory, effective immediately. Roughly a month later, North Carolina introduced a similar voter ID law.[107] Other states indicated a willingness to follow in the same direction.

Many democratic elections across the globe are tainted by some form of voter intimidation (race-based or otherwise). However, America is unique in another practice that disproportionately strips the right to vote from nonwhites. The United States is the only democracy that disenfranchises felons *as well as ex-felons*. Sociologists estimate that 5.3 million American citizens (one adult in every forty) are denied the right to vote because of felony convictions. Most of these people are ex-felons, individuals who have served their time. In the abstract, felon disenfranchisement has nothing to do with race; however, on closer inspection, we discover a clear connection between felon disenfranchisement and racial domination. For one, when we examine when states adopted laws denying felons voting rights, we notice that many states did so after the ratification of the Fifteenth Amendment, which gave black men the right to vote. From inception, felon disenfranchisement was conceived as an effective way to diminish nonwhite political power. This was especially true for newly manumitted slaves. As the prison emerged to replace the slave plantation as the major social institution used to disempower African Americans, blacks were imprisoned, and therefore disenfranchised, at much higher rates than whites. Indeed, as Jeff Manza and Christopher Uggen demonstrate in *Locked Out: Felon Disenfranchisement and American Democracy*, states where blacks constituted a significant proportion of the prison population were more likely to adopt and expand felon disenfranchisement laws than states where the black prison population was relatively small.[108]

On this account, things have not changed much. Because the criminal justice system, which we discuss at length in Chapter 6, is guided by, and works

FIGURE 3.6 STATES' POLICIES ON VOTING RESTRICTIONS FOR CONVICTED FELONS

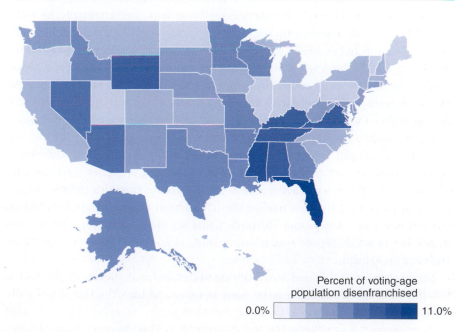

Percent of voting-age
population disenfranchised

0.0%   11.0%

In some states, felons who can no longer vote make up a sizeable percentage of the population.

to reinforce, racial domination, blacks and Hispanics are imprisoned at disproportionately high rates. Just as they were a century ago, nonwhites, and blacks in particular, are the people most severely affected by today's felon disenfranchisement laws. Nationwide, suffrage rights have been denied to at least one in seven black men. In the states with the highest black disenfranchisement rates, as many as *one in four* black men cannot vote.[109] These are troubling statistics for a democracy that prides itself on the principle of universal suffrage. And lest we think the proportion of disenfranchised felons and ex-felons is inconsequential, we need only remember the 2000 presidential race. To win, the Republican nominee, George W. Bush, had to carry Florida—the country's leader in felon disenfranchisement with over 1.1 million citizens (10 percent of the constituency) denied the right to vote. Like in other states, a disproportionate number of these disenfranchised citizens were African American: 293,000, to be exact, of whom 205,000 had completed their sentences. This amounted to 19 percent of the black electorate. Political analysts estimate that had these former felons been allowed to vote, the Democratic nominee, Al Gore, would have carried Florida, thereby clinching the presidency.[110]

ELECTIONS AND IMPLICIT RACIAL APPEALS

It was 1988, and, according to all the polls, Massachusetts governor Michael Dukakis would be the next president of the United States. Dukakis was pummeling his Republican opponent, George H. W. Bush. The Republicans needed something to sink Dukakis, and they would find it after assembling a thirty-person focus group of swing voters, people who had voted for Reagan but were planning to vote for Dukakis in the upcoming election. The moderator began reviewing the governor's political record, asking for participants' reactions, and eventually, he hit on an issue that struck a nerve with the focus group. A young black man named Willie Horton, a convicted murderer serving a life sentence in a Massachusetts prison, had escaped while on a weekend furlough. Ten months later, Horton had broken into the home of a white couple, beating and stabbing Cliff Barnes and raping his fiancée, Angela Miller. On hearing this story, focus group participants recoiled in disgust. Fifteen of the thirty voters changed their minds: they no longer would support Dukakis. The Republicans had found what they were looking for.[111]

Bush soon began repeating Horton's story, using it to accuse Dukakis of being "soft on crime." Bush mentioned Horton during speeches, and the news media covered the story heavily, repeatedly displaying Horton's picture: a large, cold-faced black man with a mature afro. Television and radio ads featured the story.[112] Republicans repeated Horton's name so much that, years after 1988, polled voters would report remembering three names about the election: Bush, Dukakis, and Horton.[113]

Bush began gaining ground. He caught up to Dukakis, and, in early October, when the story was receiving the heaviest news coverage, he took the lead. During this time, no one—not the media or either political party—mentioned race. Instead, the Horton story was about crime and liberal policy. This changed in late October, when Jesse Jackson accused the Bush campaign of tapping into whites' fears of blacks. Once race was mentioned, Bush's ratings began to drop, but it was too late. In an upset victory, Bush won the presidency, and, in the end, all parties involved admitted that he would not have prevailed without the help of the heinous acts of Willie Horton.[114]

There is substantial evidence that Bush's campaign intentionally used Horton's image as a racially motivated appeal to garner white votes. From day one, Bush aides were fully aware of Horton's race.[115] Indeed, several other white criminals had escaped from the Massachusetts furlough program and had committed violent crimes, yet they never were mentioned by the Republicans.[116] Even the name "Willie Horton" was a Republican creation, coined by Bush's campaign manager, Lee Atwater, who changed William Horton (the name Horton went by) into the boyish "Willie."[117] This does not mean that all right-wing political appeals are racially motivated. Had the Bush campaign featured one of the white furlough escapees to criticize Dukakis and to promote Bush as a "law and order" candidate, it would not have been a racial appeal. But this strategy might not have packed the same punch.

Atwater recognized the power of the implicit racial appeal. In 1981, while working in the Reagan White House, Atwater gave an interview in which he articulated in plain terms the transformation of racial politics from overt to covert messages. "You start out in 1954 by saying, 'Nigger, nigger, nigger.'" Atwater explained. "By 1968 you can't say 'nigger'—that hurts you, backfires. So you say stuff like forced busing, states' rights, and all that stuff, and you're getting so abstract. Now [later on], you're talking about cutting taxes, and all these things you're talking about are totally economic things and a byproduct of them is, blacks get hurt worse than whites. . . . 'We want to cut this,' is much more abstract than even the busing thing, and a hell of a lot more abstract than 'Nigger, nigger.'"[118]

As we have already seen in this chapter, this country's political system is deeply divided by race. Since the partisan realignment, our two-party system has been driven and organized around racial issues: the Democratic Party has secured loyalty from most nonwhites, while the Republican Party has become virtually an all-white organization. Thus, Republicans have much to gain by ignoring nonwhite citizens and attracting white voters through racial appeals. However, since the Civil Rights Movement, racism has been outwardly decried by most Americans. In these times, nobody wants to be labeled a racist or to get behind a politician who is labeled as such. Today's politicians no longer can employ explicit racist appeals to win support in the ways they could forty years ago. (During the 1970 Alabama gubernatorial race, a group called Committees for [George] Wallace displayed newspaper ads with a young blonde girl sitting on a beach surrounded by seven grinning black teenage boys, accompanied by the caption, "This Could be Alabama Four Years From Now.")[119] Those who do employ such appeals—as Pat Buchanan also did in his 1996 bid for the presidency, advocating strict immigration controls because most immigrants "are not English-speaking white people from Western Europe [but] Spanish-speaking brown and black people from Mexico, Latin America, and the Caribbean"—usually do not ascend to the highest posts. This fact testifies to the attenuation of overt racism in American politics.[120]

In short, politicians hoping to secure whites' support by "playing the race card" must do so through implicit racial appeals, or what have been called "dog whistles." These convey hidden messages inaudible to many but readily "heard" and understood by numerous others, in whom are generated powerful, race-based responses.[121] Crucial to dog whistle politics is its unique combination of deniability and effectiveness. In the words of political scientist Tali Mendelberg, "The power of implicitly racial appeals today is due to the coexistence of two contradictory elements in American politics: powerful egalitarian norms about race, and a party system based on the cleavage of race. Politicians convey racial messages implicitly when two contradictory conditions hold: (1) they wish to avoid violating the norm of racial equality, and (2) they face incentives to mobilize racially resentful white voters."[122]

White voters need not be outspoken racists for racial appeals to resonate with them. Indeed, research suggests that implicit racial appeals can backfire when they are rendered explicit, when voters recognize the appeals as fundamentally racial in content.[123] What implicit racial appeals rely on are white voters' deep-seated racialized dispositions—habits, feelings, and convictions that sometimes rest beneath the level of consciousness. These dispositions are conditioned by major social institutions (schools, families, religious institutions), which themselves are products of a history of racial domination. Our racialized dispositions may lie relatively dormant until triggered by suggestive images (a mug shot of a black man) or coded language ("welfare queen," "urban unrest," "illegal immigrants," "Islamic terrorists").

Bush was not the first politician to use implicit racial appeals—nor was he the last. During Tennessee's 2006 Senate race, the Republican National Committee released a commercial targeting the Democratic nominee, Harold Ford, who would have been the first southern black man elected to the Senate since Reconstruction. At one point in the ad, an attractive white woman with blond hair giggles, "I met Harold at the Playboy party!" The commercial ends with the white woman winking at the camera and whispering suggestively, "Harold, call me." The commercial tapped into an enduring taboo—sexual relations between black men and white women—one seen as especially scandalous in southern states. Ford lost the election. Democrats, too, have relied on implicit racial appeals to gain a political edge. Hillary Clinton's remarks during the 2008 presidential primaries, at a time when she was locked in a heated battle with Obama, are a case in point. "I have a much broader base to build a winning coalition on," she noted in an interview, citing a recent poll that she said, "found how Senator Obama's support among working, hard-working Americans, white Americans, is weakening again, and how whites in both [Indiana and North Carolina] who had not completed college were supporting me." Clinton's equation of "hard-working Americans" with "white Americans" struck many as a form of intentional dog whistling.[124]

Ian Haney-López has noted, in his book *Dog Whistle Politics*, that racial dog whistling comprises three important moves: "a punch that jabs race into the conversation through thinly veiled references to threatening nonwhites . . .; a parry that slaps away charges of racial pandering, often by emphasizing the lack of any direct reference to a racial group or any use of an epithet; and finally a kick that savages the critic for opportunistically alleging racial victimization. The complex jujitsu of racial dog whistling lies at the center of a new way of talking about race that constantly emphasizes racial divisions, heatedly denies that it does any such thing, and then presents itself as a target of self-serving charges of racism."[125] The "punch" entails references, for example, to "food stamps," a form of social provision widely identified in white Americans' minds with African Americans (even though a majority of its beneficiaries are poor whites). Hence during the 2012 Republican primaries, candidate Newt Gingrich frequently referred to Obama as "the most successful food stamp president in American history." "Parry" involves the assertion that no racial allusion was intended. "Dog whistle politics trades . . . in studied ambiguity, where the lack of a smoking-gun racial epithet allows for proclamations of innocence." When Gingrich was challenged about his comments at a Republican presidential debate (and as the audience booed the very question), he denied that they had a racial basis, then added, "The fact is that more people have been put on food stamps under Barack Obama than any other president in history." As Haney-López observes, "[Gingrich] reacted with studied indignation—he was shocked that anyone would see race in his comments. But the barbed point of those three words—food stamp president—was to link Obama to indolent blacks on welfare, and to communicate that Gingrich would stand with hardworking whites who earn paychecks."[126] Finally, "kick" entails a swift shift from defense to offense: "When accused of racism, turn the tables and accuse your accuser of injecting race into the conversation."[127] Hence the suggestion that any white liberals or nonwhites who tie coded racial appeals to race themselves are the real racists, that they engage in race-baiting and in "playing the race card." Hence also the invocation of terms such as "reverse racism." These three rhetorical moves are played out frequently in today's political and racial discourse.

By their very nature—their implicitness—racial dog whistles are almost impossible to prove, and they always can be denied as being racial. But we all are familiar with the use of indirect, coded language in everyday life, whether it be in allusions to physical appearance, class upbringing, or sexual attractiveness. There are ways to signal things without "really" saying them. Politicians know the data just as well as political scientists; they know that racial attitudes guide voting behavior. Given this, as well as the history—and effectiveness—of racial appeals in American politics, is there good reason to believe that implicit racial appeals do not make an appearance in public discourse? "Because post–Civil Rights racial norms disallow the open expression of racial views," writes Eduardo Bonilla-Silva, "whites have developed a concealed way of voicing them."[128]

THE LONGING FOR COLOR-BLIND POLITICS

America—it is undeniable—is better off because of the Civil Rights Movement. The movement pushed the nation, kicking and screaming, several steps closer to the dream of establishing a democracy without racial hypocrisy and injustice. The gains of the movement, and the sacrifices of its champions, cannot be ignored. Because of them, racial domination has been dealt a massive blow.

The political field is complex and many-sided, however, and, despite the ongoing work of many social movements struggling for civil rights, the worldwide fight against racism has run into new obstacles in recent years. One reason for this is the changing nature of racial politics. Specifically, countries once built on racial domination now are claiming to be rid of race. "The successes of antiracist and antico-lonialist movements in recent decades are being transformed into new patterns of racial inequality and injustice," writes sociologist Howard Winant. "The 'new world racial system,' in sharp contrast to the old structures of explicit colonialism and state-sponsored segregation, now presents itself as 'beyond race,' 'color-blind,' multicultural, and postracial."[129]

Our discussion of dog whistle politics suggests some of the contours of the new racial situation, at least here in the United States. Much of our politics now is a matter not of outright segregationism or explicit bigotry, but rather of implicit triggering of deep-seated, not always self-conscious racial fears and antagonisms. Often the very persons who respond to it are loath to admit they are driven by racial considerations at all. Yet the political field is racially divided through and through. Racial progress will be impeded so long as we fail to uncover the mechanisms through which race continues to affect politics—and through which politics, in turn, continues to support racial injustice and domination. As Tocqueville put it in *Democracy in America*, a new science of politics indeed is needed for our new age.

THE BIG PICTURE

Chapter 3: Politics

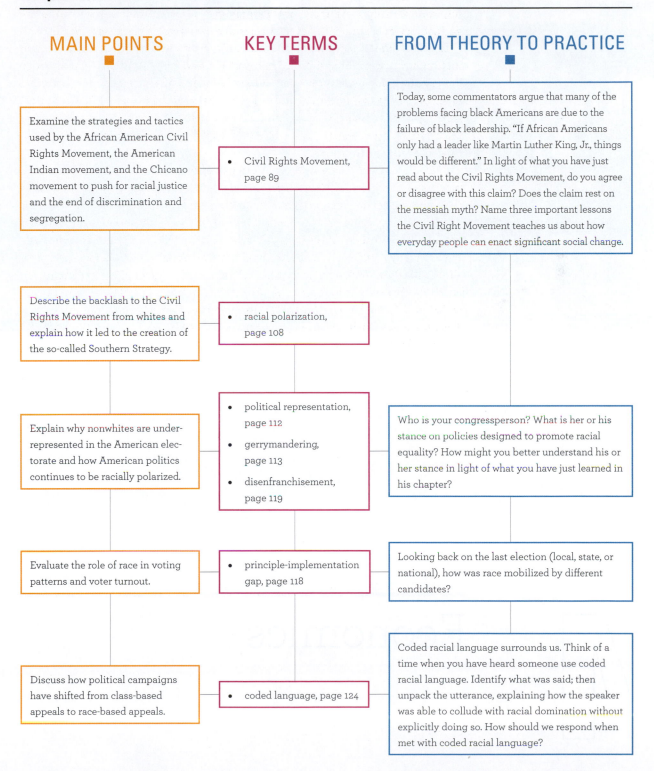

MAIN POINTS

Examine the strategies and tactics used by the African American Civil Rights Movement, the American Indian movement, and the Chicano movement to push for racial justice and the end of discrimination and segregation.

Describe the backlash to the Civil Rights Movement from whites and explain how it led to the creation of the so-called Southern Strategy.

Explain why nonwhites are under-represented in the American electorate and how American politics continues to be racially polarized.

Evaluate the role of race in voting patterns and voter turnout.

Discuss how political campaigns have shifted from class-based appeals to race-based appeals.

KEY TERMS

- Civil Rights Movement, page 89

- racial polarization, page 108

- political representation, page 112
- gerrymandering, page 113
- disenfranchisement, page 119

- principle-implementation gap, page 118

- coded language, page 124

FROM THEORY TO PRACTICE

Today, some commentators argue that many of the problems facing black Americans are due to the failure of black leadership. "If African Americans only had a leader like Martin Luther King, Jr., things would be different." In light of what you have just read about the Civil Rights Movement, do you agree or disagree with this claim? Does the claim rest on the messiah myth? Name three important lessons the Civil Right Movement teaches us about how everyday people can enact significant social change.

Who is your congressperson? What is her or his stance on policies designed to promote racial equality? How might you better understand his or her stance in light of what you have just learned in his chapter?

Looking back on the last election (local, state, or national), how was race mobilized by different candidates?

Coded racial language surrounds us. Think of a time when you have heard someone use coded racial language. Identify what was said; then unpack the utterance, explaining how the speaker was able to collude with racial domination without explicitly doing so. How should we respond when met with coded racial language?

Economics

MAIN POINTS

- Describe how President Franklin D. Roosevelt's antipoverty programs failed to decrease the economic division between whites and nonwhites.

- Explain how historical and contemporary institutional racism has extended significant income and wealth gaps between whites and nonwhites.

- Examine the explanations for why most poor Americans are white but African Americans, Hispanics, and American Indians are more likely than whites to be poor.

- Discuss why racial discrimination persists in today's job market.

- Compare who actually benefits from the welfare system in the United States with racial attitudes that many have regarding welfare.

- Understand what affirmative action policies are designed to do and examine the evidence for whether they are successful.

America, it often is said, is the most affluent nation on the planet. If we define affluence by a country's Gross National Income, the sum of the country's total value of goods and services and of funds garnered from other countries, then there is no questioning America's dominance. In a world of money, America reigns colossal.[1] However, if we define affluence not by the accumulation of wealth but by the distribution of wealth, America ranks far from the top. The numbers are startling. In the 1950s, the top 4 percent of American wage earners made, cumulatively, the same total as the bottom 35 percent of the country's workers. Today, the top 5 percent bring in the same amount as more than 80 percent of the country's lowest-paid workers, while the bottom 20 percent of earners collect only 3.2 percent of the country's income.[2] If money is time, consider this: while it takes a chief executive of a U.S. company an average of 3 hours to make $1,000, it takes the janitor who cleans that executive's office roughly 103 hours to earn the same amount. It would take the waitress who serves the executive dinner and the cashier who rings up his groceries even longer.[3]

America's accumulation of riches is matched only by the drastically uneven ways those riches are distributed.[4] Luxurious abundance and abundant destitution, the sublime and the slum, coexist in bright contrast. What role does race play in creating and maintaining such economic inequality?

This chapter concentrates on the workings of race in the economic field. It begins by analyzing changes that took place during the twentieth century, changes that systematically excluded people of color from American prosperity. Turning its attention to the present day, it then examines income and wealth disparities by race before investigating racialized poverty and affluence. Next, it focuses on labor market dynamics, concentrating on hiring practices, labor organizing, promotions, and the multicultural workplace. It concludes with an extended discussion of policy measures designed to confront racialized economic inequality: welfare and affirmative action.

ECONOMIC RACISM FROM THE NEW DEAL TO REAGANOMICS

American Indians never received compensation for being uprooted from their land, for being imprisoned on reservations, or for having their indigenous economies gobbled up by European settlers. Mexican Americans never were compensated for being deported to Mexico during the late nineteenth and early twentieth centuries, nor were they repaid for being dispossessed of their homes and land through the 1862 Homestead Act. Japanese American victims of internment camps did receive monetary reparations, but many were not allowed to claim rightful ownership of lands stripped from them in the wake of the Pearl Harbor bombings, lands that today (especially in California) are among the most wealth-producing in the nation. African Americans were denied reparations for slavery promised them. Consequentially, as America rolled into the twentieth century, many of its nonwhite citizens struggled through poverty, trying to make a life amid the rubble left from years of economic warfare.

Things were better for whites but not radically so. The Great Depression began in the fall of 1929, ushering in a period of severe economic deprivation. From the stock

Before World War II, when the South became more industrialized, all manufacturing jobs were limited to whites.

market crash of 1929 to America's entrance into World War II in 1941, thousands of Americans, of all colors, lost their jobs. When Japan bombed Pearl Harbor, most whites stood a far throw from middle-class security. But then things started to change. As the country marched into war, unemployment almost disappeared as new manufacturing jobs were developed. With thousands of white men fighting overseas, women and nonwhites were allowed to work in positions previously denied them.

World War II revived the American economy and launched the country into the roaring fifties. Americans prospered, but not equally. During these times of economic uplift, the economic gap between whites and nonwhites did not shrink or maintain its shape (which would imply that all people rose at the same pace). Instead, the racial gap increased, substantially.[5] What happened?

When Affirmative Action was White

Responding to the Great Depression, President Franklin D. Roosevelt initiated several programs dealing with welfare, work, and war designed to uplift Americans. Together, these programs came to be known as the New Deal. To date, no antipoverty program in the history of America has come close to matching those of the New Deal, which birthed unemployment insurance, the minimum wage, workday limitations, and, with the Social Security Act of 1935, one of the country's most significant pieces of social legislation, old age insurance. During the development of New Deal policies, the southern arm of the Democratic Party was a powerful force in the House and Senate. These white men acted as a separate party within the Democratic Party, a party that was willing to back New Deal policies only if they did not threaten the racial hierarchy of the South. By securing a disproportionate number of committee seats and flexing their political muscle, southern Democrats forced northern Democrats into a devil's bargain: "Either you design New Deal policies in such a way that Jim Crow remains perched atop his roost, or we will align with the Republicans and veto them." Northern Democrats gave in, barring nonwhites access to social spending programs.[6]

Many nonwhites were denied access to the New Deal. This was accomplished by disqualifying certain jobs, those dominated by nonwhite workers, from the policy. For instance, many southern black men, who constituted a full 40 percent of southern agricultural workers during the 1930s, could not benefit from these programs because farm workers did not qualify. Neither did maids, a profession dominated at that time by black women. As a result, the majority of blacks— 65 percent nationwide and up to 80 percent in some parts of the South—could not take advantage of the benefits offered by the Social Security Act.[7] The act was designed to discriminate; it functioned, in the words of NAACP spokesperson Charles Houston, "like a sieve with holes just big enough for the majority of Negroes to fall through."[8]

The New Deal mandated a standardized minimum wage, imposed work hour limitations, and provided a climate in which unions could flourish. But, again, southern Democrats refused to extend these rights to blacks and other nonwhite citizens. James Mark Wilcox, a representative from Florida, spoke for his fellow white southerners when he said, "We may rest assured, therefore, that when we turn over to a federal bureau or board the power to fix wages, it will prescribe the same wage for the Negro that it prescribes for the white man. Now, such a plan might work in some sections of the United States, but those of us who know the true situation know that it just will not work in the South. You cannot put the Negro and the white man on the same basis and get away with it."[9]

During World War II, the labor force began to change. Nonwhites made inroads into manufacturing jobs, and the South grew more industrialized. This meant that many nonwhites for the first time had access to New Deal work policies. This worried southern Democrats, who responded by backing Republican-led antilabor legislation. This new alliance led to the passage of the 1947 Taft-Hartley Act, which diminished union power. The ability to organize was important to working-class Americans, whose interests the southern Democrats often strove to protect—but not if that meant weakening the racial hierarchies of the old Confederacy.[10]

World War II rearranged American racial dynamics in several ways. It ignited anti-Asian, particularly anti-Japanese, sentiment—a process encouraged by government-sponsored propaganda and internment camps. At the same time, it allowed Jews and white Catholics, groups that previously had been ostracized from the American mainstream, to move closer to the center of American society. As anti-Semitism raged horrifically in Europe, it began quieting down in America. Jews

The GI Bill, which helped millions of veterans buy homes, go to college, and obtain unemployment insurance, was not equally available to veterans of color.

began enlisting in the military in record numbers and were treated to the perks of first-class citizenship. Thousands of other nonwhite men also attempted to enlist. Many, however, were denied on the basis of their race. It was only during the final throes of the war, when the American military found itself short on manpower, that it began admitting nonwhites into its ranks in substantial numbers.[11]

With respect to widening racial inequalities, more important than the war itself was the legislation that followed it, legislation designed for veterans returning home. By all standards, the Selective Service Readjustment Act—the GI Bill of Rights—was massive. In the three decades that followed the war, the United States spent more than $95 billion on the bill—almost $270 billion in today's dollars—making it the single most comprehensive set of social benefits ever issued by the federal government under a unified initiative. Using the GI Bill, millions of veterans bought homes, went to college, got by on unemployment insurance, financed small businesses, and purchased farmland. College enrollment shot up, nearly tripling between the beginning of the war and the 1950s. According to one source, America "gained more than 400,000 engineers, 200,000 teachers, 90,000 scientists, 60,000 doctors, and 22,000 dentists."[12] The dream of buying a home, which before the war was a luxury enjoyed only by the wealthy, became a reality for everyday Americans. In the decade that followed the war, over 13 million new homes were erected, nearly 40 percent of which were funded by veteran mortgages.[13] The GI Bill, more than any other program, forged the American middle class.

But, again, these benefits were not extended with equal generosity to nonwhites. The drafters of the GI Bill, many of whom were southern Democrats, left the administration of the bill up to state and local authorities. This meant that the distribution of veteran benefits was left in the hands of local Veteran Affairs offices, private banks, or universities—many of which were staffed by people who wished to uphold the racial order. Many banks made it a policy to deny small business loans and home mortgages to black and Latino veterans. Major colleges and universities barred black veterans from entry, leaving historically black colleges—underfunded at the time— to shoulder the burden. Nearly all black veterans who used the GI Bill's educational benefits did so at these segregated institutions. And nonwhite veterans who applied for job assistance were channeled into menial and unskilled professions. Of the jobs filled by Mississippi veterans by 1946, 86 percent of skilled and semiskilled posts were taken by whites, while 92 percent of the unskilled jobs were staffed by blacks.[14]

Why did economic and educational inequalities between whites and nonwhites increase rather than decrease during and after World War II, a time when the country was lifting itself out of the Great Depression and flourishing economically? Because, answers political scientist Ira Katznelson, "at the very moment when a wide array of public policies was providing most white Americans with valuable tools to advance their social welfare—insure their old age, get good jobs, acquire economic security, build assets, and gain middle-class status—most black Americans were left behind or left out. Affirmative action then was white."[15]

The End of Industrialization

Although the standard of living for many nonwhites improved because of the New Deal, the majority remained locked into low-wage work. Nonwhite affirmative action programs launched in the 1960s and 1970s allowed people of color to make inroads into white-collar professions, but many remained at the bottom rungs of the labor market. During the 1980s, the upward economic momentum propelled by industrialization following World War II came to a halt. Manufacturing jobs began disappearing from the Northeast and Midwest, a process known as deindustrialization.[16]

The factory was giving way to a service economy, one based on finance, sales, transportation, personal care, and technical advances. This new service economy featured many high-end jobs, but it also included low-end ones: more janitors to clean the IT (i.e., information technology) workers' desks or to empty the trash from the business managers' offices. This move toward a service economy would only widen the racial income gap. Deindustrialization was particularly hard on blacks and Puerto Ricans. To take but one example, between 1979 and 1984, half of all black men working in durable-goods manufacturing in major Midwest metropolises lost their jobs.[17] And out-of-work blacks often had a difficult time finding work in the service sector; in fact, whites were four times more likely to be employed full time in service industries than blacks.[18]

The economy was not the only thing changing. Federal assistance also was being altered dramatically under the leadership of Ronald Reagan. If Roosevelt opened the floodgates of federally mandated social benefits, Reagan built a dam. A staunch individualist, Reagan felt that the government should not interfere in the workings of the economy. The market should rule itself, he believed, which meant that all forms of social benefits—especially liberal policies ushered in by the New Deal— should be dismantled. Welfare spending was rolled back.[19]

Reagan championed the doctrine of supply-side economics, or Reaganomics, as it came to be known. The chain of reasoning ran like this: once the government pulls out of the market, primarily by cutting taxes to the wealthy, the wealthy will invest the money they usually dedicated to taxes into new capital ventures, which in turn will lead to cheaper production, which in turn will lead to lower prices and increased demand, thereby expanding the economy. Tax cuts will leave the federal government worse off, decreasing its ability to carry out social programs; however, there will be less of a need for these programs because low- and moderate-income workers will profit alongside the wealthy. How so? New capital investments developed by wealthy beneficiaries of tax cuts will create jobs, thereby allowing the riches at the top level to "trickle down" to the less fortunate at the bottom.[20]

During the 1980s manufacturing jobs began disappearing from the Northeast and Midwest. How did deindustrialization widen the racial income gap?

What was the result of Reagan's new economic strategy? The wealthy prospered under the program: the top 10 percent profited from a 5 percent tax cut, while the top 1 percent enjoyed a 15 percent cut, which brought about a 60 percent income increase. Those in the middle—between the fiftieth and ninetieth income percentiles—were relatively unaffected. But the bottom 50 percent actually suffered from tax *increases*, and the poorest fifth of Americans watched their incomes drop an average of 10 percent. Poor people of color were among the hardest hit. In the early 1980s, the poorest black families lost 18 percent of their family income. Many had to get by on less than $100 a week.[21] As a result, the distance separating America's elites from its poor increased substantially, as did the wage gap between nonwhites (namely, blacks and Hispanics) and whites.[22]

INCOME AND WEALTH DISPARITIES

We now turn to examining the most recent data on income and wealth disparities. By income, we mean wages and salaries earned from employment, retirement, or government aid. By wealth, we mean owned assets that yield monetary return, such as stocks and bonds, savings accounts, houses and real estate, and business and farm ownership. Income comes from your job, while most wealth comes from intergenerational transfers (that is, passed down from one generation to the next). You use your income (your paycheck from work) to buy groceries, diapers, and school supplies. You use your wealth (the funds accrued from your money-generating assets) to secure a desired standard of living for you and your family and perhaps to wield political influence. With income, you work for your money; with wealth, your money works for you.[23]

Income Inequality

In 2009, the median household income of Hispanics was $38,039 and the median income for Native Americans was $35,062. It was $32,358 for black households and $51,861 for white households. A median is the middle number in a set of ranked numbers. (The median of the set 1, 2, 3 is 2.) So, if you made every American family line up by race (a Native American line, a white line, and so forth) and income earnings (richest to poorest), and if you picked the family exactly in the middle of the white line, that family would be $13,822 richer than the families in the middle of the Hispanic line, $16,799 richer than the families in the middle of the Native American line, and $19,503 richer than the families in the middle of the black line.[24] These gaps narrow considerably when we account for important characteristics, such as education, employment experience, immigrant status, and hours worked; however, the gaps do not disappear. This means that on average a white worker will make more than a black or

FIGURE 4.1 2009 MEDIAN HOUSEHOLD INCOME BY RACE

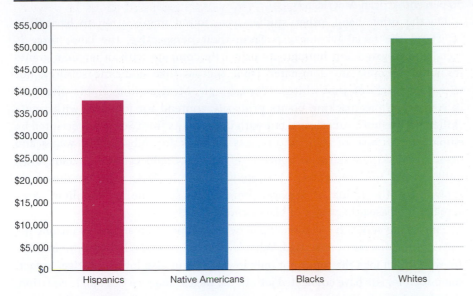

Despite working the same hours, white workers make more than their black and Hispanic peers.

Hispanic worker, even if all these people work exactly the same hours, possess exactly the same work experience, and hold exactly the same educational credentials.[25]

One explanation claims that high levels of immigration lead to racial disparities in income levels. The idea goes like this: Immigrants from poor countries flock to the United States searching for a better life. Because they came from poverty, they are willing to work for substandard wages. This attracts employers longing for the cheapest labor available. Soon, employers replace native-born workers with an immigrant labor force. This leaves many workers unemployed and drives down wages on the bottom rung of the income sector, thereby widening the gap between the working poor (many of whom are nonwhite) and the well off (many of whom are white). It also sours relations between nonwhites and immigrant groups.[26]

The evidence for this theory is mixed. On the one hand, there is evidence that low-income African Americans do lose out in the labor market because of increased competition with immigrants. Immigration flows drive up the unemployment rate of low-education African Americans, some studies have found, in part because black applicants to low-wage jobs are less likely to receive positive evaluations from potential employers.[27] As law professor Carol Swain has argued, "I don't believe there are any jobs that Americans won't take, and that includes agricultural jobs. [Illegal immigration] hurts low-skilled, low-wage workers of all races, but blacks are harmed the most because they're disproportionately low-skilled."[28] Some real-life examples bear out these arguments. Amid workforce raids by Immigration and Customs Enforcement, in 2008 the North Carolina poultry producer House of Raeford Farms began replacing immigrants with native-born workers at all its plants. In a year's time, House of Raeford's flagship production line in Raeford, North Carolina, went from more than 80 percent Latino to 70 percent African American.[29]

On the other hand, other studies have found immigration to have little effect on the racial income gap. From their perspective, the labor force is racially segregated and immigrants primarily compete with other immigrants for jobs in immigrant-dominated labor sectors (like domestic service), not with poor blacks or poor whites.[30] For example, Mexican immigrants who work in Nebraskan meatpacking plants primarily contend for jobs not with semi-skilled native-born Americans, but with immigrants from Somalia, recruited by employers because of their willingness to work for substandard wages and on account of their status as political refugees not subject to immigrant raids, unlike many undocumented Mexican workers.[31] In fact, some studies have shown that the influx of Mexican immigrants in some metropolitan areas actually increases the wages of blacks and whites.[32]

The debate about the relationship between immigration and racial income inequality remains far from settled. What is clear, however, is that many nonwhites are working in jobs that offer not only lower pay but also lower prestige. In fact, some sociologists have connected job status, wages, and race in a single equation, claiming that when a job becomes associated with a dominated racial group—just as domestic service is equated with Latinas or New York City taxi driving is equated with Arab American men—that job loses status. Once a job's status declines, so too do its wages. The influx of nonwhites into certain sectors of the labor market pulls down both wages and status.[33] Certain jobs become connected with certain racial groups and often become the subject of ridicule and humiliation. Recently, on one college campus, white students attending *Cinco de Mayo* parties dressed up like Mexican janitors and gardeners. At another party thrown at the University of Delaware, students dressed as Mexican landscapists, wearing shirts with the names Pedro or Julio on the front, and, on the back: "Spic and Span Gardening."[34]

Wealth Inequality

Although income inequality is still with us, the gap between white wages and nonwhite wages has been narrowing. The same cannot be said of wealth inequality. In fact, the wealth gap between whites and many nonwhite groups is growing. Between 1984 and 2009, for example, the wealth gap between white and black families nearly tripled, from a median net worth of $85,000 to $236,500.[35] The median net worth for black households in 2011 ($6,446) was lower than it was in 1984 ($7,150), while white households' median net worth was almost 11 percent higher, adjusting for inflation. Married black households with high incomes have, on average, less wealth than low-earning married white households.[36] In other words, poor whites

America's accumulation of riches is matched only by the drastically uneven ways those riches are distributed.

possess *more* wealth than well-off blacks. Today white families are on average six times more wealthy than black and Hispanic families ($632,000 versus $103,000).[37] Substantial racialized wealth inequality remains after accounting for human capital characteristics (education, salaries, family status).

To understand wealth disparities across race, we must look first to the past. Recall what we said in Chapter 1: racial advantages and disadvantages accumulate over generations. This means that today's wealth inequality is a concrete result of yesterday's racism. In whites' healthy assets, as compared to the sparse wealth of most people of color, we see the legacies of slavery, colonization, and "the Indian Problem"; we see the hundred years that ran from the Civil War to the Civil Rights Movement, during which people of color were barred from participating completely in business or commerce; we see government policies that uplifted poor whites while leaving poor nonwhites behind; and we see decades of meager wages, bad schools, and sharecropping.[38] For most of its history, the American market has been anything but "free."

This is especially important since most wealth is passed down from one generation to the next. This is truer today than ever before. In 1900, 39 percent of America's wealthiest people came from wealthy families. By 1950, 68 percent of the richest people came from wealthy backgrounds. By 1970, it was nearly impossible to work your way into wealth, since 82 percent of the wealthiest were born into fortune, and only 4 percent climbed up from the lower rungs of the social ladder.[39] Nevertheless, most Americans believe that wealth is a result of hard work, pluck, personal drive, or superior talent. In a recent survey, the most popular response to the question "What makes someone wealthy?" was "Hard work and initiative."[40] Hard work can pay off, to be sure—but rich families tend to pay better. "It is not usual," remarked the American sociologist C. Wright Mills, "and it never has been the dominant fact, to create a great American fortune merely by nursing a little business into a big one. It is not usual and never has been the dominant fact carefully to accumulate your way to the top in a slow, bureaucratic crawl. It is difficult to climb to the top, and many who try fall by the way. It is easier and much safer to be born there."[41]

Past forms of discrimination are not the only explanation for today's racialized wealth disparities. Present-day institutional racism also plays a large part. First, banks are more likely to offer credit to whites than to nonwhites. According to a study conducted by the Federal Reserve, commercial banks turn down black and Hispanic applicants two to three times more often than white applicants. In fact, the study concluded that the poorest white applicant has a better chance of getting her or his mortgage application approved than the highest paid black applicant.[42]

Second, nonwhites who do manage to secure a mortgage loan often pay higher interest rates than whites. In normal times, blacks pay half a percentage point more on loans than whites do. Although this may not look like much, it amounts to blacks who take out a twenty-five-year mortgage being deprived of $4,000. This adds up. Social scientists predict that the current generation of black homeowners will pay an extra $21.5 billion to banks—the penalty one pays for being black.[43]

FIGURE 4.2 **AVERAGE FAMILY WEALTH BY RACE AND ETHNICITY, 1983–2010**

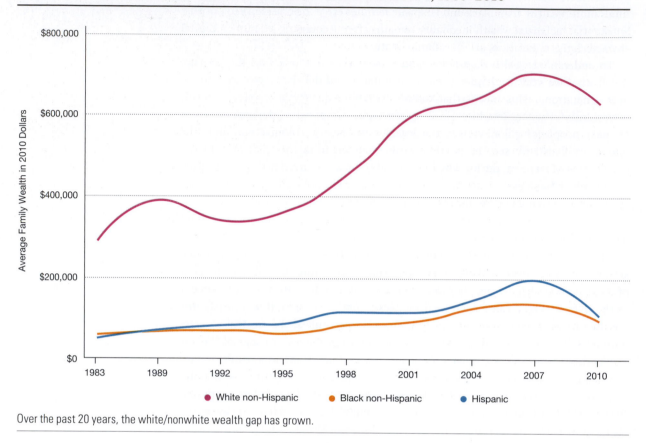

Over the past 20 years, the white/nonwhite wealth gap has grown.

During the housing spike, nonwhites were more likely to be offered high-interest subprime mortgages than whites, and when the housing bubble burst and foreclosures began sweeping the nation in 2007, they were disproportionately affected, losing their homes at extremely high rates, their credit scores plummeting.[44] In fact, recent research by the sociologists Jacob Rugh and Douglas Massey shows that racial segregation was a contributing cause of the foreclosure crisis. Blacks and Hispanics living in highly segregated neighborhoods were differentially targeted by the subprime lending industry specializing in risky loans. Cities with higher levels of racial segregation experienced higher levels of foreclosures, even after controlling for housing market characteristics. The authors write, "Ongoing residential segregation and a historical dearth of access to mortgage credit in U.S. urban areas combined to create ideal conditions for predatory lending to poor minority group members in poor minority neighborhoods. This racialized the ensuing foreclosure crisis and focused its negative consequences disproportionately on black borrowers and home owners."[45] The foreclosure crisis and ensuing recession resulted in a drastic loss of wealth for black and Hispanic families. Between 2007 and 2010, the average white family experienced an 11 percent reduction in wealth; the average black family experienced a 31 percent reduction; and the average Hispanic family lost 44 percent of its wealth.[46]

Yet another way in which institutional racism hinders nonwhites from obtaining wealth has to do with property values. Put bluntly, homes of a given size, design, and age in nonwhite or racially integrated communities do not accrue as much value as similar homes in white communities.[47]

As we have just seen, banks impede nonwhites' access to homeownership through three mechanisms: by disproportionately denying loans to nonwhite applicants; by charging nonwhites higher interest rates; and by devaluing homes in nonwhite neighborhoods. It is noteworthy that, because some banks refuse to do business with well-qualified nonwhite home buyers, they work against their economic interests. Denying nonwhites home loans simply because they are nonwhite is not a strategy dictated by the logic of the market; it makes sense only according to the reasoning of racism. Consider the fact that in twenty-seven years only 10 applicants out of 3,900 who secured loans through the Nehemiah Homes—a program in New York's outer boroughs that constructs and sells homes to working poor people, a disproportionate number of whom are nonwhite—have defaulted on their loans.[48] Our economy is far from color-blind and does not exist in its own world, somehow cordoned off from the realities of race. Class cannot be understood apart from race, and race cannot be comprehended apart from class.

A home in San Antonio faces imminent foreclosure.

CHASING THE AMERICAN DREAM: POVERTY AND AFFLUENCE

With over 46 million Americans living in poverty, America's poor population is far greater than that of other developed countries.[49] Roughly 15 percent of American citizens live below the poverty line.[50] This means that their income is not enough to sustain a decent standard of living, what is called a poverty threshold. According to the U.S. Bureau of the Census, in 2013 the poverty threshold for a single person under the age of 65 was $11,490; it was $23,550 for a family made up of a couple and their two children.[51] If these people earn less than their respective thresholds, they are said to be below the poverty line. Almost one in six Americans struggles through such hardship.

Most poor Americans are white. But if we compare proportions by race, we see that only 13 percent of whites are poor, while 35 percent of Hispanics, American Indians, and blacks live below the poverty line. Between 12 and 18 percent of Asian Americans live in poverty.[52] African Americans, Hispanics, and American Indians are twice as likely to be poor as whites. When we explore ethnic variation in poverty levels within racial categories, we notice marked differences. Of Hispanics, Mexican Americans and Puerto Ricans are much more likely to be poor than Cuban

Americans. Of Asians, Southeast Asians are much more likely to live down-and-out than Filipinos, Japanese, or Indian Americans. In fact, first-generation Laotian and Cambodian families have a 61 percent poverty rate, first-generation Chinese and Vietnamese families have a 25 percent poverty rate, and first-generation Filipino families have only a 10 percent poverty rate.[53]

The Causes of Poverty

What causes poverty? "The poor themselves," some answer back. Many Americans rationalize poverty in their midst by attributing it to negative characteristics of poor people: their laziness, incompetence, or lack of education.[54] At least since medieval times, people have blamed the poor, and especially the so-called undeserving poor (able-bodied people out of work), for their plight. Americans are no different in this respect.[55]

We even have invented a slew of pejorative labels that downgrade and stigmatize poor people. "White trash" is an epithet reserved for impoverished, rural (and usually southern) whites that began circulating in northern newspapers and books in the 1850s. Recently, it has regained popularity, along with "hick," "hillbilly," and "redneck."[56] "Underclass" was coined in 1962 by Gunnar Myrdal, a Swedish economist who used the term to describe the throngs of "unemployed unemployables" pushed out of work by the motors of deindustrialization. But journalists and popular writers quickly picked up the term, racializing it by applying it to poor inner-city blacks.[57] "White trash" brings to mind something that is dirty and polluted, something that does not belong in a safe and clean society. "Underclass" conjures up a group of people below (or under) society, a group that should be cordoned off, kept low, and ostracized.[58] Both epithets evoke

FIGURE 4.3 **POVERTY RATE BY RACE/ETHNICITY**

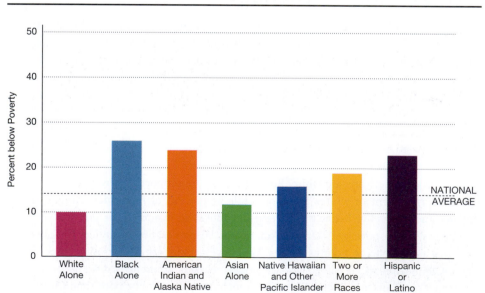

the idea of a threat precisely because these labels speak to behavioral traits more than economic ones do. "Most interpreters of the 'underclass,'" writes historian Robin Kelley, "treat behavior as not only a symptom from culture but also as the determinant for class. In simple terms, what makes the 'underclass' a class is members' common behavior—not their income, their poverty level, or the kind of work they do. It is a definition of class driven more by moral panic than by systemic analysis."[59]

Poverty cannot be explained solely by concentrating on the behavior of those suffering through it. We all make bad decisions. For some those decisions can be rather costly. (Privilege might best be defined as one's ability to screw up and get away with it.) To understand the causes of poverty, we must deploy a sociological imagination, taking into account things that are bigger than individuals, things such as social structures and historical changes. "True compassion," said Martin Luther King, Jr., "is more than flinging a coin to a beggar; it understands that an edifice which produces beggars needs restructuring."[60] Social scientists have identified many structural causes of poverty. We highlight three here.

First, modern-day capitalism produces a pool of unemployed laborers. A natural side effect of market capitalism is the fact that the number of people willing to work far exceeds the number of job vacancies. Economists call it "natural unemployment." In 2013, America's unemployment rate fluctuated around 7.5 percent—that's 11.3 million people.[61] Many people are unemployed as a result of outsourcing, downsizing, and layoffs.[62]

Second, deindustrialization made conditions of poverty worse. Midlevel occupations, such as factory work, have sharply declined, resulting in an economy shaped like an hourglass, with opportunities at the very top (in professional posts) and at the very bottom (in the low-wage service sector) but little sustainable work in the middle.[63] As a result, millions of Americans are counted among the working poor: people who have secured regular work that does not provide them with the means to lift themselves out of poverty. Here we find the garment worker who cannot afford the dresses she sews, the maid who will never be able to stay in the hotel she cleans, the medical transcriptionist who has not been to a doctor in years, the bank clerk whose balance is in the red. Today, fully one-third of the breadwinners of American families make less than $10 an hour; 20 percent make less than $8 an hour, and 12 percent make less than $6 an hour.[64] With wages like these, they cannot hope to pull their family out of poverty. Getting by is hard enough.

The third structural origin of American poverty is found in the country's safety net. Social spending in America dedicated to lessening economic difficulty—food stamps, housing subsidies, aid to needy families, Medicaid, and Social Security—has been rolled back in recent years. In fact, with the exception of Japan, America dedicates a smaller percentage of its wealth to antipoverty programs than any other developed country.[65] Studies have shown that such programs drastically reduce a country's poor population. If Germany, the Netherlands, and the United States did not offer any assistance to the poor, all three countries would have a 30 percent poverty rate. After assistance, Germany has a 4.3 percent rate and the Netherlands a 7.4 percent rate. American welfare programs, meager in comparison, bring about a smaller drop, resulting in a 15 percent poverty rate, more than double that of Germany and the Netherlands.[66]

Black Poverty, Black Affluence

Most poor whites live in areas where the majority of their neighbors are not poor. The same is true for only 15 percent of poor blacks and 20 percent of poor Hispanics. Conversely, whereas only 7 percent of poor whites live in extremely impoverished areas (with poverty rates at or above 40 percent), 32 percent of Hispanics and 40 percent of blacks live in such neighborhoods.[67] One study finds that the number of social establishments—places such as banks, grocery stores, pharmacies, restaurants, and childcare centers—increases as a neighborhood's poverty level increases but decreases as a neighborhood's proportion of blacks increases. In other words, it is not poor neighborhoods that are lacking these establishments but poor *black* neighborhoods.[68] "To be a poor man is hard, but to be a poor race in a land of dollars is the very bottom of hardships."[69]

In the black ghetto—a racial institution marked by social isolation and economic vulnerability first formed when blacks emigrated north during the early twentieth century—poverty is more concentrated and everyday establishments are scarce. What is more, its isolated residents suffer from pandemic unemployment and are cut off from social networks of people who could tell them about employment opportunities and help them get jobs. People who live outside the ghetto, and who are connected to job networks, often find out about jobs in the inner city faster than the people who actually live there.[70]

During the latter decades of the twentieth century, inner-city poverty in ghetto neighborhoods became more severe and more concentrated.[71] Social scientists have advanced three interlocking explanations.[72] The first, often referred to as the spatial mismatch thesis, holds that jobs that employed large numbers of semi-skilled black workers—manufacturing jobs—were moved in large numbers from the central city to the suburbs at the end of the twentieth century. From the end of World War II until the beginning of the 1970s, central cities in the biggest metropolitan areas lost 880,000 manufacturing jobs and 867,000 positions in retail and wholesale trade, while these cities' suburbs gained millions of jobs in these industries. Large cities began to look like donuts with job opportunities concentrated in the (mainly white) suburbs and a drastic dearth or absence of opportunities in the (mainly nonwhite) central city. This resulted in massive unemployment rates and concentrated poverty.[73]

The second explanation has to do with residential segregation, a topic to which we shall return in Chapter 5. Many blacks who wanted to leave the ghetto and who had the means to do so simply couldn't because of entrenched racial segregation and the virtual absence of fair housing policy enforcement. Writing in 1945, St. Clair Drake and Horace Cayton, authors of *Black Metropolis*, summed up the problem concisely: "The impecunious immigrant, once he gets on his feet, may . . . move into an area of second-settlement. Even the vice-lord or gangster, after he makes his pile, may lose himself in a respectable neighborhood. Negroes, regardless of their affluence or respectability, wear the badge of color. They are expected to stay in the Black Belt."[74] What is more, housing policy financed the suburbanization of America—offering large tax breaks for businesses relocating to the suburbs and subsidizing suburban housing developments—but by and large restricted these boosts to white citizens. Indeed, the Federal Housing Authority operated under the assumption that integrated neighborhoods would drive down property values. Hence, we read in its *Underwriting Manual* from the period: "If a neighborhood is to retain stability, it is necessary that properties shall continue to be occupied by the same social and racial classes."[75]

As a result, during the first half of the twentieth century, many black neighborhoods were integrated along class lines: the educated were neighbors to the uneducated; the white-collar home abutted the blue-collar lawn. However, the Civil Rights Movement broke down legally enforced barriers to residential mobility, and many middle-class black families moved out of the central city. This is the third explanation for the concentration and exacerbation of racialized poverty in the ghetto. Black inner-city neighborhoods experienced a kind of brain drain, where the more educated, wealthy, and privileged left behind families who constituted "the truly disadvantaged," to borrow a phrase from sociologist William Julius Wilson.[76] The declining presence of middle-class blacks, writes Wilson, "deprives ghetto neighborhoods of key resources, including structural resources (such as residents with income to sustain neighborhood services) and cultural resources (such as conventional role models for neighborhood children)."[77] Recently, however, researchers have challenged this point, arguing that most middle-class blacks live not interspersed throughout predominantly white suburbs, but in predominantly black middle-class neighborhoods usually positioned between black ghettos and white neighborhoods.

"The ghetto . . . is not bereft of role models and institutions," observes sociologist Mary Pattillo-McCoy. "What is missing are jobs that pay a decent wage, health care, decent affordable housing, and effective educations."[78]

The black middle class receives much less attention from journalists, reporters, and scholars than do the black poor, despite the fact that the majority of blacks are not poor. Although a black elite has existed since slavery and Reconstruction, the black middle class did not begin to flourish until the 1960s, after the Civil Rights Movement. Like the white middle class, the black middle class largely was formed through government action: civil rights legislation that eroded legally enforced barriers to upward advancement as well as the de-whitening of affirmative action programs.

Before 1960, less than 10 percent of the black population could be considered middle class, with only 385,586 black women and men in the entire country working as business owners, professionals, or officials. By the end of the 1980s, that percentage had grown to 45 percent, with over a million blacks employed in such professions.[79] Over the last thirty years, black enterprises have multiplied at an impressive rate. In 1973, the combined sales of the top 100 black-owned businesses came to $473 million; in 2012, that total amounted to over $19.1 billion. Between 2002 and 2007, black-owned firms grew by 60.5 percent; today there are over 1 million black-owned businesses in the United States.[80] Black-owned banks, such as OneUnited Bank and Broadway Federal, have prospered and are reaching out to black neighborhoods, as are black-owned insurance companies, newspapers, and computer industries. Over 200 black women and men have ascended to the upper ranks of Fortune 500 companies.[81]

FIGURE 4.4 THE EFFECT OF A CRIMINAL RECORD FOR BLACK AND WHITE JOB APPLICANTS

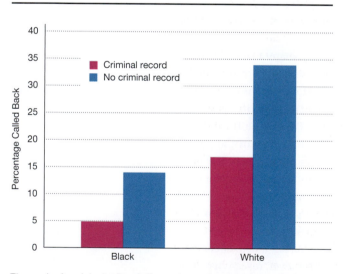

The work of sociologist Devah Pager shows that among men looking for work, whites with a criminal record do better on the job market than blacks without one.

Despite these impressive gains, we must not make the mistake of thinking that black affluence is identical to white affluence. The bulk of the black middle class belongs to the *lower* middle class. Although there are successful black surgeons and stockbrokers aplenty, most black middle-class women and men work in sales or as clerks or public-service workers, garnering much lower wages than professionals belonging to the upper middle class.[82] And, as we already have seen, white middle-class families tend to have much more wealth than black middle-class families—even if the families have similar incomes. One study compared white and black middle-class families and found that, should they need to dip into their reserves to make ends meet—say, a company goes out of business—the typical white family could survive at the poverty line for a whole year. The typical black family would not last a month.[83]

Black middle-class families also must confront challenges that many white middle-class families do not. Some have argued that while poor blacks suffer from economic exploitation and social isolation, middle-class blacks suffer "in a spiritual sense," as E. Franklin Frazier put it in *Black Bourgeoisie*.[84] Affluent blacks, having succeeded in life—having graduated from college, secured a stable job, purchased a home, and stored some money away in savings—continue to be plagued by racism.

Since the fall of slavery, some blacks have held tight to the belief that once they obtain some professional and financial success, whites will extend to them their respect and friendship. Booker T. Washington, a powerful black political leader who gained fame around the turn of the twentieth century, once addressed a crowd saying that whenever he had "seen a black man who was succeeding in business, who was a taxpayer, and who possessed intelligence and high character, that individual was treated with the highest respect by the members of the white race."[85] But blacks soon came to realize the hollowness of such statements. Now they could afford a home, but realtors refused to show them properties outside the black area of town. Now they had earned a college degree, but companies would not hire them. Now they had worked diligently and loyally, but the promotion was offered to someone else. Cut after cut after cut—these everyday acts of violence can result in a spiritual suffering brought on by the realization that something as unreasonable as racism cannot always be won over by reason. Something that seeks to dehumanize a people does not routinely wither and die when those people assert their humanity. Middle-class blacks have learned that money can help them ascend to very high places, but it cannot lift them above the veil of racism.

American Indian Reservations

The central city is not the only site of American destitution; poverty also is pervasive in many rural communities. Since their creation, American Indian reservations have been wracked by extreme rural poverty. The median household income for American Indians on reservations is roughly 66 percent of the U.S. average, and the poverty rate is almost twice the national average. The Pine Ridge Indian Reservation in South Dakota has a shocking 75 percent unemployment rate, and its per capita income is only a quarter of the national average. Although the Crow Indian Reservation houses one of the largest coal reserves in the world, most of those living on the reservation face bleak economic conditions: over 50 percent of tribal members receive some public assistance. By and large, American Indian reservations are plagued by dire poverty, joblessness, and poor living conditions.[86]

Some tribes, however, are prospering. With a popular golf resort, developed construction industries, and flourishing plastic, automotive, and electronics manufacturing plants, the Choctaw Tribe is the second-largest employer in Mississippi, generating over $170 million dollars in annual wages and supplying 12,000 jobs. Not only are most Choctaws employed, but the tribe provides jobs for over 6,000 black and white workers in surrounding counties. Northern Arizona's White Mountain Apache Tribe runs a ski resort, manages prime logging forests, employs hundreds of workers at a busy sawmill, and brings in revenue with hunting and fishing tourism. Like the Choctaw, the Apache's economic prosperity has spilled over into non-Indian communities, benefiting those in surrounding areas. And the Salish and Kootenai tribes, living on Montana's Flathead Reservation, have built up successful tourism, agricultural, and retail enterprises. The tribes' unemployment rate is lower than the state's average, and non-Indians seeking a solid education often apply to the tribal college.[87]

So why are some tribes beating poverty while others are beaten by it? Indian gaming is a popular answer. Since 1998, roughly 200 of the 559 federally recognized tribes have ventured into gaming, and some tribes have profited considerably. But this is rare. The top 13 percent of Indian casinos account for 60 percent of Indian gaming revenue, which means that an elite group of tribes—namely, those with prime locations—are doing well, while most are drawing in unimpressive profits. Indian gaming is not a viable economic strategy for isolated tribes located in the backcountry, and some Indian nations have outlawed casinos on their land for fear that they would erode traditional culture and breed gambling addiction. And Indian gaming usually comes with a high cost: it tends to chip away at tribes' political sovereignty. This is a serious drawback, because sovereignty seems to be connected directly with Indian economic sustainability and advancement.[88]

Tribal sovereignty means the power of Indian tribes to act as semiautonomous states, designing and running their own system of governance. Since 1970 the federal government, responding to the American Indian political resurgence discussed briefly in Chapter 3, began recognizing tribes' right to self-rule. "Indian peoples are Nations, not minorities," David Wilkens once asserted.[89] Tribal sovereignty, or "Indian self-determination," allowed many tribes to chart their own course on matters of economic development, political decision making, and the management of natural resources. As a result, several tribes exercising their sovereignty have developed new economic initiatives and have invested in reservation communities, ensuring that American Indian resources benefit American Indian people instead of outside investors. And tribal sovereignty works best, studies have demonstrated, when Indian nations develop proficient institutions rooted in the cultural foundations of the tribe. Indian culture is itself a valuable resource to Indian nations working toward independence, because tribes that align their political governance with their heritage seem to be the most successful.[90]

The Pueblo de Cochiti of New Mexico is one such tribe. Operating under a traditional form of rule, the tribe's top six positions are chosen every year by the Cochiti chief spiritual leader, the Cacique. Though this form of government operates without a constitution, it does include a very sophisticated system of checks and balances. If the lieutenant governor finds that spiritual leaders are abusing their power, he can exercise immediate impeachment rights. Policy development is guided by the Pueblo Council, made up of forty male tribal members. And the Cacique himself—who, though he is the most powerful

Ogala Sioux Leon Brave Heart, 22 years-old, faces a bleak future on the reservation without a federal college grant.

member of the tribe, often occupies a more humble position in the economic sector—is forbidden to use any Cochiti money for his own enrichment. This system of governance serves the Cochiti well today, as the tribe is a paragon of economic success. Operating a retirement community, a marina, a golf course, and a number of other profitable enterprises, it boasts one of the lowest unemployment rates in all of Indian country.[91]

Some American Indian tribes are beginning to overcome poverty that has riddled reservations since their inception. Much work, however, remains to be done. In the final analysis, the economic problems in Indian country are perhaps best confronted by political solutions—not the "quick fix" of Indian gaming, despite all the glitter and controversy. "Economic development on Indian reservations is first and foremost a political problem," write sociologists Stephen Cornell and Joseph Kalt. "At the heart of it lie sovereignty and the governing institutions through which sovereignty can be effectively exercised. . . . It is increasingly evident that the best way to perpetuate reservation poverty is to undermine tribal sovereignty. The best way to overcome reservation poverty is to support tribal sovereignty."[92]

The Struggles of Immigrants

Immigrants are another group disproportionately affected by poverty. Over the last forty years, the poverty level for children of immigrants—who make up no less than one in five U.S. children—has increased, rising from 12 percent in 1970 to 30 percent in 2012.[93] And things are markedly worse for those who do not carry naturalization papers.[94]

As we discussed in Chapter 2, the United States maintained strict limitations on immigration throughout most of the twentieth century. Certain groups—such as Italians—came under quota restrictions, while other groups—namely, people from Japan, China, Korea, and other parts of Asia and the Pacific Rim—were barred from entry altogether. The Immigration and Nationality Act of 1965, drafted in the wake of the Civil Rights Movement, changed all this by abolishing national-origin quotas. Although the act established limitations on the number of visas allotted each year to most immigrants (distributed on a first-come, first-served basis), it did not limit family reunification visas, which allowed immigrants with family members in the United States to be admitted. Fifteen years later, the 1980 Refugee Act was ratified. This act provided political asylum for refugees and asylees victimized on the basis of their race, religion, nationality, political affiliation, or group membership.

These two acts drastically changed immigrant flows to America and fundamentally reshaped the landscape of social, political, cultural, and economic life in this country. Immigrants from Latin America—Mexico in particular—and Asia began coming to America in large numbers, as did refugees, asylees, and undocumented migrants from many parts of the globe. Many immigrants from Mexico, finally reunited with their families, came with little education and little money in their pockets. Today, Mexican immigrants rank among the poorest immigration groups, with a 35 percent poverty rate for first-generation children.[95] Vietnamese, Hmong, Cambodian, and Laotian families fled their countries during the Vietnam War and the subsequent American bombings of

Cambodia. In 1975, roughly 150,000 refugees were airlifted out of Vietnam, and over 85,000 were relocated to the United States. Many of these refugees' homes had been firebombed and their property burned or stolen—and in America most remained in poverty.[96]

There is no monolithic "immigrant experience" or natural sequence through which those fresh off the boat assimilate to American society. Rather, immigrants are absorbed into different segments of the American landscape. Some assimilate into the upper classes, some into the lower classes. The body of thought that explores these processes is called segmented assimilation theory. Sociologists Alejandro Portes and Min Zhou describe three common pathways through which immigrants adapt to American society. "One of them replicates the time-honored portrayal of growing acculturation and parallel integration into the white middle-class; a second leads straight into the opposite direction to permanent poverty and assimilation into the underclass; still a third associates rapid economic advancement with deliberate preservation of the immigrant community's values and tight solidarity."[97] In other words, new immigrants join the ranks of the economically privileged, the economically downtrodden, or the moderately prosperous ethnic economy. There is no so-called Middle America into which immigrants enter after a process of assimilation. Because American society is divided along all sorts of lines, on arrival new immigrants are met with a range of divides and are sorted into them accordingly. The important question is this: What determines their American experience? Why do some immigrants climb upward while others slide down into the depths of poverty?

To answer this question we must look first to the shape of the American economy, just as we did when examining the causes of American poverty in general. Stable blue-collar jobs with decent wages, jobs that traditionally have been attractive to newly arrived immigrants, are now scarce. And the gap between dream jobs in the professional sector and lousy jobs in the service sector continues to widen, such that at workers at the bottom of the market have virtually no chance of climbing upward. Mobility ladders simply don't reach that high. Consequently, many immigrants who come without college degrees, let alone high school diplomas, must work in low-wage industries offering little opportunity for economic advancement. That idea so cherished in the American imagination—the poor immigrant working her or his way to a life of comfort—is becoming less and less a reality in America's hourglass-shaped economy.[98]

However, for those elite immigrants who arrive with wealth, college degrees, and specialized skills, lucrative jobs often await. Thus, to understand divergent immigrant trajectories, we must examine not only the shape of the U.S. economy but also the skills, education, and training—in a phrase, the class privileges—immigrants bring with them. Speaking generally, immigrants from India, China, Africa, Western Europe, and Canada tend to be well educated and to have a higher proportion of professionals and managers in their midst. Those from the Caribbean, El Salvador, Mexico, and other Latin American countries tend to have little education and are represented disproportionately in low-wage work. Once they master the English language (if they haven't done so already), highly skilled immigrants who received an education in their mother country usually have little trouble securing professional posts as engineers, mathematicians, scientists, and teachers.[99] We should point out, however, that a college degree from a foreign country is not as valued as a U.S. education. A recent study found that similarly educated native-born whites, Asian Americans, and Asian immigrants educated in the United States have similar incomes, but Asian immigrants educated in their home countries earn 16 percent less than do these three groups.[100]

To the job opportunities found at the very top and the very bottom of the labor market, immigrants have added a third option: employment in the ethnic enclave. An ethnic enclave is a semiautonomous economy, large or small, that is owned, operated, and managed by members of the same immigrant or ethnic community. In New York City, Dominican immigrants have created an entrepreneurial enclave complete with its own restaurants, travel agencies, and Spanish-speaking newspapers. Here one also finds informal finance agencies called *financieras* that allocate loans and grant credit to Dominicans who are not able to secure them through mainstream banking channels. *Financieras* award loans, which usually are accompanied by low interest rates, based on a person's reputation in the community and her or his personal and familial connections. The same is true in the Cuban enclaves of Miami, where many Cuban-owned businesses were started from "character loans," loans made by agencies in the Cuban community to other Cubans. Salvadoran immigrants in Los Angeles and Washington, D.C., have cultivated a growing ethnic enclave as well, one based on transnational enterprises: American goods are shipped to El Salvador, while Salvadoran food, clothing, music, and cultural goods are transported to the United States.[101]

Immigrant women are key players in enclave economies. Roughly 70 percent of foreign-born Chinese women are employed—twenty-four percentage points higher than foreign-born European women and sixteen percentage points higher than native-born white women. This is not because Chinese immigrant women have an abundance of class privileges, but in spite of this: they have drastically low levels of education (with fewer than half completing high school) and low English proficiency. Many first-generation Chinese women work in Chinatown-based jobs, such as New York City's garment industry, which employs over half of all working Chinese women in the city. In fact, roughly 70 percent of all garments sewn in New York City were sewn by the hands of immigrant Chinese women. Many of these women work six days a week for less

A Cuban café on 8th street in the district of Little Havana in Miami.

than minimum wage, bending over machines and, paid by the piece, working as fast as they can. Garment workers often compare their wages not to those of other Americans, but to what they would earn in China for comparable work. Since their wages in the United States are higher than Chinese wages and since few economic opportunities are available beyond the enclave, Chinatown's garment industry is not in want of eager workers. On top of working in the garment shops, immigrant Chinese women are expected (and expect of themselves) to support their husbands and to raise their children. They are responsible for the bulk of the domestic labor—cooking, cleaning, grocery shopping, and childcare. Doubly disadvantaged, these women hold in one hand the demands of a menial job and in the other the demands of a family.[102]

Some studies have shown that immigrants who work in ethnic enclaves earn more money than those with similar education and skills employed in the mainstream economy. For instance, self-employed Asian immigrants earn $6 per hour more than other immigrants with similar education and skills.[103] And low-interest character loans requiring little collateral, a creation of the ethnic enclave, have been used by hundreds of immigrants to start their own bookstore, restaurant, or bodega. These findings lead some researchers to conclude that "enclaves are no mere ghetto where foreigners huddle together eking out a living from marginal activities. Instead, ethnic enterprise can be an effective avenue for economic mobility."[104]

Some studies, however, argue that ethnic enclaves impede immigrants' upward mobility. Finding that enclave-employed immigrants are not better off than those working elsewhere, earning low wages and sometimes facing unfair working conditions, some scholars have labeled enclaves "ethnic mobility traps." Researchers have observed that San Francisco's Chinatown is controlled by a small group of elite clans who often bar from their enterprise immigrants unwilling to adopt their conservative political opinions. Others have noted that the Cuban enclave in Miami benefits men more than women.[105] Social scientists have not yet resolved what has come to be known as the "enclave economy debate." At best, we can conclude only that ethnic enclaves seem to offer newly arrived immigrants looking for reliable work a mixed bag of advantages and disadvantages.

Besides the structure of the economy, the class privileges (or lack thereof) of immigrants, and ethnic enclaves, there is a final mechanism that determines how well immigrants fare in America: racial privileges.[106] On coming to America, immigrants immediately are confronted with its racial order. They are branded with foreign racial classifications—Indonesians, Cambodians, and Koreans become "Asian"; Russian Jews, Croatians, and Germans become "white"—which affects their economic trajectories. Plainly, taking into account class privileges, such as education and job training, immigrants classified as white or Asian tend to do better than immigrants classified as Hispanic or black. Recently, researchers found 21 percent of first-generation immigrants classified as white to be poor; the same was true of 24 percent of those classified as black, 27 percent of those classified as Asian, and 41 percent of those classified as Hispanic. When they looked at the economic standing of the children of immigrants, they noticed that many were not as poor are their

Roughly 70 percent of all garments sewn in New York City are sewn by immigrant Chinese women.

parents. But they also noticed that some racial groups fared better than others. For whites and Asians, the poverty rate dropped more than half, whereas it declined less than a third for blacks and Hispanics. When the researchers observed the economic conditions of the children of children of immigrants, "the third generation," they were confronted with a shocking finding: the poverty rate for Asians declined further, it remained the same for whites and Hispanics, but it *increased* by 26 percentage points for blacks. By and large, third-generation black immigrants were poorer than were their grandparents, who emigrated from Haiti, the West Indies, or South Africa.[107] The American dream of poor immigrants carving out a better life, if not for themselves then at least for their children, comes more easily to those classified near the privileged end of America's racial hierarchy.

Recognizing this, many immigrants resist Americanized racial classification by emphasizing their "immigrant-ness." For instance, West Indian parents often cultivate in their children an island accent so they might take advantage of employment opportunities not offered their African American peers.[108] Such adaptive strategies are rewarded by employers, many of whom would rather hire immigrants than native-born Hispanics or blacks. The irony of this racialized process is that immigrants who refuse to assimilate are rewarded. This is why sociologist Mary Waters observes that "we should not just be asking as a society, 'How can we structure our immigration policy and our institutions to facilitate immigrants adopting our civic culture and becoming American?' We should also be asking, 'What can we do about the pervasive inequalities in American life that often mean that becoming black American or Mexican American leads to a less bright future than remaining an immigrant?'"[109]

Although the labor market continues to be marred by racial inequality, nonwhites have made impressive advances in the professional realm.

LABOR MARKET DYNAMICS

Getting a Job

The unemployment rate has fluctuated greatly over the past fifty years. It decreased from 1950 to 1960, only to increase sharply through the 1970s, peak in the early 1980s, and climb slowly down until 1990. It increased slightly in the early 1990s but decreased for the remainder of the decade. Despite all this fluctuation, one thing has remained the same: the nonwhite unemployment rate consistently has been double that of whites. If you remove blacks from the equation, the difference shrinks considerably. In 2013, the unemployment rate was 6.4 percent for whites, 13.2 percent for blacks, 9.1 percent for Hispanics, and 5.4 percent for Asian Americans.[110] What can explain these racial disparities—and blacks' high rates of unemployment in particular?

Americans debating this question have divided into two camps. On one side there are those who believe that "impersonal market forces" explain racial inequalities in the labor force. "It's not racism per se," argues this camp. "Nonwhites are disadvantaged in terms of lower wages and higher unemployment rates because they don't have the necessary schooling or skills to compete in today's economy. If nonwhites had the same training as whites, things would even out." On the other side are those who explain racial inequalities by institutional racism. "Blacks and Hispanics have higher unemployment rates because they are denied job opportunities solely on the basis of their skin color," argues this camp. "To understand racial cleavages in the workforce, we must pay attention to persistent discrimination." Because each camp sees the world differently, each has its own policy recommendations. Those who believe that the problem lies in impersonal market forces hold that the solution lies in job training programs and inner-city education. Those who believe that discrimination is the problem claim that education is not enough; they advocate civil rights legislation, affirmative action programs, and "diversity education" in the workplace.[111] Which camp is right?

Social scientists have amassed libraries full of data that conclusively and convincingly show that qualified Hispanics and blacks seeking jobs are passed over for white applicants. One study found that employers were three to four times more likely to offer whites a job than equally qualified blacks or Hispanics. In another study, nearly half of employers interviewed in four major cities criticized blacks' skills and work ethic, while Hispanics and Asians, praised for their "immigrant work ethic," were not evaluated nearly so negatively.[112] As we mentioned in the preceding section, some employers would rather hire immigrants than native-born people of color. A white supervisor who oversees the hiring procedures for a service firm confessed to one interviewer: "The Polish immigrants that I know and know of are more highly motivated than the Hispanics. The Hispanics share in some of the problems that the blacks do."[113] Some firms recruit directly from white immigrant populations, advertising openings in German- or Polish-language papers instead of in the local English paper.

In another study, 185 employers based in Chicago were asked if they believe different racial groups have different work ethics. Half claimed they noticed no difference or refused to categorize their workers in such a fashion. But 38 percent claimed that blacks have the weakest work ethic out of all groups, and 8 percent placed both blacks and Hispanics at the bottom of the ranking. No employer reserved this demeaning evaluation for whites.[114]

Audit studies are an especially powerful way to determine if and how discrimination affects hiring decisions. These studies send paired actors to apply for real jobs. The actors are equal in every way aside from race.[115] In one experiment, economists Marianne Bertrand and Sendhil Mullainathan responded to 1,300 help-wanted ads by submitting résumés from phantom job applicants. The résumés reported similar skill levels, education, and experience but differed on one account: the names. Some were assigned names common among blacks (like Lakisha and Jamal); others were assigned names common among whites (like Emily and Greg). The results? Compared to applicants with black-sounding names, those with white-sounding names were 50 percent more likely to be called for an interview.[116]

In another creative audit experiment, sociologist Devah Pager sent four men to apply for 350 low-skill jobs in Milwaukee. Two white men made up one pair; two black men formed another. Within each pair, one applicant reported having been convicted of a felony drug charge. Besides race and criminal record, the actors as applicants were identical on all other measures. Pager found that 34 percent of whites without a criminal record received callbacks from the employer, but the same was true of only 17 percent of whites with a criminal record. And only 14 percent of black applicants without a criminal record, and 5 percent with a record, received callbacks. In other words, whites convicted of selling drugs were more likely to land a job than were blacks with no criminal history![117]

Taken together, these studies offer strong evidence that institutionalized racism denies qualified blacks and Latinos job opportunities. The "discrimination matters" camp is right. Does this mean that the "impersonal market forces" camp is wrong? Yes and no. They are wrong to think the market is detached from society. Since the economy is embedded in social relations, as we already have seen, an argument touting the explanatory superiority of class instead of race is flawed from the get-go. However, this camp is right to stress how a good education, networks of employed friends and family members, and skill training disproportionately are denied to nonwhites.[118]

Disadvantage breeds disadvantage. Since blacks and Latinos are discriminated against when applying for jobs, many have a spotty work history. Since they have a spotty work history, they are less attractive to employers. Again, if institutional racism channels many blacks and Hispanics into periods of unemployment or low-wage work, then they will have a difficult time cultivating within their children a middle class disposition—those ineffable "soft skills" such as social graces and professional communicative styles, often bound up with white privilege—for which employers often look.[119] And they will not be able to help their family and friends secure employment in good-paying work, which is precisely what social scientists have found.[120]

We cannot understand racial inequalities within the workforce without accounting for the pernicious fact of discrimination. But neither should we forget that racial domination, having a long and established career, has robbed many nonwhites of opportunities to build up class privileges: education, soft skills, job training, and connections to powerful people. The source of the problem is threefold: a history of racialized opportunity hoarding, modern-day racial discrimination at the point of hiring, and institutional racism at work in other fields of life.

Racial Antagonism and Interracialism in a Split Labor Market

In the industrial northern cities of the 1920s and 1930s, blacks, many of them men who recently had emigrated from the South, began securing jobs as meatpackers, steelworkers, bricklayers, and carpenters. By some estimates, the black unemployment rate in northern and western cities at this time was significantly lower than the white rate. Why were black workers more attractive to employers? Because they were more exploitable. Compared to whites, blacks worked longer hours for lower wages. During this time, many "whites only" unions barred blacks from membership, and some spokespeople in the black community, persuaded by capitalists who owned the factories, discouraged blacks from organizing as workers. Unorganized, black workers had no bargaining power. They could not demand from their employers better wages or improved working conditions, nor could they strike if their employers paid them no mind.[121]

Seeking lower labor costs, employers often replaced white workers with blacks, who came to be known as "strike insurance" to some company owners.[122] And

When Tyson workers at the Jefferson, Wisconsin plant went on strike during contract negotiations, African Americans were bused in to replace the striking workers.

when white workers went on strike, blacks often were used as strikebreakers. During the Great Steel Strike of 1919—when over a quarter million steelworkers walked out of their jobs when their companies refused to raise their wages and shorten their workday—some 40,000 black workers were brought in to weaken the strike. Many were imported from the rural South. In large part because of this, employers crippled the strike, forcing the steelworkers to return to the same dangerous conditions for the same meager wages.[123] Racialized strikebreaking occurs to this day. In 2004, when workers at the Tyson Foods meat processing plant in Jefferson, Wisconsin, were forced to strike when the company initiated wage cuts and withdrew benefit packages, African Americans from the nearby town of Beloit were bused in to replace the striking workers.

These dynamics depend on a split labor market. "To be split," writes sociologist Edna Bonacich, "a labor market must contain at least two groups of workers whose price of labor differs for the same work, or would differ if they did the same work."[124] According to Bonacich, a split labor market is steered by the struggles of three groups: the business elite, higher-paid labor, and cheap labor. The business elite own and run the companies and seek the cheapest labor possible. The higher-paid labor work in these companies and, through union organizing, have secured a decent wage and fair working conditions. However, higher-paid labor lives in constant threat of cheap labor, which the business elite can hire to cut costs. Because the division between higher-paid labor and cheap labor corresponds to racial divisions, competition between the two labor groups can heighten racial antagonism. Today, for instance, the fact that some employers would rather hire undocumented workers on the cheap than native-born union members helps to stir up anti-immigrant sentiment.

At the same time, some unions have begun actively recruiting Mexican immigrants, documented or otherwise. After losing many jobs to nonunionized workers, a significant number of whom were undocumented immigrants, the United Brotherhood of Carpenters and Joiners have started to reach out to immigrants. "If you want [your union] to grow, you have to represent the people who are doing the work," says one Colorado union leader.[125] Just as competition for jobs can lead to racial antagonism, organizing across the color line to secure fair and honest working conditions can encourage the process of forming a racially integrated political community that works toward a common goal.[126]

In the split labor market, the business elite can employ racial division on behalf of worker exploitation, pitting one group against another to thwart interracial worker solidarity and to keep the price of labor low. If workers participate in these racial struggles, forming prejudices against Chinese workers (as in the late nineteenth century), black workers (as in the early twentieth century), or Mexican workers (as in the present day), they tend to blame other exploited workers for their exploitation. If, however, workers refuse to play by the rules of this game and instead build interracial coalitions, as did the Hawaiian working class (more on this in Chapter 11), they can commit their energies to confronting the structural conditions that produce economic vulnerability and poor working conditions. A split labor market dependent on racial cleavages disadvantages *all* workers.

By exploring the racial dynamics of a split labor market, we are better able to understand one of the causes of interpersonal racism. Interpersonal racism shapes and is shaped by institutional racism in the economic field. In the words of Herbert Blumer, "race prejudice exists basically in a sense of group position rather than in a set of feelings which members of one racial group have toward the members of another racial group. This different way of viewing race prejudice shifts study and analysis from a preoccupation with feelings as lodged in individuals to a concern with the relationship of racial groups."[127] Specifically, racial antagonism is heightened when we begin to believe that in order to grasp hold of society's resources—jobs, safe neighborhoods, good education—we must engage in a competition with other racialized groups. And if we perceive those resources to be scarce, studies have shown, we are more likely to harbor racial resentment toward other groups.[128]

Power and Privilege in the Workplace

Recent studies exploring middle-class occupations have found that blacks are nearly twice as likely to be laid off as whites, a difference that could not be explained by conventional measures, such as seniority or education. In other words, race is the main explanation as to why blacks working in white-collar professions are the first to be fired.[129] With respect to promotions, women and people of color—with similar years of schooling and similar years working for a company—are less likely to hold positions of authority than their white male counterparts. In fact, relative to blacks and Hispanics, whites are twice as likely to be supervisors—controlling budgets, wielding power over hiring and firing decisions, instructing subordinates—while Asians seem to be on par with whites on this score.[130]

Many nonwhites who have ascended to positions of authority tend to be low-level supervisors overseeing other nonwhites and, relative to white men, cut off from social ties and communication channels that otherwise could connect them to opportunities, resources, and influential people.[131] Standing out against other (mostly white male) supervisors, nonwhites in positions of power, especially those placed there as tokens, often are subjected to intense monitoring and scrutiny. Many feel isolated and weighted down by performance pressures. They are cut off from other nonwhite workers because of their superiority and cut off from other superiors because of their race.[132]

In general, black, Latina, and Asian women fill low-status and low-paying positions relative to white women and nonwhite men. And women of color are rewarded less for their education and job experience than are white men, white women, or men of color. In fact, if black women were paid as much as white men with similar credentials, they would earn on average $7,000 more per year.[133] Just as a country's financial exchange rate fluctuates depending on its position in the global economy, so, too, one's human capital exchange rate is determined by one's position in the American racial and gender orders.[134]

On entering the workplace, white women, men of color, and women of color (to varying degrees) are met with glass ceilings—unspoken obstacles to advancement.[135] Glass ceilings seem more prevalent (and thicker) the further one climbs up the corporate hierarchy. Although there are some exceptions to this rule, the highest positions of power continue to be dominated by white men.[136] It goes without saying that glass ceilings result in serious consequences. One study estimated that barriers to career promotion account for one-third of the income gap between black and white men.[137]

Women of color disproportionately fill low-status and low-paying positions.

So what keeps glass ceilings in place? Sociologists have identified a process known as homosocial reproduction. Put simply, authorities tend to fill positions of power with people like themselves. As Rosabeth Moss Kanter put it in *Men and Women of the Corporation*, organizational rules are much more formalized and clear at the bottom of the organizational hierarchy.[138] Things are murkier at the top. For instance, a software company might guarantee you will advance to a managerial position after five years of work. There are no such guarantees when it comes to appointing the company's vice president. Because of this, high-level supervisors can show great discretion in staffing supervisory positions; they often do so by excluding, often unintentionally, qualified candidates whose gender or racial identity differs from their own. A white man's chances of securing a supervisory position are doubled if his supervisor (the one doing the promoting) is also a white man. The same pattern holds for nonwhites. For instance, the odds of a black woman advancing to a high-level supervisory position increase dramatically if her supervisor is black. Homosocial reproduction is practiced by whites and nonwhites alike. However, because they are disproportionately represented in positions of power, only white men can do so with some regularity. In other words, "ingroup favoritism may be universal, but opportunities to practice it are not."[139]

WELFARE

The final two sections of this chapter take up two policies that greatly affect racial dynamics in the economic field: welfare and affirmative action. The purpose of these last two sections is to see what social science has to say about these policies in employment. (We review the literature on affirmative action in education in Chapter 7.) With respect to welfare, we address three questions: Why is American welfare the size it is? Who's on welfare? And does welfare lead to dependency?

By welfare, we mean government provisions intended to help disadvantaged people, including those who are poor, elderly, war veterans, unemployed, and disabled. In-kind welfare programs allocate resources for specific needs, such as food, medical care, or housing. These include food stamps, Medicaid, and housing subsidies. Cash programs, by contrast, provide recipients with regular income. These include Temporary Assistance for Needy Families (TANF), Social Security, and general assistance.

Why Is American Welfare the Size It Is?

Earlier in this chapter, we compared American social spending to that of other developed countries and discovered that Japan is the only industrialized country that devotes a smaller portion of its wealth to welfare programs. Why does America lag behind other industrialized nations in welfare spending? Historians have found that America's welfare state can be understood only when we explore the relationship between the development of social spending programs and race. Because New Deal programs only worsened racial inequalities, President Johnson hoped to initiate new welfare programs that promoted racial equality. Through his War on Poverty, launched in the 1960s, Johnson began targeting inner-city ghettos by implementing school improvements, housing allowances, job training, and community action programs. These initiatives were taken up by leaders involved in the Civil Rights Movement, leaders who recognized that racial justice had to be accompanied by economic justice. "What good is it to be allowed to eat in a restaurant if you can't afford a hamburger?" King once asked.[140] When antipoverty programs became intertwined with antiracism movements—and especially after affirmative action was legislated—whites (including working-class and poor whites) began turning away from the Democratic Party and their new policies. The white backlash mounted as suburban homeowners resisted integration and beat back fair-housing laws.

On entering the White House, Nixon sought to cater to the growing white hostility aimed at nonwhites and antipoverty programs, to reach the "forgotten Americans," as he liked to call them. He shifted the welfare focus away from programs that targeted America's urban poor. Although the far-reaching programs of the War on Poverty would have helped many poor people, white and nonwhite alike, they were thwarted by racial divisions and white backlash. "The long-term legacy of coupling social policy to racial issues has diminished America's ability to stem the decline of the inner cities and to protect the family," laments Jill Quadagno in *The Color of Welfare*.[141]

Since the War on Poverty, welfare spending has continued to be rolled back. In 1996, President Bill Clinton, making good on his promise to "end welfare as we know it," ended America's largest cash assistance program, Aid to Families with Dependent Children (AFDC), replacing it with TANF. TANF placed strict restrictions on how long recipients could collect welfare: two years while unemployed and only five years over a lifetime. Clinton's act, tellingly titled the Personal Responsibility and Work Opportunity Reconciliation Act, stressed individual responsibility, moral uprightness, and a good work ethic.[142] Cash assistance caseloads have fallen from 12.3 million recipients per month in 1996 to 4.5 million in 2011. Today, only one in ten adults living below the poverty line receives cash assistance in the form of welfare.[143] On the other hand, some federal programs have grown substantially over the last two decades, namely, the Earned Income Tax Credit and the Supplemental Nutrition Assistance Program (or food stamps).

TANF has pushed many single mothers into the workforce.[144] Are they better off? Many poor single mothers pressed into low-wage work through the welfare-to-work programs earned more income than they did while on welfare. Their official poverty levels *decreased*. But their material hardship *increased* because those returning to work had to pay for childcare and transportation, and most lost Medicaid benefits and had their food stamps and housing subsidies cut. As a consequence, single mothers working in the service sector found themselves worse off than those relying primarily on welfare, even if their incomes were larger.[145]

Who's on Welfare?

Depending on your socioeconomic background, you might be surprised to learn that most Americans have benefited from welfare during some point in their lives. This statement holds true even if we forget about the more universal welfare programs such as Social Security and veterans' assistance (which are not based on recipients' incomes) and concentrate solely on means-tested programs such as food stamps, TANF, and Medicaid (which are income based). Two-thirds of all Americans collect means-tested public assistance during some point in their lives, 63 percent of them receiving Medicaid, 52 percent food stamps, and 13 percent cash assistance.[146]

Many people receive assistance through TANF, including single mothers, refugees, recently unemployed workers, new immigrants, and poor families living in urban and rural areas. Of those receiving TANF, 33 percent are black, 31 percent are white, 29 percent are Hispanic, 2 percent are Asian, and 1 percent are Native American.[147] Given the historical legacy of economic racism and present-day processes of discrimination, we should not be surprised to learn that blacks and Hispanics are overrepresented on welfare lists, accounting for nearly half of all first-time TANF recipients.[148] What is more, several studies have shown that black and Hispanic women were just as likely as white women to hold continual employment after leaving welfare—yet also more likely than white women to return to welfare.[149]

Social scientists have provided four reasons for this discrepancy. First, poor black and Hispanic women are less likely to have a solid education and to cohabitate or marry than white women are, characteristics associated with longer welfare assistance.[150] Second, and more important, the networks enveloping white women—supportive family and friends—usually are more privileged than those enveloping nonwhite women. Accordingly, white women looking to lift themselves out of poverty are better able to take advantage of their "private safety net"— money from parents, lovers, or friends—than are women of color, whose social resources are less bountiful.[151] Third, studies have shown that white single mothers receive assistance from several different kinds of programs (including Social Security, veteran's payments, and unemployment compensation) at much higher rates than single mothers of color, who rely heavily on TANF.[152] The fourth explanation has to do with obstacles women of color face in the labor market. As we already have described, nonwhites face unequal access to good wages and positions of power. One study found that the average salary of a black woman with a college degree is $25,914, while it is $28,266 for a white man with only a high school diploma.[153] If college-educated black women face such unfair discrimination in earnings, imagine the bleak prospects facing black women with little education.

Does Welfare Lead to Dependency?

Much public debate on welfare has revolved around this question. Clinton thought that welfare made people dependent on the government, as do many Americans today. In fact, studies tracing media coverage on social spending since the 1930s have concluded that the concept of dependency has played a leading role in structuring the welfare debate.[154] Does welfare deplete one's drive to work? Studies have shown that most welfare recipients work while on welfare and after welfare. Indeed they must, as one often cannot survive by relying on welfare alone. The majority of single mothers on welfare must supplement their TANF benefits with other income to make ends meet.[155] Many do so through "care work," watching over children or taking in an ailing friend or family member.[156]

Some evidence suggests that members of the inner-city poor experience a difficult time shifting from welfare to work, but most people collect welfare only for short periods of time.[157] One study found that the majority of welfare recipients do not stay on welfare for more than one year. Another study conducted before TANF (when one could stay on welfare for longer periods of time) concluded that a minority of recipients (30 percent) stayed on welfare for more than two years. The uncertainty and skimpy pay of low-wage work does force many poor families to return to welfare after having left it—90 percent of those who use welfare during some point in their life will do so again—but this pattern is explained less by the psychological state of welfare dependence than by the realities of living and laboring at the bottom of the income ladder. Far from being a means whereby people can eke out an existence without working, welfare is a form of assistance that families rely on between jobs or when struggling through a family emergency.[158]

Despite thin evidence of "welfare dependency" as well as the fact that a small minority of poor families receive welfare in the form of cash assistance, politicians and the popular press continue to slander welfare recipients. When Clinton's welfare reform act was being debated on the floor of Congress, two congressmen made speeches comparing welfare recipients to wild animals who had lost their ability to survive in the wild. And President Reagan often spoke of Cadillac-driving "welfare queens" with "a tax-free income of over $150,000."[159] Media reporters have portrayed welfare recipients in an unflattering light as well, as lazy and lascivious. Some have blackened the welfare rolls, as if African Americans were the only beneficiaries of social spending.[160]

Many Americans see welfare as a racialized policy. In his book *Why Americans Hate Welfare*, Martin Gilens marshals an impressive amount of data to demonstrate that most whites despise welfare because they assume that the majority of welfare recipients are "lazy blacks," undeserving of the government's help. Another study found that in states with large white populations, whites who stereotyped blacks and Hispanics as lazy were less willing to spend money on welfare than those who did not. And according to a large social survey, 59 percent of whites polled believed that most blacks would rather collect a welfare check than work for a living. Forty-six percent felt the same way about Hispanics, while 18 percent characterized Asians in this light. Only 3 percent believed that, given the chance, most whites would choose welfare over work.[161] These startling statistics reveal that many white Americans not only consider blacks and Hispanics to be welfare dependent but incorrectly assume that welfare is a policy that benefits only nonwhites.

WHEN AFFIRMATIVE ACTION WASN'T WHITE

A recent study reported that one-third of those polled admitted they did not know the meaning of affirmative action.[162] Affirmative action has been misconstrued in the media and distorted by politicians, who disparage the controversial program to court voters. In the following sections, we address four key questions: What is affirmative action? Does it help those it was intended to help? Does it hurt white men? And, finally, is affirmative action an affront to the American ideal of meritocracy?

Before we march forward, we should pause and look back. Affirmative action is not new. As we learned at the beginning of this chapter, white affirmative action was instituted with the New Deal. And some have rightly pointed out that it is much older than that: "It is strange and peculiar, arbitrary and incorrect, to suggest that affirmative action began in the summer of 1961 when President John F. Kennedy issued Executive Order 10925. . . . The more accurate beginning date for this legal and public policy is 1641. This is when the fledgling jurisdictions that would later become the first states began to specify in law that rights to property, ownership of goods and services, and the right to vote would be restricted by race and gender. In 1790, Congress formally restricted citizenship via naturalization to 'white persons,' a restriction that remained in place until 1952. Understood in this way, affirmative action has been in effect for 360 years, not 39."[163] What is new, then, is nonwhite and nonmale affirmative action.

What Is Affirmative Action?

Affirmative action (in its current nonwhite and nonmale form) is an umbrella term referring to a collection of policies and practices designed to address past wrongs, institutional racism, and sexism by offering people of color and women both employment and educational opportunities. Such policies and practices encourage employers seeking to create integrated institutions to consider race, ethnicity, and gender in their hiring, admittance, and other decisions. In so doing, they seek proactively to redress historic patterns of domination, to combat present-day discrimination, and to ensure equal access to opportunities.[164]

School busing, race-based outreach, setting aside contracts for nonwhite- and female-run firms, and monitoring workforces' underrepresentation of people of color and women are all programs that can be classified as affirmative action. It is helpful to conceptualize affirmative action policies on a continuum, where on one end are rigid quotas (extremely rare) and on the other end are companies that have taken positive steps against discrimination. Between these extremes is where most affirmative action programs lie. Here we find "preference systems," or systems of "social restitution," that give qualified white women and nonwhite women and men a slight advantage over equally qualified white men in hiring and promotion. Here we also find recruitment strategies that target underrepresented groups, and self-examination programs, where employers scrutinize their workplace representation. Affirmative action programs differ from antidiscrimination laws in that the former are proactive—they attempt to prevent discrimination from occurring—while the latter are reactive: they redress specific people who have been victimized by discrimination.[165]

Modern-day affirmative action programs can be traced back to 1941, when President Franklin D. Roosevelt criminalized racial discrimination in government and war industries. His executive order largely was ignored, because it carried no sanctions for violators. That changed in 1961, when Kennedy, through Executive Order 10925, mandated that federal contractors take proactive steps—that is, "affirmative action," a term he coined—to treat prospective and current workers equally, regardless of race, color, or national origin. The Civil Rights Act of 1964 cme three years later; its Title VII forbade employers from discriminating on the basis of race, sex, religion, color, or national origin. President Johnson followed Kennedy's lead one year after that with Executive Order 11246, which added women to the list of protected groups and created the Office for Federal Contract Compliance (which would later become the Office for Federal Contract Compliance Programs, OFCCP). President Nixon contributed as well, requiring firms with at least $50,000 in federal contracts and at least fifty employees to submit written affirmative action plans accompanied by benchmarks and timetables.[166]

None of these legal policies defined affirmative action as quota systems. In fact, quotas are illegal under OFCCP guidelines: "In seeking to achieve its goals, a [contractor] is never required to (1) hire a person who does not have the qualifications needed to perform the job successfully; (2) hire an unqualified person in preference to another applicant who is qualified; (3) hire a less qualified person in preference to a more qualified person."[167] Despite popular opinions to the contrary, affirmative action required of federal contractors does not allow quotas or the hiring of unqualified applicants.

Importantly, federally mandated affirmative action rules apply only to companies that conduct a fair amount of business with the federal government, about 3 percent of American firms. Captured in this small percentage are relatively large firms employing about 20 percent of the country's workforce. But there are other types of affirmative action programs, including policies regulating public employees and court-ordered affirmative action. With court-ordered affirmative action, federal courts can require companies found guilty of practicing discrimination to implement affirmative action programs. If the company's practices are excessive, courts can order the company to develop and monitor quotas, although this is uncommon. Finally, some companies, hoping to allay the threat of litigation or to promote good business practices, voluntarily enforce on themselves affirmative action guidelines. It is hard to say how many of America's corporations have adopted affirmative action. By some estimates, 71 percent of firms have some sort of affirmative action plan, while others have found that fewer than half practice affirmative action. We might conclude that although some companies voluntarily practice affirmative action, many have shifted to a less aggressive "diversity management" model, which we discuss in Chapter 11.[168]

Does Affirmative Action Help Those It Was Intended to Help?

Affirmative action has increased the representation of white women and nonwhite women and men in employment, and it has decreased the levels of occupational segregation by impressive margins. Firms that contracted with the federal government in 1980 (and thereby were subjected to federally mandated affirmative action programs) increased their nonwhite workforce by 25 percent more than firms that did not. Big-city firms that took affirmative action measures in hiring were 10 percent more likely to hire women and 20 percent more likely to hire black men than firms that did not. Affirmative action has increased the representation of nonwhite women and men and white women in the public service sector as well. The military carried out a successful affirmative action campaign to recruit nonwhites into commanding ranks. And between 1970 and 1990 the number of nonwhite men and women and white women in the police force rose dramatically: from 10,000 to 97,000 for nonwhites, and from 2,000 to 20,000 for women.[169]

What is more, affirmative action seems to have benefited not only members of disadvantaged communities, but the disadvantaged communities themselves. Affirmative action programs have helped to produce hundreds of nonwhite doctors, who are much more likely to practice in nonwhite communities than their white counterparts. Graduates admitted to one medical school under affirmative action guidelines were more likely to serve patients living in underserved communities— the inner city and poor rural areas—than students who were not.[170]

Despite these gains, some have wondered whether affirmative action comes at too high a cost, namely, that it imprints on its recipients a stigma of self-doubt. But over 90 percent of women and 75 percent of blacks feel that affirmative action has not played a role in their employment opportunities. And some evidence suggests that affirmative action has helped, not handicapped, the self-esteem of nonwhite women and men as well as white women. By expanding their occupational opportunities, affirmative action has raised the aspirations of those previously relegated to menial work.[171]

This does not rule out that some coworkers might stigmatize their nonwhite and female peers as "affirmative action hires." But research has found that most women and nonwhites do not feel their coworkers doubt their abilities because of affirmative action. Only 1 percent of women executives felt their experience with affirmative action was completely negative, while 22 percent felt it affected their careers in both positive and negative ways.[172] Plus, owing to the legacy of racial and gender-based discrimination, many would look down on nonwhites and women even if affirmative action did not exist.

Some have argued that those hired and promoted by affirmative action are unqualified. What does social science say? Several studies examining job performance evaluations have concluded that affirmative action hires do just as well as those not hired by affirmative action. One study of police officers hired through affirmative action, for example, found that black women perform at the level of white male officers. And firms that operate with affirmative action protocols perform no differently (in terms of profit margins, growth, and so forth) than firms that do not. Indeed, some research suggests that companies with solid affirmative action plans reap bigger profit margins than companies with poor records of recruiting women and nonwhites.[173]

Not only is the practice of hiring unqualified workers through affirmative action disconfirmed by research, but it also is illegal. Passing over a qualified white candidate for an unqualified nonwhite candidate is discrimination and punishable under federal law. Affirmative action is not designed to work like this. Rather, affirmative action encourages employers to take race and gender into account when choosing from a pool of qualified applicants. Or, to put it another way, it encourages employers not to discriminate against qualified white women and nonwhite men and women.

Far from suggesting that affirmative action reserves job positions for unqualified individuals, some social scientists have argued that the policy selects out the most privileged members of disadvantaged populations. "It is important to recognize," writes William Julius Wilson, "that in modern industrial society the removal of racial barriers creates the greatest opportunities for the better-trained, talented, and educated segments of the minority population—those who have been crippled the least by the weight of past discrimination."[174] If this is true, then the problem is not that unqualified people are staffing positions but that a large proportion of nonwhites lacking qualification—a good education, job training, network connections—virtually are unaffected by affirmative action. That poor and uneducated members of disadvantaged populations are passed over by race- and gender-based affirmative action has led some to argue that those policies should be complemented by class-based programs.[175]

Does Affirmative Action Hurt White Men?

Affirmative action has helped nonwhite women and men to secure employment opportunities previously denied them, and it certainly has helped white women, who by some accounts are its biggest beneficiaries. But has it done so at the expense of white men? Many white Americans believe this to be true. When asked who was most likely to face discrimination at work, survey respondents picked whites over blacks by two to one. And 40 percent of people participating in a recent poll thought whites being disadvantaged by affirmative action was a bigger problem than blacks being disadvantaged by race-based discrimination.[176] Are these fears justified?

The evidence suggests they are not. First, as we already have seen, racial discrimination unfairly targeting nonwhites continues to influence hiring and promotion decisions. The findings from social-scientific studies demonstrate that employers regularly pass over equally or better qualified nonwhites to hire whites. Second, compared to nonwhites, whites are much less likely to believe they were denied a job or promotion on account of their race. One study found that 16 percent of blacks and 8 percent of Hispanics claimed to have been refused pay increases or promotions because of their race; only 3 percent of whites felt likewise.[177] Third, whites rarely file complaints citing "reverse discrimination." Courts reject almost all reverse discrimination cases as without merit. Perhaps we see such a small number of reverse discrimination cases because white men do not report being victimized. If this were true, we would expect whites to underreport instances of other forms of discrimination too. But this is not the case. With respect to discrimination cases based on age or health status, whites file complaints in impressive numbers.[178]

If affirmative action provides discipline and structure to employment practices that previously operated willy-nilly, relying heavily on personal connections, it may help white men more than is often recognized. In the words of sociologist Barbara Reskin, "White men are helped by affirmative action more often than they are hurt. It encourages employers to formalize hiring and to move away from the old boy network when thinking about people for jobs."[179] Affirmative action does provide a boon to qualified white women and nonwhite men and women over equally qualified white men. In some cases, it also may give qualified white men a fighting chance against less qualified applicants who previously would have landed the job through cronyism.

Is Affirmative Action an Affront to American Meritocracy?

Many have argued that affirmative action threatens an important American value: that of meritocracy, the notion that one succeeds only on the basis of her or his own abilities. This idea relies on three assumptions. The first is that people get ahead in life solely by virtue of their own talents, skills, and work ethic. Our analyses of white affirmative action and racial inequalities in wealth show that this rarely is the case. (Many of us who have received some sort of help practice a self-imposed amnesia, reassuring ourselves that we got to where we are solely by our own merits.)

The second assumption is that race and gender preferences are the only kinds of preferences in the world. In truth, the preferences advanced by affirmative action, which seeks to redress past and current wrongs, join hundreds of other kinds of preferences in employment—many of them, to be sure, justified by less admirable reasons. One thinks of sons who inherit their father's business, legacies admitted to Ivy League universities because their parents are contributing alumni, or homeowners who enjoy tax breaks. Are we bothered by preferences or preferences based on race and gender?[180]

The third assumption holds that employment practices without affirmative action are more merit based than those with it. But evidence documenting ongoing racial discrimination challenges this assumption. Here is yet another instance where whiteness (and masculinity) operates as an invisible norm. When a well-qualified white man lands a job, it is because he is well qualified. When a well-qualified Arab American woman lands a job, it is because of her race and gender. Too often we forget that white men—qualified or otherwise—sometimes receive jobs, promotions, and pay raises precisely because of *their* race and gender.

Does affirmative action threaten meritocracy, or does it strive to protect it by replacing a system rife with race and gender biases with a system that rewards one's skills, abilities, education, and talent regardless of their race or gender? To quote Reskin once more, "An essential part of affirmative action is the replacement of subjective and biased personnel practices with practices that treat all prospective and actual workers uniformly. . . . Although many Americans would prefer a labor market that never takes race or gender into account, as long as employers and employment practices routinely discriminate against minorities and women, the choice is not between meritocracy and affirmative action, it is between discrimination and affirmative action."[181]

THE VALUE OF INCONVENIENT FACTS

A recent poll reported that half of white Americans believe the average black American is financially as well off as the average white.[182] Indeed, many whites doubt the realities of racial subjugation altogether and think that America offers each of us an equal shot at success. This is just one of the many reasons why social science can be so very helpful. It disillusions us of long-held assumptions and makes us better aware of life circumstances we previously had been inclined to deny. Economic inequality and racial inequality are closely interconnected, and the linkages between them are difficult to tease out. But make sense of them we must, for economic inequality rooted in racial domination is an affront to the American Dream and a reminder of how just hard we still must work to realize—to make true—our national self-image as a land of equal opportunity for all.

THE BIG PICTURE
Chapter 4: Economics

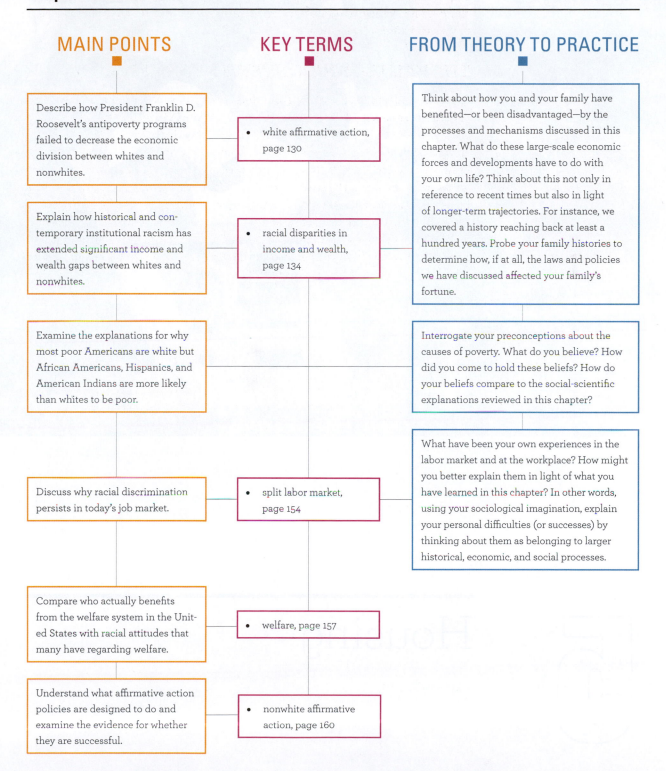

MAIN POINTS

Describe how President Franklin D. Roosevelt's antipoverty programs failed to decrease the economic division between whites and nonwhites.

Explain how historical and contemporary institutional racism has extended significant income and wealth gaps between whites and nonwhites.

Examine the explanations for why most poor Americans are white but African Americans, Hispanics, and American Indians are more likely than whites to be poor.

Discuss why racial discrimination persists in today's job market.

Compare who actually benefits from the welfare system in the United States with racial attitudes that many have regarding welfare.

Understand what affirmative action policies are designed to do and examine the evidence for whether they are successful.

KEY TERMS

- white affirmative action, page 130

- racial disparities in income and wealth, page 134

- split labor market, page 154

- welfare, page 157

- nonwhite affirmative action, page 160

FROM THEORY TO PRACTICE

Think about how you and your family have benefited—or been disadvantaged—by the processes and mechanisms discussed in this chapter. What do these large-scale economic forces and developments have to do with your own life? Think about this not only in reference to recent times but also in light of longer-term trajectories. For instance, we covered a history reaching back at least a hundred years. Probe your family histories to determine how, if at all, the laws and policies we have discussed affected your family's fortune.

Interrogate your preconceptions about the causes of poverty. What do you believe? How did you come to hold these beliefs? How do your beliefs compare to the social-scientific explanations reviewed in this chapter?

What have been your own experiences in the labor market and at the workplace? How might you better explain them in light of what you have learned in this chapter? In other words, using your sociological imagination, explain your personal difficulties (or successes) by thinking about them as belonging to larger historical, economic, and social processes.

5 Housing

MAIN POINTS

- Describe how urbanization, housing shortages, the migration of whites to suburbs, and urban unrest led to the rise of racialized neighborhoods.

- Explain why most Americans continue to live in racially segregated neighborhoods.

- Discuss how the lack of housing assistance combined with flat incomes at the bottom of the economic distribution and rising housing costs have disproportionately affected families in poor, minority neighborhoods.

- Examine how poverty levels, unemployment rates, and demographic changes have transformed the suburbs since the 1990s.

- Learn more about the ways environmental racism disadvantages nonwhite rural communities, particularly those on American Indian reservations.

One of the most pernicious images of America is that the country is white. To attribute to whites a certain ownership over this country, even if it isn't done on purpose, is to amputate from our collective memory the fact that nonwhites always have belonged to it—to its industry and progress, its culture and spirit, its suffering and celebration. Nowhere is this more important than in the careful analysis of how race works within the residential field.

This chapter takes up that analysis with a historical overview of the racial struggles over housing that took place during the twentieth century, explaining the changing demographic contours of cities, the origins of black ghettos, and white flight from the inner city. It then moves into the present day by discussing the causes and consequences of racial segregation before analyzing how race works in four major residential areas: ghettoes, cities, suburbs, and rural areas. A home, we know, is more than bricks and mortar. It is the cultural and spiritual center of the family, a dwelling steeped in significance and meaning. Where you live is intimately connected to thoughts of who you are as well as your life chances. And in America, the geography and dynamics of the residential field are in large part driven by, and drive, race.

RACIAL STRUGGLES OVER RESIDENCE IN TWENTIETH-CENTURY AMERICA

Many of us might guess that America was more racially segregated at the conclusion of the Civil War than today. But the opposite is true. Throughout the nineteenth century, whites and nonwhites lived relatively close together, interacting with one another on a daily basis. In northern cities, whites and blacks lived side by side; in southern cities, black servants and sharecroppers lived close to their white employers, either on their land or in alleys connected to main streets. By and large, there were no "black areas of town" before the 1900s. To be sure, many nonwhites excluded from participating fully in the labor market tended to live in the poorest areas of town, but so, too, did poor whites and new immigrant groups from eastern Europe. The segregation levels in major cities during the nineteenth century, however, were less than half of what they are today. In 1890, the average black person living in Milwaukee resided in a neighborhood that was 1 percent black; today, the average black person living in Milwaukee resides in a neighborhood that is 66 percent black. The same pattern holds for cities across the country.[1] At the beginning of the twentieth century, most blacks residing in northern cities lived in neighborhoods that were majority white; by the end of the century, most lived in neighborhoods that were majority black.[2] What happened?

The Racialization of Neighborhoods

The racial and economic landscape of American cities underwent dramatic changes as the twentieth century unfurled. The rise of industrialism, which facilitated the rise of cities, attracted thousands of people—immigrants, blacks, Mexicans, whites, Asians—to roiling metropolises. As they poured into cities, some ethnic groups tended to cluster together in neighborhoods, many living in crowded, dilapidated slums. Irish, German, Polish, Swedish, Persian, Italian, and Hungarian families lived in cordoned-off areas with such names as the Irish Kilgubbin, Polish Hamtramck, and Hungarian Delray. Chinatowns emerged in some cities, as did black belts, where African American families lived together. As groups grew in numbers and moved into different neighborhoods, ethnic conflicts sparked between Greeks and Persians, blacks and Sicilians, and Chinese and Germans, to name just a few. As Harvey Zorbaugh described it, writing in 1929, "While the Irish and Swedish had gotten on well as neighbors, neither could or would live peacefully with the Sicilian. There was considerable friction, especially among the children of the two races. The play parks were the scenes of many a 'battle' when the Irish boys would attempt to run out the Italian, and alley garbage cans were stripped of their covers which served as shields in these encounters."[3]

As the twentieth century marched forward, prosperous European immigrant families were able to move out of the slums and assimilate into the white American mainstream. Meanwhile, those who wore the badge of otherness—the "racial uniform," in the words of American sociologist Robert Park—were forbidden by law and custom to live anywhere else.[4] As European Americans of the "new immigration" were further enveloped by whiteness, ethnic distinctions between Italians, Irish, Hungarians, and so forth became less salient. So, too, did ethnic distinctions among neighborhoods, such that by the 1920s many neighborhoods based on close-knit ethnic affiliations gave way to urban divisions based on race and class. Little Italy, Hungarian Town, and the Norwegian village melted into white sections of town, a transition that made the racial contrast between nonwhite and white neighborhoods even more stark.[5]

Migration and Urbanization

As cities grew, they became racially more diverse. Employment opportunities in manufacturing and in agriculture inspired many Mexican families to move north. The U.S. government endorsed Mexican migration, and factory employers actively recruited Mexican Americans and Mexican immigrants, who by and large could be hired at cheaper rates than whites.

However, as the economy began to take a turn for the worse, a turn that resulted in the Great Depression of the 1930s, whites started blaming Mexicans for widespread unemployment and economic scarcity. White anger targeting Mexicans soon materialized into government policy. In what became known as Mexican Repatriation Programs, thousands of Mexican families were rounded up and sent via train back to Mexico. All too often, those who conducted the roundups did not differentiate between Mexican Americans and Mexican nationals. More than half the people shipped back to Mexico were U.S. citizens. Repatriation proved an especially painful experience for Mexican families, who lost their jobs, property, and livelihood. Families were separated, and many were forced to live in poverty-stricken borderlands. By the end of the 1930s, roughly 2 million people—over one-third the overall population of people of Mexican heritage—forcibly were removed from American soil.[6] Recognizing the suffering induced by repatriation programs, the state of California, which alone deported roughly 400,000 American citizens and legal residents of Mexican ancestry, offered an official apology—in 2005. "The state of California," the act read, "apologizes . . . for the fundamental violations of . . . basic civil liberties and constitutional rights during the period of illegal deportation and coerced emigration."[7]

Thirteen thousand Mexicans were sent back to their native country by the Los Angeles County Charities Department on August 21, 1931. By the end of the 1930s almost 2 million people were relocated to Mexico.

If Mexican Repatriation Programs were intended to evict Mexicans en masse from America, policies targeting Native Americans were designed to have the opposite effect: to advance programs of assimilation and tribal dissolution. During the Great Depression, poverty crushed many families living on reservations, and it continued to do so during the World War II years. To combat this suffering, policymakers advanced programs to relocate thousands of Native Americans to urban centers, hoping they could prosper from the economic uplift that took hold after the war. They also hoped that indigenous peoples, once removed from their respective reservations, would shed their "Indian-ness" and be fully incorporated into "mainstream American society." From 1950 to 1970, thousands of indigenous people moved to Detroit, Seattle, Chicago, and other metropolises. Los Angeles served host to the largest American Indian population, with 60,000 indigenous residents. By 1990, more than 60 percent of American Indians were residing in cities.[8]

American Indian urbanization proceeded in lockstep with processes of tribal termination. In 1953, Congress enacted legislation that divested the federal government of trust responsibilities to Indian country. State governments were given legal jurisdiction over Indian reservations, and between 1953 and 1973, 109 tribes were terminated in the eyes of the federal government. Protection was lifted from over 1 million acres of land formerly entrusted to tribes, and thousands of Native Americans were stripped of their (legally recognized) tribal affiliations, including those people who belonged to Wisconsin's Menominee Tribe and Oregon's

Jacob Lawrence's *The Migration Series, Panel No.1* depicts the great migration north by southern African Americans during World War I.

Klamath Tribe. Tribal termination policies were slowed during the Kennedy years and abandoned by the Nixon administration in the wake of the American Indian movement, yet the effects of twenty years of wiping out political sovereignty and tribal ownership of economic resources still are felt today.[9]

The beginning of the twentieth century also witnessed a massive movement of blacks from the rural South to the urban North. As southern slavery gave way to sharecropping, Jim Crow segregation, and racial terrorism, many blacks sought to flee to better conditions. A decline in the price of cotton resulted in job shortages in southern agriculture. At the same time, World War I sharply reduced European immigration, cutting off northern industry's main source of cheap labor and creating massive job vacancies in growing Midwest metropolises. These two economic shifts encouraged many blacks to head north to Chicago, New York, Cleveland, Detroit, and other cities in search of better work and a safer life for their children. In his poem "The South," Langston Hughes effectively captured the sentiment of many African Americans during this period. Referring to "The lazy, laughing south with blood on its mouth," he wrote, "And I, who am black, would love her, but she spits in my face; and I, who am black, would give her many rare gifts, but she turns her back upon me. So now I seek the North—the cold-faced North. For she, they say, is a kinder mistress. And in her house my children may escape the spell of the South."[10] Between 1910 and 1930, over 1.5 million African Americans traveled north; another 3 million followed between 1940 and 1960—a movement known as the Great Migration.[11]

But these sojourners encountered a new face of racism, one enforced not so much by the mob violence of the Ku Klux Klan as by the antiseptic arm of the law. Some towns, primarily in northern and western states, forbade African Americans and other nonwhite groups from living there. Townspeople hung signs that warned nonwhites to be out of town by sundown: "Nigger, don't let the sun set on YOU in Hawthorne" read a sign posted in Hawthorne, California, in the 1930s. These towns came to be known as "sundown towns" and to function as all-white communities. By one estimate, between 1890 and 1960, "probably a majority of all incorporated places kept out African Americans." Chinese Americans, Native Americans, and Jewish Americans also were subjected to sunset restrictions.[12]

In large cities, blacks were cordoned off to restricted districts, rundown slums that quickly became overcrowded. Isolated from the surrounding city, these slums began to see more crime and disease, as well as poverty, since many blacks who secured jobs worked in menial and dangerous positions. Blacks were kept a safe distance from the surrounding white population, whose antislavery sentiments during the Civil War in no way translated into prointegrationism after the fall of the Confederacy.[13] As the folk saying went, "The South doesn't care how close a Negro gets just so he doesn't get too high; the North doesn't care how high he gets just so he doesn't get too close."[14]

A sundown town sign, forbidding nonwhites after dark.

Tensions between blacks and whites heated up, sometimes exploding into racial uprisings or riots that were a recurrent feature of the first half of the twentieth century. One of the worst uprisings took place in Chicago during the summer of 1919. One hot July day, a seventeen-year-old black teenager swam to the "white side" of a bathing beach and was pelted with rocks by white swimmers. In the altercation that ensued between blacks and whites, the teenager—his name was Eugene Williams—drowned. This sparked a weeklong uprising that left 38 people dead (23 blacks and 15 whites), 500 injured, and 1,000 homeless. The Chicago riot was just one of many that took place during the summer of 1919, a summer that later would aptly be called the Red Summer. Uprisings continued throughout the interwar years, involving whites, blacks, and Hispanics. One of the bloodiest uprisings of the century took place in Detroit during June 1943. Fights between white and black youth escalated into three days' fighting, shooting, and looting. When things died down, thirty-four people lay dead, most of them black.[15]

The Origins of the Ghetto

Major U.S. cities experienced housing shortages lasting from the Great Depression to the mid-1940s. While these shortages were painful for many whites, conditions were worse for nonwhite populations forced to live in teeming slums. Simply put, most houses were built strictly for white inhabitants. In 1947, 92 percent of Detroit's housing units were for whites only.[16] Federal law not only permitted racial segregation; it *encouraged* it, since lawmakers feared that integrated neighborhoods would result in unrest that would drive down property values. The Federal Housing Administration denied loans to many nonwhites, regardless of their financial or veteran standing, and real estate brokers refused to show nonwhites homes outside "designated areas."[17] According to one analyst, "the Federal Housing Administration and the Veterans Administration financed more than $120 billion worth of new housing between 1934 and 1962, but less than 2 percent of this real estate was available to nonwhite families—and most of that small amount was located in segregated areas."[18] By 1940, thanks to the discriminatory efforts of the federal government and the housing market, racial residential segregation was widespread.

Some white home sellers made matters worse by including in the deeds to their property *covenants,* which sought to uphold the "desirable residential characteristics" of a neighborhood. Covenants could restrict the purchase of land or property to certain religious or racial groups. "This property shall not be occupied by any person except those of the Caucasian race," a typical covenant might read. Although covenants were rendered legally unbinding in 1948, they still could be included in property deeds and remained effective. Even if the courts no longer enforced covenants, banks refused to subsidize contractors looking to build homes for nonwhites on land deemed "for whites only," and realtors who violated racial covenants risked being boycotted by whites.[19] Nonwhites not only were denied a place to live beyond

said Tracts to a corporation or association formed by residents or owners of property in Innis Arden No. 2, or to a corporation or association formed by residents or owners of Innis Arden, for community purposes, in the activities of which corporation or association residents of Innis Arden No. 2 shall have the right to participate, subject to reasonable restrictions and requirements imposed by such corporation or association.

14. *RACIAL RESTRICTIONS*...No property in said addition shall at any time be sold, conveyed, rented or leased in whole or in part to any person or persons not of the White or Caucausian race. No person other than one of the White or Caucausian race shall be permitted to occupy any property in said addition or portion thereof or building thereon except a domestic servant actually employed by a person of the White or Caucausian race where the latter is an occupant of such property.

15. *ANIMALS.* No hogs, cattle, horses, sheep, goats, or or similar livestock shall be permitted or maintained on said property at any time. Chicken hens, pigeons, rabbits and other similar small livestock, not exceeding a total of twenty-five in number, shall be permitted but must be kept on the premises of the owner. Not more than one dog and cat may be kept for each building site. No pen, yard, run, hutch, coop or other structure or area for the housing and keeping of the above described poultry or animals shall be built or maintaied closer

In the 1940s racial restrictions were written into contracts, forbidding non-White people from owning a particular property.

majority nonwhite areas but also were systematically denied the ability to purchase homes within those areas. Lenders refused to offer mortgages and home loans in nonwhite neighborhoods through a discriminatory practice known as "redlining." The word derives its name from lenders' practice of taking a city map and drawing in red ink a border around nonwhite neighborhoods, marking them as too risky for loans or subsidies.[20]

There was good money to be made in the exclusion of nonwhites from the private housing market. To save money, slumlords ignored housing repairs and building occupancy codes, a combination that proved deadly during times when faulty electric wiring could set ablaze a house swelling with people. Landlords also divided their properties into multiple apartments, charging their nonwhite occupants inflated rents. In 1960, the median black rent payment was $76 per month, whereas the median white rent payment was $64 per month, even though whites were living in much better conditions.[21]

"The process of housing segregation set into motion a chain reaction that reinforced patterns of racial inequality," observes historian Thomas Sugrue, speaking of blacks in postwar Detroit. "Blacks were poorer than whites, and they had to pay more for housing, thus deepening their relative impoverishment. In addition, they were confined to the city's oldest housing stock, in most need of ongoing maintenance, repair, and rehabilitation. But they could not get loans to improve their properties. As a result, their houses deteriorated. City officials, looking at the poor housing stock in black neighborhoods, condemned many areas as blighted, and destroyed much extant housing to build highways, hospitals, housing projects, and a civic center complex, further limiting the housing options for blacks. Moreover, the decaying neighborhoods offered seemingly convincing evidence to white homeowners that blacks would ruin any white neighborhood that they moved into. Finally, neighborhood deterioration seemed definitive proof to bankers that blacks indeed were a poor credit risk, and justified disinvestment in predominantly nonwhite neighborhoods."[22]

Housing opportunities for nonwhites were strained even further by urban development projects undertaken after World War II. Cities' infrastructure was ill suited to accommodate their steady growth. Highways had to be installed; hospitals to be erected; sewage processing plants to be built. City planners in Detroit, Milwaukee, New York, and other major cities destroyed entire nonwhite communities, complete with mass eviction orders. In fact, some saw highway development as "a handy device for razing slums."[23]

Some residents who owned property in areas designated for highway construction were forced to leave before selling their property—for who would want to buy a house that would be bulldozed in a week's time? And dozens of African American and Puerto Rican neighborhoods were razed, not to make way for a new expressway but in the name of "urban renewal." As historian Robert Caro has noted, urban renewal was unique, not only in scope—an enormous venture with costs soaring into the billions—but also in philosophy, because it was the first time in the country's history that the "government was given the right to seize an individual's property not for its own use but for reassignment to another individual for *his* use and profit."[24] Proponents of urban renewal programs were motivated by a desire to breathe new life into the ailing inner city and to better the living conditions of slum dwellers, but they also were attracted to large profits to be made by the erection of luxury apartments, art museums, and toll roads.[25]

The mid-twentieth century was the age of the wrecking ball, which crashed through windows and walls that once housed families struggling against the big city and smashed neighborhoods that had stood for generations. Urban renewal programs obliterated entire blocks of areas city planners called "slums"—most of them occupied by nonwhites—and millions of people lost their homes. In New York City alone, between 1946 and 1953, Robert Moses, the powerful and infamous city planner, evicted "not thousands of people or ten thousands but hundreds of thousands from their homes and tore the homes down."[26] Overwhelmingly, Moses, and dozens of city planners like him—planners who, in fact, flocked to Moses's table to learn how to toss people out of their homes to make way for this stadium or that expressway—replaced the housing he destroyed not with apartments for the poor, but with high-rises for the rich. Residents of areas marked for destruction—the cities' most economically vulnerable and racially marginal—were expected to find another place to live, sometimes with and sometimes without the government's help. In a tight housing market in which only a handful of neighborhoods were open to nonwhites, slum dwellers did the only thing they could: they packed themselves into other racial slums, worsening the already poor living conditions there.[27]

White Fight and White Flight

Disadvantage bred disadvantage to create the American ghetto. But as the Civil Rights Movement gained steam, racial segregation lost its legal foothold. In the late 1960s, civil rights activists in cities across America marched for "open housing." They sought to bring an end to legalized housing discrimination. But resistance was strong. A supermajority in both houses had helped President Johnson pass the Civil Rights Act of 1964 and the Voting Rights Act of 1965, but legislators backed by real estate lobbies had refused to get behind his open housing law. What moved the hand of

The mid-twentieth century saw the obliteration of areas city planners called "slums," most of them occupied by nonwhites. Millions of people lost their homes.

Congress was the murder of Martin Luther King, Jr., on April 4, 1968, and the urban uprisings that followed his assassination. "Shocked that the nation's leading advocate of nonviolence had been brutally slain," historian Patrick Jones writes, "and reeling from the massive wave of urban violence that followed, Congress quickly moved to pass the 1968 Civil Rights Act, which featured a strong open housing measure."[28]

The Civil Rights Act was the last landmark piece of legislation that resulted from the Civil Rights Movement. Title VIII of the act, known as the Fair Housing Act, provided federal enforcement to prohibit housing discrimination on the basis of race, religion, or national origin. Later amendments also prohibited discrimination on the basis of gender, disability status, or family composition.

Legalized segregation dismantled, nonwhites who could move out of the ghetto did so. Nonwhite communities previously segregated by race soon became segregated by race *and* class, as economic fault lines within black, Asian, and Hispanic communities were made more prominent. In many respects, the liberation of middle-class nonwhites from segregated areas resulted in the decay of tightly knit, economically diverse nonwhite communities. Those left behind were such communities' poorest of the poor.

Many whites at the time thought that nonwhites would bring drugs, sexual immorality, and crime into their neighborhoods and would cause property values to plummet. Some described the migration of nonwhites into their neighborhoods with the language of war. They spoke, that is, of being "invaded," "taken over," or "threatened," as well as of the need to "defend" and "protect" their homes, families, and livelihoods.[29] Testifying in front of a Senate committee in 1963, a local politician captured the sentiment of many white families: "When integration strikes a previously all-white neighborhood . . . there will be an immediate rise in crime and violence[,] . . . of vice, of prostitution, of gambling and dope. . . . [Racially mixed neighborhoods] will succumb to blight and decay, and the residents will suffer the loss of their homes and savings."[30]

Broadly speaking, whites reacted to the racial integration of their neighborhoods in two ways: by picking up and moving or by slugging it out with newcomers—that is, by fleeing or fighting. Fearing racial integration, many whites who had the means to do so sold their houses in the city and fled to the suburbs, a migratory process known as "white flight." White flight had begun in the 1950s, spurred on by suburbanization. Whites who could afford it followed factory jobs as the latter relocated from the city center to the suburbs and surrounding small towns. But white outward migration peaked in the wake of the Civil Rights Movement—migration spurred on not by job loss, but by racial fear.

This fear was exploited by real estate agents who spotted a chance to cash in on neighborhood integration. "Blockbusting" agents, as they became known, learned to stir up whites' fear of integration. They might pay a black woman to walk her baby through a white neighborhood, giving off the image that she lived there. Or they might sell a house to an Asian family and publicize it widely. Once word spread that the neighborhood was being "taken over," agents would post fliers and call homeowners, encouraging them to sell their homes before things got worse. One blockbuster paid a pair of black children to travel door to door in a white neighborhood delivering fliers that read, "Now is the best time to sell your house—you know that."[31] As a result, many panicking whites sold their homes to real estate agents at below-market rates. The agents, in turn, would sell that house to nonwhite families hungry for decent housing at above-market rates, thereby collecting a large profit. If nonwhite families could not secure a home loan, blockbusting agents often would step in, offering loans at inflated interest rates.

As blacks and Asians moved in, whites moved out and were welcomed in small towns and suburban communities. In fact, the federal government endorsed white migration to the suburbs through loan programs administered by the Federal Housing Administration and the Veterans Administration. As discussed in Chapter 4, these programs provided, for the first time in American history, the opportunity for many working white families to own a home. In some areas it became cheaper to buy a house in the suburbs than to rent one in the central city.[32] When we consider this fact, as well as rampant white fear of nonwhites' "taking over" cities, we should not be surprised to learn that neighborhoods changed rapidly in their racial composition, from completely white to completely black in only a few years. Whites poured out of Atlanta so quickly that the city, once nicknamed "The City Too Busy to Hate," earned a new title: "The City Too Busy Moving to Hate."[33] As whites fled, they took their accumulated wealth with them, depleting the cities' tax base. Soon, city centers, spaces that just a few decades before had housed massive factories and bustled with the vibrancy of urban life, were hollowed out and abandoned by thousands of white homeowners, as well as better-off nonwhite families. In 1940 only one-third of all metropolitan residents lived in the suburbs; by 1970 the majority of them did.[34]

But not all white people left their neighborhoods during this time. Working-class white homeowners and European immigrants, who had poured their life savings into their homes and whose grasp on homeownership was more tenuous than that of their middle-class counterparts, could not afford to flee the city. Instead, on facing racial immigration, they chose to ward off nonwhite families through intimidation tactics, protests, and violence—a strategy that can be labeled "white fight." Neighborhood homeowners' associations were employed as political vehicles through which white homeowners could "defend their property" from encroaching nonwhite populations. Signs were posted throughout neighborhoods reading "Whites Only" or "All White." In 1945—the year American soldiers liberated Jewish concentration camps throughout Germany and Poland—white homeowners in one Midwestern city hung signs that read, "Negroes moving here will be burned. Signed, Neighbors."[35]

When a nonwhite family moved into a previously all-white neighborhood, white residents often reacted with protests and organized violence. When that did not work, protests often escalated into vandalism, and vandalism escalated into terrorism. Whites threw rocks through windows, poured gasoline on front lawns, dumped rotting garbage on porches, and pulled down

A sign from white Americans "defending" their neighborhood.

fences. In some cases, they lit newly purchased houses on fire or planted a burning cross—the terrifying emblem of the KKK—on the front lawn. Sometimes, the houses of new nonwhite residents, as well as the offices of their real estate officer, were firebombed. Young people regularly participated in these acts. In most cases, they were responsible for spreading the word about events and for adding a special dose of verve and spit to the rallies.[36]

Not all whites reacted with such vehemence. Some sold their homes to nonwhites, despite their neighbors' pleas. Compared to other whites, those belonging to Jewish communities were far less likely actively to resist nonwhite "intrusion."[37] White antiracists fought for racial integration and against the white backlash. They worked for the multiracial NAACP to dissolve the legal standing of segregation and formed new organizations, like the Detroit Interracial Committee, that urged whites to "join the fight against religious and racial hate."[38] Some white religious leaders, like Milwaukee's James Groppi, a Catholic priest who organized several protests against residential segregation in one of the nation's most segregated cities, stood up against white resistance.[39]

In many other cases, however, whites fought tooth and nail, risking prison time to preserve the color line.[40] Although some nonwhite families stood firm in the face of harassment, in many cases whites' efforts drove nonwhites back to run down and segregated neighborhoods.

Like most people during the Civil Rights Movement, the majority of nonwhites simply wanted to live a "normal life."

Urban Unrest

By the 1960s, American cities had undergone rapid transitions—economic, racial, and political. Not only were native-born nonwhite populations growing and expanding out of concentrated areas, but the abolition of national-origin quotas (as discussed in Chapter 4) resulted in immigrants from Asia and Latin America streaming into the country by the thousands. American Indians continued to relocate to the cities, and so did Mexican Americans, settling primarily in border towns and urban areas of the Southwest. But despite these changes, racial segregation remained stubbornly entrenched. The expansion of nonwhite neighborhoods did not translate necessarily into integrated neighborhoods. As one group moved in, the other group moved out—if not to the suburbs, then to another area of the city. And many nonwhite city dwellers—victims of years of economic exploitation, housing discrimination, and the compounding effects of racial domination—remained trapped in their respective ghettos, areas that had deteriorated only because of the flight of jobs and the middle class to the city's outskirts. Sociologists writing in 1962 observed that many blacks living in northern cities "live[d] in essentially the same places that their predecessors lived during the 1930s—the only difference [was] that[,] due to increasing numbers, they occup[ied] more space centered around their traditional quarters."[41]

The violent enforcement of racial segregation and degradation continued to relegate nonwhites to neighborhoods stripped of city services, bereft of jobs, ignored by politicians, and simmering with a sentiment of discontent. In the mid-1960s, many of these neighborhoods exploded. The majority of these racial uprisings took place in poor black neighborhoods and, unlike the uprisings that took place earlier in the century, were started by black residents. Harlem, which according to one of its residents at the time "needed something to smash," hosted a racial uprising in 1964; a year later, the weeklong Watts uprising of Los Angeles resulted in the deaths of thirty-four people (twenty-five of whom were black) and over 1,000 injuries; and Detroit served host to a vicious uprising in 1967, one that left forty-three dead (most of them shot by police) and over 2,500 buildings looted and burned.[42] And as we mentioned earlier in this chapter, after King was assassinated in 1968, uprisings erupted all across the nation. Throughout the mid- to late 1960s, in one major city after another, black neighborhoods went up in flames. Many Americans were certain that in these uprisings a second civil war was brewing.

These uprisings were not merely criminal or destructive acts; they were expressions of rage and suffering caused by a racist system. Many started as protests against police action within the black community. The insurgents targeted for destruction white-owned businesses in black neighborhoods, stores that refused to hire blacks, and institutions that mistreated blacks.[43] The majority of whites surveyed in 1968 felt the uprisings mainly were caused by "looters and undesirables." Nearly half of all blacks surveyed believed the uprisings were a reaction to "discrimination and unfair treatment."[44]

While many blacks disagreed with the uprisings, arguing that racial progress would best be achieved by more conventional means, others felt more radical

On the second night of Harlem's racial uprising, two African American girls flee police officers in Brooklyn.

action was needed. A growing sense of black militancy was taking hold in urban black communities, or what came to be known as the Black Power Movement (which we discuss in more detail in Chapter 9). Many insurgents, the majority of whom were young black men, were fed up with white supremacy. "People keep calling it a riot," recalls Tommy Jacquette, who at twenty-one years of age participated in the Watts revolt. "But we call it a revolt because it had a legitimate purpose. It was a response to police brutality and social exploitation of a community and of a people, and we would no more call this a riot than Jewish people would call the extermination of the Jewish people 'relocation.' . . . People said that we burned down our community. No, we didn't. We had a revolt in our community against those people who were in here trying to exploit and oppress us. We did not own this community. We did not own the businesses in this community. We did not own the majority of the housing in this community. Some people want to know if I think it was really worth it. I think any time people stand up for their rights, it's worth it."[45]

The racial uprisings not only brought the plight of the urban black poor to the forefront of American discourse; they also directly resulted in policies aimed at improving conditions in the ghetto. Government programs such as welfare payments, low-income housing subsidies, and job programs were initiated, as were summer programs for young people, often referred to as "riot insurance."[46] The uprisings brought about another consequence as well: the ratcheting up of police repression in the black community, a topic we take up in Chapter 6.

In their song "Loaded Gun," American Steel, the Oakland-based punk band, scream: "I didn't see Watts burn, but I felt the embers." So it is for us today. Our cities and suburbs—as well as our small towns—have been forged in the fires of Watts, Harlem, Detroit, and other cities that hosted racial uprisings, as they have by white flight and fight, immigration patterns, housing discrimination, and urban renewal.[47] In the history of American housing, we see, too, the origins of present-day racial segregation and disadvantage. Because of the intimate connection between homeownership and wealth accumulation, the unequal distribution of wealth discussed in Chapter 4 is explained in large part by the housing struggles reviewed here. Because many assets, especially those rooted in real estate, are passed down from one generation to the next—property usually is inherited—the wealth and financial security many whites enjoy today are a direct consequence of government restrictions and business practices that systematically excluded nonwhites from stable homeownership during the second half of the twentieth century.

Throughout the twentieth century, many whites blamed nonwhites for their problems, allowing the real culprits—job loss brought on by deindustrialization, the housing shortage that came after World War II—to escape scrutiny. Casting a backward glance at the history of housing in twentieth-century America reveals not a smooth transition or a "natural" progression, but a bloody struggle over the right to live where one wishes—the very ownership of America. And at the plinth of this struggle lies the color line, pitting the principles of American democracy against the practices of racial intolerance.[48]

RACIAL SEGREGATION

How racially segregated are America's neighborhoods today? To answer this question, we need a good measure of segregation. Racial segregation can be measured by the degree to which certain racial groups are distributed throughout the city. For instance, if a city had a 20 percent Asian population, then in a city with no racial segregation, each neighborhood would be 20 percent Asian. The degree of segregation, therefore, can be gauged by the percentage of a certain racial group that would have to move into other neighborhoods to obtain zero segregation. If in our city of 20 percent Asians a neighborhood is 40 percent Asian, then to achieve perfect integration, 20 percent of those people would have to move into a neighborhood where the Asian population is below 20 percent.[49] Imagine that a city is a grid of boxes, each box representing a neighborhood. Now imagine that you are given a bag of multicolored marbles: white marbles represent your white population, black marbles your black population, and so forth. To model perfect integration, you would need to gather all your white marbles and drop them, one by one, into each box until they run out, repeating this step with your other marbles. If you did that, your segregation level would be zero. If, however, you decided to dump all your black marbles into a few connected boxes and all your white marbles into different boxes, you could model a very high level of segregation. Which model does America resemble?

FIGURE 5.1 DIMENSIONS OF SPATIAL SEGREGATION

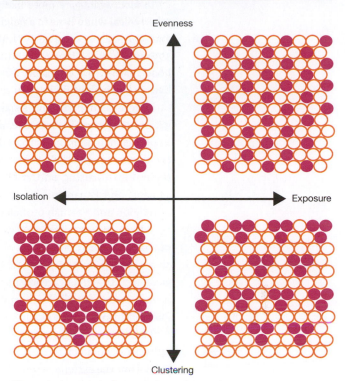

Theoretical patterns of segregation or integration.

Segregation has declined in some metropolitan areas (mostly in multicultural cities of the West and Southwest) and smaller towns since the 1970s. Between 1990 and 2010, the share of metropolitan census tracts that are racially integrated increased from 20 percent to 30 percent.[50] Even more encouraging is the finding that 75 percent of neighborhoods that were integrated in the 1980s remained so a decade later. Whites and nonwhites committed to the principle of integration have helped to build up stable, multiracial neighborhoods.[51]

And yet, most Americans continue to live in racially segregated neighborhoods. In many areas, the majority of the entire black population would have to move into different neighborhoods to achieve perfect integration. Northern cities, such as Detroit, Chicago, Milwaukee, and Gary, are the most segregated in America, where our segregation measure reaches 80 percent to 90 percent.[52] If blacks are segregated to such a severe degree in cities, then so, too, are whites. Many times when people speak of segregation, they speak of neighborhoods with a high concentration of blacks or Hispanics, failing to realize that those neighborhoods exist only because there also are neighborhoods with a high concentration of whites. An all-white section of the city is no more "natural" than an all-black one; each exists because of the other.

In fact, whites are more likely to live in segregated neighborhoods. In U.S. cities, "the typical white lives in a neighborhood that is 75% white, 8% black, 11% Hispanic, and 5% Asian. . . . The typical black lives in a neighborhood that is 45% black, 35% white, 15% Hispanic, and 4% Asian. The typical Hispanic lives in a neighborhood that is 46% Hispanic, 35% white, 11% black and 7% Asian. The typical Asian lives in a neighborhood that is 22% Asian, 49% white, 9% black, and 19% Hispanic."[53]

Different Hispanic and Asian ethnic groups experience different levels of segregation. Filipinos, Vietnamese, and Indian Americans are more segregated and live in poorer neighborhoods than do Chinese, Japanese, and Korean Americans.[54] And the degree to which Hispanics are segregated depends in large part on the color of their skin. Focusing on Caribbean Hispanics, such as Puerto Ricans, Dominicans, Cubans, and Panamanians—groups that share many cultural characteristics (such as religion and Spanish proficiency) but vary greatly with respect to skin tone (from very light to very dark)—researchers have found that dark-skinned Hispanics are much more segregated than light-skinned Hispanics. In ten metropolitan areas, 52 percent of light-skinned Hispanics would have to move to achieve perfect integration. That percentage jumps to 72 percent for brown-skinned Hispanics and soars to 80 percent for black Hispanics.[55] And many black Hispanics, especially those of Puerto Rican descent, live in poorer neighborhoods than light-skinned Hispanics.[56]

The fact that Asians and Hispanics are less segregated than African Americans reflects not so much the former two groups' extreme integration into white neighborhoods, but the extreme segregation of African Americans. In twenty-nine cities, which contain no less than 40 percent of the entire black population, blacks are isolated to

FIGURE 5.2 **DIVERSITY EXPERIENCES IN EACH GROUP'S TYPICAL NEIGHBORHOOD, 2010**

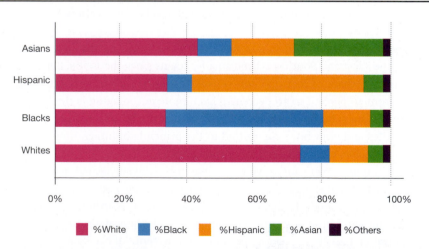

Although Americans of all different races end up living in racially segregated neighborhoods, white people are significantly more likely to do so.

Source: American Communities Projects, Brown University

such an acute degree that most of them live only within "black areas of town."[57] The segregation of black Americans living in these cities is so severe that Douglas Massey and Nancy Denton, authors of *American Apartheid*, refer to it as "hypersegregation," a term describing the observation that "black Americans in these metropolitan areas live within large, continuous settlements of densely inhabited neighborhoods that are packed tightly around the urban core. . . . No other group in the contemporary United States comes close to this level of isolation within urban society."[58]

The Role of Economic Factors

What causes racial segregation? Perhaps what on the surface looks like racial segregation is segregation based on economic factors, that is, because on average whites are more wealthy than nonwhites. Perhaps racial segregation is caused not by mechanisms of racial domination, but by class-based inequalities. If this is true, then racial segregation would disappear the higher one climbed up the economic ladder. This idea, however, is not borne out by evidence. In northern cities, blacks remain highly segregated from whites, regardless of income. Blacks making more than $50,000 a year are just as segregated as those making minimum wage. Middle-class Latinos are slightly less segregated than poor Latinos: in Los Angeles, for instance, where Hispanics constitute 45 percent of the population, 64 percent of the poor Latino population would have to relocate to achieve perfect integration, while 50 percent of the middle-class Latino population would have to do so. Economic inequalities matter, but they alone cannot explain racial segregation—especially the hypersegregation of African Americans, the most affluent of whom are more segregated than the poorest Hispanics in the country's largest Latino barrio. Economic explanations also cannot account for the fact that racial segregation persists in affluent suburbs.[59]

The Role of Personal Choice

What about personal choice? In a survey, two-thirds of Milwaukee residents claimed that the reason their city was so segregated was because "people of different races choose to live in communities with people of their own race."[60] To what extent were they right? Are black people segregated simply because of their desire to live in black neighborhoods? By and large, the answer is no. Most African Americans strongly endorse the ideal of integration. Consider the findings of the Detroit Area Survey. In this study, conducted in the 1990s, white and black people were shown maps of hypothetical neighborhoods that varied in terms of racial composition: dwellings that housed black families were colored black; those that housed white families were colored white. Those who participated in the study were asked how they felt about the different neighborhoods and in which neighborhoods they would choose to live. The majority of blacks said their ideal neighborhood was 50 percent black and 50 percent white; when asked about their preference, many emphasized the importance of racial cooperation and collaboration. Blacks also showed a strong aversion to segregated neighborhoods: 30 percent would not move into an all-black neighborhood and, fearing they would be unwelcome (or, worse, would be met with hostility), 60 percent were unwilling to move to an all-white neighborhood.[61]

While blacks are strong proponents of integration, whites are advocates of segregation. A quarter of whites who participated in the Detroit Area Survey reported that a single black neighbor would make them uncomfortable. Regarding a neighborhood that was one-third black, 73 percent of whites would refuse to travel there, 57 percent would feel uncomfortable, and a full 40 percent would move away if they lived there. When shown a neighborhood that was 50 percent black and 50 percent white, 84 percent of whites would not enter that area, while 64 percent would move away, and 72 percent would feel uncomfortable. In other words, the neighborhood that most blacks would want to move to—one with an even balance of black and white folks—is the one that whites would want to move away from. These whites, echoing the sentiments of whites across the twentieth century, feel that having even a handful of black neighbors would drive down property values and increase neighborhood crime.[62] Since this famous study, numerous others have re-affirmed the finding that modern racial segregation does not solely reflect personal preferences.[63]

Racial segregation *is* caused in part by personal choice: it is the choices not of Puerto Ricans to live with other Puerto Ricans or blacks with other blacks, but of whites to live with other whites that matters the most. Just as they did in the twentieth century, some whites will go to great lengths to avoid racial integration at the neighborhood level, from lashing out in violence at their nonwhite neighbors—roughly half of all Chicago's hate crimes today occur in white neighborhoods undergoing a process of integration—to paying outlandish mortgages and suffering lengthy commutes to live in predominantly white suburbs.[64] This is why observers have claimed that ending America's racial segregation will require "a moral commitment that white America has historically lacked."[65] It will require a moral commitment to render hollow and worthy of reproach the joke that circulates in segregated white neighborhoods: "What is a word that starts with 'n' and ends with 'r' that you should never call a black person? . . . 'Neighbor.'"[66]

FIGURE 5.3 **WHITE PARTICIPANTS IN THE DETROIT AREA STUDY**

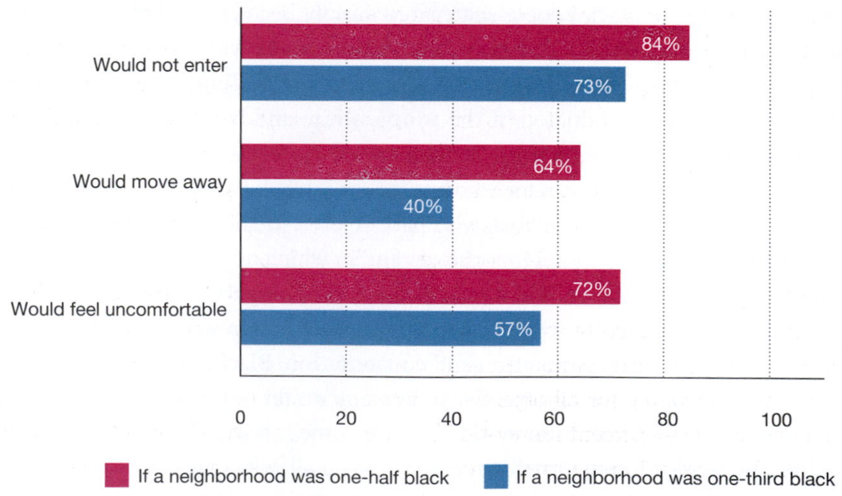

Percentage of whites responding to questions about integrated neighborhoods. Whites are unlikely to want to move into a neighborhood with an even balance of black and white residents.

The Role of Housing Discrimination

Social scientists also have explained racial segregation by analyzing the mechanisms of housing discrimination.[67] Through the employment of audit studies, where paired actors, equal in every way aside from race, approach a realtor as prospective home buyers or renters, researchers have gathered evidence documenting compounding and multisided discrimination against nonwhites. According to a massive audit study conducting by the U.S. Department of Housing and Urban Development, Hispanics and blacks looking for housing faced high levels of discrimination (which occurred in 50 percent of their interactions with realtors and landlords), as did Asians (who faced discrimination in 20 percent of cases) and Native Americans (who faced discrimination in 30 percent of cases).[68] Although housing discrimination has been outlawed since the Fair Housing Act of 1968, it is clear from such studies that it continues, albeit in more covert and underhanded ways.

Several audit studies have documented the practice of realtors falsely informing prospective nonwhite clients that the houses or apartments they noticed in an advertisement have just been rented or sold. One study documented the practice of a Chicago-based developer who worked only with whites; blacks were *always* told no properties were available, whereas whites were shown properties the majority of the time.[69] According to another study, prospective black home buyers were informed of 65 homes for every 100 shown to whites.[70] Yet another study found that between 60 percent and 90 percent of houses and apartments displayed to whites are never shown to blacks.[71] In addition, a good number of realtors often show nonwhites only those homes located in nonwhite or integrated areas, leading them away from majority-white neighborhoods—a practice known as "steering."[72] One analyst found that Hispanic and black home seekers encounter steering between 30 percent and 40 percent of the time, while white home seekers are often discouraged from buying in integrated neighborhoods.[73] Real estate offices advertise homes in majority-nonwhite or integrated neighborhoods at far lower rates than they do homes located in middle-class white neighborhoods, a pattern that persists even after taking into account the economic profile of the neighborhoods.[74]

Social scientists also have documented gender discrimination in housing, a dynamic that makes things especially difficult for women of color. Not only are women sometimes denied loans or charged higher rents on the basis of their sex, but they also are disproportionately victimized by sexual harassment. Landlords and building managers may agree to fix a repair or waive a late fee in exchange for sexual favors or may threaten a tenant with eviction unless she "is nice to him."[75] What is more, on learning that a woman is in an abusive relationship, landlords have been known to reject her rental application or evict her.[76]

For their part, banks and loan companies, as we learned in Chapter 4, reinforce racial segregation. Regularly, nonwhites, even those with impressive financial portfolios, are denied mortgage loans and receive poor credit ratings. One study found that even "after controlling for all objective indicators for applicant risk, lenders still rejected minorities 56 percent more often than otherwise identical whites."[77] According to political scientist Karen Orren, since the 1960s, life insurance companies virtually have abandoned the city, choosing instead to offer mortgage loans almost exclusively to suburban properties.[78] And many banks, continuing a more clandestine kind of redlining, refuse to finance homes in nonwhite and integrated neighborhoods.

FIGURE 5.4 **THE CONSEQUENCES OF SEGREGATION**

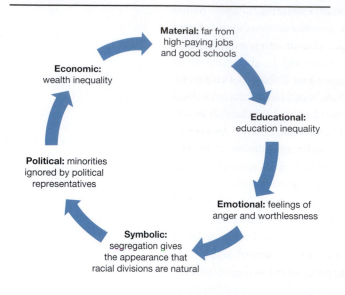

Interestingly, banks seem most hesitant to invest in areas undergoing racial change—distributing loans at high volumes in majority-white areas, moderate volumes in majority-black areas, and low volumes in racially mixed areas—a practice directly at odds with the principle of racial integration.[79]

The Consequences of Segregation

The consequences of segregation are multisided and complex. First, racial segregation takes an economic toll. Because banks often deny qualified nonwhites home loans, nonwhite home seekers must secure mortgages with inflated interest rates and high monthly payments. And because realtors steer nonwhites away from affluent white neighborhoods, many nonwhites end up purchasing homes that are not worth as much as comparable homes in white neighborhoods. In fact, studies have shown that black homeowners actually are penalized for purchasing a home: the average black homeowner resides in a neighborhood that is more segregated and less prosperous than that of the average black renter.[80] And in his study of housing discrimination, John Yinger estimates that each time a black or Hispanic person looks for housing, she or he, met with all the mechanisms of discrimination discussed earlier, pays an average "discrimination tax" of $3,000.[81]

Added to the economic disadvantages attached to housing in segregated neighborhoods are the disadvantages associated with one's proximity to well-paying jobs. Opportunities for work are abundant in some areas—namely, booming suburbs that have flourished since the white flight of the 1960s—and virtually nonexistent in others. Nonwhites clustered together in isolated city centers live in gutted-out areas cut off from the economic mainstream.[82] In many overlapping ways, therefore, racial segregation directly reproduces racialized poverty.

Racial segregation also affects people's living conditions. Forced to live in neighborhoods bereft of normal institutions (like grocery stores and banks), housed in old, dilapidated structures in a state of disrepair, and miles away from the nearest hospital or medical clinic, residents in poor, nonwhite neighborhoods experience a quality of life resembling nothing like the American ideals of comfort and security. To a lesser degree, this is true even of some middle-class black families, who live in neighborhoods with higher crime rates and lower property values than those of their white counterparts who earn the same amount of money.[83]

Racial segregation also has political consequences. If nonwhites are clustered only in certain areas of the city, they can be more or less ignored by political representatives who focus their energies on other areas. Although segregation can help nonwhites elect nonwhite representatives, as we learned in Chapter 3, by the same token it can marginalize nonwhites in the political arena. The segregation of nonwhites therefore erodes hope of coalition building and interracial collaboration in the political field, on both local and national levels.[84]

Students' performance in school does not go unaffected by racial segregation. Children and young people living in run-down segregated neighborhoods must attend poor schools with teaching shortages and few resources. Roughly half of all property tax revenue is used for public elementary and secondary education.[85] Because property tax is dictated by property values, affluent neighborhoods with soaring property values will enjoy a plump tax base from which schools can draw, while poor neighborhoods with abysmal property values will have a paltry tax base. This means that schools that service students in nonwhite low-income areas will be forced to operate with a much smaller budget than will schools housed in affluent white neighborhoods; they will have less money for field trips, textbooks, computers, and competitive teachers' salaries. It is small wonder, then, that black and Latino students living in highly segregated ghettos perform worse in school than black and Latino students from poor families living in more affluent neighborhoods. For many students living in racially isolated neighborhoods, doing well in school takes a back seat to staying safe, avoiding street crime and gangs, navigating the drug scene, and making ends meet.[86]

Besides such material consequences, racial segregation also brings about symbolic consequences. By dividing cities along racial dimensions, racial segregation gives off the appearance that racial divisions are real, natural, and unchanging. The geographic segregation in cities encourages a kind of mental segregation, one that reinforces and reifies the racial order. As one historian has put it, "in the very act of defining the boundaries of the 'ghetto,' whites also continually defined and reinforced the boundaries of race."[87]

And, last, we cannot forget the deep emotional costs of racial segregation. "The people of Harlem know they are living there because white people do not think they are good enough to live anywhere else," wrote James Baldwin in 1960. "No amount of 'improvement' can sweeten this fact. . . . A ghetto can be improved in one way only: out of existence."[88] "Housing is no abstract social and political problem, but an extension of man's personality," remarked American sociologist Kenneth Clark in 1965. "If the Negro has to identify with a rat-infested tenement, his sense of personal inadequacy and inferiority, already aggravated by job discrimination and other forms of humiliations, is reinforced by the physical reality around him. . . . A house is a concrete symbol of what the person is worth."[89]

Economic, material, political, educational, symbolic, and emotional—the consequences of racial segregation are mighty and many. But if racial segregation disadvantages some, it advantages others. If inner-city blacks are cut off from well-paying jobs, whites living in the suburbs are well connected to corporate America; if Mexicans living in crowded barrios are ignored by their political representatives, whites throughout the suburbs, with their healthy tax base, can more easily catch hold of the politician's ear; if Native Americans relegated to isolated and impoverished reservations are burdened by a sense of inferiority, whites living the good life might come to possess, perhaps without their knowledge, a sense of entitlement. It is incorrect to assume that every white gain translates into nonwhite loss—or vice versa. However, it is equally inadequate to speak of the disadvantages faced by people of color living in segregated neighborhoods without at the same time calling to mind the advantages enjoyed by whites living in equally segregated communities.

THE CITY

Unaffordable America

Public housing—government-owned units provided at low rates to poor residents—always has played a large part in reinforcing racial segregation in cities. Public housing arose after World War II as a response to the country's housing shortage. At first, many white and black families stayed in public housing units for short periods of time. However, as urban renewal projects were visited upon ghetto areas and thousands of poor blacks, evicted from their homes, were channeled into already swelling slum areas, public housing "was now meant to collect the ghetto residents left homeless by the urban renewal bulldozers."[90] To make room for these displaced newcomers, cities erected towering public housing units—Chicago's Robert Taylor homes once housed as many as 20,000 tenants—always in the isolated ghetto and, more often than not, "bleak, sterile, and cheap—expressive of patronizing condescension in every line."[91] Unlike many European states, which provide public housing in the form of financial housing subsidies to poor families, American public housing tends to consist of these inner-city projects.

Yet we should bear in mind that most low-income Americans do *not* benefit from public housing. In fact, the vast majority of low-income families live unassisted in the private market. Since the Nixon administration that began in 1969, policymakers have withdrawn funding from housing programs for the needy on the grounds that the private housing market is the best provider of shelter. Towering public housing that once defined ghetto neighborhoods—Chicago's Robert Taylor Homes, St. Louis's Pruitt-Igoe Homes, Atlanta's McDaniel-Glenn Homes—has been destroyed. Public housing inventory has fallen by roughly 20 percent since 1991.[92] In an average year in the 1980s, 161,000 additional households (as compared to the previous year) received subsidies in the form of public housing, vouchers, or some other kind of assistance. Since 1995, in an average year only 3,000 did.[93]

Only one in four households that qualify for housing assistance receives it. The lack of housing assistance combined with flat incomes at the bottom of the economic distribution and rising housing costs since 2000 have resulted in more and more renting families devoting large chunks of their income to housing costs. Because they have been disproportionately excluded both from good jobs and from the mortgage market, most African American and Latino families rent their housing—and accordingly have been disproportionately affected by the rise of rent burden.[94] As research by Matthew Desmond (an author of this book) shows, the percentage of black and Latino renters dedicating less than a third of their income to housing costs has declined over the last twenty years, but the percentage dedicating over half their income has risen. Today, roughly one in four black and Latino renting families spends at least half their income on housing.[95]

As a result, eviction has become commonplace in poor, minority neighborhoods. Desmond's research shows that in the city of Milwaukee, landlords evicted roughly 16,000 adults and children from 6,000 units in an average year. That's sixteen evictions a day. To place these figures in perspective, consider that the number of families evicted in Milwaukee in an average *year* is equivalent to the number of families forced out of public housing in Chicago, a city with approximately five times the population, over the course of a *decade*. Almost half of Milwaukee's evictions take place in predominantly black inner-city neighborhoods. With roughly one in fourteen renter-occupied households evicted annually, eviction is frankly commonplace in Milwaukee's black ghetto.[96]

The consequences of eviction are many and severe. Eviction decreases one's chances of securing decent and affordable housing because landlords often turn away applicants with a recent eviction record. And it can prevent families from benefiting from affordable housing programs, as the housing authority often regards an eviction as a strike against an applicant. Eviction often brings about prolonged periods of homelessness and increases poor families' material hardship. Recent research has linked eviction to job loss, depression, residential instability, and relocating to poorer, more violent neighborhoods. Women in poor minority neighborhoods disproportionately experience eviction and its consequences. In poor black neighborhoods, women are more than twice as likely to be evicted as men. If incarceration has become typical in the lives of men from impoverished black neighborhoods, eviction has become typical in the lives of women from these neighborhoods.[97]

An eviction team removes the belongings of a tenant who was forced from her apartment. She had been unable to work the year prior because of a medical condition.

Advanced Marginality: The Ghetto

It is fitting to end our section on race in the city by returning to the ghetto, that institution, formed by fear and racism, in which the metropolis's "urban outcasts" live. In Chapter 4, we defined the ghetto as a racial institution marked by social isolation and economic vulnerability first formed when blacks migrated north during the early twentieth century. To this we might add Massey and Denton's observation that "a ghetto is a set of neighborhoods that are exclusively inhabited by members of one group, within which virtually all members of that group live."[98] By this definition, African Americans are the only group in the history of the United States that have experienced ghettoization. Even early European immigrants, who clustered together in Germantowns and Little Italys, did not experience ghettoization to the degree that blacks experience it today. There are poor white neighborhoods, Hispanic barrios, and Chinatowns aplenty. But a ghetto is not defined exclusively by its poverty, nor, as we have already seen, are all kinds of poverty the same.

The defining characteristic of a ghetto is not economic destitution, but advanced marginality. Advanced marginality refers to the severe spatial and social segregation of the ghetto's residents, marked by their amputation from America's economic prosperity, national security, collective imagination and memory, and state services.[99] The ghetto first originated in medieval Europe as an area of the city where Jews were cordoned off from the rest of the population. In fact, the word "ghetto" comes from an Italian word meaning "the part of a city to which Jews are restricted."[100] And it is this restriction, this social isolation, that is the essence of the ghetto.

The ghetto we find today, primarily in northern cities, does not resemble the ghetto of the mid-twentieth century. The ghetto of midcentury might be called the "the communal ghetto." Owing to legalized segregation, virtually all African Americans—no matter their title, profession, or economic standing—lived there. The ghetto was economically diverse, had its own economy, and functioned as a safe space for blacks who were unwelcomed in other areas of town. After legalized segregation fell, middle- and upper-class blacks fled the ghetto, leaving behind only low-income families. The "hyperghetto" of today is a territory segregated by race *and* class—and is a site of extreme concentration of poverty, crime, and other social maladies. Other neighborhoods may be racially segregated or economically deprived. But the hyperghetto is marked by extreme levels of both African American segregation and acutely concentrated disadvantage.[101]

Ethnic Enclaves

Immigration has been and remains an urban phenomenon. Of the thousands of immigrants who come to the United States each year, most settle in large "receiving" or "gateway cities," such as Miami, Los Angeles, New York, Dallas, Chicago, Houston, and San Francisco. Through international communication channels, immigrants in the sending countries learn where pockets of immigrants from their country have settled. Although not as segregated as African Americans—or, for that matter, European immigrants of the nineteenth century—today's immigrants are a fairly segregated lot, many clustering together in ethnic enclaves.[102]

Are ethnic enclaves transitional neighborhoods in which new immigrants live until they gain enough footing in American society to move out, or are they more established communities, where multiple generations of immigrants live even though they do not have to? The answer, social scientists have learned, is "both."

Ethnic enclaves, such as Manhattan's Koreatown (pictured), create communities which can either help or hinder immigrant populations.

According to the spatial assimilation thesis, advanced by American sociologist Douglas Massey, new immigrants self-segregate in enclaves and rely on the enclave economy for their start.[103] After some time in the enclave, immigrants, having acquired savings and improved their English skills, look for a new place to live, one that can offer a higher standard of living. In this view, ethnic enclaves are a stopping point for immigrants—some of whom face high rates of housing discrimination—on their way to economic and cultural assimilation.[104]

According to another view, the ethnic community thesis, ethnic enclaves are sought out by immigrants who could afford to live elsewhere. Some immigrants prefer living in areas where a good number of their neighbors eat the same food, celebrate the same holidays, and speak their native language.[105] Although most ethnic neighborhoods are underprivileged, some are quite well off. The Vietnamese and Japanese enclaves of inner-city Los Angeles, for example, are at least as affluent as the other neighborhoods where Vietnamese and Japanese families live. The same is true of New York City's Afro-Caribbean, Filipino, and Indian American enclaves.[106]

Within ethnic enclaves—indeed, within neighborhoods of all varieties—we find those who could live elsewhere but who, attracted to their enclave's cultural life, choose not to; those who wish to live elsewhere but are trapped within it; and those who use the enclave as a launching pad from which to ascend.[107]

Interracial Conflict: Blacks and Koreans

Immigrants always have added to the pulse and vibrancy of American urban life. Take today's Korean immigrants, the immigrant group with the highest rate of self-employment in the United States. Many cities owe their dry cleaners and nail salons, fish markets and fresh-flower stands, and neighborhood grocery stores to Korean entrepreneurs. For over a hundred years, immigrant groups have established businesses in the inner city. Throughout the twentieth century, Jewish shopkeepers were a regular fixture in the center of town. But as their children inherited not just the opportunities their parents had worked so hard to provide but also the opportunities involved in being welcomed deeper into the ranks of whiteness, they took leave of their shops, opening up in turn new opportunities for streams of other ethnic immigrants. Koreans have filled the business niche left by Jewish shopkeepers, and many have opened up shop in the black ghetto, because they can afford to live there and because they do not have to compete with large corporations, which are much more interested in the deeper pockets of suburban residents.[108]

Many black ghetto residents, however, view Korean shopkeepers with a fair degree of animus and resentment. Many poor blacks feel that Korean entrepreneurs have taken their jobs, while others feel generally mistreated and disrespected by shopkeepers. We are met with this tension when comedian Dave Chappelle jokes, "Now I would never say I hate all Korean people. I haven't met all Korean people. That hate talk's for savages. But even though I don't generalize, I do do percentages and averages. So far I hate one out of five Koreans I've met."[109] Conflicts between black patrons and Korean store owners often are colored by racist language, with each party exchanging epithets.

Black-Korean conflict boiled over in the early 1990s. In 1991, a Korean merchant shot and killed a black teenager in South Central Los Angeles. A year later, Los Angeles went up in flames as insurgents of all racial identities took to the streets after four white police officers, who had been caught on videotape beating a twenty-five-year-old motorist named Rodney King, were acquitted. As the smoke settled from the country's first multiethnic uprising, fifty-two people had been killed and millions of dollars' worth of property had been destroyed. Korean store owners were hit the hardest, suffering almost half of the total property damage—roughly $400 million.[110]

A Korean-American store owner stands vigil on the roof of his grocery store in the Koreatown area of Los Angeles during the three days of violence following the acquittal of the four Los Angeles police officers accused of beating Rodney King.

Nearly 8 million people in the United States live in gated communities.

Urban conflict and tension between minority groups can be found in today's cities just as it could have been found there a century ago between Italians and Germans, Catholics and Protestants. The distrust that different racial and ethnic groups living in poor urban neighborhoods harbor toward one another is matched only by the interests and struggles shared by these groups.

THE SUBURBS

America's sprawling suburbs originated as a racial creation, and they remain one today. Suburban development was fueled by white fear: fear of racial integration, of plummeting property values, and—most of all—of violent crime. In their distance from city centers, their cul-de-sacs and dead-end roads, their stringent zoning laws, and their lack of public transportation, the suburbs purposefully are constructed to promote isolation from city dwellers and their "vices." Nowhere is this better exemplified than in gated communities, which have flourished since the 1970s. As their name suggests, gated communities, where nearly 8 million Americans reside, are residential areas fortified by high walls and security forces. To enter, pedestrians, bicyclists, and motorists must pass through a large gate, sometimes enabled by round-the-clock guards and surveillance cameras. No longer only a luxury of the elite, middle-class gated communities are now springing up all over suburbia.[111]

Americans often view urban life as made up of "chocolate cities and vanilla suburbs," as funk master George Clinton once put it, and associate multiracial cities with poverty and crime and white suburbs with affluence and safety. After eating at Sylvia's, a famous soul food restaurant located in the heart of Harlem, Fox News commentator Bill O'Reilly announced that he "couldn't get over the fact" that Sylvia's was like any other restaurant. "It was like going into an Italian restaurant in an all-white suburb in the sense of people were sitting there, and they were ordering and having fun," O'Reilly said. "And there wasn't any kind of craziness at all."[112] Embedded within this comment is the implication that black city areas are distinctly different, especially in terms of order and civility, from all-white suburbs.

The suburbs, however, are neither all affluent nor all white. In fact, since the 1990s, poverty has been on the rise in many suburbs. Between 2000 and 2010, suburban poverty levels rose an astonishing 53 percent.[113] Indeed, many cities have attempted to entice upper-class individuals to newly renovated central-city areas by pushing out poor families, who in turn have relocated to the inner rings of the suburbs. The result has been the beginnings of "suburban ghettos," areas with extremely high poverty and unemployment rates, detached from social services and employment opportunities.[114]

In 2010, 78 percent of whites, 62 percent of Asians, 59 percent of Hispanics, and 51 percent of blacks lived in the suburbs.[115] Most nonwhites migrating to the suburbs moved into areas already populated by nonwhites and areas undergoing racial change. Suburban areas with small nonwhite populations experienced higher levels of integration, while segregation is more trenchant in areas with large non-white populations. Typically, black Americans with ample bank accounts do not move from segregated urban areas to integrated suburbs, but from one black neighborhood to another. To pluck one statistic from many: 60 percent of black households earning over $75,000 live in majority-black neighborhoods. The same pattern is true, though to a lesser extent, of Hispanic and Asian Americans.[116]

Because many middle-class black neighborhoods abut poor black neighborhoods, middle-class residents often shop at the same stores, play in the same parks, and walk down the same streets as poor blacks living a few blocks away. Some middle-class blacks attempt to erect clear boundaries between themselves and their downtrodden neighbors (and hence have been labeled "buppies," a combination of black and yuppie). Others, however, have forged alliances with poor members of the black community, together participating in church fund-raisers or community education projects. Accordingly, many of the social problems that fester in the ghetto have crept into middle-class black neighborhoods, which are less affluent and have higher crime rates than middle-class white neighborhoods (or even many poor white neighborhoods). On the whole, middle-class blacks are just as segregated from whites—and, in turn, from good schools, well-funded social service agencies, and grocery stories with fair prices and fresh produce—as are poor blacks.[117]

At the same time, middle-class black families often oscillate between black and white communities, navigating racial boundaries at different times and for different reasons. Career-driven blacks may work in a majority-white corporate world but worship in a majority-black church. Black children from well-off families may attend a majority-white prep school during the weekday and play on a majority-black inner-city Little League team on the weekends.[118] However, other middle-class black families, especially those sprinkled across majority-white suburbs, may remain culturally and spatially isolated from other black families. Black adolescents brought up in such areas often describe themselves as "raised white," such that they do not identify with African American history, culture, or communities. Indeed, biracial adolescents raised in white suburbs often identify as white until they get to college, where they undergo a reracialization orchestrated by their peers, professors, and guidance counselors. As one biracial woman attending the University of California—Berkeley explained, "Before I came to Cal I was white. I was all white culturally. . . . Here I am perceived as black. I'm treated as black so I don't have a problem with being black. . . . But it's a difficult situation. It's really hard."[119] Comments like these attest to the fluidity of racial categories, as well as to the importance of place in molding those categories.

Growing numbers of immigrant families live and work in the suburbs. In fact, almost half of new immigrants who arrived in the 1990s settled in suburban areas. In Los Angeles, which, along with New York, is home to the largest and most diverse collection of immigrant communities in the nation, there are more Mexican, Chinese, Filipino, Korean, Japanese, and Vietnamese citizens and immigrants living in the suburbs than in the inner city. Large Cuban communities thrive in the suburbs of New Jersey, and Salvadoran enclaves are nestled beyond the city limits throughout southern California. Although not as affluent as many white suburbs, suburban ethnic communities provide a higher standard of living than do inner-city ethnic enclaves and other urban neighborhoods.[120]

One of the largest and most diverse Asian American communities is found in the suburban cities that made up the San Gabriel Valley, east of Los Angeles. First settled by Asian workers in the mid-nineteenth century, the San Gabriel Valley is home to the eight cities in the United States with the highest proportions of Chinese Americans as well as to thousands of Japanese, Filipino, South Asian, and Japanese Americans. Public libraries and schools in the area have embraced Asian cultures as well as the principles of multilingualism and multiculturalism, with some high schools incorporating Mandarin language courses into their curriculum. As one observer has commented, many Asian American youth living in San Gabriel Valley "do not know they are 'supposed to' major in engineering and not in sports," and a significant number of the area's young people, Asian and non-Asian alike, are "multilingual, multiracial, and multicultural . . . [and] comfortable in diversity."[121]

RURAL AMERICA

Most of this chapter has focused on urban life, and for good reason: most Americans live in metropolitan areas.[122] However, racial dynamics also affect the lives of millions of people living in rural areas, the residents of American Indian reservations, farmlands, and small towns. In fact, many rural areas are just as racially segregated as their urban counterparts; what is more, many rural nonwhites live "in close proximity to the historical remnants of institutions explicitly created to conquer, oppress, and maintain their subordinate position in society."[123] For this reason, the remainder of this chapter is devoted to unpacking the racial dynamics of residence in rural America.

Colonias and Bordertowns

Since the early 1900s, American agriculture has relied on the busy hands and sturdy backs of migrant laborers, who were willing to work for below-market wages. In fact, between 1942 and 1964, the U.S. government recruited Mexican nationals for agricultural work through the Bracero program, which granted them temporary residence in the United States. Over 4.5 million Mexicans worked in the United States through this program, willing to bend and sweat and pick in the fields for substandard wages. They often lived in crowded and hot dwellings, with bunk beds stacked on top of one another. Called "legalized slavery," the Bracero program was outlawed the same year the Civil Rights Act was ratified; however, the working and housing conditions for today's migrant workers—the overwhelming majority of them Mexican immigrants working in the rural West—have not improved much.[124]

Between 1990 and 2000, the proportion of Mexican immigrants working in agricultural fields nearly doubled.[125] Small settlements, called *colonias*, have sprung up around the fields where migrant workers toil. Many *colonias* are made up of low-cost housing or, in some cases, lines of dilapidated shacks built of pieces of discarded sheet metal, old tires, and scrap wood. Their residents are isolated—culturally, linguistically, economically, and politically—from the neighboring white communities, including the farmhouses of their employers; many suffer from a lack of social services and basic medicine. Although *colonias* house significant numbers of Mexican immigrants, many are made up of native-born Mexican Americans. In South Texas, for instance, roughly two-thirds of *colonia* residents are American citizens.[126]

The desolate towns nesting against the 2,000-mile border separating the United States from Mexico are some of the poorest areas in the country. Star County, Texas, has one of the highest poverty rates in the nation.[127] Mexican Americans and Mexican immigrants who populate the borderland face limited economic opportunities and accept positions in America's growing low-wage market. Many Mexican American families have moved north, to the upper Midwest and other parts of the country, in search of more opportunity.[128]

A woman watches her two children play in front of their home in a *colonia* just northwest of McAllen, Texas.

Life on the Reservation—and Environmental Racism

A large proportion of America's indigenous population lives on reservations.[129] These are anything but one-dimensional settings. They vary along economic, cultural, religious, linguistic, and political lines. There also is immense variation within Indian nations, caused (among other things) by differentiations built into tribal structure: separate clans, traditions, and villages. On examining the history of the Cherokee Nation, one sociologist noted that because the tribe's language changed from village to village, as did its customs, rituals, and everyday practices, it is more accurate to speak of "many different Cherokee populations," as opposed to a single, monochrome tribe.[130]

Those who never have set foot on an American Indian reservation might carry in their minds a great many misconceptions of reservation life. Indeed, many non—Indian Americans seem to view Indians as somehow locked in time, living on reservations the same way their ancestors lived centuries ago. Reacting to the frequency of these stereotypes, a joke circulating on an Indian listserv in 2002 read, "Things Native Americans Can Say to a White Person upon First Meeting One: (1) Where's your powdered wig? (2) Do you live in a covered wagon? (3) What's the meaning behind the square dance? (4) What's your feeling about riverboat casinos? Do they really help or are they just a short-term fix? (5) I learned all about your people's ways in the Boy Scouts."[131] Just as it would be absurd to ask a white person these questions, it would be equally absurd to ask a resident of an Indian reservation, "Where's your headdress?" or "Do you live in a tepee?" More accurately, like most other Americans, many Native Americans live with one foot in the present and the other in the past. Many members of the Navajo Nation, for instance, live in modern homes decorated with traditional hand-woven rugs, pottery, and sand paintings; in their back yards, next to the trampoline and propane grill, sits a hogan, a small, dome-shaped wood and mud structure, which serves as a ceremonial site.

Many firms have offered millions of dollars for the right to pollute Indian reservations.

Among the many problems facing American Indian reservations in the twenty-first century, environmental racism ranks among the most pressing. Environmental racism can be defined as any environmental policy, practice, or directive that disproportionately disadvantages (intentionally or unintentionally) nonwhite communities.[132] Native American lands have been targeted for radioactive dumpsites, incinerators, and erosive mining operations. According to one source, over 300 reservations are threatened by environmental hazards, from chemical waste to dangerous air emissions, clear-cutting, and strip-mining. Faced with stringent environmental regulations, waste disposal firms have looked to Native American reservations, which are not subject to state laws regarding dumping. Hoping to buy off corrupt tribal leaders or to exploit the economic vulnerability of reservation inhabitants, these firms have offered thousands, even millions, of dollars for the right to pollute Indian country.[133]

Consider the case of the Skull Valley Band of Goshutes, located on reservation land in northern Utah. Only a couple dozen tribal members live on the impoverished reservation, and it is not hard to see why. "To the southwest lies the Dugway Proving Ground, where the U.S. government develops chemical and biological weapons. To the east is one of the world's largest nerve-gas incinerators. To the north is a giant magnesium plant, a major polluter. To the northwest sit a hazardous-waste incinerator and a toxic-waste landfill. The tribe's only profitable business is a municipal garbage dump serving Salt Lake City."[134] In 2006, tribal members were approached with a proposition by Private Fuel Storage, a consortium representing nuclear utilities. In exchange for $100 million in fees to be dished out over a span of forty years, the Skull Valley reservation would agree to store nearly all the country's radioactive waste, roughly 44,000 tons. The payoffs were obvious, as were the risks—nothing short of the permanent poisoning of their lands—and tribal members disagreed on the plan and finally rejected it.[135] To debate whether or not residents of the Skull Valley reservation should have taken the deal is an important exercise. Equally important, however, is a sociological exercise that forces us to question why these Native Americans must choose between rural poverty and radioactive waste. What past and present economic, social, cultural, and political forces combine to produce this devil's bargain?

American Indians living on reservations are exposed to some of the worst air and water pollution in the country. As a result, they are at high risk of contracting cancer and lung diseases, of dying at a young age, and of giving birth to babies with defects. Compared to the national average, Native Americans living on reservations are 2.8 times more likely to die of diabetes, for example.[136] When we learn that doctors can identify industry pollutants in the milk of nursing mothers living on the Akwesasne Mohawk reservation in upstate New York, we begin to understand one reason why many Indian babies are born prematurely and weigh less than the national average—and why the infant mortality rate on reservations is 1.2 times the national average.[137]

Native Americans have formed coalitions to resist environmental racism. In 1999, residents of the Eastern Navajo reservation appealed to the Nuclear Regulatory Commission to put an end to ongoing uranium mining. California's Mohave Nation and Nevada's Western Shoshone battled against proposals to build radioactive waste dumps on tribal land. And interracial coalitions aimed at combating such problems have emerged since American Indians are not the only group that suffers from environmental racism. After taking economic attributes into account, Latino and black urban neighborhoods are far more likely to experience environmental hazards than their white counterparts. The majority of large hazardous waste landfills are located in nonwhite neighborhoods; in 2000, as many as three out of five African Americans lived in areas with toxic waste dumps, and more than 46 percent of all public housing units were located within a mile's radius of factories emitting toxic gases.[138]

Poor rural black communities, especially those located in the Deep South, also have been sacrificed to house the nation's waste. In a document prepared for the United Nations, sociologist Robert Bullard wrote, "The Lower Mississippi River Industrial Corridor has over 125 companies that manufacture a range of products including fertilizers, gasoline, paints and plastics. Environmentalists and local residents have dubbed this corridor 'Cancer Alley,' and tax breaks given to polluting industries have created few jobs at a high cost. This is particularly true in Louisiana. . . . In the 1990s, Louisiana wiped off the books $3.1 billion in property taxes to polluting companies. The state's top five polluters have received $111 million over the past decade."[139] Over thirty petrochemical and industrial plants are located within a two-mile radius of Mossville, Louisiana, a rural black community. According to a study carried out by the U.S. Department of Health and Human Services, dioxin levels in Mossville residents are extremely high. A deadly substance, dioxin can cause cancer, hormone disruption, and severe birth defects.[140]

We now know who suffers from environmental racism. But who benefits from it? Companies that profit directly from creating pollution (such as chemical or plastic manufacturers) or by disposing of it (such as those involved in the waste processing industry)—as well as corrupt politicians more interested in funding their campaigns than in the livelihoods of their most vulnerable constituents—undeniably are beneficiaries of environmental racism. But there is another beneficiary as well. If you live as the average American does, you use up roughly twenty tons of raw materials each year, consuming ten times more than the average Chinese citizen and thirty times more than the average person living in India.[141] Where does all our garbage go? Is the place you now live powered by coal or nuclear energy plants? If so, who is forced to breathe the coal emissions that power your television set? Where does the radioactive waste from your nuclear energy plant get buried? If you are privileged enough to live in a neighborhood that does not house garbage incinerators or sewage plants, an area that does not abut nuclear waste dumps or factories spouting toxic gases into the air, but you continue to gobble up resources, then, when asked, "Who benefits from environmental racism?" we must answer, "I do."

The Changing Face of Rural White America

Poor rural white communities face many of the same problems that affect poor nonwhite communities. Small villages throughout Kentucky and Virginia have been victimized by environmental devastation, including illegal dumping and strip mining that has caused flash flooding. Poor whites living in rural America often are isolated from mainstream economic opportunities, overlooked by their government leaders, and constrained to live in inadequate housing. Like poor blacks living in the projects, poor rural whites living in trailer parks also are marked with a stigma, a "blemish of place," which threatens to erode their sense of self-worth and dignity.[142] Trailer parks, it is commonly held, are where "rednecks," "hicks," and "white trash" live; they are breeding grounds for deviant behavior, poor hygiene, and lazy talking. And poor rural whites—especially those of the Deep South—often are stereotyped as bitterly intolerant, harboring violently racist attitudes associated only with zealots of the KKK. This is an old belief, one that existed before the Civil War, and it divides rich from poor, civil from uncivil, North from South. As W. J. Cash wrote in 1960, there exists among ordinary people, from North and South, "a profound conviction that the South is another land, sharply differentiated from the rest of the American nation, and exhibiting within itself remarkable homogeneity."[143]

The world of poor rural whites has been turned into a kind of backward and bigoted world, one that outsiders enjoy pointing to with a smirk or a condescending shake of the head. In debasing poor rural whites, other Americans—affluent and city-dwelling whites and nonwhites alike—can conveniently avoid inspecting their own racist attitudes and dispositions. "I'm not a racist," they say. "If you want to see racism, talk to a redneck." In truth, interpersonal racism is not concentrated in backwoods white towns but is found throughout America, in all communities, white and nonwhite alike. And as long as we peg the poor rural white as the American bigot, we can avoid the painful exercise of asking how racial domination thrives in our own communities and families, and even in our own thinking.[144]

Today, many rural middle-class white communities no longer are able to avoid confronting their own racial modes of thinking and acting, primarily because immigration patterns are transforming the racial landscape of previously majority-white towns. Some small towns that only ten years ago hosted small pockets of nonwhites now are adjusting to growing nonwhite populations as well as to cultural change. Grocery stores are beginning to stock Chinese food; Wal-Mart is beginning to follow English announcements with ones in Spanish; Middle Eastern restaurants are appearing on Main Street. The reactions from white residents have been diverse and, at times, disquieting.

Poor rural whites are often thought of as racist "rednecks," but this stereotype ignores the deep poverty suffered by many individuals in rural communities.

Lewiston, Maine, an inland town of 36,000 located in the whitest state in the Union, recently has experienced an influx of Somali immigrants. Between 2001 and 2002, roughly 1,200 Somalis moved to Lewiston; that number doubled over the next five years, until Lewiston had the highest per capita Somali concentration in the United States. The Somalis, many of whom were refugees, were attracted to Lewiston's low cost of living, its tradition of racial and religious tolerance (most Somalis are practicing Muslims), its good schools, and its social services. But some of Lewiston's white residents resented the immigrants, assuming they were disproportionately draining the town's resources. This sentiment was made official in a letter, penned by the city's mayor, asking the elders of the Somali community to discourage their friends and family members from moving to the town. "The Somali community must exercise some discipline and reduce the stress on our limited finances and our generosity," the mayor wrote. "Our city is maxed-out financially, physically, and emotionally." The Somali residents of "Little Mogadishu" felt unfairly blamed for the town's financial hardships, responding to the mayor's letter with reminders of their own contributions to Lewiston.

The mayor's letter, however, began a string of events—including a rally held by a white supremacist group and a man rolling a severed pig's head down the center aisle of a local mosque during an evening prayer service—that stoked the coals of racial hostility, dividing Somali residents from their white neighbors.[145] But even in this charged atmosphere, non-Somali antiracists, nonwhite and white alike, took stands against interracial hostility and intolerance. While the hate group rally drew only 30 people, roughly 5,000 turned out for the counterprotest held on the same day, a "diversity rally" that condemned racial hatred.[146]

Like Lewiston, the 37,000-person town of Carpentersville, Illinois, has experienced drastic changes in its racial demography. In 1990, Hispanics made up 17 percent of the town's population; today, they constitute more than half. Although most of the town's Hispanic families are American citizens, some of Carpentersville's white residents have reacted to their rising Hispanic population by voicing opposition to illegal immigration. In a recent election, candidates calling themselves "The All American Team" won seats to Carpentersville's board of trustees by vowing to penalize landlords who rented to undocumented workers, as well as businesses that employed them. Before the election, a flier printed by a supporter of the All American Team was circulated throughout the town. It read,

> Are you tired of waiting to pay for your groceries while Illegal Aliens pay with food stamps and then go outside and get in a $40,000 car? . . . Are you tired of reading that another Illegal Alien was arrested for drug dealing? Are you tired of having to push 1 for English? . . . Are you tired of not being able to use Carpenter Park on the weekend, because it is overrun by Illegal Aliens? Are you tired of seeing the Mexican Flag flown above our Flag? If you are as tired as me then let's get out and Vote for the: All American Team."[147]

In 2007, the newly elected All American Team passed an ordinance making English the official language of Carpentersville. This ordinance forbids the printing of various city notices, including warning signs and local regulations, in both Spanish and English, and would discourage city employees, including police officers, from speaking Spanish. As a result of these moves, the racial climate in Carpentersville has grown more toothy and intolerant. Many of the town's Hispanic residents feel unwelcome and under attack. For them, white residents are not taking on illegal immigration but are mounting an assault on Hispanic culture and language. Many whites, however, feel that the town's Hispanic population is not assimilating fast enough. "They want the American dream, but they don't want to assimilate," declared one member of the All American Team. "Immigrants are what made this country great, but the immigrants of yesterday and the immigrants of today are totally different people. They don't have the love of this country in their hearts."[148]

Carpentersville is not the only place that has passed or proposed English-only resolutions, and thirty-two states list English as their official language. Other state and local governments have passed laws designed, in one observer's words, to "make life miserable for illegal immigrants in the hope that they will have no choice but to return to their countries of origin."[149] (This strategy has become known as "self-deportation.") Indeed, many of these laws are having their desired effect. Undocumented immigrants, many of whom have worked in the town for years, are leaving Carpentersville, because they fear deportation more than ever before. Even Mexican American citizens are leaving, because they feel unwanted. In this way, English-only ordinances and other laws targeting the Hispanic population can be interpreted as a new tactic of white fight.

TOWARD AN INTEGRATED AMERICA

Focusing on the workings of racial domination in the residential field, this chapter has underscored the continuing persistence of racial segregation, as well as problems and privileges unequally distributed to different communities on the basis of their racial makeup. These social ills are old and established but, as we have learned, have not been with us forever. Nor must they remain this way. But we still have a long way to go before we arrive at an America that is truly integrated. Listen to James Baldwin once more: "It is a terrible and inexorable law that one cannot deny the humanity of another without diminishing one's own: in the face of one's victim, one sees oneself. Walk through the streets of Harlem and see what we, this nation, have become."[150]

THE BIG PICTURE

Chapter 5: Housing

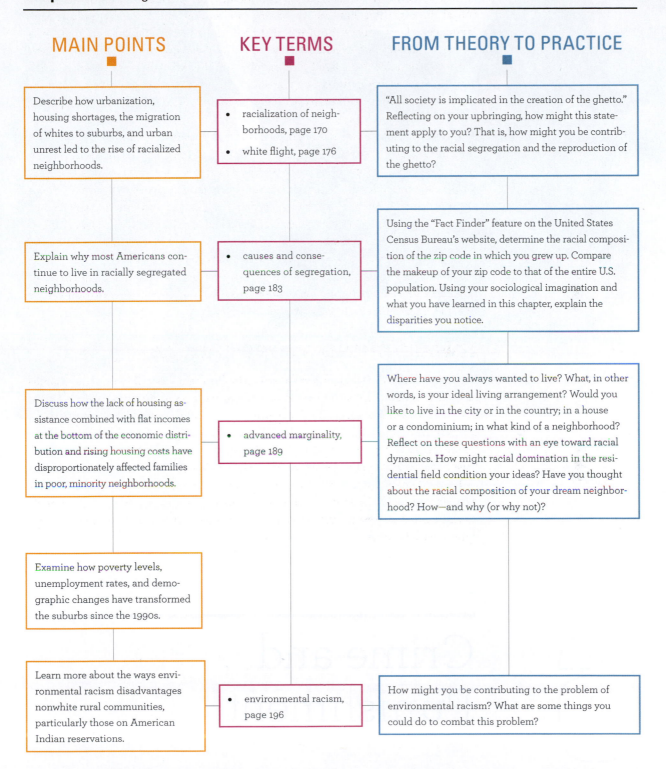

MAIN POINTS	KEY TERMS	FROM THEORY TO PRACTICE
Describe how urbanization, housing shortages, the migration of whites to suburbs, and urban unrest led to the rise of racialized neighborhoods.	• racialization of neighborhoods, page 170 • white flight, page 176	"All society is implicated in the creation of the ghetto." Reflecting on your upbringing, how might this statement apply to you? That is, how might you be contributing to the racial segregation and the reproduction of the ghetto?
Explain why most Americans continue to live in racially segregated neighborhoods.	• causes and consequences of segregation, page 183	Using the "Fact Finder" feature on the United States Census Bureau's website, determine the racial composition of the zip code in which you grew up. Compare the makeup of your zip code to that of the entire U.S. population. Using your sociological imagination and what you have learned in this chapter, explain the disparities you notice.
Discuss how the lack of housing assistance combined with flat incomes at the bottom of the economic distribution and rising housing costs have disproportionately affected families in poor, minority neighborhoods.	• advanced marginality, page 189	Where have you always wanted to live? What, in other words, is your ideal living arrangement? Would you like to live in the city or in the country; in a house or a condominium; in what kind of a neighborhood? Reflect on these questions with an eye toward racial dynamics. How might racial domination in the residential field condition your ideas? Have you thought about the racial composition of your dream neighborhood? How—and why (or why not)?
Examine how poverty levels, unemployment rates, and demographic changes have transformed the suburbs since the 1990s.		
Learn more about the ways environmental racism disadvantages nonwhite rural communities, particularly those on American Indian reservations.	• environmental racism, page 196	How might you be contributing to the problem of environmental racism? What are some things you could do to combat this problem?

6

Crime and Punishment

MAIN POINTS

- Recognize the role of the late-twentieth-century prison boom in the creation of the stark racial disparities now seen within the U.S. incarcerated population.

- Discuss the ways that Americans' fear of crime is strongly connected to their racial identity, their racial attitudes, and the racial makeup of their neighborhood.

- Understand why members of different racial groups are more likely to commit or be victims of crime.

- Learn how racial disparities in the prison population are driven in large part by severe criminal sentencing practices that give lengthy prison terms for nonviolent offenses as well as by new policing techniques that disproportionately affect poor minority communities.

No subject requires a higher level of critical thinking, a more unwavering commitment to rational assessment, than the subject of crime. If we wish to think deeply about it—and to develop effective ways of addressing it—we must resist accepting as truth the prepackaged collection of assumptions, statements, and beliefs we commonly (and sometimes carelessly) attach to issues of illegal behavior and punishment. This requires reevaluating those dangers that seem to trouble us the most and taking note of all the other dangers we dismiss because of our selective focus. It also means rethinking the very essence of "crime" and evaluating why, although many things inflict harm, only some are outlawed. Likewise, the way we fight crime deserves rethinking. America's "get tough on crime" approach is relatively new and, of the many methods designed to decrease crime, may be among the least effective. We also should develop complex appraisals of all the actors found in the legal realm—lawyers, police officers, victims, and criminals—and even force ourselves to construct multidimensional depictions of those who have committed acts that horrify us. Carrying out monstrous deeds does not necessarily make someone a monster; to paraphrase Helen Prejean, everyone is more than the worst thing they have ever done.[1]

The phrase "Justice is blind" suggests that the legal field is somehow detached from normal society, that it floats above society's prejudices. As critical thinkers, we need to focus our attention on the multiple ways in which race—as well as class and gender—operates as a central organizing principle of the criminal justice system. Let us, therefore, approach the hot topic of crime with cool heads, for arriving at a more rational and rigorous understanding of race, crime, and punishment can help liberate our thinking from the clutches of fear, thereby helping us to make better decisions as we work to create a more just democracy. Toward such an end, this chapter starts with a historical overview that traces the development of America's prison boom. After that, it explores the workings of race in the legal field in three related sections: fear, crime, and punishment.

THE RISE OF THE AMERICAN PRISON

Early conceptions and practices of justice, crime, and punishment were formed under conditions of colonialism and slavery. Indigenous systems of justice were overshadowed by European ones, which criminalized tribal practices. (Not even certain dances and idioms were exempt from such criminalization.) Enslaved Africans were excluded from the protection of the law, which did not recognize as rape the sexual assault of a slave girl by a white man or classify as murder the accidental killing of a slave at the hands of his master. From its inception, American law permitted nonwhites to be brutalized, dehumanized, and killed. It is within this contradiction—the simultaneous extension of liberty and the retrenchment of justice, the exaltation of freedom for most but at the expense of some—that the American justice system was forged.

The Lynch Mob and the Prison Labor Camp

After the fall of slavery, two important institutions arose to control and confine nonwhites, and African Americans in particular. The first was the lynch mob. Sometimes the lynch mob operated in cahoots with local law enforcement; other times its rabid masses simply overpowered sheriff's deputies attempting to protect their captives long enough that they might receive a fair trial. The mob would break into the jail cell, dragging the trembling black man outside, and with impunity torture

Between 1880 and 1930, lynch mobs murdered over 2,300 black men, women, and children that we know of.

him to death. Between 1880 and 1930, lynch mobs murdered over 2,300 black men (and women and children) whom we know of.[2] The broader white public justified the practice of lynching in a number of ways, one of which was by arguing that it kept white women safe from the black male rapist. "There is only one crime that warrants lynching," declared Bill Tillman of South Carolina, "and Governor as I am, I would lead a mob to lynch the negro who ravishes a white woman."[3] The majority of black men accused of rape, castrated and hung from dogwood limbs, were innocent. A good number of accusations were brought forth, not by the supposed victim of rape, but by her husband or brother or someone in the community. Indeed, many white women, constrained by southern manners, were told to keep quiet as others used these women's bodies as a pretext for leveling a scourge against black men.

Although many whites believed lynch mobs were carrying forth swift and effective justice on the body of a rapist, most lynch mobs were not motivated by this crime. Or, to put it another way, the southern white man's definition of "rape," as it applied to black men, hardly could have been broader. As W. J. Cash has observed, "What Southerners felt . . . was that any assertion of any kind on the part of the Negro constituted in a perfectly real manner an attack on the Southern woman. What they saw, more or less consciously, in the conditions of Reconstruction was a passage toward a condition for her as degrading, in their view, as rape itself."[4] Accordingly, when Ida B. Wells, a black woman who defiantly and indefatigably stood up against the institution of the lynch mob, researched southern lynchings, she found that most black men were killed not because they had been accused of rape but because they had been found to be too "uppity." They refused to take their hat off in front of a white woman; they winked at her; they laughed behind her back.[5] Nonetheless, the lynch mob thrived on the widespread fear that black men were violent, lecherous predators, a fear that spread during Reconstruction and is with us still. The lynch mob upheld white supremacy by letting blacks know they could not find refuge in the law. And it upheld white patriarchy by cultivating within white women a dread of the black male rapist, a dread that increased white women's dependency on their white male protectors.[6]

Alongside the lynch mob, a second important institution arose after emancipation: the prison. Although prisons long had been a feature of American society, they took on a new function after the fall of slavery, namely, to reenslave thousands of black workers recently released from bondage. New laws were drafted to target poor blacks, ensuring they would be segregated from white society. Vagabond laws were

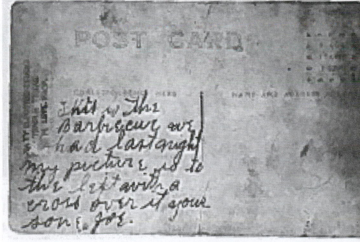

Photograph of a lynching made into a postcard that one white onlooker mailed home to his parents.

adopted in state after state after the Civil War. These laws outlawed begging and loitering. In short, they transformed the poor into the criminal, who, for simply panhandling—or even looking for work—could be sent to jail or a hard labor camp. Under many vagabond laws, a panhandler could be imprisoned for six months and was not offered the right to a jury trial.[7] Formerly institutions that warehoused mostly white offenders, prisons began teeming with black ex-slaves, many of whom were arrested under vagabond laws.[8] To meet the labor shortage once filled by enslaved workers and poor whites (many of whom perished in the Civil War), and to uphold an economic system built on racial domination, southern prisons introduced "convict leasing" programs, which forced prisoners to work for no pay. Once again, black men returned in shackles to the cotton fields, the swamps, and the roadsides, sometimes chained to white prisoners. Historians have found that prison labor camps were just as inhumane as were conditions under slavery. At Mississippi's Parchman Prison Farm, for instance, one out of every six prisoners died under the cruel work conditions; in fact, according to historian David Oshinsky, "not a single leased convict ever lived long enough to serve a sentence of ten years or more."[9] Such harsh conditions were remembered in Johnny Cash's song "Going to Memphis":

> Well I brought me a little water in a Mr. Prince Albert can;
> But the bossman caught me drinkin' it, and I believe he broke my hand;
> Another boy is down, the shovel burned him out;
> Let me stand on his body, to see what the shoutin's about.

The Prison Boom

As the twentieth century rumbled forward, lynching and racialized terrorism died down and convict labor was curtailed, mainly because of protests by unions, which could not compete with prisoners' cheap labor. Race relations in America were improving. Then Japanese fighter pilots bombed Pearl Harbor in 1941, causing prejudice and paranoia directed at Japanese Americans to boil over. Japanese Americans were seen as "the enemy within our borders," as spies and traitors. A year later, President Franklin D. Roosevelt ordered the internment of all Japanese Americans living on the Pacific Coast. In the years that followed, over 110,000 people of Japanese ancestry, most of them American citizens, were made to leave their communities and workplaces and to live in "exclusionary zones," which resembled modern-day refugee camps, often in desolate areas. Among the detained were over 30,000 children. According to one report from 1943, the internment camps were made of "tarpaper covered barracks of simple frame construction without plumbing or cooking facilities of any kind." In January 1945, the internment order was rescinded, and the Japanese American families held in

Juvenile convicts at work in the fields in a Southern chain gang.

the camps were given $25 and a bus ticket home. In the years that followed, the U.S. government would officially apologize for the policy, distributing over $1.6 billion in reparations to Japanese Americans who had suffered internment (or to their children).[10]

Internment camps were bulldozed. The chain gang, meanwhile, became a relic of yore. Lynching was criminalized. But the prison remained. In the 1970s, experts began to question incarceration as an effective way of fighting crime and reducing recidivism (repeat offending). A growing consensus among experts in the legal field was that more rehabilitative measures needed to be put in place—and that an effective anticrime strategy must attack the problem at its roots, focusing on social conditions that foster deviant behavior, such as poverty and institutional racism.[11] The prison was coming under strict criticism as an expensive, unhelpful, and inherently racist institution. It is curious, then, that during that same time, America's prison population did not shrink but grew—and by leaps and bounds. In fact, the rapid expansion of American incarceration, which began in the early 1970s and continues to this day, can only be described as a prison boom.

A Japanese American man speaks to fellow internees at a relocation camp in Puyallup, Washington.

The numbers are unprecedented. Between 1925 and 1975, the prison population remained the same, fluctuating between 100,000 and 200,000 prisoners. But around 1975, the prison population began to skyrocket and by 2000 had reached 1,400,000. From 1970 to 2003, moreover, the number of state and federal prisons did not double or triple or even quadruple; it grew *sevenfold* (see Figure 6.1). In 2003, over 7 million people—what amounts to the entire population of Switzerland—were under the supervision of the criminal justice system (on probation or parole, or in jail or prison).[12]

Although America does not suffer from higher crime rates than other industrialized countries, it was the only country to experience a prison boom of this magnitude. Between 1983 and 2001, the prison population in several other industrialized countries grew only marginally. The United Kingdom's prison population per 100,000 citizens increased from 87 to 126; in Italy it increased from 65 to 95; in Sweden from 65 to 68. In some countries, such as Germany, Denmark, and Austria, the prison population decreased. In the United States, however, the prison population grew from 275 per 100,000 citizens in 1983 to 686 per 100,000 in 2001. California alone houses more inmates than France, Great Britain, Germany, Japan, Singapore, and the Netherlands *combined*.[13] Today, with a prison population of almost 2.3 million, if one also includes people in county jails and juvenile detention (a rate of roughly 1 person per 135 behind bars), the United States incarcerates more of its citizens than any other nation on earth.[14] China has the second-highest number of people incarcerated (1.65 million). But compared to the United States' prison population, China's is smaller by roughly 650,000, even though its general population exceeds ours by more than 1 billion.[15]

FIGURE 6.1 INCARCERATION RATES

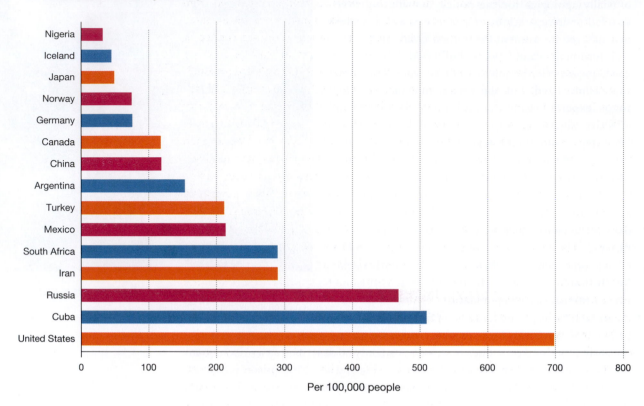

Incarceration Rates by Country

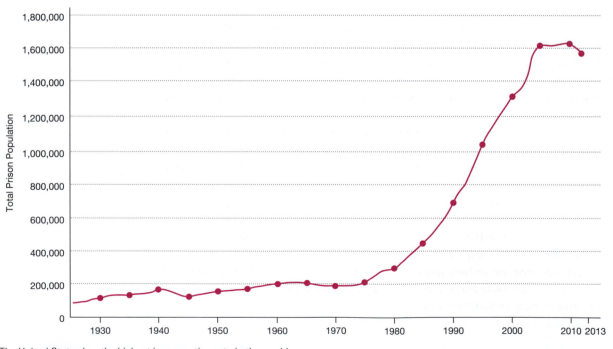

State and Federal Prison Population in the United States, 1925–2013

The United States has the highest incarceration rate in the world.

The Color of America's Incarcerated

By international standards, American women are incarcerated at a very steep rate. In fact, between 1980 and 2011, the number of women behind bars jumped from 15,118 to 111,387, a 587 percent increase! In 2011, black women were incarcerated at 2.5 times the rate of white women, and Hispanic women were incarcerated at 1.4 times the rate of white women. The majority of women in state prisons are mothers. One in twenty-five women is pregnant when admitted to a state prison.[16]

Although women are being incarcerated at historically high rates, they still account for only 6.7 percent of the nation's prison population.[17] The vast majority of those behind bars are men. Relative to other countries, America's white male population is incarcerated at a steep rate, one that exceeds the total incarceration rates of most industrialized countries. But the brunt of the prison boom has been borne by America's nonwhite male populations—specifically, by its poor, under-educated black and Hispanic men. Blacks and Hispanics account for approximately 25 percent of the U.S. population but 58 percent of all prisoners. Hispanic men are three times—and black men nearly eight times—more likely than white men to be in prison. If African Americans and Hispanics were incarcerated at the same rate as whites, America's prison and jail population would be cut in half. *One in six* black men has been incarcerated as of 2011.[18] For poor, young black men, the prison cell has become an all-too-familiar institution—just as familiar, in fact, as the college campus, the military base, or the factory floor.[19]

The imprisonment rate for young men of color who drop out of high school is especially high. In 1980, 2 percent of all white male dropouts between the ages of twenty and forty were in prison or jail; in 2000, that number jumped to 7 percent. For Hispanics, 3 percent of male high school dropouts between the ages of twenty and forty were in prison or jail in 1980, and 6 percent were incarcerated in 2000. For African Americans, the percent increase is breathtaking: In 1980, one of ten high school dropouts between the ages of twenty and forty was in jail or prison. In 2000, *one of three* black male dropouts that age was behind bars. The incarceration rate of young black men who dropped out of high school was nearly fifty times the national average.[20] The majority of all state prisoners—roughly 70 percent—have not finished high school.[21] According to a study by sociologist Becky Pettit, if you are a black man without a high school diploma, on any given day you have a higher likelihood of being in prison or jail than of working.[22]

By the end of the twentieth century, hundreds of thousands of America's poor had passed through the prison system. A white man born after World War II (that is, around 1945–1949) who later dropped out of high school had a 4 percent chance of serving time in prison sometime in his life; however, a white man born after the Civil Rights Movement (that is, around 1965–1969) who later dropped out of high school had an 11 percent chance of doing time. By contrast, a black man born after World War II who later dropped out of high school had a 17 percent chance of serving time in prison, whereas a black man born after the Civil Rights Movement who later dropped out of high school had nothing short of a 60 percent chance of being locked up at some point in his life.[23] If these statistics have not alarmed you, we suggest you go back and read them again.

FIGURE 6.2 **LIFETIME LIKELIHOOD OF IMPRISONMENT**

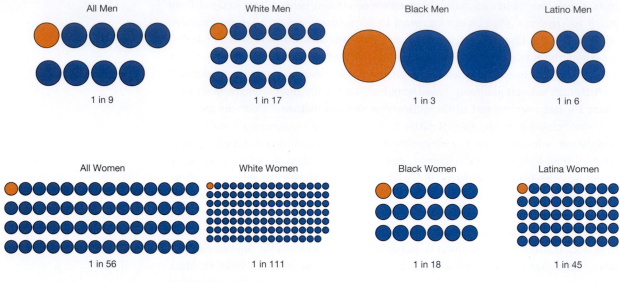

There are large racial disparities in America's prison population.

Severe Sentencing

Why did America's prison population multiply so quickly and by such an enormous measure? Rising crime rates certainly are part of the answer. Between 1965 and 1980, the homicide rate in America doubled before generally following a downward trend between 1981 and 2000.[24] However, most of the prison boom cannot be explained by rising crime rates. First, most people incarcerated during the prison boom were non-violent offenders (e.g., people who dealt drugs). Although there was a spike in murder rates after 1965, the prison boom is not a reflection of a significant increase of convicted murderers. Second, for the most part, overall crime rates remained the same, and even decreased, during the prison boom. America's youth from poor neighborhoods were not committing more crime in 2000 than they were in 1980. In a 1980 survey, 18.5 percent of poor white male teenagers and 17.5 percent of poor black teenagers confessed to having attacked someone with the intention of seriously injuring or killing them that year. In 2000, only 17 percent of poor white teenagers and 14 percent of poor black teenagers confessed to doing so. In the same way, people were stealing, selling drugs, and damaging property at lower rates in 2000 than in 1980 even though more people were being locked up in newly erected prisons.[25] And the chances of being murdered were far greater during several points in the nineteenth century than at the height of the prison boom. One study has concluded that only 12 percent of the rise of incarceration rates between 1980 and 1996 was driven by increases in the crime rate; the other 88 percent was caused by changes in sentencing policies.[26]

What changed during the prison boom was not so much the crime rate but the way crime was punished; namely, it was punished more harshly. Arrest rates climbed at a record pace, and sentences grew more severe. Although violent crime fell between 1990 and 2001, the chances a suspect would be arrested for a violent crime doubled. Between 1965 and 2001, drug arrests quadrupled, hitting black and Puerto Rican men especially hard. Does this mean that drug use increased between 1965 and 2001 and that black men were more likely to use and sell drugs? The evidence leads us to answer no to both questions. Between 1979 and 2000, drug use among young adults declined by 10 percent, and according to surveys of high school seniors, white students during this time reported using more drugs than black students. In fact, scholars who have analyzed emergency room records have discovered that, compared to blacks, whites were two to three times more likely to be rushed to the emergency room for drug-related problems.[27]

Not only did arrest rates, especially for drug-related offenses, shoot upward during the prison boom, but several other changes were put into effect to harshen criminal sentencing. Parole was limited severely or abolished entirely. Mandatory minimum sentences—including for those convicted of nonviolent crimes—were enforced. During the 1970s, several laws were passed attaching a life sentence to those found guilty of selling hard drugs, as well as to those possessing more than an ounce of cocaine or heroin. Draconian sentencing policies continued through the 1990s, most notably with three-strikes laws. Three-strikes laws intensified punishment for repeat offenses, with many such laws imposing a life sentence for the third offense. California's 1994 three-strikes law doubled the sentence for the second offense and mandated life in prison for the third, even for nonviolent crimes such as minor fraud and drug possession. By 2000, twenty-four states had adopted three-strikes laws similar to California's.[28] Why did criminal sentencing take such a mean turn? The answer lies in the rise of the "law and order" politician.

The Rise of the "Law and Order" Politician

Opinion polls from the mid-1960s show that most Americans did not list crime as among the nation's most pressing concerns. The Vietnam War and civil rights were what occupied most Americans' minds at the time. Nevertheless, the Republican Party, beginning with Barry Goldwater's 1964 presidential bid, started to focus on crime as a central issue. "Tonight there is violence in our streets," Goldwater boomed during his acceptance speech as the Republican nominee. "History shows us that nothing prepares the way for tyranny more than the failure of public officials to keep the streets safe from bullies and marauders."[29] Although Goldwater was defeated, he planted a seed among Republicans, a seed that would soon blossom into a new kind of politics.

Richard Nixon launched a "war on crime" to protect Americans from those who "increasingly threaten our cities, our homes, and our lives." Ronald Reagan followed by initiating a "war on drugs," introducing harsher penalties for those found guilty of possessing and selling drugs. And George H. W. Bush won the White House after exposing his opponent, Michael Dukakis, as "soft on crime," marshaling the infamous Willie Horton case to drive home his point. Republicans governed states with the steepest growth in prison populations. To take but one example: when Republican John Ashcroft was governor of Missouri between 1985 and 1993, the state's prison population increased by 80 percent. Ashcroft slashed state services by over $1 billion, while allocating over $100 million to new prison construction.[30]

FIGURE 6.3 DRUG ARREST RATE VS. REPORTED DRUG USE

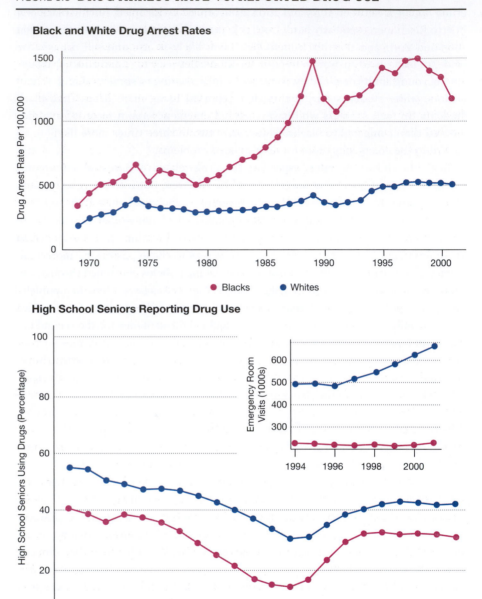

Black and White Drug Arrest Rates

High School Seniors Reporting Drug Use

African Americans report lower drug use than white Americans, but are far more likely to be arrested for drug crimes.

Rapidly, the terms of political debate were altered in such a way that "tough on crime" stances, which called for repressive punishments, were counterposed to more rehabilitative stances, which focused on the root causes of crime. In fact, many conservative politicians argued that social welfare programs actually helped to cause crime.

"The solution to the crime problem," Nixon would declare, "is not the quadrupling of funds for any governmental war on poverty but more convictions."[31] America's concern with rehabilitation and the war on poverty became eclipsed by a war on crime and an ardent pursuit of punitive measures. Once this frame took root in public thought and debate, it became virtually impossible for candidates—Democrats included—to get elected to public office without promising to crack down on crime. President Clinton became an avid supporter of three-strikes laws, and his Violent Crime Control and Law Enforcement Act of 1994 allocated nearly $10 billion for the construction of new prisons and mandated life sentences for third-time offenders.[32]

Prisons have transformed regional economies by employing thousands of correctional officers, wardens, and other workers. They also have expanded America's cheap labor force, as inmates are put to work at third world wages, making everything from clothing to be sold at Nordstrom department stores to graduation caps and gowns.[33] Indeed, entire prisons now are operated by private companies. Although the government operates most prisons, private prisons have been on the rise since the mid-1980s. Today, over half the states rely on for-profit prisons, where roughly 128,000 inmates are housed each year.[34]

More than any other set of policies, those introduced by the war on drugs helped to fuel the prison boom and wreak devastation on African American communities. Between 1981 and 2001, national drug control spending increased from less than $2 billion to over $18 billion. More and more police officers were dispatched to poor, nonwhite communities to arrest street-level dope slingers—despite the fact that drug use declined during the 1980s and nonwhites were not using drugs at drastically higher rates than whites. Thousands of young nonwhites from poor communities were arrested for drug-related offenses. Law enforcement officers targeted ghetto neighborhoods for a number of reasons, including because their drug transactions often took place in public areas—street corners, parks—and were easier to spot than drug transactions in more affluent neighborhoods, since these often occurred in private settings.

Nonwhite neighborhoods also were targeted because of America's established tradition of linking nonwhites with drug use. As Michael Tonry writes in *Malign Neglect*, "Through [the twentieth century] in periods of high intolerance of drug use, minority group stereotypes have been associated with deviant drug use. Early in this century, even though mainstream women were the model category of opiate users, Chinese opium smokers and opium dens were among the images invoked by opponents of drug use. . . . In the 1920s, it was blacks and cocaine. In the 1930s, images of Mexicans and marijuana were prominent in the antimarijuana movements that culminated in the Marijuana Tax Act of 1937 and the many states prohibiting marijuana use. In the antidrug hysteria of the 1980s, crack cocaine, the emblematic drug of the latest 'war,' is associated in public imagery with disadvantaged minority residents of the inner cities."[35]

Repressing the Civil Rights Movement

Why did politicians focus on crime as the main problem plaguing America when most Americans did not view it as a major problem? And why did the focus on crime resonate with so many Americans once it was introduced? The answer to both of these questions lies in part with the white backlash against the Civil Rights

Movement. It is no coincidence that the prison boom began shortly after the main thrust of the Civil Rights Movement came to an end. In fact, the former fact helps explain the latter.

Often, when politicians mentioned "violence in the streets," they were not speaking of mugging and assault (which had not increased dramatically), but were using coded language to decry civil disobedience tactics of civil rights activists. Since the beginning of the Civil Rights Movement, politicians criticized protesters as "criminals," "hoodlums," and "troublemakers."[36] In a real sense, such labels were accurate, for activists often got their point across by breaking laws, such as by refusing to follow segregation regulations. By dismantling racist systems that had structured American society for years, the Civil Rights Movement made many whites uneasy. This unease intensified as legalized racial segregation fell, causing whites to cross paths more frequently with nonwhites, and peaked during the racial uprisings of the late 1960s. Unlike many African Americans, most white Americans did not understand the uprisings as political acts against demoralizing ghetto conditions, but as criminal acts of vandalism and violence.[37] As a result, when politicians began speaking against crime in the streets, many whites knew precisely to what they were referring and endorsed platforms promising to "punish criminals" and "restore order to our troubled society."

Many racial uprisings began as a response to police brutality and unfair treatment, and the police responded in kind. Expenditures for "riot control" and domestic surveillance programs expanded once the uprisings got underway. Studies have shown that during the 1970s, police funding increased dramatically in cities with large black populations and in those that had hosted major uprisings and strongly supported the Civil Rights Movement.[38] To suppress the uprisings, law enforcement officers began to treat poor, black communities as "danger zones," subjecting those neighborhoods to a high level of surveillance. However, after the riots were quelled, police presence did not die down, but remained steady and even increased. Instead of arresting rioters, police officers began arresting *potential* rioters: young black men.[39]

Perhaps the primary, if unspoken, intent of law and order policies was to repress the Civil Rights Movement, especially potential rioters. On that score, these policies had their desired effect. As for their more overt motives—to decrease crime and the distribution of drugs—law and order policies had a more marginal effect.[40] The war on crime and on drugs, it seems, defeated something—but not criminal activity or drug trafficking.

FEAR

Although crime rates fell during the 1990s, six out of ten Americans believed they were rising. And although drug use dropped among high school students during that decade, most Americans listed drugs as the greatest danger threatening the country's youth. And with a rampant fear of crime came a call for harsher penalties. According to a national survey, 85 percent of Americans feel that current sentencing guidelines do not deal "harshly enough with criminals," and 70 percent feel that the country should spend more money on the crime problem.[41] In 1998, four in ten Americans reported they would be afraid to walk by themselves within

A man backs away as law enforcement officials close in on him during protests over the death of Michael Brown in Ferguson, Missouri.

a mile radius of their home. In 2010, that rate was still four in ten, even though violent crime had fallen steadily in the intervening years.[42] This section explores some of the causes and consequences of America's fear of crime, analyzing how these fears are informed by race and, by marshaling recent social-scientific evidence, holding these fears up to the light of rational assessment.

Criminalizing Darkness

Numerous studies have shown that one's fear of crime is strongly connected to one's racial identity, one's racial attitudes, and the racial makeup of one's neighborhood. After surveying undergraduate students at two Midwestern universities, one criminologist concluded that, compared to their nonwhite counterparts, white students were more likely to list crime among the nation's most serious problems and to fear being victimized by a crime.[43] And time and again, studies have produced convincing evidence of a robust link between the proportion of blacks and Hispanics in a neighborhood and fear of crime.[44] In fact, social scientists have found that the racial composition of a neighborhood—as well as the perceived composition of a neighborhood (that is, how many nonwhites people think live nearby, regardless of how many actually do)—are more powerful predictors of one's fear of crime than actual crime rates.

After comparing neighborhoods with identical crime rates, sociologists Lincoln Quillian and Devah Pager concluded that people who live in areas with a higher proportion of young black men think their neighborhood is plagued with more crime than those who live in majority-white areas.[45] Another study demonstrated that whites living in a multicultural section of the country and Hispanics living in a predominantly white section are more likely to fear being victimized by a crime when they think blacks and Hispanics live nearby.[46] This study reminds us that a racialized fear of crime does not affect whites alone. Members belonging to racial groups feared by the larger white society can adopt the attitudes of their host society and come to fear members of their own group.

Besides America's racial history, what explains these fears? The media is a popular answer—and for good reason. When asked why they felt America had a crime problem, over 75 percent of survey respondents referred to stories they had seen in the media. Between 1990 and 1998, America's murder rate fell by 20 percent, but during this time, the number of stories about murder airing on network newscasts increased by 600 percent.[47] And although young black men are far more likely to be victims of murder than members of other groups are, the media focused a disproportionate amount of attention on white and female victims.[48]

Although the media certainly bear some responsibility for promoting a fear of blacks and Hispanics, the media also have played a large role in debunking such fears. What is more, the media are in the business of spreading all kinds of fears (the obesity epidemic, deadly bacteria strains, poisoned Halloween candy), but only a handful stick.[49] Why are some fears fleeting while others are stubbornly durable? Mary Douglas, the British anthropologist, points out that all societies have at their disposal a vast array of threats on which to focus, and in most cases, the threats to which a society directs its attention do not necessarily carry the highest degree of objective danger. (After all, Americans wring their hands over avian flu, which has killed a total of zero Americans, but worry little about the common flu, which kills an average of 36,000 Americans each year—so little, in fact, that many forget to get their annual vaccination.)[50] Certain threats are overlooked, while others receive a great deal of attention, either because they offend the fundamental values of society or because they facilitate the continued stigmatization and exclusion of marginalized groups.[51] The fear of being victimized by nonwhite men fulfills both those requirements.

The stigmatizing of Hispanics and, especially, of blacks as criminals is deeply entrenched in America's collective consciousness, so much so that Americans' fear of crime has more to do with *blackness* than with crime itself. Survey data have shown that Americans, whites and nonwhites alike, believe blacks to be more prone to violence than nonblacks.[52] Because Americans so often comprehend crime through blackness, and blackness through crime, blackness, as conceived by nonblack America, is in a sense itself a crime—not in the metaphorical sense but in the very literal sense of something that "offends strong and definite states of the collective conscience," to borrow Émile Durkheim's definition.[53] Richard Wright, the great American novelist, understood this. Of America's black men, the novelist wrote, "Excluded from, and unassimilated in our society . . . every sunrise and sunset makes him guilty of subversive actions. Every movement of his body an unconscious protest. . . . Every glance of the eye is a threat. *His very existence is a crime against the state!*"[54]

Might this help explain why many whites, especially those who harbor anti-black and anti-Hispanic prejudices, are avid supporters of law and order policies? Compared to their nonwhite peers, white undergraduates are more likely to support harsher punishments for criminals. According to one study, only half of white students felt that rehabilitation should be a main goal of the criminal justice system, but two-thirds of nonwhite students felt this way. The same study reported that 50 percent of white students support the death penalty, whereas only 29 percent of their nonwhite peers do.[55] And several studies have concluded that, as whites' interpersonal racism against blacks and Hispanics grows, so too does their support of punitive policies. Holding constant other important measures, whites' prejudice has been linked to their support of the death penalty, excessive force used by police officers, longer prison sentences, warrantless searches of young men of color, and spending tax dollars to fight crime.[56]

Do Immigrants Increase Crime?

On the morning of April 16, 2007, students at Virginia Tech awoke to the sound of gunfire. Seung-Hui Cho, a twenty-three-year-old English major armed with a .22-caliber semiautomatic handgun and a 9-millimeter Glock, marched onto campus and began a shooting rampage. When it was over, thirty-three people lay dead, as did Cho, having committed suicide as the police approached. So far, this massacre is the deadliest school shooting in American history.[57]

Almost six years later to the day, on April 15, 2013, two homemade bombs exploded near the finish line of the Boston Marathon, killing three people and injuring over 260 others. Two Chechen immigrants, Dzhokhar and Tamerlan Tsarnaev, were identified as the bombing suspects. While on the run, the brothers allegedly killed one police officer and injured another in a shootout that left Tamerlan dead. Dzhokhar, twenty years old, would be found and arrested the next day.

Most school shootings in the United States are carried out by young white men, as are many acts of domestic terrorism (e.g., the Oklahoma City Bombing and lynchings by the KKK). But in the aftermath of the Virginia Tech shooting and the Boston Marathon bombings, some Americans attempted to make sense of these seemingly senseless events by focusing not only on Cho's or the Tsarnaev brothers' access to firearms and explosives or their mental state but also on their immigrant status. Some conservative politicians reacted to the Boston Marathon bombings by calling for a freeze on immigration reform.[58] And after the Virginia Tech massacre, some observers noted that Cho had emigrated from South Korea at the age of eight and asked, "Would the Virginia Tech killings have occurred if America's immigration laws were stricter?" Patrick Buchanan, a conservative spokesperson, drew a direct connection between the Virginia Tech shooting and immigration: "Cho was among the 864,000 Koreans here as a result of the Immigration Act of 1965, which threw the nation's doors open to the greatest invasion in history, an invasion opposed by a majority of our people. Thirty-six million, almost all from countries whose peoples have never fully assimilated in any Western country, now live in our midst. Cho was one of them. . . . What happened in Blacksburg [Virginia] cannot be divorced from what's been happening to America since the immigration act brought tens of millions of strangers to these shores, even as the old bonds of national community began to disintegrate and dissolve in the social revolutions of the 1960s. 'In our diversity is our strength!' So we are endlessly lectured. But are we really a better, safer, freer, happier, more united and caring country than before, against our will, we became what Theodore Roosevelt called 'a polyglot boarding house for the world'[?]"[59]

Although Buchanan's views are extreme, they resonate with a question that Americans have been asking for over a century: Do immigrants make the country less safe? Many seem to think so. According to a recent poll, 73 percent of Americans believe that immigrants are "somewhat" or "very likely" to increase crime.[60] President George W. Bush, considered liberal on issues of immigration by his Republican peers, declared in a 2006 speech that illegal immigration "strains state and local budgets and brings crime to our communities."[61]

Just as they helped to create a "crime problem," politicians recently have fashioned an "immigration problem," intensifying anti-immigrant sentiment that disproportionately targets those from Latin American, Asian, and Middle Eastern countries. Driven by the "tough on crime" logic applied to the criminal justice system, U.S. immigration policies have grown more punitive in recent years. Social rights and benefits have been withdrawn from undocumented immigrants, and immigration authorities have relied more heavily on the use of detention, just as juridical authorities increased their dependence on incarceration. Immigration raids, detentions, and deportations increased sixfold between 2000 and 2010.[62] President Obama has deported more undocumented immigrants than any other president. Over 2 million people have been deported under this administration—more than all deportations prior to 1997.[63] Some of the most extreme immigrant raids have taken place in southwestern cities. In 2008, for example, Maricopa County sheriffs, along with volunteer members of the sheriffs' "posse," carried out high-profile immigrant raids in Phoenix and its neighboring townships, arresting dozens of people at their homes and workplaces. One raid began at 2 A.M., when strike force members, armed with semiautomatic weapons and police dogs, stormed local businesses and government buildings, including the public library and the City Hall of Mesa, Arizona, looking for undocumented immigrants working as janitors.[64]

Punishments for violating immigration law have grown more severe. The 1996 Anti-Terrorism and Effective Death Penalty Act broadened the list of criminal acts that warranted deportation for noncitizens; the 1996 Welfare Reform Act denied even legal immigrants many public benefits; and the 2001 PATRIOT Act, discussed in detail in the ensuing section, denied noncitizens many basic civil rights. Today, those who reenter the United States after being deported are subject to two years' imprisonment, those who reenter after being deported for breaking the law are subject to ten years in prison, and those who have been convicted of an aggravated felony who reenter after being deported can be imprisoned for twenty years.[65]

Many of these policy shifts have been driven by the fear that immigrants, documented and undocumented, increase America's crime rate. However, social-scientific research has arrived at the opposite conclusion, finding that immigrants make America safer. After searching through homicide records in cities with large immigrant populations, criminologist Ramiro Martinez found that border cities, such as El Paso and San Diego, are some of the safest metropolitan areas in the country. Despite their high levels of poverty, many immigrant communities in large cities—Haitian neighborhoods in Miami, Mexican barrios in Houston—have strikingly low crime rates.[66] Other studies have found that cities that experienced the largest increases in immigration between 1990 and 2000 experienced the largest decreases in violent crime during that time and that urban neighborhoods with a higher proportion of immigrants had lower crime rates after controlling for poverty.[67]

FIGURE 6.4 IMMIGRATION RATES AND HOMICIDE TRENDS

U.S Totals in 3-Year Averages

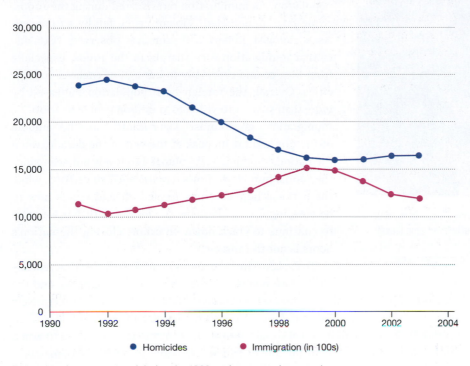

● Homicides   ● Immigration (in 100s)

As immigration rates soared during the 1990s, crime rates plummeted.

It is true that violence in Mexico has increased in recent years. Gangs and violent crime plague some border communities. But the problem of powerful drug cartels and escalating violence in Mexico is distinct from the question of the relationship between crime and immigration in the United States. Although violence sometimes spills over the border, much of it remains in Mexico. The majority of immigrants to the United States are not working for drug cartels, but are striking out in search of new opportunities for themselves and their children. In fact, recent studies have concluded that youth of Mexican descent commit far less violent crime than do white or black youth, and analysts have attributed this gap to immigrants from Mexico. One study found that first-generation immigrants (that is, immigrants who were born in another country and who came to the United States) were 45 percent less likely to participate in a violent crime than were third-generation Americans (those born in the United States to parents who are U.S. citizens). Comparing immigrants to whites and blacks of similar class backgrounds, researchers also found that immigrants are less likely to participate in many different kinds of criminal behavior, from gang fights and selling drugs to arson and mugging. In fact, those who live in immigrant neighborhoods, regardless of racial identity or immigrant status, are less likely to commit crimes than those who do not.[68]

Smugglers frequently use cars to bring illegal immigrants into the U.S. because of increased efforts to stop illegal crossings on foot.

Noting these trends, some social scientists have argued that a sizable proportion of the crime drop that occurred in the 1990s can be attributed to the swelling immigrant population. As immigration rates soared during the 1990s, crime rates plummeted. Violent crime fell by 57 percent. As sociologist Robert Sampson has observed, "Consider that immigration rose sharply in the 1990s, especially from Mexico and especially to immigrant enclaves in large cities. Overall, the foreign-born population increased by more than 50% in 10 years, to 31 million people in 2000.... Immigration grew most significantly in the middle of the 90s and hit its peak at the end of the decade, when the national homicide rate plunged to levels not seen since the 1960s. Immigrant flows have receded since 2001, while the national homicide rate leveled off and seems now to be creeping up. . . . Perhaps the lesson is that if we want to continue to crack down on crime, closing the nation's doors is not the answer."[69]

To explain why immigrants commit so little crime, sociologists have pointed to their high rates of marriage and the presence of professionals in immigrant neighborhoods, as both factors are negatively associated with crime. They also have observed that immigrant neighborhoods often operate under a code of informal social control, which encourages neighbors to watch out for one another and to be mindful of criminal activity.[70] In other words, members of immigrant neighborhoods have accepted as part of their civic duty the shared task of keeping their sidewalks safe. By casting "eyes upon the street," immigrants participate in what Jane Jacobs believed to be the best strategy for upholding safety in an urban environment. "The first thing to understand," wrote Jacobs, "is that the public peace—the sidewalk and street peace—of cities is not kept primarily by the police, necessary as police are. It is kept primarily by an intricate, almost unconscious, network of voluntary controls and standards among the people themselves, and enforced by the people themselves."[71]

Since so much evidence points to the conclusion that immigrants, documented and undocumented, make America safer, one must wonder why so many Americans fear an "immigrant invasion" and why politicians continue to draft laws designed to make immigrants' lives harder. Like blackness, foreignness (and ethnic markers connected to foreignness, such as speaking Spanish) has become intertwined with our notions of criminality, so much so that immigration itself is conceived as a criminal act, as something that offends the American consciousness. It is small wonder, then, that just as antiblack and anti-Hispanic prejudices are strongly associated with one's support of punitive policies, interpersonal racism directed at nonwhites, and at Mexicans in particular, is strongly associated with anti-immigration policies.[72]

The Arabization of Terrorism

America, like many countries, has been the victim of numerous terrorist attacks. In 1993, terrorists attacked the World Trade Center, killing 6 people and wounding

1,000 more; in 1995, terrorists bombed the Federal Building in Oklahoma City, killing 168 people; and in 1998, the U.S. embassies in Kenya and Tanzania were firebombed, leaving 4,000 injured and over 200 dead. But for many Americans, the threat of terrorism became much more imminent and terrifying after the attacks on September 11, 2001, which sent the twin towers of the World Trade Center crashing to the ground in a cloud of grey ash and smoke. Nearly 3,000 people lost their lives, including 343 firefighters and 23 police officers.[73]

Anyone who has watched the footage of the September 11 attacks knows that terrorism is something to fear. The terrorists' prime objective, after all, is to draw blood. And immediately after the events, fear coursed quickly through the American body politic.[74] Arab Americans suffered from a double helping of fear, because not only did they join all Americans in worrying about repeat attacks; they also dreaded repression from the American government as well as assaults from their fellow non-Arab citizens. Their fears were justified.

In the weeks following the attacks, men and women of Arab descent—as well as those perceived to be Arabs (Indian American Hindu Sikhs, for example)—were victims of workplace discrimination, racist threats, assaults, and even murder. In 2001, the FBI reported that crimes directed at Muslims increased seventeenfold, while Arab groups registered over 2,000 events where Americans lashed out at "Arab-looking" people after September 11. The American-Arab Antidiscrimination Committee reported that in the nine weeks after September 11, over 700 violent attacks directed at Arab Americans took place. Of those events, 66 percent involved physical or psychological attacks, 27 percent consisted of acts of arson or vandalism, 22 percent included hate mail and bomb threats, 16 percent were beatings, and 1 percent entailed hate-motivated murder. (Many of the 700 total attacks included more than one of these elements, which is why the percentages add up to more than 100.) There was, for instance, Mark Stoman of Dallas, who walked into a line of convenience stores and shot clerks from Pakistan, India, and Bangladesh. There was James Herrick of Salt Lake City, who set ablaze a Pakistani restaurant. There was Patrick Cunningham of Seattle, who opened fire on people worshipping in a mosque.[75] In the weeks following September 11, America was not safe for its Arab citizens.

Despite these violent outbursts, many Americans, according to opinion poll data, viewed Arab Americans with a fair degree of tolerance and understanding, acknowledging that an entire group of people could not be blamed for the actions of a few wrapped in similar-looking skin who lived on the opposite end of the earth. And many continue actively to deny anti-Arab prejudice: 51 percent have "favorable" views of Muslim Americans, and as many as 80 percent believe that "Arab-Americans, Muslims, and immigrants from the Middle East are being singled out unfairly by people in this country."[76] However, in the months and years following September 11, non-Arab Americans' interpersonal racism toward Arab

In a very real sense, Arab Americans are invisible in discussions of the "war on terrorism."

Americans grew, and today, the average American is more likely to harbor anti-Arab prejudices than in 2001. According to recent polls, 25 percent of Americans harbor "unfavorable" views of Muslim Americans; 33 percent believe that Arab Americans are "more sympathetic to terrorists"; and 44 percent confess to having less trust in Arab Americans after September 11. These views break down sharply along political lines. According to a 2012 poll, 48 percent of Republicans harbor "unfavorable" views toward Arab Americans, compared to 20 percent of Democrats.[77]

For a good number of Americans, the face of a "terrorist" is the face of an Arab, and that anti-Arab prejudice has risen since the September 11 attacks. Why did anti-Arab prejudice increase, rather than decrease, in the months following the attacks? The answer lies in the ways Arabs have been depicted in the political field as well as in the press. The categories of Arab, Muslim, and Middle Eastern have been rendered synonymous, a maneuver that overlooks the fact that most Muslims around the world are neither Arab nor Middle Eastern (but reside in Southeast Asia) and that flattens the historical and cultural differences between Middle Easterners who do not consider themselves Arab (such as Turks or Persians) and Middle Easterners who do (such as Palestinians).[78] Scholars have concluded that Arabs often are portrayed in films as bestial, violent villains. One study analyzed more than 900 films and found that, with few exceptions, Arabs were represented as "Public Enemy #1—as brutal, heartless, uncivilized religious fanatics and as money-mad cultural 'others' bent on terrorizing civilized Westerners, especially Christians and Jews."[79] And politicians, for their part, often saddle Arabs with negative qualities.[80]

As a result, since September 11 a bipolar discursive frame has calcified, one that pits America against "the Arab world." Positive qualities are attached to the American side of the frame, while negative characteristics are assigned to the Arab side. In fact, in this polarized way of thinking, the positive qualities are set against (and gain their essence from) their mirror images, such that if the Arab world is violent, America is peaceful; if the Arab world is irrational, America is rational; if "they" are freedom-hating, "we" are freedom-loving.[81] Where, then, do Arab Americans fall in this schema? Are they "we" or "they"? In a very real sense, Arab Americans are invisible in discussions of the "war on terrorism." One hears much of Americans and much of Arabs, but very little attention has been devoted to the nation's 3 million Arab American citizens.[82] Because of this—and because racial identities are so powerful that they often trump other identities (such as those based on nationality)—Arab Americans often are stripped of their "Americanness" and associated with the Arab/terrorist side of the bipolar discursive frame.[83]

One final thought deserves mention. Today, Americans are told that the events of September 11 constitute the first time in history that a terrorist attack of that magnitude was visited upon American soil. Having surveyed the history of racial domination in America, we know better. America's indigenous peoples were brought mercilessly under the heel of Western colonizing forces. The Mexican Repatriation Programs could accurately be classified as organized kidnapping. Black America has been plagued by a most brutal and bloody terrorism, which has included the Middle Passage, slavery, and lynch mobs. The Ku Klux Klan resembles a terrorist organization much as al-Qaeda does. Post-September 11 America is set apart not by the *presence* of terrorism but by the *victims* of it. As applied to modern times, the term "age of terror" is historically inaccurate, for terrorism in America is anything but a modern development.[84] Perhaps the African American comedian Earthquake put it best when he remarked, "Many people wonder why I'm not tripping after the terrorist attacks in New York and D.C. I'm a niggah—I've been dealing with terrorists all my life!"[85]

CRIME

Having reviewed racialized fear of crime in America, we turn now to examining crime itself. We begin by discussing drug trafficking and street gangs. We then examine offenses often overlooked in public discussions of crime: white-collar crimes and crimes of corporations. Finally, we turn our attention to more violent crimes, including violence against women and homicide. Along the way, we offer explanations for crime by employing, as always, sociological analysis grounded in current research.

Drug Trafficking

The combined forms of enterprise classified as criminal under current law can be said to constitute the underground economy. By some estimates, each year four out of five Americans buy something through the underground economy.[86] Without a doubt, the largest and highest-yielding industry within the underground economy is the drug trade. It is estimated that illegal drugs account for roughly 8 percent of worldwide trade, grossing between $300 billion and $400 billion every year, more than the combined global revenues of textiles, clothing, iron, and steel.[87]

According to the *National Survey on Drug Use and Health*, in 2012 about 24 million Americans over the age of twelve used drugs each month. Of those, 62.8 percent smoked marijuana, and 20 percent took painkillers. An additional 1.6 million people used cocaine, 1.1 million took hallucinogens, and roughly 670,000 shot heroin into their veins. American Indians had the highest rates of drug use, with 12.7 percent using drugs at least once a month. Blacks and whites had the second-highest rate (11.3 percent and 9.2 percent), followed by Hispanics (8.3 percent) and Asian Americans (3.7 percent).[88]

Many Americans associate drug trafficking with urban street gangs, the members of which are vital players in the underground economy. Because many gangs are based in racially segregated urban neighborhoods, they mobilize race as a principle for forming group boundaries and identities. Across America, one can find white gangs (including skinheads and biker gangs), black gangs (including those that gained wide recognition in the 1980s, such as Los Angeles's Bloods and Crips), Latino gangs (including Chicago's Latin Kings), Asian gangs (including the Chinese Mafia), and others. Modern cities are populated with equal numbers of black and white gangs.[89] Because immigrant youth often rely on gangs as avenues through which to carve out an American identity, we also find gangs in immigrant enclaves, including Salvadoran enclaves in San Fernando, Vietnamese communities in Southern California, the Kurdish section of Nashville, and the Italian and Irish sections of New York City.[90]

There are a number of reasons why people join gangs. For some, like the sons and daughters of immigrants, the gang is an institution in which they can ground their identity. For others, the gang offers economic opportunity, namely, through the drug trade. Most gangs, however, avoid the drug trade, as well as other entrepreneurial opportunities within the underground economy. For the most part, gang-driven drug trafficking operations are unorganized, small-scale ventures that rarely expand beyond the confines of a neighborhood.[91] Some also do not pay well. After combing the books of a Chicago drug gang, a pair of scholars discovered that the average low-level dope slinger worked approximately twenty hours a week for $200 a week, a pay rate below the federal minimum wage.[92]

Still, for impoverished ghetto residents, the underground economy offers a viable way to earn a living, however meager, where few opportunities exist. Just as down-and-out Irish, Italian, and Jewish immigrants of the early twentieth century sold drugs and bootlegged alcohol to get by, some of today's most marginalized citizens earn a buck the same way.[93] The underground drug economy provides economic livelihood in the desolate ghetto, an area abandoned by steady jobs and disowned by state services, and enables its employees to avoid the tedious (and often humiliating) work found in the licit low-wage service sector.[94]

The American ghetto has created a form of economic activity—"hustling"—of which selling drugs and gang activity are only a small part. "The demands of the ghetto require an economy utterly different from what most of America can imagine," writes sociologist Sudhir Venkatesh in *Off the Books*. "The barber may rent his back room to a prostitute; the mechanic works out of an alley; the preacher gets donations from a gang leader; and everyone has a hand in keeping the streets tolerable and keeping the goods and services flowing. . . . With few well-paying full-time jobs available in the neighborhood and with access only to the most menial jobs elsewhere in the city, [the ghetto] resident may turn to hustling as a temporary means to keep food on the table, clothes on a child's back, and rent paid up."[95]

White-Collar Crime

Of course, illegal entrepreneurship is not specific to the ghetto. Technological crimes, such as computer hacking, fraud, identity theft, environmental law violations, tax evasion, bribery, counterfeiting, money laundering, and embezzling are found in affluent communities and wealthy corporations. Edwin Sutherland coined the term "white-collar crime" to refer to these illegal acts. "White collar crime," wrote Sutherland, is "crime committed by a person of respectability and high social status in the course of his occupation. . . . Persons of the upper socioeconomic class engage in much criminal behavior; [and] this criminal behavior differs from the criminal behavior of the lower socioeconomic class principally in the administrative procedures which are used in dealing with the offenders."[96] Sutherland advanced this definition to focus our attention on the upper echelons of the criminal world, illegal acts committed by more privileged members of society. Just as drug trafficking is not specific to the inner city, white-collar crime does not thrive only in the suburbs; however, because many white-collar crimes require a certain degree of expertise and education, most are committed by middle-class citizens. Relative to those who participate in street-level criminal behavior, white-collar criminals are three times more likely to have steady employment, five times more likely to own a home, and eight times more likely to have more than $10,000 in assets.[97]

White-collar crime has increased over the last thirty years. In 1970, crimes of fraud cost Americans around $5 billion; in 1990, they cost them around $100 billion.[98] It is estimated that the white-collar crime industry grosses between $300 billion and $660 billion each year, far outpacing revenue gleaned from America's street crime.[99] Most people arrested for white-collar crimes are white. In fact, Americans seem to associate white-collar crime with whites and street-level crime with blacks and Hispanics. In studies simulating decisions made by jurors, psychologists have found that people presented with different criminal scenarios are more likely to favor harsher sentences for whites convicted of embezzlement than blacks convicted of the same crime but are more likely to prefer the harsher sentence for blacks convicted of robbery than for whites convicted of the same crime.[100] In other words, when our categories dividing crimes of privilege from crimes of poverty correspond to our racial categories separating racially privileged from racially dominated groups, we are more likely to punish crimes we understand to be "racially typical."

Thinking about white-collar crime brings to mind various acts perpetrated in corporate America that, although they inflict harm, remain perfectly legal or do not result in stiff penalties. Financial crimes, for example, were committed in the lead-up to the financial collapse of 2008 and the Great Recession that followed—and those crimes still have not been prosecuted and punished. Corporations, meantime, have been allowed to dump toxic waste in some communities and to emit toxic pollutants that can cause serious diseases. Drug companies are allowed to market pills whose side effects include stroke and loss of breath, but the possession of marijuana can fetch a prison term. Our energies expended on worrying about the murderer lurking in the night might be better directed at evaluating our workplace conditions, since Americans are three times more likely to die of occupational hazards than of homicide. Indeed, every hour, two Americans will be killed by a murderer, whereas three will be slain by their job. Why, we might ask, is the corporate supervisor who, by ignoring safety precautions in the name of profit, directly is responsible for a mine caving in and killing ten men merely fined or fired, but the crazed man who guns down ten people in a shopping mall receives the death penalty? Both actions, after all, resulted in the death of ten innocent people. Is corporate oversight that results in deadly consequences that much different from first-degree homicide? No corporation intentionally desires to kill its workers, of course, but organizations that bypass safety regulations know full well they are playing with people's lives. Accordingly, is not the corporation's wager pitting profit against people akin to the murderer's intent of inflicting harm?[101]

We commit these questions to you. As you grapple with them, we encourage you to call into question criminalization processes and their relation to systems of economic exploitation and racial domination. There

Family and friends of the 29 men killed in the Upper Big Branch mine explosion view the granite monument in Whitesville, West Virginia.

is great power in the act of defining the crime, of labeling certain things criminal while overlooking others that are just as harmful. In recent years, social thinkers have documented the ascendancy of neoliberalism, a form of social organization in which the dynamics of the market are given priority over other concerns.[102] In a society governed by neoliberalism, all sorts of dehumanizing, harmful, and deadly acts can masquerade as legitimate or normal, hiding behind phrases such as "It's not personal; it's just business" or "the bottom line." Not everything that harms is criminalized.

Violence against Women

In recent years, Americans often have pointed out abuses against women in other countries (especially those in the Middle East, Africa, and parts of Asia), thereby giving the impression that women in the United States rarely are victimized by violence. Violence against women, however, is one of our nation's most pervasive crimes. Domestic abuse is among America's most common forms of violence. More than 6 million women are abused by their partners each year, and in some studies as many as one in four women report being recently beaten. Every day, three women are killed by their husbands or boyfriends.[103]

American women continue to be terrorized by rape. Over 600 women are raped each day. It is estimated that one in five women will be raped sometime in her life, and we have reason to believe that this ratio is underestimated, since as many as 60 percent of sexual assaults are not reported to the police. Almost half of all rape victims are assaulted before their eighteenth birthday.[104] College women especially are at risk, with 25 percent of all rapes taking place on college campuses. Far from being perpetrated by strangers, most rapes are committed by persons whom the victims know—their friends, boyfriends, husbands, or relatives.[105]

Although women throughout society suffer from violent attacks—and although researchers have found that, after accounting for income, race is not significantly correlated with rates of domestic abuse—poor women, immigrants, and women of color are victimized at disproportionately high rates.[106] Native American women are abused at twice the rate of black and white women. And between 40 percent and 60 percent of Asian women are beaten at some point during their lives. Compared to black women, white women are nearly twice as likely to be killed by an intimate partner; however, the leading cause of death for black women between the ages of fifteen and twenty-four is partner homicide.[107]

A woman's risk of partner abuse increases the more isolated she is from the wider society, and immigrant women are perhaps the most isolated in America. Often living thousands of miles away from their families, unfamiliar with American laws and customs, coping with limited English proficiency, and sometimes connected to their communities only through their husbands, abused immigrant women have few places to turn for help. (Indeed, some cultural traditions, like purdah—the strict segregation of the sexes that is observed in some immigrant and Muslim American communities and that, in some cases, inhibits women from leaving the house—further isolates immigrant women.) Many cannot seek help from their in-laws, who tend to side with the husband or, worse, to perpetrate violence themselves. Sociologist Margaret Abraham has observed that, in South Asian immigrant communities, older women are delegated the responsibility of "controlling young women."

As such, wives are sometimes abused not only by their husbands but also by their mothers-in-law and other relatives.[108]

If they are undocumented immigrants, women may refuse to report their abuse to the authorities, because they fear that doing so would lead to their deportation. Moreover, American immigration law helps to trap in abusive relationships women who come to the United States to marry. To guard against fraudulent marriages, where an immigrant marries a U.S. citizen or permanent resident only to obtain citizenship, the Immigration and Naturalization Service (INS) does not allow immigrants even to apply for permanent residency until they have been married for a minimum of two years. Although this stipulation is waived for women who can prove their husbands are abusing them, many immigrant women do not have access to the kind of evidence required by the INS, such as police affidavits or reports from social workers.[109] And some domestic violence shelters, for their part, make matters worse by turning away abused women who cannot speak English. The fact that many shelters are located in white neighborhoods makes it that much harder for immigrant women, many of whom do not have driver's licenses (let alone a car), to seek refuge there.[110]

Like immigrant women, many physically and sexually abused American women of color do not have equal access to protection or justice. As we learned earlier in this chapter, the widespread fear of the black male rapist with the white female victim has resulted in black men being looked on as violent threats. However, that same trope also has facilitated the systematic disregard for black female rape victims. Law scholars who have sifted through sentencing records have found that men who rape black women are punished less severely than those who victimize Latina and white women. One study that evaluated sentencing decisions for rape cases found that black men convicted of raping white women received the harshest sentences, while black men convicted of raping black women received the lightest. According to another study, while men, nonwhite and white alike, found guilty of raping Latina women served an average term of five years, and men convicted of raping white women served an average of ten years, men convicted of raping black women served an average sentence of only two years.[111] In these sentencing discrepancies, we observe the American racial hierarchy and the systematic devaluation of Latina and especially black women victims.

We notice this, too, in the heightened media coverage white victims of rape receive, especially if their assailant is black, as compared to the relatively skimpy coverage of black victims. We might ask, for example, why the brutal beating and rape of a white female jogger in New York City's Central Park allegedly by a group of young black men was national news, but the equally brutal gang rape of a young black woman who, in the same week, was assaulted on top of a four-story building before being thrown off the roof received little attention.[112] Moreover, even when cataloguing black-on-black violence, the media tend to highlight only the violence visited on black males and hence once again to overlook the abuses of black women.[113] This self-imposed blindness continues despite the fact that in a significant proportion of cases, the victims of young men convicted of homicide actually happen to be men who had beaten the assailants' mothers.[114]

Not only are black women victims devalued in the courts and ignored by the media; they often are silenced by other members of the black community. Because women are abused more often than not by those they know, most black women are victimized by black men, just as most white women are victimized by white men, and Asian women by Asian men. Accordingly, black women often are faced with a difficult decision after being raped or beaten: Should I speak out against my attacker and risk reinforcing the stereotype of violent black men, risk him being carted off by the police, or should I remain silent and risk being abused again, while my attacker goes unpunished? "In all of their lives in America," writes Nellie McKay, "black women have felt torn between the loyalties that bind them to race on the one hand, and sex on the other. Choosing one or the other, of course, means taking sides against the self, yet they have almost always chosen race over the other: a sacrifice of their self-hood as women and of full humanity, in favor of the race."[115] Such are the workings not only of physical violence but also of the symbolic violence of which we spoke in Chapter 1.

In many cases, when a black man is charged with violating a black woman, members of the black community rally around the black man under the banner of "racial solidarity"—or in the words of Katheryn Russell-Brown, "black protectionism"—drowning out the lone voice of the victim with shouts decrying racial biases in the criminal justice system.[116] When boxer Mike Tyson was accused of raping Desiree Washington, a young black woman, many prominent African Americans, eager to quash the "black male rapist" trope, rushed to Tyson's side. Although black men continue to be falsely accused of rape, black women are far more likely to be raped than black men are to come under false allegations. Why, then, did so few voice support for Washington or, beyond that, speak out against the systematic oppression of women of color?[117] Cornel West has argued that "the idea of black people closing ranks against hostile white Americans reinforces black male power exercised over black women . . . in order to preserve the black social order under circumstances of quite literal attack and symbolic assault."[118]

Homicide

Although the United States' crime rate is not dramatically higher than that of other industrialized countries, its murder rate is. Between 16,000 and 17,000 Americans are murdered each year—that's around forty-five murders every day.[119] Russia and Brazil have higher murder rates, as do Mexico and Estonia, but when it comes to murder, the United States beats out almost all other developed nations. In fact, when it comes to gun-related murder, the United States tops the list of developed countries. Switzerland and Turkey are tied for third on the list. But the United States has four times as many gun-related homicides per capita as Switzerland and Turkey.[120]

When we compare murder victimization rates by race, the differences are unsettling. Between 1980 and 2008, victimization rates for white adults (between the ages of twenty-five and forty-four) decreased steadily. By 2008, the victimization ratio per 100,000 people was 4.5 for whites. That rate was 27.8 per 100,000 for African American adults, whose victimization rates decreased in the early 1980s, increased between 1985 and 1993, and decreased thereafter until 2003, when they began to rise again.[121]

Comparisons among young people (ages ten through twenty-four) reveal even starker differences. Today, roughly 3 white male youth per 100,000 are murdered; the same is true of Asian American male youth. That ratio is 13.5 per 100,000 for Hispanic male youth, and 18 per 100,000 for Native American male youth. The homicide rate for black male youth, however, towers over that of all other groups.

Almost 52 black male youth in 100,000 are murdered every year.[122] In other words, black male youth are over 17 times more likely to be murdered than white or Asian male youth; 3.8 times more likely than Hispanic male youth; and 2.8 times more likely than Native American male youth. Murder is the leading cause of death among black male youth.[123] According to one study, "the murder rate for black men is double that of American soldiers in World War II."[124] Why?

Memorial mural to a dead friend on the Lower East Side of New York City.

Popular answers abound. Many people fear that violence in the media—on television, music, and video games—is directly linked to murder rates. They have good reason to be concerned. By the age of eighteen, the average American has viewed over 40,000 murders acted out on the television screen. But she also has been exposed to an equal number of kind and generous acts, as sitcom and movie characters constantly are involved in good deeds. Given this, shall we argue that the media encourage acts of benevolence? There is not much evidence that media violence causes actual violence. Nor can blood-soaked television or video games help explain racial disparities in murder rates (since there is no reason to believe that black youth watch more violent programming than nonblack youth) or, for that matter, the much higher homicide rate in the United States as compared with other countries, which air equally violent movies and television shows.[125]

Perhaps our answer lies in the fact that Americans own roughly a quarter of a *billion* guns and have more guns stolen each year (around 300,000) than many other industrialized countries have gun owners.[126] With the introduction of semiautomatic and automatic weapons, as well as high-caliber bullets, guns have grown more deadly in recent years, and firearm dealers are found in every corner of the nation. In fact, America, a nation of automobiles, has more licensed firearm dealers than gas stations.[127] There is little doubt that America's homicide rate would be lower if its citizens were not so well armed. In seven out of ten homicides, guns are used as the murder weapon, and 70 percent of victims are killed by a single gunshot, which suggests that had the murderer been forced to use a less lethal weapon, many victims still would be alive today. The proliferation of guns might help explain why America's murder rate is high by international standards, but because there is little reason to believe that guns are more prevalent in black neighborhoods, access to firearms does little to explain racial disparities in murder rates.[128]

To understand why black youth fall victim to murder at such high rates, social scientists convincingly have shown that we must examine the brutal inequalities and overlapping hardships that define the African American ghetto. The evidence points to a single, clear conclusion: violent crime thrives in neighborhoods wracked by compounding structural disadvantages. What matters is not so much individual-level disadvantage—we gain little by comparing one poor individual with another, or one individual from a broken home with another—but structural disadvantage observed at the neighborhood level.[129] Structural disadvantage refers to the concentrated accumulation of overlapping and mutually reinforcing social problems in a single residential area. These problems include a disproportionate number of jobless adults, poor schools, and single-parent households, as well as high degrees of social isolation, racial segregation, and chronic poverty.

If the rate of murder is unparalleled within black communities, it is because so, too, is the level of structural disadvantage. Studies comparing black and Hispanic neighborhoods have shown that the latter are located closer to more prosperous white neighborhoods, have better relations with law enforcement officials, have fewer single-family households, and overall have lower levels of structural disadvantage.[130] Similarly, when researchers have compared black and white neighborhoods with equal levels of structural disadvantage, they have found no significant difference in homicide rates.[131] And because the discrepancies in homicide rates across race largely are explained by examining neighborhood-level differences—ecological dissimilarity, we might call it—we should hardly be surprised to learn that black youth who live outside majority-black neighborhoods have the same rates of offending as white youth.[132] "The combination of urban poverty and family disruption is so strong," write Robert Sampson and Lydia Bean, "that the 'worst' urban neighborhoods in which Whites reside are considerably better off than those of the average Black community. . . . Racial segregation exposes African-American youth to neighborhoods with higher risk factors and fewer protective factors for violence than neighborhoods where youth from other groups live."[133] As a result, many poor whites who come from broken homes or who are unemployed (factors associated with violent crime) live in areas with steady levels of family stability and employment. The same is not true of poor blacks living in urban areas. As we have already learned, black poverty is not the same as white poverty.

Crime-ridden streets have bred a spirit of fear and distrust in many black neighborhoods, a spirit that dissolves community relationships and modes of informal social control. Recall that informal social control can effectively attenuate violent crime by ensuring that little problems do not boil up into bigger ones and by encouraging neighbors to look out for one another. Although researchers have documented a high degree of social control in other poor neighborhoods, especially those of immigrants, they have observed that poor black inner-city dwellers often are isolated from one another, primarily because of a widespread fear of victimization.[134]

To adapt to the extreme structural disadvantage found within the ghetto, many young black teenagers develop cultural dispositions and attitudes that promote (and even normalize) violent crime. According to sociologist Elijah Anderson, black youth living in poor inner-city neighborhoods operate under a "code of the street," which requires them to present themselves as aggressive, hard menaces who are not to be trifled with and who, at a second's notice, will "act a fool" and resort to violence.[135] Young people abiding by such a code earn respect from their peers through acts of courage and aggression. To the man who hits on a rival's girlfriend, throws the first punch, or pulls the trigger go "the props," "the juice." Disrespected, in the fullest sense of the term, by mainstream white society, poor black youth create their own ways of allocating respect and honor, but these ways serve to breed only violence and to reproduce the conditions of their own domination—again, symbolic violence.[136] That said, we should bear in mind that the code of the street is not endorsed solely by black youth. "The important thing to note about the subculture that ensnares [young black men] is that it is not disconnected from the mainstream culture," writes sociologist Orlando Patterson. "To the contrary, it has powerful support from some of America's largest corporations. Hip-hop, professional basketball, and homeboy fashions are as American as cherry pie. Young white Americans are very much into these things, but selectively; they know when it is time to turn off Fifty Cent and get out the SAT prep book."[137]

The code of the street and the dissolution of informal social control both help explain why blacks, and young blacks especially, have such high rates of homicide, but both these factors must be understood, above all, as induced by the extreme structural disadvantage that makes the black ghetto distinct from other poor neighborhoods in America. Years of research have yielded the firm conclusion that social problems related to homicide are rooted in enduring systems of inequality: notably, economic marginality and racial segregation. For example, people who were abused as children are far more likely to commit a violent crime than those who were not, but child abuse is prevalent in neighborhoods reeling from chronic poverty and endemic unemployment.[138] America—and black America, in particular—has a violent crime problem. And because the problem is environmental, not individual, in nature, so, too, must be the solution. A weed will spring up again and again unless it is pulled up by the roots.

PUNISHMENT

The last major section of this chapter takes up punishment, the nation's reactions to crime and its methods of combating it. The ensuing discussions follow the process of punishment through the criminal justice system, beginning with policing strategies and with profiling and racial disparities in arrest rates and then moving into sentencing decisions. The section ends where the chapter began, namely, with prisons, exploring the high costs of mass incarceration and evaluating how effective prisons are when it comes to decreasing crime.

American Police State

Most people arrested in the United States are white. In 2010, 9.1 million white people were arrested, compared to 3.6 million black people.[139] But Hispanics and African Americans are arrested at much higher rates than whites. According to statistics released by the FBI, 13 blacks in 100 are arrested annually, whereas only 5 whites in 100 are. In some states, the difference is much more exaggerated. In Wisconsin, for example, where only 6 whites out of 100 are arrested each year, that ratio shoots up to 41 out of 100 for blacks.[140] Racial disparities in arrest rates vary widely by criminal offense as well. Federal data released in 2013 show that blacks are nearly four times as likely as whites to be arrested for marijuana possession, even though blacks and whites use the drug at similar rates.[141] What explains these wide discrepancies?

Although some of the difference in arrest rates undoubtedly is attributed to the high rates of violent crime found in distressed nonwhite neighborhoods, a good proportion is caused by institutional racism operating at multiple levels of the criminal justice system.[142] Ever since the racial uprisings of the 1960s, poor, nonwhite urban neighborhoods have been subjected to heightened surveillance and police repression. What held true for cities that experienced major uprisings around the middle of the twentieth century remains true today: metropolitan areas with sizable black populations have larger police forces and bigger crime-fighting budgets than cities with fewer black residents. More detailed analyses have demonstrated that on a national level, police forces grow in proportion to cities' level of racial residential segregation as well as to whites' fear of crime.[143] Sociologist Alice Goffman conducted an in-depth ethnography, beginning in 2002, of one urban ghetto neighborhood in Philadelphia. Although this was not even among the poorest or most crime-ridden neighborhoods in the city, she reports that, nonetheless, "by 2002, police curfews had been established around the area for those under age eighteen, and police video cameras had been placed on major streets. In the first eighteen months that I spent in the neighborhood, at least once a day I watched the police stop pedestrians or people in cars, search them, run their names for warrants, ask them to come in for questioning, or make an arrest. In that same eighteen-month period, I watched the police break down doors, search houses, and question, arrest, or chase people through houses fifty-two times. Nine times, police helicopters circled overhead and beamed searchlights onto local streets. I noted blocks taped off and traffic redirected as police searched for evidence—or, in police language, 'secured a crime scene'—seventeen times. Fourteen times during my first eighteen months of near daily observation, I watched the police punch, choke, kick, stomp on, or beat young men with their nightsticks."[144]

Owing to the criminalization of dark skin, blacks, Mexicans, and Puerto Ricans are singled out as potential criminals at a much higher rate than Asians and whites. One study found that whites are six times less likely than blacks and four times less likely than Hispanics to be stopped by the police. Consider New York City's controversial "stop and frisk" policy. The policy allows police officers to stop pedestrians and search them for weapons and drugs. Over half a million people are stopped and frisked by the police each year in New York City, and a disproportionate number are African American or Latino. In 2011, blacks and Latinos accounted for over 50 percent of those stopped in seventy of seventy-six of New York City's police precincts. In thirty-three precincts, they accounted for more than 90 percent of stops—and this was not always because those precincts were located in minority neighborhoods. Blacks and Latinos make up only 8 percent of the population in the 6th Precinct, but they accounted for 77 percent of police stops in 2011. Less than 2 percent of all stops resulted in a weapon being found.[145]

African Americans have grown so used to being pulled over by the police that many speak of

Policemen stop and frisk a group of young men who were loitering in a known drug selling area in Orange, New Jersey.

being stopped on account of DWB: "driving while black."[146] Perhaps more disconcerting is the fact that once pulled over, black and Hispanic drivers are more likely than are their white counterparts to be searched, fined, and arrested. A New Jersey–based study found that the majority of cars searched during traffic stops belonged to nonwhite drivers (70 percent), and a high percentage of drivers searched subsequently were arrested. Many police officers, the study went on to say, intentionally targeted blacks and Latinos because, statistically, they have higher arrest rates.[147] Thus, through a self-reinforcing cycle of disadvantage, racial profiling results in more nonwhites being arrested, and high levels of nonwhite arrest rates are marshaled as evidence to justify racial profiling.

What some white people have a difficult time understanding is that for many people of color, the police are anything but guardians. As African American comedian Dave Chappelle has observed, "The premise of reasonable doubt for a Black person and for a White person are two separate things. For a White person, the idea that the police planted evidence is ridiculous: 'The police are here to serve and protect us!' Yeah *you*. But to a Black person, it's not ridiculous. The FBI followed Martin Luther King around! Was he a threat to America?"[148]

Many nonwhite Americans, especially those brought up in poor communities, are taught from childhood that the police—not to mention judges, lawyers, parole officers, social workers, prison guards, and all others in the legal field—bring violence and harm, unfair treatment and repression. The police, after all, historically have served as the primary guardians of white supremacy, called on to track down runaway slaves, to kill Native Americans who refused to stay cooped up in their reservations, to enforce Jim Crow segregation, and to unleash attack dogs on civil rights marchers. Even so, African Americans and Latinos desire the protection of the police just as much as anyone else. A recent survey asked respondents if they would call the police and file a report had their house been burglarized and if they believed their complaint would be taken seriously. The vast majority of both white and black respondents—90 and 93 percent, respectively—said they would call the police. However, only 35 percent of blacks expected to be taken seriously, compared with 60 percent of whites.[149]

According to the Bureau of Justice, police officers are more likely to use force on black and Hispanic citizens than on their white counterparts.[150] Police brutality has been inflicted on blacks and Hispanics—sometimes in lethal doses. In 1992, Malice Green, a black man, was beaten to death by two white police officers after he resisted arrest. In 1997, Abner Louima, an immigrant from Haiti, was arrested outside a Brooklyn nightclub and taken to a police station, where he was beaten, tortured, and sodomized with a broomstick by New York City police officers. In 1999, four plainclothes police officers fired forty-one shots at Amadou Diallo, a twenty-three-year-old West African immigrant, who they believed to be holding a gun. When they approached Diallo's bullet-ridden, dead body, officers discovered he had been gripping his wallet. In 2003, Ousmane Zongo, another unarmed young West African immigrant, stumbled upon a CD pirating sting operation and was shot four times—twice in the back—by a New York City police officer. And in 2006, undercover police officers unleashed a barrage of gunfire at Sean Bell, a twenty-three-year-old African American man, and two of his friends. The officers sprayed bullets into Bell's car and surrounding houses. Bell and his two friends, none of whom were armed, were leaving a strip club (one the police had been investigating), celebrating Bell's final hours of bachelorhood. Sean Bell never made it to the church the following morning. His bride-turned-widow accepted Bell's surname days after she laid him in the ground.[151]

On February 26, 2012, Trayvon Martin was shot and killed by George Zimmerman in Sanford, Florida, a city of roughly 50,000 residents. Martin, a seventeen-year-old black high school student, was walking alone to his father's house, wearing a dark hoodie and carrying a bag of Skittles and a can of Arizona Iced Tea he had just bought at a convenience store. Zimmerman, a twenty-eight-year-old volunteer neighborhood watch coordinator and light-skinned Hispanic (his father is white and his mother Peruvian), spotted Martin and began following him. "We've had some break-ins in my neighborhood, and there's a real suspicious guy," Zimmerman told a 911 dispatcher. "This guy looks like he is up to no good or he is on drugs or something." When the dispatcher learned that Zimmerman was trailing Martin, she replied, "We don't need you to do that." What happened next is a matter of dispute. But here is what is known: Zimmerman ignored the dispatcher's request and continued to follow Martin. At some point, Zimmerman got out of his car and approached the boy. Martin, who weighed 158 pounds, was unarmed. Zimmerman, who weighed 185 pounds, was carrying a 9-millimeter semiautomatic pistol. The two engaged in a violent encounter that ended with Zimmerman shooting Martin point-blank in the chest.

Police soon arrived at the scene. Zimmerman was treated for head injuries, questioned for five hours, and released. The police did not arrest Zimmerman, who was licensed to carry a firearm, because they thought he had a right to shoot and kill Martin under Florida's "Stand Your Ground" law, an amped-up self-defense statute. Traditional self-defense law mandates the obligation to flee to safety, if able, before using deadly force against an attacker; this is known as the "duty to retreat." Stand Your Ground laws take this duty off the table.

After massive and widespread protest calling for Zimmerman's arrest, he was finally charged with murder. Although Zimmerman originally avoided arrest based on Stand Your Ground, his defense team did not rely on this statute during his trial, presumably because that would open up the possibility that Trayvon Martin had a right to "stand his ground" as well. Zimmerman's defense team argued he had a right to shoot and kill Martin based on conventional self-defense protections. A jury lacking a single black juror acquitted Zimmerman of all charges.[152]

According to the law, when Zimmerman pleaded self-defense, the burden of proof rested on him. It was up to him to prove he shot Martin because he reasonably feared for his life, even though Martin was unarmed, almost thirty pounds lighter, and a child. But Zimmerman never took the stand. This raises the question, why did people believe him? Why did the police and the jury think Zimmerman was right in seeing Martin as a dangerous threat?

To acquit Zimmerman was, in effect, to convict Martin in death; to find him not innocent or victimized, but menacing and threatening to such a degree that killing him was not against the law. How is it possible that someone who is wholly innocent is blamed for his own death by law enforcers, judges, and a jury? Given the history of antiblack racism in the United States in general—and the history of typing young black men as criminals in particular—Zimmerman did not have to do much to convince others that a young black man was a threat.

There are many details of the confrontation between Martin and Zimmerman that we will never fully know. Who threw the first punch? Was Martin getting the best of Zimmerman in a scuffle? But, as sociologist Lawrence Bobo observed, "The most elemental facts of this case will never change. A teenager went out to buy Skittles and iced tea. At some point, he was confronted by a man with a gun who killed him. There is no universe I understand where this can be declared a noncriminal act. Not in a sane, just and racism-free universe."[153]

Protesters hold "Justice for Trayvon" signs during a march and rally for Trayvon Martin in Sanford, Florida.

After such killings, it is tempting to shovel blame solely on the shoulders of the police officers—or, in Zimmerman's case, a neighborhood watch volunteer—calling them "racist" or "incompetent" and demanding their resignation. But focusing only on the officers permits us to avoid examining the circumstances in all their complexity. Millions of people play a part in criminalizing darkness—from the elderly white woman terrified of her black neighbors to the young black teenager who refers to himself as a "thug"—and this contributes to racial disparities in arrest rates and the killing of innocent men and boys of color. To blame "racist hot heads" is to blot out the many ways in which our complicity maintains a system that facilitates racially motivated brutality. Likewise, to point our fingers solely at the victims, assuming they "must have done something wrong," is to misidentify the wrongdoer, to criminalize the innocent.

Unjust Sentencing

Scythian, an ancient Greek philosopher, once likened laws to spider webs, as "they catch the weak and the small, but the strong and powerful break through them."[154] Indeed, as it stands now, the American legal system is biased by design, heavily tilted against the poor. Because nonwhites from disadvantaged communities are arrested at higher rates relative to whites, and because most of these accused people are flat broke, they are forced to rely on public defenders, who tend to be overworked, underpaid, and unable to afford potentially useful resources such as DNA tests or expert witnesses. Public defenders have very poor records: whereas private attorneys win over half their cases, public defenders achieve a not guilty verdict only 11 percent of the time; while private attorneys force the courts to dismiss 48 percent of their cases, public defenders get only 11 percent of their cases dropped.[155] Some public defenders, burdened by their caseloads, hastily push for plea deals, to which many defendants, seeing no better option, reluctantly agree. These facts remain even (and especially) in capital cases, forcing one journalist to quip, "Some people go to traffic court with better prepared lawyers than many murder defendants get."[156]

The strong arm of the law often reserves its harshest blows for nonwhite offenders. Consider Georgia law, which allows courts to hand down a life sentence for repeat drug offenses, even if both offenses are minor ones (such as simple possession). Between 1990 and 1995, 573 repeat offenders were sentenced to life under this law, but only 13 of them were white. Fifteen percent of black repeat offenders but only 3 percent of white repeat offenders were put away for life. Compared to whites who commit similar crimes, nonwhite juvenile offenders are more likely to be tried as adults, are more likely to receive tougher punishments, and are more likely to be viewed as "inherently criminal" by their parole officers. Blacks arrested for aggravated assault are jailed nearly a third longer than whites arrested for the exact same offense—a discrepancy brought to the nation's attention during the trial of six young black teenagers arrested for assaulting a white teenager in Jena, Louisiana.[157]

Outside the local high school in Jena (population 3,000), a tree once stood that was known as the "white tree," so named because according to local convention, only white students were allowed to sit under it. The day after a black student defied the unspoken law in September 2007, white students hung three nooses on the tree, sending a threatening message to black students, one that harkened back to the days of the lynch mob. Tension between whites and blacks mounted, and, later in the school year, when a young white high school student taunted black students with racial epithets and jeers, a group of black students beat

Jena, Louisiana's High School's "white tree" was so named because only white students were allowed to sit under it.

him unconscious. The victim of the assault was taken to the hospital and released a few hours later. Six black male students were arrested and charged—not with assault but with attempted murder, a sentence grievously disproportional to the crime. Thousands of people descended on the little Louisiana town to protest, marching on behalf of "the Jena 6," as they came to be known. As a result, charges were scaled back to aggravated second-degree battery and conspiracy to commit aggravated second-degree battery. According to Louisiana law, what distinguishes "aggravated" battery from simply battery is employment of a weapon. The prosecutor in the Jena 6 case argued that the tennis shoes worn by one of the black assailants were dangerous weapons, and the jury accepted this argument.[158]

After the case received national attention that sparked weeks of protests, charges against five of the Jena 6 were reduced to simply battery. The five defendants entered pleas of no contest, and each had to pay a $500 fine. The remaining defendant, Mychal Bell, who was sixteen at the time of his arrest, pled guilty to a reduced battery charge and served eighteen months in a juvenile facility. The white students who hung the nooses on the tree were punished with only a few days' suspension.[159] The events of Jena, Louisiana, represent but a small piece of a larger problem: justice, far from being blind, systematically disadvantages poor nonwhites, especially young black men.[160]

Nowhere is institutional racism within the criminal justice system more cruel than in death penalty sentencing. After taking into account dozens of other factors (including previous offenses and the heinousness of the crime), numerous studies have concluded that of all people accused of committing capital offenses, blacks are more likely to be sentenced to death than whites. Moreover, people accused of killing whites are four times more likely to receive the death sentence than those accused of killing blacks.[161] Since 1973, 143 people have been found innocent and released from death row. Of those, 60 are black, 61 are white, and 18 are Hispanic. This pattern mirrors that of all exonerations. Since 1989, 311 people have been found innocent based on DNA evidence, including the five blacks originally charged in the infamous Central Park jogger case, discussed earlier. Of the 311, 193 are black, 94 are white, and 22 are Hispanic.[162] These figures suggest that America is imprisoning—and even killing—innocent men and women, a disproportionate number of whom are black.

Because racial domination systematically tilts the scales of justice against people of color, many blacks and Hispanics, especially those living in poor neighborhoods, have little faith in the criminal justice system.[163] It is clear how nonwhites' views of the criminal justice system are affected by racial inequality. But does racial domination affect whites' views? Absolutely. The very fact that many whites view the criminal justice system as unbiased and fair reflects their racial privilege, the privilege of knowing that in no time in American history has the system been used as a machine of oppression against people with their skin color; that people who look like them are not racially profiled; that whiteness is not riveted to images of violence and criminality, as is blackness; that most police officers are white and have good relationships with white communities; that, should they stand trial, their whiteness will not result in a harsher sentence; and that, in a jury trial, they can rest assured they will be judged by "a panel of their peers."

The Many Costs of Mass Incarceration

We began this chapter by discussing the prison boom and the racial imbalance of America's prison population, and we explored the social mechanisms that help account for this gross discrepancy. It is fitting, therefore, to conclude this chapter by examining the consequences of imprisonment, for offenders and ex-offenders, as well as for society as a whole.

For over fifty years, researchers have warned us about the negative psychological effects of incarceration. The experience of confinement, of caging, can exert very powerful effects on one's mental state. This is especially true of the 25,000 inmates

According to recent statistics, America is imprisoning a disproportionate number of poor black men.

imprisoned in supermaximum facilities.[164] Living in a concrete seven-by-fourteen-foot cell, the inmate held in supermax spends twenty-three hours a day locked down. He or she eats all meals in solitude and, although they may be dimmed, his or her cell lights are never shut off. Such conditions often drive prisoners to suicide or insanity. Medical researchers have demonstrated that prisoners subjected to solitary confinement can become delirious and hallucinatory in as little as forty-eight hours. Historian Alfred McCoy calls solitary confinement "no-touch torture," saying, "it sends prisoners in one of two directions: catatonia or rage."[165]

If they survive prison, offenders are met with a whole host of problems once released. There are, first, political consequences, as many no longer are allowed to participate in the most fundamental right of citizenship, the right to vote (as we discussed in Chapter 3). There also are severe economic costs of being branded with a criminal record. Many licensed or professional occupations in health care or the public sector disqualify all applicants with criminal records, and a good number of employers simply refuse to hire ex-convicts, especially men of color with felony convictions. One study found that a criminal record reduces one's chances of landing a job by 50 percent to 60 percent.[166]

Because budgets for educational and vocational training have been rolled back in recent years, prisoners have little hope of gaining job skills while doing time. And because prisoners are cut off from the larger society, their connections to stably employed friends and family members, people who could connect them to job opportunities, diminish the longer they are behind bars. As a result, many women and men with criminal records have a very difficult time securing well-paying, full-time jobs. Add to this the fact that ex-offenders are denied many types of social services, such as food stamps, public housing, Medicaid, and government-based financial aid for college, and we can begin to understand how difficult it can be for someone recently released from prison to turn her or his life around. We can thereby begin to grasp the direct connection between incarceration and chronic poverty.[167]

Compared to those who have never been incarcerated, ex-convicts have lower wages, employment rates, and annual incomes. Incarceration results in a 15 percent reduction in hourly wage rates across the board, and those who have been incarcerated work an average of eight fewer weeks a year than if they had never been convicted. An ex-convict earns 30 percent to 40 percent less each year than a person with the same job skills and education. A black man who dropped out of high school earns roughly $9,000 a year, but a black man who dropped out of high school and has a criminal record earns roughly $5,700 a year. Since the *majority* of black male dropouts will be incarcerated at some point in their lives, the economic consequences of incarceration are intimately linked to the persistence of racialized poverty. In fact, if no African Americans were incarcerated, no fewer than one-fifth of all poor blacks would be lifted out of poverty.[168]

Incarceration also wreaks havoc on the family, as wives must cope without their husbands, children without their mothers. Incarcerated parents miss out on key events in children's lives—their first steps, major holidays, soccer games, graduations—which erodes the bond between parent and child. If it is the father who is incarcerated, the newly single mother often is forced to make ends meet by working several jobs and cannot afford to spend extended amounts of time supervising her children or helping them with homework. As a result, many children from single-parent homes fare worse in school and are at a higher risk of developing behavioral problems than their peers from two-parent households. If it is the single mother who is incarcerated, her parental rights may be revoked and her children may become wards of the state, shuffled through the foster care system.

Incarceration often tears families apart. Although the divorce rate for men inside and outside prison is the same (50 percent), most marriages involving an incarcerated partner end in less than seven years, a full decade before the national rate of seventeen years. Couples with children are at a high risk of splitting if the father is locked up. By one estimate, America would enjoy 20 percent to 30 percent more marriages if it did not incarcerate a single person. And men with criminal records seem to have a difficult time getting married after their sentence expires. Just as they are "marked" by employers who refuse to hire them, they are "marked" by potential mates who refuse to marry them. By the age of thirty-five, roughly 80 percent of men who have never been incarcerated are married; the same is true of only 40 percent of men with a record.[169]

Incarceration also comes with a hefty price tag. It costs approximately $30,000 a year to incarcerate one person. In a nation with a prison population exceeding 2 million, this amounts to over $60 billion a year. If we add in the costs of policing, legal processing, court fees, and all the other expenses of the criminal justice system, we are met with the realization that America spends an extravagant $110 billion a year to fight crime.[170] This money could otherwise be directed at building schools, decreasing pollution, raising teachers' salaries, or funding job skill programs in the inner city. Indeed, as the prison system has swelled, the United States has rolled back social spending. In 1973, states spent 2 percent of their budgets on police and corrections and 5.5 percent on cash assistance to the poor; in 2013, cash assistance programs accounted for a little more than 1 percent of state expenditures, and police and corrections accounted for roughly 4.5 percent.[171]

Do Prisons Make Us Safer?

However devastating the effects of incarceration on the lives and families of offenders, and however much damage the criminal justice system does to our strivings toward racial justice, and however high a price we all pay for having the world's largest prison population, many Americans still would approve of incarcerating thousands of people each year if that kept them safer. So, the million-dollar question is, do prisons decrease crime? The crime drop America has been enjoying for the last twenty-five years coincided with the prison boom. Did the boom cause the drop?

As sociologist Bruce Western has argued, there are three ways prisons may reduce crime. "Inmates who participate in prison education or treatment programs might be rehabilitated, and turn away from crime after they are released. Prisons might simply incapacitate offenders, locking them away to prevent crime in society. Finally, prisons might deter those who would commit crime were it not for the threat of incarceration."[172] So, prisons will make us safer if they effectively *rehabilitate* offenders, *incapacitate* lawbreakers, or *deter* people from committing crime. Let us examine each in turn.

Since the rise of "law and order" politics and the implementation of harsher sentences, prisons have abandoned their original mission—to rehabilitate those who have committed crimes—and instead have become punishing and warehousing institutions. Evidence suggests that rehabilitation programs reduce recidivism; however, since funding for such programs has been scaled back, there is little proof that prisons decrease crime by rehabilitating offenders.[173] In fact, some have argued that prisons produce more crime. If an ex-offender cannot find steady work after his release, he might resort to stealing appliances or selling drugs to get by. If an ex-offender's marriage dissolved while he was in the pen, he might find community in the friends he socialized with before his arrest, friends perhaps involved in the criminal underworld. The criminal justice system spends far less money and effort reintegrating ex-offenders into society than it does punishing them. The result is that a good number of the hundreds of thousands of people released from prison each year "return to their old ways."[174] After all, they just left a parallel society filled with offenders, a place where first-time offenders were introduced to career criminals, where friendships between gang members and drug dealers were forged and solidified. A person might enter prison as a man who committed a single crime and leave it as a hardened criminal, as if being released from prison were akin to graduating from crime school.

If prisons do not rehabilitate offenders, perhaps they decrease crime simply by taking criminals off the streets—that is, by incapacitating them. This line of reasoning would make sense if most people behind bars were career criminals responsible for multiple offenses. Although many prisoners have carried out dozens of crimes, a good number are first-time offenders. What is more, street-level drug dealers easily are replaced after they are arrested, resulting in a diminished incapacitation effect. As Western puts it, "locking up drug offenders does not avert serious crime."[175] It appears that incapacitation decreases the crime rate only by a modest degree.[176]

Lastly, we might argue that prisons function as a strong deterrent for would-be criminals. If prisons are to have a deterrent effect, someone contemplating a crime must weigh the rewards of the crime (say, $5,000 for stealing a car) against the punishment (say, three years in prison for grand theft auto) and decide against committing the crime specifically because the punishment outweighs the reward. There is no denying that prisons deter some people from committing a crime. But how strong is the effect? It appears not as strong as many people tend to think. Surveys of prisoners reveal that one in three people convicted of a felony confesses to having never considered the punishment when committing the crime. Indeed, many offenders literally were out of their minds when they broke the law: 30 percent of state convicts confess to having been on drugs when they committed their crimes, and another 17 percent committed the offenses in order to get money for drugs.[177]

For all these reasons, the effect of mass incarceration on the crime drop is much more modest than many Americans believe. It is difficult to parse out the effect of incarceration on crime from the effect of crime on incarceration. But if evidence indicates that the three mechanisms by which incarceration is supposed to lower crime are less effective than originally thought, we might suspect the effect of mass incarceration on the crime drop to be modest. And indeed the best available evidence indicates that the prison boom can account for only 2 percent to 5 percent of the crime drop. In other words, "more than nine-tenths of the decline in serious crime through the 1990s would have happened even without the prison boom."[178]

THINGS ARE NOT WHAT THEY SEEM

A rational assessment of race and crime, one that marshals the usefulness of social science to judge the validity of popular claims, often leads to surprising discoveries. By holding in abeyance the emotional reactions unleashed during discussions of crime and punishment, choosing instead to study the thing carefully and objectively, we are presented with facts that flip conventional wisdom on its head. Crime is not forever on the rise; immigrants do not cause crime, but make the streets safer; we have more to fear from unsafe working conditions than from the crazed murderer lurking in the darkness; prisons may do more harm than good when it comes to decreasing crime. Perhaps Gaston Bachelard was right in saying, "The first impression is not a fundamental truth."[179]

If many things believed to be threatening (for example, immigrants) actually make us safer, and if many things believed to be protective (for instance, prisons) actually increase our risks of harm, then, as critically minded sociological thinkers, we are obliged to rethink the crime problem and its solutions. This requires, first, reconsidering the dangers to which our minds and money should be devoted. The high homicide rates in poor urban neighborhoods certainly deserve attention, but so, too, do rampant violence against women and offenses carried out by corporations. Indeed, the sociological thinker must be willing to question the very definition of "crime" itself.

Second, we must rethink conventional solutions to fighting crime, solutions, as we have just seen, that may bring about harmful unintended consequences. We must denaturalize incarceration as the one and only means of punishment.[180]

This precisely has been the goal of the anti-incarceration movement. Thoroughly multiracial and made up of citizens of all ages, this movement has criticized America's reliance on the prison as the primary method through which punishments are dealt.

Finally, we must examine how our racialized fears erode the hope of a multicultural democracy rooted in interracial alliances. The more we fear one another, looking on each other as potential threats, enemies, and terrorists, the slimmer are our chances of reaching out to one another to help build the society in which we wish to live. Fear causes us to lock our doors; it keeps us from walking across the block and introducing ourselves to our neighbors. It causes us to divert our eyes, to clutch our purses, to change seats on an airplane when confronted with people whose very skin tone marks them as criminals. Psychologists have shown that we pay a high price for racialized fear, the price of walking through life filled with unhealthy doses of guilt, shame, anxiety, and depression.[181] The nation as a whole pays a high price as well—for racialized fear withers away the promise of American community, and it makes a mockery of justice.

THE BIG PICTURE

Chapter 6: Crime and Punishment

MAIN POINTS ■	KEY TERMS ■	FROM THEORY TO PRACTICE ■

Recognize the role of the late-twentieth-century prison boom in the creation of the stark racial disparities now seen within the U.S. incarcerated population.

- racial terrorism, page 177
- mass incarceration, page 207

Think about a police officer. Write down five adjectives you think accurately describe her or him. Having done that, reflect on how your views of a police officer are informed by America's racial past. Reflect, too, on how your upbringing might have informed your outlook.

Discuss the ways that Americans' fear of crime is strongly connected to their racial identity, their racial attitudes, and the racial makeup of their neighborhood.

- fear of crime, page 214

Understand why members of different racial groups are more likely to commit or be victims of crime.

- underground economy, page 224
- white-collar crime, page 224

- In this chapter we learned that, in many cases, the voices of women of color are silenced in debates about crime, especially those concerning domestic violence and rape. Reflecting on public discussions of crime and punishment, name another group whose voice is silenced. How is this group ignored? Why do you think this is so? How might fully including this group in public debate help us reach new understandings?

- Think of something that is harmful but not criminalized (for example, actions carried out by state officials). Offer a sociologically informed explanation for why these actions are not criminalized. When doing so, be sure to identify who is disproportionately affected by the harmful actions and who benefits from their not being criminalized. Additionally, determine how this helps to support systems of domination.

Learn how racial disparities in the prison population are driven in large part by severe criminal sentencing practices that give lengthy prison terms for nonviolent offenses as well as by new policing techniques that disproportionately affect poor minority communities.

- police state, page 231
- deterrent effect, page 240

- A young man is found guilty of possessing 5 grams of crack cocaine and is therefore eligible to serve a minimum sentence of five years in prison. This is his first offense. Assuming the role of the judge with absolute sentencing powers—and pretending for a moment that judges are not bound by draconian mandatory minimum sentencing cues—offer an alternative to incarceration. That is, what other punishment, besides prison, might be suitable in this case? And why would it preferable to the conventional sentence of incarceration?

7 Education

MAIN POINTS

- Describe how education policies of the twentieth century attempted to force racial groups to assimilate into Anglo-American culture or systematically exclude them from white society through segregation.

- Examine the ways that whiteness often pervades the curriculum and college life.

- Explain why the racial education gap—separating whites and Asians, on the one hand, and African Americans, Hispanics, and Native Americans, on the other—has shrunk in recent years at the secondary level but has increased at the postsecondary level.

- Discuss how affirmative action operates in higher education and whether it has changed the racial disparities it was intended to reduce.

Study after study has concluded that individuals who have more education make more money, have more stable relationships, and live longer and healthier lives. Education, it seems, increases one's chances of experiencing a thriving, successful life. Not only that, but education makes civic debate and democracy possible. That was as true in the mid-nineteenth century, when Alexis de Tocqueville wrote of America, "The first duty imposed on those who now direct society is to *educate democracy*. . . . A new political science is needed for a world itself quite new," as it is today, when in 2007 Harvard president Drew Gilpin Faust declared that "education is the engine that makes American democracy work."[1]

If a democratic society cannot function properly without education, it is because education provides us with tools to comprehend, and therefore critically to assess, the economic, social, cultural, and political forces that govern our lives. It also allows us to employ our sociological imagination to better understand ourselves. Freedom, therefore—which for a society means unencumbered democracy and for an individual the capacity for self-knowledge and self-mastery—arrives only on the back of education.[2]

But today, education is not granted freely and equally to all citizens. Nor are educational institutions somehow immune to sources of division based on class, religion, sexuality, gender, or race. This chapter explains how race matters in the field of education. It begins with a historical overview of racial struggles over education across the twentieth century. Then, it turns to analyzing the many ways in which whiteness informs what and how we are taught. Next, it underscores racial inequalities in education, proposes sociological explanations for those inequalities, and evaluates a potential remedy for them: affirmative action. Racial inequality and injustice within the educational field is a topic that should concern us all—for nothing short of our very minds and freedoms is at stake.

"I HAVE A RIGHT TO THINK!": RACIAL BATTLES OVER EDUCATION, 1900–1970

This section serves as a reminder, however brief, of the racial struggles that took place within the educational field during the tumultuous twentieth century, a

The School for Native Americans in Albuquerque, NM (pictured), like many schools of its kind, attempted to anglicize Native Americans.

reminder that the right to think was something young people, like many of you, risked their lives for, a right we would do well not to take for granted.

The Colonizer's Education: Indian Boarding Schools

As we learned in Chapter 2, at the beginning of the twentieth century, whites sought new ways to "civilize"—that is, to Anglicize—America's indigenous people. Education would become a primary civilizing machine. American Indian parents were forced to send their children to boarding schools run by Christian missionaries and, later on, by the federal government. If parents refused (and many did), they were pressured by military power, threatened with imprisonment, or denied food rations. Hundreds of Indian children were sent to boarding schools, where their hair was cut and their traditional garb traded in for English-style clothes.[3] In her memoir, *The School Days of an Indian Girl*, Zitkala-Sa recalls the traumatic experience of having her long hair sheared: "Our mothers had taught us that only unskilled warriors who were captured had their hair shingled by the enemy. Among our people, short hair was worn by mourners, and shingled hair by cowards! . . . I was carried downstairs and tied fast in a chair. I cried aloud, shaking my head all the while until I felt the cold blades of the scissors against my neck, and heard them gnaw off one of my thick braids. Then I lost my spirit. . . . In my anguish I moaned for my mother, but no one came to comfort me. Not a soul reasoned quietly with me, as my own mother used to do; for now I was only one of many little animals driven by a herder."[4]

A boarding school's primary objective was to strip American Indian students of all their Indianness, to force them to assimilate into Anglo-American society and culture through strict discipline. Schools often were built a good distance from reservations, and parental visits were discouraged. Students were forbidden to speak in their native tongue or to practice their religion. Infractions were subject to harsh punishment, as one student remembered: "If everybody knew part of their language or even spoke any Indian terms you would be spanked for it. . . . You were brought in front of everybody and when you lined up in the morning before you go to breakfast, they would call you out, they would have you pull your pants down, grab your ankles and they would spank you in front of everybody so everybody could view it."[5] American Indian children were taught, day after day, that their way of life, and that of their parents and grandparents, was silly, backward—evil.

Many students were thoroughly indoctrinated into whiteness and, on returning home, appeared alien to their family members and others in the community. Others, however, resisted cultural reeducation. Students ran away from the schools, practiced outlawed ceremonies in secret, and whispered to one another in their native language. Some even mounted organized rebellions not only against schools'

Tom Tomlino, an American Indian, before and after attending an Indian boarding school.

colonialist project but also against their pitiful conditions.[6] When government researcher Lewis Meriam published *The Problem of Indian Administration* in 1928, he brought to the public's attention what many American Indian students already knew: "that the provisions for the care of the Indian children in boarding schools are grossly inadequate."[7] In 2008—with the discovery of mass graves at former boarding schools located in Canada, containing hundreds if not thousands of bodies of children, some of whom, many believe, were punished to death—we learned what many American Indians long had suspected: that the abuses suffered by American Indian children at boarding schools were much worse than even those documented in Meriam's scathing report.[8]

Meriam's report—which, besides pointing out the sorry conditions of boarding schools, called attention to their inability to educate students—caught the government's attention, and things began to change. In 1933, John Collier, a white man, became the Commissioner on Indian Affairs and began reforming Indian education. Collier loosened the grip of Anglo-American colonialist education, encouraging bilingualism in boarding schools, replacing far-off schools with day schools on reservations, and making sure that schools provided students with a safe and healthy environment. He even introduced Native American literature, poetry, and philosophy into schools' curriculum through new textbooks written in collaboration with tribal elders.[9]

Despite these important changes, American Indians did not regain full control over the education of their children until the Civil Rights Era. In 1966, the first

Historic photograph of Creek children of all ages posing in front of their boarding school.

Indian-controlled school was established on the Navajo reservation, and three years later (on that same reservation) the first tribal college, Navajo Community College, was founded. Whereas education historically had been "for Indians," these schools represented education "by Indians." Today, in many reservation schools, tribal language is taught besides English, and Native American folklore and literature are read along with the likes of Mark Twain and Jane Austen.[10]

The effects of colonialist education are still felt across Indian country, though, especially in tribes whose culture and language virtually were wiped out and whose religion and traditions continue to be viewed as primitive relics, things to be displayed in a museum. Indeed, many today point to misrepresentations of American Indians in textbooks and popular movies, as well as in national myths about the country's indigenous population, and justly claim that Indian education—in the broadest sense of the word—has not yet fully been wrenched from the colonizers' grip.

"Spoiling Field Hands": Early African American Education

While American Indians were being forced to conform to white society at the beginning of the twentieth century, African Americans were being excluded from it. After Reconstruction, whites, especially southern whites, actively resisted educating blacks, who only a generation before had been released from bondage. The thought of even a negligible portion of their taxes being devoted to building black schoolhouses so infuriated many whites that they refused to approve *any* school taxes, strangling blacks' education even at the expense of their own children's. Whites knew that if blacks were granted access to the world of learning, it would be difficult to exploit them as a cheap labor source. "Educate a nigger and you spoil a good field hand," the old saying went. Education would expand blacks' horizons, allowing them to seek out a livelihood other than the menial one they were forced to accept under sharecropping and other exploitative systems.[11]

Additionally, if blacks were educated, whites would incur a symbolic cost. Whites, especially poor whites, who constantly sought ways to distinguish themselves from blacks, understood, to quote the famous abolitionist and educational advocate Horace Mann, that education was "the great equalizer." "The poorer classes of whites," Gunnar Myrdal observed in *An American Dilemma*, "are in competition with Negroes for jobs and for social status. One of the things that demarcate them as superior and increase the future potentialities of their children is the fact that white children in publicly supported school buses are taken to fine consolidated schools while often Negro children are given only what amounts to a sham education in dilapidated one-room schools or old Negro churches by underpaid, badly trained Negro teachers."[12]

As a result of whites' enduring opposition to educating blacks, "the question was not so much what kind of education blacks were going to receive but whether they would receive any education at all."[13] Recognizing the precarious state of black education, an African American reformer by the name of Booker T. Washington, whom we met briefly in Chapter 4, offered whites a compromise. Born in a rundown Virginia shack to a slave mother and a white father he never knew, Washington climbed the rungs of the social ladder, becoming his era's most powerful black leader. His breakout moment came in 1895, when he delivered a famous speech at the Atlanta Cotton States and Industrial Exposition, his "Atlanta Compromise," as it came to be known. In this speech, Washington made two concessions. The first was that allowing blacks full access to political power, the fundamental idea of Reconstruction, had been a mistake; the second was that blacks did not strive to be equal to whites. He advised blacks to dedicate themselves to working hard, even in the lowest sectors of society,

Booker T. Washington's "Atlanta Compromise" speech responded to the question of what to do about the abysmal social and economic conditions of blacks in the South.

instead of fighting for equal rights. In turn, he asked whites to treat blacks fairly. The races, said Washington, were to be separate but cooperative: "In all things that are purely social we can be as separate as the fingers, yet as one hand in all things essential to mutual progress."[14]

Washington's compromise rang beautifully in whites' ears, and they rewarded him in kind by providing him with the philanthropic support and political backing necessary to institute his program of "industrial education," which he did in earnest at Tuskegee Institute, an all-black school he founded in 1880. Industrial education amounted to vocational training, as Washington—a man who pulled himself "up from slavery," as he liked to say—believed that the solution to "the race problem" was for blacks to accept their dominated position and to work hard in jobs reserved for them.[15]

As soon as it was introduced, the doctrine of industrial education came under attack from black leaders. Many believed that Washington's program served racial domination and legitimized an unjust educational system, where whites received the best training while blacks were prepared for tedious and backbreaking work. Others pointed out the growing inequality between white and black schools. Still others worried about the psychological damage Washington was inflicting on the minds of black youth by essentially teaching them to accept white society's message about their inferiority.[16]

One of Washington's most outspoken critics was W. E. B. Du Bois, a thinker we have quoted on multiple occasions in earlier chapters. The first African American to graduate with a PhD from Harvard, Du Bois was a scholar of deep erudition and passion, a prolific writer who published works of history, sociology, poetry, and fiction. He also was a tireless political activist, who cofounded the NAACP and edited its magazine, *The Crisis*. An intellectual's intellectual, Du Bois believed that blacks were

"One ever feels his twoness—an American, a Negro; two souls, two thoughts, two unreconciled strivings; two warring ideals in one dark body, whose dogged strength alone keeps it from being torn asunder." —W.E.B. Du Bois

entitled to much more than what Washington's humble industrial education offered. He believed that black education should be no different from white education. In *The Souls of Black Folk*, Du Bois wrote, "Shall we teach them trades, or train them in liberal arts? Neither and both: teach the workers to work and the thinkers to think; make carpenters of carpenters, and philosophers of philosophers, and fops of fools."[17] Du Bois himself took great comfort in the fact that the life of the mind was not bound by color. "I sit with Shakespeare and he winces not," he once wrote. "Across the color-line I move arm in arm with Balzac and Dumas, where smiling men and welcoming women glide in gilded halls."[18]

Du Bois also chastised Washington for perpetuating a kind of symbolic violence, for failing to criticize white supremacy. "Mr. Washington represents in Negro thought the old attitude of adjustment and submission. . . . His doctrine has tended to make the whites, North and South, shift the burden of the Negro problem to the Negro's shoulders and stand aside as critical and rather pessimistic spectators; when in fact the burden belongs to the nation, and the hands of none of us are clean if we bend not our energies to righting these wrongs."[19] To Du Bois, blacks would never arrive at freedom by toiling quietly in the lowliest parts of a society. Rather, the brightest and most talented members of the race—"the talented tenth," he liked to call them—should educate themselves in order to uplift all blacks.[20]

Today, Washington's platform strikes many of us as inadequate. But we must remember the racial context in which he worked and recognize, too, that the words he uttered to white folks (especially those with deep pockets) most likely reflected a political strategy rather than his true feelings. After all, the students of Tuskegee Institute not only learned to work; they also learned to read. Washington accommodated white supremacy to save black education. Du Bois, however, refused to grant white supremacy any such accommodation. Thus, the state of black education at the beginning of the twentieth century was defined by two opposing camps—industrial education and equal education—championed by two powerful black leaders.

Looking back, neither program provided the struggling black masses a means to organize against racism. Washington preached submission and hard work, while Du Bois, who very much believed in fighting against injustice, advanced a program that was rather elitist. All the while, African Americans were hungry for full access to education. Wrote one commentator at the time, "The eagerness of the coloured people for a chance to send their children to school is something astonishing and pathetic. They will submit to all sorts of inconveniences in order that their children may get education."[21] With the dawning of the Civil Rights Movement, blacks' yearning for education would be more fully realized.

"Separate Is Not Equal": School Desegregation

Both those striving to overthrow white supremacy and those struggling to uphold it recognized in education the potential to spark political protest. Of northern capitalists funding black education in the South, one senator bemoaned, "What the North is sending South is not money but dynamite; this education is ruining our Negroes! They're demanding equality."[22] Education, thought many whites, threatened their way of life—and they were right. As nonwhite education coughed and sputtered along—teachers making do with beat-up and outdated textbooks, holding class in dilapidated and segregated schoolhouses—voices of resistance began to ring out. "Education is the kindling of a flame," as Socrates had noted long ago.

Beginning in the 1930s, the NAACP launched an aggressive campaign against legalized school segregation. Led by a forward-thinking and sharp-minded lawyer named Thurgood Marshall (who, as we know, later would become the first African American to sit on the Supreme Court), the NAACP won several legal victories.[23] Other organizations, too, would join the fight. In 1945, the League of United Latin American Citizens came to the aid of five families who, in *Mendez v. Westminster School District*, challenged the segregation of Mexican American students in California. The U.S. District Court of Los Angeles ruled in favor of the families, and its decision was upheld in 1947 by San Francisco's Ninth District Court of Appeals. *Mendez v. Westminster* allowed Earl Warren—then governor of California and later to become Chief Justice of the U.S. Supreme Court and author of the *Brown v. Board of Education* decision—to sign into law a bill repealing the segregation of all students in the state, including African and Asian Americans. Additionally, the case provided a precedent for *Brown*: not only did a federal court rule that "the segregation of Mexican Americans in public schools was a violation of the state law," but also it impressed on NAACP lawyers the importance of marshaling social-scientific evidence to criticize the segregationists' key idea (and motto): "separate but equal."[24]

Using previous legal victories as the building blocks of a larger case, the NAACP filed several lawsuits on behalf of black parents, whose children were denied entry to white schools throughout the country. In 1952, the Supreme Court agreed to hear five of these cases, consolidated under the lead case's title, *Brown v. Board of Education*. Employing strategies used in *Mendez*, the NAACP marshaled an impressive array of evidence challenging the "equal" pillar of the "separate but equal" doctrine. Black and white schools were separate, but they were anything but equal, Thurgood Marshall argued. The court

African American student Linda Brown sits in her segregated classroom at the Monroe School before *Brown v. Board of Education* made school segregation illegal.

Handwriting On The Wall

agreed. In a unanimous decision handed down in 1954, the court ruled on behalf of the NAACP, dismantling the legal basis of racial segregation. "In the field of public education," read Chief Justice Warren, "the doctrine of separate but equal has no place. Separate educational facilities are inherently unequal."[25]

The Supreme Court's decision required segregated schools to be phased out. But instead of matching their strong ruling with equally strong benchmarks and timelines for change, the Court balked, vaguely suggesting that states comply with *Brown* with "all deliberate speed." This gave southern whites time to mount a defiant backlash against school desegregation. They formed citizens' councils and went on the offensive. They tried to abolish public education outright and encouraged whites to start private, all-white institutions. When this strategy failed, they initiated a set of legislative acts dealing with "public placement." These acts permitted racial integration in theory but made actual integration almost impossible by erecting a maze of bureaucratic requirements and procedures through which nonwhite students had to navigate if they hoped to transfer to white schools. Last, citizens' councils lobbied state legislatures to take down the NAACP, a strategy that was enormously effective, as we learned in Chapter 3.[26] Frustrated by the poor enforcement of *Brown*, a decision "heeded with all deliberate delay," as Martin Luther King, Jr., would write, "The phrase 'all deliberate speed' did not mean that another century should be allowed to unfold before we release the Negro children from the narrow pigeonhole of the segregated schools; it meant that, giving some courtesy and consideration to the need for softening old attitudes and outdated customs, democracy must press ahead out of the past of ignorance and intolerance, and into the present of educational opportunity and moral freedom."[27]

Press ahead it did. In the face of white hostility, nonwhites persisted and, as in much of the Civil Rights Movement, change was carried forward on the shoulders of the youth. Nonwhite students across the nation gathered their courage and stepped into formerly white-only schools filled with hostile students, bitter teachers, and unforgiving principals. Among them were nine black teenagers selected by the NAACP (on account of their impressive academic records) to desegregate Little Rock Central High. Members of the Arkansas Citizens' Council lined up and blocked the entrance, an act supported by the state's governor, Orval Faubus, who deployed the National Guard to aid the segregationists. This state-sponsored defiance of *Brown* emboldened whites, who formed mobs to intimidate black students attempting to integrate. The Little Rock Nine, as they came to be known, were able to set foot in Central High only when President Eisenhower provided them with an armed military escort, the 101st Airborne.[28] What followed was a year of terror for the Little Rock Nine, one defined by ongoing verbal and physical attacks, including acid being thrown in the face of fifteen-year-old Melba Patillo Beals, a brutal encounter Beals has recorded in her memoir, *Warriors Don't Cry*.[29]

School integration came slowly to the nation and more slowly still to the South. By one estimate, substantial integration did not occur in the South until ten to fifteen years after *Brown*.[30] But change did come. By 1975, the percentage of black children attending all-black schools in the South had dropped to 18 percent, and nearly half the black children of that region were enrolled in majority-white schools. These are impressive numbers by any measure, considering that just twenty years earlier, schools had been almost absolutely segregated.[31] That said, *Brown* did not once and for all plunge a stake in the heart of legal segregation.

Because courts understood racial segregation as a matter of discrimination (for example, where qualified nonwhite applicants are turned away strictly on the basis of their race), they failed fully to grasp the complexity of the problem and, therefore, did not develop effective and enduring desegregation initiatives. Operating under the individualistic fallacy, the courts outlawed intentional school segregation, but not school segregation caused by systemic racism operating in other realms of social life—most consequentially, the residential field. This was most clearly seen in the 1974 case *Milliken v. Bradley*, in which a divided U.S. Supreme Court ruled that integrating schools by busing students between the black inner city and the white suburbs was unacceptable and not mandated by *Brown*, since schools forced to participate had not violated the law by actively discriminating against students. The Court ruled, in other words, that racial school segregation attributed to intentional acts of discrimination was unlawful, but racial school segregation attributed to residential segregation was not.[32]

The 1970s and 1980s witnessed continued efforts to desegregate *within* school districts, but these efforts were weakened by vigorous resistance, including by white ethnics, who joined in protests and even, in some cases, rioted against compulsory busing. Boston saw some of the most unsettling violence, with multiple deadly or near-deadly incidents involving mob actions by white ethnics (especially Italian and Irish Americans) as well as retaliatory violence by black youth.[33] Struggles against busing also were carried out indirectly through large-scale white flight into outlying suburbs and through movement of many remaining white children out of the public schools into private and parochial schools. This same pattern repeated itself across the country. By the late 1980s, many formerly embattled urban school districts were finding themselves serving a greatly diminished student population—and one that was increasingly nonwhite. And in many cases, those schools became run-down and underfunded. Because America's neighborhoods and school districts remain

Elizabeth Eckford, one of the nine black students whose integration into Little Rock's Central High School was ordered by a Federal Court, ignores the hostile screams and stares of fellow students on her first day of school.

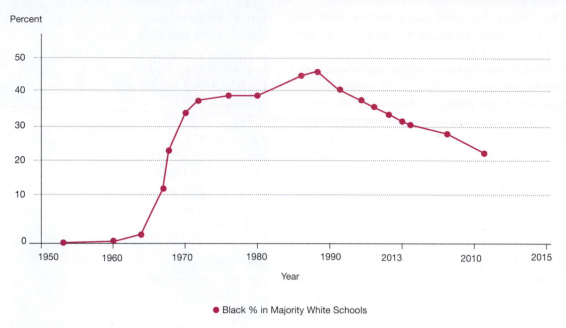

Due to poor enforcement of integration legislation, America's schools remain segregated by race.

Source: U.S. Department of Education, National Center for Education Statistics, Common Core of Data (CCD), Public Elementary/Secondary School Universe Survey Data. Data prior to 1991 obtained from the analysis of the Office of Civil Rights data in Orfield, G. (1983). *Public School Desegregation in the United States,* 1968-1980. Washington, D.C.: Joint Center for Political Studies.

segregated by race, and because school segregation is a direct reflection of residential segregation, our schools today remain separate and unequal.

WHITENESS IN EDUCATION

Whiteness, as you might recall from our introductory chapter, is racial domination normalized. How, then, is racial domination normalized in our curriculum, classrooms, and campuses? This section addresses this question, focusing on how certain racialized practices and bodies of knowledge camouflage themselves under the guise of normalcy. In doing so, this section focuses primarily on college education, although the points advanced in the following pages certainly are applicable at the primary and secondary levels. We have decided to focus on college education in order to highlight the world in which you are now a part and to help you critically to evaluate your classes, dorm rooms, and sorority parties with a fine-tuned sociological imagination.

Whiteness in the Curriculum

Du Bois was an ardent critic of the many ways in which whiteness blunts scientific progress and distorts truths about the world. After reviewing the history of Reconstruction he concluded in 1935 that "with a determination unparalleled in science, the mass of American writers have started out so to distort the facts of the greatest critical period of American history as to prove right wrong and wrong right." They did this, Du Bois continued, by bending historical facts to accommodate racial domination, so much so, in fact, that history became nothing more than propaganda for white supremacy.[34] Just as he feared, the distortions promoted by historians made their way into state-approved textbooks that justified slavery, criticized Reconstruction, and mourned the fall of the South, books that circulated well into the 1950s.[35]

Much has changed since Du Bois's time, but much also has remained the same. One still finds today Eurocentric historical accounts that consider the stories and experiences of Americans of European descent central to our knowledge of American history and those of non-European Americans marginal. Fundamental to the historical account of the birth of the United States is the signing of the Declaration of Independence (but not the governance of the Iroquois Nation, from which many principles of democracy were borrowed by American statesmen); Abraham Lincoln's Emancipation Proclamation (but not slave revolts); and the labor of white meatpackers, brewers, and steelers (but not so much Asian American railroad workers).[36]

Eurocentric history not only silences the voices of nonwhites; it also tends to dull the sharp edge of past injustices. One need only read one of the many books or watch one of the many movies on the Civil War to discover how some historical accounts gloss over the hell that was slavery, preferring to entertain a nostalgia for the South's "good old days"; one need only peruse one of the hundreds of books on American immigration to learn much of "immigrant gumption, hard work, and determination" and little of anti-immigrant violence and discrimination.[37] The fact that more Americans know of Martin Luther King, Jr., than of Emmett Till, or of Thanksgiving dinner between pilgrims and Native Americans than of the Indian Wars, speaks to how whiteness in our historical imagination considers past wrongs something to be "forgotten, distorted, skimmed over."[38]

Or consider how whiteness informs the field of literature. Until very recently, the Western literary canon—the collection of works consecrated as "classics"—comprised almost entirely works by white men. Although works by white authors largely were considered universal, able to capture the experiences of all people, works by nonwhites were considered specialized and particular—they captured "a perspective." An analysis of literary works themselves, moreover, reveals that a fictionalized, nonwhite presence is essential to many white novelists' and poets' understanding of American-ness.[39] In *Playing in the Dark: Whiteness and the Literary Imagination,* Toni Morrison demonstrates how white writers have depicted blacks as savage and dimwitted to create an image of whiteness as essentially civilized and intelligent—that is, as blackness's mirror image.

In Mark Twain's *Adventures of Huckleberry Finn,* Jim helps Huck realize Huck's freedom.

It is only through Mark Twain's enslavement of Jim, a black slave, that Huck Finn was able to experience freedom. And Ernest Hemingway made white women pure and beautiful by depicting black women as predatory and inhuman.[40] Blackness was sullied to make whiteness shine clean and unblemished. "Africanism," writes Morrison, "is the vehicle by which the American self knows itself as not enslaved, but free; not repulsive, but desirable; not helpless, but licensed and powerful; not history-less, but historical; not damned, but innocent; not a blind accident of evolution, but a progressive fulfillment of destiny."[41]

Consider, too, how whiteness affects the field of anthropology. The anthropologist's method—ethnography, the practice of embedding oneself in a foreign culture so as to learn about it—has helped to normalize whiteness. America's nonwhite groups traditionally have been treated as objects of study, as exotic cultures within our nation, worthy of observation and scrutiny. White communities, in contrast, communities from which many anthropologists come, have been considered uninteresting and domestic—in a word, normal. Anthropologists have treated Native American communities as especially important settings for research. One can find literally hundreds of anthropological books on tribal communities. In many of these works, Native Americans are treated as vestiges of a bygone era, as "genuine" only if they uphold their ancestors' cultural practices and lifestyles. Of anthropologists, Vine Deloria, Jr., has observed, "Indians must be redefined in terms that white men will accept, even if that means re-Indianizing them according to a white man's idea of what they were like in the past and should logically become in the future. . . . [But] would [a school board] submit to a group of Indians coming to Boston and telling [Bostonians] what a modern Irishman was like?"[42]

Whiteness even can be found in progressive intellectual movements, such as feminism. Women of color feminists, for example, long have criticized the mainstream women's movement for claiming to speak for "all women" while ignoring the unique struggles of women of color. A defining characteristic of feminist discourse, women of color feminists have argued, is the assumption that all women experience the same troubles, regardless of race, class, or sexuality. However, to fully understand and combat sexism, we must explore how it intersects, and feeds on, other systems of domination, those grounded in racial difference or economic inequality, for example. As Chandra Mohanty has noted in *Feminism without Borders*, mainstream feminist scholarship that fails to reflect on the ways whiteness influences its thought "inadvertently produces Western women as the only legitimate subjects of struggle, while Third World women are heard as fragmented, inarticulate voices in (and from) the dark."[43]

Recently, nonwhite and white scholars alike have taken steps to expose whiteness in intellectual thought. And their efforts have yielded impressive results. But the challenge remains, to quote Mohanty once more, of "decoloniz[ing] our disciplinary and pedagogical practices."[44] This would require paying special attention to how texts treat (or refuse even to talk about) race, how authors write primarily to a white audience, how scientists use metaphors that draw on the white (and male) experience, how philosophers flatten different racialized histories and struggles under the umbrella of "universal humanity," how intellectual accomplishments of Europeans still are considered the standard against which all works must be measured, and so forth.

Whiteness on College Campuses

Leaving family and hometown to attend college can be a painful and frightening experience, especially for first-generation college students and those from small towns or religious communities.[45] The transition also can be trying for students of color attending majority-white universities.[46] White students from rural America often view their college town as the most diverse place they have lived, whereas students of color from cities with sizable nonwhite populations often view the same town as the whitest place they have lived. Many students of color feel unwelcome, isolated, and bereft of community on predominately white campuses—and experience a significant culture shock during their first year. For their part, white students, studies have shown, often feel uncomfortable around their nonwhite peers, a sentiment that can cause them to avoid interacting with students of color or, in some cases, to treat them with hostility.[47] In a survey of students from ten universities, 33 percent of students of color reported experiencing harassment, compared to 22 percent of white students. And 31 percent of students of color felt the classroom climate was unwelcoming for underrepresented students, but only 21.2 percent of white students felt the same way.[48]

Universities often prioritize certain groups' history, culture, and needs over others'. For instance, because most universities do not honor Jewish holidays, many Jewish students who wish to attend religious services are forced to miss class during Yom Kippur and other holy days during the Jewish High Holidays. And Jewish students who wish to remain kosher usually have to find their meals someplace other than the convenient cafeteria frequented by their non-Jewish peers.[49] Native Americans attending universities with Indian mascots, such as the University of Illinois (Fighting Illini) or Florida State University (Seminoles), must put up with humiliating and contorted caricatures of Native Americans. Some colleges cancel classes in honor of Martin Luther King Day, but others refuse. "In this multicultural society, it's impossible to honor everyone's holidays," one might say. That may be true, but at the very least, we should ask whose culture and traditions are honored and whose are brushed aside.

Some of you already may have picked up on certain ways whiteness helps to guide your classroom discussions, especially those about race. Think about the class for which you are reading this book. In your classroom conversations, which students talk with confidence, and which keep quiet? If your classroom is like others around the nation, then most likely there is a group of nonwhite students who do a good deal of the talking and a contingent of white students who don't seem to have much to say.[50] Why? While many nonwhite students grow up talking about race, many white students did not. Accordingly, white students sometimes find themselves uncomfortable in classroom discussions about race, fearing they will say something ignorant or offensive and hear it from their

Native Americans attending universities with Indian mascots must put up with humiliating and contorted caricatures of Native Americans.

peers. Other times, white students, immersed in their assumed racelessness, are surprised to learn that they, too, can be the objects of stereotypes and narrow thinking.[51]

In many classrooms, nonwhite students are dubbed as (or, sometimes, dub themselves) the "real experts" on racism, as if whites—whose ancestors literally *invented* race—had nothing to do with it. This bias is manifest most obviously (and offensively) when a white professor asks a nonwhite student to speak for all members of his or her racial or ethnic group. "Samir, tell us," the professor might say, "how do Arab Americans feel about the war on terrorism?" If Samir is feeling feisty, he might reply, "I don't know. Why don't you go and ask America's 3.7 million citizens of Arab descent? I can, however, tell you what *I* think." Only whiteness allows the professor to pose such a question, to ask Samir to act as the voice of "his people," as if Arab Americans had but one voice, unified on every issue. Would a white student ever be asked to speak on behalf of all white people?

Research has shown that students of color receive differential treatment during their college careers, treatment that can have negative effects on their academic records. Educators asked to evaluate similarly performing white and nonwhite students often give nonwhite students lower marks. In one experiment, teachers were asked to examine the definitions students attached to words and to evaluate those students' verbal skills. Researchers did not vary the definitions but did vary the race of the students. Rating identical definitions, teachers attached poorer grades to black students.[52] Studies such as this (and many others with similar findings) suggest that nonwhite students do not receive the same returns for their academic investments, relative to their white peers.

The situation is all the more unfair to women of color, because sexism often clouds educators' judgment of female students' potential. Many studies have found that educators view women as less intelligent than men. One experiment, for example, distributed résumés of young psychologists to established psychologists. Like the verbal skill experiment, the résumés were identical except that some were assigned male names, others female names. Overwhelmingly, the psychologists evaluated the male résumés more favorably.[53]

Whiteness not only informs classroom dynamics and academic evaluations; it also can be found in other aspects of college life. Many college students find dorm life to be stressful and uncomfortable, but the situation can be intensified for nonwhite students in predominantly white dorms. A young Puerto Rican might be asked repeatedly on what sports team he plays. A Latina student from the big city might be asked if she grew up in the projects. An Asian American student struggling through his chemistry class might be told that Asians are supposed to be good at science. A Native American student might join her friends at a Halloween party only to find that one partygoer is dressed like an "Indian."[54] Indeed, an entire book could be written on how racial stereotypes, quietly veiled during most days of the year, suddenly burst confidently and clumsily to the surface in full view on Halloween night and during other masquerade events. In 2007, white students attending California's Santa Clara University hosted a "South of the Border" party and dressed up as Hispanic janitors, gardeners, and pregnant teenagers.[55] In January 2014, a fraternity at Arizona State University

Stereotyping

threw a party to commemorate Martin Luther King, Jr.'s birthday, during which nonblack students wore loose basketball jerseys, flashed gang signs, and drank from hollowed-out watermelons.[56]

And, as we have mentioned before, hate crimes are not uncommon occurrences on college campuses. According to one FBI report, half of all surveyed colleges and universities documented on-campus hate crimes during the previous year.[57] Consider the events that unfolded on the campus of San Jose State University in the fall of 2013. A black freshman was tormented by his white roommates, who hung up a Confederate flag and a picture of Hitler, wrote "nigger" on the room's white board, and placed a bike lock around the black student's neck.[58]

And yet, college campuses are precisely where some of the best antiracist work is being carried out. For every student who commits a racist hate crime on campus, there are antiracists who demonstrate against such events. If antiracist activism has slowed around the country in other fields of life, it has proliferated on college campuses, thanks in large part to the commitment of white and nonwhite antiracists and student leaders.

EDUCATIONAL INEQUALITY

Compared to whites and Asians, blacks, Hispanics, and Native Americans are much more likely to drop out of high school. According to the U.S. Department of Education, the dropout rate among public high school students in 2012 was 7 percent for Asians, 15 percent for whites, 24 percent for Hispanics, 32 percent for Native Americans, and 32 percent for blacks.[59] Some students who drop out of high school later return and graduate or obtain the equivalent of a high school diploma (e.g., passing the GED). Another way to view the data, then, is to examine the percentage of twenty-five- to twenty-nine-year-olds who have received at least a high school diploma or its equivalent. In 2013, roughly 95 percent of whites and Asians and 90 percent of African Americans in that age range received at least a high school diploma or its equivalent. The same was true for only 76 percent of Hispanics. When last measured, the white-Hispanic education gap for secondary education was eighteen percentage points. Although this is sizable, it is a significant reduction from what it was a generation ago. In 1990, for example, the white-Hispanic education gap for high school completion was thirty-two percentage points.[60]

The shrinking gap separating high school completion rates of whites and Asians, on the one hand, and African Americans, Hispanics, and Native Americans, on the other, is encouraging. However, in today's economy a high school diploma does not open up the same employment opportunities as in generations past. While the incomes of those with a high school education have stagnated in recent years, the incomes of those with a college degree have grown. A key question, then, is, to what degree do we observe racial disparities in college completion rates?

Regrettably, as the education gap has shrunk in recent years at the secondary level, it has increased at the postsecondary level. Between 1990 and 2013, the percentage of twenty-five- to twenty-nine-year olds who had attained at least a bachelor's degree increased from 43 to 58 percent for Asian Americans, from 26 to 40 percent for whites, from 13 to 20 percent for blacks, and from 8 to 16 percent

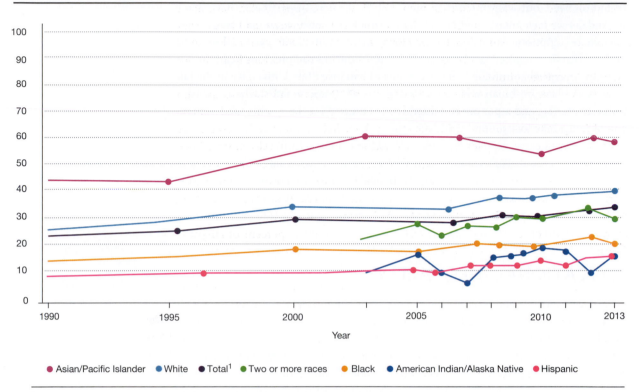

● Asian/Pacific Islander ● White ● Total[1] ● Two or more races ● Black ● American Indian/Alaska Native ● Hispanic

[1]Included in the total, but not shown separately, are estimates for persons from other racial/ethnic groups.
NOTE: Race categories exclude persons of Hispanic ethnicity. Prior to 2005, data on American Indians/Alaska Natives and persons of two or more races were not available.
Source U.S. Department of Commerce, Census Bureau, Current Population Survey (CPS), "Annual Social and Economic Supplement," selected years, 1990–2013. See *Digest of Education Statistics 2013*, table 104.20.

for Hispanics. College graduation rates are up across the board, but this actually has widened educational disparities. Between 1990 and 2013, the white-black college graduation gap increased to twenty from thirteen percentage points, and the white-Hispanic graduation gap increased to twenty-five from eighteen percentage points.[61]

Importantly, there also is considerable variation within racial groups with respect to educational attainment and achievement. Research has concluded that Mexican Americans score lower on standardized tests, possess lower educational aspirations and expectations, and complete college at lower rates than do Cubans, Dominicans, or Puerto Ricans. Southeast Asians and Pacific Islanders lag behind their Korean, Japanese, Indian, and Chinese peers in all measures of educational success—a fact often lost on policymakers and school administrators, who tend to ignore disadvantaged Asian groups while implementing programs addressing racial inequalities. Gender differences persist as well, with women graduating from college at slightly higher rates than men.[62] Black women, in particular, have made impressive strides in the educational field in the last twenty years, and today, they have more ambitious educational aspirations, graduate from college at higher rates, and earn higher marks than black men, a trend with enormous ramifications for African American culture.[63]

What explains racial inequalities in education? "Poverty and the unequal distribution of wealth," we might reply. Indeed, economic inequality and educational inequality are wound tightly together, such that one helps determine the other and vice versa. Studies have shown that students with highly educated and wealthy parents are advantaged in school. And, in many cases, racial disparities in education shrink considerably once researchers account for economic inequality. Parents' financial assets help students pay for school supplies, computers, field trips, private tutors, college tuition, and a whole gamut of things that constitute the ticket price of a solid education. For example, in 2011 only 58 percent of Hispanic households had the Internet, compared to 76 percent of whites and 83 percent of Asian households.[64]

The role of economic inequality in explaining racial disparities in education cannot be underestimated.[65] But the economic explanation is not the only one supported by research. And since we already have devoted an early chapter to explaining racialized economic inequality (see Chapter 4), we now focus on three other explanations that help us understand racial inequality in education, explanations that center on the family, culture, and schools.

The Role of the Family

A family can provide students not only with material resources but also with immaterial resources that help them get ahead in school. How do parents pass along to their children noneconomic resources—skills, beliefs, knowledge, dispositions, network contacts—that advantage them in the educational field? And how might that help us better understand racial inequality?

Cultural Capital If we refer to parents' financial resources as "economic capital," we also can refer to the degree to which they introduce their children to cultural information and practices that will advantage them later in life as "cultural capital." Cultural capital can be defined as the sum total of one's knowledge of established and exalted cultural activities and practices.[66] Your knowledge of certain cultural topics (such as classical music or French Impressionism) and cultural practices (such as how to dress properly for a dinner party or how to sound confident and smart when discussing politics) can benefit you in the educational realm. Just as one type of currency can be exchanged for another—dollars for Euros, yen for pesos—cultural knowledge can be exchanged for educational achievement (graduating from an elite school) or economic advancement (landing a dream job).

Obtaining cultural capital at a young age can pay off later on in life.

We say "established and exalted cultural activities and practices" when defining cultural capital because not all cultural knowledge behaves as capital. You can be the foremost expert in electric music and know just how to act at a Daft Punk concert, but that won't get you very far in college. But your knowledge of Greek philosophy and your ability to debate Plato might. Cultural capital has mostly to do with one's experience with and understanding of "high-brow" culture, such as opera, art, classical music, and canonical literature; it also has to do with one's facility in spoken and written English.[67]

A person's background—especially her class and ethnic upbringing—provides her with different degrees of cultural capital, which, in turn, helps her to reproduce her social position. Many people from wealthy homes are endowed, from a very young age, with large amounts of cultural capital—they visit museums, are taught to play the piano, and learn the language and etiquette of the elite class—which allows them to fit into the upper echelons of society. And if those from more humble origins seem uncomfortable at black tie events or uncertain during classroom debates, it is because, unlike their more well-to-do peers, they have not inherited significant amounts of such cultural capital.[68] Cultural capital not only helps one to navigate certain situations and to distinguish between "refined" and "vulgar" conduct; it also marks the person who does the navigating, indicating what sort of a person she is, how "well-groomed" she might be.[69]

Researchers have found that even before children are out of diapers, they acquire certain advantages and disadvantages associated with their parents' social standing. Child psychologists Betty Hart and Todd Risley took a hard look at the way parents talk to their young children, and they discovered that middle-class parents direct an average of 487 utterances at their children per hour, whereas parents on welfare direct only 178 utterances per hour. Middle-class parents not only talk to their children more; they also are more encouraging. By age three, the average middle-class child has been offered roughly 500,000 encouragements and 80,000 discouragements. Those numbers are reversed for poor children, who by age three have heard roughly 75,000 encouragements and 200,000 discouragements. Hart and Risley went on to demonstrate that how frequently and positively parents converse with their children is tied not only to childhood language competence and intelligence—by age three, the average middle-class child knows 1,110 words and has an IQ of 117, while the average poor child knows only 525 words and has an IQ of 79—but also to subsequent success in school.[70]

Other studies have shown how parents consciously and unconsciously work to nurture within their children certain cultural competences. In her book *Unequal Childhoods,* sociologist Annette Lareau argues that parenting styles unique to middle-class households better prepare children for success in the academic and business worlds. Working-class parents, she observes, set clear boundaries between adults and children and encourage long stretches of child-initiated play and leisure time, whereas middle-class parents tend to provide their children with several regimented activities (soccer practice, ballet lessons, choir rehearsal) and teach them to regard adults as their equals. The result? Middle-class children obtain a sense of entitlement and confidence, and they quickly learn how to question and challenge adults, qualities that greatly advantage them in the classroom.[71] Thus, "the disadvantages that poverty imposes on children aren't primarily about material goods. The real advantages that middle-class children gain come from more elusive processes: the language that their parents use, the attitudes toward life that they convey."[72]

A child in possession of large amounts of cultural capital becomes endowed with characteristics that encourage academic success. She develops a disposition that evokes respect and admiration from teachers and peers—a certain way of standing and sitting, of talking and listening, a class-specific posture and essence. Not only this, but she has a well-tuned sense of informal practices, a certain know-how, that gives her a boost. She has better access to the "hidden curriculum," that collection of unspoken "values, dispositions, social and behavioral expectations . . . essential to satisfactory progression through school."[73] The hidden curriculum comprises anything from knowing how to email your professors to responding in class to a question to which you don't know the answer. A student with a middle-class sense of entitlement might feel comfortable challenging her grade on a paper, but a student with a more working-class disposition perhaps thinks, "What you see is what you get."[74] It is small wonder that studies have documented a direct correlation between cultural capital and academic achievement (test scores and grades).[75]

Because parents with more schooling and economic capital tend to have more cultural capital, and because white and Asian parents tend to have more schooling and economic capital than do black, Hispanic, and Native American parents, we can begin to understand how the unequal distribution of cultural capital helps to reproduce racial inequalities. However, the story is more complicated than that. It is not only the case that racial privilege is accompanied by economic privilege, as we discussed in Chapter 4; it also is the case that the consumption of cultural activities varies by race. All families "do culture" in one way or another, but studies have shown that Asian, but even moreso white, families tend to participate in more activities that foster cultural capital. That is, white families are more likely than nonwhite families to attend classical music concerts and opera, to frequent museums, and to enroll their kids in ballet classes. Such variation remains even after accounting for differences in parental education.[76]

This provokes the question: who gets to decide which cultural practices can be cashed in as "capital" and which cannot? One answer is that racial domination gets to decide. By and large, it is your familiarity with *Eurocentric* art, literature, language, and history that garners cultural capital. Whiteness educates cultural capital, and cultural capital upholds whiteness. Noting this does not make Picasso less brilliant or opera less beautiful. But it should make us appreciate why only specific kinds of cultural knowledge can be "cashed in," thereby helping to produce racial inequalities in education.

Familism may be a double-edged sword with respect to its impact on school performance, advantaging students in some respects while disadvantaging them in others.

Social Capital The family can be a key source of another type of capital as well: social capital. If cultural capital has to do with *what* you know, social capital refers to *whom* you know. It is the sum of all resources one accrues by virtue of being connected to a network of people.[77] *Familism* is a specific variant of social capital having to do with one's attachment to, and reliance on, family-based relationships.[78]

Many researchers have explored the relationship between social capital, especially familism, and educational success. By and large, they have discovered that students benefit greatly from extended family ties. Psychologists have found that familism produces positive psychological effects, while educational scholars argue that familism can mitigate the negative experiences associated with belonging to a dominated racial group.[79] Several studies have documented a positive relationship between social capital and high school and college completion among at-risk youth. Others have noted that as students' social capital increases, so too do their educational aspirations and ambition.[80]

Familism, studies have shown, also is an important component of Hispanic culture. Hispanics value interdependence, as well as family support and obligations, more than other racial or ethnic groups; they report higher degrees of familial cohesion and assist family members in instrumental ways to a greater degree than do other racial or ethnic groups; they also live in denser kinship networks than other racial or ethnic groups.[81] After examining how familism affects Hispanic students in school, researchers have documented a positive relationship. High academic performance of Hispanic students has been linked to social capital provided by family networks, as family members help students to complete their homework and to make informed educational decisions.[82]

But familism also may serve as an impediment to students' educational success. American sociologist Alejandro Portes has pointed out that families with dense network ties—who often place weighty demands on their talented and privileged members and value group conformity—can stifle high achievers' motivation and accomplishments. Indeed, some researchers have attributed the poor performance of Hispanic students to the unique demands placed on them by their parents, demands that might include caring for their siblings or grandparents or working to supplement the family income.[83]

Social capital—and familism, in particular—may be a double-edged sword with respect to its impact on school performance, advantaging students in some respects while disadvantaging them in others. Social capital works best when combined with other forms of capital. A student well connected to economically downtrodden and poorly educated family members will benefit less than one connected to a network rich in cultural and economic capital. You know the game. If your father graduated from a prestigious university and remembers his alma mater when donating money, the school's admissions board might take a long, hard look at your application. If your aunt is the CEO of an architecture firm, you might not have to worry about securing a good job after college. People belonging to racial groups that have been, and currently are being, excluded from elite networks might not receive much return from their familistic ties, while the racially privileged, connected to networks in which advantage has accumulated over generations, might reap healthy gains. Successful Americans often assure themselves that, as the old saying goes, they "pulled themselves up by their own bootstraps." But if we take a closer look, usually we notice that many hands, at one time or another, have pulled at those bootstraps.

The Role of Culture

"Culture," an elusive concept if there ever was one, has to do with the realm of meaning-making, symbols, and traditions. "Cultural patterns," said the great American anthropologist Clifford Geertz, "provide a template or blueprint for the organization of social psychological processes, much as genetic systems provide such a template for the organization of organic processes. . . . The reason such symbolic templates are necessary is that, as has often been remarked, human behavior is inherently extremely plastic."[84] How, then, does culture affect racial inequalities in education—and how does it not?

Does Culture Help Explain Asian American Educational Achievement? By any measure, Asian Americans have the highest rates of educational attainment in the nation—and by a significant margin. For example, the Asian-white college graduation gap for people between the ages of twenty-five and twenty-nine has remained around eighteen percentage points since 1990. In other words, the gap between Asian and white college completion rates is equivalent to the gap between white and black college completion rates. Unlike all other groups, the *majority* of Asian Americans between the ages of twenty-five and twenty-nine have graduated from college. And one in five has obtained a master's degree or higher, compared to one in eleven whites, and one in thirty black and Hispanic twenty-five- to twenty-nine-year-olds.[85]

Does "culture" contribute to the high rates of Asian American educational attainment? In part, yes. Asian American parents often play a considerable role in boosting their children's educational expectations and pushing them to achieve those goals. This appears especially true among East Asian immigrant parents, including those with small incomes, who "generally have high educational expectations for their children, talk to them often about their progress toward their expectations, find ways to marshal supplemental resources to help them, such as by sending them to Chinese schools after school, on weekends, and during school breaks, and make concrete plans for the future, such as by saving for college."[86]

But Asian American parents who have been in America for generations also seem to place a high value on educational success—so much so, in fact, that some judge their success as a parent based on their children's educational achievement.[87] As a result, many Asian American parents push their children to work in school. One study found that Asian American high school juniors studied six hours more per week than their white peers. Another found that while only 40 percent of white and Hispanic high school students did homework for at least five days a week, over two-thirds of Asian American high schoolers did.[88] Psychologists have posited that the educational expectations of Asian American households may be driven by the Confucian conviction that life should be spent striving toward perfection, as Confucian ideas cast a long shadow over East Asian cultures. As one observer put it, "transmitted down through the generations, this 'moral mandate' for self-improvement 'has tremendous motivational impact.'"[89]

That said, we also should be mindful of the social and historical circumstances unique to different racial and ethnic groups. Historically, certain racial groups were brought to the United States against their will—through the slave trade—or were rendered "minorities" through the workings of colonialism, while others voluntarily migrated here. This distinction between "involuntary" and "voluntary minorities"—and we note that some racial or ethnic groups fit snugly into neither of these categories—also is important to understanding modern-day differences across racial categories. Additionally, the economic privileges of voluntary minorities, privileges often accrued in immigrants' home countries, translate into other kinds of privileges, including educational success. A significant number of East Asian immigrants came to America with healthy amounts of economic and cultural capital. They had college degrees and savings accounts and applied for professional jobs. As a result, they were significantly advantaged relative to nonwhite groups that had been systematically excluded from the ranks of the American middle class.[90] A recent study found that 50 to 80 percent of foreign-born fathers from Japan, Korea, Hong Kong, Taiwan, India, and Pakistan were college graduates, but only 4 to 10 percent of fathers from Mexico and the Caribbean were.[91]

The Model Minority Ever since the nineteenth century, white America has regarded its Asian inhabitants as constituting a "model minority." After the Civil War, a Baton Rouge newspaper compared Chinese immigrants to blacks, saying the former "were more obedient and industrious than the negro, work as well without an overseer, and at the same time are more cleanly in their habits."[92] The model minority image was reborn near the end of the Civil Rights Era, when in 1966 William Peterson published an article in the *New York Times Sunday Magazine* entitled "Success Story, Japanese-American Style." "By any criterion of citizenship that we choose," he wrote, "the Japanese Americans are better than any group in our society, including native-born whites." Peterson referred to African Americans and Hispanic Americans, by contrast, as "problem minorities."[93] Peterson's article was widely circulated and read, and since then, Asian Americans have been depicted in the popular press as America's most successful nonwhite group. *Time, Newsweek,* and 60 Minutes have dubbed Asians "model minorities"; *Fortune* magazine has called them "superminorities"; and *The New Republic* has claimed "the triumph of Asians" is "America's greatest success story." Journalists rave that Asian Americans are "winning all the science prizes," "outperforming others at school and work," and even "outwhiting whites."[94]

To think of Asian Americans in terms of the stereotype of the model minority is to think of them, first and foremost, as whiz kids, extremely gifted in school (especially when it comes to the more technical disciplines, such as physics, math, and computer science), disciplined beyond their age, geeky and quirky, quiet and polite. If anything, this description seems positive, even flattering. But are there such things as "positive" stereotypes—or are there only stereotypes, oversimplified ways of thinking that can result in harmful consequences for the people they target? For Asian Americans, the burden to succeed sometimes can result in a lose-lose situation. If they succeed—if they claim the coveted science prize or win the spelling bee—some non–Asian Americans may think, "Well, of course they won. They're Asian." But if they lose, many people might think, "Why didn't they win? They're Asian." In both scenarios, Asian Americans' racial attributes take precedence over their personhood.

Some Asian Americans consider the educational success of their child a marker of their success as a parent.

Every "positive" stereotypical statement also invokes its antipode. The saying "Blacks are good athletes" can mean "Black aren't very intelligent." The claim "Jews are excellent at managing money" can mean "Jews are stingy and greedy." In the same way, all claims attaching a glorifying attribute to Asian Americans inevitably affix a degrading attribute as well. In the words of Frank Wu, author of *Yellow*, "To be intelligent is to be calculating and too clever; to be gifted in math and science is to be mechanical and not creative, lacking interpersonal skills and leadership potential. To be polite is to be inscrutable and submissive. To be hard working is to be an unfair competitor for regular human beings and not a well-rounded, likable individual."[95]

For some Asian Americans, the pressure to live up to the model minority image is too heavy a cross to bear. Young Asian American women—faced with parental and societal pressures to be perfect students as well as perfect women, girlfriends, and wives—commit suicide at alarmingly high rates. High school and college-aged Asian American women have the highest suicide rates of women in any racial group. In fact, suicide is the second-leading cause of the death of Asian American women between the ages of fifteen and twenty-four.[96]

Fear of Asian American overachievement has caused a good deal of anxiety on college campuses among non-Asian students, white and nonwhite alike. Students at MIT joke that the acronym of their university stands for "Made in Taiwan," not Massachusetts Institute of Technology. Some white University of California—Los Angeles students claim that UCLA stands for "United Caucasians Lost among Asians." Students at the University of California—Berkeley were greeted with the words "Stop the Asian Hordes" spray-painted on the Engineering School's walls, while a former student body president of that university once remarked, "Some students say that if they see too many Asians in a class, they are not going to take it because the curve will be too high." A newspaper reporter quoted a non-Asian Yale student remarking, "If you are weak in math or science and find yourself assigned to a class with a majority of Asian kids, the only thing to do is transfer to a different section."[97] Because they view Asians as academically gifted or especially driven, some non-Asian students treat them as a threat to their academic success and future prosperity.

Oppositional Culture The work of anthropologist John Ogbu has greatly influenced how social scientists conceive of the relationship between cultural practices and racial inequalities in education. Ogbu believed that many involuntary minorities have developed an oppositional culture, a collection of linguistic, behavioral, aesthetic, and spiritual attitudes and practices formed in direct opposition to mainstream white culture. Oppositional culture is structured by powerful historical forces. Black oppositional culture, for example, is rooted in slave times, when enslaved Africans developed a specific style of talking and joking, a repertoire of folkloric, musical, and religious practices that helped them cope with the pains of slavery. Savvy to the fact that whites, who denied them access to white culture and prohibited them from reading and writing, held to a set of assumptions about how blacks "should" talk and act, many enslaved Africans learned how to "code switch," how to exude a persona of servitude in front of whites, while back at slave quarters freely criticizing and mocking whites and their oppressive system.[98] As the Ethiopian proverb goes, "When the great lord passes, the wise peasant bows deeply and silently farts."[99]

After the fall of slavery, African Americans continued to navigate between the dominant white society and the marginalized black community. In the process, they formed a cultural identity that directly negated the mainstream white society, which had caused so much of their suffering. This oppositional culture, argue Ogbu and others, is a major part of African American culture today and, what is more, might disadvantage blacks and other involuntary minorities in school. Specifically, Ogbu has argued that black and Latino students do not aspire to excel in school because if they did, they would be viewed by their peers as "selling out" or "acting white." It is not so much that these students deny the importance of a good education as that they are unwilling to adopt certain behaviors, perceived as uniquely "white," which would allow them to do well in the white-dominated educational realm: speaking "standard English," for example.[100] A Mexican American student who refuses to mix Spanish with English (that is, to talk "Spanglish") might face ridicule from his friends, and a black student who trades in her dark hoodie for a starched blouse from The Gap might find herself invited to fewer and fewer parties. According to a recent survey, 22 percent of Hispanic students polled claimed that "my friends make fun of people who try to do well in school," whereas only 13 percent of whites reported likewise.[101]

Ogbu's theory of oppositional culture—first put forward in the 1970s—has received mixed support. Scholars have found that young nonwhites' identities simply do not hinge on an oppositional culture mindset, that blacks and Hispanics feel no pressure to reject so-called white values.[102] A recent study of over 11,000 students, for example, concluded that African Americans are just as engaged in school as are their white counterparts. Another discovered that pressures against "acting white" are found only in schools with a high percentage of nonwhites and low-income students enrolled in college preparation courses.[103]

In her book, *Keepin' It Real: School Success beyond Black and White*, sociologist Prudence Carter developed a theory of race, culture, and schooling that modifies Ogbu's concept of "acting white." Drawing on ten months of in-depth study of high school students living in Yonkers, New York, Carter argues that some black and Latino students "perform blackness" or "act Spanish" but that doing so does not mean being apathetic toward school. "Resistance to 'acting white,'" she observes, "for many African-American students is about maintaining cultural identity, not about embracing and rejecting the dominant standards of achievement. . . . Resistance to 'acting white' refers to [students'] refusal to adhere to the cultural default setting in U.S. society . . . [,] the generic American, white, middle-class patterns of speech and mannerisms, dress and physical appearance, and tastes in music and art forms."[104]

However, problems arise for black and Latino students when their teachers do not deem their cultural attitudes and practices appropriate and positive. Many educators favor Eurocentric knowledge and cultural styles over non-Eurocentric ones, even if the latter are not avowedly anti-intellectual. Consider the example of a young black man from a poor, inner-city high school who excels in his classes and wins a scholarship to a top university. He is just as talented and smart as his classmates, and he works hard to finish all his homework. But he begins to feel alienated by much of the material assigned in class, Eurocentric material that does not resonate with his experience, spark his imagination, or incite his passion. He has been surprised and angered by some things his classmates have said about African Americans, troubled that his professors have relegated "the African American experience" to only a single class week, and disappointed that he has not had the opportunity to read more black writers and poets. He begins to grow disillusioned with college, and the question "How does this matter to my friends and family back home?" plagues him—but he puts his head down and tries to get through it.[105]

On campus, he dresses in the style of his home neighborhood—baggy jeans, an oversized t-shirt, a gold necklace, a clean baseball cap cocked to the side. His demeanor is the "cool pose" of the street, which he and his friends adopted as teenagers, and his language is sprinkled with slang. Based on his expressions of blackness, as well as his lack of enthusiasm for the (Eurocentric) curriculum, his professors associate the young man's style and language with underperformance. Indeed, seated next to a young Asian American woman who wears collared shirts, slacks, and glasses, who sits up straight and raises her hand confidently, who looks you in the eye, our young black student "looks," to his professors, like a slacker. They evaluate him accordingly.[106]

Sadly, the student comes to believe that his low marks are accurate evaluations of his capabilities; that he, not the university, is the problem. "I'm not cut out for this," he thinks. A self-fulfilling cycle thus takes hold, as doubts about failure lead to actual failure.

In this example, it is not the student's cultural attributes per se that are the problem, but the educational institution's interpretation of those attributes. Did our student disengage from school, or the school from him?

Stereotype Threat Racial dynamics can infect the unconscious—the domain of unreflective habits, tendencies, and dispositions—such that we end up reproducing inequality without even knowing it. This is precisely the finding generated by a collection of fascinating psychological studies that confirm the existence of what has come to be known as "stereotype threat."

The notion of stereotype threat derives from the work of Claude Steele and Joshua Aronson. Steele and Aronson set out to determine how elusive and abstract stereotypes meted out very concrete consequences in the lives of members of stereotyped groups. They reasoned that a negative stereotype about your racial group makes you conscious of the fact that any of your actions that happen to align with that stereotype end up verifying the stereotype, making it more real in the eyes of others and, perhaps, even of yourself. Stereotype threat, therefore, "is being at risk of confirming, as self-characteristic, a negative stereotype about one's group."[107] Members of dominant groups rarely experience this threat, while it holds great sway over the conscious and unconscious behavior of members of marginalized groups.

For example, whenever black students undertake an intellectual task, they face the threat of confirming demeaning stereotypes about the intellectual capability of African Americans. This threat, hypothesized Steele and Aronson, can interfere with blacks' intellectual performance. To test this hypothesis, the psychologists developed a series of simple experiments. In one, they gave black and white undergraduates at Stanford University a thirty-minute test based on questions drawn from the Graduate Record Examination (the test you take to get into graduate school). Steele and Aronson believed that telling students that the test measures intellectual ability would trigger in black students the stereotype threat, the anxiety that should they do poorly, their results could be used to confirm the stereotype that blacks are intellectually inferior to whites. To find out if this really would happen, the researchers divided the students into two groups, both of which comprised white and black students. Group 1 was told that the test was "a laboratory problem-solving task," and Group 2 was told that it measured their "intellectual ability." The results were startling. In Group 1, black and white test scores were indistinguishable, as were the scores for whites in both groups. However, blacks in Group 2 scored much lower than did whites and blacks in Group 1. The conclusion was clear: "Making African-American participants vulnerable to judgments by negative

FIGURE 7.3 **EFFECTS OF STEREOTYPE THREAT**

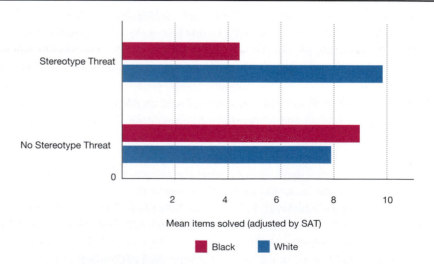

Mean items solved (adjusted by SAT)

■ Black   ■ White

Black and white students performed similarly on tests when no stereotypes were triggered, but black students performed considerably worse when they were.

stereotypes about their group's intellectual ability depressed their standardized test performance relative to White participants, while conditions designed to alleviate this threat improved their performance, equating the two groups."[108]

Steele and Aronson further verified the presence—and power—of stereotype threat in another experiment. This time, instead of manipulating what the test was said to measure (for example, intelligence or not), they primed race by asking students in one group to list their race before taking the test and omitting this step for students in another group. When race was not primed, black and white test scores were virtually identical; but when race was primed, blacks scored significantly lower than whites. Simply reminding black students of their racial identity—and the negative stereotypes that accompany it—awakened stereotype threat and reduced their performance.[109]

Since the publication of Steele and Aronson's groundbreaking work, the stereotype threat hypothesis has been confirmed by hundreds of studies and has been applied to other groups. Medical researchers have concluded that blacks taking tests where stereotype threat was activated have higher blood pressure and lower scores than whites and blacks taking tests under conditions where the threat was not.[110] Hispanics, women, and students from poor families have been found to be subject to stereotype threat.[111] Even whites can experience stereotype threat, when comparing themselves to Asian students. In a recent study, Aronson found that white men taking a mathematics examination scored considerably worse when they were told prior to the examination that Asians typically outperform whites on such tests.[112] Collectively, these studies offer indisputable evidence that students, even if they fail to realize it, are corrupted by stereotypes others have of them. This is a burden disproportionately borne by African American, Hispanic, and Native American students—as well as by women. The crippling consequences of stereotype threat are yet another example of the role culture plays in reproducing racial inequalities in education.

The Role of Schools

Although one's family and culture can play a deciding role in broadening or narrowing one's educational horizons, schools themselves are perhaps the most powerful institution with respect to generating educational inequalities. The American school system is plagued by "savage inequalities," inequalities marked on one end by affluent schools that lavish their students with pedigrees, cultural capital, network connections, and the finest education and on the other by ghetto schools, dilapidated, mired in poverty, and frequently vexed by violence.[113] The situation is powerfully captured in a two-line poem penned by a high school student attending one of New York City's poorest schools:

America the beautiful,
Who are you beautiful for?[114]

Students Advantaged, Students Betrayed Picture your high school. Perhaps you attended a state-of-the-art suburban school, one, in fact, that prompted your parents to move to that new subdivision. Maybe you went to a small, rural high school with a graduating class of thirty. Perhaps you are from an inner-city school, or one on the U.S.-Mexican border, where the teachers looked tired and nothing—nothing—was new. Did your high school have new textbooks and nice laboratory equipment? Did it offer art classes with plenty of supplies and take you on field trips to museums and concerts and historical landmarks? Were your teachers competent, experienced, qualified, and well compensated? Was it exceptional that you went off to college, or did most of your classmates do that as well? Answering questions such as these will provide you with a glimpse into the educational advantages you acquired (or did not acquire) as a result of the kind of school you attended.

As we already have learned, *Brown v. Board of Education* did not abolish school segregation: fifty years later, schools still are drastically segregated and unequal.[115] In fact, social scientists have documented a nationwide movement of *educational resegregation*, which has left today's schools even more segregated than during the time of *Brown v. Board of Education*.[116] The average white student attends a school that is majority-white. The average black student attends a school that is majority-black. The average Hispanic student attends a school that is majority-Hispanic.[117] Like residential segregation, racial segregation in schools is connected to a whole host of social problems.

Uncertified teachers disproportionately are found in poor, majority-nonwhite schools. And such schools often have a difficult time retaining even those teachers (ghetto schools have a remarkably high teacher turnover rate). By contrast, teachers who attended the most prestigious universities, who have more teaching experience, and who earn higher test scores primarily teach white, economically privileged

TABLE 7.1 **ASIAN-AMERICAN GROUPS, EDUCATION AND INCOME**

Educational Attainment and Average Income of Asian-American Groups, 2005

Group	% of Adults With at Least 4-Year Degree	Average Income
Asian Indian	68%	$66,000
Korean	54%	$52,000
Pakistani, Bangladeshi, Sri Lankan	54%	$48,000
Chinese	53%	$56,000
Filipino	48%	$46,000
Japanese	44%	$59,000
Indonesian, Malaysian, Thai	44%	$40,000
Vietnamese	25%	$41,000
Native Hawaiian, Pacific Islander	17%	$38,000
Cambodian, Laotian, Hmong	13%	$32,000

Amount Set Aside for Higher Education by Asian-American Families, by Group

Group	None	Up to $10,000	$10,001-$20,000	>$20,000
Southeast Asian	12%	73%	4%	8%
Filipino	3%	51%	10%	32%
South Asian	6%	34%	17%	22%
Korean	3%	40%	17%	42%
Chinese	9%	31%	22%	37%
Japanese	6%	41%	23%	27%

SOURCE: Scott Jaschik. The original story and user comments can be viewed online at http://insidehighered.com/news/2007/07/27/asians.

students. In Illinois, four out of five schools with very high minority populations (more than 90 percent) placed in the bottom quartile for teacher quality, but only 10 percent of low-minority schools were in the same quartile. In Wisconsin, half of all teachers in schools with large nonwhite populations have five or fewer years of experience, whereas only one in five teachers at schools with low-minority schools does.[118]

We can hardly blame the teachers for such discrepancies. The vast majority of states offer no incentives for teaching in poor, nonwhite schools. As a result, the nation's best teachers get hired where they are needed the least, accepting jobs in affluent, majority-white institutions. In a nation that continually stresses the importance of education, teachers are among America's lowest-paid professionals. And the situation is worse in poorer states with large nonwhite populations, states that allocate a pitifully low proportion of their annual budget to education.[119]

In some of the nation's worst schools, it is all teachers can do to maintain order. Keeping their students safe necessarily takes precedence over education, as the festering problems of the ghetto—its poverty and joblessness, its crime and violence—seep through the walls of the school. Bowen Paulle conducted participant-observation research in one of the toughest, most crime-ridden schools in the South Bronx (New York City) during the 1990s. He observed that the effects of school violence do not easily fade away once the outward violence is gone. "The anxiety related to threats and episodic outbursts of brutal violence," he wrote, "was always both 'out there,' in the educational settings, and 'in there,' beneath the flesh of the exposed."[120] The violence gets under students' skins, into their very bones, and remains there as a depository of fear, insecurity, and intimidation, long outlasting the fights and stabbings, the shouting and gunshots.

Author and teacher Jonathan Kozol set out to evaluate the state of education in inner-city America. He toured the country, talking with students and teachers in Camden, New Jersey; San Antonio, Texas; and other city centers. His discoveries were shocking. Kozol found schools whose gyms had been flooded with sewage because of broken plumbing and whose classrooms were sweltering owing to poor heating systems. He found ramshackle biology labs, supply closets without any paper, four computers in a school of 600, and a school so poor it could not afford to put goalposts on its football field. During Kozol's tour of East St. Louis, a young reporter told him, "The ultimate terror for white people is to leave the highway by mistake and find themselves in East St. Louis. People speak of getting lost in East St. Louis as a nightmare. The nightmare to me is that they never leave that highway so they never know what life is like for all the children here. They *ought* to get off that highway. The nightmare isn't in their heads. It's a real place. There are children living here."[121]

Far too many ghetto, reservation, and barrio schools—third world institutions smack dab in the center of the world's wealthiest nation—do little to prepare their students for college or even for vocational training. On the other end of the spectrum, affluent schools, which include not only elite private institutions—some of which charge as much as $40,000 per year for tuition, are staffed by teachers holding PhDs, and shuttle their students into Ivy League colleges at alarmingly high rates—but also public high schools in wealthy suburbs, open wide the doors of privilege.

In his book *Privilege*, sociologist Shamus Khan presents an intimate account of life at St. Paul's School in Concord, New Hampshire—one of the most prestigious

How do the differences between schools deepen the inequalities between the privileged and the poor?

and wealthy high schools in the nation. At St. Paul's, students learn much more than Greek and Latin. They also learn—more importantly—how to carry themselves, how to feel at ease in just about any social situation. In classrooms they are asked to think about both *Beowulf* and *Jaws*, classical music and rap. "Rather than mobilizing what we might think of as 'elite knowledge' to mark themselves as distinct—epic poetry, fine art and music, classical learning—the new [adolescent] elite" are trained to "display a kind of radical egalitarianism in their tastes. . . . This elite ease is an embodied interactional resource." If we look at seemingly mundane acts of everyday life—talking, posture, eating, dating—we can see "how privilege becomes inscribed upon the bodies of students and how students are able to display their privilege through their interactions. In being embodied, privilege is not seen as a product of differences in opportunities but instead as a skill, talent, capacity—'who you are.' Students from St. Paul's appear to naturally have what it takes to be successful. This helps hide durable inequality by naturalizing socially produced distinctions." It also helps St. Paul graduates to "fit" comfortably in other elite spaces, like Harvard, the college they are *most likely* to attend.[122]

Tracking "American high schools are racist," declared Tom Vander Ark, executive director for education at the Gates Foundation. "It's not that most teachers are; it's the institution—the basic architecture."[123] One final mechanism of inequality—one grafted into schools' very architecture—deserves special mention here: tracking. Tracking is the practice of sorting students into different tracks, ostensibly according to their ability. A typical tracking system features four tracks: honors/accelerated, college preparation, vocational, and remedial. Students' future opportunities—the extent to which they will go to college, enroll in the armed services, find a job straight out of high school, or drop out—are determined largely by the track to which they are assigned.

Studies have found that tracking—intentionally or unintentionally—produces racial inequality. Researchers have found that whites and Asians disproportionately are represented in higher tracks (accelerated and college prep), while African Americans, Hispanics, and Native Americans disproportionately are clustered in lower ones (vocational and remedial). Racialized tracking remains even after students' cognitive ability and class backgrounds are taken into account. And studies have shown that as a school's racial diversity increases, the chances that blacks and Hispanics will be assigned to higher tracks decreases. This suggests that in schools with sizable nonwhite populations, upper-level tracks function as a collection of "white and Asian classes," while lower-level tracks are reserved for blacks and Hispanics.[124]

How is this possible? How is it that nonwhite and non-Asian students are over-represented in vocational and remedial tracks when schools have developed objective measures to evaluate students' ability? One answer is that whiteness can muddy teachers' evaluations of Native American, Hispanic, and African American students. According to survey research, a significant proportion of white teachers harbor prejudicial attitudes, and some evidence suggests that white teachers often overlook Native American, Hispanic, and African American students' abilities, instead emphasizing their academic weaknesses and disciplinary infractions.[125] "Clearly," write sociologists Samuel Lucas and Mark Berends, "teachers are in a position to sponsor a child for upward mobility or to ignore evidence of a child's promise. . . . Teachers of different races [may] not only interpret students' performances differently but, in actuality, *literally see different performances*."[126]

Accelerated and college prep classes not only groom students for college; they also stimulate and mature them intellectually.[127] But, again, we see an unequal distribution of opportunity—and the wastefulness of racial division. When we consider the inequality *between* schools (inner-city schools versus suburban schools) and the inequality created *within* schools (maintained through tracking and other mechanisms), we cannot help but be overcome by all the potential and talent and ingenuity lost. Think of all the spirit and passion snuffed out by the harsh realities of the reservation, the ghetto, the barrio, the trailer park; of all the bright and motivated students assigned to classes that do not enable them to reach their full potential.

COMBATING EDUCATIONAL INEQUALITY: THE CASE OF AFFIRMATIVE ACTION

The final section of this chapter is dedicated to a program designed to combat racial inequality in the educational field: affirmative action. We already have addressed at length affirmative action in employment in Chapter 4 and, accordingly, offer only a brief discussion here. But affirmative action is such a controversial program that often it overshadows other important issues pertaining to racial inequalities in the educational field, issues such as whiteness in the curriculum and the causes and consequences of achievement gaps.[128] In this final section, we pose three questions we should answer before arriving at a conclusion about affirmative action. First, are we sure we know what affirmative action is? Second, does affirmative action unfairly handicap deserving whites and Asians? Third, does America still need a program designed to ameliorate racial inequalities in education, and if so, is affirmative action the best one for the job?

How Does Affirmative Action in Education Work?

In Chapter 4 we defined affirmative action as "an umbrella term referring to a collection of policies and practices designed to address past wrongs, institutional racism, and sexism by offering people of color and women both employment and educational opportunities." Many Americans overestimate two features of affirmative action: its prevalence and its power. With respect to its prevalence, affirmative action is not used in all colleges and universities. A significant number of colleges—some 75 percent by one estimate—place no weight on race or gender as a positive criterion of admission. Most schools that do not employ affirmative action programs are nonselective institutions that accept most applicants. Selective institutions, in contrast, those with competitive admissions, are the schools more likely to rely on some type of affirmative action.[129]

How do colleges and universities "do" affirmative action? Affirmative action does not rely on quota systems but can take many different forms. When employed in college admissions, it means, simply, giving people who belong to groups that are disproportionately underrepresented an edge over members of groups that are not. This usually amounts to selecting a woman or nonwhite applicant from a pool of equally qualified applicants or, in a stronger version, selecting a woman or nonwhite applicant whose application is slightly weaker than those of her or his male or white counterparts. Affirmative action does not typically entail selecting a woman or nonwhite applicant over male or white applicants whose records are substantially better, nor does it mean choosing unqualified people over qualified ones. There may be sound reasons to criticize affirmative action, but suggesting that it admits into top universities unqualified applicants at the expense of qualified ones is not one of them.[130]

How Does Affirmative Action Affect Whites and Asians?

In some cases, giving "targeted minorities" an edge in admissions procedures only increases the scores of students who would have been accepted without affirmative action; in other cases, the edge is fundamental to students being accepted; and in still other cases, the edge is not enough. To be sure, elite schools with affirmative action policies reject large numbers of African Americans, Hispanics, and Native Americans, along with sizable numbers of Asian and white applicants. But what, more specifically, are the consequences of affirmative action for whites and Asians, who in most cases do not qualify for affirmative action programs? After thirty years of affirmative action, whites and Asians apply to, enroll in, and graduate from college at higher rates than Native Americans, African Americans, and Hispanics; such disparities only widen when we examine selective institutions. It is true that some whites and Asians who would have been accepted at certain colleges and universities are denied entry because of affirmative action policies. It is equally true that they probably make up a relatively small proportion of applicants. According to one account, "Very few white and Asian students are actually bumped [because of racial considerations], and many of them get into alternative elite institutions of equal stature."[131]

In fact, it is far more likely that a qualified white or Asian applicant will be rejected from a top university because her or his spot was reserved for an academically mediocre but socially privileged white applicant with ties to the university. Roughly one in seven Ivy League students is a *legacy*, a child of alumni. Admissions data from the top thirty colleges in the nation reveal that legacies have a 45 percent greater chance of being admitted—that's the equivalent of 160 additional SAT points. And numerous studies have shown that legacies are significantly less qualified than other students (including affirmative action applicants) on virtually every measure of academic ability. Roughly 15 percent of freshmen enrolled in

America's top universities are white students who failed to satisfy their university's minimum requirements. Harvard admits fewer than 6 percent of all applicants but 30 percent of legacies, the average of which scored lower on standardized tests than the average nonlegacy student who was admitted.[132] White students who benefited from legacy preferences are nearly twice as prevalent on college campuses as nonwhites who benefited from affirmative action. "Rather than promoting social mobility," observes Peter Schmidt, author of *Color and Money: How Rich White Kids Are Winning the War over College Affirmative Action*, "our nation's selective colleges appear to be thwarting it, by turning away applicants who have excelled given their circumstances and offering second chances to wealthy and connected young people who have squandered many of the advantages life has offered them."[133]

There are cases where a deserving student's spot at a prestigious university is given to a less deserving student—but in the majority of cases, this is not because of affirmative action, but because of admissions policies that give legacies a boost. It is not affirmative action but legacy-favoring practices that deny a significant number of qualified students—white and nonwhite alike—a place at the table. Every university, it seems, has its price.

Is Affirmative Action the Most Effective Program?

Is affirmative action the most effective program to confront racial inequalities in education? One way to address this question is to ask, if affirmative action went away, what would happen? The answer, we know from real-life situations, is that college enrollment of underrepresented groups would decrease substantially. For example, when the University of California banned race-conscious admissions practices, the percentage of black freshmen decreased by 50 percent in a single year.[134]

Even if affirmative action is working, is it effective enough? As we mentioned in Chapter 4, some have argued that the biggest beneficiaries of affirmative action have been white women, followed by middle- to upper-class blacks and Hispanics. "Minority members from the most advantaged families . . . reap disproportionate benefits from policies of affirmative action based solely on their group membership," writes sociologist William Julius Wilson.[135] Although this claim has not gone unchallenged, there is good reason to believe that affirmative action programs do little to aid the thousands of nonwhites who each year are born into dire poverty.

Some policymakers have proposed a type of affirmative action based not on race or gender but on class. Because nonwhite populations disproportionately are victims of poverty, proponents of income-based affirmative action postulate that such programs will alleviate both class- and race-based inequality. But when schools have transitioned from race-based to class-based affirmative action programs, the racial diversity of their student body has declined. The reason? There are many more poor whites than poor nonwhites (in raw numbers), even if the percentage of poor African Americans, Latinos, and Native Americans exceeds that of whites. This is why economist Thomas Kane has suggested that an income-based affirmative action program would have to be six times the size of current race-based programs to admit a similar number of African Americans.[136]

Others have suggested that what needs to change is not affirmative action but how colleges evaluate their applicants. As sociologist Jerome Karable has observed, a society's conception of "merit" tends to be defined by its dominant groups, who tender a definition that aligns with their interests.[137] When colleges and universities put special emphasis on test scores, they propagate a measure of merit that benefits economically privileged white and Asian students—students who are tracked in accelerated classes, who can afford SAT tutors and Kaplan courses, and who are not affected very much by stereotype threat. Accordingly, studies have suggested that placing more emphasis on performance-based measures of merit, such as class rank, would greatly alleviate colleges' reliance on race-based affirmative action programs while still allowing them to pursue diversity.[138]

One last issue about affirmative action deserves mention. Some have suggested that affirmative action forces all nonwhite students, whether admitted under race-conscious admissions policies or not, to bear a heavy psychological burden. Their self-confidence might suffer as they consider the possibility that perhaps they are "not good enough" to be enrolled in their college. By and large, however, the evidence suggests that by providing nonwhites with access to higher education, affirmative action can boost their self-esteem. If we were truly worried about students' self-esteem, we might show greater concern for white students, whose racial privilege has, since they were children, provided them with advantages much more numerous and powerful than any affirmative action program ever conceived or implemented.[139]

THE BENEFITS OF A MULTICULTURAL LEARNING ENVIRONMENT

If we hope to confront racial inequality and injustice in our schools and universities, then we must continue the work of confronting whiteness in the curriculum, classroom, and college campus, and we must develop new, radical ideas for combating this problem. We must do so not only in the name of racial justice but also because a racially democratic learning environment, one that welcomes students from diverse backgrounds and encourages a wide variety of ideas, is beneficial to the intellectual development of all students.

Some critics of multicultural education have suggested it "lowers the bar." But all the evidence leads us to the opposite conclusion. Young men and women who engage actively with people from racial and ethnic groups other than their own, who are introduced to a variety of viewpoints on the world, who are taught how to identify and deconstruct racial domination, and who are exposed to intercultural training *make better students*. A college campus that encourages racial diversity within its student body is a campus that strives to shape students into mature, critical thinkers. Not only this, but a racially democratic education better prepares students to participate competently in America's workforce and democracy, both of which grow more racially diverse by the day.

THE BIG PICTURE

Chapter 7: Education

MAIN POINTS	KEY TERMS	FROM THEORY TO PRACTICE

Describe how education policies of the twentieth century attempted to force racial groups to assimilate into Anglo-American culture or systematically exclude them from white society through segregation.

- boarding schools, page 246
- separate is not equal, page 251

Examine the ways that whiteness often pervades the curriculum and college life.

- eurocentric curriculum, page 255

Identify at least one way whiteness informs your major field of study or one of the classes in which you currently are enrolled. Explain precisely how racial domination is normalized; offer at least one consequence of this normalization; and advance at least one suggestion for how whiteness might be effectively confronted.

Explain why the racial education gap—separating whites and Asians, on the one hand, and African Americans, Hispanics, and Native Americans, on the other—has shrunk in recent years at the secondary level but has increased at the postsecondary level.

- education gap, page 259
- cultural and social capital, page 261
- model minority, page 266

Think about your high school. How did it confer or fail to confer on you advantages that have helped in your transition to college? In light of what you have learned in this chapter, evaluate your high school experience, paying special mind to how racial domination might have informed your school and your experience.

Discuss how affirmative action operates in higher education and whether it has changed the racial disparities it was intended to reduce.

- Stereotype threat, page 269

- Research your college or university's affirmative action policy. What is your institution's stance with respect to using race as a criterion in admissions? Write a letter to the administrator in charge of affirmative action, explaining why you support or disagree with your college or university's policy. In your letter, be sure to justify your argument by drawing on what you learned in this chapter about affirmative action.

8 Aesthetics

MAIN POINTS

- Examine the ways that whites held a virtual monopoly over the dominant images of beauty, genius, and art for most of American history.

- Discuss how art represents racial groups and racial domination and how artists can challenge racial stereotypes and strive for racial justice.

- Describe the ways that whiteness guides artists and critics as they decide what should be classified as "art" and what should not.

- Explain how artistic divisions—those separating, say, different styles of dance, musical tastes, fashion senses, or schools of art—can be racialized and lead to an unequal distribution of cultural capital.

- Learn to recognize when cultural appropriation occurs and how to distinguish between racist appropriation and antiracist appropriation.

This chapter examines racial domination in the aesthetic realm, that sphere of society where artistic goods, such as painting, photography, sculpture, dance, stage performance, literature, poetry, music, fashion, and cinema, are produced and consumed. In today's media-connected world, television, movies, and music videos wield considerable power over our modes of thought. And so-called high art (art that is found in museums and opera houses) influences our perceptions of brilliance and the beautiful, as well as our interpretations of the past, evidenced by the fact that more people get their history by visiting museums than by reading books.[1] When you consider the thousands of ways movies, photographs, music videos, and so many other cultural goods influence what we think about and how we think about it, the ways they open and close our minds to imaginative possibilities, how they represent our social world and its problems, and how they reproduce or challenge the norms of dominant groups, there is no denying the importance of aesthetics to race in America.[2]

How, then, should we sociological thinkers approach the study of art? For starters, we should resist "spiritualizing" art by treating it as somehow detached from (and lifted above) social reality. Art must be situated within the social contexts in which it was created and scrutinized as a reflection of those contexts. "Flowers," wrote American philosopher John Dewey, "can be enjoyed without knowing about the interactions of soil, air, moisture, and seeds of which they are the result. But they cannot be *understood* without taking just these interactions into account."[3]

Analyzing a wide variety of art forms, this chapter examines how art influences the racial order and how the racial order influences art. This chapter begins with a brief historical overview of the workings of race in the aesthetic field during the last 150 years. It then turns to the modern day by exploring three rich topics: representation, racialization, and cultural appropriation. If "the job of the artist is always to deepen the mystery," as Francis Bacon once said, then the job of the sociologist is to demystify that mystery and, specifically, to unpack the multiple ways art fights for racial domination or racial democracy.

RACE AND ART IN NINETEENTH- AND TWENTIETH-CENTURY AMERICA

Throughout most of the nineteenth and twentieth centuries, whites dominated the American and European aesthetic fields. Art was associated with the white, educated, leisure class. Indeed, some art forms—the novel, for instance—were invented during the eighteenth century to entertain the idle upper class, its ranks swelling on account of the advance of capitalism. Nonwhites, economically and socially dominated, were denied access to fine art. Most could not afford the entrance fee to museums, and for those few who could, most museums were closed on Sundays, the only days off for many nonwhite laborers. Moreover, it was virtually impossible for a talented artist of color to be admitted to one of the nation's professional schools of art.[4] And most others—the would-be consumers of art—were deprived of the sort of knowledge that would allow them to get much out of the art they experienced, even were they capable of spending their weekend days strolling leisurely through museum galleries.

The Reign of Minstrelsy

In past centuries, whites held a virtual monopoly over the dominant images of beauty, genius, and art. As a result, white artists could misrepresent nonwhites with impunity, portraying them in the most distorted ways. For example, throughout the eighteenth and nineteenth centuries, neoclassical European and American sculptors represented Cleopatra—the famous Egyptian queen—as a white woman. They also chose as their favorite medium white marble, an intentional (and racialized) choice that, in their eyes, served to exalt purity and fidelity.[5] Neoclassical painters, too, associated white skin with the beautiful and the good. Consider *The Great Bath at Bursa* (1885) by French artist Jean-Léon Gérôme, a contemporary (and critic) of Manet and other impressionist painters. In this painting, Gérôme depicted a Turkish bath house filled with nude white women. In the middle of the canvas, one such woman leans elegantly on a partially clothed black woman, who is guiding her. To the painting's white viewers, the very presence of the black female body had the effect of sexualizing the white women, who, had the artist not inserted the black figure, might instead have evoked the essence of wholesomeness and cleanliness. To provide added emphasis to the contrast, Gérôme intertwined the two women: a white hand drapes softly on a black shoulder, and a black arm wraps gently around a white waist. And in this fleshly marriage, skin on skin, he portrayed the entanglement of pure with polluted, civilized with primitive—the sexualized racial order as personified in two women.

Jean-Léon Gérôme's *The Great Bath at Bursa* portrayed the sexualized racial order as personified in two women: the very presence of the black female body had the effect of sexualizing the white women, in the eyes of white viewers.

Particularly unsettling exhibits known as human zoos became immensely popular during the nineteenth and twentieth centuries. In these exhibits, which toured America and Europe and drew large crowds at World's Fairs, nonwhite people from so-called primitive cultures were put on display. The people usually were shown in their "natural habitat"— primitive surroundings designers thought were most "authentic"—sometimes wearing very little or no clothing. The 1889 World's Fair, held in Paris and attended by roughly 28 million people, displayed no fewer than 400 Africans in a "Negro village," the fair's most popular attraction.[6]

Human zoos were intended to demonstrate the supposed natural superiority of the white race. Similarly, through the minstrel shows, which ruled the American stage between 1830 and 1910 (so much so that entire theaters, with names such as Ethiopian House, were dedicated solely to minstrelsy), whites controlled the dominant image of blackness. Performed by white actors in blackface (and, for a brief stint after the Civil War, by black actors as well), minstrel shows purported to represent authentic African American life. Actors blackened their skin by applying burnt cork or shoe polish and enlarged their lips with red makeup. Minstrel shows featured a collection of stock characters that portrayed blacks as lazy, ignorant, subservient, buffoonish, and childish. There was the dandy—the presumptuous, "uppity" black—and his mirror image, the slave, happy and content in his chains. There also was the caretaking mammy figure (think Aunt Jemima), the lascivious mulatto seductress, and the "old darky," stupid but musical. As the abolitionist movement gained steam, minstrel shows became avowedly proslavery and portrayed black slaves as content and earnest, eager to please their white masters. Some minstrel songs even celebrated lynching, as actors sang of blacks who were "roasted, fished for, smoked like tobacco, peeled like potatoes, planted in the soil, or dried up and hung as advertisements."[7]

Through an exaggerated way of speaking, costume, makeup, postures, and movement, the minstrel show became a grotesque mockery of blackness on which members of the white audience could project their anxiety and confusion, their patronizing affection and hatred. The minstrel show perfectly fulfilled the racist fantasy because it was nothing less than blackness under complete white control. It was blackness possessed by a white body, blackness excreted from the white (social) body in the shape of a minstrel.[8] Although minstrel shows died out after the early twentieth century, "minstrelsy"—white control of the representation of blackness in particular and nonwhiteness in general—carried on throughout the twentieth century. Blacks continued to be depicted as ignorant and silly in radio and television shows like *Amos 'n' Andy*, a popular minstrel-inspired show (created by

Al Jolson (1886–1950), an American entertainer, was a famous blackface minstrel.

two white men) that made its television debut in the 1950s. Native Americans, for their part, were cast as cruel, savage, and primitive in American western movies and successful television shows, many of which still air on cable and satellite channels today, and South Asians were typed as erotic, spiritual, and irrational in children's books, vaudeville shows, circus acts, and movies (such as the 1942 version of *Jungle Book*).[9]

Voices from the Underground

But art cannot be colonized. Even under the most oppressive of conditions, dominated groups create and imagine; they sing and write, carve and dance. Jews played music within their dark and crowded chambers at Auschwitz and Dachau; America's indigenous people refused to put an end to the Ghost Dance, even after their white colonizers forbade it; and enslaved Africans wrote and sang songs while bending and sweating in the cotton fields of Georgia and Mississippi.

Consider the career of African American music. To express their anguish, enslaved Africans sang spirituals. Often slow and melodious, these dirges (Du Bois called them "sorrow songs") often cried out to God for deliverance:

> The blind man stood on the road and cried,
> The blind man stood on the road and cried,
> Cryin', "Oh, my Lord, save me,"
> The blind man stood on the road and cried.[10]

Some heart-wrenching spirituals went so far as to present suicide as a way to escape slavery. Others, however, were filled with hope as well as with calls for freedom (for example, "Go Down Moses"). "The Negro folk-song—the rhythmic cry of the slave—stands today not simply as the sole American music but as the most beautiful expression of human experience born this side of the seas."[11] So Du Bois wrote in 1903.

Spirituals expressed explicitly contradictory emotions. To be the victim of racial domination was to curse that domination's cruelty and in the next breath to laugh at its senselessness. Despair and hope, apathy and perseverance—these emotional states lived side by side in the spirituals and, indeed, are a unique characteristic of African American music. Nowhere is this more apparent than in the blues, a musical form that evolved from spirituals in the early twentieth century. Consider Nina Simone's "Mississippi Goddamn," a song that is completely comedy and completely tragedy from first note to last.[12] As James Baldwin, a fan of and mentor to Simone, once teasingly said, "In all jazz, and especially in the blues, there is something tart and ironic, authoritative and double-edged. White Americans seem to feel that happy songs are *happy* and sad songs are *sad*, and that, God help us, is exactly the way most white Americans sing them. . . . Only people who have been 'down the line,' as the song puts it, know what this music is about."[13] It often is said that blacks gave America the blues. We must remember that it is the other way around. The blues represent a response to racial domination, a comingling of contradictory passions, a marriage of sorrow and laughter.

In the mid-twentieth century, bebop arose as the dominant strain of jazz music. (Think Charlie Parker, Thelonious Monk, and Dizzy Gillespie.) As philosopher Cornel West observes, their music was "not only a reaction to the white-dominated, melody-obsessed 'swing jazz'; [it also was] a creative musical response to the major shift in sensibilities and moods in Afro-America after World War II."[14] Notice here the triple reading in which West engages: an aesthetic reading (black jazz as a response to white jazz); a political reading (the social currents that stirred after the defeat of Nazi Germany); and, implicitly, a racial reading (bebop as a distinctly African American art form).

Meanwhile, the blues continued to gain in popularity, and such musicians as Louis Armstrong, Duke Ellington, and Miles Davis began playing to large audiences. As they did so, white musicians took notice and began to incorporate the blues into their repertoire. Soon, headlining musicians—from Bob Dylan to the Rolling Stones—were trying their hand at the blues, a musical appropriation that made some African Americans applaud and others cringe. Poet Langston Hughes cringed, bemoaning,

> You've taken my blues and gone.
> You sing 'em on Broadway
> And you sing 'em in Hollywood Bowl
> And you mixed 'em up with symphonies
> And you fixed 'em
> So they don't sound like me.[15]

In the minds of Hughes and others, the white appropriation of the blues disconnected the music from the social conditions—white racism—in which it was grounded and, in doing so, cheapened it. In the words of music historian Craig Werner, "When the Stones called out for satisfaction, they meant yesterday. When Otis Redding and Aretha Franklin covered the song, their responses carried the weight of hundreds of years."[16]

The white sanitation of the blues, some argued, dulled their jagged edge and glossed over past and present forms of suffering to which they spoke. Indeed, even if Dylan and the Stones did not see things this way, whites have a long history of borrowing art forms associated with nonwhites in the interest of white supremacy. As Dexter Hawkins, a white academic, put it in 1875, "The strength of [Anglo-Saxon] blood is manifest in the fact that it crosses with all cognate races, and takes up and absorbs their good qualities without losing its own identity."[17] As Hawkins's words attest, whites for centuries have been able to accept and appreciate nonwhite art forms without accepting and appreciating those who created them, resulting in a contradiction between the inclusion of nonwhite, especially African American, *culture* and the simultaneous rejection and marginalization of nonwhite *people*.[18]

The Rise of Multiculturalism

As the twentieth century rolled forward, things began to change. Nonwhite artists began to move from margin to center. For example, Spanish radio, which began in the 1920s, grew into a formidable enterprise serving the Southwest's growing Mexican American population.[19] Asian American painting—the works of Japanese-born Yasuo Kuniyoshi, for example—began appearing in art museums. And artistic movements—for instance, the blossoming of black literary and artistic life that took place throughout the 1920s and 1930s, known today as the Harlem Renaissance—challenged the whiteness of artistic life. At first, many nonwhite artists had to rely on white sponsors for financial backing. Such uneasy collaboration often bridled nonwhites' artistic freedom and blunted their political edge. Not only this, but many a book publisher, movie producer, and theater owner shied away from avowedly antiracist works that, in their minds, would not turn a profit.[20]

Nonwhite artists were gaining admiration and acclaim, but because whites still controlled the levers of artistic production, many nonwhite artists did not gain full control over their art or, for that matter, over their representations of racism or nonwhite groups. Bit by bit, however, nonwhite artists broke through. Asian American musicians and conductors, such as Yo-Yo Ma, the highly acclaimed cello prodigy, and Seiji Ozawa, who directed the Boston Symphony Orchestra from 1973 to 2002, shook up the world of classical music. African American playwrights such as August Wilson (who won two Pulitzer Prizes) and Lorraine Hansberry (whose *A Raisin in the Sun* was the first play written by a black woman to run on Broadway) emerged as respected dramatists whose plays confronted racism and plumbed the depths of Black America. Television sitcoms featuring Jewish characters and depicting Jewish life flourished in the 1970s and grew by leaps and bounds in the 1990s.[21] And in the realm of comedy, nonwhite comedians pushed the envelope and forced their audiences to confront racism. In the wake of the Civil Rights Movement, African American comedian Richard Pryor made audiences laugh and squirm with his unapologetic, irreverent humor that found ample material in America's sticky "race problem." "The truth is gonna be funny," he wrote in his 1995 autobiography, "but it's gonna scare folks."[22]

RACIAL REPRESENTATION IN ART

Turning now to the present day, this section confronts the topic of racial representation in the aesthetic field. How does art represent racial groups and racial domination? How do fashion, television, music, photography, and other art forms present us with a racialized image of the social world? How might these images affect the racial order? These are the questions we address over the next several pages. As we will see, art can reflect, support, or challenge racial domination; it can be driven by white, racist, or antiracist aesthetics. As we navigate among the images and sounds that meet our eyes and ears on a daily basis, we should be diligent in deciphering how art represents racial domination and certain racial and ethnic groups. Is, for example, television programming defined more by the white, racist, or antiracist aesthetic? Certainly all three aesthetics are found on television, but which is more prevalent—and why?

The White Aesthetic

Detecting whiteness in art often means paying attention to absences. It means seeing the unseen, listening to silences. This requires our constantly asking ourselves on viewing a piece of art, "What—or who—is missing?" Images of whiteness often are understated and subtle. They rely on an unspoken edict that treats the white body and the white experience as normal, an edict that, for some of us, connects with our innermost presuppositions about the world. As art historian Martin Berger has observed, "Images do not persuade us to internalize racial values embedded within them, so much as they confirm meanings for which the discourses and structures of our society have predisposed us."[23] If this is the case, then our task should be critically to examine whiteness in art so as to better understand how our deep-seated racial dispositions fail to treat nonwhite experiences as a *central* part of American life.

Consider the world of haute couture, high fashion. When the Spring 2014 collections of the Western world's most influential designers—from Prada and Balenciaga to Chloé and Chanel—premiered across America and Europe, the vast majority of the displayed clothing hung on skinny white bodies. Some organizers of fashion shows believe that "one black girl" is enough. Some fashion agencies openly discriminate against nonwhites, sending modeling firms requests for "Caucasian models only." But the fashion world is beginning to change, if slowly. Eighty percent of runway looks in 2014 still involved white models, but in 2008, 87 percent did.[24]

Denying nonwhite women access to the runway strictly on the basis of their skin color is certainly unfair, but this kind of discrimination reaches beyond the models themselves to the dominant definition of beauty. In the words of one commentator, "It is not just a handful of genetically gifted young women who are hurt by this exclusion [that favors white models]. Vast numbers of consumers draw their information about fashion and identity from runways, along with cues about what, at any given moment, the culture decrees are the new contours of beauty and style."[25] Nonwhite children learn from a very young age that to be white is to be pretty and desirable, which is why, as psychologists long have shown, upon being given the choice between a white doll and a black one, African American preschool and elementary school children are more likely to choose the white one. And when asked to color a sketch of a person using a color that matches their own skin, these children frequently do not select an accurate match, but a crayon a shade or two lighter than their own skin tone.[26]

Non-white children learn from a young age to prefer white skin.

Blepharoplasty surgery on an Asian-American woman makes their eyes look rounder and more "white."

These internalized biases do not necessarily fade with age. According to the American Society of Plastic Surgeons, ethnic plastic surgery has increased by over 65 percent since 2000, with nose jobs being the most common procedure among African Americans, Asian Americans, and Hispanics. Of the nearly half million Asian Americans on whom cosmetic surgery was performed, many underwent double-eyelid procedures meant to make their eyes look rounder—less "Asian."[27] "In the bathroom one night, I used a toothpick to push up my epicanthic folds," writes Vietnamese American Andrew Lam. "They held for a few seconds, giving me the appearance of rounder eyes, and a glimpse of what I might look like with double eyelids. I had contemplated cosmetic surgery, and for a few months, even saved money for the purpose." Lam never went through with the surgery, although he was constantly bombarded by advertisements for such a procedure: "One only needs to open a Vietnamese magazine or newspaper in San Jose or Orange County to see the onslaught of ads for cosmetic surgery. . . . In the online business directory of the *Nguoi Viet Daily News*, based in Southern California where the largest Vietnamese population in the United States resides, there are more than 50 local listings for cosmetic surgery."[28]

Whiteness informs not only high fashion, which only an elite handful of people can afford, but also more everyday fashion—the kind of clothes worn by your classmates and maybe by you. Let's talk about Abercrombie and Fitch. A company that began supplying outdoor gear in 1892, Abercrombie and Fitch today is a major fashion retailer targeting young consumers. The company owes its success less to the quality of its products than to its ability to peddle an image, to market a brand. And its success is attributed to tapping into young people's deep yearning to be included among "the beautiful people," who in Abercrombie and Fitch's eyes constitute the white leisure class. "Surely we know that people are not buying 'Abercrombie' for the clothes," writes Dwight McBride. "The catalogue isn't even about featuring those, after all. People buy 'Abercrombie' to purchase membership into a lifestyle. . . . In order for such a marketing strategy to work, in all of the diverse ways that this one clearly does, the consumer must necessarily bring to his or her understanding of A&F . . . a fundamentally racist belief that this lifestyle—this young, white, natural, all-American, upper-class lifestyle— being offered by the label is what we all either are, aspire to be, or are hopelessly alienated from ever being."[29]

If Abercrombie and Fitch continues to flourish, it is because it has learned how to bottle up and sell white privilege by manufacturing a "look." (Or, as *New York Post* fashion columnist Lisa Marsh has observed, Abercrombie and Fitch's "aggressive lifestyle marketing makes you feel like you're buying a polo shirt and getting the horse and summer house on Martha's Vineyard with it."[30]) This look can be spotted in its catalogue, in its larger-than-life posters featuring mostly white models, and especially in its store clerks, or "brand reps." Brand reps are hired only if they have the "A&F look," an embodiment of the celebration of whiteness on which the company thrives, and, indeed, they can be fired if they cease to embody it.[31] In 2005, Abercrombie and Fitch was ordered to pay $40 million to a group of African Americans, Asian Americans, and Hispanics who, together, filed a discrimination lawsuit against the retail giant. But has anything changed?

Consider these racialized patterns. Marketing research has found that whites consistently are overrepresented in commercials.[32] In the same way, some television shows and movies with all-white or majority-white casts enjoy enormous success. Think, for instance, of *Game of Thrones*, *Girls*, and *Seinfeld*. Then there are comic strips, the vast majority of which feature exclusively white characters, from *Family Circus*, which represents a white middle-class worldview, to *Wizard of Id*, which depicts white characters fumbling about in the Middle Ages as if nonwhites didn't exist back then. Not a single frame in Bill Watterson's *Calvin and Hobbes*, which enjoyed a decade-long run as a syndicated daily from 1985 to 1995 and resulted in several book-length collections, featured a nonwhite character.

Art that fails to include nonwhites represents the world as a white world. And if nonwhites do not exist, then neither does racial inequality. *The Brady Bunch*, which ran from 1969 to 1974, depicted an idyllic white family beset by the most minor problems—like finding a prom date—while black neighborhoods in major cities erupted in racial uprisings. The disconnection between the show's depiction of tranquil American life and the fires that burned through Watts and Harlem and Detroit was startling. Since that time, nonwhite actors have made inroads in television and film—just as nonwhite cartoonists have enjoyed broader coverage— but it takes but a moment's reflection to realize how many all-white or nearly all-white shows (e.g., *The O.C.*) are divorced from the pressing problems facing nonwhite communities today (e.g., mass incarceration, housing unaffordability, joblessness). Even nonwhite artists feel industry pressure to dull their art by removing all social commentary. The Brooklyn-based rapper Talib Kweli speaks to this pressure in his song "I Try":

> Tryin' to bring your struggle to life;
> The label want a song about a bubbly life.
> I have trouble tryin' to write some shit
> To BANG in the club through the night
> When people suffer tonight.[33]

One thinks, too, of country music. Although country music long has marketed itself as the music of the "American working man," there are very few recent country ballads dealing with racial discrimination in the labor force, racialized wage inequalities, or the oppressive conditions under which migrant workers toil. On the contrary, many songs romanticize white racism. For example, Toby Keith's duet with Willie Nelson, "Beer for my Horses"—the video for which includes a black prostitute and a black homeless man urinating in public— glorifies lynching. As one journalist accurately has observed of the song, "During the days when Toby Keith's 'Grandpappy' stalked the Jim Crow South, lynching was an institutional method of terror employed against blacks to maintain white supremacy."[34]

Even less aggressive songs, ones that reminisce about "the good old days," are steeped in whiteness. Rascal Flatts's song "Mayberry," the name of the fictional 1920s North Carolina town in which *The Andy Griffith Show* was set, nostalgically recalls a past era in which life was simpler and better. But a song like this prompts us to ask: For whom were the "good old days" good? Could it be true that only whites can "miss Mayberry"? Regardless of whether country artists recognize this or not, many of their songs breed a kind of racial nostalgia, a yearning among whites for a time when their position over nonwhites was much surer than it is today.[35]

Racial nostalgia looms large in the American imagination. To find its visual incarnation, we need look no farther than the paintings of Norman Rockwell. An extremely popular and successful artist, Rockwell is best known for his paintings of "typical American life"—some of his favorite subjects being children, families, and patriotism—paintings that in the beginning of the twentieth century adorned *The Saturday Evening Post* and that now can be found on calendars, posters, and coffee mugs and, of course, in museums. A study of Rockwell's life's work reveals that in his eyes, "typical American life" was white. Not only white, but happy too; American life was bereft of troubles (aside from war, which took place on foreign soil). White people are ice skating in one painting; white people are raking leaves in another. In others, white people are praying or drinking tea or being paid a visit by Santa Claus or being protected by white soldiers. Race was not completely off Rockwell's radar (he composed at least two paintings that dealt with racial segregation), but by and large this thoroughly American artist—perhaps *the* twentieth-century artist of America— represented his country as a white utopia where neither people of color nor trouble was to be found.

Norman Rockwell might not have sought to represent whiteness in his paintings any more than did the members of Rascal Flatts in "Mayberry." But that is precisely the point. By treating "white" as the unexamined artistic default category, the white aesthetic tries to lay claim to "the universal." However, as Pierre Bourdieu has pointed out, "a number of universalistic manifestos or universal prescriptions are no more than the product of (unconscious) universalizing of the particular case. . . . To grant 'humanity' to all, but in a purely formal way, is to exclude from it, under an appearance of humanism, all those who are deprived of the means of realizing it."[36]

Art is a two-way street between artist and audience, and artists alone are not wholly responsible for the perpetuation of the whiteness aesthetic. We, their audience, also play a part by expecting whiteness and voicing our disapproval when that expectation is not met. Consider how fans responded to the movie adaptation of Suzanne Collins's enormously popular *The Hunger Games* trilogy. Many were upset, even outraged, that black actors were cast in the roles of Rue and Thresh, even though both characters are described in the books as having "dark brown skin." Dozens of fans voiced their outrage on Twitter:

- "why does rue have to be black not gonna lie kinda ruined the movie" @maggie_mcd11
- "EWW rue is black?? I'm not watching" @Joe_Longley
- "call me racist but when I found out rue was black her death wasn't as sad" @jashperparas

As one journalist noted, "The posts go on and on and on. It's not just a couple of tweets, it's not just a coincidence. There's an underlying rage, coming out as overt prejudice and plain old racism."[37] So pervasive is the white aesthetic that a good number of readers read whiteness into characters described as nonwhite in the very books they cherished. When the movie's casting challenged their image, many reacted with blatant anger and disgust. For many of us, whiteness in books, movies, and art is not simply something authors, actors, and artists give us; it also is something we expect and sometimes demand.

The Racist Aesthetic

If the white aesthetic seeks to normalize whiteness, the racist aesthetic seeks to depict people of color in negative ways. If the white aesthetic ignores people of color, the racist aesthetic represents them—but never in their full humanity. Rather, it distorts and stereotypes; it infantilizes and demonizes. And its ubiquity today demonstrates that nonwhites, regardless of their presence in the aesthetic field, have yet to gain full control over the representations of themselves.

The racist aesthetic can be found all over the art world, from high fashion to pop culture. In 2012, the lingerie retailer Victoria's Secret released its "Go East" collection, which included a piece called "Sexy Little Geisha." Taking traditional Japanese women entertainers as a model, the piece included an "Eastern-inspired" floral print along with a fan, chopsticks, and an obi belt. One observer noted that such a product fed into hypereroticized stereotypes of Asian women and "fulfill[ed] our fantasies of a safe and non-threatening, mysterious East." The retailer Urban Outfitters has a long tradition of selling clothing that has upset several ethnic groups, from Mexican Americans (with a shirt that reads, "New Mexico: Cleaner than Regular Mexico") to Irish Americans (with an assortment of items linking Irishness with drunkenness).[38]

Lest we think this is a trend found only in shopping malls catering to young people, the racist aesthetic also can be found in the world of haute couture. In its spring 2013 collection, the luxury fashion brand Dolce and Gabbana made

A Model and her Blackamoor earrings in Dolce and Gabbana's Spring 2013 collection.

wide use of Blackamoor imagery. White models walked runways with giant earrings of turbaned dark black faces or burlap frocks imprinted with the face of slavelike African women. Blackamoor imagery as "European decorative exotica" dates back to the seventeenth century, when enslaved Africans were dressed in colorful garb as symbols of wealth and luxury. The images can be striking and beautiful, but they also are rooted in slave culture and white supremacy.[39]

What about new media? The Internet is full of user-generated videos of poor black people speaking to local news crews in a vernacular some people find amusing. Cleveland's Charles Ramsey rescued three kidnapped women. He told news reporters that he used to barbeque with the kidnapper: "We eat ribs and whatnot." When asked about the looks on the kidnapped women's faces, he said, "I knew something was wrong when a little pretty white girl ran into a black man's arms. Something is wrong here. Dead giveaway." YouTube subscribers put Mr. Ramsey's words to music and auto-tuned them, making songs available on iTunes. These videos have been viewed millions of times, briefly making Ramsey an online sensation. "The catch phrases are humorous," one observer said, "but they also shine a light on the harsh realities that Ramsey and his like face on a regular basis. . . . Finding humor in the turn of phrase of a lower class black population is, of course, hardly a recent phenomenon. *Amos 'n' Andy*, a radio and television sitcom where white actors portrayed stereotypical black characters, was very popular from the 1920s to the 1950s. In this day and age, we like to think that we're no longer like that, that we've moved on as a society to shun this type of entertainment. The fact is, these online videos are essentially a modern day minstrel show . . . , which turn[s] the likes of . . . Ramsey [and others] into 'musical negroes.'"[40] Maybe this assessment is too harsh, but is there a stark difference between videos like "Dead Give Away" (over 22 million views on YouTube) or "Bed Intruder Song" (over 122 million views) or "Ain't Nobody Got Time for That" (over 46 million views)—all parodies of poor black folk by whites—and white actors putting on blackface and mimicking "black speak"?

Take, for example, comedy. Many stand-up comedians promote a racist aesthetic. Amid America's fascination with the war on terror, Jeff Dunham, the popular and talented ventriloquist, created a puppet character named Achmed the Dead Terrorist. Achmed is a skeleton, all that remains of a suicide bomber, with a turban wrapped around his skull. He talks with a heavy Middle Eastern accent and berates the audience with the phrase, "Silence! I kill you!" Through Achmed—a "harmless" toy—Dunham is able to caricature Arabs and Islam. He stereotypes Mexican Americans as well—exaggerating their "ethnicness"—with his puppet José Jalapeño, a sombrero-topped jalapeño pepper with a long black mustache. African Americans don't escape his ridicule, either. They are represented by Sweet Daddy D, a black pimp in flashy clothing. Through Dunham's puppets, Arabs, Mexican Americans, and African Americans are represented only through their most stereotypical, pejorative—and emphatically *nonwhite*—properties.

Jeff Dunham with his puppet character Achmed the Dead Terrorist.

Much racist humor thrives off its shock value. In this way, it resembles the work of "shock jocks" of talk radio shows, which are full of racial slurs and over-the-top offensive language. Some shock radio shows, such as Chicago's Mancow's Morning Madhouse or New York's El Vacilón de la Mañana, each day draw tens of thousands of listeners. Members of this immense audience tune in to hear their favorite personalities ridicule Muslims, Jews, women, gays, immigrants, and people of color. Shock jock Don Imus made headlines in 2007 for calling the black women on the Rutgers women's basketball team "nappy-headed hos." As this sexist and racist comment was circulated over the Internet and on news channels, members of the public voiced their outrage. Imus apologized and was fired by CBS Radio. Eight months later, however, he returned to the airwaves and seemed to have little trouble securing business advertisers and high-powered guests.[41] Shock jocks often justify their offensive humor by claiming, in the words of New York–based radio host Nick Di Paolo, that they "take shots at everybody." This certainly is untrue, for whites—as a racial group—rarely are the butt of jokes, unlike Native Americans, African Americans, and Chinese, Mexican, and Arab immigrants. But even if such a comment were accurate, would it excuse the racist content of shock humor? Does a dig pitched at a privileged group pack the same punch as one targeting an underprivileged group?

If you are a regular television viewer or movie buff, you probably already are aware of the racist aesthetic's prevalence in popular culture. Nonwhite actors often are cast in stereotypical roles. Native American actors, for example, usually appear on screen only as Indians doing "Indian things," as opposed to modern-day executives, athletes, or members of a suburban family. And when Hollywood does attempt to depict Indian life, it often grossly misrepresents tribal ceremonies, showing Indians performing dog-eating or wrist-cutting rituals, or using ceremonies of one tribe to (mis)represent another.[42] Arab American actors have it equally bad, as they often are depicted as enraged Muslim terrorists. Iranian American actor Maz Jobrani explains that his career started out with auditions "for terrorist role after terrorist role." He refused to play the game and has turned down many (well-paying) roles that depict Arabs as uncomplicated, violent savages, including the terrorist mastermind of Fox's show *24*, which boasts of 15 million viewers. When viewers see a white villain, Jobrani explains, they think, "Wow, that American's crazy," but on seeing an Iranian American villain, they think, "Man, those Iranians are crazy."[43]

Countless other examples abound. One thinks, for example, of the endless association of goodness with whiteness and of evil with blackness in the *Lord of the Rings* trilogy. Gandalf, the "white wizard," rides a white horse (Shadofax) and helps the heroes defend the white folks of Rohan and the "White City" of Minan Tirith against the ruthless Uruks, "tall, black, and muscular [creatures] with long, coarse hair that resembles dreadlocks."[44] And Anime, the collection of animated video games, playing cards, television shows, and movies that originated in Japan and now has blossomed into a global enterprise, does not avoid the racist aesthetic. The Nintendo-owned *Pokémon* series features a character named Jynx that is modeled after minstrel caricatures of African Americans. With its blackface and exaggerated lips and breasts, Jynx's main weapon of attack is its sexuality—its sensual dance and "lovely kiss"—which links blackness to hypereroticism. Similarly, *Dragon Ball Z* features Mr. Popo, a blackfaced genie whose head is wrapped in a bejeweled turban. Mr. Popo has been described as a "loyal servant" willing to please, resembling, top-to-bottom, the slaves of minstrel shows.[45]

The racist aesthetic misrepresents not only people of color but also the very nature of racial domination. It does so in at least three ways. First, it whitewashes history to blunt the sharp edge of past wrongs and replaces nonwhite heroes with white ones. In the film *Mississippi Burning*, for example, two white FBI agents investigate the slayings of Goodman, Schwerner, and Chaney, the three civil rights workers killed in 1964. The white agents crack the case single-handedly, and justice is served. Thus, the film turns the Civil Rights Movement's "historical enemies—the racist FBI which harassed and sabotaged the movement—into the film's heroes, while turning the historical heroes—the thousands of African Americans who marched and braved beatings and imprisonment and sometimes death—into the supporting cast, passive victim-observers waiting for official White rescue."[46] Indeed, as several film critics have observed, the white male savior of seemingly helpless nonwhite communities is a common trope in movies, one that perhaps began with the 1962 classic *To Kill a Mockingbird*. Think, for example, of *Black Hawk Down*, *Three Kings*, *The Matrix*, and *Avatar*, to list but a few.[47]

The second way the racist aesthetic distorts racial domination is by pretending it does not exist. Rather than exclude altogether nonwhites and their troubles (like a Norman Rockwell painting), the racist aesthetic includes nonwhites but excludes racism. Society is depicted as a kind of racial utopia: racial inequalities are nonexistent and the history of racial oppression is long forgotten and forgiven. This is why racial domination never seems a problem between the two lead characters of the *Lethal Weapon* series: Murtaugh, the straight-laced, married black middle-class cop played by Danny Glover, and Riggs, the psychotic, alcoholic divorced white cop played by Mel Gibson. "In [interracial] buddy films such as *Lethal Weapon*," writes anthropologist John Jackson, Jr., "black middle-classness (that is, moral, behavioral, ethical conservatism) and white male marginality combine to depict race without engaging the entrenched discourses of racial difference found in the real world beyond the reel world."[48]

But perhaps the most invidious way the racist aesthetic warps the true nature of race is by depicting it as a purely *psychological* issue. It reduces racial domination to interpersonal racism—racist attitudes and prejudice—while ignoring institutional racism. Consider the movie *Crash*, which won the Oscar for Best Picture in 2005. *Crash* features a multiethnic cast and grapples with racial and class-based tensions in Los Angeles. Tempers flare between a racist white police officer and black citizens, a wealthy white woman and her Hispanic maid, an Iranian storeowner and a tattooed Hispanic family man, and so the movie goes. Viewers are berated with one jarringly racist exchange and insult after another and, in the end, walk away with the impression that virtually everybody is a racist and that racism is violent and visible and quite conscious. *Crash* should be commended for attempting to confront racial divides, but it should be criticized for doing so in such an elementary and misleading fashion, presenting racism as just a collection of mean attitudes and opinions possessed by whites and nonwhites alike. The movie makes little mention of historical and institutional racism, apart from which interpersonal racism ceases to exist. Even more troubling is the film's tendency to represent racism as something that affects all people equally; having reviewed a mass of sociological evidence in the previous chapters, we know better.[49]

The Antiracist Aesthetic

Just as art can be used on behalf of racial domination, it can be marshaled on behalf of racial justice. Indeed, art always has functioned as a primary "weapon of the weak," a mode of defense against racial tyranny.[50] Subversive art is propelled by the antiracist aesthetic, an artistic approach that seeks somehow to throw a wrench into the grinding gears of racism. This can be accomplished in several ways.

Instead of ignoring America's brutal past, or twisting history to cast racist whites in a positive light, antiracist art forces its audience to confront American racial history honestly and courageously. This is the impulse behind Kara Walker's powerful artwork. An African American woman and one of the youngest recipients of the MacArthur "Genius" Award, Walker specializes in room-sized installations featuring silhouetted depictions of African Americans and whites during slavery. Her pieces often feature unsettling images, such as white-on-black violence, the rape of enslaved African girls by older white men, black suicide, and infanticide. The silhouetted shapes command the eye and force you to study them in such a way that you find yourself asking, "Is that really what I see?" and then, "Did that really happen?" Walker's work is a direct assault on racial nostalgia and leaves its viewers angered and ashamed, even nauseous.[51] In a similar way, Japanese American artist Michi Itami confronts the history of Japanese internment camps. In his computer-generated photo collage *The Irony of Being American*, Itami overlays three pictures of his father—one in traditional Japanese dress, one in a business suit, and one in his Army uniform—against a picture of Manzanar, the internment camp where he and his family were held captive.[52]

Darkytown Rebellion by Kara Walker.

Subversive art also can provide a direct response to the racist aesthetic, correcting distorted representations of nonwhites. Some Native American artists, for example, have responded sardonically to the pervasive tendency to depict Native Americans as relics of the past. Jimmie Durham's *On Loan from the Museum of the American Indian* displays his personal belongings as museum relics to mock scientists' and artists' all-too-frequent tendency to portray American Indians only as anthropological subjects to be gazed upon and studied. A photograph of Durham's mother and father is placed against black paper and labeled "The Indian's Parents (frontal view)." Even more confrontational is James Luna's *The Artifact Piece*. This installation features the artist himself, a member of the Luiseño Nation, lying face-up on a bed of sand in a museum case. The displayed Luna is marked with a nametag and other labels that draw attention to his scars, including ones received from bouts of "excessive drinking."[53] These two humorous pieces parody the racist aesthetic to ridicule it: American Indians present their belongings—or, in Luna's case, their selves—as ancient relics stuck in the past in order to demonstrate the absurdity of such a view.

The white aesthetic has not gone unscrutinized by antiracist art. Recently, several artists from across the aesthetic field have attempted to call attention to whiteness through their work.[54] One thinks, for example, of Nikki Lee. A young, Korean-born artist based in New York, Lee specializes in embedding herself in American subcultures, adopting their dress, postures, and behaviors and then having herself photographed. (One of her works is reproduced in Chapter 1.) For her *Yuppie Project*, Lee immersed herself in the fast-paced, white-dominated world of Wall Street professionals and emerged with photographs that render whiteness visible. Lee captured the relationship between white privilege and affluence by underscoring the yuppies' expensive clothing, their country-club camaraderie, and their racial exclusivity.[55] In her photographs, whiteness is represented not as the norm but as a curious, tangible something to be objectified and placed in specific social and historical contexts.

The world of poetry always has been—and remains—a hotbed of the antiracist aesthetic. From the pens of poets such as Audre Lorde, Sonia Sanchez, and Sekou Sundiata have come the sternest abominations of all forms of oppression. And spoken-word poets, those who perform their work on stage, recently have emerged as some of the most outspoken critics of racial domination. (Indeed, the spoken-word scene is one of the most multicultural, democratic, and critically minded spaces in contemporary America.) For instance, in the poem "In America," Palestinian American poet Suheir Hammad links contemporary American society to its colonial past, pointing out that readers are "standing on stolen land" regardless of where they are reading the poem.[56]

Although television programs and movies slowly but steadily have integrated an antiracist aesthetic into their repertoires—think, for example, of the stereotypes that are turned on their heads in *Grey's Anatomy* or the diversity of the cast of *Orange Is the New Black*—comedians are perhaps popular culture's most creative critics of racism. The "Axis of Evil" comedy troupe, made up of performers of Middle Eastern descent, calls attention to the ways Arab Americans suffer at the hands of racial domination; Margaret Cho's edgy humor takes homophobia and sexism and anti-immigrant sentiment to task; and Dave Chappelle's sketch comedy and stand-up routines scrutinize race relations. Through his character Clayton Bigsby—a blind black man who believes himself to be white and who is an outspoken white supremacist—Chappelle finds a clever and hilarious way to belittle bigotry.

And, of course, the antiracist aesthetic courses through the lyrics of some forms of music. It seeps through the songs of Woody Guthrie, a white American and folk legend from Great Depression times. A staunch defender of workers' and immigrants' rights, when Guthrie learned of an airplane crash that killed Mexican migrants being deported from California back to Mexico, migrants referred to only as "deportees" in the news coverage, he grew incensed and, in response, wrote "Deportee," an indictment of the exploitation of immigrants.

The *corrido*, a Mexican folk ballad that tells a story, has for years been used to chronicle Mexican history. Today, many Mexican immigrants have embraced *corridos* and have begun to write tunes that document their current struggles. Responding to America's repressive anti-immigrant policies, for example, Jose Garcia reaches for his accordion and sings,

> Now they are putting up barriers in front of us so we
> don't return;
> But that is not going to block us from crossing the
> United States,
> We leap them like deer; we go under them like moles[57]

Band members play a corrido in Caldwell, Idaho, June 2007. Corridos have long telegraphed the melancholy of Mexico's northern frontier. But modern corridos have also been inspired by everyday occurrences and current events, with some written about the Kennedys, crops, floods and truck stops.

Rapper Nicki Minaj performs onstage at the 2014 American Music Awards.

The Promise and Pitfalls of Hip-Hop

Until now we have said little about hip-hop, that cultural movement that combines music, break-dancing, graffiti, deejaying, fashion, and poetry into one distinctive style. Hip-hop is one of the most influential art forms today. It also is one of the most controversial. Indeed, hip-hop is chock full of racial and sexual messages that deserve to be dissected with care through intersectional analysis. The descendent of jazz, black rhetoric, African drumming, quick-tongued poetry, and humor, rap—which stands for "rhythm and poetry"—originated in the black ghetto. This unrelentingly urban art form exploded a few brief months after Harlem's Sugarhill Gang released "Rapper's Delight" in 1979 and since then has bloomed into a global enterprise worth billions. Today, hip-hop music likely will be remembered as the defining musical movement of this generation. In every consecutive year since 1999, rap has been the second best-selling music category (behind rock).[58] Cornel West calls rap music "the musical expression of the paradoxical cry of desperation and celebration of the black underclass."[59] For Trisha Rose, author of the celebrated book *Black Noise: Rap Music and Black Culture in Contemporary America*, rap represents "the central cultural vehicle for open social reflection on poverty, fear of adulthood, the desire for absent fathers, frustrations about black male sexism, female sexual desires, daily rituals of life as an unemployed teen hustler, safe sex, raw anger, violence, and childhood memories."[60]

Although hip-hop began as a beat-thumping voice of protest, many have claimed it has ceased to be a positive force. It has become commonplace for rappers to pepper their songs with violent and unblushing homophobic and misogynistic lyrics. And their videos, many of which accurately can be classified as soft-core pornography (especially the "uncensored versions" that appear on YouTube), often reduce women to mere sexual objects who exist solely to satisfy men's sensual desires. Is it any wonder that sociologists have found African Americans who listen to rap to be more likely to harbor homophobic and misogynistic attitudes than those who do not?[61]

Add to this the violent lyrics of many popular rap artists, lyrics that some politicians have used to justify police crackdowns in black neighborhoods, as well as hip-hop's hypermaterialism, its emphasis on "getting paid" and living luxuriously, manifest in ostentatious displays of gold and diamonds, fancy cars, and expensive liquor in hip-hop videos, and one can begin to understand why some prominent African Americans, such as the Reverends Delman Coates and Calvin Butts, have called for an all-out boycott of hip-hop music.[62] At best, this brand of hip-hop fails to function as a cultural movement that advances the cause of social justice; at worst, it helps to support racial domination and masculine (not to mention heterosexual) domination by depicting black men as ultraviolent killers and black women as at-your-service sexual objects.[63]

And yet, hip-hop perhaps is the most outspokenly defiant and powerful voice for racial justice emanating from the aesthetic field. Self-packaged gangsta rappers are not representative of hip-hop's rich diversity. Indeed, progressive-minded rappers sing out against racial and class-based domination and criticize the exploitation of women. Referencing the dilapidated state of American ghettos, the Seattle-based Blue Scholars rap in "Back Home,"

> And they say "progress," but the fact is
> Dr. Martin Luther King's legacy is lookin'
> Like the streets we named after 'em:
> Permanently under construction
> The people hustlin'
> Despite the pain and sufferin'.[64]

Some of the harshest critics of hip-hop's sexism, materialism, and violence are hip-hop artists. (Go listen to Lauryn Hill or Saul Williams or Hopsin.) They demonstrate clearly that hip-hop has a "socially conscious" dimension. Like all art forms, it is not one-dimensional; it encompasses both racist and antiracist aesthetics. Indeed, rappers themselves are far from one-dimensional. One thinks immediately of Tupac Shakur, who alternated between uncritical acceptance of gangsta motifs and highly critical-minded social commentary. Or of Eminem, who in one verse makes light of violence against women while in another scathingly indicts racial domination, pointing out, as he does in "The Way I Am," that shootings in white suburban schools shock America while black-on-black inner-city violence hardly is considered newsworthy.[65]

A weapon against racial domination, hip-hop is full of great promise—and great disappointment. The important sociological question is this: What social forces act on hip-hop to turn it away from, or toward, its political roots? Corporate pressure certainly is one answer. Major record labels and television stations—many of which have to answer to powerful (and often white) corporate executives—often pressure hip-hop artists to abandon calls for liberation and justice in favor of indulgent consumerism and sexism.[66] And music promoters also have found a way to "merchandise dissent," to turn the idea of "revolution" itself into a depoliticized commodity.[67] In mainstream hip-hop, that is, "revolution" often is reduced to getting rich: stick it to "The Man" by buying a Bentley.

Besides examining how corporate and economic forces influence the course of hip-hop, we also should examine if and how hip-hop unfairly is singled out for criticism because it is a distinctly black art form. After all, sexist and violent lyrics are not unique to hip-hop. Country western singers, for example, have penned violent lyrics at least since Johnny Cash. "Early in the morning, while making the rounds / I took a shot of cocaine, and I shot my woman down," Cash sings in "Cocaine Blues." In "Attitude Adjustment," Hank Williams, Jr., gives his girlfriend an "adjustment on the top of her head." In rock music, Neil Young shoots his baby "Down by the River"; the Beatles threaten a woman with death if she ever cheats in "Run for Your Life."[68] It is not simply the content of offensive rap lyrics that results in hip-hop's being labeled the country's "most dangerous music." It is how those offensive lyrics bring to the surface America's longstanding fear of black men.[69]

THE RACIALIZATION OF ART WORLDS

The preceding section dealt with the artistic representation of race or how art depicts racial groups and racism. This section deals with the racialization of the aesthetic field or how racial domination guides and structures artistic production and consumption.

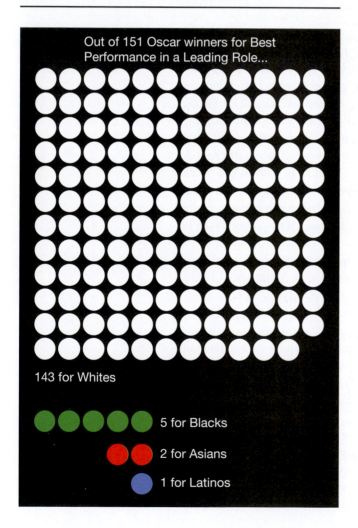

FIGURE 8.1 **OSCAR WINNER BY RACE**

Out of 151 Oscar winners for Best Performance in a Leading Role...

143 for Whites

5 for Blacks

2 for Asians

1 for Latinos

Gustave Flaubert, the famous French novelist, once complained, "One does not write what one wants."[70] What did he mean? That artists—who often profess to being liberated individuals beholden to nothing and no one—are constrained by the structures of the aesthetic field. The artist's world is not set off from society but is grafted, head to heel, to the social world and its problems.

The Power of the White Gaze

Despite many significant inroads made by nonwhites into Hollywood, the music industry, art museums, and other cultural institutions, whites continue to wield significant control over the arts. As in sports, nonwhites constitute many of the players and performers but few of those who hold the power: owners, curators, producers, directors, or scriptwriters. Studies have concluded that nonwhites are underrepresented in "each and every aspect" of the entertainment industry. Over 80 percent of all television episodes shot in the 2012–2013 season were directed by white people, and 91 percent of the directors in Los Angeles and New York City who are registered with the Directors' Guild of America (the strongest union in the film and TV industry) are white.[71] With the exception of Taiwan-born Ang Lee, Mexican-born Alfonso Cuarón, and Kathryn Bigelow, a white woman, every single recipient of the Academy Award for Best Director has been a white man.[72] And nonwhite filmmakers often have to work with a shoestring budget, as Hollywood producers, who are more than willing to pour millions into summer action blockbusters, seem hesitant to fund films written and produced by nonwhites.[73]

Or consider the corporate domination of radio. Have you ever driven across the country and wondered why many of the radio stations in California sound like the ones in Nebraska, which sound like the ones in North Carolina? It is a safe bet that the similarity is a result of the fact that the same company that owns the radio stations in California owns the ones in Nebraska and North Carolina, too. Clear Channel Communications, one of the nation's largest media conglomerates, owns over 1,000 full-power AM and FM radio stations, not to mention twelve XM Satellite radio channels and over thirty television stations. In other words, roughly one in ten radio stations in the United States is a Clear Channel station.[74] Clear Channel's dominance of the airwaves leaves little room for more critically minded music or political viewpoints that challenge the racial status quo, which is why the Black Eyed Peas and Nicki Minaj are played over and over but many radio listeners have never heard of Aesop Rock.

Whites also are overrepresented in positions of power in art museums, constituting a sizable portion of museum trustees, curators, and directors. It is beyond dispute that artists of color and artworks that challenge racism now make frequent appearances in major art museums. But it also is beyond dispute that such museums are bastions of Eurocentrism. In most museums, white European and American artists are the ones most prominently displayed. Museums that wish to provide visitors with a thoroughly non-Eurocentric art education must get by on decidedly less impressive budgets, which is why we tend to find such museums tucked away in small, usually unremarkable buildings and staffed by a cadre of committed volunteers. They tell a different story, yes, but their voice is far softer than the one that booms from New York's Metropolitan Museum of Art or the Art Institute of Chicago.[75]

As nonwhites continue to be excluded from the highest seats of artistic power, control, and visibility, it is small wonder that whiteness continues to infuse our conception of the beautiful. Whiteness guides artists and critics as they decide what should be classified as "art" and what should not. The best-known mid-twentieth-century sociologist of music, Theodor Adorno, infamously dismissed (black-dominated) jazz as one of "many varieties of rhythmic-spatial music . . . 'sprouting forth everywhere as though they are rooted in nature,'" even as he lavished praise on (white-dominated) classical music for being "expressive-dynamic."[76] Only Duke Ellington earned his grudging respect—but solely on account of Ellington's "tasteful" appropriation of musical ideas already found in compositions by Claude Debussy and Maurice Ravel. In many cases, creations by nonwhites are revered as "art" only when respected white critics—or white establishments or elite artists—revere them as such. To take but another example, African masks and sculpture have been around for centuries, but it was only after famous European artists such as Picasso and Matisse began including African masks in their paintings that the masks appeared to the white-dominated art world as "art."[77] In this case, white artists borrowed images from the nonwhite (indeed, non-Western) world and refurbished that image through an established artistic medium (modernist painting) to incorporate it into the artistic canon.

In other cases, ordinary artifacts and tools created by nonwhites to meet every-day needs are "discovered" by white art critics. For years, the black women of Gee's Bend, a poverty-stricken patch of Alabama, made quilts out of discarded cloth and rags. The quilts were stunning—colorful and complex, the material sewed and cut by hand—and eventually were discovered by museum curators. In 2002, Houston's Museum of Fine Arts devoted an impressive exhibition to the quilts of Gee's Bend, an exhibition that gripped the nation's attention. Soon, they were shown in some of the nation's most prominent museums and impressive art books were dedicated to them. The (white) discovery of the Gee's Bend quilts did not make them more beautiful or special, but it did in a way make them "art." Once the quilts were hung in Houston's Museum of Fine Arts, they became, as the museum director put it, "works of art that just happened to be made for utilitarian purposes."[78]

With little effort other examples could be highlighted—from the pottery of Native America to the crafts of the Pacific Islands—demonstrating the control cultural elites exercise over the definition of "art." When "folk art" or "outsider art" (these are art historians' terms) are deemed important by these cultural gatekeepers, important enough to be exhibited in museums, important enough to be studied and purchased at high prices, we are able to catch a glimpse of how whiteness conditions their aesthetic decisions. After all, in a majority of cases, art created outside the normal boundaries of an art world—by people who reside outside the normal boundaries of society—is deemed "naïve art." A beautiful handmade quilt made by a poor black woman of Alabama is art; a beautiful handmade quilt made by a middle-class white grandmother is not. Why? Because the beauty of "naïve art" is found in its *exotic*—not normal, not white—characteristics. It is found in its Africanism, its Orientalism, its primitivism, all of which come to us filtered though the white aesthetic.[79] As the dominant and normative artistic judgment that pervades the aesthetic field, the unexamined artistic default category, the white aesthetic normalizes whiteness by exoticizing nonwhiteness.

Just as the white aesthetic can turn an ordinary quilt into a masterpiece, it can reward artists whose work supports it and punish artists whose work it finds threatening. The 2014 Grammy Award for the Best Rap Album was awarded to Macklemore and Ryan Lewis, a white Seattle-based duo, for "The Heist," an album many do not consider rap at all. Macklemore beat out several black artists, including Kanye West, Jay-Z, and, perhaps most surprisingly, the Compton-based Kendrick Lamar, whose "Good Kid, m.A.A.d. City" many considered the defining rap album of the decade. We can debate which album is the best, but it is difficult to view this Grammy in terms not explicitly racialized. Macklemore himself realized this, which is why many believe he told Lamar after the award, "You got robbed. I wanted you to win."[80]

The distribution of awards is but one indicator of how institutions within the aesthetic field award nonwhite artists when they do not challenge the dominant, white representation of the social world. One also could analyze artists' fame and fortune. The distance between nonwhite musical artists who do not challenge the racial status quo and those who do—measured, for example, by the prominence of their music videos on MTV or their songs on the radio, how easily one can find their songs, how often they are featured in *Rolling Stone*, and their net worth—is considerable.

Indeed, the white aesthetic is so powerful that few artists can escape it. Even those who wish to challenge it are forced to acknowledge it. To quote Cornel West once more, the African American artist driven by an antiracist aesthetic "still seems too preoccupied with how black folk appear to the white normative gaze, too obsessed with showing white people how sophisticated they are, how worthy [they are] of white validation and recognition. . . . The irony of the view of black art as protest . . . [is that] it reduces black people to mere reactors to white power."[81] If artists represent nonwhites only as the un-stereotype, they end up responding to white representations of nonwhiteness.[82] To wrest free of the white gaze, artists must depict nonwhites in their full and complex humanity rather than representing them in the soft glow of romanticism, as only their stereotype's mirror image: *not* criminals, *not* impoverished, and so on. In painting, Horace Pippin, the self-trained African American artist, achieves such a goal, "portray[ing] black people as 'fully themselves'—that is, as they are outside of the white normative gaze that requires elaborate masks and intricate posturing for black survival and sanity."[83] In literature, one also thinks of Zora Neale Hurston; in film, of Oscar Micheaux.[84]

In the aesthetic field, works and performances that do not align with the white aesthetic tend to be marginalized, pushed to the side. Artists who refuse to "sell out" often do not enjoy the perks of artistic success—wealth, fame, long-running television shows, lavish record deals, prominent museum exhibits—as often as those artists who do. Faced with the tension that long has defined the aesthetic field— that between art and money, authenticity and profitability, truth and clichés— artists must choose to what extent, if at all, they will sell out, most of them fully aware of the consequences of their decision.

Alternative viewpoints are relegated to low-budget media sources found on the edges of the aesthetic field: low-power pirate radio stations, ethnic newspapers and websites, a museum that relies on donations (as opposed to government funding) and makes do in a small building on the "bad side" of town.[85] Never in the history of humankind have shouts of protest against racial domination been completely silenced, and today, in some artistic corners, they perhaps are louder than ever. But sometimes it is hard to be heard above all the noise.

The Racial Structures of the Aesthetic Sphere

Artistic divisions—those separating, say, different styles of dance, musical tastes, fashion senses, or schools of art—map onto racial divisions. Or, as cultural sociologist William Roy has put it, "boundaries between aesthetic genres correspond to social boundaries between groups."[86] In the 1930s, country music was so explicitly connected to whiteness that the KKK hosted fiddle contests. Rhythm and blues, by contrast, was linked to blackness, so much so that rhythm and blues records were first called "race records."[87] With respect to this specific division, not much has changed. Country western, along with polka and rock-and-roll, continues to be associated with whites, while rhythm and blues, hip-hop, gospel, funk, and soul are associated with blacks. Other musical tastes are racially coded as well: cumbia, salsa, and reggaetón, for example, are connected to Latino culture. Indeed, the distribution of musical instruments is related to the distribution of racial groups: the steel guitar with whites; the pipa with Chinese Americans; the sitar with Indian Americans.

How are racial divisions on display in your neighborhood grocery store?

In poetry, traditional written poetry is associated with whites, modern spoken-word poetry with non-whites. In dance, the world of classical ballet is inhabited almost exclusively by white dancers, Latinos tend to be overrepresented on the floors of salsa clubs, and modern dance often features African Americans and African influences. Cooking certainly should be considered an aesthetic expression, and we see racial divisions here, too: white chefs and consumers are overrepresented in the organic food movement—as well as in high cuisine restaurants—while soul food is considered a thoroughly black culinary art form. Whiteness can be spotted in grocery stores, where some items—such as tortillas and salsa, chow mein and soy sauce—are grouped in the "ethnic foods" aisle, while other, equally "ethnic" items—for example, spaghetti sauce and French baguettes—are not labeled as such.

Racial divisions are quite apparent in television programming. For years now, television producers have targeted specific racial or ethnic groups with programs supposedly designed to speak to those groups' unique needs and lifestyles. Because it focuses on a narrow segment of society, this practice has become known as "narrowcasting" (as opposed to "broadcasting," which targets a general audience). The result is a kind of artistic segregation, where "black programs" are pitched at black viewers, "Jewish programs" at Jewish viewers, "Hispanic programs" at Hispanic viewers, and so forth. Indeed, in multicultural metropolises, such as Los Angeles and New York, one can find weekly programs aired in Assyrian, Armenian, Persian, and Hebrew. Entire television networks are dedicated to narrowcasting, such as the Jewish TV Network, Black Entertainment Television, and American-owned Spanish-language stations, such as Telemundo and Univision.[88]

Like all racial divisions, those found within the aesthetic field are never fixed, impenetrable, or complete. Nor are such divisions timeless. If one were to conduct a historical analysis of the aesthetic field, one would quickly discover how art forms associated, say, with blacks are taken up by whites and then abandoned by blacks. The banjo used to be known as a "Negro instrument"; now it is associated with whites and bluegrass.[89] The piano used to be reserved for the white-dominated world of classical music, but it was "jazzed up," so to speak, by such black artists as Duke Ellington and Ray Charles. Lindy hop swing dance was popularized in the 1920s by blacks in Harlem. It fell out of style after World War II but roared back onto the cultural scene in the 1990s, this time as an art form populated by young white professionals.[90] Or consider folk music, which began as the voice of white nationalism before being refashioned in the 1930s as the sound of a multiracial labor movement. It crumbled under the pressures of consumer culture during the 1950s, only to be resurrected again in the 1960s, but this time as an art form predominantly played and listened to by whites.[91]

Because aesthetic choices can be used to signal and enforce social differences—to divide "us" from "them"—the shifting nature of artistic tastes across racial boundaries often is propelled by identity struggles and power relations. Speaking of the role fashion plays in signaling class divisions, German sociologist Georg Simmel observed, "Just as soon as the lower classes begin to copy their style, thereby crossing the line of demarcation the upper classes have drawn and destroying the uniformity of their coherence, the upper classes turn away from this style and adopt a new one, which in its turn differentiates them from the masses; and thus the game goes merrily on."[92] Simmel's point is not exclusive to fashion or to economic divisions. It can be applied to racial divisions and to all kinds of aesthetic choices. When blacks "invade" a traditionally white art form, many whites abandon that art form for something new. The reverse also is true: many blacks turn their backs on a traditionally black art form when it is taken up by too many whites.[93] Jazz itself, once seen as the quintessential black art form, has come to have predominantly white audiences in recent decades, as blacks have moved on to hip-hop and other musical forms.

Highbrow and Lowbrow Culture

The racialization and reracialization of art worlds comes with consequences. For one, not every art form awards its practitioners the same amount of cultural capital. You might recall that in the previous chapter we defined cultural capital as "the sum total of one's knowledge of established and revered cultural activities and practices" and demonstrated how cultural capital can be exchanged for other varieties of capital (for example, economic, political, and educational). So-called highbrow culture, the collection of art forms associated with an upper-class taste and lifestyle, is rich in cultural capital, while "lowbrow culture" or "popular culture," art forms considered more ordinary and associated with the tastes and lifestyles of "the masses," is more or less bereft of it. Ballet, opera, classical music, sculpture, and abstract painting are considered highbrow art forms, while club dancing, popular music, and stand-up comedy are considered lowbrow art forms. In fashion, it is the difference between tailored items plucked fresh off the Milan runway and clothes purchased at the local mall. In cuisine, it is the difference between foie gras and a cheeseburger or between a 1989 Haut Brion and a Budweiser.[94]

The distinction between highbrow and lowbrow corresponds to the distinction between traditionally white and traditionally nonwhite art forms. Indeed, the origin of this artistic division is rooted in racial and class divisions of the nineteenth century. As historian Lawrence Levine has documented, as English cities grew larger and more diverse (owing to processes of immigration and urbanization), the members of the upper class needed to devise a way to set themselves apart from (and above) the masses. One way they did so was by transforming the performing arts. No longer would Shakespearean plays be performed alongside comedy routines and trained animal acts, and no longer were audience members allowed to partake in rowdy behavior (for instance, by booing inept actors). By the end of the nineteenth century, the upper class had claimed certain art forms as its own, had developed certain behaviors

Classical music, historically a form of entertainment for all classes of people, has been deemed highbrow.

to accompany those art forms (for example, sitting quietly, no tobacco spitting), and had elevated these forms above other ones.[95] Soon, cultural organizations linked to upper-class taste, such as the symphony orchestra and the art museum, arose and provided an institutional existence to the distinction between highbrow and lowbrow culture.

When this distinction was imported to the United States, it took on a specifically racialized meaning. The new upper-class ideal that came to define the culture and conduct of highbrow art—"orderly, regulated, learned, prosperous, 'civilized'"—became associated with white audiences, while lowbrow behaviors, such as heckling or calling to a friend from across the room, were associated with nonwhite audiences.[96] Affluent whites (as well as whites who wished to appear affluent) approached highbrow art with reverence and stillness, with coolness and calm; poorer nonwhites, in contrast, tended to approach lowbrow art with much more bravado and vim, with honest appraisals uttered aloud.Such behavioral differences remain today, which helps explain why it is not unusual to hear nonblacks voice discomfort when African American movie- or theatergoers participate more vocally during the show.[97]

Just as it was designed to do in the nineteenth century, today the binary coding scheme separating white/highbrow culture from nonwhite/lowbrow culture is marshaled as a mechanism of inclusion and exclusion. Thus fashion statements rooted in African American history and culture—Afros, dashikis, and even flamboyant and colorful suits rooted in the fashion style of the Southern black church—are deemed "inappropriate" for the professional world. American Airlines, Hyatt, and, as recently as 2014, the U.S. military are but three organizations that at one time forbade their employees from wearing braids, a hairstyle traditionally worn by black women. The Hyatt went so far as to label braids an "extreme and unusual hair style."[98] Hip-hop fashion in particular has been so deeply linked to negative behavior that it has been banned by several companies. The NBA dress code, for example, forbids its players from wearing "chains, pendants, or medallions" over their clothes, "headgear of any kind," and "sunglasses while indoors" when engaging in team or league business. And some bars and restaurants explicitly forbid their patrons from donning clothes associated with hip-hop fashion.

Nonwhite audiences face barriers when attempting to access traditionally white highbrow culture. If nonwhites are disproportionately impoverished, as we learned in Chapter 4, then they also are disproportionately denied access to many highbrow art forms and their cultural capital. Opera tickets and violin lessons are expensive. So are locally grown vegetables, which is why the organic food movement (as much an aesthetic movement as a political or nutritional one) appeals mainly to white, middle-class people who can afford to pay $2.15 for a California-grown organic cucumber or $5 for an unprocessed loaf of bread.[99] And besides, to the palates of many poor folks, that fancy bread tastes funny. They develop, in other words, distaste for the things they cannot afford; social barriers to highbrow food, culture, and art are transformed into legitimate tastes. If you cannot afford to eat at expensive restaurants, you adapt (perhaps without even knowing it), twisting that structural barrier into a personal choice.[100]

Although certain art museums might be relatively accessible today in terms of the price of admission, they continue to be frequented not by working-class people, at least proportionately speaking, but by (white) middle- and upper-class audiences. Why? Because only the latter are equipped by the cultivation they have received in their family lives and schooling to understand and appreciate the (primarily Eurocentric) art they encounter there. Others experience only discomfort and say to themselves, "This place isn't for the likes of me."

Who appreciates modern art and who says, it's "not for them"?

Even nonwhite artists face significant barriers, both explicit and implicit, when seeking to access majority-white art worlds. Talented black dancers, for example, often are denied a position in ballet companies, and many black ballet dancers who have secured a spot feel isolated and singled out against the white backdrop of their fellow dancers. As former black dancer Victoria Johnson confessed, "It's hard to be the only black dancer. You feel separate, and you feel neglected in a certain sense, and it's not that people are trying to make you feel bad, but it's just obviously around you. Everyone else can make a bond by similarity, and you have to make an effort, and making an effort makes you wonder, 'Am I not being true to myself?' It's hard to be strong enough to be in that environment and to not feel wrong."[101]

The racial structures of the aesthetic field, therefore, associate certain art forms with certain racial or ethnic groups and assign to different art forms various degrees of cultural capital. Some of the most sophisticated sociological research on this topic has found that highly educated people do not reject all forms of lowbrow culture; instead, they tend to reject only those low-status art forms most appreciated by people with the lowest levels of education.[102] When it comes to music, for example, sociologist Bethany Bryson has found that highly educated people tend to profess liking everything but rap, heavy metal, country, and gospel music, musical genres most closely associated with low education.[103] Education, then, promotes cultural tolerance but only to a point. And it is in people's artistic *dislikes* that we best are able to detect how they erect symbolic boundaries between themselves and people they hope to keep at a safe distance. There is a racial element to all of this. Indeed, studies have shown that compared with people who are fairly tolerant of other racial groups, people who harbor racial prejudice are more likely to reject art forms associated with nonwhite groups, such as Latin music, reggae, gospel, and rap.[104] As we mentioned in our discussion of hip-hop, the rejection of certain (racialized) artistic forms can function as coded language, as a method of putting down certain groups without sounding like a racist.[105] You can express animus against poor whites by claiming to hate NASCAR or monster truck rallies; you can express your anti-Mexican attitudes by observing that Mexican food is disgusting and that Mexican music is simplistic.

In the aesthetic field, then, one confronts a race-based audience segmentation rooted in race-based social divisions.[106] However, taking note of the racial cleavages within the aesthetic field should not blind us to the fact that artistic production is—and always has been—a thoroughly multicultural and multiethnic undertaking. Artistic forms and tastes glide and float across color lines. Aesthetic styles overlap and bleed into one another. Although typically thought of as black music, jazz found inspiration and guidance in the compositions of white military bands. Rock has been categorized as white music, despite the fact that in its early days it drew heavily on rhythm and blues and gospel.[107] Recently, Native American modernist painters have represented traditional Indian images through techniques borrowed from European artistic movements, and, as we noted above, European artists, such as Picasso, borrowed artistic images from African cultures. Romare Bearden, the great African American artist, was influenced not only by scenes from his Harlem neighborhood but also by Mexican muralists and French cubists.[108]

Entire musical genres are based on the premise of cross-cultural convergence. Reggaetón, for example, mixes hip-hop, Electronica, reggae, and dancehall influences with bomba, merengue, and other Latin American musical traditions. And dozens of artists have made a name for themselves specifically by transcending racial divisions within the aesthetic field.[109] Music, like many American art forms, reflects the country's multicultural mosaic.

CULTURAL APPROPRIATION

If American art is, in some way or another, a kind of multiracial hybridization—a creolized cultural concoction—can we even speak in terms of "Puerto Rican art" or "Hopi art"? Is there no such thing as Jewish humor, Latin dance, or Irish food? If art forms considered black borrow from those considered white or Asian or French, is there such a thing as a "black aesthetic" or, for that matter, an "Asian American aesthetic" or a "white aesthetic? The answer is yes. Racialized aesthetics stem from the different ways racial groups have been incorporated into American society. Because Native American history is different from Asian American history, and because Native Americans experience different struggles today than Asian Americans do, it should not surprise us that there exists a Native American aesthetic that differs from an Asian-American aesthetic. One theme that helps define Asian American poetry, for example, is that of dislocation, the experience of being a perpetual foreigner in America. And the large number of Columbus and Custer jokes that circulate through Indian country are properly understood as constituting Native American humor.[110]

Claiming that racialized aesthetics exist doesn't imply that they are isolated from one another. In our multicultural society—indeed, our multicultural world—such a claim is untenable. Nor does it suggest that, say, the Asian

American aesthetic is simple and monolithic. Indeed, assuming that certain racial groups must have a unified aesthetic or no aesthetic at all implies that nonwhite groups are homogeneous blobs, void of diversity and internal differences. As one Asian American art critic has pointed out, "When we speak of Euro-American aesthetics, there is room for diversity and a myriad of cultural influences, many of which came from Asia and other parts of the world. But suddenly when we speak of the possibility of an Asian-American aesthetic, it must either be monolithic or not viable."[111]

When is it appropriate to appropriate another group's culture? Does doing so belittle or celebrate the appropriated group's music, style, or fashion? Does cultural appropriation lead to a more liberated, multicultural democracy, or is it another mechanism of racial inequality and unfairness?

Making Sense of Cultural Appropriation

Cultural appropriation occurs when members of one ethnic or racial group adopt a cultural product associated with another.[112] Asian fashion has been widely appropriated by non-Asians, as evidenced by the proliferation of Chinese character tattoos and, in the world of women's fashion, Japanese kimonos and Indian saris.[113] Native American art forms and traditions—or at least *representations* of Native American art forms and traditions—have been employed by the Boy Scouts of America, New Age gurus, and non-Indian artists.

One of the most referenced examples of cultural appropriation is the nonblack (and especially white) adaptation of African American culture in general and hip-hop culture in particular. Hip-hop styles, such as tilted caps, baggy clothes, and hip sayings—styles rooted in the predominantly low-income black urban experience—have been picked up by nonblacks, many of whom have never set foot in a ghetto. Since the rapid expansion of hip-hop, many have wondered about its appeal to nonblack youth, especially white middle-class suburban youth. *Why Do White Kids Love Hip-Hop?*, asks Bakari Kitwana in his recent book. He tenders several answers: hip-hop connects with youth's feelings of alienation and their antiestablishment leanings; it allows them to nourish their fascination with black culture; and, on the flip side, it has been very intentional about reaching wider audiences. "As much as white kids chose hip-hop, hip-hop chose white America."[114]

Let us intervene in this debate as sociologists, ever ready to *question* conventional questions. Why do we need to know why young nonblack people love hip-hop? Wondering why whites or Asian Americans connect with hip-hop implies, first, that hip-hop still has not reached the status of "true art," a musical expression that can be enjoyed by everyone. The reason we do not ask why Asian Americans love classical music, even though most classical music originally was composed for white upper-class audiences, is in part that we treat classical music as pure (read: highbrow) art that transcends racial boundaries. But, clearly, one of the reasons nonblacks listen to Jay-Z and Kendrick Lamar is that their music is fresh and exciting and important. What is more, asking why white kids appreciate hip-hop implies that whites should not love hip-hop and that blacks should. Not only does this stance advance some overarching generalizations about white and black people, it imposes an artificial racial segregation on the aesthetic field.

The point we are driving at is this: it is too simplistic to comprehend cultural appropriation as a kind of "ethnic theft" which *always* occurs when insider culture is performed by outsider bodies. It certainly is true that white Americans do not daily bear the weight of racial discrimination on their shoulders, but it equally is true that such vast diversity exists within nonwhite racial groups that claims like "only blacks can truly understand hip-hop" only help flatten that diversity. Who has a better chance of understanding the black mother in Alice Walker's short story "Everyday Use" (a character who tends a small farm and "can kill and clean a hog as mercilessly as a man"), a black man from an affluent suburb or a young Latina from a poor family, who grew up butchering livestock?[115] Or as one Cherokee leader has expressed it, "I've seen some full-blooded Indians, that I *know* are full-blooded Indians, that are *not* Indians. They don't care about Indian culture, they don't attend Indian functions. . . . I see a blonde-headed person, blue-eyed, that attends ceremonial things and goes to different tribal affairs and things like that. And they try to uphold the Indian tradition. To me, that's a real Indian."[116]

Cultural appropriation, in other words, is not simply about *who* is doing the appropriating but *how* they are doing it. We can distinguish between cultural appropriation that denigrates and that which appreciates; that which supports a racist aesthetic and that which contributes to the antiracist aesthetic. "There is a difference," writes Kitwana, "between 'cultural banditry,' appropriation that comes in the form of an outsider ripping off another culture, and 'acknowledged appropriation,' where the outsider emulates a culture *and* redefines it, while acknowledging its roots."[117]

Racist Appropriation

If some nonwhites are offended by cultural appropriation, it is because for years their art has been used against them, co-opted by cultural outsiders who twist and distort, malign and fragment their art so as better to exploit, dehumanize, and dominate the very people that art was intended to heal. Racist appropriation employs a variety of methods. One is a strategic amnesia. Here, the appropriators not only refuse to credit the racial or ethnic group responsible for the appropriated art form, they also attempt to completely detach that art form from the racial or ethnic group that brought it into the world. One encounters this, for example, in *le jazz*, that peculiar concoction, part classical music and part pseudo-African chic, that briefly was popular in Paris during the 1920s; "there is no need to belabor the point," writes music historian Alex Ross, "that *le jazz* was condescending toward its African-American sources. [Its leading composers] were enjoying a one-night stand with a dark-skinned form, and they had no intention of striking up a conversation with it the following day."[118] A few decades later, white popular singers appropriated rock music from black performers such as Chuck Berry, B. B. King, and Count Basie—and whitewashed it to such an extent that today the genre is associated with whites and often is misunderstood as originating from white performers, which is why Elvis Presley is considered "the King of Rock and Roll" and Eric Clapton is regarded widely as the country's leading blues guitarist.[119] Mos Def in "Rock N Roll" puts it this way: "You may dig on the Rolling Stones / But they ain't come up with that style on they own."[120]

In deracializing and reracializing an art form, racist appropriation denies nonwhite groups the ability to profit from their creations. Given the pronounced race-based economic inequalities in America, whites who get rich off an art form co-opted from nonwhites, especially from poor nonwhites, steal not only culture but resources and revenue as well. Additionally, when a successful art form is appropriated from the group in which it originated, that group loses control over the form and, by extension, the ways it is represented. Racist appropriation can be used to exoticize the nonwhite groups and, therefore, to contribute to their status as Other. "Within commodity culture," writes bell hooks, "ethnicity becomes spice, seasoning that can liven up the dull dish that is mainstream white culture. . . . Should youth of any other color not know how to move closer to the Other, or how to get in touch with the 'primitive,' consumer culture promises to show the way. . . . Encounters with Otherness are clearly marked as more exciting, more intense, and more threatening. The lure is the combination of pleasure and danger."[121] Thus, the white appropriation of Native American culture can entrap Indianness in representations of the primitive, just as the appropriation of Asian American culture can bind Asianness to foreignness—thereby contributing to both groups' continued alienation from mainstream America.

American retailers have reduced the kaffiyeh, a scarf symbolizing Palestinian nationalism, to a trendy accessory divorced from its historical and political significance.

When an image slips out of your hand, the very image you created to dismantle racial domination can be used by those who seek to uphold it or, more commonly, who do not give it a second thought. Racist appropriation of an art form or of a cultural style weakens its political power, sometimes to the point of impotence. (Recall, for example, the discursive co-optation, discussed in Chapter 3, practiced by whites who opposed the Civil Rights Movement.) Equally destructive, racist appropriation can be used as a new form of colonization, where white supremacy is strengthened by the appropriation and purposeful degradation of nonwhite cultures. The result is a kind of modern-day minstrelsy, where nonwhite culture is represented by and for the white gaze.[122] And if the appropriated image comes to overpower the original image—as is usually the case—then the distorted representation of, say, black culture soon is widely regarded as an accurate reflection of black culture. Representation becomes misrecognized as reality.

What disrespectful appropriators often fail to realize (and this is the crux of the matter) is this: because nonwhite art often is a cry against oppression and suffering—black spirituals were a sigh of anguish in the face of slave tyranny; hip-hop emerged in an era of mass incarceration as the voice of abandoned black masses huddled together in America's desolate city centers—those who co-opt that art without acknowledging the suffering that helped inspire it do violence to the artists who created it and the people they represent. The essence of racist appropriation is the act of taking "everything but the burden," of enjoying the pleasure without even recognizing the pain.[123]

> Saw whites clap during a sacred dance
> Saw young blonde hippie boy with a red stone pipe
> My eyes burned him up
> He smiled *This is a Sioux pipe* he said from his sportscar
> *Yes* I hiss *I'm wondering how you got it*
> *& the name is Lakota not Sioux*
> *I'll tell you* he said all friendly and liberal as only
> Those with no pain can be
> I turned away Can't charm me can't bear to know . . .
> Today was a day like TB
> you cough & cough trying to get it out
> all that comes
> is blood & spit
>
> Chrystos, "Today Was a Bad Day Like TB"[124]

Antiracist Appropriation

Do nonwhite groups appropriate white culture? Absolutely. But when appropriation flows in this direction, it does not bring about the same (negative) consequences. That is, when white culture is appropriated by nonwhites, whites as a group do not suffer (materially or symbolically) because of it. Whites have not experienced years of cultural humiliation and debasement or been depicted in a superficial or dehumanizing light. Never in the history of America were whites kidnapped and transported to boarding schools, where they were told that white culture was evil, as were Native Americans; never have a group of powerful nonwhites appeared in "whiteface" and mocked white culture to loud applause, as African Americans were mocked in minstrel shows; and never have grotesque images of whites committing anti-American acts been displayed on posters that hung in American towns, as were those of Japanese Americans during World War II. The white appropriation of nonwhite culture connects with this history of racial domination; the same cannot be said of the nonwhite appropriation of white culture. Cultural appropriation may flow both ways, but in nearly every case raced-based power and privilege are asserted in but one direction.

That said, there are respectful ways to appropriate another group's culture. Antiracist appropriation refuses to deracialize or dehistoricize the art form that inspires it, but gives credit where credit is due. It does not distort or malign the image in mocking ways; it refuses to use the image in the interest of racial domination. The antiracist artist (or consumer of art) acknowledges the suffering caused by racial domination and, importantly, the role she or he might play in upholding that suffering. And if an artist makes money off an appropriated art form, she or he reinvests some of that money in the nonwhite communities from which the art was borrowed.

"No human culture," writes African American literary critic Henry Louis Gates, Jr., "is inaccessible to someone who makes the effort to understand, to learn, to inhabit another world."[125] Gates's observation is reaffirmed by the many who have accurately and justly represented another culture in their artwork. Tony Hillerman, a white novelist, set many of his books on the Navajo (or Dineh) reservation and was awarded the Special Friend of the Dineh Award by the Navajo Nation for "authentically portraying the strength and dignity of traditional Navajo culture."[126] Similarly, the Yankton Nation of South Dakota allowed a non-Indian, who had been adopted by a Yankton family, learned to speak their language, and participated in tribal culture, to market his artwork as "Indian produced."[127] And unlike other white artists who have incorporated hip-hop styles and sounds into their music, "Eminem comes across as someone who cares as much (if not more) about maintaining the overall integrity of hip-hop culture as he does about his commercial success."[128]

Debates about cultural authenticity and appropriation can be especially complex and even disheartening for people who claim multiracial heritage. "If I belong to two worlds," they might wonder, "does this mean I am doomed to be loyal to neither, inauthentic by birthright?" Can a woman, for instance, whose mother is Oneida and whose father is white label her pottery "Oneida art"? Should a man whose mother is Cuban and whose father is Chinese express a kind of ethnic authenticity by learning Spanish or Mandarin? Should the children of African American and Jewish parents celebrate Hanukkah or Kwanzaa? Questions such as these can leave biracial and multiracial people feeling confused and frustrated just as, in the opposite direction, they can provoke creative action that blurs racial boundaries and forecasts multicultural possibilities.[129]

Even more ironically, claims about the cultural authenticity of a certain art form—claims reacting against cultural appropriation—can bring about the death of that art form. As "real Indian art" comes to rely more and more on a cultural preservationist ethic, Indian culture becomes smothered by the weight of unchanging tradition. Because traditional storytellers risk being labeled un-Indian if their tales diverge too far from the well-worn path, Indian poetry and literacy, reduced to simple imitation, can become void of creativity. As sociologist Eva Marie Garroutee has stated, "The logic of cultural 'authenticity' may initially support the identity claims of individuals and tribes, only later to destroy them, along with the culture in which they arose."[130] In Ceremony, novelist Leslie Marmon Silko, of white, Mexican, and Laguna Pueblo heritage, captures eloquently the tension between tradition and progress as it relates to Native American practices. "The people nowadays have an idea about the ceremonies," she writes. "They think the ceremonies must be performed exactly as they have always been done. . . . But long ago when the people were given these ceremonies, the changing began, if only in the aging of the yellow gourd rattle or the shrinking of the skin around the eagle's claw, if only in the different voices from generation to generation, singing the chants. . . . The people mistrust this greatly, but only this growth keeps the ceremonies strong. . . . Things which don't shift and grow are dead things."[131]

And from where, we might ask, do our own ideas of "cultural authenticity" come? From no other source than the European colonizer. White explorers charted distant lands in search of "primitive" cultures "uncontaminated" by outside sources; they wanted to set their eyes upon the "authentic" art of these cultures. The notion of cultural authenticity was invented within the context of the colonial enterprise; it was developed to satisfy the white gaze. Accordingly, it carries with it colonialist assumptions, those that divide the world into rigid racial groups and that attribute to those groups certain practices and behaviors.[132] And what about our concept of "cultural ownership"? Where does that originate? As philosopher Kwame Anthony Appiah has observed, our idea of "cultural ownership" sprouts directly from Western notions of intellectual-property law, which originally was designed to benefit the interests of corporate owners: "Talk of cultural patrimony ends up embracing the sort of hyper-stringent doctrine of property rights . . . that we normally associate with international capital. . . . In the name of authenticity, [we] would extend this peculiarly Western, and modern, conception of ownership to every corner of the earth. The vision is of a cultural landscape consisting of Disney Inc. and the Coca-Cola Company, for sure; but also of Ashanti Inc., Navajo Inc., Maorin Inc., Norway Inc.: All rights reserved."[133]

THE SOCIOLOGY OF ART, THE ART OF SOCIOLOGY

We have traversed the aesthetic field, discussing poetry, literature, painting, dance, performance, television, cinema, photography, fashion, and many varieties of music. In so doing, we have learned that racial dynamics are found within all art worlds, even if the artists and consumers of those worlds fail to recognize this. Perhaps, too, we have been reminded of the unquestionable, enduring, and prophetic importance of art. The power that media hold over our thinking is breathtaking; our only hope of preserving a clear and accurate understanding of the world is to interrogate all the representations delivered daily to us at breakneck speed. Passive consumption is not an option, for all art, in some way or another, is political.

Edgar Degas, the famous French impressionist painter, once said, "Painting is easy when you don't know how, but very difficult when you do." The same could be said of sociology. Anyone can look at a painting or a television program or any other piece of art and venture a guess as to how that art form affects the racial order, just as they can (and often do) overlook the art form's racial implications altogether. But it takes a trained eye to conduct a thorough socioanalysis of art, placing it in its overlapping historical and social contexts and deciphering precisely how the art in question affects racial domination (if it supports a white, racist, or antiracist aesthetic) and how racial domination might have affected it. The sociological eye also pays attention to the included and the excluded; it notes the excesses, silences, and omissions when conducting a racial analysis of art. In this chapter, we have provided you with some guidance for effectively objectifying the artistic representations that meet you every day, so that you can better understand the social world and your position within it.

THE BIG PICTURE

Chapter 8: Aesthetics

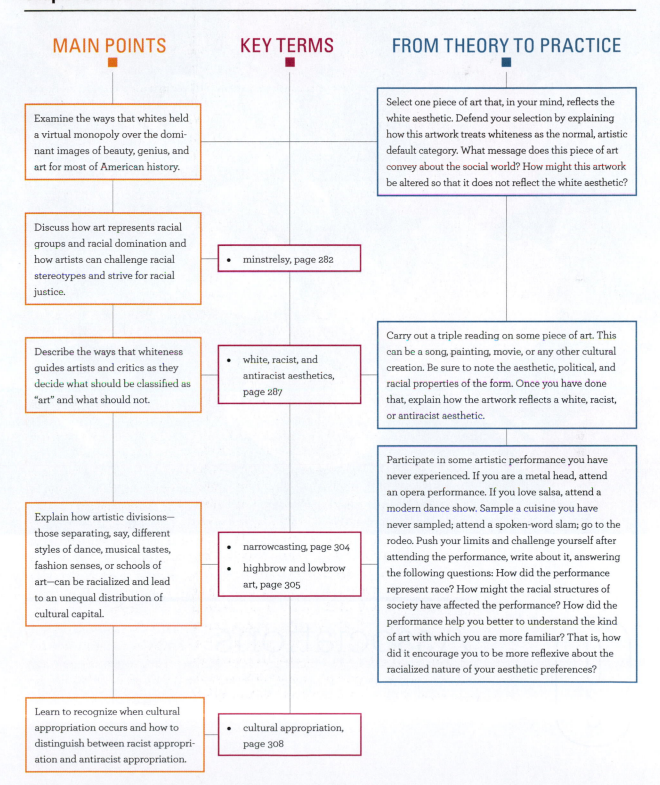

MAIN POINTS

Examine the ways that whites held a virtual monopoly over the dominant images of beauty, genius, and art for most of American history.

Discuss how art represents racial groups and racial domination and how artists can challenge racial stereotypes and strive for racial justice.

Describe the ways that whiteness guides artists and critics as they decide what should be classified as "art" and what should not.

Explain how artistic divisions—those separating, say, different styles of dance, musical tastes, fashion senses, or schools of art—can be racialized and lead to an unequal distribution of cultural capital.

Learn to recognize when cultural appropriation occurs and how to distinguish between racist appropriation and antiracist appropriation.

KEY TERMS

- minstrelsy, page 282

- white, racist, and antiracist aesthetics, page 287

- narrowcasting, page 304
- highbrow and lowbrow art, page 305

- cultural appropriation, page 308

FROM THEORY TO PRACTICE

Select one piece of art that, in your mind, reflects the white aesthetic. Defend your selection by explaining how this artwork treats whiteness as the normal, artistic default category. What message does this piece of art convey about the social world? How might this artwork be altered so that it does not reflect the white aesthetic?

Carry out a triple reading on some piece of art. This can be a song, painting, movie, or any other cultural creation. Be sure to note the aesthetic, political, and racial properties of the form. Once you have done that, explain how the artwork reflects a white, racist, or antiracist aesthetic.

Participate in some artistic performance you have never experienced. If you are a metal head, attend an opera performance. If you love salsa, attend a modern dance show. Sample a cuisine you have never sampled; attend a spoken-word slam; go to the rodeo. Push your limits and challenge yourself after attending the performance, write about it, answering the following questions: How did the performance represent race? How might the racial structures of society have affected the performance? How did the performance help you better to understand the kind of art with which you are more familiar? That is, how did it encourage you to be more reflexive about the racialized nature of your aesthetic preferences?

9 Associations

MAIN POINTS

- Examine how associational life has reflected racial segregation in America and how labor unions and ethnic nationalist groups have responded differently to racial discrimination.

- Explain the racial discrepancies in civil participation between whites and nonwhites. Why are people of color less likely to join voluntary associations or participate in community activities?

- Describe who joins hate groups and how they organize and recruit members.

- Discuss how the Internet can be a source of virtual racism as well as of virtual empowerment that facilitates multiracial coalition building.

- Understand why religious life continues to be one of the most racialized areas of American society.

"A rich vegetation of associations and organizations for worth-while causes is an American characteristic. Americans are great 'joiners,' and they enjoy 'campaigns' and 'drives' for membership or contributions. Social clubs are plentiful, and even they are taken with a seriousness difficult for a stranger to understand. . . . It is natural for the ordinary American, when he sees something that is wrong, to feel not only that 'there should be a law against it' but also that an organization should be founded to combat it."[1]

So wrote the Swedish social scientist Gunnar Myrdal in 1944. Myrdal later would call associations the "salt of American politics." Associations, in other words, are the stuff of democracy. For Alexis de Tocqueville, another European who, a century earlier, had much to say about America, associational life helped to cultivate in Americans a spirit of civic virtue and responsibility. "It is difficult to force a man out of himself," Tocqueville wrote, "and get him to take an interest in the affairs of the whole state. [But] the free institutions of the United States and the political rights enjoyed there provide a thousand continual reminders to every citizen that he lives in society. At every moment they bring his mind back to this idea, that it is the duty as well as the interest of men to be useful to their fellows."[2]

The importance of associations to healthy democracy cannot be overstated. They are the lifeblood of civil society and the very embodiment of community. A government "of the people, for the people, and by the people" requires that its citizens connect with one another—that they work and struggle and deliberate together. American citizenship is predicated on the community bonds its people forge with each other. Those bonds, however, have not always been—and are not always now—the fraternal sort of which Tocqueville spoke so highly. Associations can exclude people from the fruits of full citizenship, just as they can force the democratic state to include them. "In truth," writes political theorist Judith Shklar, quoting the historian James Kellner, "from the nation's beginnings as an independent republic, Americans were torn by 'glaring inconsistencies between their professed principles of citizenship and their deep-seated desire to exclude certain groups permanently from the privileges of membership.' These tensions constitute the real history of its citizens."[3]

This chapter examines how race affects associational life. We have explored the workings of many associations in previous chapters—from political organizations and neighborhood-based groups to educational and artistic guilds—but have not yet fully unpacked the rich complexity of society's associational realm. In this sphere of society, we find social clubs, religious organizations, voluntary associations, and (in the age of the Internet) even virtual associations. Here are Elks Clubs, Masonic Lodges, and Odd Fellows Halls; college feminist societies, fraternities, and sororities; community garden groups and Girl Scout troops. Here, too, are neo-Nazis and Klansmen and NAACP members and all sorts of religious followers, including Hasidic Jews, Methodists, Catholics, Sunni Muslims, and Vaishnava Hindus. We begin with a backward glance that places American organizations in a historical context, examining, specifically, the struggles toward and away from racial integration. We then investigate how voluntary organizations affect and are affected by the racial order and their importance for sustaining a multiethnic democracy. Finally, we focus on three kinds of organizations extremely important to the career of racial inequalities today: hate groups, Internet-based associations, and religious communities.

THE ORDEAL OF INTEGRATION AND THE RISE OF ETHNIC NATIONALISM

After the fall of slavery, African Americans and other nonwhite citizens began to reach higher social and economic status. Some worked their way out of poverty; others reunited with family members; still others made inroads into political life. America's racial order, which to many eyes appeared rather secure and settled just a few years before the Civil War, was changing at dizzying speeds. "And whites responded to this increasing diversity and the rising black middle class with fear, violent reprisals, and state legislation—their floundering attempts to build a new racial order," observes historian Grace Elizabeth Hale. "Whites created the culture of segregation in large part to counter black success, to make a myth of absolute racial difference, to stop the rising."[4]

With the union intact and slavery abolished, racial segregation arose as one of American society's central organizing principles. It reconfigured the geography of the nation's neighborhoods and it came to dominate all areas of life—including associational life.[5] As Lillian Smith reflected in her stirring book *Killers of the Dream*, "Every little southern town is a fine stage-set for Southern Tradition to use as it teaches its children the twisting turning dance of segregation. Few words are needed for there are signs everywhere. *White . . . colored . . . white . . . colored . . .* over doors of railroad and bus stations, over doors of public toilets, over doors of theaters, over drinking fountains. . . . There are the signs without words: big white church on Main Street, little unpainted colored church on the rim of town; big white school, little ramshackly colored school; big white house, little unpainted cabins; white graveyard with marble shafts, colored graveyard with mounds of dirt."[6]

The Segregated Community

After the Civil War, America was wounded and reeling. Its towns, especially those south of the Mason-Dixon Line, burnt and leveled by battles, needed to be rebuilt. Its national community, which had lost no less than 2 percent of its population—620,000 men, "the same number as those lost in all of America's other wars from the Revolution through Korea combined"—needed to be resurrected and patched back together.[7] In the North, associations proliferated: between 1861 and 1865, men and women formed organizations dedicated to the wartime effort, and those committed to community service continued to spread long after the fighting stopped. The white chapters of the Independent Order of Odd Fellows, for example, doubled their number of lodges between 1865 and 1895, while the black chapters experienced an even more impressive increase. In 1865 black northern chapters of the Odd Fellows had only five lodges per 100,000 people; in 1895 they had over thirty lodges per 100,000.[8] And new associations continued to be formed. Between 1895 and 1899, whites established roughly forty new national organizations, and white ethnics, such as Irish and Polish Americans, established approximately twenty new groups.[9] Southern whites, in contrast, devastated by the fall of the Confederacy, lagged behind northern whites and blacks when it came to building associations. "As losers in the great conflict over demarcation of American nationhood, white southerners found it harder than the victorious northerners to organize or participate in large-scale civic endeavors in the postwar era."[10] There was, however, one major exception: the 1865 founding of the Ku Klux Klan.

FIGURE 9.1 **WHITE AND BLACK ODD FELLOWS LODGES IN THE NORTH AND SOUTH BEFORE, DURING, AND AFTER THE CIVIL WAR**

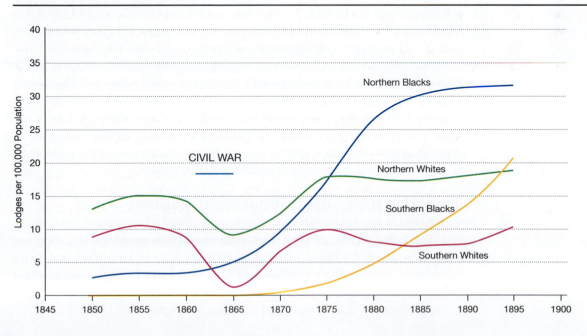

Only white male citizens could be members of the Elk Lodge. Some performed in blackface.

Although the Klan's racial terrorism was extreme (if widely accepted by white Protestants), many other new organizations, across the nation, were formed with the explicit purpose of promoting racial and ethnic conflict. Irish associations were established to wage battle with Italian ones; Protestant groups struggled against Catholic societies. And many social clubs limited their membership to white men. The Elks' membership pamphlet, *What It Means to Be an Elk*, was typical in its declaration that "membership in the Order is limited to white male citizens of the United States...who believe in the existence of God."[11] The same was true of most trade unions, churches, business associations, professional societies, and political groups.[12]

As a result, nonwhite organizations sprouted up alongside white ones, as did women's groups alongside those reserved for men. Consider the rise of African American societies. When whites refused to admit blacks into the Masonic Lodge in 1775, blacks formed their own chapter, inaugurating a pattern that would continue throughout the 1800s and into the twentieth century, when dozens of African American fraternal societies were established. "As the largest and most extensive sector of popularly rooted social organizations next to churches," write political scientist Theda Skocpol and colleagues in *What a Mighty Power We Can Be*, "African American fraternal lodges and federations likewise nurtured African American solidarity and supported many instances of civil rights advocacy from the nineteenth century, through the post–Civil War and Jim Crow periods, and down to eruption of Civil Rights militancy. . . . In times and places where blacks had few chances to create well-capitalized business enterprises, African American fraternal orders expressed and fostered entrepreneurial talents, paid wages to black employees, and allowed blacks to use dues payments to amass considerable institutional capital. As of the early 1920s, more than 60 nationally visible 'secret and fraternal organizations' had about 2.2 million members and owned $20 million worth of property."[13]

Toward Integration: Associational Coalition Building

Associational life bent itself to accommodate America's newfound edict of racial segregation. Blacks attended black churches; whites attended white churches; Hispanics attended Hispanic churches; and so on. There were black and Asian American Boy Scout Troops and segregated military brigades, barbershops, corner stores, and restaurants. There were Mexican unions in the copper industry, black miners' unions, and United Hebrew Trades that came up beside the dominant, white, non-Jewish ones.

But in the wake of racial segregation, a movement toward integration also began to take shape within associational life. Political societies, such as the Commission on Interracial Coalition, which arose alongside the NAACP, practiced integration in membership and leadership. Veterans' associations, such as the Grand Army of the Republic, the Veterans of Foreign Wars, and the American Legion, allowed nonwhite veterans to join integrated chapters in the North.[14] African American women in the Young Women's Christian Association (YWCA) fought to integrate their organization. Beginning in 1920, black women began to organize and challenge the YWCA's stance on racial segregation and eventually helped to transform the YWCA from a progressive-minded but segregated organization to one that "put racial justice at the centre of its mission." The YWCA adopted an interracial charter in 1946. As the twentieth century pushed forward, the YWCA transformed itself into an antiracist and fully integrated organization, a transformation symbolized by a new slogan it adopted in 2002: "Eliminating Racism; Empowering Women."[15]

"In times and places where blacks had few chances to create well-capitalized business enterprises, African American fraternal orders expressed and fostered entrepreneurial talents, paid wages to black employees, and allowed blacks to use dues payments to amass considerable institutional capital." – Theda Skocpol

Even some labor unions, traditional mainstays of nonwhite exclusion and racial segregation, joined the movement toward integration. As early as 1892, one local of the United Mine Workers of America not only allowed nonwhites and Eastern European immigrants to join, it also selected "one Hungarian, one [African American], one Polander, one Slav, and one white" to serve as officers.[16] White workers were starting to come around to the idea that their interests and those of nonwhite workers were bound together. As one mid-twentieth-century steelworker put it, "You must forget that the man working beside you is a 'Nigger,' Jew, or 'Pollock.' The man working beside you, be he negro, Jew, or Pollock, is a working man like yourself."[17] Indeed, the inclusion of nonwhites into traditionally white unions challenged the dominant image of nonwhites as strikebreakers and discouraged white workers from "[jeopardizing] class solidarity by exhibiting racial antagonism."[18]

After the Civil Rights Movement, many associations erased racially exclusive language from their constitutions and charters, and some actively pursued racial integration. In the 1960s, many Boy Scout troops were desegregated, and in 1970, the Parent-Teacher Association (PTA), which had always practiced segregation, forbade its chapters from limiting membership to white parents only.[19] Slowly but surely, whites embraced integration. In 1977, only 42 percent of surveyed whites said they would try to change the rules of their club if it excluded blacks. By 1993, 67 percent of whites said they would. Nonwhites, who are most disadvantaged by segregation, always have been stronger proponents of integration. When blacks were asked in 1993 if they would try to change the rules of a social club to which they belonged so that whites were allowed to join, 86 percent answered yes.[20]

Away from Integration: The Case for Ethnic Nationalism

In the same way they resisted integrated neighborhoods, many whites opposed the integration of their associations. But just as a small if committed cadre of whites fought *for* racial integration, a small but committed cadre of nonwhites fought *against* it. For these nonwhites, racial integration did not lead to liberation, but only to more oppression. Racial segregation and complete independence from whites was the only answer. This ideological movement has come to be known as "ethnic nationalism"; its ambassadors resist cultural and social assimilation and instead champion self-determination, race pride, separatism, and, in some cases, the creation of an independent nation based on racial identity. Here one thinks of nonwhite ethnic nationalist movements, including the American Indian push for sovereignty and Chicano nationalism (or *Chicanismo*). The most influential of these was black nationalism.[21]

The roots of black nationalism stretch clear back to the early days of slavery. Black nationalism's political philosophy was prevalent in nineteenth-century African American thought, but it was not until the early twentieth century that black nationalism gained momentum, secured a significant following, and captured the nation's (and the FBI's) attention.[22] In 1918, Booker T. Washington had been dead for three years; many African Americans were yearning for a new leader; and a Jamaican immigrant by the name of Marcus Garvey was earning a name for himself in Harlem. Garvey was a masterful orator, one who could "throw his voice around three corners without batting an eyelash," as one admirer put it.[23] And the message Garvey advocated with such force and eloquence was that of black nationalism.

Garvey was the founding mastermind behind and primary spokesperson for the United Negro Improvement Association (UNIA), which in its heyday (1920–1921) most likely had more members than the NAACP. (And, unlike the NAACP, the UNIA placed women in positions of leadership and was entirely led, financed, and staffed by blacks.) For Garvey and the UNIA, the solution to antiblack racism could be found only within the collective strength of the black community. Garvey encouraged African Americans to view themselves as Africans first—as people who had had their culture, history, language, identity, and pride stripped from them—and as Americans second. Although other black leaders criticized racist notions of black inferiority and worked to instill in blacks a

Marcus Garvey's UNIA Parade in Harlem, New York, 1924.

sense of dignity, it was Garvey who most compellingly and unequivocally argued that blacks all over the world constituted a powerful *nation* with a proud past and a heroic future. Garvey did not think blacks were equal to whites; he thought blacks were better than whites.[24] "They tell us that God is white," he bellowed. "That is a lie. They tell us that all of His angels are white, too. To my mind, everything that is devilish is white. They told us that the devil was a black man. There isn't a greater devil in the world than the white man."[25] It was Garvey who popularized the term "white devil."

Garvey's ethnic chauvinism—or excessive loyalty toward and belief in the superiority of a racial or ethnic group—was central to his black nationalist platform. And it was in the principles of black chauvinism, a direct reversal of white supremacy, that Garvey grounded his anti-integrationist stance. Garvey vied for the complete separation of the races: "This is going to be a 'white man's country,' sooner or later, and the best thing possibly we can do is [to] find a black man's country."[26] Black nationalism was not a movement for equal rights; it was a movement for *black power*, for black-owned businesses and a black-run government with a black military behind it. How, precisely, this vision was to be fulfilled was never fully articulated. Several times, Garvey went so far as to promote a repatriation plan, where all people of African descent would return to Africa to help liberate the continent from white colonialism. "Africa for the Africans, home and abroad," so read the UNIA slogan.[27]

In his anti-integrationist convictions, Garvey had much in common with outspoken white supremacists. Fully aware of this fact, Garvey arranged secret meetings with Edward Clarke, the Imperial Wizard of the KKK. Garvey lost considerable support once news of this unholy alliance spread throughout African American communities. A "Garvey Must Go" campaign was launched in 1922; a year later, Garvey was convicted of mail fraud; in 1925 he was deported to Jamaica, never to set foot again on American soil.[28]

Black nationalism would lay dormant until the 1960s, when urban centers erupted in racial uprisings. Some northern black ghetto-dwellers were growing impatient with Martin Luther King, Jr., and the failure of the Southern Christian Leadership Conference (SCLC) to achieve in the North the political victories it had enjoyed in the South. It was during his visits to Chicago, New York, and other northern cities that King most fully realized that a minority of blacks disagreed with his philosophy of nonviolence and that some even were ready to employ armed resistance on behalf of the black liberation struggle. They were ready to rally behind another leader, one who would energize a movement that bared more teeth than King's integrationist platform. Malcolm X would become that leader.

Malcolm Little was born in 1925 into hardscrabble poverty. Whereas King grew up in a stable and supportive family, Malcolm's family was riddled with hardship. When Malcolm was six, his father was killed in a car accident. A few years later, when his mother was committed to a mental institution, Malcolm was shuffled between relatives and foster parents before, as a young adult, getting caught up in a life of drugs and crime. Convicted of burglary, he was imprisoned between 1946 and 1952, and it was in prison that Malcolm remade himself. He began to read voraciously and converted to the Nation of Islam, a small, black separatist religious sect then led by Elijah Muhammad. He abandoned his last name—one that belonged to his ancestors' slave master—and replaced it with the letter X, which stood for his real African name which was "destroyed during slavery." Once released, Malcolm X helped bring about a powerful resurgence of black nationalism.[29]

If Garvey had the UNIA, Malcolm X had the Nation of Islam, which promoted racial pride, isolation, and self-discipline. (Unlike the UNIA, however, the Nation of Islam was by and large dominated by men.[30]) Like Garvey, Malcolm X was a skilled elocutionist; also like Garvey, he criticized integration—"We believe that separation is the best way and the only sensible way, not integration," he said in 1963—and advanced a kind of ethnic chauvinism, which tended to downplay or altogether disregard the actions of white antiracists. Like Garvey, Malcolm X sometimes referred to whites as "snakes" and "devils."

Drawing great inspiration from the uprisings of colonized people in Africa, Asia, and Latin America—uprisings he understood as together constituting a global revolt of nonwhites against white supremacy—Malcolm X condemned nonviolent protest as weak and ineffective, even cowardly, and argued that violence could play an important role in bringing freedom to African Americans. "Nationalism is the wave of the present and the future," he said. "It is *nationalism* that is bringing freedom to oppressed people around the world. . . . The Africans didn't get it by sitting in. They didn't get it by waiting in. They didn't get it by singing, 'We Shall Overcome.' They got it through *nationalism*, and you and I will get it through nationalism."[31]

"The purpose of our organization," Malcolm X famously declared, "of Afro-American unity, which has the same aim and objective to fight whoever gets in our way[,] . . . is to bring about the complete independence of people of African descent, . . . to bring about the freedom of these people *by any means necessary*." This phrase—"by any means necessary"—caused a chill to run up the spines of many white Americans. Although Malcolm X's defense of violence was not new—enslaved African Americans (such as Nat Turner) as well as white abolitionists (such as John Brown) had advocated and practiced armed self-defense, and racist whites long had subscribed to the same position—it did break with the "turn the other cheek" message championed by King.[32]

Malcolm X eventually would break with the Nation of Islam and some of its separatist leanings. After converting to orthodox Islam, he partook in the Hajj, the sacred pilgrimage to Mecca, and upon seeing Muslims of all races and nationalities come together, after catching a glimpse of the promise of multiracial unity and harmony, he began to rethink his promotion of ethnic chauvinism. The full impact and development of Malcolm X's modified views toward black nationalism never would be realized, as he was shot and killed on February 21, 1965, just a few months before his fortieth birthday.[33]

Malcolm X talks to a woman inside Temple 7, a halal restaurant in Harlem patronized by black Muslims.

The majority of blacks during Malcolm X's time believed more in the promise of and movement toward integration than in black nationalism. In 1966, 88 percent of blacks polled approved of Martin Luther King, Jr., and 55 percent approved of the SCLC; by contrast, only 12 percent approved of Elijah Muhammad, and 9 percent backed the Nation of Islam.[34] Nevertheless, a good many blacks identified with and respected black nationalism, even if they rejected the movement's more militant elements. In the words of James Farmer, "Deep in the heart of every black adult lives some of Malcolm and some of King, side by side."[35]

On the one hand, black nationalism failed. A separate black nation never came to be, and racial integration has become the desired goal. But on the other hand, the movement struck a tremendous blow to the symbolic violence inflicted upon the psyches of black people. Speaking of Malcolm X, African American actor Ossie Davis remembers, "He scared the hell out of us, bred as we are to caution, to hypocrisy in the presence of white folks, to the smile that never fades. . . . He would make you angry as hell, but he would also make you proud. It was impossible to remain defensive and apologetic about being a Negro in his presence. He wouldn't let you."[36]

CIVIL SOCIETY IN A MULTIRACIAL DEMOCRACY

"Citizens cannot leave politics just to politicians," reasons German novelist Günter Grass.[37] By participating in associational life—or in civil society: that area of life where we find public debate, community organizing, and citizen-led political mobilization—citizens can help to chart the course of history. From its inception, America has developed a diverse and active civil society, bursting forth with a rich variety of associations. As Gabriel Almond and Sidney Verba demonstrated in their influential book *The Civic Culture*, compared with citizens in other Western countries, a significantly higher percentage of Americans belong to associations.[38] And America's healthy civil society, a number of social scientists have concluded, has been primarily responsible for bringing about the nation's stable and developed democracy. What, then, is the state of today's all-important civil society? How does racial division thwart the development of genuine community and racial democracy? And what can we do about it?

Racial Variation in Civic Participation

Whites have higher rates of civil engagement, whereas people of color are less likely to join voluntary associations and to participate in community activities. As one pair of researchers plainly state, "On average, Whites participate in the most organizations, followed by Blacks, Latinos, and Asians."[39] Nonwhites also exhibit lower degrees of social trust, a fundamental prerequisite of community building. One study found that while 41 percent of whites believe that "most people can be trusted," only 20 percent of African Americans and 12 percent of Latinos feel likewise.[40] Speaking of the racial divisions in her community, one resident of the Mississippi Delta observed, "Everything here is segregated. There is no social interaction between the races, and *no trust*. Whites say you can't trust blacks, and blacks say the same thing about whites."[41] Such racial discrepancies

FIGURE 9.2 CIVIC INVOLVEMENT BY HIGH- AND LOW-INCOME GROUPS

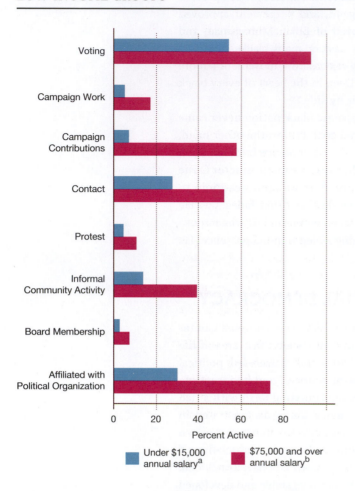

Percent Active

■ Under $15,000 annual salary[a]   ■ $75,000 and over annual salary[b]

in civil participation are disturbing because they suggest that nonwhites' interests may be underrepresented in the public debate and that civil society may be developing in an uneven and dysfunctional fashion.[42]

Studies have shown that racialized economic inequality is the primary force behind most of racial variation in associational life. Participating in associational life takes time (attending meetings, organizing events) and money (paying dues, making financial contributions to campaigns), which is why the affluent are overrepresented in civil society. Forty percent of people with annual incomes of $75,000 or higher but only 15 percent of people with annual incomes under $15,000 are involved in some informal community activity. Seventy-five percent of people with annual incomes of $75,000 or higher are affiliated with a political organization; the same is true of only 25 percent of people with annual incomes under $15,000. Only with respect to religious attendance and church membership do the poor participate at similar rates as middle- and upper-class citizens.[43]

Because the poor do not participate in community organizations as much as the affluent and because nonwhites are disproportionately wracked by poverty, we should expect racial variation in associational life to dissipate to a significant degree once economic differences are accounted for. This expectation is precisely what researchers have found. Once economic differences are taken into account, Latinos are just as likely, and blacks even more likely, to participate in voluntary associations as whites.[44] In fact, several analysts have observed that many African Americans are "super joiners."[45]

Unlike blacks and Latinos, however, Asians participate in associational life at significantly lower rates than whites do, regardless of economic differences. There are other factors, then, besides economic differences driving racial variation in civic participation. According to recent sociological research, those factors seem to be associated with the immigrant experience. One's English proficiency and one's time of arrival in the United States can affect one's level of civic participation. Once these factors are accounted for, the gap between Asian and white participation rates narrows, and Latinos seem even more involved than whites in associational life.[46] Indeed, social scientists have found high levels of community building in immigrant enclaves.[47] Sociologist Min Zhou has documented a rise of voluntary associations in New York's

Chinatown, associations designed to help new immigrants adjust to American society. These organizations, such as the Chinese Consolidated Benevolent Association and the Chinese-American Planning Council—not to mention the many Buddhist temples and Christian churches sprinkled throughout the enclave—oversee English-language classes, career training, and cultural events. They have played a vital role in strengthening community and helping immigrants integrate into American life.[48]

Homophily in Associational Life

With whom do you choose to associate? Do your friendship networks, social clubs, and favorite spots to hang out mostly consist of people who share your skin color? Researchers studying social networks long have documented the phenomenon of homophily. Literally meaning "love of the same," "homophily" refers to the practice of associating with people like you. "Birds of a feather flock together," as the old adage goes. Homophily applies to age, religion, education, and occupation, but, as one group of sociologists concluded after reviewing over 100 studies that document homophilous associations, "homophily in race and ethnicity creates the *strongest divides* in our personal environments."[49] You are more likely to associate regularly with people of different class standings, educational levels, and religions than with people of different racial or ethnic groups.

Race-based homophily is found in a wide variety of associations, from our most intimate relationships (e.g., marriage) and institutional associations (e.g., coworkers, schoolmates) to very informal ties that connect people who simply "know about" each other or are seen in public together. Only 8 percent of Americans report having a close confidant, with whom they can discuss "important matters," who does not share their race or ethnic identity. Social patterns resulting in the racial segregation of associational life begin in childhood and continue over the life course, with white Americans exhibiting the highest levels of racial homophily.[50]

By and large, today's associations remain racially segregated, but today's associational segregation is maintained not so much through active and open discrimination as through a softer kind of exclusion. Whites who belong to a majority-white Rotary Club, for example, might keep their club white, not by turning down nonwhite applications, but by actively recruiting women and men from their own social circles (for example, their families, work, or religious institutions), circles that, because of the homophily principle, most likely also are white. They are not pushing "enemies" away so much as they are pulling friends in.[51] Sociologists have referred to this kind of dynamic as boundary work.

Do your friendship networks mostly consist of people who share your skin color?

"Boundary work" refers to the multiple ways people create, uphold, and traverse social boundaries that separate familiar from unfamiliar, welcome from unwelcome, "us" from "them." The key idea gleaned from the social science of boundary work is that racial and ethnic groups can understand one another as possessing distinct cultures and lifestyles only if they actively distinguish themselves from other groups. To be Persian American is, at base, to be *not*—Arab American, *not*-black, *not*-white, and so forth. Boundary work is the collection of practices by which people maintain or challenge racial relations of exclusivity and inclusivity.[52] And one of the primary sites of boundary work is the associational field.

More oten than not, formal associations, such as churches and social clubs, only deepen—rather than defy—racial divisions. One thinks of the English-only movement, a collection of white-led political organizations that seek to outlaw the use of any language other than English in public settings and on government documents and to make English the official language of towns, states, and the nation. The English-only movement has gained steam in recent years, riding the tide of a growing anti-immigrant sentiment, and in thirty-one states English is the official language—an unwelcoming symbolic gesture targeting immigrant communities in general and Spanish speakers in particular, as linguistic boundaries map onto racial ones.[53] At the same time, other organizations have criticized the English-only movement. The Linguistic Society of America, for example, decries English-only measures "on the grounds that they are based on misconceptions about the role of a common language in establishing political unity, and that they are inconsistent with basic American traditions of linguistic tolerance."[54]

Other examples of formal associations contributing to racial boundary work abound. Think of the clear-cut racial segregation that marks your college or university's sororities and fraternities. Or consider the boundary work carried out by America's Christian churches. "We must face the fact that the church is still the most segregated major institution in America," said Martin Luther King, Jr. "At 11:00 on Sunday morning, when we stand and sing that Christ has no east or west, we stand at the most segregated hour in this nation." If there are two kinds of social capital—a homophilous kind that *binds* you to "your people" and a heterophilous kind that *bridges* racial cleavages—then most formal associations dole out the binding kind.

The same is true of more informal associations, those that do not hand out membership cards or charge dues but nevertheless are as important to civil society as their more formal counterparts. Here one thinks of boundary work executed by bars and nightclubs and the social (and racial) significance of the phrase, "This is my kind of place."[55] One thinks, too, of how different ethnic ceremonies, from Quinceañeras and Bar Mitzvahs to Puerto Rican Pride parades and Polish Day festivities, reinforce boundaries. And, of course, if we conceive of social boundaries with an intersectional imagination, we realize the many ways in which formal and informal associations reinforce class, gender, sexual, and religious boundaries that further divide racial and ethnic communities. Elite social clubs of the black upper class—such as Jack and Jill of America, a private, invitation-only club that caters to children of wealthy black families—help to distinguish affluent African Americans from poor blacks.[56] And certain religious institutions, such as the Mormon Church or Amish communities, provide their majority-white congregants with practices and beliefs that separate men from women.

Sporting associations—communities of players and fans—are an important part of the nation's associational life. But athletic divisions map onto racial divisions, too. Fans use coded language at times to signal racial boundaries through sports affiliations. In Chicago, the Cubs are associated with the city's (white and affluent) northern neighborhoods, while the White Sox are associated with its (nonwhite and poorer) southern districts. In the Bay Area, the 49ers are connected to white and affluent San Francisco, while the Raiders are linked to black and not-so-affluent Oakland.

Our associations, then, remain homophilous and highly segregated. But this may be starting to change. The value of multiculturalism is prized by this generation—your generation—much more than generations past. In the political field, one can find racially integrated organizations fighting for a living wage, health care, or sustainable agriculture; in integrated neighborhoods, community-based associations gather together people of different racial or ethnic heritage to cultivate community and respond to criminal activity; and on college campuses multicultural student coalitions often have a visible (if still marginal) presence. Integrated associations, like integrated neighborhoods, are not the norm—not even close—but they may be proliferating. Racial integration of the associational field will not come through a Supreme Court decision or a federally mandated policy; it will come only if people like you take up its charge, influencing the organizations to which you belong and the company you keep.

Ethnic ceremonies, such as quinceañeras and debutante balls, celebrate cultural heritage.

Racial Domination and the Decline of Social Capital

What, we now ask, is the status of our civil society more generally? Dysfunctional and anemic, answers political scientist Robert Putnam in his modern classic, *Bowling Alone: The Collapse and Revival of American Community*. According to Putnam, the current generation (*your* generation, if you are a "traditional" college student who came straight to college from high school) is less interconnected and less engaged in community affairs than the one that came before. And *that* generation (your parents' generation, if you are a traditional college student) was less interconnected than the previous one. In other words, since the end of the Civil Rights Movement, social capital has declined in America. Since the 1960s, "Americans have become perhaps 10%–15% less likely to voice our views publicly by running for office or writing Congress or the local newspaper, 15%–20% less interested in politics and public affairs, roughly 25% less likely to vote, roughly 35% less likely to attend public meetings, both partisan and nonpartisan, and roughly 40% less engaged in party politics and indeed in political and civic organizations of all sorts."[57] Church congregations, bridge clubs, socialist societies, community outreach coalitions, and organizations of all hues have thinned and in some cases dissolved altogether. In Putnam's view, one informed by an impressive array of evidence, we are becoming more disconnected from and distrustful of one another. Civil society is in trouble.

What social forces are responsible for the weakening of civil society? Social scientists have pointed to many, including the rise of television, the mass movement of women into the labor force, and the lengthening of the workweek. Of particular interest to our purposes, analysts have demonstrated at least two of the social forces in which race plays a role.

First, the suburbanization of America, a process pushed along by white fear and flight, has contributed to the erosion of social capital. Putnam himself recognized this: "Far from seeking small-town connectedness, suburbanites [keep] to themselves, asking little of their neighbors and expecting little in return."[58] The suburbanite values privacy and self-sufficiency, confirming the historian of city planning Lewis Mumford's observation that "the romantic suburb was a collective attempt to live a private life."[59] Here homeowners' associations, with their strict rules and penalties, have emerged as the primary, if not exclusive, community organization in suburban neighborhoods. What is more, the suburbanite simply might not think he has time to participate in associational life on account of his daily commute. Suburbanization helped to create the commute by expanding the distance separating work from home. Today, the average American spends twenty-five minutes each day commuting to work. That's more than 100 hours a year.[60]

As America has become more racially segregated and suburbanized, it has become more racially diverse as well, and this brings us to the second way in which racial life influences social capital. Several studies have concluded that social capital and trust for fellow Americans are lower in more racially diverse communities.[61] Membership in associations lags in metropolitan areas with greater amounts of racial and ethnic integration and economic inequality. Likewise, nonwhites who live in majority-white suburbs are less involved in community

FIGURE 9.3 SOCIAL CAPITAL AND CIVIC ENGAGEMENT BY GENERATION (EDUCATION CONTROLLED)

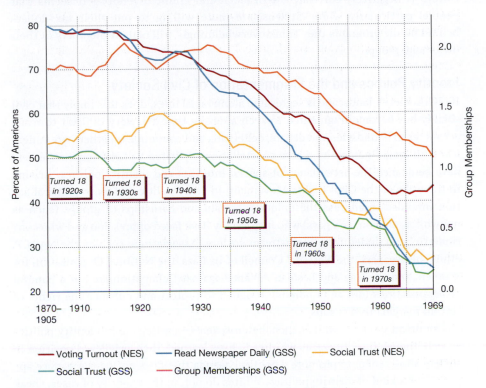

By many indicators, social trust and political participation declined in America.

organizing than those who live in majority-nonwhite areas. The proliferation of associations and the degree of social trust are highest in states with racially homogeneous populations (such as Minnesota and Maine) and lowest in states with racially heterogeneous populations (Mississippi and New Mexico). These findings make sense given the homophilous nature of social networks. If whites are more likely to associate with other whites, blacks with blacks, Latinos with Latinos, and so forth, then we would expect to observe an increase in social capital in areas that facilitate the formation of segregated associations. In the words of political scientist Rodney Hero, because "social capital is inevitably easier to foster within homogeneous communities[,] . . . there is a deep tension between diversity and connectedness."[62]

Not only are Americans less willing to associate with and to trust people of other racial and ethnic groups, they also are less likely to support public programs (such as education and welfare) that they think will disproportionately benefit members of other racial and ethnic groups. In Florida, for example, the average taxpayer is a white senior citizen, but the average public school student is a Latino child. In this state, white taxpayers voice considerably less support for public school expenditures than those in states where most taxpayers and public school students are white. Economists have amassed a good deal of evidence for the "Florida Effect" in other states as well, finding that support for public services (from trash pickup and sewer systems to road maintenance and education) is negatively correlated with racial and ethnic diversity.[63] It seems that people, particularly white citizens, are more willing to put their tax dollars behind public programs they think overwhelmingly will benefit members of their own racial group.

Identity Politics and the Fragmentation of Civil Society

If civil society's landscape is segregated along racial lines, does this imply that civil society has become fragmented to such a degree that it is very difficult to reach across racial boundaries and debate, deliberate, and commune together? Are Americans no longer guided by a core constellation of shared values? Some observers have bemoaned the ascendancy of special interests and identity politics. Arising in the wake of the Civil Rights Movement, identity politics refers to political action intended to address the unique interests and hardships of groups (such as nonwhites, women, and gays) who historically have faced oppression and who continue to be excluded from mainstream society. Associations such as the NAACP, ethnic newspapers, the National Council of La Raza, the National Organization for Women, and the Gay and Lesbian Alliance against Defamation are but a handful of organizations (out of hundreds) designed to protect and enhance the rights of certain marginalized groups.

Dominant groups—whites, men, heterosexuals—participate in identity politics as well, though oftentimes, as we already have learned, their privileged position in society allows them to promote a political agenda that does not on the surface appear to be a kind of identity politics. Whites do not, in the majority of cases, speak of advocating for "white rights" or of "serving the white community" in the same way that some nonwhite groups advocate for, say, "immigrant rights" or "serving the South Asian community." However, the silence of some white politicians in the face of racial injustice—the fact that they avoid altogether discussing racial inequalities or championing antiracist programs—is a form of identity politics.

Some critics believe identity politics is responsible for splintering civil society.[64] They worry that the growing number of Americans who live in racially homogeneous communities may be "willing to protect [only] their own lifestyles but are unlikely to express interest in broader issues of national importance," resulting in a civil society that resembles a collection of warring camps where "diverse groups have so little in common that they are unable to come to agreement at all."[65] The increasing fragmentation of identity politics, some argue, may cause some Americans to become disillusioned and cynical and to withdraw from civil society altogether.

Are such worries justified? The evidence suggests they are not. Despite what is happening in Washington, Americans' political attitudes and interests are not becoming more polarized; in fact, on moral, social, economic, and political issues there is impressive congruence. While so-called culture wars may wage among political elites and media pundits, at the ground level everyday Americans of all racial identities agree on many important issues.[66] We have our differences, but we have much more in common than many people believe. Most of us, regardless of our racial identity, gender, or class upbringing, believe that all people should be provided equal opportunity to succeed, that everyone should be treated equally under the law, and that freedom is a fundamental human right.[67]

Americans of all stripes see eye-to-eye on many core issues, and yet, today, there are more organizations associated with specific racial or ethnic groups than ever before. Even if associations are dwindling, one has little trouble locating political, social, and professional groups that cater to specific racial and ethnic communities. In the last fifty years, for example, Chinese associations in the United States have increased by over 300 percent, and now nearly a quarter of the world's Chinese associations are located in America.[68] And on college campuses, one finds Native American coalitions, African American sororities, Thai American student organizations, Hillel (the nationwide Jewish student organization), Korean Christian Fellowships, the Muslim Student Association, and the Movimiento Estudiantil Chicano de Aztlán (MEChA), to list but a few. The prevalence of such organizations has provoked some to ask, "In this day and age, one that places great value on the concept of multiculturalism, are race- and ethnicity-based organizations still necessary?"

Usually this question is directed at associations that represent nonwhite groups and interests, but organizations that do not refer to themselves as white organizations nonetheless exist as such. The Christian Coalition of America claims to represent all conservative Christians, even though its membership rolls are made up primarily of middle-class whites. Civil War reenactors, who wear historic uniforms and stage mock battles (thereby participating in one of the fastest-growing hobbies in America)—and who overwhelmingly want to "fight" for the Confederacy—do not limit their membership to whites only, although very few nonwhites participate in their events.[69] And one only need glance at those big group pictures of fraternity and sorority houses to see how "normal" Greek organizations mostly comprise white students from affluent families.

Whites, just like other racial and ethnic groups, have many associations that cater to their specific interests, even if the word "white" does not appear in their names. The difference is that many nonwhite groups were formed specifically to help dismantle racial inequalities. Nonwhite professional associations, such as the Society of Black Lawyers, the Association of Asian Probation Staff, the Native American Journalist Association, and the Cuban-American Certified Public Accountants, provide support, mentoring, and training to nonwhites working in organizations structured by institutional racism.[70] Nonwhite campus organizations provide nonwhite students, especially those attending majority-white institutions, a safe and comfortable space.[71] And the ethnic press—newspapers, magazines, websites, and blogs that take as their primary audience certain racial or ethnic groups—holds the mainstream

White men reenacting a scene from the Civil War.

(primarily white) news media accountable; increases the visibility of nonwhites in civil society; and addresses issues of particular importance to nonwhite communities often ignored in the popular press (for example, migrant workers' rights; Native Americans' health care; inner-city poverty).[72]

Nonwhite associations also can provide nonwhites with temporary solace from a society that privileges and prioritizes whiteness. This is why many middle-class nonwhite families choose to worship and socialize with friends and family members belonging to their own racial or ethnic group, even if they spend most of their workweek with whites.[73] Consider, for example, black barbershops and beauty parlors—staples of urban black communities. Not only are most mainstream (white) hair salons incapable of cutting and styling black hair, but black barbershops and beauty parlors also provide their African American clientele with a thoroughly black space, a protected space, set apart from the surrounding society. Historically, barbershops and beauty parlors have functioned as key gathering places in black neighborhoods. As Rev. Wyatt Walker, one of Martin Luther King, Jr.'s, top advisors, once put it, barbershops and beauty parlors were "the second-best means of communication" in the black community, second only to the church.[74]

Some nonwhite associations only exacerbate racial tensions and sour relationships between, say, immigrants and native-born Americans, blacks and Hispanics (the so-called Black-Brown divide), or even antiracist whites and antiracist people of color, thereby decelerating the racial justice movement.[75] And sometimes such associations encourage their members to obsess over racial and ethnic differences at the expense of ignoring racial domination and economic injustice. As a result, their focus is diverted away from life-and-death issues—for example, racialized poverty on American Indian reservations, institutional racism within the criminal justice system, and the exploitation of Mexican migrant workers—and toward "celebrating diversity."[76] That said, white associations, which refuse to refer to themselves as such, are even more responsible for maintaining racial divisions within associational life. Compared with their white counterparts, nonwhites are more likely to favor integration. If this is true, then critics of identity politics, who often blame nonwhite associations for the culture wars they believe to be fractionalizing the civil sphere, have misplaced their animus.

What Is "Political Correctness"?

Some commentators have suggested that American civil society is now guided by an ethic of "political correctness," which discourages free thought and honest debate, because people are afraid to offend their fellow citizens or, worst of all, to be labeled as "racists." In its most recent incarnation, "political correctness" usually refers to discourse that, while designed to minimize offense to marginalized groups, ends up censoring certain speech or attitudes deemed off-limits. Political correctness, so the logic goes, forbids you to say what is truly on your mind. Former President George H. W. Bush spoke of a left-wing movement of political correctness, a movement to "declare certain topics off-limits, certain expressions off-limits, even certain gestures off-limits."[77] Speaking at American University in 2000, conservative spokesperson Bill Lind had this to say about political correctness: "For the first time in our history, Americans have to be fearful of what they say, of what they write, and of what they think. They have to be afraid of using the wrong word, a word denounced as offensive or insensitive, or racist, sexist, or homophobic."[78]

Who, exactly, does Mr. Lind have in mind when he references Americans who, *for the first time in history*, have to watch what they say? He cannot have African Americans in mind. They have had to choose their words carefully since slavery and Reconstruction, when blacks were lynched for saying the wrong thing. He cannot be thinking of Native Americans either, because Indian children were beaten at boarding schools if they spoke their native tongue and Indian adults were killed during the Indian Wars if they practiced certain ceremonies. He cannot be thinking of Hispanic Americans fluent in Spanish, a language that a national movement is attempting to ban from schools and government offices. Perhaps, then, Mr. Lind is speaking only of white Americans. But whites who spoke out against racial domination also had to pay a high price. Bill Moore, the postal worker we met in Chapter 1, gave his life to the Civil Rights Movement; John Brown, a white abolitionist who advocated arming enslaved Africans, was hanged for treason.[79]

To whom, then, is Mr. Lind referring? Who are those Americans who "for the first time in our history have to be fearful of what they say"? They are those who advocated for a kind of white identity politics; it is their voices that have come under attack. The Civil Rights Movement has transformed American discourse in such a way that, for the first time in American history, a significant number of Americans, white and nonwhite, consider racial domination evil.[80] As one sociologist has observed, "By 1970, a new normative climate in the area of race relations had emerged in the United States. . . . Whites, South as well as North, who discriminated became 'racist' rather than regular guys."[81] In post–Civil Rights America, civil society has widened to include a cacophony of voices and opinions. It is not marred by a silencing code of political correctness, but by an impressive diversity of opinions. (This certainly includes the loud contingent complaining about "political correctness.") This is the mark of a healthy and flourishing associational field.

FIGURE 9.4

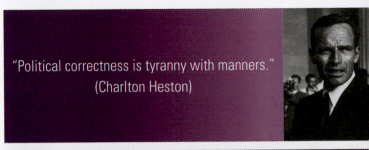

"Political correctness is tyranny with manners."
(Charlton Heston)

"What I think the political correctness debate is really about is the power to be able to define. The definers want the power to name. And the defined are now taking that power away from them."
(Toni Morrison)

FIGURE 9.5 **PHRASES "POLITICAL CORRECTNESS" AND "WHITE POWER" USED IN BOOKS BETWEEN 1800 AND 2008**

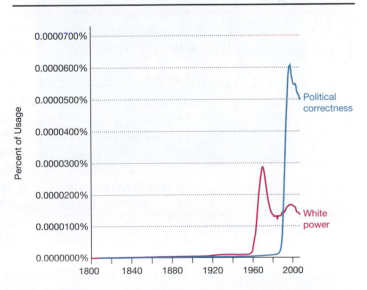

HATE GROUPS

Racist hate groups present a threat to a multiracial democratic society: skinheads, neo-Nazis, the KKK. Closely tied with avowedly racist hate groups are white nationalist organizations, which believe whites to be superior to African Americans and Hispanics and vie for a separate, exclusively white country. With names such as Euro-American Student Union, Institute for Historical Review, the Conservative Citizens Council, and the New Century Foundation, white nationalist groups might not appear to be hate groups at first blush, but they thrive on racist and anti-Semitic beliefs. Although it has been almost ninety years since the heyday of hate groups—the KKK and its offshoots had more than 5 million members in the 1920s—some have pointed to a recent resurgence in hate groups and hate crimes. According to the Southern Poverty Law Center, there were 939 active hate groups in the United States in 2013, up from 708 in 2002.[82]

Organized Racism

More than an exaggerated form of everyday racism, the kind of extraordinary or organized racism cultivated by hate groups is more intensified and commanding. It is ordered by a unifying racist philosophy that demonizes specific "enemies" and advances certain goals aimed at promoting the white race.[83] Hate groups are "filled with evil conspiracies and righteous crusades."[84] In the minds of hate group members, Jews and nonwhites are responsible for most of the world's problems. "The difference between everyday [racism found in routine life] and extraordinary racism [found in hate groups]," writes Kathleen Blee, a leading sociologist of hate groups, "is the difference between being prejudiced against Jews and believing that there is a Jewish conspiracy that determines the fate of individual Aryans, or between thinking that African Americans are inferior to whites and seeing African Americans as an imminent threat to the white race."[85]

Many hate groups believe that the Holocaust was a hoax, that Martin Luther King, Jr., was a fraud, and that the accomplishments of white culture have been blotted out in the mainstream historical record.[86] Mirroring the strategies of the white backlash that helped extinguish the Civil Rights Movement, hate groups regularly co-opt the discourse of nonwhite organizations. Parodying the NAACP, some white racists have founded chapters of the National Association for the Advancement of White People (NAAWP), while the white nationalist movement borrows much of its rhetoric from black nationalism.

The practices of hate groups are many and diverse. On one end of the spectrum are white

Philip Guston's 1969 oil painting, *Edge of Town*. Guston said of the hooded Klan figures that appear in many of his paintings, "They are self-portraits. I perceive myself as being behind the hood... I almost tried to imagine that I was living with the Klan. What would it be like to be evil?"

nationalists who hope to energize a social movement aimed at establishing a white nation. White nationalism primarily is a symbolic movement channeled through leaders, magazines, music, and even comic books. "We believe that we as white people, as European-Americans, have the right to pursue our destiny without interference from other races," states Don Black, founder of the racist website stormfront.org, perhaps the Internet's most popular hate site.[87] On the other end of the spectrum are hate groups steeped in a culture of violence. Vandalism, arson, assault, and even murder and terrorism are the lifeblood of these groups. Violence rests at the core of the white supremacist movement. It is a panacea for its problems and, in the movement's apocalyptic vision of an imminent race war, to which many active racists look forward, violence will bring about the triumph of the white race.[88] For example, Hal Turner, a neo-Nazi radio host, proclaimed in 2006, "All of you who think there's a peaceful solution to these invaders are wrong. We're going to have to start killing these people. I advocate using extreme violence against illegal aliens."[89]

As the debate over immigration has intensified and as people's fear of being "invaded" by Mexican migrants has expanded and deepened, hate groups have responded by lashing out at immigrants and Hispanics (regardless of their immigrant status). In 2004, Hispanics were the targets in 17 percent of reported hate crimes; by 2012, that percentage had jumped to 30 percent.[90] There was Pedro Corzo, a Cuban American who worked as a regional manager for Del Monte Produce in Dateland, Arizona. In January 2004, he was shot and killed by two young white men from Missouri. The killers, sixteen-year-old Joshua Aston and his twenty-four-year-old cousin Justin Harrison, shaved their heads and set out on a trek through southern Arizona with the specific intent of murdering Mexicans. There was José Gonzales, a U.S. citizen who in September 2007 returned to his home in Avon Park, Florida, to find his car and garage destroyed by fire and "Fuck Puerto Rico" spray-painted on the garage walls. Gonzales, a car mechanic, lost thousands of dollars' worth of tools in the fire. And there was David Ritcheson, a sixteen-year-old Latino teenager who in April 2006 was attacked by two skinheads after allegedly trying to kiss a white teenaged girl at a party. The two assailants, yelling racial epithets and "White Power!," broke Ritcheson's jaw, knocked him unconscious, burned him with cigarettes, attempted to carve a swastika into his chest, poured bleach on him, and, finally, violently sodomized him with a patio umbrella pole. It took thirty surgeries before Ritcheson, who was confined to a wheelchair and forced to use a colostomy bag, was able to return to school. The attack left him so emotionally and psychologically scarred that a year later he committed suicide by jumping from a cruise ship into the Gulf of Mexico.[91]

These attacks harm not only the direct victims of racial violence but also their families, friends, and, indeed, fellow members of their racial or ethnic groups. When an Arab American is beaten specifically because he is an Arab American, it puts all Arab Americans on notice; it lets them know there are organized people out there who want to hurt them. White Americans—at least those who are heterosexual, white, and male—rarely experience the weight and pain of this realization.[92]

Who Joins Hate Groups?

Despite popular representations of hate group members as poor, uneducated whites from rural America, white supremacist groups draw from all regions of society. When Kathleen Blee conducted her in-depth study of women involved in the white supremacist movement—women are prominent in the movement and often are targeted for recruitment by hate groups—she discovered that most were neither poor nor uneducated but possessed college degrees, came from middle-class stable homes, and held steady jobs, working as nurses, engineers, teachers, therapists, and librarians.[93] Others have verified Blee's observation, finding that hate groups have pitched their message to a broad audience and have been somewhat successful, even incorporating highly educated and affluent people into their ranks.[94] The economist Seth Stephens-Davidowitz analyzed tens of thousands of profiles on stormfront.com and found that many of the site's members were not that different than he was. Stormfront users are young, political junkies, and frequent readers of the *New York Times*. "Perhaps it was my own naïveté," Stephens-Davidowitz writes, "but I would have imagined white nationalists inhabiting a different universe from that of my friends and me. Instead, they have long threads praising 'Breaking Bad' and discussing the comparative merits of online dating sites, like Plenty of Fish and OkCupid."[95]

Hate groups thrive off the erroneous idea that race relations are a kind of zero-sum game, where nonwhite advancement always results in white loss. Matthew Hale, the former head of a white supremacist group called the World Church of the Creator (now the Creativity Movement)—and a convicted felon currently serving a forty-year sentence for conspiracy to commit murder—has expressed it this way: "The more that the other races obtain, the more white people feel that it's being obtained at their own expense."[96]

FIGURE 9.6 **WHITE NATIONALISM IN THE UNITED STATES**

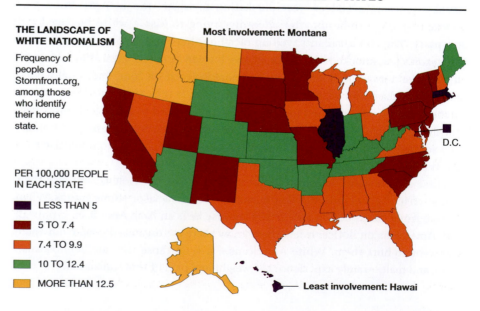

THE LANDSCAPE OF WHITE NATIONALISM

Frequency of people on Stormfront.org, among those who identify their home state.

Most involvement: Montana

D.C.

PER 100,000 PEOPLE IN EACH STATE

- LESS THAN 5
- 5 TO 7.4
- 7.4 TO 9.9
- 10 TO 12.4
- MORE THAN 12.5

Least involvement: Hawai

Whites also are pulled into the hate movement by various recruitment techniques. Leaflets, speakers, 'zines, music, children's books, and face-to-face conversations all are employed by hate groups in pursuit of new members. The Internet quickly has become one of hate groups' favorite recruiting tools. In 1995, there were only a handful of websites dedicated to white supremacy; today, there are hundreds. Estimates of the number of hate group websites range from 600 to over 2,000.[97] Cheap and efficient, the Internet is the ideal medium through which hate groups can channel their message around the globe. Because it allows people to camouflage their true identity behind screen names, hate group members are able to post seething racist diatribes without compromising their relationships with unsuspecting neighbors or coworkers. And because cyberspace virtually is unregulated, functioning as a kind of free speech haven where anything goes, where information is unfiltered and rarely is screened for accuracy, white supremacists are able to disseminate their distortions with impunity.[98]

Some hate groups' websites have pages dedicated to children and teens, who are presented with games, music, and "history" lessons. The kids' page on stormfront.org, for example, reads, "My name is Derek. I am 11 years old and I am the webmaster of kids.stormfront.org. I used to be in public school, it is a shame how many white minds are wasted in that system. I am now in home school. I no longer get beat up by *gangs* of nonwhites and I spend most of my day learning, instead of tutoring the slowest kids in my class."[99] More commonly, however, hate groups' websites attempt to attract young, college-aged women and men. According to one study, nearly half of all extremist websites contain multimedia presentations (music, videos, and downloads of speeches) that appeal to the younger generation.[100]

More underhandedly, hate groups have created dozens of websites that at first glance do not appear to be hosted by hate groups. Rather, they present themselves as "natural information sites" where one can learn about American history and society. While researching a term paper on, say, the Holocaust, affirmative action, or slavery, you might pull up a white supremacist website without even knowing it, one that offers an "alternative interpretation" of certain events. Stormfront.org sponsors a page (dedicated to Martin Luther King, Jr.) that mirrors the site hosted by the King Center. Stormfront's site is slick, professional, and bereft of white supremacist symbols. Indeed, the website is housed at the innocent address www.martinlutherking.org. It purports to offer a "true historical examination" of King's legacy (one that makes him out to be a communist, a drunk, and a rapist) and even displays downloads of "flyers to pass out at your school."[101]

"The Internet," observes hate group expert Mark Potok, "is allowing the White Supremacy movement to reach into places it has never reached before— middle and upper middle-class, college bound teens. The movement is terribly interested in developing the leadership cadre of tomorrow."[102] In his view, "The movement is interested not so much in developing street thugs who beat up people in bars, but [in] college-bound teens who live in middle-class and upper-class homes."[103]

That said, the power of the white supremacist and white nationalist movements should not be overstated. Despite their inflated Internet presence, their true numbers are relatively small (for many hate groups, the leader's house doubles as "headquarters"), and their leaders are relatively powerless (before going to jail, Matthew Hale, whom we met earlier in this chapter, lived in the basement of his parents' house).[104] The white supremacist movement is built on a foundation of lies. And try as it might to repackage its rhetoric or to revamp its image, a movement of lies is bound to tumble, like a house of cards, under the weight of the truth.

CYBER COMMUNITIES

The power and influence of the Internet are indisputable. In its relatively short existence, the World Wide Web already has emerged as *the* primary source of information. Open-source websites such as Wikipedia blur the lines between teacher and student, allowing browsers to play the role of expert, and journalism as we know it is undergoing a massive overhaul thanks to the rise of the Internet. Many have pointed to the Internet's potential to energize and strengthen democracy. Indeed, the technologists who helped develop it had precisely this in mind. The Internet, they forecasted, would foster free expression, allowing anyone to speak her or his mind to audiences around the globe. It would strengthen civil society, enabling people to transcend geographic boundaries and work together. And it would democratize knowledge, bringing all that is known within the click of a mouse. Many of these predictions have become reality, as the Internet seems to be a powerful democratic tool. How do we know? "From the most closed regimes like Iraq and Cuba to the more open ones like China and Iran, authoritarian governments have sought in numerous ways to shut out the Internet or to limit its effects on their populations. What better proof could there be that the Net nourishes democracy?"[105] How does racial division affect virtual associations, and how have people marshaled the Internet to combat it?

The Digital Divide

Before we can discuss how race affects virtual associations, we must examine who, on account of their not having regular access to the Internet, is excluded from these associations in the first place. Studies have shown that nonwhite citizens disproportionately are less likely to own computers and to have regular access to the Internet than their white peers. Compared with African American and Hispanic households, Asian and white households are much more likely to own a computer and have Internet access. As of 2011, fewer than 58 percent of black and Hispanic households had Internet access, compared with 76 percent of white households.[106] Regular Internet use is sparse in some immigrant communities (non-English speakers have very low rates of computer ownership and home Internet access), as it is in many poor rural areas, such as American Indian reservations, impoverished white communities, and rural black towns scattered throughout the Mississippi Delta.

That which separates those with regular and unfettered home access to the Internet from those without it—the split between people with and without twenty-four-hour access to valuable information, educational software, social networking websites, local and national news, and medical advice—has been termed the "digital divide."[107] If you are an average college student, then you have regular access to the Internet and probably log on every day. Think how different your life would be without it! You would be locked out of libraries upon libraries of vital information, not to mention the entire middle-class professional world, which nowadays does much of its business online. You would be cut off from friends and family members, too, who more and more have come to rely on email and social networking sites to stay in touch.

Sociologist Daniel Bell called knowledge and information the "major structural features of post-industrial society."[108] Those without equal access to this knowledge and information would be left behind by a society in which knowledge is power. The digital divide between the technical class and the "digital underclass" is a serious problem.[109] "The computer is not a toy; it is a site of wealth, power and influence, now and in the future. . . . [For this reason, people of color and those with few resources] cannot afford to be excluded from this new medium. To do so will [put them at] risk [of] becoming the information poor. It will be not to count; to be locked out of full participation in society in the same way that illiterate people have been disenfranchised in a print world."[110]

Virtual Racism

Those privileged enough to have regular Internet access are admitted into a parallel universe teeming with virtual associations and cyber communities. There are large associations, such as eBay and YouTube communities, as well as more specialized ones, including chat rooms and electronic bulletin boards. MUDs (Multi-User Domains) and MOOs (MUD Object Oriented), primarily text-based interactive sites that allow people to talk and play games with one another, paved the way for MMORPGs (Massively Multiplayer Online Role-Playing Games) that bring thousands of players together from across the globe. One such role-playing game, *World of Warcraft*, is so popular that Dell sells a computer system designed specifically for it; China, worried its citizens were growing addicted to the game, imposed mandatory limits on the amount of time one can spend playing.[111] Other MMORPGs, such as the popular *Second Life*, allow players to live in a virtual world, complete with virtual property one can buy and sell, as well as virtual jobs, parties, sex, and, of course, virtual characters known as avatars, "your persona in the virtual word."[112]

But these online habitats do not transcend real-life social problems. Several studies have documented the prevalence of racism in cyber communities, even (and especially) in well-traveled, mainstream websites.[113] Consider YouTube. On this site, racism is perpetrated much more regularly by users who respond to videos than by those who post them. It is rare to find a well-viewed video that grapples somewhat critically with the topic of race without also seeing a number of blatantly racist comments directed at the person who posted the video or, as is usually the case, at a racial or ethnic group in general. When YouTube featured several videos in honor of Black History Month in 2008, among which was a video of a speech by Malcolm X and one of a poem entitled "A Black Woman's Smile," several members of the YouTube community responded with hate. Speaking of Damon

Wayans, YouTube's guest editor, Gnomewarrior86 wrote, "How did this monkey learn how to speak?" and Wwk99xp3du commented, "I am sick of all these filthy niggers dirtying up our country. Go back to Africa you dirty niggers." Hiding behind their screen names, protected by complete anonymity, users such as these are able to pollute one of the Internet's most popular websites with hate speech they most likely never would dare use offline.

If you confront someone who believes that racism is dead, simply suggest they spend thirty minutes perusing YouTube. Chat rooms, too, can be sites where racist transactions take place. For instance, researchers who surveyed teens found that 20 percent of white respondents and 29 percent of African American respondents experienced individual discrimination in online chat rooms, and 71 percent of all respondents had witnessed racist comments made in online chat rooms.[114]

Because one often does not know your racial identity online, many Internet users have come to regard whiteness as the virtual norm. Chat room participants sometimes make assumptions about one's racial identity, especially if one "presents white" by the way one types. As a Korean American woman who participates in LambdaMOO, a popular chat room with thousands of users, complained, "I never outright . . . said I was Asian, because I felt that IRL [in real life] people already have stereotypes and felt that it would be at least as bad here. . . . But then it bugs me that people just assume you're white if you don't say otherwise."[115]

This woman underscores a fascinating virtual dilemma: whether or not to reveal one's racial identity. Although light-skinned people of color have passed (with varying degrees of success) as whites for centuries, the Internet allows all people, regardless of their phenotype, to trade their offline racial identity for a different online one. Online, an Arab American man can pass as a white woman, just as a white woman can pass as a Native American teenager. Virtual associations, then, encourage a form of racial tourism where players can, through various avatars, temporarily slip into another skin just as vacationers can temporarily travel to a foreign country.

On the one hand, racial tourism can denaturalize racial categories and might provide people with a kind of racial freedom that offline life does not permit. On the other hand, too often racial tourism reinforces racial divides through stereotypes. For example, many white men who pass as Asians do so by relying on exotic caricatures, accentuating the foreignness of their avatars by, for instance, confining them to the popular Asian stereotypes of samurais or geishas. One white American man on LambdaMOO passed as the avatar Geisha Girl, a "petite Japanese girl in her 20s . . . [who] has devoted her entire life to perfecting the tea ceremony and mastering the art of lovemaking . . . [and who] has spent her entire life in the pursuit of erotic experiences."[116] Noting the (ironic) social disconnect between virtual race relations and real race relations, communications

Virtual associations can encourage a form of racial tourism, whereby players, through various avatars, temporarily slip into another's skin.

professor Lisa Nakamura writes in *Cybertypes*, "Peopling the virtual landscape with samurai, homeboys, and sexy Latina women confirms a vision of ethnicity from which many in the offline world are struggling to distance themselves."[117]

Virtual Empowerment

Although a good number of cyber communities are rife with racism, many others facilitate multiracial coalition building. Antiracist movements have relied on the Internet to circulate information around the world and to increase their visibility in civil society.[118] A committed group of black women, for example, have attempted to improve the health and life quality of underserved populations by using the Internet to close the gap between medical professionals, technical experts, and patients, creating sites such as sisternetonline.org. Native American nations have built websites devoted to their history, culture, and governance. And antiracist organizations have constructed websites such as whiteantiracist.org and tolerance.org to join in the struggle against racial inequality.[119]

The Internet also has been marshaled to reconnect members of diasporic communities, communities of people or ethnic groups that have been fractured, displaced, and scattered around the world on account of warfare, colonialism, or the slave trade. Thus Vietnamese and Hmong Americans who immigrated to the United States during the Vietnam War might use the Internet to reconnect with friends and family members on the other side of the Pacific. Jews whose parents fled Europe during the Holocaust might reach out to fellow Jews in Israel or Russia in an attempt to patch the Jewish community back together. One scholar has examined how Filipino Americans negotiate and create their ethnic identity through the Internet by entering into (virtual) community with women and men in the Philippines. She has observed how "members of the diaspora established what Filipino identity means with people back home and how people at home forged an identity with members of the diaspora."[120]

In a similar vein, Native Hawaiians have relied on the Internet to preserve their native culture and language. Twenty years ago, those who spoke the Hawaiian language numbered only in the hundreds, and most speakers were elderly. To avoid the extinction of their language, some Hawaiians started a language revitalization movement, an extension of the larger Hawaiian cultural identity movement that came to the fore in the 1970s and that revived indigenous traditions such as hula, oral chanting, and canoeing. As early as 1994, Hawaiian teachers built an electronic bulletin board, named *Leoki* (Hawaiian for "powerful voice"), devoted to the Hawaiian language. *Leoki* has spread throughout the archipelago and beyond, allowing users to converse in Hawaiian through email, live chats, and virtual conferences.[121] The Internet, then, has helped resuscitate the Hawaiian language—and unique perspectives and worldviews connected to that language—and it could help save other endangered languages as well, thousands of which are projected to fade away within the next century.[122]

The promise of forging multiracial, multinational communities on the Internet is immense. In effect, the Internet has shrunk the world to the size of your computer screen, and this is its most important contribution to civil society. Even websites like YouTube, where racist comments abound, may help move us one step closer to a racial democracy simply by bringing people together who otherwise never would have met. The Internet enables people of different racial identities and nationalities to interact and enter into conversation with one another. Whether or not those conversations will divide or unite, repair or tear down, heal or wound is up to you. As the old Hawaiian saying goes, "*I ka ʻōlelo no ke ola, i ka ʻōlelo ke make*" (In the language there is life; in the language there is death).[123]

RELIGIOUS ASSOCIATIONS

If America is a nation of joiners, it also is a nation of believers. American atheists constitute only 1.6 percent of the population. By contrast, atheists make up the majority in other Western countries, constituting over 80 percent of the population in Sweden and Denmark, for example. America overwhelmingly is a Christian nation, with approximately 78 percent of all adults following the Christian faith. On any given Sunday, as few as 20 percent and as many as 40 percent of Americans attend a Christian church service. An additional 4.7 percent of Americans practice other religions: 1.7 percent of Americans are Jewish and fewer than 1 percent are Buddhist or Muslim. Almost 15 percent of Americans identify as "agnostic" or "nothing in particular" when it comes to religion.[124]

Religious Illiteracy and Intolerance

Given that America is one of the most religious nations in the Western world, it is surprising how confused many Americans are when it comes to religion. The majority of Americans cannot name five of the Ten Commandments, one of the Gospels, or the five books of the Torah.[125] Although Americans have focused much of their political thought and attention on Islam and the Middle East since September 11, 2001, ignorance of Islam is rampant. Case in point: when U.S. Representative Silvestre Reyes, head of the House Intelligence Committee—which oversees the sixteen government agencies, including the CIA and FBI, that make up the U.S. Intelligence Community—was asked if the al-Qaeda terrorist group was associated with Sunni or Shiite Muslims, he failed to answer correctly (the correct answer is Sunni).[126] In the words of religious studies professor Stephen Prothero, although America is "one of the most religious places on earth," it is also "a nation of religious illiterates."[127]

Where there is ignorance, intolerance never is far behind. Anti-Muslim prejudice and attacks increased in the aftermath of September 11.[128] According to recent polls, whereas 96 percent of Americans would vote for a black presidential candidate, and 95 percent would vote for a woman, only 58 percent would vote for a Muslim.[129] In the words of one commentator, "Calling someone a Muslim is still a slur."[130] Mosques have been vandalized and ridiculed. When Craig Baker, a white man living in Katy, Texas, discovered that his town's Islamic Association planned to erect a mosque next to his property, he projected his outrage by hosting pig races and grilling sausage every Friday evening, the holiest day of the week on the Muslim calendar. One hundred people showed up to the first pig race, despite heavy rain. Although Baker's bigoted display was rooted in a misunderstanding of Islam—Muslims do not despise pigs; they simply refrain from eating them—he managed to get his message across.[131]

To capture widespread fear and discrimination of Muslims in Western countries, observers have coined a new term: "Islamophobia." Muslims are more likely than Jews, Mormons, Christians, or Americans of other any other religious groups to report having experienced racial or religious discrimination in 2014. Almost one in two Muslim Americans have reported recent discrimination, compared with 30 percent of Mormons and 18 percent of Protestants. And today Arab Americans (52 percent) are more likely to report recent experiences with discrimination than Hispanics (48 percent) or African Americans (45 percent).[132] Statistics such as these—combined with the ubiquitous profiling in airports—have led comedians and political pundits to remark that "Arabs are the new blacks."[133]

Although anti-Semitism has declined significantly in recent years, Jews continue to face discrimination and assaults. Spokesmen for the Nation of Islam, such as Louis Farrakhan and Abdul Muhammad, have made anti-Semitic speeches, including one delivered by Muhammad in which he claimed that "the so-called Jew . . . is sucking our blood in the black community."[134] Such remarks exacerbate the already strained relationships between African Americans and Jews.[135] One also can point to instances of institutional anti-Semitism, such as when the city council of Fort Collins, Colorado—home of Colorado State University—refused to allow a local rabbi to display a nine-foot-tall menorah near the city square, even though the town prominently displayed a Christmas tree and other Christmas decorations during the winter holiday season.[136]

(Top) Anti-Semitic vandalism, Brooklyn, New York. (Bottom) Flyer depicting slain Muslim students from Chapel Hill.

Religious intolerance, then, is yet another force that tears at the fabric of civil society, dividing Christian from Muslim, Muslim from Jew, and so forth. It is a vector we must consider in our intersectional analyses, for failing to account for the many complex ways in which religious conviction drives social action is fundamentally to misinterpret the social world.

Racialization of the Religious Sphere

Does the religious sphere mirror society's racial segregation, or does it buck the tide? By and large, religious associations do not overcome racial divides; in fact, the opposite is true. Religious life is racialized to a high degree. Certain religions, denominations within religions, and places of worship within denominations correspond to certain racial and ethnic groups. Let's start with Christianity. If a church is considered multiracial if no more than 80 percent of its members belong to a single racial group, then only one in ten American churches is multiracial. As sociologist Michael Emerson observes, "[Christian] congregations are approximately 10 times less racially diverse than are the neighborhoods in which they reside."[137] According to a recent study, 43 percent of Christian churches do not have *a single member* from another racial group, and many others have only a very small percentage. Sunday morning remains, as it did fifty years ago, one of society's most racially segregated hours.[138]

The racial segregation of Christian congregations has led to the development of traditionally white, black, Hispanic, Asian American, and Native American churches, each with its own unique rituals, practices, and styles of worship. Many white congregations, such as Southern Baptist, Presbyterian, and Lutheran churches, follow either a traditional style of worship, where old hymns are sung, or a more modern variant, complete with a contemporary Christian band. Services tend to be quite professional and regimented, and congregants tend to listen quietly and attentively. The black church, however, has since slavery been defined by an energetic, emotional, and "spirit-led" style of worship. The southern revival, the black choir, the fiery preacher, who between proclamations wipes the sweat off her or his brow, and the "call and response" style of service, peppered with audience members' shouts of "Amen" and "Preach it!" all are emblematic practices found within the black church.[139]

The Pentecostal Revival Church in the Flatbush section of Brooklyn, New York.

For years the black church has functioned as the nexus of African American life, and today it continues to serve that role in many communities. This is one reason why African Americans perhaps are the nation's most religious racial group.[140] Indeed, a number of scholars have observed that many residents of poor black neighborhoods are "overchurched," meaning that "African Americans [possess] far more churches than they [can] keep up or that [can] be useful in ameliorating the social and economic conditions of the Black population."[141] In many black ghettos across the country, one can find literally dozens of small congregations—storefront churches, home churches, churches that congregate outside—each fitting itself to different populations within the black community and together reflecting the "kaleidoscopic expression of Black subcultures."[142] Such observations lend some credibility to the depressing cliché that all one finds in rundown neighborhoods are liquor stores and churches. The *Boston Globe* described one of Boston's toughest neighborhoods as follows: "The Four Corners area . . . [comprises] o supermarkets; o bakeries; o hardware stores; o accounting offices; 11 religious organizations; [and] 14 vacant storefronts."[143]

The majority of Latinos, for their part, are Catholic (55 percent). Another 22 percent classify themselves as Protestant and 18 percent are unaffiliated.[144] Within Latino Christianity, one finds divisions along ethnic lines—distinct Puerto Rican, Cuban, and Mexican parishes—as well as along generational divides: first-generation immigrants are more likely to be Catholic, while third-generation Latinos are over-represented in Protestant denominations.[145] The Latino presence in the Catholic Church is so commanding that it is common to hear commentators speak of the "Hispanicization of American Catholicism." However, the percentage of Latinos who are Catholic has declined steadily in recent years. In the early 2000s, roughly seven in ten Hispanics were Catholic. Today, the ratio is roughly five in ten. To better connect with immigrant congregants, Masses around the country are delivered in Spanish. The priests at Los Angeles's St. Thomas The Apostle Parish went so far as to incorporate mariachi bands (in full regalia) into their services.[146]

Ethnic churches associated with Asian and Arab Americans also are a common feature of America's Christian landscape. Most Arab Americans are Christian, not Muslim, as is often assumed. According to one study, 35 percent of Arab Americans are Catholic, 18 percent are Eastern Orthodox (one of the world's largest Christian denominations), and 10 percent are Protestant. Another 13 percent have no religious affiliation, and 24 percent are Muslim. Maronite Christians from Lebanon, Coptic Christians from Egypt, and Chaldeans from Iraq have established ethnic churches.[147] Forty-two percent of Asian Americans are Christian as well, with 22 percent identifying as Protestant and 19 percent as Catholic. Among Asian Americans, variants of Christian denominations are associated with different ethnic groups. For example, the majority of Filipino Americans are Catholic (65 percent); the majority of Korean Americans are Protestant (61 percent).[148] Many of these Asian American believers belong not to multiracial congregations but to Filipino or Korean churches, or even to more encompassing Asian American churches, formed around a pan-Asian congregation instead of a particular ethnic group.[149]

Native Americans, too, have developed their own variant of Christianity. From the 1880s to the 1940s, the U.S. government prohibited Native Americans from practicing their traditional religions. During this time, missionaries spread Christianity throughout Indian country. Some tribes, such as Oklahoma's "Five Civilized Tribes"—the Cherokee, Creek, Choctaw, Seminole, and Chickasaw—converted to Christianity early on. (Anglo-European colonists gave them the name "Five Civilized Tribes" because the tribes adopted many of the colonists' customs.) Many members of these tribes integrated into their newfound Christian faith rituals and practices that dated back to pre-Columbian times. The result was the Native American Church, a pan-Indian religious organization that blends mainstream Christianity with indigenous beliefs and traditions.[150] (One scholar has estimated it is roughly 80 percent Christian and 20 percent traditional.[151]) Not only does it encourage medicine men to conduct traditional healings, it also (and more controversially) employs peyote in some of its ceremonies. A spineless cactus indigenous to the Southwest, peyote is eaten or drunk during all-night religious ceremonies. Although some non-Indians have labeled peyote a narcotic, many Native Americans see it as a kind of medicine or sacrament.[152]

The last fifty years have witnessed a resurgence of Native American traditional practices, not just those sewn into Christian belief systems but also those that constitute their own religion. Navajo medicine men work beside non-Indian doctors, who practice modern medicine; Apache Crown Dancers hold a special place in their tribe's religious life; New York's Iroquois Nation conducts religious ceremonies by making use of masks and wampum belts; and after the government lifted its prohibition on the Sun Dance, some Northern Plains tribes have reinstituted the ceremony, which requires participants to abstain from food and to suffer through considerable pain as their chest or back is pierced. Perhaps more than any other tribe, "the Pueblos stand out as the most consistent and persistent of the nation's Indian groups in continuing their old ways."[153] During especially important ceremonies, Pueblos often place barricades on the roads leading into their reservation towns so that outsiders cannot enter. Although there is great variety in Indian country when it comes to traditional religions, one can identify several shared themes and practices that together constitute a unique Indian spirituality and cosmology, including an intimate connection to nature and sacred lands, dancing, and powwows (North American Indian ceremonies involving food, singing, and dancing).[154]

Turning now to Buddhism, we see that 53 percent of America's practicing Buddhists are white and 32 percent are Asian American.[155] As in other religions, different Buddhist sects correspond to different ethnic groups. Thus Laotian, Cambodian, Thai, and Sri Lankan Buddhists tend to practice Theravada Buddhism, whereas those with family trees planted in China, Vietnam, or Japan usually practice Mahayana Buddhism. Many Asian immigrants have conformed their Buddhism to the American workweek. Whereas Buddhist temples are an everyday meeting place in many immigrants' home countries, they primarily are frequented only on the weekends in America.[156]

As for Islam, over 60 percent of Muslims in America are born outside the United States, coming from over seventy-seven different countries. Pakistan accounts for 9 percent of America's Muslim population, while the Middle East and North Africa account for 26 percent. While Americans of South Asian descent, who identify ethnically as Pakistani, Indian, Bangladeshi, and Afghan, account for 16 percent of American Muslims, 37 percent of America's Muslim population was born in the United States.[157] Additionally about 24 percent of Muslims in America are African Americans.[158] Although the majority of mosques have one dominant ethnic group, they are more racially diverse than other religious organizations.

The abbot at Wat Pa in Chandler, Arizona collects food from a parishioner in the ordination hall during Makha Bucha day services.

Ninety percent of all American mosques have at least some Arab Americans and some Americans of South Asian heritage. The Nation of Islam, however, remains exclusively black.[159]

American Judaism is the whitest of all the nation's major religions. As historian Eric Goldstein makes clear in *The Price of Whiteness: Jews, Race, and American Identity*, the relationship between Jewish ethnicity and whiteness always has been uncertain and filled with tension. Throughout the nineteenth and twentieth centuries, Jews worked both to insert themselves into the white mainstream and to preserve their distinct cultural identity. As a result, they always have teetered on the outer boundaries of whiteness, a position they occupy to this day.[160] Although Latinos and African Americans have converted to Judaism in small numbers, most Jews (92 percent) are white.[161] In Judaism, the overlap between religion and ethnicity is nearly complete. Although one can be ethnically Jewish and religiously atheist (or Christian or Buddhist), Jewish ethnicity (its food, clothing, holidays, language) is rooted in Jewish religion. Jewishness encompasses religious, cultural, ethnic, and national elements, though these elements, of course, are not found in every person who identifies as a Jew.

Explaining Racial Homophily in Religious Life

After surveying religious associations in America, we are met with the conclusion that they are marked by high levels of racial and ethnic segregation. As sociologists Michael Emerson and Karen Chai Kim have noted, "Despite the racial integration that has been occurring in other institutions, the vast majority of the more than 300,000 religious congregations—*the largest and most active voluntary associations*—involve members who are of the same race."[162] But why?

One reason is that religious associations behave as other associations in civil society do, following the homophily principle. Since religious groups spring from (most likely racially homophilous) social networks and connections based in (most likely racially segregated) neighborhoods, it is not surprising that most reflect preexisting racial divides.[163] Another reason for racial segregation in religious life is that certain religious cultures and habits unintentionally widen racial divisions. Although the white evangelical Christian community has taken impressive steps since the 1980s toward racial reconciliation, a good number of white churches have failed seriously to address racial domination. Why? Because most white evangelicals understand racism only on the interpersonal, not the institutional, level.[164] "Despite devoting considerable time and energy to solving the problem of racial division," write the authors of *Divided by Faith*, "white evangelicalism likely does more to perpetuate the racialized society than to reduce it. . . . [This is because] for white evangelicals, the 'race problem' is not racial inequality, and it is not systematic, institutionalized injustice. Rather, white evangelicals view the race problem as (1) prejudiced individuals, resulting in poor relationships and sin, (2) others trying to make it a group or systematic issue when it is not, or (3) a fabrication of the self-interested."[165]

Nonwhite Christians—as well as white members of multiracial churches—generally have a more systematic understanding of racism, one that accounts for

Although the majority of mosques have one dominant ethnic group, they are more racially diverse than other religious organizations.

its institutional properties. And both groups are more likely to advance antiracist solutions pitched at structural inequality. As a result, when white and nonwhite Christians talk about racism, many times they are working with very different understandings of the term and, by extension, what a proper Christian response to racial divisions should entail. Indeed, in a recent survey only 4 percent of white Protestants named racism a key issue that should concern Christians, compared with one-third of black Protestants, a quarter of whom listed racism as *the* most important problem Christians should address.[166]

Many nonwhite places of worship do their part to contribute to these divisions as well. Most Native Americans view their traditional religions as theirs and theirs alone and discourage non-Indians from participating. Many black churches prioritize the black experience, thereby excluding nonblacks. And some ethnic churches perpetuate a kind of ethnic chauvinism that encourages congregants to distance themselves from less successful immigrants, from "those kind" of Arabs, "those kind" of Mexicans.[167]

Religion and Racial and Ethnic Identity

As the preceding examples demonstrate, religious associations are connected to, and used to promote and preserve, certain racial and ethnic identities. Places of worship that cater to new immigrants, for example, allow them to form friendships with fellow immigrants who speak their language and enjoy similar kinds of food. They also play a large part in preserving immigrant culture. Korean churches conduct their services in Korean, observe Korean holidays, and offer Korean-language classes for children. Just as Irish and Italian culture, language, and music were preserved through Catholic parishes during the beginning of the twentieth century, Mexican, Cuban, and Puerto Rican culture thrive in many Catholic parishes. In many neighborhoods, the Greek Orthodox parish, Hindu temple, or Lebanese church is the only major institution that strives to preserve certain ethnic cultures and languages.[168]

For minority groups, the church, mosque, temple, or synagogue often functions as a refuge. Religious associations provide valuable social services. They supply new immigrants with information on naturalization, health care, education, and jobs, which in part is why immigrants tend to become more religious in the United States than they were in their home country.[169] What is more, religious associations provide those denied honor by the surrounding society with social status and prestige. An unemployed Native American may be looked on as a respected spiritual leader on the reservation; a black man who works as an underappreciated middle manager may be an admired deacon in the National Baptist Convention.[170]

Religious associations also can be powerful agents of social change and political mobilization. Recall that Native American spirituality helped America's indigenous people resist white colonialism, just as it informed the American Indian movement that rose up in the late 1960s. And the importance of the black church to the Civil Rights Movement cannot be overstated: its congregants served as activists, its preachers as some of the movement's most important voices, its buildings as central meeting spots.[171] Many mainline and predominantly white churches have adopted an antiracist stance and have developed programs to confront racial injustice.

Multiracial religious services are on the rise.

Religious associations have played a significant role in defending immigrant rights. For example, Jews, Baptists, Catholics, Quakers, Unitarian Universalists, and other religious groups came together in the early 1980s to form the sanctuary movement. This interfaith coalition was devoted to providing sanctuary (that is, religious-based asylum) to families suffering from political turmoil and violence that had erupted in some Central American countries. Sanctuary was offered in direct defiance of U.S. immigration law, which resulted in some activists being arrested. Today, the sanctuary movement is spearheaded by the Catholic Church and works to protect undocumented immigrants from deportation.[172] Latino churchgoers think their churches should be actively involved in protecting immigrants. In fact, 74 percent believe their church should provide help to undocumented immigrants even when doing so is illegal.[173] And in 2014, when the number of child migrants fleeing to America from violence and poverty in Honduras and other Latin American countries soared to crisis levels, religious leaders argued for their inclusion and provision. After Cardinal Timothy Dolan, archbishop of New York, learned that busloads of immigrant mothers and children had been turned away by angry white protesters shouting, "Go home!" he said the episode was "un-American," "unbiblical," and "inhumane."[174] "I think the church will always side with the rights of people to live where it's best for them to live," remarked Monsignor John Moretta, pastor of Los Angeles's Church of the Resurrection. "We took that position when the Irish came and when the Italians came, and now we are doing the same with the Latinos."[175]

We should emphasize, by way of conclusion, that not all of America's religious organizations are monoracial; some congregations are quite multiracial and exist as a powerful force for integration. How, then, do these religious associations swim against the tide? Sociologists have offered several answers, but the most important one has to do with organizational priorities. Synagogues, churches, mosques, and temples that make concerted and serious efforts to diversify their congregations often are successful. One thinks of the American Catholic Church, which circulated a letter in 1984 urging its priests to "broaden the embrace" to new immigrant communities. Today, the Catholic Church is one of the most racially integrated religious organizations, with the average parish made up of at least three racial and ethnic groups. One thinks, too, of the new evangelical movement, a mainline Christian movement that stresses social justice and interracial solidarity. Many new evangelical congregations are multiracial, including 35 percent of megachurches (those with a weekly attendance that exceeds 2,000 people).[176]

Religious associations can affect today's racial order in a variety of ways. Analysts have shown that whites who attend multiracial religious services harbor less prejudice toward nonwhites than those who attend all-white or majority-white services.[177] Others have demonstrated that Conservative Protestant congregations contribute to residential racial segregation, whereas Mainline Protestant churches, as well as most Jewish and Muslim congregations, contribute to neighborhood integration.[178] Still others have asserted that religious associations can strengthen civil society by joining people together, fighting against injustice and exploitation, encouraging altruism and community service, helping the poor, and meeting people's emotional needs.[179] Religious associations are a powerful force in today's racial order, just as they have been ever since the founding of the country.

AMERICAN PROMISE

In Alexis de Tocqueville's view, the strength and vitality of America's voluntary associations constituted the foremost safeguard of its freedom. Today, from our reflexive and critical perspective, we can see that although robust and vibrant in many ways, the American associational field continues to be marred by profound racial divisions. The ideals of public-spiritedness, citizenship, and community that so inspired Tocqueville, not to mention later observers of the American scene such as Gunnar Myrdal, never will be realized so long as our civil society is rent with racial separations and discord. We have accordingly stressed throughout this chapter the need to bring out the full democratic potential in our associational life, to bridge racial divides in civil society and to establish a more genuine solidarity in our community organizations, social clubs, and religious congregations. Think how much more powerful civil society would be if we evicted racial domination from its midst, how much louder and clearer our democratic voices would grow. Much work remains to be done. In our associational field reside some of the deepest obstacles to the realization of a racially just society. But there, too, can be found some of its greatest promise.

THE BIG PICTURE
Chapter 9: Associations

MAIN POINTS

KEY TERMS

FROM THEORY TO PRACTICE

Examine how associational life has reflected racial segregation in America and how labor unions and ethnic nationalist groups have responded differently to racial discrimination.

- ethnic nationalism, page 322
- homophily, page 327

- With whom do you choose to associate? Pick an association (religious institution, knitting circle, intramural team) to which you belong and analyze it in terms of its racial and ethnic composition. Who is present and who is absent? Why? Address these questions by drawing on the information in this chapter.

Explain the racial discrepancies in civil participation between whites and nonwhites. Why are people of color less likely to join voluntary associations or participate in community activities?

- identity politics, page 332
- civil society, page 332
- political correctness, page 334

- Strike up a conversation with someone—stranger or friend—specifically asking her or his opinion on identity politics or "political correctness." (You may or may not choose to tell this person you are doing this for a class assignment.) Afterward, analyze her opinions with a sociological imagination, paying special attention to how her beliefs rely on certain assumptions about racial domination. How does she conceive of identity politics or "political correctness"? On what assumptions about the nature of social reality do her opinions rest? To what extent do you agree or disagree with her positions?

Describe who joins hate groups and how they organize and recruit members.

- hate groups, page 336

Discuss how the Internet can be a source of virtual racism as well as of virtual empowerment that facilitates multiracial coalition building.

- digital divide, page 340

Visit a webpage that functions as a kind of cyber community—that is, any webpage that allows users to interact and post comments—and conduct a racial analysis. How is racial domination challenged or upheld by members of that cyber community? How do members assert, distort, or conceal their racial identity? What might this community tell us about the workings of racial domination on the Internet?

Understand why religious life continues to be one of the most racialized areas of American society.

- religious associations, page 344

10 Intimate Life

MAIN POINTS

- Understand how racial domination has wreaked havoc on many nonwhite families and interracial couples—through such means as separating parents from children, limiting the immigration of spouses and children, and forbidding marriages between races.

- Learn about the reasons for the significant racial differences in rates of marriage, divorce, and out-of-wedlock birth.

- Examine the racial dynamics that inform everyday interactions, such as the way we greet each other, and how these racial dynamics often cause misunderstanding and frustration.

- Recognize the ways that each person's identity is made up of multiple intersecting features, such as race, gender, religion, sexuality, and class.

- Explain how race is both *marked* through America's racial taxonomy and *made* through hundreds and thousands of practices: gestures, sayings, tastes, ways of walking, religious convictions, and opinions.

The ancient Greeks had a saying: "Know thyself." By this, they meant that we must submit to self-evaluation, exploring our innermost thoughts and desires as well as the people closest to us, if we ever hope to understand the world around us—let alone gain some control over our lives.[1] Rigorous reflexivity provides some limited but real power over the forces that would control our imaginations and actions. At the very least, it allows us rationally to assess and perhaps to alter how those forces affect our thinking and behavior. "The true freedom that sociology offers," wrote Bourdieu, "is to give us a small chance of knowing what game we play and of minimizing the ways in which we are manipulated by the forces of the field in which we evolved, as well as by the embodied social forces that operate from within us."[2]

To this end, we here analyze sociologically those aspects of our daily lives that so often avoid socioanalysis: our families and ourselves. We begin with a survey of the history of the family, reaching all the way back to colonial and slavery times and tracking the emergence of interracial and same-sex couples. We then survey the sociology of race and the family, providing explanations for racial variation in marriage and divorce rates, examining the dynamics of interracial marriage, and focusing on the hardships associated with single motherhood. In the last section, we take up such topics as the racialized nature of the self and the miscommunications that occur within interracial relationships, intersectionality, and the idea of "racial authenticity."

THE FAMILY SINCE COLONIALISM AND SLAVERY

Today, a good many of us—but certainly not all—are encouraged to marry the person we love. And most of us believe that people over the age of eighteen should make their own decisions and that the family should not be dominated by the husband. Such ideas are quite new in the American context. In colonial times, the family—certainly the white family—functioned quite differently. Marriages, governed more by economic practicalities than by romance, required parental permission. Because a daughter was thought to belong to her father, in the same way that a gun or a horse belonged to him, she was "given away" at the marriage ceremony in exchange for the groom's promise of financial support, a ritual that continues to this day.[3]

Before World War II, most white women were excluded from the formal labor market. Those few who did work outside the home were paid paltry wages. Indeed, most were not even paid, as many employers refused to pay women directly, choosing instead to pay their husbands. Forced to rely on men to survive, many women were pressured into unhappy marriages (just as many gays and lesbians were pressured into unhappy heterosexual unions) and were controlled by their husbands. This gendered system designated public life (that is, work and politics) as male and private life (that is, child rearing and housework) as female. And even today, though things are beginning to change, some people believe that a heterosexual and monoracial marriage, made up of a breadwinning husband and a stay-at-home mom, is a kind of natural and timeless creation. We must remember that this model of the "ideal family" took a considerable amount of social engineering to perfect. It is neither natural nor timeless, but originated in America's Puritan past.[4]

The Black Family under Slavery

Since colonial times, racial domination has wreaked havoc on many nonwhite families. Native American boarding schools separated parents from their children, sometimes, tragically, forever. Citizenship laws that forbade Asian women, and later all Asian immigrants, from entering the country inhibited significantly the development of Asian American families and communities. And Mexican Repatriation Programs ripped husband from wife, brother from sister, daughter from mother. But perhaps no other nonwhite group suffered from a systematic attack on the institution of the family as much as blacks did under slavery.

A slave family, circa 1850.

If the white family was held up as a powerful and sacred union before the nineteenth century, the black family was not even considered a family under slavery. If slavery allowed white masters to assume absolute control over their enslaved Africans and if fatherhood in those times required, at minimum, a man to protect and to provide for his wife and children, then we must conclude that slavery all but completely abolished the role of husband and father for most enslaved black men. A slave could not provide for his wife and children (let alone for himself); he could not prevent his wife from being ripped from his arms and shipped to another plantation; he usually could not stop his master from beating his son or raping his daughter.[5] The historian Willie Lee Rose recalls the case of Jacob, a young slave, who was beaten unrelentingly by his master. When Jacob sought comfort and advice from his father, the latter replied, "Go back to your work and be a good boy, for I cannot do anything for you."[6]

Black motherhood, too, was denied under slavery. Some slave women were forced to sleep not near their husbands or children, but "on the floor at the foot of a mistress's bed (increasing the chances they would sooner or later be bribed, seduced, or forced into sexual relations with the master)."[7] A slave woman did not have control over her sexuality or her reproductive capabilities: her womb belonged to her white master. So, too, did her breasts, for in many cases lactating mothers had to feed their masters' wives' white babies before nursing their own children. Long before the lactating period was over, slave women were forced back to the fields, their infants placed in "nurseries where their care was in the hands of slaves either too infirm, too old, or too young to work elsewhere."[8] As a result, children were malnourished and many did not survive. Those who did survive could be beaten, sexually molested, put to work, and forced to watch their parents endure the same treatment. Many were shipped to other plantations and never again saw their mothers or fathers.[9] "Because of the omnipresent threat of forced separation by sale, gift, or bequest, the [slave] family was not 'stable,'" writes Jacqueline Jones—with considerable understatement.[10]

White domination of the black body and black family was so total during these times that some historians convincingly have argued that on many plantations what existed was not a slave "family" in the conventional sense of the term, but rather a "reproductive unit" controlled by the master, who desired as many offspring as possible. Slavery made it impossible for slaves to love their spouses and children unreservedly and without hesitation. Toni Morrison captures this sad truth in her novel *Beloved*. As Sethe and Paul D, both former slaves, sit and talk, Sethe recalls her escape from bondage: "Look like I loved em more after I got here. Or maybe I couldn't love em proper in Kentucky because they wasn't mine to love." The narrator tells us Paul D's thoughts: "So you protected yourself and loved small. . . . Anything bigger wouldn't do. A woman, a child, a brother—a big love like that would split you wide open in Alfred, Georgia. He knew exactly what she meant: to get to a place where you could love anything you chose—not to need permission for desire—well now, *that* was freedom."[11]

After emancipation, some blacks, especially those in the South recently freed from bondage, continued reproductive and familial strategies they devised to survive slavery. While somewhat practical under such an oppressive environment, these strategies—having large families, for example—would prove disastrous after emancipation. In 1900, the average African American family in the rural South had eight children. With so many mouths to feed and with so few opportunities for economic advancement, many black families had a difficult time lifting themselves out of poverty. Facing this desperate situation, they accepted the neoslavery terms of sharecropping.[12]

In contrast, other black families adopted the dominant model of family government at the time. Instead of being the nonfather and the nonhusband, roles thrust on them during slavery, many black men now assumed a paternalistic and patriarchal role as head of the household. Black women were to be controlled and protected, lauded as homemakers and caretakers; they were to be treated, that is, like white women. Patriarchy, then, came to define many black families, just as it had defined white families since colonial times. But unlike white women, many black women, who for centuries had not been treated like "dainty ladies," refused to accept their newfound place in the shadows of their husbands. Ironically, under the vicious system of slavery black women had experienced a kind of gender equality— they often worked alongside black men, picking cotton, harvesting rice, swinging axes—and many were not about to allow one kind of freedom (emancipation) to usher in another kind of oppression (patriarchy). This situation bred a tense spirit of distrust and contempt between black men and women and birthed the stereo-type of the "black matriarch."[13]

White control of the black family would continue throughout the twentieth century, most heinously in the form of forced sterilizations sometimes applied to unknowing black women (as well as to Native American women). "For sever-al decades," writes Dorothy Roberts in *Killing the Black Body: Race, Reproduction, and the Meaning of Liberty*, "peaking in the 1970s, government-sponsored family-planning programs not only encouraged Black women to use birth control but coerced them into being sterilized. While slave masters forced Black women to bear children for profit, more recent policies have sought to reduce Black women's fertility. . . . During the 1970s sterilization became the most rapidly growing form of birth control in the United States, rising from 200,000 cases in 1970 to over 700,000 in 1980. It was a common belief among Blacks in the South that Black women were routinely sterilized without their informed consent and for no valid medical reason. Teaching hospitals performed unnecessary hysterectomies on poor Black women as practice for their medical residents. This sort of abuse was so widespread in the South that these operations came to be known as 'Mississippi appendectomies.'"[14]

Brave New Families: The Emergence of Interracial and Same-Sex Unions

Before the Civil War, some white communities were tolerant of interracial marriages between free blacks and whites. Historians believe that interracial sex was common during the colonial period, when black and white servants worked side-by-side and entered into relationships with one another. But as blacks descended into chattel slavery, white landowners sought to separate white indentured servants from per-manent black slaves (lest they join together in open rebellion) by outlawing inter-racial unions. This gave rise to antimiscegenation laws that criminalized interracial marriage and sex.[15] These laws applied not only to black-white unions but to nearly all romantic and sexual intercourse that traversed the color line and that might lead to "race mixing." On the West Coast, for example, relationships between whites and Asians were of particular concern to defenders of the racial status quo.[16]

Of course, in practice antimiscegenation laws applied only to *consenting adults* who longed to be together; white slave masters who had their way with enslaved black women—and children—ignored antimiscegenation statutes. When African

American novelist and critic James Baldwin responded to a question that obsessed white America during the 1960s—"Would you want *your* daughter to marry one?"— he did so with the kind of penetrating deftness that defined his career. Addressing a white man, he said, "You're not worried about me marrying *your* daughter—you're worried about me marrying your *wife's* daughter. I've been marrying *your* daughter since the days of slavery."[17]

Interracial relationships continued to decline after the fall of slavery. Biracial children posed no threat to slavery because the "one-drop rule" classified all people with African American blood as black and, therefore, subject to bondage. But biracial children did pose a threat to the order of racial segregation that arose postemancipation, an order that attempted to create a bipolar racial system that rigidly separated whites from blacks. During Jim Crow segregation, more antimiscegenation statutes were passed into law, and the lynch mob arose to "protect white women's purity" (and to uphold white patriarchy, as we learned in Chapter 6). The fact that black men often were lynched on fabricated rape charges or simply for whistling at white women, as was the case for young Emmett Till, and the fact that many lynchings involved castration indicate that the fear of black male sexuality and miscegenation fueled the reign of white terrorism that lasted clear into the twentieth century. As Jim Crow segregation reached its peak near the beginning of the twentieth century, interracial marriages fell to their lowest point in U.S. history.[18]

But throughout the twentieth century the family would be remade. Two events, in particular, helped erode parental influence over children as well as masculine dominance over women and thereby reorganized America's gender regime. The first was the Great Depression, which sent thousands of men to the unemployment line and diminished their role as breadwinner. Women and children had to join men in helping make ends meet, forcing men to relinquish total control over family finances. The second event was World War II. With a significant portion of the male workforce fighting overseas, women en masse had to pick up the slack. White women, who for centuries had been relegated to the home, marched to the factories to work in assembly lines and contribute to the war effort. Nonwhite women, much more familiar with working outside the home than their white counterparts, worked in the factories as well, often performing

Rosie the Riveter represented the American women who worked in factories and shipyards during World War II. Nonwhite women were familiar with work outside of the home long before the 1940s.

the dirtiest and most dangerous tasks. They also filled the void left by the absence of white women in the home, soon becoming overrepresented in the domestic service sector. Significantly, the flood of women into the labor force during the war challenged the demeaning idea that women were unable to do "men's work."[19]

America's military men were helping to reinvent the family as well. Thousands of miles away from the demands of their families, gay soldiers were able to express their sexuality in ways that before had been denied them. As one historian has argued, "Once they left the constraints of family life and watchful neighbors, many recruits were surprised to find that military service gave them opportunities to begin a 'coming-out' process. . . . The massive mobilization for World War II relaxed the social constraints of peacetime that had kept gay men and women unaware of themselves and each other."[20]

Not only this, but some heterosexual soldiers of color engaged in relationships with white European women, relationships that would have been strictly forbidden by antimiscegenation policies in the United States.[21] When the war ended, America had entered a new age in the career of the family. As the century marched into the 1960s and beyond, the sexual revolution unfolded; the gay rights movement gained steam; the women's rights movement found new energy and launched "a full-scale attack on the exploitative and stultifying effects of women's confinement and dependency as homemaker"; and the Civil Rights Movement gained power and helped alter the course of the nation.[22]

In 1967, the Supreme Court ruled antimiscegenation laws unconstitutional in *Loving v. Virginia*, marking a significant civil rights victory. At the time of the decision, interracial marriage was illegal in as many

FIGURE 10.1 PERCENTAGE OF AMERICANS FAVORING INTERRACIAL MARRIAGE

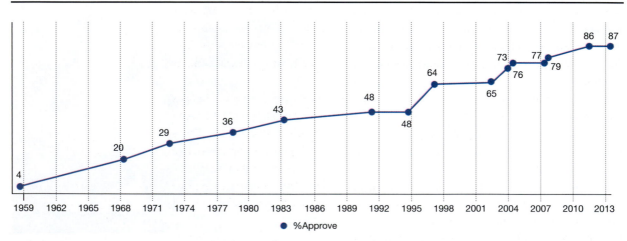

1958 wording: "...marriages between white and colored people"
1968-78 wording: "...marriages between whites and nonwhites"

Support for interracial marriage has increased steadily over the years.

as sixteen states. Mildred Loving (an African American woman) and Richard Perry Loving (a white man) were residents of Virginia and had gotten married in 1958 in the District of Columbia, having left Virginia to evade the Racial Integrity Act, a state law banning marriages between any white person and any nonwhite person. Upon their return to Virginia, they were charged with violation of the ban. They were caught sleeping in their bed by a group of police officers who invaded their home in hopes of finding them having sex. In their defense, Ms. Loving pointed to a marriage certificate on their bedroom wall. Rather than defending them, it became evidence the police needed for a criminal charge, for according to Virginia code, interracial couples were prohibited from marrying out of state and then returning to Virginia. Miscegenation was a felony, punishable by a prison sentence of between one and five years. The Lovings were sentenced to one year in prison, with the sentence suspended on condition the couple leave Virginia. The Supreme Court ruled in their favor some eight years later, ending all race-based restrictions on marriage in U.S. law.

Married couple Mildred and Richard Loving embrace after the court, in a unanimous verdict, overturned Virginia's anti-miscegenation statute, which had resulted in the Lovings' arrests shortly after their 1958 marriage.

After the *Loving* decision, Americans began to marry across racial lines in record numbers. Interracial marriage increased tenfold between 1960 and 1990.[23] In 1960, there were only 55,000 black-white married couples (living mostly in the North, where interracial marriage was permitted). In 2000, there were over 331,000 black-white marriages. Similarly, between 1960 and 2000, Asian-white marriages increased from 49,000 to 579,000. There were fewer than 280,000 Hispanic-white married couples in 1970; in 2000 there were well over 1.5 million. Compared with whites and other nonwhite groups, American Indians have the highest rates of intermarriage. The majority of American Indians are married to non-Indians.[24]

Rates of interracial and interethnic marriage continue to grow. Opposite-sex interracial or interethnic married couple households grew by 28 percent between 2000 and 2010. Today, they constitute 9.5 percent of American households. Rates of opposite-sex interracial or interethnic marriage are highest in western and southwestern states, as well as Hawaii and Alaska.[25] Roughly 15 percent of new marriages in 2010 were between people with different racial or ethnic identities. As one study reported, "Among newlyweds in 2010, 9% of whites, 17% of blacks, 26% of Hispanics, and 28% of Asians married out."[26]

Same-sex couples actually have the highest rates of interracial unions. While almost one in ten different-sex married couples are in interracial unions, almost one in five (married and unmarried) same-sex couples are. In Hawaii, half of all same-sex couples are interracial; in California, roughly a third are.[27]

FIGURE 10.2 BLACK-WHITE MARRIAGES 1970–2010

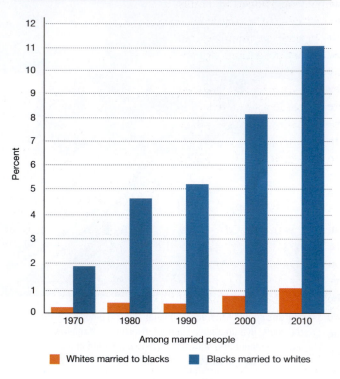

Among married people

■ Whites married to blacks ■ Blacks married to whites

Source: U.S. Census Bureau 2008 and 2010a.

A higher percentage of blacks are married to whites than whites to blacks, but interracial marriage among both groups is growing.

Today the United States is home to over 4.8 million interracially married couples; that's one in twelve. Men and women involved in interracial marriages have demonstrated that love does not respect racial divides. And as the familial landscape has shifted, so too have Americans' attitudes about marriage. In 1958, 96 percent of whites disapproved of interracial marriage; by 1997, that percentage had dropped to 33 percent.[28] A study published in 2012 found that two-thirds of Americans said it "would be fine" if a family member married outside his or her racial or ethnic group. Only one-third held this belief in 1986.[29]

RACE AND THE FAMILY TODAY

The family: so much could be said. Some of us attach words such as love, support, and safety to our family; others of us attach such words as pain, isolation, and violence. The family can be a refuge from the burdens of society, just as it can be a space where certain forms of domination thrive. Feminists long have drawn our attention to the hundreds of ways women are disadvantaged within the traditional family arrangement that places men at the helm. The sexual division of labor not only infiltrates the economic field, such that certain jobs (such as nurse and receptionist) are classified as female while others (such as firefighter and engineer) "belong" to males; it also structures family life, such that women are assigned the lion's share of the housework and child care. For women who work a paying job in addition to doing their housework and caring for their children, unpaid housework and childcare—work often not recognized as such—can amount to a "second shift." After the first shift ends at your job, your second shift begins at home, where you cook dinner, clean house, and take care of your children.[30]

If mainstream feminists have criticized patriarchy, women-of-color feminists have confronted the overlapping modes of oppression that affect them—in particular, the intersection between masculine and racial domination. Women-of-color feminists have chided mainstream civil rights leaders for at times silencing women's voices and ignoring their needs, just as they have criticized the mainstream feminist movement for assuming that the needs of white and nonwhite women are identical. The stereotypes that latch onto white women are different from those that latch onto Arab American, Asian American, Hispanic, Native American, and

African American women. And women of color face unique problems created by the overlapping systems of race and gender. For example, conditioned by family members and friends to put their needs below those of "the race," many women of color keep quiet about sexism or domestic violence in their communities out of fear of being labeled "race traitors" for speaking out against the actions of non-white men.[31]

We would do well to remember these points as we evaluate critically the ways in which race affects family life. We begin with a discussion of racial differences in marriage rates and then turn to the topics of interracial relationships and mixed marriages, then to divorce. Last, we explore the racialized aspects of out-of-wedlock births and single motherhood, focusing in particular on the hardships of raising a child alone.

Explaining Racial Differences in Marriage Rates

The United States has one of the highest marriage rates in the world, ranking fifteenth overall.[32] For many Americans, marriage brings stability, companionship, and social status, as well as economic perks that come from tax breaks and (for many) two incomes. But racial groups do not marry at similar rates. Some groups have strikingly low rates of marriage, and although rates of marriage have declined for all Americans over the last forty years, some racial groups have experienced more significant declines than others. In 1975, over 60 percent of white women between the ages of twenty and twenty-four were married; by 1998, that percentage had fallen to 32 percent. Similarly, almost 50 percent of black women that same age were married in 1975, but only 15 percent were in 1998. There were virtually no racial differences in marriage rates between 1880 and 1950. During those seventy years, roughly 60 percent of women from all racial and ethnic groups were married. After 1950, marriage rates declined for everyone, but the decline has been most dramatic for African American women, who between 1950 and 2010 experienced a 60 percent decline in the proportion of woman married.[33] Today, black women are least likely to marry, compared with other groups. Some analysts estimate that only one in three will marry in their lifetime. At the opposite end of the spectrum are Asian American women, who have the highest marriage rates. In 2010, only 26 percent of black women were married, compared with 42 percent of Hispanic women, 50 percent of white women, and 56 percent of Asian American women.[34] How do we make sense of these drastic differences? Why do such a large proportion of African Americans today never marry?

FIGURE 10.3 FIRST MARRIAGES PER 1,000 NEVER-MARRIED WOMEN, 2010

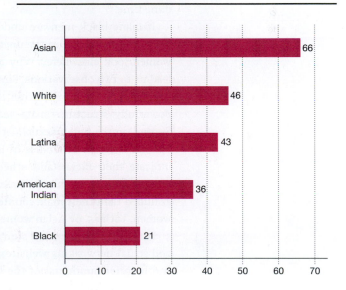

Do our answers lie in the fact that certain groups are more likely to cohabitate, that is, to live together as committed romantic partners but not as husband and wife? Cohabitation between heterosexual couples has risen steadily in recent years, so much so, in fact, that today the majority of marriages begin as cohabitating relationships. However, there are virtually no racial differences in cohabitation rates.[35] Our answers lie elsewhere.

Let's begin by thinking about the labor market, which is structured in such a way as to advantage Hispanics and disadvantage African Americans with respect to marriage. Although roughly the same proportion of Hispanics and blacks live below the poverty line, Hispanic men (including recent immigrants) are employed at much higher rates than black men (for reasons discussed in Chapter 4). Because a man with stable employment is a much better "catch" than one without a job, Hispanic men are advantaged when it comes to marriage relative to black men.[36] Indeed, a number of scholars have documented how the disappearance of stable employment opportunities from the inner city has resulted in the growth of a population of black men who are not "marriage material." For William Julius Wilson, job flight has created "a long-term decline in the proportion of black men, and particularly young black men, who are in a position to support a family."[37]

The black male marriage pool has been diminished even further by America's prison boom. Racial disparities in imprisonment, as we already have learned, are enormous. Black men are eight times more likely to be in prison than white men. In 2007, one in fifteen black men was behind bars, as was one in nine black men of marrying age (between twenty and thirty-four)![38] In poor black communities that are intensely policed, black women outnumber black men by sizable margins. In one such neighborhood in Washington, D.C., for example, there are only sixty-two men for every 100 women. And once they are released, many men with criminal records do not reenter the marriage pool since many women, concerned about their reputations and husband's job prospects, do not want to marry someone who has done time.[39]

If many black men are underrepresented in the "marriage pool" because they are overrepresented on the unemployment rolls or in prison, then why don't black women look elsewhere? Why don't they marry nonblack men? These questions lead us to two observations. First, although interracial marriage is on the rise, most Americans still marry within their own racial or ethnic group. Racial homophily powerfully structures mate-searching behavior, especially among heterosexuals. Second, in the heterosexual dating and marriage game, many black women are left behind. A series of studies of Internet dating, for example, in which daters could indicate their racial (and other) preferences and exclude members of particular groups, found that "black women are the only female minority group who are more excluded than their male counterparts. They are also far more excluded than white women, Latinas, or Asian women."[40]

For example, in a recent study drawing on data from one of the largest U.S. dating and social networking websites, Ken-Hou Lin of the University of Texas–Austin and Jennifer Lundquist of the University of Massachusetts–Amherst found that race matters when it comes to responding to requests from users of the dating interface.[41] Women tend to respond only to requests from men of a similar or more dominant racial status. White women tend to respond only to requests from white men, Hispanic women from Hispanic and white men, and so forth. Nonblack men are not so rigid in their responses except when it comes to black women. Neither white, Asian American, nor Hispanic men respond regularly to requests from black women. Significantly, the researchers found that socioeconomic differences, like education, do not explain away the race effect. "White men and white women with a college degree," they wrote, "are more likely to contact and to respond to white daters without a college degree than they are to black daters with a college degree."

This dating pattern has resulted in friction and resentment between black and nonblack women (particularly when the latter women remain completely oblivious to these dynamics), as well as between light-skinned and dark-skinned black women.[42] And it has made many black women feel utterly rejected. "You have to be a black black woman to really understand," one college student observed. "Like when the African-American students' group has a dance, all the men rush to dance with the light-skinned women. All of us black black women are left standing around, like leftovers."[43] Gloria Wade-Gayles, an African American scholar and critic, has put the matter this way: "We feel abandoned. We feel abandoned because we have been abandoned in so many ways, by so many people, and for so many centuries. We are the group of women furthest removed from the concept of beauty and femininity which invades every spot on the planet, and, as a result, we are taught not to like ourselves. . . . The truth is we experience a pain unique to us as a group when black men marry white women and even when they don't. It is a pain our mothers knew and their mothers before them."[44]

FIGURE 10.4 ONLINE DATING RESPONSES, BY RACE

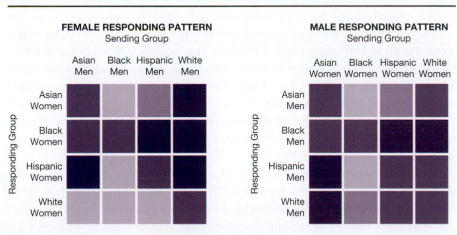

Studies of online dating websites show that race is a more important determinant of romantic preferences than education or other key factors. Men and women responded most frequently to requests from people of a similar or dominant racial status (dark purple in the grids above). People with the lowest response rates are light purple.

Interracial Marriage

Many consider interracial marriage a barometer for racial progress and social integration. Although interracial marriage has increased over the years, as we pointed out earlier, it still accounts for only a small fraction of all U.S. marriages. And there are considerable differences in interracial marriage across racial boundaries. Let us ponder again that, "among newlyweds in 2010, 9% of whites, 17% of blacks, 26% of Hispanics and 28% of Asians married out."[45] While whites are the least likely group to intermarry, Native Americans are the most likely, with nearly 60 percent of all Native Americans married to non-Indians. After Native Americans, Asian Americans are the most likely to intermarry, then Hispanics, then African Americans. Additionally, there are noticeable gender differences for interracial marriage rates, especially for blacks and Asian Americans. "About 24% of all black male newlyweds in 2010 married outside their race, compared with just 9% of black female newlyweds. Among Asians, the gender pattern runs the other way. About 36% of Asian female newlyweds married outside their race in 2010, compared with just 17% of Asian male newlyweds."[46]

There are countless reasons why people traverse racial borders to marry, including the simplest and most powerful explanation of all: they found someone to love. But some interracial relationships are driven more by a negative dynamic than by a positive one. That is, some people form an aversion to dating and marrying within their race. We already have seen how this applies to some black men. Some women and men raised in immigrant families with a domineering father or mother, too, might seek a partner outside their racial or ethnic group so as not to revisit the problems of their parents' marriage. For example, heterosexual Asian American women often look for non-Asian partners because they believe many Asian men are sexist. The study of Internet daters mentioned above found that Asian women were conspicuous among all groups for their preference to date outside their racial category—that is, to exclude Asian men as potential dates. Asian males were highly excluded by all groups, including Asian women.[47] Similarly, some Asian American men refuse to date Asian women because they want to break away from the traditional "Asian family" mold. Importantly, each also may find the other unattractive. When researchers in a different study interviewed Asian American women and men in interracial marriages, they found that "women reported they found Asian-American men physically unattractive, conservative, and boring. . . . Male interviewees complained that Asian-American women were workaholics and too serious about relationships. They claimed that [these] women weren't vivacious and were too laden with Asian baggage."[48]

"I'm all for interracial marriage, but what about the children?" This question comes up time and again in discussions of mixed-raced unions. In fact, most Americans who disapprove of interracial marriage cite "concerns for children produced by those unions" as one of the primary justifications for their disapproval.[49] Do biracial children have it harder than children from intraracial couples? Not necessarily. As Ronne Hartfield writes in *Another Way Home*, the popular notion of "confused and troubled" biracial children overlooks "stories about the ordinary lives of the vast number of people of color who have occupied the zone of mixed race with ease and sanity for several generations."[50] It certainly is true that some biracial individuals wrestle with racial identity issues as they transition into adulthood, but psychological research leads us to conclude that their struggles are not worse or more complicated than those faced by other nonwhites whose parents share a racial identity.[51] Plus, if young biracial adults do have a hard time coming to terms with their racial makeup, what needs to change, interracial marriage patterns or the system of racial domination that is the root source of their anguish?

Some biracial and multiracial women and men have grown justifiably tired of people assuming they are confused because of being half this and part that.[52] One biracial student named Kimberly uses humor to shine light on the assumptions that buttress this train of thought: "People come up to me and they'll say, 'Do you get confused between being black and white?' I say, 'Well, yeah, you know some mornings I wake up with this craving for fried chicken, and other mornings I just can't get the beat.'" Kimberly goes on to explain her retort, saying, "I want them to see how narrow-minded they're being. What do you think? One day I like fried

FIGURE 10.5 U.S. MULTIRACIAL POPULATION MAP

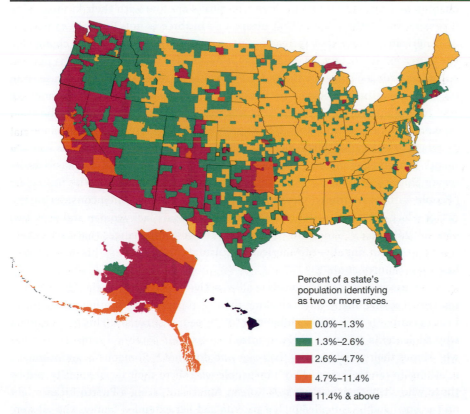

Percent of a state's population identifying as two or more races.

- 0.0%–1.3%
- 1.3%–2.6%
- 2.6%–4.7%
- 4.7%–11.4%
- 11.4% & above

Individuals claiming multiracial heritage are growing in number, especially in Hawaii, the West, and Southwest.

chicken, and the next I don't? It's not like that."[53] In other words, the idea that biracial and multiracial people are doomed to a life of ethnic confusion assumes it is more "natural" to belong to only one race and that one's actions and lifestyle are dictated completely by one's racial identity.[54] Neither of these assumptions holds water.

What is more, people like Kimberly, those who claim multiracial heritage, are growing in number. As we mentioned in Chapter 2, one in twenty people under the age of eighteen claims multiracial heritage.[55] Such projections have led to another popular question in conversations about interracial marriage: "If we all are multiracial, is racism on its way out?" Unfortunately, things are not so simple, and there is little evidence that racism can be bred out of our society.

First, there is nothing new about interracial unions and multiracial people. Recall that interracial sex and multiracial offspring were common during colonial times and slavery. No one would argue that those were eras of racial harmony. Second, racism can shape-shift and adjust to demographic changes. It can make—and has made—room in its wide enterprise for degrading multiracial people. Consider the long list of mean epithets reserved for them: from half-breed, zebra, banana, and coconut to sellout, race traitor, and wannabe. Third, interracial marriage is far from universally accepted in the United States. Earlier in this chapter we learned that two in three Americans are fine with their kin marrying across racial or ethnic lines. That means one in three is not. Roughly 43 percent of Americans believe that increasing interracial marriage has been a change for the better in our society, 44 percent say it has made no difference, and 11 percent say it has been a change for the worse.[56] Until 2000, Alabama did not erase from its state constitution (legally nonbinding but symbolically powerful) language prohibiting interracial marriage. When it did, 40 percent of voters in the state objected.[57] And prior to a 2015 U.S. Supreme Court decision declaring same-sex marriage to be a right, thirty-one states had added to their constitutions amendments banning gay marriage. After New York City elected Bill de Blasio as its mayor in 2013, *Washington Post* editorialist Richard Cohen wrote the following: "People with conventional views must repress a gag reflex when considering the mayor-elect of New York—a white man married to a black woman and with two biracial children. . . . This family represents the cultural changes that have enveloped parts—but not all—of America. To cultural conservatives, this doesn't look like their country at all."[58]

Some parents, white and nonwhite alike, actively discourage their children from interracial dating, many times cloaking their own prejudices or ethnic chauvinism in a concern over mixed-race children or "other people's" racism. This helps explain why adolescents are more likely to introduce to their parents a romantic partner who shares their racial identity than one who does not.[59] Someone in an interracial relationship can feel rejected both by people who share their racial identity and by those who share their partner's. A Korean American dating a Puerto Rican might on the one hand be ridiculed by her parents and her extended family, who all were hoping she'd meet a "nice Korean boy," and on the other hand feel awkward and out of place around her boyfriend's Puerto Rican friends and family.

Doing the (Racial) Work

Given this hostile climate, it is not surprising that psychologists have documented an association between interracial relationships and high levels of distress, finding, in particular, that Native Americans, white women married to nonwhite men, and Hispanics with nonwhite (but non-Hispanic) spouses have elevated levels of stress and anxiety.[60] What, then, is needed to make an interracial relationship last? If you desire a fulfilling interracial relationship, then, simply, you must be willing to *do the work*. Interracial relationships require each person to engage in a fair amount of cultural labor. If you want to grow more intimate with your Jewish partner, you should learn about Jewish history and culture. If you are dating a Mexican American whose family speaks Spanish at home, then, in the interest of growing closer to your partner and her or his family, you should take Spanish lessons. If you desire to grow closer to a second-generation Arab American, you should make the effort to learn more about where his relatives migrated from—their country's history, culture, and mores—but do so respectfully and with humility. If you are getting serious with a white person, you should strive to get in touch with her or his white identity. Cultural labor requires broadening your cultural competence, stepping out of your comfort zone, and trying as much as possible to adopt another perspective on the world.

Some whites never experience being victimized by interpersonal and institutional racism until they begin dating a nonwhite person. Sociologist Heather Dalmage, a white woman married to a black man, explains her experiences: "As an interracially married woman, my experiences are vastly different from other white women. Things like being seated in the back of restaurants, being denied loans, being steered out of white neighborhoods when we search for housing, being pulled over for no reason, and facing hostility from racist whites are experiences most whites never contend with. Because of my experiences, I no longer take white privilege for granted, and in some cases I am no longer seen as a white by other whites."[61] Dalmage has been treated to a first-rate education in racism through her marriage. And in order fully to understand her husband—let alone the world in which she herself lives—she has had to do the (racial) work, to divest her white privilege and to come to expect unfair treatment.

We cannot overemphasize the importance of cultural labor. It is a principle that applies to any meaningful relationship that traverses racial boundaries—not only romances and marriages but also friendships and professional associations. It applies as well to parents raising biracial or adopted children whose racial identities differ from their own. A white woman who adopts a black baby, for example, must learn how to braid and style black hair; she must learn to provide her child with tools to defend herself from racial slights; she must know what to do when the child comes home crying after being called "dirty"; she must be vigilant about her whiteness.[62] This mother, in short, must do some serious cultural labor, learning and relearning. But then again, in our multiracial society, one that grows more diverse by the day, aren't we all required to do the (racial) work? Isn't it rather unacceptable—not to mention thoroughly unpatriotic—to walk through life unaffected by other people's histories and hardships, their joys and jokes and experiences?

"We are learning," as Jane Addams once said, "that a standard of social ethics is not attained by travelling a sequestered byway, but by mixing on the thronged and common road where all must turn out for one another, and at least see the size of one another's burden."[63] We heartily agree. And we wager that many of you would agree as well.

Divorce

If the United States has a fairly high marriage rate, it has an enormously high divorce rate, ranking second only to Aruba in the number of divorces per 1,000 people.[64] Divorce rates have risen since the 1970s, but like marriage rates, they fluctuate widely across race. Immigrant families, for one, experience relatively high levels of divorce. Characterized by change and adjustment, immigrant families are a blending of the old and the new, an amalgamation of influences rooted in both the sending country and the receiving nation. Oftentimes, these families' very definition of what constitutes a "family" must bend to U.S. law and custom. For example, social service agencies narrow Hmong immigrants' notions of a family from extended kin networks of aunts, uncles, cousins, and grandparents to the nuclear family model.[65] And many immigrant parents are surprised and angered by the fact that in America they are not allowed to discipline their children "with the rod," a fact that immigrant children learn quickly. In her research on West African immigrants, sociologist Mary Waters found that these parents "believe that physical punishment is the best way to deal with a child who has misbehaved. They are shocked that this is unacceptable in the United States and consistently told us that it was one of the most disturbing aspects of living [here]."[66]

The biggest threat to the immigrant family is the process of immigration itself. In the majority of cases, immigrant families migrate in bits and spurts. Sometimes one parent migrates first, under an occupational visa, sending for her children and spouse later. Other times, children go ahead of their parents to live with relatives or friends, or to attend a boarding school, their parents following when they are able. One recent study found that 85 percent of immigrant youth are separated from one or both of their parents during the immigration process.[67] A family that begins to immigrate to the United States may not be reunited for years.[68] And when families do reconnect, ties between spouses may have frayed in transit. They may become weaker still when parents, forced to find jobs in the immigrant labor market, begin working long hours for meager pay. The immigrant process—demanding, fracturing, all-consuming—unravels a good number of families.

African American marriages are twice as likely to end in divorce as those of whites and native-born Mexican Americans.[69] Why? Again, a significant part of the answer lies in the fact that African Americans disproportionately are incarcerated and impoverished. Incarceration greatly increases the risk of divorce, as does inner-city poverty.[70] As the sociological ethnographer Elliot Liebow explained in *Tally's Corner*, speaking of unemployed black men, "By itself, the plain fact of supporting one's wife and children defines the principal obligation of a husband [for these men]. . . . Few married men, however, do in fact support their families over sustained periods of time. Money is chronically in short supply and chronically a source of dissension in the home. . . . Thus, marriage is an occasion of failure. To stay married is to live with your failure, to be confronted by it day in and day out. It is to live in a world whose standards of manliness are forever beyond one's reach, where one is continuously tested and challenged and continuously found wanting."[71]

If financial hardship and imprisonment can wreak havoc on a marriage, so too can high levels of spousal dissimilarity. Opposites might attract, but many do not stay married. Social scientists have argued that couples with high levels of incompatibility with respect to socioeconomic differences, conflicting views on gender roles, different degrees of educational attainment, and a large age gap are at higher risk of divorce. And studies have shown that black couples exhibit greater spousal dissimilarity than nonblack couples in these key areas.[72] One reason for this is the small African American marriage pool we discussed earlier: the fewer the choices of potential mates, the greater the chances of incompatibility. Another reason is the historically conditioned incongruence between the ways in which black men and women understand gender roles, an incongruence whose genesis is located in the destruction of the black family under slavery.

Added to poverty, incarceration, and spousal dissimilarity is yet another explanation for the high black divorce rate: the psychological strain of racism. Here is an analogy: A soldier is ordered to leave his family to be deployed in a war zone. Once there, he sees terrible things, does terrible things, and has terrible things done to him. He then returns home to his family, changed. War transformed that marriage from a stable union to a tragically unstable one. Divorce, once considered something that happens to other people, seems imminent. Now consider a black couple. Over the years they collect war stories of their own: job discrimination, police harassment, working but never getting ahead, sending their children to rundown schools, everyday cuts because of their skin color—a slight here, a denied opportunity there. Things add up, as numerous studies that have documented the psychological costs of racism attest.[73] These psychological costs can harm a marriage.

Out-of-Wedlock Births

Relative to other major industrialized countries, the United States ranks near the middle when it comes to the proportion of out-of-wedlock births. Countries such as Iceland, Sweden, Norway, Britain, and France have higher percentages of babies born outside of wedlock than countries like Canada, Ireland, Portugal, Greece, and Japan.[74] Since 1995, one in three babies has been born to an unmarried mother in the United States (in 1950, the rate was one in twenty).[75] In 2011, out-of-wedlock births accounted for 41 percent of all births in the United States.[76] Out-of-wedlock births steadily have increased over the last few decades. In fact, the number of American children living in single-parent homes nearly doubled between 1960 and 2010. In 1970, only 12 percent of all children lived with one parent; in 2000, 25 percent of children did.[77] Today, a third of all American children are not being raised by two parents, the majority of whom live in single-mother households.[78]

At least since the presidency of Ronald Reagan, single mothers have been stereotyped as immoral delinquents who have more children in order to collect bigger welfare checks. (Absent fathers, however, are mentioned less frequently, a silence that assumes single mothers somehow acted alone in the creation of their babies.) But the truth is that single mothers are "a remarkably diverse group who have arrived at single parenthood through divergent, and often class-segregated paths."[79]

According to one study, most single mothers are in their early twenties (11 percent are under age eighteen); most are poor and have very little education (over 30 percent lack a high school diploma); and, in most cases, the mother and father are in a committed relationship at the time of the birth, although many separate afterward.[80] Racial differences in out-of-wedlock births are considerable and well documented. With 67 percent of births occurring outside of marriage, African Americans have the highest rate of out-of-wedlock births—and by a wide margin. Forty-one percent of Hispanic births occur outside marriage, as do 26 percent of white births. At 11 percent, Asian Americans have the lowest rate of out-of-wedlock births.[81] The majority of white mothers are married (13 percent are single and 12 percent are cohabitating); for black mothers, the pattern is reversed: most are single. Eighty-nine percent of all teenage births occur outside of marriage. One in seven American women will give birth before her twentieth birthday. Teenage mothers—the majority of whom give birth when they are eighteen or older—constitute 10 percent of all white adolescent women (ages fifteen through nineteen), 21 percent of black adolescent women, and 24 percent of Hispanic adolescent women.[82]

What is going on? Before getting to that, let us say a brief word about the statistic that nearly 70 percent of black children are born outside of marriage. This statistic has been used by people—both within and outside the black community—to make claims about the moral character of black America today. On

FIGURE 10.6 TRENDS IN TEENAGE BIRTH RATES BY RACE, 1990–2012

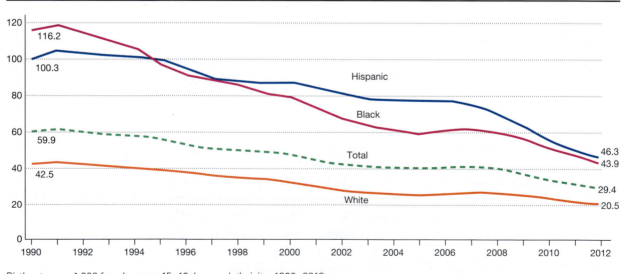

Birth rates per 1,000 females ages 15–19, by race/ethnicity, 1990–2012.

Source: National Center for Health Statistics

The O'Reilly Factor, Fox News contributor Bernie Goldberg said the out-of-wedlock birthrate among African Americans is "embarrassing," continuing, "In the entire recorded history of the planet, there has never been a greater voluntary abandonment of men from their children than there is today in black America."[83] Whether you ascribe to this position or not, understanding should preempt interpretation, so let's recognize two things about the out-of-wedlock births statistic. First, while the number of unmarried black women has climbed over the years, the birthrate among unmarried black women has plummeted. In fact, today, the birthrate for unmarried black women is the lowest it has been in forty years. Many black women are choosing not to marry, but many of those unmarried women also are choosing not to have children or to have fewer of them. Second, the rate of out-of-wedlock births among African Americans is driven by unmarried *and* married births: out-of-wedlock birthrate = unmarried births / (unmarried + married births). This means that the rate will get bigger if increasing numbers of *married* African Americans chose not to have children. This is exactly what has happened. The birthrate for married black women has fallen dramatically since 1980, dropping at a faster rate than the birthrate for unmarried black women. Observing these trends, Ta-Nehisi Coates has said, "Whereas at one point married black women were having more kids than married white women, they are now having less.... People who are truly concerned about the percentage of out-of-wedlock births would do well to hector married black women for moral duty to churn out babies in the manner of their glorious foremothers. But no one would do that. Because it would be absurd."[84]

FIGURE 10.7 BIRTHRATE FOR BLACK AND WHITE UNMARRIED WOMEN, 1969–2009

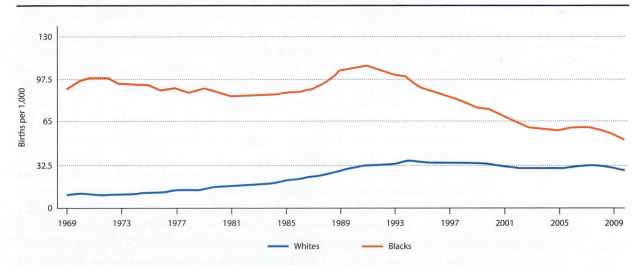

The birth rate for unmarried African American women has declined since the 1990s.

Source: National Center for Health Statistics

That said, what are the causes of racial discrepancies in single-mother house-holds? Once again, two of America's most powerful racial institutions—the economy and the prison—have something to do with it. For all racial groups, "the prevalence of fatherhood among prisoners is almost identical to that on the outside." The consequence is that groups imprisoned at higher rates—Latinos and especially blacks—also will have larger numbers of children with incarcerated fathers. Nationwide, 3 percent of children are in this position. A little over 1 percent of white children have incarcerated dads; for Latino children, the percentage is 3.5 percent. But *one in eleven* black children—over a million children—has a father behind bars.[85] By extracting the father from the home and community, imprisonment plays a large role in creating single-mother households.

Others have linked out-of-wedlock births to poverty, which is disproportionately experienced by blacks and Hispanics. States with more poverty have more out-of-wedlock births. Combining the percentage of women without a high school degree in a state with its median income explains 67 percent of the variation in out-of-wedlock births among states.[86] However, as we have repeated throughout this chapter, racialized economic inequalities cannot fully explain why nonwhite women, especially black women, are so much more likely to have children outside of marriage than are Asian Americans or whites. "Most of the world's peoples are poor, far poorer than Afro-Americans, but do not experience the marital and familial problems that Afro-Americans do," writes Patterson. "Millions of chronically unemployed men live on the verge of starvation, in urban squalor all over Asia and Latin America, without abandoning their wives and children. In America itself, the three-quarters of a century of urban semighetto poverty experienced by the postfamine Irish, and the present condition of the Latino minority[,] . . . have not resulted in men's massive abandonment of their wives and children."[87] Other answers to our question lurk, ones having to do with racial differences in attitudes toward sex and childbearing.

One answer highlights the sexual strategies of some poor black men, namely, their practice of impregnating multiple women over their lifetimes. Seventeen percent of fathers have multiple children with different women, and black men account for a disproportionate number of those children. One-third of black fathers have had children by two or more women, relative to 16 percent of Latino fathers and 5 percent of white fathers.[88] If a man has children by more than one woman, then at least one of those women is raising the child alone or with a stepparent. Indeed, research has suggested that some men who have children by different women spend very little time with any of their children.[89]

The special value some groups place on motherhood is another explanation for racial differences in out-of-wedlock birthrates. "In the ghetto," observes American sociologist Kenneth Clark, "the meaning of the illegitimate child is not ultimate disgrace. There is not a demand for abortion or for surrender of the child that one finds in more privileged communities. In the middle class, the disgrace of illegitimacy is tied to person and family aspirations. In lower-class families, however, the girl loses only some of her already limited options by having an illegitimate child; she is not going to make a 'better marriage' or improve her economic and social status either way. On the contrary, a child is symbolic of the fact that she is a woman, and she may gain from having something of her own. Nor is the boy who fathers an illegitimate child going to lose, for where is he going? The path to any higher status seems closed to him in any case."[90]

Sociologists Kathryn Edin and Maria Kefalas interviewed over 160 young, urban, and poor single mothers to understand why so many remain unmarried after having children and why they decide to have children even when caring for them may require living hand to mouth. They found that single mothers do not devalue or scorn marriage. On the contrary, they revere it, so much so, in fact, that they refuse to trade vows until they are certain the marriage will last. "The poor women we talked to," Edin and Kefalas write in *Promises I Can Keep: Why Poor Women Put Motherhood before Marriage*, "insist [that marriage] means lifelong commitment. In a surprising reversal of the middle-class norm, they believe it is better to have children outside of marriage than to marry unwisely only to get divorced later."[91] If these single mothers value a stable marriage but in the end conclude it is too risky—because their child's father, who once wooed them with the line "I want to have a baby with you," now cannot find a job, goes to prison, abuses drugs, or blows his monthly paycheck on stereo equipment—they view parenthood as a "promise they can keep." These women "seldom view out-of-wedlock birth as a mark of personal failure, but instead see it as an act of valor."[92] They understand childbearing as a central part of their womanhood and their worth. Edin and Kefalas sum up their main argument: "While the poor women we interviewed saw marriage as a luxury, something they aspired to but feared they might never achieve, they judged children to be a necessity, an absolutely essential part of a young woman's life, the chief source of identity and meaning."[93]

"[Many poor single mothers must] choose between a welfare system that [pays] far too little to provide for their basic needs and a labor market that [offers] them little more than they could have gotten by staying home." —Kathryn Edin and Laura Lein

The Consequences of Single Motherhood

The major consequences of single motherhood are many. Out-of-wedlock pregnancy decreases teenage women's chances of graduating from high school as well as their likelihood of marrying in the future. And children raised by single mothers, despite their mothers' best efforts, are disadvantaged in a number of ways. They are less likely to be healthy, more likely to have children in their teens, and, when they get older, more likely to have trouble finding steady employment. Children from single-parent households also are more likely to acquire behavioral and psychological problems, to do worse in school, and not to go to college than their peers raised by both biological parents.[94]

Many—but certainly not all—of these negative consequences stem not from the one-parent family structure per se, but from the economic disadvantage that accompanies marital disruption and single motherhood. In 2003, only 64 percent of custodial mothers possessed a child support order, and of those, only 45 percent received the full amount they were due.[95] It is estimated that over 90 percent of poor noncustodial fathers pay no formal child support. Fathers who contribute little to nothing, low earnings, poor employment status, a lack of affordable childcare, meager public assistance programs, and low levels of wealth result in single-mother families ranking below all other major demographic groups on the economic ladder.[96] Children of single mothers are five times more likely to live below the poverty line than those raised by married parents. Sociologists have referred to the swelling ranks of single mothers among the poor—the fact that increasing numbers live "one sick child away from destitution"—as the feminization of poverty.[97]

Some low-income single mothers rely on welfare to get by. But since 1996, when President Bill Clinton reformed welfare, elected as he was on the promise that he would "end welfare as we know it," the number of poor Americans who receive welfare has fallen dramatically. Cash assistance caseloads have fallen from 12.3 million recipients per month in 1996 to 4.5 million in 2011. Today, only one in ten adults living below the poverty line receives cash assistance in the form of welfare.[98] By contrast, some federal programs have grown substantially over the last two decades, namely, the Earned Income Tax Credit and the Supplemental Nutrition Assistance Program (colloquially: food stamps). Large-scale changes in federal poverty policy have created new winners and losers. Some low-income families now fare much better; others fare much worse.

FIGURE 10.8 **PERCENTAGE OF U.S. POPULATION IN POVERTY, 1960–2011, BY FAMILY TYPE**

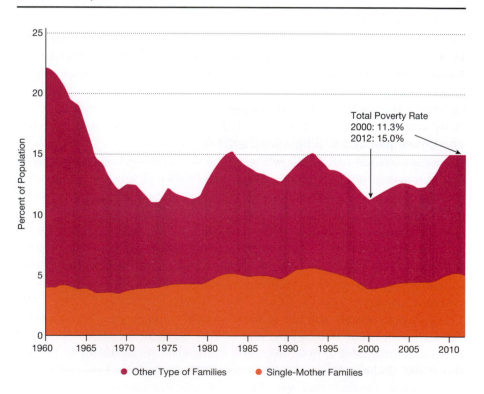

To the extent that they have a choice, single mothers choosing between welfare and work can find themselves between a rock and a hard place. Theirs is a choice between "a welfare system that [pays] far too little to provide for their basic needs and a labor market that [offers] them little more than they could have gotten by staying home."[99] Because most single parents lack the wherewithal to pay for educational expenses (such as private tutoring, textbooks, computers, college tuition, and so forth), their children play with a handicap in school and, by extension, in the labor market. Recognizing the severity of single mothers' financial situations, researchers have shown that the negative effect on children's life chances of living with a single mother declines significantly when income is held constant.[100]

THE SELF AND IDENTITY FORMATION

Finally, we arrive at a discussion of the self. With this section on the most intimate of all sociological topics—your identity and psychology, your emotions and innermost thoughts—we bring our survey of racial life in America to a close. We start with a discussion of common misunderstandings that occur during interracial communication, misunderstandings that push us farther apart. We then examine variations in racial identity, moving from an examination of the interaction order to an analysis of the complexities of intersectionality. We conclude by interrogating the idea of "racial authenticity," of being true to one's ethnic or racial heritage, including in that discussion the choice of some whites to reject whiteness for an alternative ethnic identity.

Interaction Troubles

The interaction order is the face-to-face domain of social life, the mezzanine level between large-scale structure and individual psychology. In this domain we find transactions between two or more persons and all those performances—breathing, standing, laughing, lying, blowing one's nose—that constitute the daily work of impression management. Here the object of study is verbal and nonverbal communication—what one "gives" and "gives off." As Erving Goffman, sociologist par excellence of the interaction order, put it, "The ultimate behavioral materials are the glances, gestures, positionings, and verbal statements that people continuously feed into the situation, whether intended or not."[101] For Goffman, the self is best described as an arrangement of social performances, the face you present to different audiences at different times.[102]

Goffman drew many parallels between society and the stage (which is why his brand of social science has been termed the dramaturgical approach). In life, there is a front stage and a back stage. The bustling restaurant kitchen, where the five-course meal is prepared among yelling chefs, banging knives, and clanging dishes, is the back stage; the quiet dining room, where waiters interact solemnly with well-dressed guests, is the front. Your own classroom, where you have adopted a certain kind of performance to impress your professor or peers, is the front stage; your dorm room, where you tell your best friend what you "really think"—or, for that matter, the hallway right outside the classroom door—is the back stage.

When it comes to the drama of race, the distinction between front stage and back stage tends to be much more distinct and clear for people of color than for whites. To put it another way, in most of life the front and back stages are almost one for whites when it comes to their racial practices. Because whiteness is the dominant and "normal" racial category in all of society's fields of life, whites need not be reflexive about their whiteness to get ahead in the world. They need not "check their whiteness at the door" to move up the corporate ladder or to excel in school. The same cannot be said for people of color. Most of the time, whites do not need to know terribly much about nonwhites to navigate society, but non-whites must know about whites to do so. "Of them," wrote Du Bois, "I am singularly clairvoyant."[103] Accordingly, many nonwhites, operating with a double vision, a double consciousness, have developed racial survival strategies to navigate white America. One strategy is "testing," the act of "feeling out" members of other racial or ethnic groups to evaluate their level of racial tolerance and understanding. Because of America's legacy of racial domination, some nonwhites are distrustful of whites—and have their guard up around whites until they are confident they are trustworthy or "down with the cause." That is, they might "wear a mask" (another survival strategy) around those who have not yet earned their confidence. An ambitious middle-class African American working in a majority white law firm, for example, might attempt to put as much distance between her and her blackness as possible. Of African Americans who join whites at the table of economic or political privilege, Patricia Williams once observed, "You need two chairs at the table, one for you, one for your blackness."[104]

Because many nonwhites think explicitly about their behaviors in these terms and because many whites do not—they do not say to themselves several times a day, "I'm white, and they're not, so I'd better do it this way"—misunderstandings are bound to happen. Consider the way we greet one another. Sociologists who study the minutiae of everyday life have demonstrated that whites and blacks engage in different greeting styles. When a white person goes to meet another, the white person usually looks to categorize the other according to their social roles. Accordingly, a white person might ask, "Where are you from? What do you do? What is your major? How old are you?" African Americans, in contrast, prefer greetings that talk about the "here and now." They like to discuss public settings that any person can clearly see and talk about. And instead of petitioning for information directly, they go fishing for it. They hint that information is desired—a practice known as "signifying"—by asking roundabout questions. For example, instead of asking, "How old are you?" an African American interlocutor might ask, "Did you just graduate from high school?"[105]

Whites find their own style of greeting natural and friendly, while some blacks see it as intrusive and prodding. They feel interrogated. In a similar way, blacks find their own greeting styles respectful and considerate of another's privacy, while some whites find it off-putting and avoidant. It leaves them cold. These innocent communication blips can easily provoke larger racial assumptions. A misfire in greeting strategies may lead whites to find blacks rude, ignorant, or prejudiced toward white people, and it may lead blacks to find whites nosy, invasive, and motivated by racial reasons ("Why do they want to know so much about me?"). These assumptions can slip into generalizations: "Black people are rude." "White people are pushy."[106]

Another common misunderstanding takes place on the job. When neither worker wants an extra work assignment, blacks are more likely to say "no" to the boss's face, while whites are more likely to say "yes" before going home and complaining about their boss to their roommates or spouses. Blacks may find whites' tendency to hide their true feelings from their supervisors dishonest—and might come to view whites as immoral and fake. Likewise, whites may interpret the way blacks turn down assignments as intimidating and offensive—and might come to view blacks as lazy and hard to handle.

Some whites find nonwhites, especially blacks and Hispanics, loud and confrontational. "They're always yelling at one another!" But many blacks and Hispanics have been taught that arguments should be handled "on the spot" and ideally settled before the conversation ends. Sometimes this requires a good deal of energy and movement, interrupting and shouting. Whites, by contrast, sometimes get nervous during a heated discussion, especially if it involves a nonwhite person; they often dread saying something offensive and being labeled a racist. They often view backing away as the diplomatic and polite thing to do.[107] Again, the tiniest things can lead to communication misfires and negative declarations about the racialized Other.

Sociologist Anne Rawls sums up the problem: although whites and nonwhites "appear to occupy the same world geographically, they rarely occupy the same interactional space. Furthermore, even today when they do more often jointly occupy interactional space, because their communities have developed in separation and their Interaction Order practices conflict, the display of moral behavior by members of one group may well look like deviant behavior to members of the other."[108] This can affect even the most critically minded and racially aware person. In his book *Race*, American journalist Studs Terkel recalls a conversation he had with a civil rights lawyer. The lawyer remembered a time when his white wife was driving through a black neighborhood: "The people at all the corners [were] all gesticulating at her. She was very frightened, quickly turned up the window and drove determinedly. She discovered, after several blocks, she was going the wrong way on a one-way street and they were trying to help her. Her assumption was that they were blacks and they were trying to get at her. Mind you, she's a very enlightened woman."[109]

Is cross-racial communication superficial at best, impossible at worst? No— *unequivocally no*. But we must do the (racial) work. Interracial and intercultural communication requires vigilant reflexivity. Instead of attributing some misunderstanding that occurs in a conversation across racial lines to some imaginary characteristics of the other group, we need to strive to extend others the benefit of the doubt. Above all, interracial communication demands a display of humility and respect, which encourages us to enter the conversation not with something to prove as much as with a desire to learn and understand.

Intersectional Identity

As we have mentioned throughout this book, your racial identity coincides with other aspects of yourself to produce a full, complex, intersectional identity. You are not "just Asian." You are also young, a student, Buddhist, a man, a brother, an urbanite, an English major, and so forth. Other aspects of your identity regulate your racial identity and vice versa. Consider the commingling of your racial identity and class background. One often hears people associate authentic blackness or Latino heritage with poverty, as if (to quote Frantz Fanon) "one is white above a certain financial level."[110] Ice Cube, for example, links "real blackness" to the ghetto in his song "True to the Game," which chastises a black suburbanite for "trying to be white or a Jew," and threatens to revoke his "ghetto pass" (that is, strip him of his blackness) if he doesn't return to the 'hood and "stop being an Uncle Tom."[111] Accordingly, some middle- and upper-class students of color, on rediscovering their cultural heritage during college, strive to downplay their class status and emphasize their race or ethnicity by, for example, learning Portuguese, growing an afro, studying the Koran, or joining a Native American coalition.[112]

Geography also is an important component of one's identity. Suburban whiteness contrasts sharply with rural whiteness, which in turn is quite different from urban whiteness. Whiteness fluctuates and shape-shifts as one moves across the country. The whiteness practiced in a Southern Louisiana town is very different than the whiteness found in San Francisco's gay-friendly Castro district. A white millionaire who made it big working as a CEO in Albuquerque most likely has a different understanding of her racial identity than one who made his money working as a pig farmer in Minnesota. Indeed, northern whites often fail to recognize their racism as racism precisely because they (still) understand racism to be a fundamentally southern phenomenon: the stuff of backwoods, rural "white trash." This dynamic predates the Civil War, when Northern whites chastised Southern whites for slavery but refused to welcome blacks into their own neighborhoods, schools, and churches.[113]

Your immigrant status, too, is an influential component of your racial or ethnic identity. A fourth-generation Mexican American most likely will have a different understanding of what it means to be Mexican than one who arrived in America just last year.[114] And within many ethnic communities, struggles take place between recent immigrants and native-born Americans. Some Asian Americans, for example, who all their lives have been treated as foreigners ("No, where are you *really* from?" "Gee, you speak good English!"), harbor anti–Asian immigrant sentiments. As sociologist Mia Tuan writes in *Forever Foreigners or Honorary Whites? The Asian Ethnic Experience Today*, some Asian Americans believe Asian immigrants fuel "the stereotypes that have contributed to their conditional status as 'honorary' but not 'legitimate' Americans." She continues, "After years of carefully cultivating good relations with their non-Asian neighbors, [Asian Americans find] themselves subject to the same hostilities as immigrants. In response, many [become] the harshest critics of the

Our identities our shaped by our race, gender, age, and other aspects of ourselves.

immigrants whom they [see] as spoiling what they had worked so hard to establish—a positive image."[115] Asian immigrants, for their part, respond by criticizing Asian Americans for being more "American" than "Asian" because, for example, they cannot speak Chinese or know little about Japanese traditions.

The intersection of race and gender is an especially powerful aspect of one's identity, one we have addressed throughout this book. Racial identity colors one's gender identity, and one's gender identity guides people's understandings of what it means to belong to a certain racial or ethnic group. Thus scholars have identified different racialized variants of masculinity, from the "cool pose" of many young black men and the machismo of some Latino men to the rural white masculinity of some "country boys."[116] Likewise, feminine identity is affected by one's racial or ethnic identity. In some communities, a "real" Chinese woman or a "real" Mexican woman takes care of the house and looks after

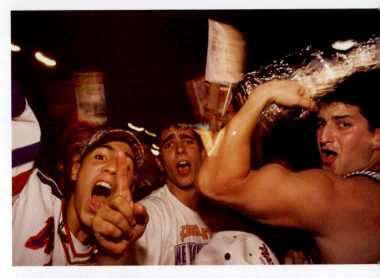

Doing race and masculinity, hockey fans celebrate their team winning the Stanley Cup.

the children. If these women do not fulfill these roles, they feel as if they are not living up to their ethnic obligations, a feeling enforced by some of their friends and family members. The racialization of Asian femininity is the dynamic behind skin-tone discrimination among some Asian Americans. That is, some Asian American women associate feminine beauty with whiteness and, accordingly, attempt to stay as white as possible. As a young Cambodian woman reflected, "My dad said one day, 'Don't wear shorts too much. You don't want to have dark legs, because no one will want to marry you.' . . . I get a lot of comments from older adults . . . like, 'Careful, you're getting so dark. You better stay out of the sun.'" Another put it even more succinctly: "Shun the sun! That's my sister's cry. Shun the sun!"[117]

"The borderlands dividing racial, ethnic, and national identities and communities constitute ethnosexual frontiers, erotic intersections that are heavily patrolled, policed, and protected, yet regularly are penetrated by individuals forging sexual links with ethnic 'others.'"[118] So writes sociologist Joane Nagel. When we examine the intersection between race and sexuality, we are struck by the observation that racial identity often is defined through certain sexual practices and performances. Immigrant families from India, for example, often construct young women's Indian sexuality explicitly by contrasting it with that of young white women. White women are depicted as feeble and promiscuous; Indian women are considered chaste, traditional, and strong.[119] And, as we already have seen, sexual fantasies—of the sexually predatory black man, the erotic Asian woman, the sexless Asian man, the pure white woman—can result in gross misrepresentations of certain racial groups and can fuel racial resentment and hatred.[120]

Studies have found that homophobia—heterosexist domination of lesbian and gay people, manifest at the institutional and interpersonal levels—is higher among African Americans and Hispanics than whites.[121] The result is that gays and lesbians of color suffer from a kind of double rejection: they are ostracized by the larger white society on account of their skin color and rejected from their racial or ethnic community on account of their sexuality.[122] Queering whitens. For many African American men, authentic black masculinity undeniably is straight. Thus Black Panther leader Eldridge Cleaver, author of *Soul on Ice*, was able to articulate forcefully the suffering caused by racial domination but was unable to grasp the unique pain experienced by gay blacks. He went so far as to call James Baldwin's homosexuality "somehow un-black"—and labeled interracial homosexual (as well as heterosexual) romantic unions a "racial death wish."[123] Black lesbians, too, often are viewed as "race traitors" and come out (of the closet) to their friends and family members only at great personal cost.[124]

Why do some heterosexual blacks understand homosexuality to be a fundamentally unblack or white phenomenon? Why is the black gay man or lesbian not simply shunned but bleached? Part of the answer lies in the fact that racial logics have sexual components, as we have been demonstrating. But another part is to be found in the historical record. "Among the myths Europeans have created about Africa," writes one historian, "the myth that homosexuality is absent or incidental is the oldest and most enduring. For Europeans, black Africans—of all the native peoples of the world—most epitomized 'primitive man.' Since primitive man is supposed to be close to nature, ruled by instinct, and culturally unsophisticated, he had to be heterosexual, his sexual energies and outlets demoted exclusively to their 'natural' purpose: biological reproduction. If black Africans were the most primitive people in all humanity . . . then they had to be the most heterosexual."[125] Thus, the idea that homosexuality is a white sexual practice is rooted in the colonialist enterprise and the transatlantic slave trade. The (black) notion that associates homosexuality with whiteness and the (white) notion that links hyper- (heterosexual) eroticism and promiscuity with blackness are two branches sprung from the same trunk.[126]

The prevalence of homophobia in some nonwhite communities leads to a larger issue: the tendency to focus on the disadvantaged components of your identity while paying little attention to the privileged ones. Many men of color talk about how they are victims of racial domination but rarely reflect on how they perpetuate sexism or homophobia. Many white lesbians fail to interrogate their white privilege because their attention is monopolized by the ways they are disadvantaged by homophobia. Middle-class women of color may be keen on the intersection of race and gender but ignore their own class privileges. Because privilege often is weightless to those who profit from it, you are most likely to select as the most important elements of your identity those that give you the most grief, downplaying your privileged memberships. Just as white people often fail to recognize their white privilege, nonwhite people can fail to recognize their heterosexual, gender, or class advantages. The result is that discussions of racism often have a male bias and discussions of sexism often have a white bias—the key point of the classic anthology *All the Women Are White, All the Blacks Are Men, but Some of Us Are Brave*.[127]

Racial Authenticity

For over 100 years now, sociologists have shown that your behavior is dictated in large part by your identity. If you identify as a Mormon, for example, you are likely to engage in a set of practices (for example, avoiding caffeine, abstaining from using foul language, going on dates with other Mormons) that align with that identity. The same is true of race.

Race is both marked and made. It is *marked* through America's racial taxonomy, which seeks to divide the nation into distinct categories. In this case, race imposes itself on you. It is *made* through hundreds and thousands of practices: gestures, sayings, tastes, ways of walking, religious convictions, opinions, and so forth. In this case, you perform race. Race as performance is "predicated on actions, on the things one does in the world, on how one behaves." As anthropologist John Jackson, Jr., notes, "You are not black because you are (in essence) black; you are black . . . because of how you act—and not just in terms of one field of behavior (say, intellectual achievement in school) but because of how you juggle and combine many differently racialized and class(ed) actions (walking, talking, laughing, watching a movie, standing, emoting, partying) in an everyday matrix of performative possibilities."[128] Because racial domination attaches to skin color, a dark-skinned person never can completely escape its clutches simply by acting "not black." But that person may choose one saying over another, one kind of clothing over another, one mode of interaction over another, because she believes such an action makes her more or less black. This is why we claim that race is both ascribed and achieved, both marked and made.[129]

Just as men often perform masculinity by professing their love of football and their contempt of ballet, we perform race and ethnicity through certain conscious and unconscious decisions. This includes speaking one's native tongue or melding English with other languages, as in the English and Spanish fusion heard in the Southwest or in the Yiddish-sprinkled English once commonly spoken in New York's Lower East Side. Some racial groups do race by staking out a virtual monopoly on certain words, ascriptions, and sayings—not to mention certain linguistic styles and bodily postures—which is why someone who does not identify as black is advised not to call a black man a "brotha" and absolutely is forbidden to call him a "nigga," even if these terms sometimes are employed with frequency and fraternity between African American friends. We perform ethnicity and race by celebrating certain holidays (for example, Kwanzaa, Juneteenth, St. Patrick's Day, Rosh Hashanah, Burns Night, or Chinese New Year) and by cultivating certain fashions (for instance, wearing dashikis, headwraps, Crucifix necklaces, burkas, kimonos, Norwegian sweaters, or kilts).[130] Those who assume that whiteness is not performed in the same way as blackness or Arabness continue to treat whiteness as the invisible norm and are only fooling themselves. Through fashion choices (think of Abercrombie and Fitch, J. Crew, or Lands' End), linguistic styles (think of Dave Chappell's impression of a white accent), and a constellation of many other racial behaviors, tastes, and practices, whiteness is executed.[131] Humor writer Christian

Frisbee sports are #110 on Christian Lander's satiric list, "Stuff White People Like."

Lander has compiled a list of "stuff white people like" that includes vintage goods, snowboarding, religions their parents don't belong to, organic food, indie music, irony, hating corporations, bumper stickers, and Frisbee sports.[132]

Such performances rely on a collection of recognizable cultural practices and beliefs that separate insiders from outsiders.[133] "We" are different from "them" because we listen to different music, eat different food, dress differently, and laugh at different jokes. A group's identity pivots on the notion of racial authenticity. Racial authenticity seeks to define the essence of Mexicanness or Arabness or whiteness by including or excluding certain behaviors from the repertoire that constitutes a group's aesthetic identity. Statements about how a "real Chinese woman" or a "real Puerto Rican man" or a "real Hmong child" should behave are statements about racial authenticity.

For many groups, racial authenticity often is bought with a pound of flesh; it is deeply tied to histories of suffering. Consider the connection between Jewish identity and the abstinence from pork. As anthropologist Mary Douglas observed, the pig is no more polluted in the Book of Leviticus than are other animals (for example, the camel and the rock badger), but the pig has come to be singled out among Jews as the filthiest of animals. Why? Because of the special historic role it has played in the humiliation and oppression of Jewish people. Greek conquerors blasphemed the God of Israel by immolating swine on Hebrew altars, and Jewish people were forced to eat pork to symbolize their submission. If they refused, and many did, they often were put to death in the most barbarous fashion. It was the Greek rulers, specifically Antiochus, who "forced into prominence the rule concerning pork as the critical symbol of group allegiance. . . . After such historic acts of heroism [on the part of those who refused to eat the flesh of swine], no wonder the avoidance of pork became a specially powerful symbol of allegiance for the Jewish people."[134] Douglas draws our attention to the intimate connection between the role of suffering in

A Jewish groom smashes the glass in his wedding ceremony, symbolizing the destruction of the Temple.

the history of a cultural practice (dietary restrictions) and the accumulation and preservation of a particular pedigree of ethnic identity (Jewish authenticity). The memory of persecution structures many other racial and ethnic practices as well, from an African American couple jumping over a broom on their wedding day (the act that solidified a union in slave times) to a Jewish groom smashing the glass in his wedding ceremony to symbolize the destruction of the Temple and thus to satisfy the Psalmist's call to "consider Jerusalem as your highest joy."

Within the African American community, there exists a cultural stock exchange of sorts, where what is being bartered and traded is black authenticity or "black sincerity," as one scholar prefers to call it.[135] We have already have alluded to the ways in which socioeconomic and sexual differences mark distinctions among blacks. Nationalism plays an important role here as well, one that allocates different amounts of black authenticity to persons of different national origins. While many blacks during the nineteenth century and even the Civil Rights Era welcomed into their ranks first- and second-generation African and Caribbean immigrants (one thinks of such black leaders as Marcus Garvey and Louis Farrakhan), today the entry fee into the field of blackness is descent not simply from slaves, but from *American* slaves. One sociologist refers to this as the "new black nativism," which, he claims, is directly responsible for "the growing tendency to define blackness in negative terms, [as] not white in upbringing, kinship, or manner."[136]

Or consider debates about who is a "real Indian." Faced with a deluge of claims to Indian identity that began in the 1960s and only increased with the advent of affirmative action programs, American Indians, more than any other group, have had to develop strict definitions of Indian authenticity to guard against "ethnic fraud." To many, true "Indianness" requires one to be frozen in time, to walk in lockstep with one's ancestors. An African American might lose some of her blackness if she secures a high-paying job in a majority-white corporation or plays in a string quartet, but some argue that the penalty is much more severe for an American Indian, who must remain culturally untouched by modernity to be considered a "real Indian" or, more harshly, an Indian at all.[137] In James Clifford's terse words, "Life as an American [means] death as an Indian."[138]

This imperative is enforced by American Indians and non-Indians alike. Some Native Americans act as "ethnic police," making sure no outsiders get in. Disturbed by "Cherokee Grandmother Syndrome," they worry about whites and other non-Indians who "discover" their indigenous heritage (or simply lay false claim to it) to gain access to Native American spirituality and culture and to qualify for tribal benefits and affirmative action programs. As a result, some Native Americans have established rules or benchmarks separating "real Indians" from "imposters."[139] And to gain a sense of how non-Indians also police Indian authenticity, one need only look to court cases in which tribes hoping to "prove their tribal identity" to white judges and juries were labeled phonies on the grounds that they had traded their horses for cars, were fond of eating at fast-food restaurants, and had taken to relying too much on modern conveniences like washers and dryers and televisions. Indeed, tribes seeking federal recognition from the Office of Federal Acknowledgement (formerly the Branch of Acknowledgement and Research) must not only

A Nez Perce woman dresses in traditional beaded cape at the Shoshone Bannock Pow Wow in Fort Hall, Idaho.

show they have been a tribe since 1900; they also must marshal evidence produced by non-Indian actors, such as anthropologists, historians, and journalists. The result, many have observed, is that "tribes whose memberships exhibit the most cultural and physical attributes of the mythical, aboriginal 'Indian' will have the greatest likelihood of being acknowledged with federal recognition."[140]

In the final analysis, struggles over racial authenticity essentially are about who is let into the "family." And any dynamic designed with the specific intent of governing behavior and including and excluding people from a community is bound to provide deep satisfaction and meaning to those "let in" as well as a painful sense of rejection for those "kept out." When American Jews attempt to get married in Israel, only to be told by the rabbinic courts that they have to "prove their Jewishness," they often leave defeated and outraged.[141] When a Chinese American woman is shunned by her family for not marrying a Chinese man, or when a third-generation Mexican American is teased by fellow Mexicans for not knowing Spanish, or when an Arab American Christian is labeled "less Arab" by his Muslim relatives, it burns and often repels people from their racial or ethnic communities. Speaking of the struggles over Indian authenticity, one sociologist has observed, "So strict and unforgiving a linkage of culture and identity often leaves Indian people with a pervasive legacy of insecurity and pain. Admitting to such sentiments, moreover, may only create more 'evidence' of one's insufficient Indianness for others to attack. . . . The judgment that 'he is not one of us' is a severe enough price that many people of Indian heritage with the potential to make significant contributions to Indian communities may choose not to participate in their traditional cultures at all, rather than risk the effort and be rejected for demonstrated lack of competence. There is probably no surer recipe for extinguishing a culture than this."[142]

What To Do with White Identity?

Whites often feel left out of conversations about racial authenticity and pride. While slogans such as "Black Power" or "Chicano Pride" strike one as empowering and appropriate, "White Power" or "White Pride" is used only by racist groups like the Skinheads. A Native American student might come to class with a button on her backpack declaring, "Indian and Proud!" But her white peers would not dare come to class with a "White and Proud!" button. Of course, when nonwhites assert a kind of racial or ethnic pride, they are driven by a fundamentally *reactionary* impulse. They are responding to structural racism. No one would need to demand "Black Power" if in reality power were evenly and justly distributed across racial groups. No one would put an "Indian Pride" bumper sticker on their truck if pride were not systematically stripped from Indians in the form of degrading social conditions (consider reservation poverty) and humiliating popular images (consider Indian mascots).

As a result, some whites simply do not know what to do with their whiteness. Many wish they could stake their identity in it, just as many of their nonwhite peers lay free claim to their nonwhiteness, but they know that doing so is not simple or innocent. Some envy nonwhites—or at least their ability to be proud of their racial identity—and may grow resentful or ashamed or confused. Yet most learn to live comfortably with their whiteness and go about their lives.

A very small but notable minority of whites strive, for a period, actively to reject their white identity. "To be outside whiteness is to be outside the cold and instrumental realm of modernity," writes one scholar attempting to capture a popular sentiment.[143] To some, whiteness is oppressive and painfully normal. Nonwhiteness, by contrast, appears liberated and cool, sexy and interesting and somehow more fully human. As an American teacher once told Fanon, "The presence of Negroes beside the whites is in a way an insurance policy on humanness. When the whites feel that they have become too mechanized, they turn to the men of color and ask them for a little human sustenance."[144]

Some whites take brief vacations from their whiteness, as in the case of those who travel to Mexico to participate in mock border-crossing expeditions, a growing tourist industry that promises participants the thrill and danger of what hundreds of real Mexican migrants experience every year. Others, as we alluded to earlier, discover that they have some nonwhite blood coursing through their veins, a heritage denied by their parents and grandparents in more overtly racist times, and strive to "reclaim" their nonwhite heritage. ("What the son wishes to forget," writes one historian, "the grandson wishes to remember."[145]) They undo their whiteness by changing their religious practices, dietary habits, and views on the family—or at least they change *how they understand* these things (once as "normal life," now as the "Cherokee way of life").[146]

And some whites—especially adolescents—attempt to break with their whiteness completely, taking on another racial or ethnic identity. In an ethnography of white students in a majority black school in Texas, Edward Morris discovered that whites often shed their whiteness for blackness. They wore their hair in cornrows, sagged their jeans, tilted their caps, wore gold chains, and spoke "black English." Some white students were so skilled at passing as nonwhites that at the beginning of his study, Morris had a hard time distinguishing the white students from their light-skinned nonwhite peers. In this school, nonwhite students used the term "white" to insult and tease those who were overly polite and nerdy. For this reason, many whites attempted to distance themselves as much as possible from their whiteness; this was doubly true of the boys, who tended to link whiteness with soft femininity. Still, this did not mean that white students lost their white privilege. Morris points out that black teachers viewed whites as good and responsible students; these teachers also were reluctant to discipline white students, though they did not hesitate to punish the latter's black and Hispanic peers.[147]

Amy Wilkins discovered similar patterns in her study of a multiracial school in Massachusetts, where some white girls turned themselves into "Puerto Rican wannabes." "The typical Puerto Rican wannabe," observes Wilkins, "rejects white middle-class cultural style, adopting an urban presentation of self associated with people of color. She wears hip-hop clothes and Puerto Rican hairstyles, drinks malt liquor, and smokes Newports. She adopts an attitude, acting tough and engaging in verbal and physical fights. And perhaps most important, she dates and has sex with Black and Puerto Rican men."[148] The Puerto Rican wannabe is criticized by whites and nonwhites alike. Whites construct the wannabes

Amy Wilkin's book *Wannabes, Goths, and Christians* explores white girls adopting the look and behaviors of the Puerto Rican students at their multiracial high school.

as "good (white) girls gone bad"; nonwhites view them as racially inauthentic and worry they are appropriating not "real" Puerto Rican culture, but a distorted stereotype of that culture, a collection of negative images and risky behavior. "By participating in behaviors associated with the urban poor and calling them Puerto Rican, the wannabes perpetuate negative stereotypes about people of color. Moreover, wannabes are seen as sacrificing white privilege in favor of Puerto Rican coolness. This trade is degrading because it implies that Puerto Ricans and Blacks devalue ambition and mainstream socioeconomic success, disparaging the efforts of those Puerto Ricans and Blacks who seek upward mobility."[149]

What does it mean when young white women wear dark lip-liner, speak Spanish, and try to become Latina? What do we make of the white teenager who calls himself "white chocolate" and "acts black"? Or, for that matter, how do we make sense of Cambodian American students who call themselves "the blacks of the Asians," address each other as "niggas," and attempt to align themselves with black students and against Latinos and whites?[150] What are the consequences of this form of racial passing or ethnic flexibility, one that involves a member of a relatively more privileged group adopting the style of members of a dominated group? It is hard to say. On the one hand, some whites who reject their whiteness for another kind of racial performance may end up degrading the racial or ethnic group whose styles they attempt to borrow, especially if their ideas of "blackness" or "Puerto Ricanness," for example, are nothing more than a shallow collection of stereotypes.[151] On the other hand, racial transgression also destabilizes racial categories and unveils their social and performative essence. In this way, it has the effect of rendering racial divisions, often viewed as hard and fast—even natural—porous and bendable. Race orders the world into neat categories; it seeks to divide and pit those divided against one another. But, in truth, none of us are 100 percent anything. We are grafted onto one another and penetrated by each other's ideas, culture, and actions. Baldwin made this point eloquently when he said, "Each of us, helplessly and forever, contains the other . . . white in black and black in white."[152]

THE PROBLEM WITH "IDENTITY"

The question of one's "true identity" occupies many young minds—and many old ones as well. In fact, the hunt for one's identity might be the quintessential college experience: hence the often-repeated refrain, "I found myself in college." Identity-based thinking and politics have their place and have been employed in the service of social justice, but some thinkers have begun to wonder just how useful the concept of identity truly is.[153] In our view, there are at least two problematic side effects of America's obsession with identity. First, talk of identity is talk about our differences, which necessarily causes further social divisions. And second, talk of identity necessarily turns our gaze inward, which may cause us to lose sight of other people's hardships. By way of conclusion, let's address each of these side effects in turn.

When we focus on identity, we focus on our differences. This encourages a person to view the world not as a reflexive thinker who has evaluated the social-scientific evidence, but as someone with a distinct identity. Thus, people often begin their sentences with phrases like "As a black women," or "Speaking as a gay man," or "For me, a recent immigrant, the truth is . . ." These kinds of identity-based statements are necessary if we are discussing different experiences, but they sometimes are used to justify questionable claims about how the world works. Consider, for example, the "insider doctrine" of which American sociologist Robert Merton spoke, a doctrine holding that only members of certain groups have access, or at least privileged access, to certain knowledge about the groups to which they belong. According to this doctrine, wrote Merton, "the Outsider, no matter how careful and talented, is excluded in principle from gaining access to the social and cultural truth. In short, [the doctrine] holds that the Outsider has a structurally imposed incapacity to comprehend alien groups, statuses, cultures, and societies."[154] One's position in the racial order conditions one's perceptions, but an insider's vantage point *in and of itself* does not lead to scientific discoveries unavailable to the outsider. After all, one would be hard pressed to find a thinker who applied the insider doctrine to members of dominant groups, that is, who actually argued that only capitalists can advance knowledgeable claims about capitalists, men about men, or whites about whites.

"No human culture," we earlier quoted Henry Louis Gates, Jr., as observing "is inaccessible to someone who makes the effort to understand, to learn to inhabit another world."[155] Scientific insight comes by way of rigorous reflexivity and research; it is not the inevitable result of one's position in society. The notion that all whites, strictly because of their whiteness, are blind to certain dimensions of racial domination, while all nonwhites, strictly because of their nonwhiteness, are keen to these dimensions, is too simplistic a proposition. And this line of thinking may result in whites, even when they are right, repeatedly ceding expertise to nonwhites when it comes to race (as if people of color were the real experts) or in nonwhite thinkers absolving themselves of reflexive practices.

We often hear the refrain "Respect differences." This is a fine refrain, one that should be heeded. But wouldn't a better one be "Fight injustice"? After all, there are some differences—those that cause injustice—that should not be respected. We should not respect violence against women, even if it is justified through "cultural or religious differences." We might have to *understand* those differences to help fight violence against women, but it is not necessary to "respect" them if respect here means leaving them be. We should not respect poverty in the same way we respect Islam or Christianity; we should strive to alleviate poverty. As Walter Benn

Michaels has said, "For thirty years, while the gap between the rich and the poor has grown larger, we've been urged to respect people's identities—as if the problem of poverty would be solved if we just appreciated the poor. . . . If we can stop thinking of the poor as people who have too little money and start thinking of them instead as people who have too little respect, then it's our attitude toward the poor, not their poverty, that becomes the problem to be solved, and we can focus our efforts of reform not on getting rid of classes but on getting rid of what we like to call classism. . . . The point is not that we should be nicer to the homeless; it's that no one should be homeless."[156]

Are we saying the poor do not deserve our respect? Of course not. What we are saying is this: to truly respect the poor, we must disrespect poverty. When we shift our focus from dismantling economic injustice and exploitation to class-based identities, antipoverty activism can dissolve into shallow talk about such identities.

The same point applies to racism, and this leads us to the second side effect of conversations that pivot on the concept of identity, namely, their tendency to be narcissistic. Identity is all about you. It's about your unique place in society and your membership in certain groups. Again, it is important to think through such issues, but it is equally important to be sure not to confine your thinking about racial domination to notions about your racial identity. The trouble starts when you begin to evaluate all racial statements by how much they offend you, a maneuver that places you at the center of the universe. Pretty soon, people learn how to talk about race without causing people to be offended, either by using a polite kind of empty talk with all the right words or by not saying anything at all. Honest dialogue—the kind that offends, sometimes—is swapped out for "diversity talk." And if you are at the center of the universe, then your hardships are the most important, and this kind of thinking leads to useless debates over "who has it worse," as well as to whites' resentment of antiracist policies they believe do not benefit them. There is more to life than you. Should we focus on differences or discrimination? Identity or injustice? "Races" or racism?

THE BIG PICTURE
Chapter 10: Intimate Life

MAIN POINTS	KEY TERMS	FROM THEORY TO PRACTICE

MAIN POINTS

Understand how racial domination has wreaked havoc on many nonwhite families and interracial couples—through such means as separating parents from children, limiting the immigration of spouses and children, and forbidding marriages between races.

KEY TERMS

- brave new families, page 358
- interracial unions, page 358

MAIN POINTS

Examine the racial dynamics that inform everyday interactions, such as the way we greet each other, and how these racial dynamics often cause misunderstanding and frustration.

KEY TERMS

- cultural labor, page 369
- interaction order, page 377

FROM THEORY TO PRACTICE

Pick one interracial or cross-cultural relationship in your life and list some steps you could take to do the cultural labor necessary to deepen and enrich that relationship. Next, pick at least one item from your list and do the (racial) work! You might, for example, go to a mosque with a Muslim coworker or to your roommate's majority-white church. You might read a memoir about growing up in a border town, or in south side Chicago, or in an ethnic enclave. And so on. Finally, write about your experiences, reflecting on this idea of doing the cultural work.

MAIN POINTS

Learn about the reasons for the significant racial differences in rates of marriage, divorce, and out-of-wedlock birth.

KEY TERMS

- marriage, page 363
- divorce, page 370
- out-of-wedlock births, page 371
- single motherhood, page 375

MAIN POINTS

Recognize the ways that each person's identity is made up of multiple intersecting features, such as race, gender, religion, sexuality, and class.

FROM THEORY TO PRACTICE

Analyze yourself with respect to racial identity formation. What stage of racial identity formation best describes where you are right now? Does one of the stages described in this chapter under the heading "racial identity formation" best express your current state of mind? Also, analyze how you may have changed to arrive at the stage you are at now. Finally, describe where you would like go in the future.

MAIN POINTS

Explain how race is both *marked* through America's racial taxonomy and *made* through hundreds and thousands of practices: gestures, sayings, tastes, ways of walking, religious convictions, and opinions.

KEY TERMS

- authenticity, page 382

FROM THEORY TO PRACTICE

Conducting an intersectional identity analysis, pinpoint one aspect of your identity which is "privileged." How might you benefit from your religious affiliation, sexuality, class background, and so forth? How does this privileged aspect of your identity coincide with your racial identity? Finally, in a reflexive fashion, explain at least one way your privileged identity might cause others to suffer and offer one way you might allay that suffering.

11 Toward Racial Democracy

MAIN POINTS

- Evaluate the strengths and weaknesses of three different responses to racial inequality: color-blindness, multiculturalism/cosmopolitanism, and racial democracy.

- Recognize the different levels where people can pursue racial democracy: the individual level, the interactional level, the institutional level, and the level of collective action.

Students of race in America primarily want to know two things. First, they want to know if our society is racist. Nearly half a century after the Civil Rights Movement, are people's life chances still affected differently according to their skin color? Or do other factors such as social class origin, gender, or perhaps even individual differences (such as intelligence, work ethic, or gumption) matter more? Second, students wish to know what our racial order ought to look like. What ideals should guide us as we move toward the future? Ought ours to be a color-blind society, in which racial differences exist but no one pays them heed? A world with no race at all? A world that celebrates multiculturalism? Or a world in which racial justice and racial democracy reign—but what would these even look like?

These questions have to do, respectively, with "what is" and "what ought to be." They ask, "What is our society like?" and "What ought it to look like?" In the preceding chapters, we have devoted extensive attention to the "is." Now, in this final chapter, we focus on the "ought": the ends we might aim to realize in the future.

Why conclude like this, not with the realities of race but with ideal solutions? The answer is that, at least in many segments of American society (but by no means all), conversations about race tend to become debates about racial ideals. No matter what the specific issue—whether it be the politics of immigration reform, affirmative action in education, racial segregation, or racial inequality in the legal system—those involved in the discussion always seem to come back to the question of ends, to how things ought to be. Our visions of "what ought to be" tend to inform our ideas of "what is."

Or, to take yet another instance of the same tendency, people tend to interpret empirical statements about race in terms of some standard or yardstick they hold dear. They might say that residential segregation is not so bad because in the ideal society, people most likely would choose to live with others of their own kind. Or they say that to teach a core curriculum is offensive because in a multicultural society (their own racial ideal), each racial group rightfully has its own canon. Oftentimes they even differ as to whether a given action or issue itself should be deemed "racial." The very choice whether or not to "racialize" an issue—to "make something about race"—means different things to different people depending on their racial ideals. This is why it is important to confront the basic assumptions we hold—and the evaluative ideals according to which we assess our racial problems or even consider them to be "racial" to begin with. If we chose not to conclude this examination of race in America by addressing what is most deeply believed in and taken for granted, then our deep-seated ideals could inform all we examine without being themselves examined.

But maybe you think that there can be no rational, systematic assessment of ends (that is, of the ideals that guide our thoughts and actions) and that these have no legitimate place in a classroom or textbook, for social inquiry only can deal with what "is." Perhaps normative ideals (matters of "what ought to be") are matters of personal preference alone. Or perhaps they are absolute truths "grounded," in one commentator's words, "on abstract, universal, timeless concepts." That inequality is natural or even part of a divine plan would be an example. In both cases—personal opinion and timeless truth—there is no point at all in discussing racial ideals.[1]

But the ends to which we aspire can be conceptualized in a very different way. We can think of them not as mere opinions on the one hand or as unquestionable truths on the other, but rather as tools or instruments to be evaluated in terms of their success in guiding conduct. If that is so, then we can test our visions of the ideal racial order "by putting them into practice," as philosopher Elizabeth Anderson has put it, or at least by reasoning them through to their likely consequences, "and seeing whether the results are satisfactory—whether they solve the problems they were designed to solve, whether we find their consequences acceptable, whether they enable successful responses to novel problems, whether living in accordance with [them] yields more satisfactory results."[2] We can envision an America informed by these ideals and ask how adequately our racial problems have been addressed in such a society.

From this point of view, we can systematically assess racial ideals in experimentalist fashion (including through thought experiments when the ideals cannot easily be put into practice) and revise them when they fail to pass the bar—the "pragmatic test." This applies even to sweeping collective ideals such as racial integration and multiculturalism. These, too, can be assessed in terms of their capacity to provide effective solutions to the problems of our racial order. That sort of assessment is what we intend to do in the pages that follow. We shall consider a range of important proposals for changing our racial lives for the better. In each case, we shall weigh the likely consequences of adopting those proposals and of seeking to realize them in the actual world. And on that basis, we shall evaluate their strengths and weaknesses.

Having explored the question of ends, we also shall take up the question of means. That is, having asked, "What are we trying to achieve?" we shall ask, "How do we achieve it?" More specifically, the second half of this chapter will be concerned with different possible means of changing racial life. It will begin with the level of individual (self-) transformation, and it will then discuss means of achieving change in interpersonal interactions, societal institutions, and various forms of collective action, such as social movements.

Racial diversity in American school classrooms is on the rise. Here, an African American boy and his Peruvian-American classmate conduct a science experiment in Schenectady, New York.

WHAT ARE THE GOALS?

So what are the ends? When it comes to race in America, what, exactly, do we want? Several answers have been proposed. One is color-blindness, the favored ideal of mainstream racial discourse. Another is multiculturalism (sometimes also called "cosmopolitanism" by philosophers). And a third is racial democracy. In what follows, we focus on these three ends. To a greater or lesser degree, color-blindness, multiculturalism (or cosmopolitanism), and racial democracy all have been proposed as plausible ways of overcoming our racial problems. What results likely would flow from seeking to realize these ideals? What projects would result from adopting one or another of them?

Our discussion in this chapter concerns collective racial ideals. However, complementary ideals for individual transformation also will be considered, for each racial ideal traverses the societal and the personal, offering guidance for reshaping selves even as it presents a vision for changing society. What kind of individuals would we find in a color-blind society? In a multicultural society? Or in one marked by racial democracy?

Color-Blindness

Color-blind thinking is central to much of American racial discourse today, and it presents itself as the genuine inheritor of the Civil Rights Movement. (The term "discourse" refers here to widely shared ways of speaking, generally in public settings, about matters of societal concern.) Indeed, color-blindness sees itself as capturing the very essence and spirit of the Civil Rights Movement, which was (or so it holds) an effort primarily to defend the dignity and autonomy of the individual rather than to advance a group agenda or to engage in a divisive politics of recognition. The discourse of color-blindness envisions a world in which race no longer serves as the basis for social stigmatization, discrimination, inequality, or injustice. It aspires to a society in which all are judged, in the famous words of Martin Luther King, Jr., "not by the color of their skin but by the content of their character."[3] The individual ought to be placed front and center, not the racialized group.

Proponents of color-blindness, as some observers have noted, "want race to disappear. For them, color-blindness is not simply a legal standard; it is a particular kind of social order, one where racial identity is irrelevant. [These proponents] believe a color-blind society can uncouple individual behavior from group identification, allowing genuine inclusion of all people. . . . Were this allowed to happen, individuals who refused to follow common moral standards would be stigmatized as individuals, not as members of a particular group."[4] Racial prejudice is condemned here in the strongest of terms, but so too

Color-blindness is a laudable ideal that many children seem to embody, but it overlooks racial inequality.

are color-conscious policies, even progressive ones, on behalf of a fairer and more just society, for to continue to think and act on the basis of race is seen as perpetuating racial division. Those who continue to "see" race at all are holding us back; obsessed with the past, they prevent us from realizing the future. In political scientist Amy Gutmann's apt summary, the color-blind ideal holds that "our society must be bound by the same morality that would be suitable to a just society. That morality . . . is fundamentally color blind, and to diverge from color blindness is to make the mistake of thinking that two wrongs make a right."[5]

The ideal of color-blindness extends its sway today in legal considerations, in discussions of social policy, and in everyday social discourse. Justice John Harlan introduced the term to American constitutional discourse in his celebrated dissent to *Plessy v. Ferguson* (1895): "In view of the Constitution," he wrote, "in the eye of the law, there is in this country no superior, dominant, ruling class of citizens. There is no caste here. Our Constitution is color-blind, and neither knows nor tolerates classes among citizens. In respect of civil rights, all citizens are equal before the law."[6] In recent times, color-blindness has become the ascendant ideal in constitutional law, as evidenced by Supreme Court rulings in landmark cases such as *Ricci v. DeStefano* (2009), which invalidated a color-conscious decision in a promotion case involving New Haven, Connecticut, firefighters; *Gratz v. Bollinger* (2003), which invalidated a color-conscious admissions policy at the University of Michigan aimed at boosting the prospects of student-of-color applicants; and *Parents Involved in Community Schools v. Seattle School District No. 1* (2007), which prohibited the assignment of students to public schools solely for the purpose of enhancing racial integration. The common theme has been a repudiation of efforts, however well meaning, to take race into account in matters of law or public policy.

In social and political life as well, the ideal of color-blindness has pushed its way to the center of the debate. The 1980s and 1990s saw a sharp rise in conservative racial commentary featuring a backlash against the "reverse discrimination" brought about by race-conscious strategies.[7] Liberal authors, too, bemoaned the "twilight of common dreams," for in their view the fight for civil and political rights had given way to shortsighted, wrongheaded struggles over identity.[8] In 2004, Barack Obama rode to political prominence by declaring at the Democratic National Convention, "There is not a black America and a white America and Latino America and Asian America—there is the United States of America."[9]

Philosopher William James once wrote, "The pragmatic method . . . is to try to interpret each notion by tracing its respective practical consequences. What difference would it practically make to any one if this notion rather than that notion were true?"[10] In that spirit, we might ask what concrete implications flow from the ideal of color-blindness. How effective is it in helping us to address our racial divides? We already have seen that in the legal and public policy domains, color-blindness demands that severe constraints be imposed on color-conscious approaches to fighting racial inequality. Affirmative action, for example, sharply is opposed by this ideal. It is portrayed as, at best, an affront to individuality, since it subsumes all its beneficiaries under a single racial characterization, "treating them as if all members of the same race were alike in some intrinsic characteristic. This is an expressive harm, an offense to people's dignity, even apart from whether the content of the stereotype is stigmatizing."[11] At worst, affirmative action is portrayed as reverse discrimination.

In place of color-conscious strategies, the ideal of color-blindness favors strictly race-neutral approaches, in particular more stringent enforcement of antidiscrimination laws. As Chief Justice John Roberts asserted in his majority opinion in *Parents Involved*, "The way to stop discrimination on the basis of race is to stop discriminating on the basis of race."[12] In other words, any policy that took race into account—whether that policy was intended to reinforce racial inequality (e.g., federal housing policy in the middle of the twentieth century) or to challenge it (e.g., affirmative action)—is wrong. Confronting discrimination and unfairness is important, but this solution falls short on some levels. Even the most vigorous attempts to enforce antidiscrimination laws fail, as Elizabeth Anderson has shown, to redress "many [other] types of conduct causing systematic

University of Michigan students protest affirmative action in front of the U.S. Supreme Court in Washington, D.C., June 23, 2003.

race-based disadvantage."[13] "Color-blind policy," she points out, "is far from sufficient to achieve the color-blind ideal. It does *nothing* to dismantle entrenched patterns of racial segregation, undermine unconscious racial stigmatization and discrimination, challenge informal practices of racial avoidance such as white flight, end coded racial appeals in politics, avoid negligence of disadvantaged racial groups in public policy, or prevent race-neutral policies with differential racial impact from being based on racially stigmatizing ideas."[14]

Specifically, color-blind policy fails to take into account forms of racial discrimination exempted in loopholes (focused on racial discrimination is practiced by private clubs); evaluative discrimination (as in soft skills or subtle habits); ostensibly nonracial discrimination that takes for granted human capital differences rooted in prior racial discrimination (e.g., in on-the-job training); unconscious and unintended racial discrimination (as in juror bias against nonwhite defendants); aversive racism under the cover of formally race-neutral policies (as in voter suppression efforts); supposedly race-neutral policies that don't have race-neutral consequences (e.g., support for cuts in school funding to avoid redistributing resources to low-income minority communities); second-order discrimination (as when crack cocaine offenders, who largely are black, are sentenced to harsher prison terms than powder cocaine offenders, who largely are white); and discrimination in peer groups, neighbors, and friends (as when communities take steps to ensure that their schools will remain racially segregated).[15]

Beyond these various sources of disadvantage, all of which evade race-neutral strategies such as stricter enforcement of antidiscrimination laws, there also are everyday forms of racism that cannot be addressed from within a color-blind framework, modes of racist thought and action that themselves, ironically, are facilitated by color-blind discourse. In *Racism without Racists*, Eduardo Bonilla-Silva surveys these new forms of "color-blind racism."[16] The ideal of color-blindness, he finds,

"Color-blind racism" protects white privilege by diminishing the saliency of race.

provides protective cover for some whites' justifying their ascendancy in the racial order while not seeming (to themselves or others) to be racist. Nonwhite people also can promote this ideal to justify their successes against the backdrop of the struggles of many other members of their racial or ethnic group or those of other nonwhite groups. By invoking classical liberal ideals of individualism, universalism, and egalitarianism, for example—all of which are race neutral—we "can appear 'reasonable' and even 'moral,' while opposing almost all practical approaches to deal with de facto racial inequality." [17] Moreover, by suggesting that racial phenomena are natural occurrences and that "they (racial minorities) do it too," whites can justify their racially motivated preferences and actions as nonracial. By asserting that racial discrimination no longer is a central dynamic in American life, they can "eliminate . . . the bulk of [racist] actions by individual whites and institutions by fiat." [18] Bonilla-Silva documents the "linguistic manners and rhetorical strategies" of color-blindness: "how to talk nasty about minorities without sounding racist." [19]

How then are we to asses color-blindness? If color-blindness is widespread and deeply rooted in American life today, this is because it entails an ideal response to skin differences in a world without race. As Gutmann has put it, "The principles that most of us learn, from childhood to maturity, are . . . color blind not because color blindness is the right response to racial injustice but rather because color blindness is the ideal morality (for an ideal society)." [20] In a perfect society—one without a history of colonization, slavery, and systematic degradation; a world without present-day racial inequalities or institutional and interpersonal racism—color-blindness would be the appropriate ethical code. But we have not inherited such a world. Hence color-blindness may be an inappropriate way of thinking about our world, an ineffective mode of response to a world itself not color-blind.

Multiculturalism and Cosmopolitanism

Much like color-blindness, multiculturalism aspires to a world in which all persons' inherent dignity as human beings is recognized. But in contrast to color-blindness, which hopes to abolish race as a relevant criterion in law, public policy, and everyday social practices, multiculturalism envisions a society in which racial diversity fully is taken into account and valued for its own sake. Before we move on to assess this ideal, let take some time to consider some history. Where did the notion come from that America's diversity is something to be cherished? What are its historical roots? Here we can usefully distinguish, following sociologist Jeffrey Alexander, between assimilation, hyphenation, and multiculturalism. [21]

Assimilation is the age-old American ideal of the melting pot, in which outgroups lose their distinctive identities over time and gradually become absorbed into a preexisting, overarching American identity. The melting pot metaphor first was used in print by a French visitor to America named J. Hector St. John de Crevecoeur in 1782. [22] But it was not until the early twentieth century that the metaphor of the melting pot became widely known in the United States. Recall that this was a time of accelerated immigration, when many new immigrants came from Southern, Central, and Eastern Europe. In 1908, a Jewish playwright named Israel Zangwill wrote a play called *The Melting Pot,* in which a character, himself an immigrant, made this noteworthy declaration: "Understand that America is God's Crucible, the great Melting-Pot where all the races of Europe are melting and reforming! A fig for your feuds and vendettas! Germans and Frenchmen, Irishmen and Englishmen, Jews and Russians—into the Crucible with you all! God is making the American." [23]

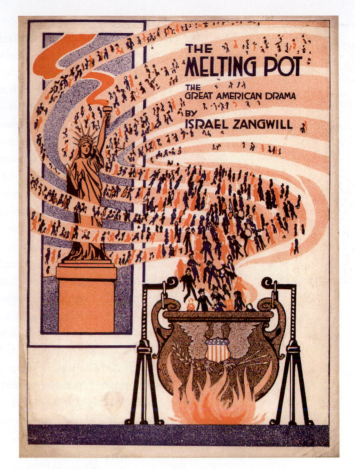

Does the "melting together" on America's shores ask everyone to change in the same way?

With the premiere of Zengwill's play, the term "melting pot" passed into the American vernacular and became an integral part of Americans' self-image. It continues to be used today. Almost from the beginning, however, there was ambiguity as to what the term meant. Was the "melting together" that was to take place a mutually transformative process, such that new arrivals on American shores would alter the cultural lives of those who had come before, just as the old-timers would transform the identities and mores of the newcomers? Or was the process to work in one direction only, with newer immigrants shedding their previous identities while the "native stock," and its dominant culture, remained unchanged?

The realities of American social life dictated that the latter would become the predominant interpretation. Assimilation would mean that "members of out-groups [would be], in principle, allowed to become members of the society on the condition that they [kept] their stigmatized qualities hidden behind the wall of private life." [24] One influential spokesperson for assimilationism was Edward A. Ross, one of the key figures of early twentieth-century American social thought. In his view, the "native stock" of white, Anglo-Saxon, British-origin Americans would become, as his critic Horace Kallen would put it, "the measure and the standard of American that the newcomer [was] to attain . . . by virtue of being heir of the oldest rooted economic settlement and spiritual tradition of the white man in America." [25]

Another spokesperson was Robert Park, noted leader of the Chicago School of urban sociology and, in his youth, a publicist and ghost-writer for Booker T. Washington. "In the relations of races," Park asserted, "there is a cycle of events which tends everywhere to repeat itself." [26] This cycle consists of four sequential stages: contact, conflict, accommodation, and assimilation. At first, when large racial groups come into contact, contestation and competition occur. Then, after some time, a certain asymmetrical, hierarchical arrangement comes to prevail—one of accommodation—in which one race is dominant and the other(s) dominated. However, in the end, assimilation results: "Every nation, upon examination, turns out to have been a more or less successful melting pot." [27] Park's view of the "race relations cycle" was less Anglo-centric and more upbeat than that of Ross. (In this respect, it recalled Zangwill's optimistic vision.) For years, sociologists would learn to think of race and ethnicity in its terms.

It is an interesting question—one we leave you to ponder—whether the assimilationist ideal persists in altered form even today. Do some Americans still believe in some variant or other of the old vision of America as a melting pot? Whatever the answer, assimilation, as a principle and an ideal, does not stand alone as a framework for incorporation. Alexander also mentions hyphenation. As he explains it, hyphenation (unlike assimilation) does tolerate outsiders' qualities and so is less rigid than assimilation. However, it also resembles assimilation in that, while tolerating outsiders' qualities, it continues to stigmatize them. What is incorporated under the model of hyphenation is the different person but not her or his different qualities. The latter still are excluded. [28]

In scholarly debates, hyphenation sometimes has gone under the banner of "cultural pluralism" and strongly anticipates multiculturalism. The idea harkens back to yet another important thinker of the early twentieth century whom we mentioned earlier in this section, Horace Kallen, who wrote about it in an essay published in 1915, "Democracy versus the Melting-Pot." Criticizing Ross's brand of assimilationism, Kallen proposed by contrast a model of "multiplicity in . . . unity, an orchestration of mankind." How many times have you heard it said of America that it is not like a melting pot but rather resembles a salad bowl? For Kallen, it was like a musical ensemble (different imagery, same idea): "As in an orchestra, every type of instrument has its specific timbre and tonality, founded in its substance and form; as every type has its appropriate theme and melody in the whole symphony, so in society each ethnic group is the natural instrument, its spirit and culture are its theme and melody, and the harmony and dissonances and discords of them all make the symphony of civilization, with this difference: a musical symphony is written before it is played; in the symphony of civilization the playing is the writing, so that there is nothing so fixed and inevitable about its progressions as in music, so that within the limits set by nature they may vary at will, and the range and variety of the harmonies may become wider and richer and more beautiful." Kallen concluded this passage—and the essay itself— with one additional sentence: "But the question is, do the dominant classes in America want such a society?" [29]

The biggest difficulty with Kallen's ideal of the hyphenated, culturally pluralistic society is that it centers itself (as had Ross's ideal of assimilationism) on a process involving only European immigrants. It has nothing to say about the massive obstacles hindering the incorporation of nonwhites into a majority-white nation. Kallen restricted his concerns, in fact, to what he termed the "Atlantic migration," leaving out of that phrase any reference at all to the Atlantic passage of millions of enslaved Africans.

Although individual members of racialized groups sometimes are labeled (or label themselves) in hyphenated terms, as in the label "Asian-American," the hyphenation model never has succeeded entirely in overcoming the problem of racism. Nor has it broken entirely free of the assimilationism against which it originally defined itself. For, as Alexander explains it, "Hyphenation is often perceived as a temporary situation, as something that will disappear as members of insider and outsider groups are absorbed into a more universal, if still culturally distinctive, national community. Hyphenated incorporation is a process, a means rather than an end."[30] These difficulties inherent in the hyphenation framework "can be overcome," Alexander continues, "only by moving beyond hyphenation to a multicultural mode that is different not only in degree but in kind."[31]

Multiculturalism breaks sharply with assimilationist logic. It welcomes both the outsider and her or his qualities. "Multiculturalism dramatically expands the range of imagined life experiences for core-group members. In doing so, it opens up the possibility not just for acceptance and toleration but for understanding and recognition. Insofar as such understandings are achieved, rigid distinctions between core and out-group members break down, and notions of the particular and the universal become much more thoroughly intertwined."[32] All people, whites and nonwhites, immigrants and native-born citizens, are not simply tolerated; they are valued and, as much as possible, are understood—their differences and similarities acknowledged, accepted, and welcomed.

Multicultural theorists have argued that the ideal America would rest on two key principles: first, that, drawn shoulder to shoulder in a common humanity with others, we have a civic responsibility to all people; second, that we must all respect one another's differences.[33] K. Anthony Appiah (who prefers the term "cosmopolitanism") puts it this way: "There are two strands that intertwine in the notion of cosmopolitanism. One is the idea that we have obligations to others, obligations that stretch beyond those to whom we are related by ties of kith and kin, or even the more formal ties of shared citizenship. The other is that we take seriously the value not just of human life but of particular human lives, which means taking an interest in the practices and beliefs that lend them significance. People are different, the cosmopolitan knows, and there is much to learn from those differences. Because there are so many human possibilities worth exploring, we neither expect nor desire that every person or every society should converge on a single mode of life."[34]

Multiculturalism recently has been given a sociological inflection—with vivid and concrete examples from everyday life—by sociologist Elijah Anderson. In *The Cosmopolitan Canopy*, he affirms the multicultural ideal in normative terms. "Exposure to

We the Peoples... is a 1984 acrylic-on-board piece by Ron Waddams.

others' humanity," he writes, "generates empathy; fears dissipate, and grounds for mutual appreciation appear." Multiculturalism should be seen "not as [a] 'time out' from normal life but as a model for what social relationships could become."[35] Anderson demonstrates, using illustrations from Philadelphia's Reading Terminal Market and Rittenhouse Square, among other sites, that cosmopolitan interactions already have become a social reality in many pockets or "islands" of contemporary racial life.[36] Cosmopolitan canopies, he writes, are "pluralistic spaces where people engage one another in a spirit of civility or even comity and goodwill. Through personal observation, [they] come casually to appreciate one another's differences and empathize with the other in a spirit of shared humanity. . . . In such settings city dwellers are encouraged to express their cosmopolitan sides while keeping their ethnocentric feelings in check."[37] Trust is established; symmetrical relations form; the notion is embraced that "the space [belongs] to all kinds of people"; strangers make "human contact" across the racial divide.[38] People learn about, and become familiar with, one another, "stretch[ing] themselves mentally, emotionally, and socially."[39] The cosmopolitan canopy can be "a profoundly humanizing experience."[40]

Anderson adds that race relations in the workplace nonetheless can be fraught with hidden tensions. Speaking of the African American experience, he notes that as "the black employee knows that on any given day he will encounter numerous white people, many of whom he is sure are racist to some degree—but to what degree, and how must this reality figure into his relationship with them?"[41] Frequently, the black employee suffers "little humiliations"—"little cuts" and "indignities"—that go unmentioned under the canopy.[42] On occasion, the canopy even is pierced by eruptions of racism, when the fabric of trust and comity is rended and the black person shockingly is reminded of a racial divide that all along was there.[43] Anderson provocatively calls these transactions "nigger moments"; psychologists have called them "racial microaggressions."[44] But despite these affronts, some subtle and others brutal, the cosmopolitan canopy survives. It is an "ongoing concern," notes Anderson, its hallmark "a certain resilience and change as it goes about meeting the exigencies of its everyday environment."[45]

Cosmopolitanism is not without its critics, many from the perspective of color-blindness. Does cosmopolitanism not erode our national culture, they ask, by encouraging us to focus not on what unites us but rather on what separates us? To this, cosmopolitans respond by saying that obsessing over our differences weakens our democratic potential and breeds animosity, yes, but any multiculturalism worthy of its name encourages us not to dwell on our differences, but rather to acknowledge and respect those differences as potential sources of wisdom and good. It seeks to draw us nearer, not to push us farther apart. It does not threaten civic community but, rather, nourishes its potential.

America always has been multicultural, although only in recent years has cosmopolitanism been valued and pursued as a normative ideal. It took an enormous labor to convince us otherwise. As Du Bois once wrote, addressing white readers, "Your country? How came it yours? Before the Pilgrims landed we were here. . . . Actively we have woven ourselves with the very warp and woof of this nation,—we fought their battles, shared their sorrow, mingled our blood with theirs, and generation after generation have pleaded with a headstrong, careless people to despise not Justice, Mercy, and Truth, lest the nation be smitten with a curse. Our song, our toil, our cheer, and warning have been given to this nation in blood-brotherhood. Are not these gifts worth the giving? Is not this work and striving? . . . Even so is the hope that sang in the songs of my fathers well sung."[46] That hope, that lonely lit candle surrounded by moonless night, passed from calloused hand to calloused hand throughout American history, is the hope of complete inclusion, recognition, and respect. *That*, in a word, is the hope of multiculturalism.

Sometimes proponents of the multicultural ideal envision a world in which all cultures are judged intrinsically worthy; all cultures are of equal value. Regrettably, this is where they begin to run into problems. At least in its strong versions, multiculturalism demands for certain cultures a level of respect they might not deserve. How much respect ought to be accorded a white supremacist (or, in some other fashion, ethnocentric) culture? In addition, multiculturalism often portrays cultures themselves in reified fashion. It is important to conceive of social groups and their cultures in more complex terms. As Nancy Fraser has pointed out, "in reifying group identity," multiculturalism, at least in these variants, "ends by obscuring the politics of cultural identification, the struggles *within* the group for the authority—and the power—to represent it."[47]

But there is a deeper, more vexing problem still. Coming to understand and appreciate one another's cultural lives is an integral part of the democratic ideal. But the flaw in multiculturalism is that democracy is not simply about recognizing others' diversity. Democracy also is about coming to a full awareness of one another's problems—of how people are treated unfairly despite the promise of full and equal inclusion—and it is about responding to those problems with just remedies. Colorblindness and multiculturalism both fail to appreciate this crucial aspect of the democratic ideal. As one critic has observed, "Multiculturalism . . . and colorblindness are not as different as they initially seem. . . . The rhetoric of multiculturalism and diversity generally acknowledges only apolitical, non-contentious differences between people. . . . Like colorblindness, [it] eschews difficult discussions of institutional racism, of economic, material, and educational inequalities across racial divides, of restitution and reparation for past injustices committed against people of color, and so on. Multicultural diversity and colorblindness work hand in hand to both see and not see racial differences, a contradictory vision that has the ultimate effect of blinding people to issues of racial (in)justice."[48]

Racial Democracy

In the abstract, racial justice means that persons of all racial groups draw returns on societal resources commensurate with the value they themselves have added to them; moreover, all are recognized in their full humanity as contributors to the social whole. In our racial order, this ideal often falls short of being realized. Racism, to put it simply, breeds injustice. Efforts at change for the better—what we might call racial reconstruction—accordingly

In a racially just society, the simultaneous extraction of immigrant labor and retraction of immigrant rights would cease, and America would develop fair policies that treat its poor immigrants as much more than simply an expendable and cheap labor force.

must take into account the real conditions of life in which the racially privileged exploit others. This does not mean they must forsake the ideals of color-blindness and multiculturalism—namely, respect for all human beings and a generous embrace of plurality and difference. It means only that they must begin from actual experience, where racial injustice is rampant, and not from an imaginary, idealized world outside experience.

Often racial injustice is perpetrated in plain sight but forgotten altogether in public discourse. Take, for instance, everyday practices of exploitation—and racial injustice—in housing, practices with a long history in the United States. During its rapid period of urbanization, America imported a model of slum exploitation originally perfected in Europe. As more and more people flocked to cities like New York and Philadelphia throughout the late eighteenth and early nineteenth centuries, urban land values soared, and landlords began subdividing their properties to make room for more renters. Cellars, attics, and storage sheds became single-room apartments, and poor families proved a profitable market even through the Panic of 1837.[49] Rents continued to rise as housing conditions deteriorated. Soon, many families, even those living in unsanitary and dangerous conditions, could not make rent. In the shadowy regions of the city, landlords quite purposefully created slums to maximize their rate of return. "Instead of being penalized for this anti-social exploitation of land," Lewis Mumford observed, "the slum landlord, on capitalist principles, was handsomely rewarded: for the values of his decayed properties, so far from being written off because of their age and disrepair, became embedded in the structure of land values and taxes."[50] The institutionalization of the black ghetto at the beginning of the twentieth century increased the exploitative possibilities of landed capital. As the black population in northern cities grew, real estate developers saw an opportunity to make handsome profits by buying up properties on the edges of the ghetto and slicing them up into flats. By law, custom, and poverty, the vast majority of blacks were excluded from purchasing their own homes, and the rise of the dual housing market allowed landlords to charge blacks higher rents for worse housing. As late as 1960, the median monthly rent in some cities was higher for blacks than for whites.[51]

And who could argue today that the urban poor are not just as exploited as in generations past? Witness not only the extractive capabilities of the private rental market, which in recent years has seen a surge in rents, but also the proliferation of pawn shops, the number of which doubled in the 1990s; the emergence of the payday lending industry, boasting of more stores across the United States than McDonalds restaurants and netting upwards of $7 billion annually in fees; and the colossal expansion of the subprime lending industry, which was generating upwards of $100 billion in annual revenues at the peak of the mid-2000s housing bubble.[52]

In the residential field, a society guided by racial justice would not be scarred by drastic segregation but

A wintertime eviction, Milwaukee, Wisconsin.

rather would promote racial integration and community. It would combat exploitation in the nation's ghettos and barrios and trailer parks. More broadly, it would strive to eliminate the problems associated with racial segregation, such as chronic poverty, educational inequality, and imbalanced political representation. It would invest in the nation's poorest communities and nourish and promote self-development and sustainable economic growth on American Indian reservations. Housing discrimination would be shut down. And it would develop cleaner and more energy-efficient ways to live, so as not to burden poor, nonwhite communities with others' trash and pollution.

What would racial justice look like in other fields of social life? Consider education. Making college more affordable would open up opportunities for thousands of people, including many people of color, who currently are excluded from the privileges many others enjoy. Why should it be limited only to those who can afford it, plus a relatively small number of underprivileged students who scrape and claw for scholarships? What is more, a racially just society would invest in its poor schools, so that the education a child receives in a wealthy suburb of Los Angeles would not be vastly superior to the one a child receives in Compton. And a racially just society would critically reconstruct its curriculum, replacing Eurocentric accounts of history, art, politics, and philosophy with a more accurate, well-rounded, and multicultural program of studies.

A society marked by racial justice and racial democracy would foster self-realization, flourishing, and growth. It would allow individuals and groups to pursue opportunities to enrich their life experience and fully to develop their own powers and capacities. It would provide members of all racial groups with equal possibilities to assume an active role in directing the social affairs in which they take part. Through such participation and the resulting formation of meaningful, trusting, solidaristic connections across racial boundaries, people would be enabled—one might say liberated—to develop their potentials and capacities. This ideal can have unanticipated consequences. For instance, it might mean that racial cultures—or particular aspects thereof—would not be preserved in their given form. Under conditions of dynamic interchange, the very ties, meanings, and sentiments associated with racial cultures might evolve. Do certain aspects of a racial culture prevent self-development and growth? If so, they must be transformed. What would be required is self-scrutiny on the part of racial groups and not merely a cosmopolitan respect for, or openness to, modes of racial life other than one's own.

What Are the Goals for Individual Transformation?

At the beginning of this chapter, we suggested that ideals of racial reconstruction have both a collective and an individual dimension. Much of the foregoing has been about the kinds of societal ends envisioned by proponents of color-blindness, multiculturalism, and racial democracy. We now turn to the individual ends associated with these ideals. What kinds of *personal* dispositions, capacities, and competences ideally are to be cultivated in racial actors? Each of the agendas for racial renovation discussed earlier in this chapter carries a different answer to this question. What might be the distinguishing characteristics of a color-blind individual, one who fails to recognize (or does not wish to acknowledge) skin color? What might be the hallmarks of a cosmopolitan individual thriving in the midst of racial diversity and difference? What sort of individual is called for by the ideal of racial democracy?

Veneration for universalistic morality and for the dignity, sacredness, and autonomy of all persons long has been at the center of the color-blindness ideal. All modern individuals ideally carry within themselves a basic reverence for others (and for themselves) fundamentally as human beings. They hold one another in an almost religious regard, cherishing one another's humanity in abstraction from all specific attributes. And they uphold their "natural duties" to each other, duties stipulated by philosopher John Rawls to "hold between persons irrespective of their institutional relationships; [to] obtain between all as equal moral persons."[53] ("In this sense," adds Rawls, "the natural duties"—among which is mutual respect—"are owed not only to definite individuals . . . but to persons generally."[54]) Color-blind individuals, however, systematically mistake raced individuals for unraced essences and racial domination for an already realized postracial order. This unwittingly helps to reproduce a racial order that denies racially minorities their fundamental humanity.

The multicultural or cosmopolitan individual, by contrast, recognizes and affirms the realities of racial difference. He or she is reflexive and self-critical, unrestricted by ethnoracial constraints on thought or action, respectful of other cultures, and compassionate toward the plight of others. He or she also is adept at moving around in different racial worlds. Sometimes as well, the cosmopolitan individual inclines toward a certain playfulness and engages in what John Stuart Mill called "experiments in living," actively pursuing a broadening of horizons, sensibilities, and sympathies.[55] While not exemplifying all these criteria in equal measure, perhaps the prototype of the multicultural or cosmopolitan individual, not in philosophy or social and political thought but in American literature, is the character Ishmael in Herman Melville's *Moby-Dick*. Over the course of several chapters, Ishmael shifts from an attitude of dread and fear toward his assigned bedfellow at the Spouter-Inn (his future shipmate on the *Pequod*), the "dark complexioned," "savage" Queequeg, to an unexpected appreciation of Queequeg's "civility and consideration."[56] "His countenance," he remarks, "yet had a something in it which was by no means disagreeable. You cannot hide the soul. Through all his unearthly tattooings, I thought I saw the traces of a simple honest heart."[57] Other positive features, too, he begins to notice in Queequeg, soon enough realizing that "I began to be sensible of strange feelings. I felt a melting in me. . . . I began to feel myself mysteriously drawn towards him. And those same things that would have repelled most others, they were the very magnets that thus drew me. I'll try a pagan friend, thought I."[58] The two characters become "bosom friends," and after some reflexive soul-searching Ishmael even joins Queequeg in a pagan ritual.[59] When the two check out of the Spouter-Inn and make their way through town together, "the people stare . . . at seeing

Portrayals of Queequeg and Ishmael in San Francisco Opera's production of Jake Heggie's adaptation of *Moby Dick*.

him and me upon such confidential terms."[60] Ishmael fully anticipates the modern cosmopolitan's willingness to cross boundaries, to be open to new modes of experience, and to participate meaningfully in others' racial life. It is only in not questioning the exploitative racial hierarchy aboard the *Pequod* that he reveals the limits of his fellow-feeling.

Many of the constitutive features of the racial democratic individual are delineated in philosopher John Dewey's writings. These include a basic faith in one another's democratic possibilities, a "faith in the capacity of the intelligence of the common man to respond with commonsense to the free play of facts and ideas"; and a "faith in the possibility of conducting disputes, controversies and conflicts as cooperative undertakings in which both parties learn by giving the other a chance to express itself, instead of having one party conquer by forceful suppression of the other."[61] Having a faith in "amicable cooperation" means being driven by an abiding concern for justice, a passion to eliminate exploitation and subjugation so that all can take part in a genuinely collaborative and mutually enriching way of life.[62] But an attitude of forgiveness also is important, for the democratic personality above all is intent on solving problems, on looking ahead rather than behind, on anticipating consequences rather than dwelling on antecedents. By extension, racial animus and vengefulness also gave way in him or her to a progressive and forward-looking spirit. Racial healing is valued over hatred, an openness to reconciliation over the impulse to condemn.

The end on which Dewey was focused was the enlargement and flourishing of the self. "*The end*," he asserted, "is growth itself."[63] The ideal individual of racial democracy deploys its creative intelligence toward the end of fashioning a more enriching experience for itself and others. We use the term "intelligence" deliberately—and in a specific, philosophic sense of that term. To philosophers, intelligence has to do with one's ability to exercise good judgment in a world full of uncertainty. As Dewey wrote, a person "is intelligent . . . in virtue of his capacity to estimate the possibilities of a situation and to act in accordance with his estimate."[64] This ability to solve the problems we confront is directly connected to our ability accurately to assess those problems and to develop different courses of action. As American sociologist Charles Cooley, a contemporary of Dewey, added, "The test of intelligence is the power to act successfully in new situations. We judge a man to be intelligent when we see that in going through the world he is not guided merely by routine or second-hand ideas, but that when he meets a fresh difficulty he thinks out a fresh line of action appropriate to it, which is justified by its success. . . . It is, then, essentially a kind of foresight, a mental reaction that anticipates the operation of the forces at work and is prepared in advance to adjust itself to them."[65]

Racial injustice relies on a tangled collection of distortions and illogic and lies sometimes misrecognized as truth. Logic, rational decision-making, and good sense—the deployment of intelligence—can shine a bright and revealing light on the obfuscations linked to racial domination; it can lay bare the true nature of the beast. Racial intelligence can promote a social climate where people desire—and need—to know the best and latest information on the pressing problems of the day, and it can lead to successful resolution of those problems. We imagine an opening of the American mind, where ideas and knowledge are treated seriously and with respect and where people realize the power of clear thinking.

HOW DO WE BRING ABOUT CHANGE?

The first part of this chapter addressed the question, What is it we wish to achieve? It settled upon an answer: racial democracy. The second part now addresses the question, How do we achieve racial democracy? Here a pessimist might reply, "It cannot be achieved. Racism is unchangeable. All our efforts at change will amount to nothing." But to this the response is clear: all experience already is change. "Becoming is an inescapable feature of life."[66] One cannot help but change the course of events, even if at times unwittingly or with limited foresight. It is not a question of *if* we change our world, but *how* we change it—for better or for worse. What, then, might be the ideal means of effecting racial reconstruction? How might racial democracy be attained? In what follows, we review four distinct levels at which change can be and, as experience has shown, already has been successfully pursued: those of the individual self, everyday interactions, established institutions, and efforts at collective action. We survey possible means of racial reconstruction at each level—some of the most potentially helpful means, but by no means an exhaustive list—and ponder their strengths and limitations. The reader should bear in mind that each set of means is interdependent with the others, and effective change in one or another alone cannot bring about the desired ends. As Tocqueville pointed out in respect to democratic liberty, not even ideal societal circumstances (he spoke of laws and institutions) can sustain a life of freedom for long in the absence of citizens imbued with public-spiritedness and a love of the common good, nor can the best "habits of the heart," as he termed them, preserve a democratic republic in the absence of the right kinds of laws and institutions.[67] So too, in a racial democracy, one ideally must establish a self-reinforcing dynamic, a virtuous cycle, extending across and subsuming all different levels. One cannot ever say that one set of means is more important than all the rest.[68]

Change at the Individual Level

At first glance, it might seem difficult to effect meaningful change at the individual level. Encrusted habits often run deep and wish and effort alone cannot easily change them.[69] Nonetheless, we *can* shed our less desirable habits, including long-established ways of thinking, feeling, perceiving, and acting that help reproduce racism. If consumed with bigotry, we can cultivate in ourselves more accepting dispositions toward other racial groups. If limited in our (self-) perceptions and strategies of action by long-entrenched cultural parochialism, we can develop capacities for deeper and more genuine mutuality. If prone to symbolic violence, we can negate this tendency toward self-negation and form more satisfying and fulfilling habits, ways of being conducive to self-development and growth.

Two potential means of change are especially noteworthy. The first is indirect. Individuals can change the settings they inhabit with the deliberate aim of putting themselves in contexts more conducive to growth and enriched experience. It is the relation between habit and habitat that matters: by altering the one, we can establish conditions for transforming the other. We already have spoken of cultural labor necessary for building bridges across racial divides and proactively fashioning more meaningful connections. But one also can insert oneself from the outset into growth-conducive contexts where cultural labor is necessary—for instance, by entering into meaningful interactions with neighbors or classmates of ethnic backgrounds other than one's own or by joining interracial, even antiracist, associations or movements. The second means of personal change is deliberate reflection. There can be "critical moments" of perplexity which in turn lead to (self-) critical thought.[70] In those moments one can pause and reconsider one's previous modes of response to a situation, in hopes of arriving at a more intelligent way forward.[71] Potentially this involves reconstructing ways of thinking, perceiving, feeling, and acting—for instance, questioning one's sense of ethnic superiority; fears of confirming demeaning stereotypes; or tendencies toward self-exclusion, the self-denying verdict that "this is not for the likes of me." At times it also involves rethinking dispositions toward racial hatred or vindictiveness. Such self-questioning, too, can result in self-enlargement and growth—and perhaps bring closer to realization the type of individual personality corresponding to the racial democratic ideal.

Several aspects of deliberate reflection merit close attention here. One is the antecedent choice even to engage in such reflection at all. As we observed in Chapter 1, many people who have the privilege of not being regularly victimized or stigmatized by racism respond to the challenges and discomforts of reflexivity with a sigh and the remark, "I'm so tired of hearing about racism!" But for self-questioning to occur, one has to get beyond "tired." One has to recognize that the complaint itself is a product of racial privilege.

Another important aspect of deliberate reflection, one required of all of us, is the sheer perseverance it necessitates. There is no conversion moment, no glorious awakening, in which, once and for all, we emerge out of darkness into light. We never can stop asking, How do I know my racial assumptions are true? How do I know the world actually works this way? How might my upbringing and racial identity be influencing my thinking? The apt metaphor here is one of training, in which day by day we discipline our thoughts, feelings, perceptions, and actions so they are not dictated without our consent by the forces of domination. And we need to train not just our mind but our bodies as well. As we have seen, racial dispositions are not merely cognitive in nature; they are deeply incorporated, even bodily modes of response for which a transformational strategy built on consciousness-raising is inadequate. How do we react when a large black man steps inside the elevator? When we spot an Arab American man in the airport security line? When we notice a white woman dressed in professional clothes, briefcase in tow? When an Asian American student raises his hand in class? These are "instinctive" responses that appear to come from somewhere deep within. Deliberate reflection has to notice, monitor, and aim at changing these undeliberate, unreflective modes of engagement.

Self-questioning rarely can bring about meaningful individual-level change without the critical, often uncomfortable intervention of others. But usually we go about it alone. The pursuit of individual transformation often involves asking ourselves if we are racist or reverse-racist. We put ourselves on trial and probe deep within for signs of guilt. If we search for guilt we usually find it, but self-reproach itself inhibits action. "Digging deep" like this often precludes putting ourselves in new circumstances conducive to inner growth and change. The result all too often is a kind of false reflexivity that errs in one of two opposite directions. On the one hand, we can search within ourselves and happily report that we are free of all prejudices. "I treat everyone the same," we might declare. "I do not have a racist bone in my body." On the other hand, we can claim, after a thorough inward-looking meditation, that we are wretches, full of prejudice: "I am so completely racist; I am helpless." One kind of dishonest exaggeration looks inside and finds an angel, seemingly immune to racial domination; the other finds a demon that welcomes racial domination without resistance. But the truth is that every one of us can locate within ourselves impulses of racism and impulses of racial enlightenment; we all are made up of a complicated blend of courage and cowardice, ignorance and intelligence.

Both forms of self-searching are dishonest; both fail to specify and alter the actual ways in which race works. Deliberate reflection only produces significant change when it takes place in a dialogical context in which internal thought processes are articulated and carried forward into action and some sort of response thereupon is received from the external environment. Friends, lovers, and fellow participants in a social movement: these are the sources of response that can help, in the manner of an ongoing experiment, to let us know if our self-questioning is on target. Often such response can be challenging and painful. But just as often, it can be rewarded.

How does individual transformation unfold? For many of us, growing up requires developing an identity. It means asking ourselves, "How should I live?" "Who am I?" Coming to terms with our racial and ethnic identity, of course, is an important part of this process. For whites, it begins often much later than it does for people of color, the vast majority of whom are socialized at a young age to understand themselves in racial terms. When whites begin to think about their racial identity, many find the process unsettling and confusing. A good many would rather think of themselves as individuals, somehow detached from the larger society, than as group members. Psychologists have identified this stage, one marked by a naïveté about racism (itself a courtesy of white privilege), as the first and most basic step in white identity formation. Unfortunately, some white people never develop beyond this stage.[72]

But many others do. They begin to understand what race means to them; they begin to come to terms with their whiteness, some through personal encounters (living with an American Indian roommate in college), others through classes like the one for which you are reading this book. Curious, they begin to pay more attention, to learn about racism. This process leads many to become aware of their racial privilege, which provokes feelings of guilt and shame.

Newly awakened, many whites made aware of racial inequality desire to fight it but don't know how. Like new religious converts, they can be zealous but unwieldy, passionate but not strategic. They tend to make their "unenlightened" friends and family members uncomfortable; the latter learn not to mention anything having to do with race in their presence. After their passion subsides, some whites begin to regress, placing the blame not on themselves or even on racism, but on people of color. "My friends are right," they say. "If there are racial inequalities today, non-white people must be at fault. After all, slavery did happen long ago, and I certainly had nothing to do with it. All this talk about racism is nonsense."[73]

By contrast, at this stage in the development of their racial identity, some other whites begin to cultivate a healthy and honest relationship with their whiteness. They begin to come to terms with the ways they are privileged simply because they are white; and they start, in a reflexive mode, to "unlearn their whiteness." They begin to interrogate attitudes they long have held about racism and people of color, and they begin spending more time in multiracial settings and with antiracist whites. They realize how they unintentionally feed racism and learn, too, how they can work against racial injustice. Here, they gain a healthy white identity. They begin to shed their guilt and to develop a "positive White identity, based in reality, not on assumed superiority."[74]

People do not move through these stages in white identity development—which proceeds from racial naïveté and confusion, through guilt and anger, to resolution and honesty—in a straight line. They do not progress through so many steps toward racial enlightenment. Rather, people move forward and backward through these stages during different points in their lives. And, we must point out, the vast majority of white people, those who never are introduced to the realities of race, never move past the first two stages.

Nonwhites, too, go through stages of racial identity development. Many begin with their own brand of naïveté, more or less unaware of racism. This innocence, however, tends to be short-lived, as many nonwhites encounter racism at a very young age. Consider this interaction told to a researcher by white parents who had adopted nonwhite children. While shopping at a mall, the family bumped into a white friend, who proceeded to ask the children what they wanted to be when they grew up. "She asked the oldest daughter, who is Asian, if she was planning to be an accountant, the youngest brother, a sturdy boy of black and Asian heritage, if he wanted to become a golfer like Tiger Woods, and the third child, a Latina girl, if she would like to grow up and become a gardener."[75]

Coming to the realization that you are nonwhite in a society marked by a long history of racism is a painful one. Many nonwhites react by immersing themselves in communities of people who share their racial identity, people who have experienced similar slights and cuts and, therefore, may understand their struggles. During this time, nonwhites might be gripped by anger and frustration at the unfairness of racism; they might grow bitter toward people who do not share their racial identity. They might also begin learning about nonwhite history and culture. Latinos, for example, might read about César Chávez and the farmworkers' movement; Arab Americans might begin studying Arabic poetry; African Americans might read up on black nationalism and black power; American Indians might begin paying more respect to their tribal language and customs.[76] For many nonwhites during this stage, their racial or ethnic identity becomes their master identity; it is what most defines their sense of self.

Just as whites pursuing a mature and healthy racial identity must recognize their privilege in order to take steps to understand themselves as more than "victimizers," nonwhites must work to rethink their blackness or Indianness or Mexicanness or Asianness or Arabness in "ways that take them beyond the role of victim."[77] They come to realize that their whole being cannot be defined by their racial identity alone. They develop a critical race consciousness that allows them to channel their animus against white supremacy in constructive ways, criticizing the systems that perpetuate racial domination. They learn to rest confidently and calmly in their nonwhite skin and resist basing their racial identity on ethnic chauvinism, which only widens racial divides.[78]

A central component of developing a nonwhite identity in a country whose past and present are scarred by racism is the formation of a "double consciousness." What Du Bois wrote about African Americans can be applied to other nonwhite groups as well: "The Negro is a sort of seventh son, born with a veil, and gifted with second-sight in this American world,—a world which yields him no true self-consciousness, but only lets him see himself through the revelation of the other world. It is a peculiar sensation, this double-consciousness, this sense of always looking at one's self through the eyes of others, of measuring one's soul by the tape of a world that looks on in amused contempt and pity. One ever feels his two-ness,—an American, a Negro: two souls, two thoughts, two unreconciled strivings; two warring ideals in one dark body, whose dogged strength alone keeps it from being torn asunder."[79]

Double consciousness, then, is a way of seeing yourself through two pairs of eyes: one pair belonging to White America, the other belonging to your racial or ethnic group. If you are an African American, it means viewing yourself as you believe nonblacks view you and as you believe blacks view you. Most white Americans never develop this kind of fractured identity because they do not have to look upon themselves with the eyes of dominated groups. This is how one sociologist explained Du Bois's famous idea: "The White American takes the role of the White other toward the self without any fundamental contradiction and thus essentially without being aware of doing so. White Americans do not take the role of Black Americans toward themselves. African Americans, on the other hand, because of the essential inequality and incompatibility between the two communities, are forced to take the role of White others toward themselves and are as a consequence uncomfortably aware of looking at themselves through the veil. . . . The African American, according to Du Bois, always is torn in two directions, held accountable to two communities."[80]

Individual-level change is at its most far-reaching when it becomes a self-reinforcing process, establishing new dispositions that are embraced, and that serve as a means toward continued reflexivity, self-development, and growth. These dispositions have to do less with deliberate reasoning and problem-solving than with an attitude of openness toward experience. They lead us always and proactively to seek out honest, searching, and dialogical ways of probing our racial blind spots. They also reach down, so to speak, into the depths of our psychical lives, into layers where the most destructive passions of racial life are to be found: spite, vengefulness, shame, and self-loathing. Self-reinforcing habits of change lead us away from such destructive passions and in the direction of empathy and love. Racial healing becomes possible when we choose potentially enriching modes of engagement over our own deeply ingrained tendencies toward fear, closure, hardness, denial, and apathy.

Individual-level change is important, yet far too much emphasis often is placed on it. Because racism manifests itself in individuals and institutions, addressing only the former usually allows institutional racism to persist. Because, as we've learned, there is a great deal more to racism than racial prejudice, there are limits to what can be expected of individual-level transformation in the striving for a racially democratic society. Still, it is morally legitimate to expect some efforts in this direction on the part of everyone, from the most to the least fortunate. It is morally legitimate, for instance, to expect white Americans to adhere to basic requirements of racial justice and to renounce as far as possible the privileges of their own whiteness. And, as philosopher Tommie Shelby has pointed out, it is equally morally legitimate to expect the ghetto poor, for their part, to live (like anyone else) by baseline standards of personal conduct. "Expecting the ghetto poor to honor their natural duties . . . does not blame the victims. The ghetto poor should not be held responsible for the appalling social conditions that have been imposed on them because of the workings of an unjust social structure, but they should be held accountable for how they choose to respond to these conditions. Demanding this basic level of moral responsibility treats them as full moral persons and as political agents in their own right." In particular, as Shelby notes, "It is reasonable to expect the ghetto poor . . . to not take courses of action that would clearly exacerbate the injustices of the system or that would increase the burdens of injustice on those in ghetto communities similarly situated. . . . Nor should they do things that would clearly make a just society more difficult to achieve."[81] Much the same would hold true for other racially subordinated individuals as well. In short, personal transformation does matter, and the more one sets one's sights on a fully realized racial democracy, the more seriously one should take the project of individual-level change.

Change at the Interactional Level

Racial reconstruction also can be pursued at the interactional level. A diversity of means are available for making interactions more racially democratic. When people with racist beliefs are confronted with an alternative view of how the world works, for instance, and thereupon grow defensive and uncomfortable, four useful techniques can be deployed for holding them accountable for their prejudices. We summarize those techniques here in the form of injunctions. First, take their prejudices seriously. Do not yell at them; do not call them "stupid" or "ignorant"; try not to get too angry. Realize that they matter, that their ideas matter too, and that their beliefs most likely are tied to their personal experience. If you want them to listen to you, then you must listen—sincerely—to them. Second, ask people questions. Questions—posed authentically, not sarcastically or presumptuously—are disarming and inviting. They also are quite natural. If someone says, "I think the Los Angeles Lakers are the best basketball team in the country," the natural response is to ask, "Why?" Similarly, if someone says, "I don't think American Indians want to climb out of poverty," it is equally natural to ask, "Why?" Questions, at bottom, are pursuers of the truth. As such, they are powerful weapons against racist beliefs.[82] Third, do your homework. How can you hope to change someone's mind if you cannot offer that person a better interpretation than the one he or she currently holds? Racism's arch-nemesis is a critically informed citizen. Finally, the worst thing you can do when you are confronted with a racist belief—other than remaining silent—is to turn the conversation into a debate you intend to "win." The goal should be a rational discussion, not a debate in the sense of a verbal sparring match. If you set out to intimidate someone or make them feel stupid, you usually will produce in them the desired effect, losing credibility and perhaps even calcifying their wrongheaded beliefs. If you truly want to change someone's mind, then you have to be willing to be vulnerable and (if appropriate) honest about your own prejudices (we are not perfect, after all). One last thing: think about the timing of your conversation. Sometimes a racist utterance is best addressed on the spot; other times, it is better to confront the person at a later juncture.

A more confrontational approach than the foregoing is laid out in the so-called race traitor literature, which calls in eyebrow-raising fashion for the "abolition" of the white race.[83] By this is meant, as a closer look reveals, nothing other than the elimination of white domination and the privileges attendant upon it—hardly a novel goal—although the means proposed for doing so are provocative. What is called for here is "disrupting" the ordinary workings of a racist order whenever and wherever they occur, even if at the cost of acrimony and discomfort.[84] The guiding orientation is not educative, but contestational, and the key idea is to prevent the smooth, unthinking operation of racial domination by throwing a wrench in the works. Such an approach would be most effective when undertaken among racially privileged whites—for instance, when one offers a racist comment and the other challenges it forthrightly and without hesitation, forcing the initial speaker to realize that racism will not go unchallenged, even among those it most clearly benefits. The race traitor approach also can be carried over, however, into interactions among nonwhites. For interactions within and across nonwhite racial or ethnic boundaries—for instance, among fellow American Indians, or between a Puerto Rican and a Dominican—also can involve an expression of racist sentiments, whether of bigotry against whites or of racism against members of other nonwhite groups. When conversation partners explicitly refuse or deny complicity with racism, the interactional power of racist speakers is reduced, and the interaction order stands a greater chance of reconstituting itself upon an antiracist basis. Intimidation may well occur, of course, and defensiveness is a likely result. But far from being unintended consequences of the disavowal of racist complicity, these are the very point of it, the very means of effecting change.

What are we to think of efforts to bring about racial reconstruction at the interactional level? What are its possibilities and limitations? By itself, at least, interaction-level change is too narrow in scope to overturn systematic racism. One cannot bring about racial democracy solely by converting minds through dialogue or even by making the operations of racial domination more arduous and conflictual. What happens, for instance, when whites interact not with other whites, or nonwhites with other nonwhites, but across the color line? Whenever Americans with different racial identities meet, a whole history of murder and slavery, colonialism and dehumanization—as well as of progress and change—stands between them.[85] Seeing another person *as* black, American Indian, or white is nothing short of seeing hundreds of years of history unfurled before our eyes. Interracial dialogue means engaging with this thing looming in one's presence. But the "thing" in question is a historically constituted relation of power that cannot be confronted solely at the dialogical level. Hence the challenges that face well-meaning whites who insist on regarding the antiracist project as basically one of face-to-face interaction. "White people who are attempting to transform their habits of white privilege should accept as fitting," notes one astute observer—perhaps a better word might have been "understandable"—"and not as 'reverse discrimination,' the angry reactions and stares that they might receive when they have entered into non-white spaces."[86] This having been said, interaction still *is* important, and there is much to be gained from effecting change at that level. It is impossible to imagine a racial democracy in which we do not engage in mutually enriching and creative interaction. Seeking to bring about such interaction is a crucial element in the effort to reconstruct our racial order.

We would be remiss here if we concluded this discussion of the means of interaction-level change without a few comments on a closely related and important topic: diversity training. Diversity management programs can be found in many workplaces across America, and they are among the most significant attempts in recent years to alter the character and tenor of interracial interactions. Diversity management is a fairly new development, one with roots in affirmative action legislation. During the early 1970s, employers woke up to the fact that they could be subjected to costly lawsuits if they discriminated against women and people of color. To decrease their risk of litigation, they established affirmative action and antidiscrimination offices. But in the 1980s, affirmative action policies were weakened by President Reagan and the Supreme Court, which forced affirmative action specialists—whose livelihoods depended on antidiscrimination efforts—to repackage their services. These specialists did so by filing back the teeth of affirmative action, in particular by doing away with more positive and proactive steps to enlarge the representation of women and people of color in the workplace. Then they spun the resultant (softer) antidiscrimination programs in a different way than before, rationalizing them not on ethical grounds—as a judicious response to centuries of racism and patriarchy—but because they made good business sense. A diverse workforce, it was reasoned, would increase a company's effectiveness and competitiveness and would expand its reach to new consumer pools. Many companies were convinced and implemented mandatory "diversity training." Affirmative action thus became diversity management.[87] Was this initiative, which came to be widely accepted, among the most effective of solutions to the problems of racial domination? Or was it widely accepted precisely because it was less effective?[88]

Many researchers have found diversity management insufficient for dismantling racism. First, diversity training seems to do nothing to bust through glass ceilings. Studies have shown that such programs leave unaltered the racial and gender mix of companies' supervisory positions.[89] Second, diversity has come to mean many things: diversity of political leanings, religious beliefs, sexual orientation, age, and so forth. As the meaning of diversity expands to incorporate more aspects of our lives, the term comes to signal human variation—not historical and structural modes of domination. "Is diversity management really just [a matter of] talking about respecting all individual differences?" asks one observer. "If so, this is problematic and cannot in its present form lead to inclusive organizations. There is a real danger in seeing differences as benign variation among people. It overlooks the role of conflict, power, dominance, and the history of how organizations are fundamentally structured by race, gender, and class."[90] Another concern is that diversity management might reify race in fallacious ways, inflating cultural differences or describing racial differences where none exist. For instance, one antidiscrimination training manual describes Latino workers as "family oriented" (versus work oriented) and suggests that blacks "react quickly to changing situations."[91] Overarching statements such as these encourage stereotypical thinking. Finally, one might ask, how could a training session that lasts less than a day—the length of half of such training sessions—have any impact on a phenomenon centuries old? The point is not that diversity management programs are useless. Some research suggests they can encourage tolerance in the workplace, and companies that have taken more serious measures—for instance, placing a permanent person or staff of people in charge of antidiscrimination programs—have created a more integrated workforce.[92] The point is that when critically analyzed, these programs are revealed to be poor substitutes for aggressive antiracist initiatives. They are but one step in the right direction, and a small step at that.[93]

Change at the Institutional Level

It will take much more than a single conversation or diversity training session adequately to address racism. And despite one's best efforts, one not always will succeed. Some people will go to their graves with their racism. After trying and trying, sometimes the only thing left to do is to move on and expend our energies elsewhere, like fighting for racial democracy at the institutional level. Why are societal institutions so very important? Because it is difficult to imagine changing patterns of racial interaction in any far-reaching way without also reconstructing the institutional frameworks within which they unfold. Among these are the economy (or, at a more microscopic level, the workplace); the state (including courts, policing, and prisons); institutions of cultural production (including the media and artistic institutions); and the fields comprising civil society (including education, religion, and the family). Rather than discuss in detail the various substantive changes required for these institutional domains to become more racially just and democratic, we focus here as elsewhere on domain-transcending means of effecting change. At the institutional level, these include devices such as antidiscrimination laws; affirmative action; a "hidden agenda" of targeting racial groups for state aid under the aegis of nonracialist policies; and efforts to change the very ways in which racial categorization, classification, and hierarchy are inscribed in institutions.

Antidiscrimination laws are among the most important measures at the institutional level for reconstructing the racial order. They address discrimination in education, housing, and the workplace in particular: key pressure points of racism. Epitomized by the Civil Rights Act of 1964, which barred racial discrimination in schools, workplaces, and public accommodations, but including as well a whole host of other legislative achievements, such as the Civil Rights Act of 1968, which prohibited racial discrimination in housing, they seek to realize across the institutional landscape the ideal of equal opportunity for all citizens. Consider the Fair Housing Act (FHA), passed by Congress in 1968. The FHA was intended to prevent discrimination by all housing providers, from landlords to lenders. Although the FHA forbids discrimination toward a number of protected groups—women, religious minorities, people with disabilities—the majority of violations involve discrimination on the basis of race. Because many people do not even realize they are being discriminated against in the housing sector—landlords may claim that available units no longer are available; real estate brokers might show a Dominican family houses only in certain areas of town—federal, state, and local institutions have taken steps to root out "hidden discrimination" by, for instance, sending testers, virtually identical in all respects save for race, to pose as potential buyers or renters. Since 1992, the Department of Justice has brought nearly 100 discrimination cases against housing providers based on evidence gleaned from these testers, recovering more than $12 million in damages.[94] Local fair housing groups also have relied on the FHA to hold discriminating landlords accountable for, say, charging Hispanics higher rent or for turning Chinese American families away. Between 1990 and 1997, local fair housing groups filed over 1,000 fair housing lawsuits and received more than $95 million in damages.[95] Still, cases alleging discrimination are far outpaced by acts of discrimination in the housing sector. The National Fair Housing Alliance estimates that each year roughly four million instances of discrimination take place against racial minorities, but only a small fraction are reported and an even smaller fraction tried. In 2007, the Department of Housing and Urban Development received 2,449 complaints of discrimination but charged only 31 of them.[96]

Some also believe affirmative action to be another important means of racial reconstruction. Philosopher Elizabeth Anderson has considered at length the different theoretical justifications for it. The most compelling of these, she has argued, is the integrative model: "Instead of waiting for injustice to happen and compensating afterward, or merely blocking discriminatory mechanisms that retain their force, [this model] . . . aims to dismantle the continuing causes of race-based injustice by practicing integration, which is an essential tool for undoing segregation and stigmatization."[97] Moreover, it has a wider scope than other alternatives that stress the potential contributions of affirmative action to institutional diversity of ideas and viewpoints. The integrative model depicts the beneficiaries of affirmative action in a nonstigmatizing way, as "partners with the practitioners of affirmative action in breaking down the barriers that block segregated groups' access to mainstream opportunities."[98] It recognizes that these partners may be among the more privileged of the underprivileged, although such a limitation it deems necessary because "successful functioning" in institutions is a requirement of "successful integration," and those who succeed are better positioned to help their less privileged peers down the line.[99] The integrative model also directly targets race as "the object of moral and instrumental concern. . . . If the problem is racial segregation, then the most direct way to remedy this problem is to practice racial integration."[100] Ultimately, affirmative action under the integrative model is concerned with advancing a racial democratic project, in which institutions truly are just and conducive to the flourishing of racial groups and individuals only insofar as they allow meritorious persons of all racial origins an equal opportunity for inclusion and meaningful participation.

"Discrimination is morally wrong, politically dangerous, industrially wasteful, and socially silly. It is the duty of whites to stop it, and to do so primarily for their own sakes." —W. E. B. Du Bois

A different means of institutional reconstruction is the so-called hidden agenda promoted by sociologist William Julius Wilson in response to the growing realization that neither antidiscrimination laws nor affirmative action has succeeded in improving the life chances of the least well-off in society. Antidiscrimination laws are inadequate for overturning cumulative inequalities that exist at the time when racial barriers are lifted and that severely hinder the most disadvantaged members of racial minorities. And affirmative action leaves virtually unaffected a large proportion of nonwhites lacking qualifications such as educational capital, job training, and network connections. "If minority members from the most advantaged families profit disproportionately from policies based on the principle of individual opportunity," writes Wilson, "they also reap disproportionate benefits from policies of affirmative action based solely on their group membership. . . . [Hence] problems of the truly disadvantaged may require *nonracial* solutions."[101] These comprise economic policies aimed at enhancing job opportunities among the least advantaged, new job training programs, and an expansion of public assistance—all measures that, unlike antidiscrimination and affirmative action efforts, benefit the general public rather than only racial minorities. "The hidden agenda for liberal policymakers," Wilson sums up, "is to improve the life chances of truly disadvantaged groups such as the ghetto underclass by emphasizing programs to which the more advantaged groups of all races and class backgrounds can positively relate."[102] Here institutional reconstruction centers on the state and economic life, its agenda aiming to benefit the underprivileged in indirect, unspoken ways, much as some models of affirmative action stress its potential to add not to the economic or educational well-being of racial minorities, but to the diversity of perspectives. Wilson's approach has important implications for racial democracy because its goal is to redress problems of racial injustice that cannot easily be remedied by race-specific policies. Ironically, however—perhaps because it recognizes the continued vehemence of racism (it speaks of a *hidden* agenda)—its strategic approach intentionally is color-blind.

One final means of racial renovation at the institutional level is symbolic reclassification. It builds on the insight that institutions embody a symbolic order, a framework of rules, categories, and boundaries, whose very structure helps to shape the workings of racial domination. For instance, the state imposes upon society a wide array of symbolic schemas, from the racial categories of the census to the quota systems of immigration law; from the delineation of "English-only" zones to the racial designations on a birth certificate. Thanks to these codifications, the state helps to naturalize racial divisions that, in fact, are socially and historically constructed. Nor is the state the only institution whose symbolic classifications matter for racial life. When universities distinguish between legacies and affirmative action applicants, when schools track students in ways that overlap with racial distinctions, and when the National Basketball Association imposes a dress code banning "hip-hop" modes of dress while endorsing conventional white fashion choices, then a great deal is done in racial life to demarcate the sacred from the profane. Struggles can be waged to call into question these symbolic divisions. And such struggles can be waged not for racial groups' discrete advantage, but on behalf of a more just and harmonious racial order.

Change at the Level of Collective Action

As history attests, of course, bold reform and transformative social change also are brought about (perhaps most consequentially) through public protest: through strikes, sustained boycotts, public demonstrations, civil disobedience, and racial uprisings. Democracy entered the world not only by means of local initiales and publics but through a revolution, and it is a revolution that Americans celebrate on the Fourth of July. Slavery was abolished because abolitionists employed revolutionary methods while agitating for slaves' freedom—and because, as Du Bois pointed out, black slaves themselves rose up in rebellion; union strikes in the first half of the twentieth century helped boost thousands of workers, including people of color, from poverty into the middle class; and segregation folded because antiracist social movements forced its hand. In 1984, Chávez reflected on a lifetime leading the farmworkers' movement. "The UFW [United Farm Workers of America]," he wrote, "was the beginning! We attacked that historical source of shame and infamy that our people in this country lived with. We attacked that injustice, not by complaining; not by seeking hand-outs; not by becoming soldiers in the War on Poverty. We organized! Farm workers acknowledge we had allowed ourselves to become victims in a democratic society—a society where majority rule and collective bargaining are supposed to be more than academic theories or political rhetoric. And by addressing this historical problem, we created confidence and pride and hope in an entire people's ability to create the future."[103] To participate in collective political action—to employ the time-honored methods of public protest—is to engage as fully and completely as possible in civil society and to refuse to "become victims in a democratic society." It is to address the challenges of racial domination on the widest scale and in the most ambitious fashion, as certainly was the case with the various racial and ethnic movements of the Civil Rights Era.

To be sure, different forms of public protest have their respective strengths and weaknesses. Urban uprisings and other such spontaneous rebellions may be necessary if only to allow "the ghetto poor to maintain their self-respect. If nothing else, such actions can be cathartic and can help the oppressed to keep from turning on each other as they seek an outlet for their justified anger."[104] These uprisings also can call attention to societal maladies all too easily ignored or dismissed by mainstream America. (Race riot reports are an important, and all too often necessary, genre of racial inquiry, and some have had significant impact.[105]) But there is no denying that these acts of rage and defiance often are self-destructive and short lived. Some believe, also, that more organized, durable movements that claim an ethnocultural basis are unsatisfactory as well—including, perhaps most famously, the Black Power Movement. They reify the racial group and proceed as though it were a reality. "The basis of black political unity," writes Shelby (although we can generalize here from blacks to all racial groups), "should not be a shared black identity, regardless of whether we understand this identity as a matter of racial essence, ethnicity, culture, or nationality."[106] It should be a common experience of racial oppression, of being stigmatized and denied the advantages racial dominants enjoy. "An oppression-centered black identity is not a matter of being anti-white or, for that matter, pro-black, but of abhorring racial injustice."[107] It is a matter, too, of individuals who have been treated unfairly because of their social classification as persons of color sharing in a concern to overturn racial injustice and to establish a more harmonious and equitable racial order. Influenced by Rawls, Shelby lends this view a liberal inflection: "This group solidarity would be understood, not as an end in itself, but as a collective strategy for bringing about a social order in which individuals can autonomously define and pursue their conception of the good life without their 'blackness' posing any limitation or burden."[108]

Perhaps most conducive to the goal of a racial democracy, however, would be a multiracial form of political contention, one embodying the very ends it hopes to realize. Multiracial movements have a long history in the United States, perhaps longer than many Americans imagine. To take but one set of examples, interracial alliances long have been crucial to workers' efforts to win rights through union mobilization. Asian American and Mexican American farmworkers, along with documented and undocumented immigrants, joined together to fight for more rights and helped to energize a movement that eventually would result in the thoroughly multiracial UFW. Chicago's white and black packinghouse workers, whom the business elite pitted against one another to drive down the price of labor, overcame racial and ethnic antagonisms to form the powerful United Packinghouse Workers of America; in 1946, this interracial union went on strike to increase workers' wages—and won.

Hawaii's racially diverse working-class movement, which united Native Hawaiian, Portuguese, Chinese, Japanese, and Filipino workers, winning better pay and the institutionalization of antidiscrimination guidelines, is another case in point.[109] After the islands of Hawaii were colonized, white settlers from Britain and America sought a cheap labor force to work the sugar plantations. They found it in Native Hawaiians and migrants from China, Japan, and the Philippines. However, by 1870 the American-led anti-Chinese movement pressured Hawaii's business elites to abandon their Chinese laborers and whiten their workforce. The elites gave in and began importing workers from Portugal. Although the Portuguese workers were not granted complete admission into Hawaii's *haole* race—the Hawaiian word (literally "foreigner") used to describe European immigrants to the islands—they were considered whiter than workers from Asia. Japanese workers were considered racially inferior and, especially after the bombing of Pearl Harbor and the ensuing construction of Japanese internment camps, were seen as anti-American. But Filipinos were thought to sit lower still than the Japanese, occupying the lowest point in Hawaii's racial hierarchy. So, the *haoles* worked to uphold white supremacy; the Portuguese hoped to be admitted to the privileged race, deriding Asian immigrants; and the Japanese joined other groups in disdaining Filipinos.[110]

But in the 1930s, things began to change. Union campaigns began to organize workers around one central idea: the fight is not against one another, but against white supremacy and worker exploitation. As one labor organizer put it, "We want you in [this union] where all brothers are alike . . . Japanese, Filipinos, Portuguese, *haoles,* and all are the same."[111] Union meetings were held in multiple languages—English, Japanese, and Ilocano—and affirmative action policies were put in place such that each racial group was well represented in union leadership. Hawaii's working class began to recast the racial system, blaming the *haole* business elites not only for exploiting their labor but also for reinforcing racial divides.

Hawaii's interracial working-class movement was tested in 1946, when sugar workers called for an all-industry strike. The business elites wouldn't budge at the bargaining table, figuring a strike would rekindle old racial divisions and smother the interracial unions. The strike, however, had the opposite effect. Workers demanded not only better pay but also antidiscrimination guidelines, a radical

A demonstration by the International Longshore and Warehouse Union. Frank Wu has written, "United by shared principles, we can create communities that are diverse and just."

proposition twenty years before the Civil Rights Act. Drawing strength and identity from their newly formed intergroup alliances, workers walked the picket lines for seventy-nine days. The employers finally conceded to their demands. Summing up the victory, a union leader declared, "It is the first time in the history of Hawaii that a strike of sugar workers on the plantations of Hawaii has ever been won. The first time in history that a strike of sugar workers has been conducted where there has been no split along racial lines."[112]

These efforts by interracial labor movements provide a compelling model today for those who would struggle for change in our racial order. "Working in multiracial coalitions of equal members," Frank Wu has written, "united by shared principles, we can create communities that are diverse and just. Together, we can reinvent the civil rights movement."[113] Perhaps, too—this might even be better—we can invent a new kind of racial justice movement altogether for the new times in which we live.

WE WHO BELIEVE IN FREEDOM

Working toward racial justice can require sacrifice; often it results in great frustration, anger, and feelings of defeat. But—ask any activist—it also will give you a deep sense of purpose and joy. When you work for something bigger than yourself, something more important than your checking account or your personal ambitions, life grows flush with meaning and importance. Do you long for a life overrunning with

"It does not require a majority to prevail but rather an irate, tireless minority keen to set brushfires in people's minds." —Samuel Adams

significance? That is a life engaged in the fight for justice. Do you want proof? Steal a glimpse of the calm, soft satisfaction in the eyes of an old civil rights foot soldier.

"There are too few of us!" one might say. But Samuel Adams, one of America's founding fathers, offers a famous and powerful refutation of that sentiment: "It does not require a majority to prevail but rather an irate, tireless minority keen to set brushfires in people's minds." It is necessary to remind ourselves time and again that during the Civil Rights Movement, the majority of white *and* nonwhite Americans stood on the sidelines while a core cadre of committed activists pushed the country forward. The same is true of most major historical events. Analysts have referred to it as the 80/20 phenomenon: the common observation that roughly 80 percent of social change is brought about by 20 percent of the population. Sociologist Mario Small has gone even further, suggesting that a community association that involves less than 1 percent of the total neighborhood population can bring about significant social change in that neighborhood. Adams was right. When a few impassioned citizens gather together around a single cause, the potential to move the world is in their hands. [114]

Sweeping racial change has come to America. Some ethnic conflicts viewed as intractable and eternal a mere 100 years ago hardly exist today. One thinks, for example, of the conflict between Protestants and Catholics, or between Irish and Italians. The historical record demonstrates that what one generation found unrealistic and impossible—idealistic—the succeeding generation made into reality. [115] "What is considered impossible today may be possible tomorrow," observe the authors of *White-Washing Race*. "It is well to remember that in the 1950s few Americans believed that a revolution in civil rights was just around the corner. Jim Crow seemed to be deeply entrenched, racial prejudice too formidable a presence in the minds of white Americans. Yet many people of all races vigorously opposed segregation anyway, not because they knew they would prevail but because they believed that doing so was morally necessary. And in the end they did prevail." [116]

Racial democracy has poked through the veil bit by bit, letting some light through with each advance, although its full potential has yet to be unleashed upon America. This book has explained how and why racial inequality persists; this chapter has explained what you can do about it. The next word is yours. We have said all we can. There is only silence without you. But in you and with you there is hope. What choice do we have but to reconstruct a new society, beautiful and right and, at last, wholly ours?

THE BIG PICTURE

Chapter 11: Toward Racial Democracy

MAIN POINTS

Evaluate the strengths and weaknesses of three different responses to racial inequality: color-blindness, multiculturalism/cosmopolitanism, and racial democracy.

Recognize the different levels where people can pursue racial democracy: the individual level, the interactional level, the institutional level, and the level of collective action.

KEY TERMS

- color-blindness, page 395
- multiculturalism, page 398
- racial democracy, page 403

- reflexivity, page 409
- changing institutions, page 416
- collective action, page 418

FROM THEORY TO PRACTICE

Imagine a racially democratic society. What would that look like? How would your daily life be different in such a society? Record your reflections.

List some ways you can work (or perhaps are working) for racial justice in your daily life. List at least one way you can change (1) yourself, (2) the people in your inner circle, (3) an institution to which you belong, and (4) your nation. As you do so, think about what kinds of resistance you might face and what you can do to overcome that resistance.

Glossary

Advanced Marginality: The severe spatial and social segregation of the ghetto's residents, marked by their amputation from America's economic prosperity, national security, collective imagination and memory, and state services.

Ahistorical Fallacy: The bold claim that most United States history, including the legacies of slavery and colonialism, is inconsequential today.

Antiracist Aesthetics: An artistic approach that seeks somehow to throw a wrench in the grinding gears of racism, forcing its audience to confront American racial history honestly and courageously.

Authenticity: Being true to one's ethnic or racial heritage, including in that discussion the choice of some whites to reject whiteness for an alternative ethnic identity.

Boarding Schools: As part of the white agenda to Anglicize America's indigenous population at the beginning of the twentieth century, American Indian parents were forced to send their children to boarding schools run by Christian missionaries and, later on, by the federal government.

Brave New Families: In 1967, the Supreme Court ruled antimiscegenation laws unconstitutional in *Loving v. Virginia*, marking a significant civil rights victory. Today the United States is home to over 4.8 million interracially married couples; that's one in twelve.

Causes and Consequences of Segregation: Throughout the nineteenth century, whites and nonwhites lived relatively close together, interacting with one another on a daily basis, but the rise of industrialism brought thousands to live in crowded, dilapidated slums. As the twentieth century marched forward, prosperous European immigrant families were able to move out of the slums and assimilate into the white American mainstream. Meanwhile, those who wore the badge of otherness—the "racial uniform," in the words of American sociologist Robert Park—were forbidden by law and custom to live anywhere else.

Changing Institutions: It is difficult to imagine changing patterns of racial interaction in any far-reaching way without also reconstructing the institutional frameworks within which they unfold.

The Civil Rights Movement: That collection of organizations and people who carried out political acts aimed at abolishing racial segregation, nonwhite disenfranchisement, and racial economic exploitation.

Civil Society: Some critics believe identity politics is responsible for splintering civil society, but in post-Civil Rights America, civil society has widened to include a cacophony of voices and opinions.

Coded Language: Indirect allusions to physical appearance, class upbringing, or sexual attractiveness; code words that give voice to dormant racialized dispositions (such as "welfare queen," "urban unrest," "illegal immigrants," "Islamic terrorists").

Collective Action: As history attests, bold reform and transformative social change also are brought about (perhaps most consequentially) through public protest: through strikes, sustained boycotts, public demonstrations, civil disobedience, and racial uprisings. To participate in collective political action—to employ the time-honored methods of public protest—is to engage as fully and completely as possible in civil society and to refuse to "become victims in a democratic society."

Colonialism: Colonialism occurs when a foreign power invades a territory and establishes enduring systems of exploitation and domination over that territory's indigenous populations.

Color Blindness: A society in which racial differences exist but no one pays them heed, a world in which race no longer serves as the basis for social stigmatization, discrimination, inequality, or injustice.

Cultural and Social Capital: Cultural capital refers to the sum total of one's knowledge of established and exalted cultural activities and practices, while social capital includes all the resources one accrues by virtue of being connected to a network of people.

Cultural Appropriation: Cultural appropriation occurs when members of one ethnic or racial group adopt a cultural product associated with another.

Cultural Labor: Interracial relationships require each person to engage in a fair amount of cultural labor, which involves learning the history and culture of one another's racial and ethnic identities. Cultural labor requires broadening your cultural competence, stepping out of your comfort zone, and trying as much as possible to adopt another perspective on the world.

Deterrent Effect: The argument that prisons function as a strong deterrent for would-be criminals.

Digital Divide: Studies have shown that nonwhite citizens disproportionately are less likely to own computers and to have regular access to the Internet than their white peers, which results in many nonwhites being excluded from virtual associations, on account of them not having regular access to the Internet.

Disenfranchisement: To deprive a group or an individual of certain privileges. Practices, which often mirror, in a softer and shrewder form, techniques deployed by southern whites during the mid-twentieth century to deter voters and revoke voting rights among racial minorities, such as voter ID laws.

Double Consciousness: An insider's vantage point, which suggests that nonwhites have a double vision as part of a racial survival strategy used to navigate white America.

Education Gap: A gap in educational opportunities that separates whites and Asians, on the one hand, and African Americans, Hispanics, and Native Americans, on the other.

Environmental Racism: Any environmental policy, practice, or directive that disproportionately disadvantages (intentionally or unintentionally) nonwhite communities.

Ethnic Nationalism: When racial integration did not lead to liberation but only to more oppression for many nonwhites, racial segregation and complete independence from whites was the only answer. Ambassadors of ethnic nationalism resist cultural and social assimilation and instead champion self-determination, race pride, separatism, and, in some cases, the creation of an independent nation based on racial identity.

Ethnicity: A shared lifestyle informed by cultural, historical, religious, and/or national affiliations.

Eugenics: A program set forth in the nineteenth century by Francis Galton to ensure genetic purity by attempting to "solve" the "natural inferiority of the lower races" through such extreme measures as forced sterilization.

Eurocentric Curriculum: Many educators favor Eurocentric knowledge and cultural styles over non-Eurocentric ones, even if the latter are not avowedly anti-intellectual.

Fear of Crime: Americans' fear of crime is strongly connected to their racial identity, racial attitudes, and the racial makeup of their neighborhood.

Fixed Fallacy: The assumption that racism is fixed, that it is immutable, constant across time and space, and that it does not develop in any way, often defining racism only by its most heinous forms, such as racial violence.

Gerrymandering: A set of processes by which elected politicians redraw and manipulate the borders of political districts to secure political advantage.

Hate Groups: Racist hate groups present a threat to a multiracial democratic society and are often closely tied with white nationalist organizations, which believe whites to be superior to African Americans and Hispanics and vie for a separate, exclusively white country.

Highbrow Art: The collection of art forms associated with an upper-class taste and lifestyle, which is rich in cultural capital.

Homophily: Literally meaning "love of the same," homophily refers to the practice of associating with people like you.

Identity Politics: Arising in the wake of the Civil Rights Movement, identity politics refers to political action intended to address the unique interests and hardships of groups (such as nonwhites, women, and gays) who historically have faced oppression and who continue to be excluded from mainstream society.

Immigration: The process of entering and establishing permanent residence in a place other than one's country of origin; during the mid-nineteenth century, immigrants flocked to America by the millions.

Individualistic Fallacy: Racism assumed to belong to the realm of ideas and attitudes; racism is only the collection of nasty thoughts a "racist individual" has about another group.

Institutional Racism: Systemic white domination of people of color, embedded and operating in corporations, universities, legal systems, political bodies, cultural life, and other social collectives.

Interaction Order: The face-to-face domain of social life, the mezzanine level between large-scale structure and individual psychology.

Interpersonal Racism: Everyday interactions and practices; either *overt*, as in old-fashioned bigotry, wherein people act out their prejudices and give direct expression to their negative attitudes guided by demeaning stereotypes of others, or *covert*, wherein it is found in the habitual, commonsensical, and ordinary practices of our lives.

Interracial Unions: Marriages between individuals of different racial or ethnic groups. Racism can shape-shift and adjust to demographic changes. It can make—and has made—room in its wide enterprise for degrading multiracial people. Some parents, white and nonwhite alike, actively discourage their children from interracial dating, many times cloaking their own prejudices or ethnic chauvinism in a concern over mixed-race children or "other people's" racism.

Intersectionality: The overlapping system of advantages and disadvantages, wherein racism intersects with other forms of domination, such as those based on gender, class, sexuality, religion, nationhood, ability, and so forth.

Legalistic Fallacy: The assumption that abolishing racist laws (racism in principle) automatically leads to the abolition of racism in everyday life (racism in practice).

Lowbrow Art: Also known as "popular culture," comprises art forms that are considered more ordinary and associated with the tastes and lifestyles of "the masses," and which is more or less bereft of cultural capital.

Manifest Destiny: The nineteenth century belief that it was God's will that the United States conquer the American continent.

Marriage and Divorce: If the U.S. has a fairly high marriage rate, it has an enormously high divorce rate, ranking second only to Aruba in the number of divorces per 1,000 people. Divorce rates have risen since the 1970s, but like marriage rates, they fluctuate widely across race.

Mass Incarceration: The prison boom and the racial imbalance of America's prison population, and the social mechanisms that help account for this gross discrepancy.

Minstrelsy: A form of popular entertainment that ruled the American stage between 1830 and 1910, in which whites performed in blackface and purported to represent authentic African-American life. Minstrel shows featured a collection of stock characters that portrayed blacks as lazy, ignorant, subservient, buffoonish, and childish.

Model Minority: Ever since the nineteenth century, white America has regarded its Asian inhabitants as constituting a "model minority." That is, "more obedient and industrious" than other minorities.

Multiculturalism: Much like color blindness, multiculturalism aspires to a world in which all persons' inherent dignity as human beings is recognized. But in contrast to color blindness, which hopes to abolish race as a relevant criterion in law, public policy, and everyday social practices, multiculturalism envisions a society in which racial diversity is taken fully into account and valued for its own sake.

Multiethnic Heritage: The category by which many Americans identify, claiming heritages from two or more ethnicities or races.

Narrowcasting: A kind of artistic segregation, in which television producers target specific racial or ethnic groups with programs supposedly designed to speak to those groups' unique needs and lifestyles, where "black programs" are pitched at black viewers, "Jewish programs" at Jewish viewers, "Hispanic programs" at Hispanic viewers, and so forth.

Nonwhite Affirmative Action: An umbrella term referring to a collection of policies and practices designed to address past wrongs, institutional racism, and sexism by offering people of color and women both employment and educational opportunities.

Out-of-Wedlock Births: Children who are born to parents who are not married at the time of the birth. In 2011, out-of-wedlock births accounted for 41% of all births in the United States. Out-of-wedlock births have increased steadily over the last few decades. In fact, the number of American children living in single-parent homes nearly doubled between 1960 and 2010. In 1970, only 12% of all children lived with one parent; in 2000, 25% of children did. Today, a third of all American children are not being raised by two parents, the majority of whom live in single-mother households.

Police State: Although some of the difference in arrest rates undoubtedly is attributed to the high rates of violent crime found in distressed nonwhite neighborhoods, a good proportion is caused by institutional racism operating at multiple levels of the criminal justice system.

Political Correctness: Some commentators have suggested that American civil society is now guided by an ethic of "political correctness," which discourages free thought and honest debate, because people are afraid to offend their fellow citizens or, worst of all, to be labeled as "racists." In its most recent incarnation, political correctness usually refers to discourse that, while designed to minimize offense to marginalized groups, ends up censoring certain speech or attitudes deemed off-limits.

Political Representation: The activity of integrating citizen perspectives and concerns in the public policy making process. Very few nonwhites are elected at the national, state, and local levels, resulting in the underrepresentation of nonwhite perspectives and concerns.

Principle-Implementation Gap: Since the Civil Rights Movement, opinion polls have shown that most white Americans consistently have accepted the *principle* of racial inclusion while rejecting any of *policy measures* designed to carry this out.

Race Is a Social Reality: The idea, as put forth by James Baldwin, that race is not a biological reality, but rather a political reality, or what we might call a social construction.

Racial Democracy: In the abstract, racial justice means that persons of all racial groups draw returns on societal resources commensurate with the value they themselves have added to them; moreover, all are recognized in their full humanity as contributors to the social whole.

Racial Demography: A society's racial categories.

Racial Disparities in Income and Wealth: The concept that, due to historical and current circumstances, certain racial groups have more income and wealth than others as a result of their race. On average, a white worker will make more than a black or Hispanic worker, even if all these people work exactly the same hours, possess exactly the same work experience, and hold exactly the same educational credentials.

Racial Polarization: A relationship between the racial identity of a voter and the way in which the voter votes. For example, the American electorate is racially polarized: the majority of whites tilt toward the Republican Party while the majority of nonwhites support the Democratic Party.

Racial Terrorism: Institutions that arose after the fall of slavery to control and confine nonwhites, and African Americans in particular; lynch mobs that masqueraded as justice and new laws that were drafted to target poor blacks, ensuring they would be segregated from white society and imprisoned.

Racialization of Neighborhoods: The rise of industrialism, which facilitated the rise of cities, attracted thousands of people—immigrants, blacks, Mexicans, whites, Asians—to roiling metropolises. As they poured into cities, some ethnic groups tended to cluster together in neighborhoods, many living in crowded, dilapidated slums.

Racist Aesthetics: If the white aesthetic seeks to normalize whiteness, the racist aesthetic seeks to depict people of color in negative ways. If the white aesthetic ignores people of color, the racist aesthetic represents them—but never in their full humanity. Rather, it distorts and stereotypes; it infantilizes and demonizes.

Reflexivity: The defensive reaction many privileged whites have to being confronted with societal racism.

Religious Associations: By and large, religious associations do not overcome racial divides; in fact, the opposite is true. Religious life is racialized to a high degree. Certain religions, denominations within religions, and places of worship within denominations correspond to certain racial and ethnic groups.

Separate Is Not Equal: The case put forth by Thurgood Marshall and the NAACP in 1954 that racially segregated schools were separate but anything but equal; the Supreme Court ruled on behalf of the NAACP, dismantling the legal basis of racial segregation.

Single Motherhood: A mother not living with a spouse or partner, who has most of the responsibilities in raising her child or children. At least since the presidency of Ronald Reagan, single mothers have been stereotyped as immoral delinquents who have more children in order to collect bigger welfare checks. But the truth is that single mothers are "a remarkably diverse group who have arrived at single parenthood through divergent, and often class-segregated paths."

Slavery: A system wherein workers are the property of their masters and are not paid for their labor.

Split Labor Force: A labor market in which there are at least two groups of workers whose price of labor differs for the same work, or would differ if they did the same work.

Stereotype Threat: A negative stereotype about a racial group can make members of that group conscious of the fact that any of their actions that happen to align with that stereotype end up verifying the stereotype, making it more real in the eyes of others and, perhaps, even of themselves; being at risk of confirming, as self-characteristic, a negative stereotype about one's group.

Tokenistic Fallacy: The assumption that the presence of people of color in influential positions is evidence of the complete eradication of racial obstacles.

Underground Economy: The combined forms of enterprise classified as criminal under current law.

Welfare: Government provisions intended to help disadvantaged people, including those who are poor, elderly, war veterans, unemployed, and disabled.

White Aesthetics: Images of whiteness often are understated and subtle. They rely on an unspoken edict that treats the white body and the white experience as normal, an edict that, for some of us, connects with our innermost presuppositions about the world.

White Affirmative Action: A series of exceptions, put forth by the southern arm of the Democratic party, which precluded a large majority of nonwhites from benefiting from Roosevelt's New Deal by disqualifying certain jobs (those dominated by nonwhite workers) from the policy.

White Flight: A migratory process whereby many whites, fearing racial integration, sold their houses in the city and fled to the suburbs.

White-Collar Crime: Illegal acts committed by more privileged members of society, often technological crimes, such as computer hacking, fraud, identity theft, environmental law violations, tax evasion, bribery, counterfeiting, money laundering, and embezzling.

Whiteness: The dominant racial category which normalizes racial domination and reproduces many cultural, political, economic, and social advantages and privileges for white people and withholds such advantages and privileges from nonwhite people.

Notes

Chapter 1: Race in the Twenty-First Century

1. Michael Brown, Martin Carnoy, Elliott Currie, Troy Duster, David Oppenheimer, Marjorie Shultz, and David Wellman, *White-Washing Race: The Myth of a Color Blind Society* (Berkeley: University of California Press, 2003); Joe R. Feagin, Hernan Vera, and Pinar Batur, *White Racism: The Basics*, 2nd ed. (New York: Routledge, 2001); Eduardo Bonilla-Silva, *Racism without Racists: Color-Blind Racism and the Persistence of Racial Inequality in the United States* (Lanham, MD: Rowman and Littlefield, 2003); Neil Gotanda, "A Critique of 'Our Constitution Is Color-Blind,'" in *Critical Race Theory: The Cutting Edge*, 2nd ed., ed. Richard Delgato and Jean Stefancic (Philadelphia: Temple University Press, 2000), 35–38.

2. Federal Bureau of Investigation, *Latest Hate Crime Statistics Report Released* (Washington, D.C., FBI, 2014).

3. U.S. Census Bureau, "Poverty rates for selected detailed race and Hispanic groups by state and place: 2007–2011," by Suzanne Macartney, Alemayehu Bishaw, and Kayla Fontenot. (Washington, DC: Government Printing office, 2013).

4. U.S. Census Bureau, "Historical Poverty Tables: Table 2, Poverty Status of People by Family Relationship, Race, and Hispanic Origin: 1959–2005" (Washington, DC: Government Printing Office, 2006); Bureau of Labor Statistics, "Employment Situation Summary: August 2006" (Washington, DC: Department of Labor, 2006); Richard Morin, "Misperceptions Cloud Whites' View of Blacks," *Washington Post*, July 11, 2001, A1; Brown et al., *White-Washing Race*, 35; Feagin, Vera, and Batur, *White Racism*, 16; Stephen Cornell and Joseph P. Kalt, eds., *What Can Tribes Do? Strategies and Institutions in American Indian Economic Development* (Los Angeles: American Indian Studies Center, 1992).

5. Jeremy Travis, Bruce Western, and Steve Redburn, eds. *The Growth of Incarceration in the United States: Exploring Causes and Consequences.* (Washington, DC: National Academies Press, 2014); Bruce Western, *Punishment and Inequality in America* (New York: Russell Sage Foundation, 2006); Bruce Western and Becky Pettit, "Black-White Wage Inequality, Employment Rates, and Incarceration," *American Journal of Sociology* 111 (2005): 553–578; Michael Tonry, *Malign Neglect: Race, Crime, and Punishment in America* (New York: Oxford University Press, 1995); Alfred Blumstein, "Racial Disproportionality of U.S. Prisons Revisited," *University of Colorado Law Review* 64 (1993): 743–760; Thomas Bonczar and Allen Beck, *Lifetime Likelihood of Going to State and Federal Prison* (Washington, DC: Bureau of Justice Statistics, 1997); Gail Chaddock, "U.S. Notches World's Highest Incarceration Rate," *Christian Science Monitor*, August 18, 2003.

6. Émile Durkheim, *The Evolution of Educational Thought* (London: Routledge and Kegan Paul, 1977 [1938]), 11.

7. Richard Alba, Rubén Rumbaut, and Karen Marotz, "A Distorted Nation: Perceptions of Racial/Ethnic Group Sizes and Attitudes toward Immigrants and Other Minorities," *Social Forces* 84 (2005): 901–919; Richard Nadeau, Richard G. Niemi, and Jeffrey Levine, "Innumeracy about Minority Populations," *Public Opinion Quarterly* 57 (1993): 332–347.

8. Shannon Harper and Barbara Reskin, "Affirmative Action at School and on the Job," *Annual Review of Sociology* 31 (2005): 357–379; David Sears, James Sidanius, and Lawrence Bobo, eds., *Racialized Politics: The Debate about Racism in America* (Chicago: University of Chicago Press, 2000).

9. Gordon W. Allport, *The Nature of Prejudice* (New York: Basic Books, 1954), 9, 191.

10. Loïc Wacquant, "For an Analytic of Racial Domination," *Political Power and Social Theory* 11 (1997): 221–234.

11. Terbert Blumer, "Race Prejudice as a Sense of Group Position," *Pacific Sociological Review* 1 (1958): 3–7; Eduardo Bonilla-Silva, "Rethinking Racism: Toward a Structural Interpretation," *American Sociological Review* 62 (1997): 465–480.

12. Brown et al., *White-Washing Race*, 43.

13. Kathryn M. Neckerman, *Schools Betrayed: Roots of Failure in Inner-City Education* (Chicago: University of Chicago Press, 2007); Jennie Oaks, *Keeping Track: How Schools Structure Inequality*, 2nd ed. (New Haven, CT: Yale University Press, 2005).

14. Douglas Harris, *Lost Learning, Forgotten Promises: A National Analysis of School Racial Segregation, Student Achievement, and "Controlled Choice" Plans* (Washington, DC: Center for American Progress, 2006); Gary Orfield with the assistance of Sara Schley, Diane Glass, and Sean Reardon, *The Growth of Segregation in American Schools: Changing Patterns of Separation and Poverty since 1968* (Washington, DC: National School Boards Association, 1993); Susan Easton, "The New Segregation: Forty Years after Brown, Cities and Suburbs Face a Rising Tide of Racial Isolation," *Harvard Education Letter* 10, January 1994.

15. Jeffrey Alexander, *The Civil Sphere* (New York: Oxford University Press, 2006); Orlando Patterson, *The Ordeal of Integration: Progress and Resentment in America's "Racial" Crisis* (New York: Basic Civitas Books, 1998).

16. Thomas Holt, *The Problem of Race in the Twenty-First Century* (Cambridge, MA: Harvard University Press, 2000), 6.

17. Howard Winant, *The World Is a Ghetto: Race and Democracy since World War II* (New York: Basic Books, 2001); Patterson, *Ordeal of Integration*; Mae Ngai, *Impossible Subjects: Illegal Aliens and the Making of Modern America* (Princeton, NJ: Princeton University Press, 2003).

18. Marc Bloch, *The Historian's Craft* (New York: Vintage, 1953), 41, emphasis added.

19. Lawrence Bobo, "Racial Attitudes and Relations at the Close of the Twentieth Century," in *America Becoming: Racial Trends and Their Consequences*, ed. Neil Smelser, William Julius Wilson, and Faith Mitchell (Washington, DC: National Academy Press, 2000), 262–299; Howard Schuman, Charlotte Steeh, Lawrence Bobo, and Maria Krysan, *Racial Attitudes in America: Trends and Interpretations*, rev. ed. (Cambridge, MA: Harvard University Press, 1997); Tomás Almaguer, *Racial Fault Lines: The Historical Origins of White Supremacy in California* (Berkeley: University of California Press, 1994).

20. Holt, *Problem of Race in the Twenty-First Century*, 20.

21. Lillian Smith, *Killers of the Dream*, rev. ed. (New York: Norton, 1961), 96.

22. Feagin et al., *White Racism*, 3.

23. See e.g., Tonry, *Malign Neglect*.

24. Joe Feagin, "The Continuing Significance of Race: Antiblack Discrimination in Public Places," *American Sociological Review* 56 (1991): 101–116.

25. Stokely Carmichael and Charles V. Hamilton, *Black Power: The Politics of Liberation in America* (New York: Random House, 1967), 5, 22.

26. Charles Lawrence, III, "The Id, the Ego, and Equal Protection: Reckoning with Unconscious Racism," *Stanford Law Review* 39 (1987): 317–388, 322, emphasis added.

27. Beverly Daniel Tatum, *"Why Are All the Black Kids Sitting Together in the Cafeteria?" and Other Conversations about Race* (New York: Basic Books, 1997), 6.

28. Pierre Bourdieu and Loïc Wacquant, *An Invitation to Reflexive Sociology* (Chicago: University of Chicago Press, 1992), 167.

29. See also Pierre Bourdieu, *Masculine Domination* (Stanford, CA: Stanford University Press, 2001 [1998]).

30. Smith, *Killers of the Dream*, 96.

31. Jean-Paul Sartre, *Anti-Semite and Jew* (New York: Grove, 1960 [1946]), 95.

32. Bourdieu, *Masculine Domination*, 37.

33. Angela Harris, "Race and Essentialism in Feminist Legal Theory," in *Critical Race Theory: The Cutting Edge*, 2nd ed., ed. Richard Delgado and Jean Stefancic (Philadelphia: Temple University Press, 2000), 261–274.

34. Kimberlé Crenshaw, "Mapping the Margins: Intersectionality, Identity Politics, and Violence against Women of Color," *Stanford Law Review* 42 (1990): 1241–1299; Chandra Mohanty, *Feminism without Borders: Decolonizing Theory, Practicing Solidarity* (Durham, NC: Duke University Press, 2003); Angela Davis, *Women, Race, and Class* (New York: Vintage, 1983); Patricia Hill Collins, *Black Feminist Thought: Knowledge, Consciousness, and the Politics of Empowerment*, 2nd ed. (New York: Routledge, 2000).

35. Feagin, "Continuing Significance of Race."

36. Sylvia Walby, "Complexity Theory, Systems Theory, and Multiple Intersecting Social Inequalities," *Philosophy of the Social Sciences* 37 (2007): 449–470; Nira Yuval-Davis, "Intersectionality and Feminist Politics," *European Journal of Women's Studies* 13 (2006): 193–209; Leslie McCall, "The Complexity of Intersectionality," *Signs: Journal of Women in Culture and Society* 30 (2005): 1771–1800.

37. Kimberlé Crenshaw, "Demarginalizing the Intersection of Race and Sex: A Black Feminist Critique of Antidiscrimination Doctrine, Feminist Theory and Antiracist Politics," *University of Chicago Legal Forum* (1989): 139–167.

38. Cf. Collins, *Black Feminist Thought*.

39. Myra Marx Ferree, "Inequality, Intersectionality and the Politics of Discourse: Framing Feminist Alliances," in *The Discursive Politics of Gender Equality: Stretching, Bending, and Policy-Making*, ed. Emanuela Lombardo, Petra Meier, and Mieke Verloo (New York: Routledge, 2009), 86–104; McCall, "Complexity of Intersectionality."

40. Cf. Mustafa Emirbayer, "Manifesto for Relational Sociology," *American Journal of Sociology* 103 (1997): 281–317; Pierre Bourdieu, *The Rules of Art: Genesis and Structure of the Literary Field* (Stanford, CA: Stanford University Press, 1996 [1992]).

41. Joseph Graves, Jr., *The Race Myth: Why We Pretend Race Exists in America* (New York: Dutton, 2004).

42. Charles Darwin, *The Descent of Man and Selection in Relation to Sex* (Chicago: Rand, McNally, 1871); M. F. Ashley Montagu, *Man's Most Dangerous Myth: The Fallacy of Race* (New York: Columbia University Press, 1942).

43. Graves, *Race Myth*, 16–17.

44. Ian Haney-López, *White by Law: The Legal Construction of Race* (New York: New York University Press, 1996); James Davis, *Who Is Black? One Nation's Definition* (University Park: Pennsylvania State University Press, 1991).

45. Oliver Cromwell Cox, *Caste, Class, and Race: A Study in Social Dynamics* (New York: Doubleday, 1948), 423. Also see Sukhadeo Thorat, ed., *Caste, Race, and Discrimination: Discourses in International Context* (Jaipur: Rawat Publications, 2004); Pauline Kolenda, *Caste, Marriage, and Inequality: Essays on North and South India* (Jaipur: Rawat Publications, 2003); Susan Bayly, *Caste, Society and Politics in India from the Eighteenth Century to the Modern Age* (New York: Cambridge University Press, 2001); Andreé Beéteille, *Caste, Class, and Power: Changing Patterns of Stratification in a Tanjore Village*, 2nd ed. (New York: Oxford University Press, 1996 [1965]).

46. Graves, *Race Myth*, 8.

47. Michael Banton, "Analytical and Folk Concepts of Race and Ethnicity," *Ethnic and Racial Studies* (1979) 2: 127–138, 130.

48. Troy Duster, "Race and Reification in Science," *Science* (2005) 307: 1050–1051.

49. John Hoberman, *Darwin's Athletes: How Sport Has Damaged Black America and Preserved the Myth of Race* (Boston: Houghton Mifflin, 1997).

50. Joseph Graves, Jr., *Emperor's New Clothes: Biological Theories of Race at the Millennium* (New Brunswick, NJ: Rutgers University Press, 2001).

51. Jim Holt, "Nobody Does It Better," *New York Times*, April 16, 2000.

52. Graves, *Race Myth*.

53. Michael Messner, "Masculinities and Athletic Careers," *Gender and Society* 3 (1989): 71–88; Harry Edwards, "The Myth of the Racially Superior Athlete," *The Black Scholar*, November 3, 1971.

54. Richard Herrnstein and Charles Murray, *The Bell Curve: Intelligence and Class Structure in American Life* (New York: The Free Press, 1994).

55. Russell Jacoby and Naomi Glauberman, eds., *The Bell Curve Debate: History, Documents, Opinions* (New York: Times Books, 1995); Steven Fraser, ed., *The Bell Curve Wars: Race, Intelligence, and the Future of America* (New York: Basic Books, 1995); Stephen Jay Gould, *The Mismeasure of Man* (New York: Norton, 1996); Claude Fisher, Michael Hout, Martín Sánchez Jankowski, Samuel Lucas, Ann Swidler, and Kim Voss, *Inequality by Design: Cracking the Bell Curve Myth* (Princeton, NJ: Princeton University Press, 1996).

56. Gould, *Mismeasure of Man*, 28.

57. Paul Pierson, *Dismantling the Welfare State? Reagan, Thatcher, and the Politics of Retrenchment* (Cambridge: Cambridge University Press, 1994); Paul Pierson, "Three Worlds of Welfare State Research," *Comparative Political Studies* 33 (2000): 791–821; Margaret Somers and Fred Block, "From Poverty to Perversity: Ideas, Markets, and Institutions over 200 Years of Welfare Debate," *American Sociological Review* 70 (2005): 260–287; Gould, *Mismeasure of Man*.

58. Gould, *Mismeasure of Man*, 60–61.

59. Feagin, Vera, and Batur, *White Racism*, ix.

60. Dalton Conley, "Universal Freckle, or How I Learned to Be White," in *The Making and Unmaking of Whiteness*, ed. Birgit Brander Rasmussen, Eric Klinenberg, Irene Nexica, and Matt Wray (Durham, NC: Duke University Press, 2001, 25–42).

61. Amanda Lewis, "'What Group?' Studying Whites and Whiteness in the Era of 'Color-Blindness,'" *Sociological Theory* 22 (2004): 623–646; Amanda Lewis, *Race in the Schoolyard: Negotiating the Color Line in Classrooms and Communities* (New Brunswick, NJ: Rutgers University Press, 2003); Ruth Frankenberg, *White Women, Race Matters: The Social Construction of Whiteness* (Minneapolis: University of Minnesota Press, 1993); Stephanie Wildman, *Privilege Revealed: How Invisible Preference Undermines America* (New York: New York University Press, 1996).

62. Toni Morrison, *Playing in the Dark: Whiteness and the Literary Imagination* (New York: Vintage, 1992), 52.

63. Frankenberg, *White Women, Race Matters*, 228–229. Also see Ruth Frankenberg, "The Mirage of an Unmarked Whiteness," in *The Making and Unmaking of Whiteness*, ed. Birgit Brander Rasmussen, Eric Klinenberg, Irene Nexica, and Matt Wray (Durham, NC: Duke University Press, 2001), 72–96.

64. Douglas Massey and Nancy Denton, *American Apartheid: Segregation and the Making of the Underclass* (Cambridge, MA: Harvard University Press, 1993); Devah Pager, "The Mark of a Criminal Record," *American Journal of Sociology* 108 (2003): 937–975; Tonry, *Malign Neglect*; Western, *Punishment and Inequality in America*; Melivin Oliver and Thomas Shapiro, *Black Wealth, White Wealth: A New Perspective on Racial Inequality* (New York: Taylor & Francis, 2006); Dalton Conley, *Being Black, Living in the Red Race, Wealth, and Social Policy in America* (Berkeley: University of California Press, 1999).

65. George Lipsitz, *Possessive Investment in Whiteness: How White People Profit from Identity Politics* (Philadelphia: Temple University Press, 1998), 8–10.

66. Peggy McIntosh, "White Privilege and Male Privilege: A Personal Account of Coming to See Correspondences through Work in Women's Studies," in *Critical White Studies: Looking behind the Mirror*, ed. Richard Delgado and Jean Stefancic (Philadelphia: Temple University Press, 1997), 291–299.

67. Brown et al., *White-Washing Race*, 22.

68. Cited in Kenneth Kinnamon and Michel Fabre, *Conversations with Richard* Wright (Jackson: University Press of Mississippi, 1993), 99.

69. Gotanda, "Critique of 'Our Constitution,'" 36.

70. K. Anthony Appiah and Amy Gutmann, *Color Conscious: The Political Morality of Race* (Princeton, NJ: Princeton University Press, 1996), 109.

71. Gotanda, "Critique of 'Our Constitution,'" 35.

72. Lipsitz, *Possessive Investment in Whiteness*, viii.

73. Cited in W. E. B. Du Bois, *Black Reconstruction in America, 1860–1880* (Cleveland, OH: Meridian, 1965 [1935]), 592–594.

74. Lipsitz, *Possessive Investment in Whiteness*, viii–ix.

75. James Baldwin, *The Fire Next Time* (New York: Vintage, 1993 [1962]), 104.

76. Pierre Bourdieu, *Language and Symbolic Power* (Cambridge, MA: Harvard University Press, 2003).

77. See, e.g., Kimberly DeCosta, *Making Multiracials: State, Family, and Market in the Redrawing of the Color Line* (Stanford, CA: Stanford University Press, 2007); Thomas Guglielmo, *White on Arrival: Italians, Race, Color, and Power in Chicago, 1890–1945* (New York: Oxford University Press, 2004); John Jackson, Jr., *Harlemworld: Doing Race and Class in Contemporary Black America* (Chicago: University of Chicago Press, 2001); Robin Sheriff, *Dreaming Equality: Color, Race, and Racism in Urban Brazil* (New Brunswick, NJ: Rutgers University Press, 2001); John Hartigan, Jr., *Racial Situations: Class Predicaments of Whiteness in Detroit* (Princeton, NJ: Princeton University Press, 1999).

78. Rogers Brubaker, and Frederick Cooper, "Beyond 'Identity,'" *Theory and Society* 29 (2000): 1–47; Mara Loveman, "Is 'Race' Essential?" *American Sociological Review* 64 (1999): 891–898.

79. Kim Williams, *Mark One or More: Civil Rights in Multiracial America* (Ann Arbor: University of Michigan Press, 2006).

80. Mary Waters, *Ethnic Options: Choosing Identities in America* (Berkeley: University of California Press, 1990); Mary Waters, *Black Identities: West Indian Immigrant Dreams and American Realities* (New York: Russell Sage Foundation, Harvard University Press, 1999).

81. Jack White, "I'm Just Who I Am," *Time*, May 5, 1997, 36.

82. J. Davis, *Who Is Black?*.

83. Allister Sparks, *The Mind of South Africa: The Story of the Rise and Fall of Apartheid* (Johannesburg: Jonathan Ball, 2006); Edward Telles, *Race in Another America: The Significance of Skin Color in Brazil* (Princeton, NJ: Princeton University Press, 2004); Thomas Stephens, *Dictionary of Latin American Racial and Ethnic Terminology* (Gainesville: University of Florida Press, 1989); Frank Dikötter, *The Discourse of Race in Modern China* (Stanford, CA: Stanford University Press, 1992); S. N. Eisenstadt, *Japanese Civilization: A Comparative View* (Chicago: University of Chicago Press, 1998); Mary Searle-Chatterjee and Ursula Sharma, *Contextualising Caste: Post-Dumontian Approaches* (Oxford: Blackwell, 1994).

84. Michel Foucault, *The History of Sexuality*, vols. 1–3 (New York: Vintage, 1999 [1984–1976]).

85. David Roediger, *Working toward Whiteness: How America's Immigrants Became White* (New York: Basic Books, 2005); David Roediger, *The Wages of Whiteness: Race and the Making of the American Working Class* (London: Verso, 1991).

86. Stuart Hall, "Race Articulation and Societies Structured in Dominance," in *Sociological Theories: Race and Colonialism*, ed. UNESCO (Paris: UNESCO, 1980, 305–345), 308. Also see Holt, *Problem of Race*; Bonilla-Silva, "Rethinking Racism."

87. Pierre Bourdieu, *Practical Reason* (Stanford, CA: Stanford University Press, 1998 [1994]), 36.

88. Cf. Ian Haney López, *White by Law: The Legal Construction of Race*, rev. and updated 10th anniversary ed. (New York: New York University Press, 2006 [1996]); Troy Duster, "The 'Morphing' Properties of Whiteness," in *The Making and Unmaking of Whiteness*, ed. Birgit Brander Rasmussen, Eric Klinenberg, Irene Nexica, and Matt Wray (Durham, NC: Duke University Press, 2001), 113–137.

89. DeCosta, *Making Multiracials*.

90. Aliya Saperstein and Andrew M. Penner, "Racial Fluidity and Inequality in the United States," *American Journal of Sociology* 118 (2012): 676–727; Jonathan Freeman, Andrew M. Penner, Aliya Saperstein, Matthias Scheutz, and Nalini Ambady, "Looking the Part: Social Status Cues Shape Race Perception," *PLoS One* 6 (2011): e25107; Andrew M. Penner and Aliya Saperstein, "How Social Status Shapes Race," *Proceedings of the National Academy of Sciences* 105 (2008): 19628–30.

91. Aliya Saperstein, "Can Losing Your Job Make You Black?" *Boston Review*, June 3, 2013.

92. Andrew Noymer, Andrew M. Penner, and Aliya Saperstein, "Cause of Death Affects Racial Classification on Death Certificates," *PLoS One* 6 (2011): e15812.

93. Baldwin, *Fire Next Time*, 104.

94. Cf. Max Weber, "Class, Status, Party," in *From Max Weber: Essays in Sociology*, ed. H. H. Gerth and C. Wright Mills (New York: Oxford University Press), 180–195.

95. Rogers Burbaker, Mara Loveman, and Peter Stamatov, "Ethnicity as Cognition," *Theory and Society* 33 (2004): 31–64; Loveman, "Is 'Race' Essential?."

96. Waters, *Ethnic Options*.

97. Conley, "Universal Freckle," 37.

98. Charles Hirschman, Richard Alba, and Reynolds Farley, "The Meaning and Measurement of Race in the U.S. Census: Glimpses into the Future," *Demography* 37 (2000): 381–393.

99. Waters, *Black Identities*, 45.

100. Ngai, *Impossible Subjects*, 7.

101. Ibid., 7–8.

102. López, *White by Law*, 1.

103. Glenn Loury, *The Anatomy of Racial Inequality* (Cambridge, MA: Harvard University Press, 2001); Christian Joppke, *Immigration and the Nation-State: The United States, Germany, and Great Britain* (Oxford: Oxford University Press, 1999); Rogers Smith, *Civic Ideals: Conflicting Visions of Citizenship in U.S. History* (New Haven, CT: Yale University Press, 1997); Judith Shklar, *American Citizenship: The Quest for Inclusion* (Cambridge, MA: Harvard University Press, 1991).

104. Irene Bloemraad, *Becoming a Citizen: Incorporating Immigrants and Refugees in the United States and Canada* (Berkeley: University of California Press, 2006).

105. C. Wright Mills, *The Sociological Imagination* (New York: Oxford University Press, 1959).

106. Bourdieu and Wacquant, *Invitation to Reflexive Sociology*, 44.

107. W. E. B. Du Bois, "The Name Negro," in *The Oxford W. E. B. Du Bois Reader*, ed. Eric Sundquist (New York: Oxford, 1996 [1928]), 70–72.

Chapter 2: The Invention of Race

1. Ivan Hannaford, *Race: The History of an Idea in the West* (Baltimore, MD: Johns Hopkins Press, 1996); Audrey Smedley, *Race in North America: Origin and Evolution of a Worldview*, 2nd ed. (Boulder, CO: Westview, 1999).

2. Pierre Bourdieu, *Masculine Domination* (Stanford, CA: Stanford University Press, 2001 [1998]); Thomas Holt, *The Problem of Race in the 21st Century* (Cambridge, MA: Harvard University Press, 2000).

3. Stuart Hall, "The West and the Rest: Discourse and Power," in *Modernity: An Introduction to Modern Societies*, ed. Stuart Hall, David Held, Don Hubert, and Kenneth Thompson (Malden, MA: Blackwell, 1996), 185–227.

4. Richard Liggio, "English Origins of Early American Racism," *Radical History Review* 3 (1976): 1–36, 8.

5. Smedley, *Race in North America*.

6. Americo Castro, *The Spaniards* (Berkeley: University of California Press, 1971); Smedley, *Race in North America*, 65.

7. Henry Kamen, *The Spanish Inquisition* (New Haven, CT: Yale University Press, 1997); Norman Roth, *Conversos, Inquisition, and the Expulsion of the Jews from Spain* (Madison: University of Wisconsin Press, 1995); Smedley, *Race in North America*; Holt, *Problem of Race in the 21st Century*.

8. Benedict Anderson, *Imagined Communities* (London: Verso, 1983).

9. David Theo Goldberg, *The Racial State* (Malden, MA: Blackwell, 2002).

10. Quoted in Hall, "West and the Rest," 207.

11. Edward Said, *Orientalism*, 25th Anniversary ed. (New York: Vintage, 1994 [1978]); Hall, "West and the Rest"; Smedley, *Race in North America*.

12. Juan Gonzalez, *Harvest of Empire: A History of Latinos in America* (New York: Viking, 2000), 6.

13. John Kicza, "First Contacts," in *A Companion to American Indian History*, ed. Philip Deloria and Neal Salisbury (Malden, MA: Blackwell, 2002), 27–45.

14. Russell Thornton, "Health, Disease, and Demography," in *A Companion to American Indian History*, ed. Philip Deloria and Neal Salisbury (Malden, MA: Blackwell, 2002), 68–84; William Denevan, ed., *The Native Population of the Americas in 1492*, 2nd ed. (Madison: University of Wisconsin Press, 1992); Russell Thornton, *American Indian Holocaust and Survival: A Population History since 1492* (Norman: University of Oklahoma Press, 1987); Woodrow Borah and Sherburne Cook, *Essays in Population History*, 3 vols. (Berkeley: University of California Press, 1971–1979).

15. Melvin Page, ed., *Colonialism: An International Social, Cultural, and Political Encyclopedia* (Santa Barbara, CA: ABC-CLIO, 2003).

16. Hall, "West and the Rest," 204.

17. Gonzalez, *Harvest of Empire*, 4.

18. Bernal Díaz del Castillo, *The Conquest of New Spain* (New York: Penguin, 1963 [1569]), 216, 235.

19. Tzvetan Todorov, *The Conquest of America: The Question of the Other* (New York: Harper and Row, 1984); Castillo, *Conquest of New Spain*.

20. Michael Meyer and William Sherman, *The Course of Mexican History* (New York: Oxford University Press, 1995); Patricia Seed, *To Love, Honor, and Obey in Colonial Mexico: Conflicts over Marriage Choice, 1574–1821* (Stanford, CA: Stanford University Press, 1988).

21. Martha Menchaca, *Recovering History, Constructing Race: The Indian, Black, and White Roots of Mexican Americans* (Austin: University of Texas Press, 2001); Meyer and Sherman, *Course of Mexican History*.

22. Menchaca, *Recovering History, Constructing Race*; Castillo, *Conquest of New Spain*.

23. Bartolomé de Las Casas, *A Short Account of the Destruction of the Indies* (New York: Penguin, 1992 [1542]), 32.

24. David Brion Davis, *Inhuman Bondage: The Rise and Fall of Slavery in the New World* (New York: Oxford University Press, 2006), 98.

25. Gonzalez, *Harvest of Empire*, 14.

26. Smedley, *Race in North America*.

27. Jack Weatherford, *Indian Givers: How the Indians of the Americas Transformed the World* (New York: Fawcett Columbine, 1988); Bruce Johnson, *Forgotten Founders: How the American Indian Helped Shape Democracy* (Boston: Harvard Common Press, 1987); Henry Steele Commager, *The Empire of Reason: How Europe Imagined and America Realized the Enlightenment* (New York: Doubleday, 1977).

28. Hall, "West and the Rest."

29. Thornton, "Health, Disease, and Demography."

30. Stephen Cornell, *The Return of the Native: American Indian Political Resurgence* (New York: Oxford University Press, 1988), 52. Also see Francis Jennings, *The Invasion of America: Indians, Colonialism, and the Cant of Conquest* (New York: Norton, 1976); Alfred Crosby, Jr., *The Columbian Exchange: Biological and Cultural Consequences of 1492* (Westport, CT: Greenwood Press, 1972).

31. David Cook, *Born to Die: Disease and New World Conquest, 1492–1650* (Cambridge: Cambridge University Press, 1998), 13.

32. Clark Larsen, "In the Wake of Columbus: Native Population Biology in the Postcontact Americas," *Yearbook of Physical Anthropology* 37 (1994): 109–154; Cary Meister, "Demographic Consequences of Euro-American Contact on Selected American Indian Populations and Their Relationship to the Demographic Transition," *Ethnohistory* 23 (1976): 161–172.

33. Hugh Dempsey, "Smallpox: Scourge of the Plains," in *Harm's Way: Disasters in Western Canada*, ed. Anthony Rasporich and Max Foran (Calgary: University of Calgary Press, 2004, 15–40), 35. Also see Barbara Alice Mann, *George Washington's War on Native America* (Westport, CT: Praeger, 2005).

34. Thornton, *American Indian Holocaust and Survival*, 42–43.

35. Jennings, *Invasion of America*, 30.

36. Bernard Bailyn, *The Peopling of British North America* (New York: Vintage, 1988); Philip Foner, *Labor and the American Revolution* (Westport, CT: Greenwood, 1976).

37. Smedley, *Race in North America*, 100–101.

38. Theodore Allen, *The Invention of the White Race*, vols. 1 and 2 (London: Verso, 1994 and 1997); David Galenson, *White Servitude in Colonial America: An Economic Analysis* (Cambridge: Cambridge University Press, 1981); Sharon Salinger, *To Serve Well and Faithfully: Labor and Indentured Servants in Pennsylvania* (New York: Heritage, 1987).

39. David Roediger, *The Wages of Whiteness: Race and the Making of the American Working Class* (London: Verso, 1991).

40. Ibid.

41. Quoted in David Brion Davis, *The Problem of Slavery in Western Culture* (Ithaca, NY: Cornell University Press, 1961), 3–4.

42. Orlando Patterson, *Slavery and Social Death: A Comparative Study* (Cambridge, MA: Harvard University Press, 1982), 340.

43. Allen, *Invention of the White Race*.

44. Cornell, *Return of the Native*, 28–32; Smedley, *Race in North America*, 104–105.

45. Smedley, *Race in North America*, 105–106.

46. Ibid., 109.

47. David Eltis, *The Rise of African Slavery in the Americas* (Cambridge: Cambridge University Press, 2000); William Pierson, *From Africa to America: African American History from the Colonial Era to the New Republic, 1526–1790* (New York: Twayne, 1996).

48. Anne Bailey, *African Voices of the Atlantic Slave Trade: Beyond the Silence and the Shame* (Boston: Beacon, 2005); Igor Kopytoff, ed., *The African Frontier: The Reproduction of Traditional African Societies* (Bloomington: Indiana University Press, 1987); David Eltis, *Economic Growth and the Ending of the Transatlantic Slave Trade* (New York: Oxford University Press, 1987); Walter Rodney, *How Europe Underdeveloped Africa* (Washington, DC: Howard University Press, 1972).

49. Hugh Thomas, *The Slave Trade: The Story of the Atlantic Slave Trade: 1440–1870* (New York: Touchstone, 1997), 415.

50. Quoted in Thomas, *Slave Trade*, 412. Also see John Newton, "A Reformed Slave Trader's Regrets, c. 1745–1754," in *The Atlantic Slave Trade*, ed. David Northrup (Lexington, MA: D.C. Heath, 1994), 80–89.

51. Malcolm Cowley and Daniel Mannix, *Black Cargoes: A History of the Atlantic Slave Trade, 1518–1862* (New York: Harold Matson, 1962); Kenneth Kiple and Brian Higgins, "Mortality Caused by Dehydration during the Middle Passage," in *The Atlantic Slave Trade: Effects on Economies, Societies, and Peoples in Africa, The Americas, and Europe*, ed. Joseph Inikori and Stanley Engerman (Durham, NC: Duke University Press, 1992), 321–338; Thomas, *Slave Trade*, 416–422.

52. Thomas, *Slave Trade*, 424.

53. George Nørregård, *Danish Settlements in West Africa, 1658–1850* (Boston: Boston University Press, 1966), 89. See also Maggie Montesinos Sale, *The Slumbering Volcano: American Slave Ship Revolts and the Production of Rebellious Masculinity* (Durham, NC: Duke University Press, 1997); Eric Taylor, "If We Must Die: A History of Shipboard Insurrections during the Slave Trade" (unpublished PhD diss., University of California–Los Angeles, 2000).

54. Winthrop Jordan, *White Over Black: American Attitudes toward the Negro, 1550–1812* (Chapel Hill: University of North Carolina Press, 1968), 366–367; Thomas, *Slave Trade*, 424.

55. David Richardson, "The Costs of Survival: The Transport of Slaves in the Middle Passage and the Profitability of the 18th-Century British Slave Trade," *Explorations in Economic History* 24 (1987): 178–196.

56. Philip Curtin, *The Atlantic Slave Trade: A Census* (Madison: University of Wisconsin Press, 1969); Paul Lovejoy, "The Volume of the Atlantic Slave Trade: A Synthesis," *Journal of African History* 23 (1982): 473–501; David Henige, "Measuring the Immeasurable: The Atlantic Slave Trade, West Africa Population and the Pyrrhonian Critic," *Journal of African History*, 27 (1986): 295–313; Joseph Inikori and Stanley Engerman, *The Atlantic Slave Trade* (Durham, NC: Duke University Press, 1992).

57. Joseph Miller, *The Way of Death: Merchant Capitalism and the Angolan Slave Trade* (Madison: University of Wisconsin Press, 1988). Also see James Rawley, *The Transatlantic Slave Trade: A History*, rev. ed. (Lincoln: University of Nebraska Press, 2005); John Thornton, *Africa and Africans in the Making of the Atlantic World, 1400–1800* (Cambridge: Cambridge University Press, 1998); Rodney, *How Europe Underdeveloped Africa*.

58. Eltis, *Rise of African Slavery in the Americas*, 11.

59. Robert Fogel, *Without Consent or Contract: The Rise and Fall of American Slavery* (New York: Norton, 1989), 29.

60. Deborah Gray White, *Let My People Go: African Americans 1804–1860* (New York: Oxford University Press, 1996); Ronald Bailey, "The Slave(ry) Trade and the Development of Capitalism in the United States: The Textile Industry in New England," in *The Atlantic Slave Trade: Effects on Economies, Societies, and Peoples in Africa, The Americas, and Europe*, ED. Joseph Inikori and Stanley Engerman (Durham, NC: Duke University Press, 1992), 205–246; Fogel, *Without Consent or Contract.*

61. Fogel, *Without Consent or Contract*, 28–29.

62. W. E. B. Du Bois, *Black Reconstruction in America* (Cleveland, OH: Meridian, 1935), 29.

63. Ibid., 700–701.

64. Pem Davidson Buck, *Worked to the Bone: Race, Class, Power, and Privilege in Kentucky* (New York: Monthly Review Press, 2001), 24.

65. William Goodell, *The American Slave Code in Theory and Practice: Its Distinctive Features Shown by Its Statutes, Judicial Decisions, and Illustrative Facts* (Ann Arbor: Scholarly Publishing Office, University of Michigan Library, 2006); Gary Nash, *Red, White, and Black: The Peoples of Early America*, 3rd ed. (Englewood Cliffs, NJ: Prentice Hall, 1992); John Blassingame, *The Slave Community: Plantation Life in the Antebellum South* (New York: Oxford University Press, 1979).

66. David Brion Davis and Steven Mintz, *The Boisterous Sea of Liberty: A Documentary History of America from Discovery Through the Civil War* (New York: Oxford University Press, 1998), 58.

67. Davis, *Who Is Black?*; Haney-López, *White by Law.*

68. Patterson, *Slavery and Social Death*, 51–96; Jordan, *White Over Black*, 103–110, 366–367.

69. Jordan, *White Over Black*, 106.

70. Elizabeth Keckley, *Behind the Scenes; or, Thirty Years a Slave and Four Years in the White House*, in *The Norton Anthology of African American Literature*, 2nd ed., ed. Henry Louis Gates, Jr., and Nellie McKay (New York: Norton, 2004, 365–384), 373.

71. Orlando Patterson, *Rituals of Blood: Consequences of Slavery in Two American Centuries* (New York: Basic Books, 1988); Eugene Genovese, *Roll, Jordan, Roll: The World the Slaves Made* (New York: Vintage, 1972).

72. Harriet Jacobs, *Incidents in the Life of a Slave Girl* (1861), in *The Norton Anthology of African American Literature*, 2nd ed., ed. Henry Louis Gates, Jr., and Nellie McKay (New York: Norton, 2004), 279–314, 294.

73. Patricia Hill Collins, *Black Sexual Politics: African Americans, Gender, and the New Racism* (New York: Routledge, 2004); David Barry Gaspar and Darlene Clark Hine, eds., *More Than Chattel: Black Women and Slavery in the Americas* (Bloomington: Indiana University Press, 1996); Deborah Gray White, *Ar'n't I a Woman? Female Slaves in the Plantation South* (New York: Norton, 1985); Jacqueline Jones, *Labor of Love, Labor of Sorrow: Black Women, Work, and the Family from Slavery to the Present* (New York: Basic Books, 1985).

74. Dorothy Roberts, *Killing the Black Body: Race, Reproduction, and the Meaning of Liberty* (New York: Pantheon, 1997), 24.

75. Jacobs, *Incidents in the Life of a Slave Girl*, 287–288.

76. Angela Davis, *Women, Race, and Class* (New York: Vintage, 1983); Roberts, *Killing the Black Body.*

77. White, *Ar'n't I a Woman?*, 188.

78. Patterson, *Slavery and Social Death*, 46.

79. James Scott, *Domination and the Arts of Resistance: Hidden Transcripts* (New Haven, CT: Yale University Press, 1990).

80. Scott, *Domination and the Arts of Resistance*; Patterson, *Slavery and Social Death.*

81. Walter Rucker, *The River Flows On: Black Resistance, Culture, and Identity Formation in Early America* (Baton Rouge: Louisiana State University Press, 2006); Eugene Genovese, *From Rebellion to Revolution: Afro-American Slave Revolts in the Making of the New World* (New York: Vintage, 1979); Herbert Aptheker, *American Negro Slave Revolts* (New York: International, 1974 [1943]).

82. Aptheker, *American Negro Slave Revolts*, 4.

83. Herbert Aptheker, *Anti-Racism in U.S. History: The First Two Hundred Years* (New York: Greenwood Press, 1994); W. E. B. Du Bois, *Darkwater: Voices from within the Veil* (New York: Dover 1999 [1920]).

84. David Reynolds, *John Brown, Abolitionist: The Man Who Killed Slavery, Sparked the Civil War, and Seeded Civil Rights* (New York: Vintage, 2006); Stanley Harrold, *The Abolitionists and the South, 1831–1861* (Lexington: University Press of Kentucky, 1995); Larry Ceplair, ed., *The Public Years of Sarah and Angelina Grimké: Selected Writings, 1835–1839* (New York: Columbia University Press, 1989); Merton Dillon, *The Abolitionists: The Growth of a Dissenting Minority* (DeKalb: Northern Illinois University Press, 1974); Russell Nye, *William Lloyd Garrison and the Humanitarian Reformers* (New York: Little Brown, 1969); Aptheker, *Anti-Racism in U.S. History.*

85. Frederick Douglass, "What to the Slave Is the Fourth of July? An Address Delivered in Rochester, New York, on 5 July 1852," in *The Norton Anthology of African American Literature*, 2nd ed., ed. Henry Louis Gates, Jr., and Nellie McKay (New York: Norton, 2004), 462–473, 468, 470.

86. Du Bois, *Darkwater*, 102.

87. Quoted in Nell Irvin Painter, *Sojourner Truth: A Life, A Symbol* (New York: Norton, 1996), 167.

88. Leslie Schwalm, *A Hard Fight for We: Women's Transition from Slavery to Freedom in South Carolina* (Urbana: University of Illinois Press, 1997); Eric Foner, *Reconstruction: America's Unfinished Revolution, 1863–1877* (New York: Perennial, 1988).

89. Du Bois, *Black Reconstruction in America*, 611.

90. Michael Vorenberg, *Final Freedom: The Civil War, the Abolition of Slavery, and the Thirteenth Amendment* (New York: Cambridge University Press, 2001); Gao Chunchang, *African Americans in the Reconstruction Era* (New York: Garland, 2000); Eric Anderson and Alfred Moss, Jr., eds., *The Facts of Reconstruction* (Baton Rouge: Louisiana State University Press, 1991).

91. Stewart Tolnay and E. M. Beck, "Black Flight: Lethal Violence and the Great Migration, 1900–1930," *Social Science History* 12 (1991): 347–370; W. J. Cash, *The Mind of the South* (New York: Knopf, 1941); Patterson, *Rituals of Blood.*

92. "Strange Fruit" was composed in 1937 by Abel Meeropol, a.k.a. Lewis Allan. Holiday first performed it two years later. See David Margolick, *Strange Fruit: The Biography of a Song* (New York: Harper Perennial, 2001).

93. Jane Dailey, Glenda Elizabeth Gilmore, and Bryant Simon, eds., *Jumpin' Jim Crow: Southern Politics from Civil War to Civil Rights* (Princeton, NJ: Princeton University Press, 2000); Glenda Elizabeth Gilmore, *Gender and Jim Crow: Women and the Politics of White Supremacy in North Carolina, 1896–1920* (Chapel Hill: University of North Carolina Press, 1996).

94. Ira Berlin, *Man Thousands Gone: The First Two Centuries of Slavery in North America* (Cambridge, MA: Harvard University Press, 1998); David Brion Davis, *Slavery and Human Progress* (New York: Oxford University Press, 1984); Eric Williams, *Capitalism and Slavery* (Chapel Hill: University of North Carolina Press, 1944).

95. Gonzalez, *Harvest of Empire.*

96. Enrique Krauze, *Mexico: Biography of Power—A History of Modern Mexico, 1810–1996* (New York: Harper Collins, 1997); Lesley Byrd Simpson, *Many Mexicos*, 4th ed. (Berkeley: University of California Press, 1996); David Weber, *The Mexican Frontier, 1821–1846: The American Southwest under Mexico* (Albuquerque: University of New Mexico Press, 1982).

97. Gonzalez, *Harvest of Empire.*

98. Quoted in Arnoldo De León, *They Called Them Greasers: Anglo Attitudes toward Mexicans in Texas, 1821–1900* (Austin: University of Texas Press, 1983), 2–3.

99. Quoted in Gonzalez, *Harvest of Empire*, 44.

100. Menchaca, *Recovering History, Constructing Race*; Weber, *Mexican Frontier.*

101. Weber, *Mexican Frontier*, 274–275; Gonzalez, *Harvest of Empire*, 44.

102. Menchaca, *Recovering History, Constructing Race*, 215–217; Jocelyn Bowden, *Spanish and Mexican Land Grants in the Chihuahua Acquisition* (El Paso: Texas Western Press, 1971).

103. Gonzalez, *Harvest of Empire*, 30.

104. Gloria Anzaldúa, *Borderlands, La Frontera: The New Mestiza*, 2nd ed. (San Francisco: Aunt Lute Books, 1987).

105. Menchaca, *Recovering History, Constructing Race*.

106. Cornell, *Return of the Native*, 40–45.

107. George Tindall, *America: A Narrative History*, 2nd ed. (New York: Norton, 1988), 423.

108. Robert Remini, *Andrew Jackson and His Indian Wars* (New York: Viking, 2001); William Anderson, ed., *Cherokee Removal: Before and After* (Athens: University of Georgia Press, 1991); John Ehle, *Trail of Tears: The Rise and Fall of the Cherokee Nation* (New York: Doubleday, 1988); Samuel Carter, *Cherokee Sunset: A Nation Betrayed* (New York: Doubleday, 1976).

109. Quoted in Ronald Takaki, *A Different Mirror: A History of Multicultural America* (Boston: Little, Brown, 1993), 97.

110. Cornell, *Return of the Native*, 59.

111. Vine Deloria, Jr., *Custer Died for Your Sins: An Indian Manifesto* (Norman: University of Oklahoma Press, 1988); Takaki, *Different Mirror*.

112. Deloria, *Custer Died for Your Sins*, 35–36.

113. Willard Hughes Rollings, "Indians and Christianity," in *A Companion to American Indian History*, ed. Philip Deloria and Neal Salisbury (Malden, MA: Blackwell, 2002), 121–138; William Coleman, *Voices of Wounded Knee* (Lincoln: University of Nebraska Press, 2000); Dee Brown, *Bury My Heart at Wounded Knee: An Indian History of the American West* (New York: Owl Books, 1971).

114. Lawrence McCaffrey, *Textures of Irish Immigration* (New York: Syracuse University Press, 1992); Naomi Cohen, *Encounter with Emancipation: The German Jews in the United States, 1830–1914* (Philadelphia: Jewish Publication Society, 1984); Lawrence McCaffrey, *The Irish Diaspora in America* (Bloomington: Indiana University Press, 1976); John Higham, *Standers in the Land: Patterns of American Nativism, 1860–1925* (New York: Atheneum, 1985 [1955]).

115. Walt Whitman, "Preface to Leaves of Grass" (1855) in *The Norton Anthology of American Literature*, vol. 1, 5th ed., ed. Nina Baym (New York: Norton, 1998, 2080–2096), 2080.

116. Said, *Orientalism*, 49.

117. Susie Lan Cassel, ed., *The Chinese in America: A History from Gold Mountain to the New Millennium* (Walnut Creek, CA: AltaMira, 2002); Gary Okihiro, *The Columbia Guide to Asian American History* (New York: Columbia University Press, 2001); Ronald Takaki, *Strangers from a Different Shore: A History of Asian Americans* (London: Little, Brown, 1989); Ronald Takaki, *Plantation Life and Labor in Hawaii* (Honolulu: University of Hawaii Press, 1983).

118. Henry Yu, *Thinking Orientals: Migration, Contact, and Exoticism in Modern America* (New York: Oxford University Press, 2001); Lucie Cheng and Edna Bonacich, eds., *Labor Immigration under Capitalism: Asian Workers in the United States before World War II* (Berkeley: University of California Press, 1984); Cassel, *Chinese in America*; Okihiro, *Columbia Guide to Asian American History*; Takaki, *Strangers from a Different Shore*.

119. *Dutch Flat Chronicles*, August 30, 1877.

120. Mia Tuan, *Forever Foreigners or Honorary Whites? The Asian Ethnic Experience Today* (New Brunswick, NJ: Rutgers University Press, 2003); Emma Gee, ed., *Counterpoint: Perspectives on Asian America* (Los Angeles: Asian American Studies Center, University of California, 1976); Stuart Creighton Miller, *The Unwelcome Immigrant: The American Image of the Chinese, 1785–1882* (Berkeley: University of California Press, 1969); Okihiro, *Columbia Guide to Asian American History*; Takaki, *Strangers from a Different Shore*.

121. Paul Ong and John Liu, "U.S. Immigration Policies and Asian Migration," in *Contemporary Asian America: A Multidisciplinary Reader*, ed. Min Zhou and James Gatewood (New York: New York University Press, 2000), 155–174; Yu, *Thinking Orientals*; Okihiro, *Columbia Guide to Asian American History*.

122. Haney-López, *White by Law*.

123. Ellwood Cubberley, *Changing Conceptions of Education* (New York: Houghton Mifflin, 1909), 14–15.

124. Ibid.

125. David Roediger, *Working toward Whiteness: How America's Immigrations Became White; The Strange Journey from Willis Island to the Suburbs* (New York: Basic Books, 2005).

126. Eric Arnesen, "Whiteness and the Historians' Imagination," *International Labor and Working-Class History* 60 (2001): 3–32; Roediger, *Wages of Whiteness*, 140; Guglielmo, *White on Arrival*.

127. Higham, *Strangers in the Land*, 158–193.

128. Neil Foley, *The White Scourge: Mexicans, Blacks, and Poor Whites in Texas Cotton Culture* (Berkeley: University of California Press, 1997), 7.

129. Donald Young, *American Minority Peoples: A Study in Racial and Cultural Conflicts in the United States* (New York: Harper & Brothers, 1932), 421.

130. Noel Ignatiev, *How the Irish Became White* (London: Routledge, 1996); Roediger, *Working toward Whiteness*.

131. Ignatiev, *How the Irish Became White*.

132. Toni Morrison, "On the Backs of Blacks," *Time*, December 2, 1993.

133. Grace Elizabeth Hale, *Making Whiteness: The Culture of Segregation in the South, 1890–1940* (New York: Viking, 1998).

134. Du Bois, *Darkwater*, 17.

135. Cornel West, "A Genealogy of Modern Racism," in *Race Critical Theories: Test and Context*, ed. Philomena Essed and David Theo Goldberg (Malden, MA: Blackwell, 2002), 99–112.

136. David Theo Goldberg, *The Racial State* (Malden, MA: Blackwell, 2002), 41–43.

137. Quoted in West, "Genealogy of Modern Racism," 106.

138. Nancy Sherman, *Making a Necessity of Virtue: Aristotle and Kant on Virtue* (Cambridge: Cambridge University Press, 1997), 234; the internal quotations are from Immanuel Kant, *Doctrine of Virtue*, part 2 of *The Metaphysics of Morals* (Philadelphia: University of Pennsylvania Press, 1964 [1797]), 472–473.

139. Robert Bernasconi, "Who Invented the Concept of Race? Kant's Role in the Enlightenment Construction of Race," in Bernasconi, *Race* (Malden, MA: Blackwell, 2001), 14; see also Emmanuel Chukwudi Eze, "The Color of Reason: The Idea of 'Race' in Kant's Anthropology," in Eze, *Postcolonial African Philosophy: A Critical Reader* (Cambridge: Blackwell, 1997), 103–131.

140. Bernasconi, "Who Invented the Concept of Race?," 14.

141. Charles W. Mills, "Kant's *Untermenschen*," University of North Carolina Colloquium Series Working Paper, italics in original. The paper was published in slightly abridged form in Andrew Valls, *Race and Racism in Modern Philosophy* (Ithaca, NY: Cornell University Press, 2005), 169–193.

142. Toni Morrison, *Playing in the Dark: Whiteness and the Literary Imagination* (New York: Vintage, 1992), xiii, xii.

143. Thomas Gossett, *Race: The History of An Idea in America* (New York: Schocken, 1965), 32–34.

144. West, "Genealogy of Modern Racism," 101.

145. Smedley, *Race in North America*, 164–165.

146. Richard Lynn, *Eugenics: A Reassessment* (Westport, CT: Praeger, 2001); Philip Reilly, *The Surgical Solution: A History of Involuntary Sterilization in the United States* (Baltimore, MD: Johns Hopkins University Press, 1991).

147. Quoted in M. F. Ashley Montagu, *Man's Most Dangerous Myth: The Fallacy of Race*, 3rd ed. (New York: Harper, 1952 [1942]), 153.

148. Daniel Kevles, *In the Name of Eugenics: Genetics and the Uses of Human Heredity* (New York: Knopf, 1985); Reilly, *Surgical Solution*.

149. Montagu, *Man's Most Dangerous Myth*, 164, 168.

150. Holt, *Problem of Race in the Twenty-First Century*, 33.

151. West, "Genealogy of Modern Racism," 108.

152. U.S. Census Bureau, "State and Country Quick Facts," 2013.

153. U.S. Census Bureau, "State and Country Quick Facts," 2013.

154. U.S. Census Bureau, "State and Country Quick Facts," 2013; National Research Council, *The New Americans: Economic, Demographic, and Fiscal Effects of Immigration* (Washington, DC: National Academy Press, 1997).

155. Sabrina Tavernise, "Whites Account for Under Half of Births in U.S.," *New York Times*, May 17, 2012.

156. Albert Camarillo, "Reflections on a Century of Immigration from Mexico to the United States," Workshop on Multidisciplinary Frameworks for the Study of Ethnicity, Migration, and Human Rights, Harvard University, October 4, 2013.

157. Jeffrey Passel and D'Vera Cohn, *U.S. Population Projections: 2005–2050* (Washington, DC: Pew Research, 2008).

158. William H. Frey, "Census Projects New 'Majority Minority' Tipping Points," Brookings Institution, December 13, 2012.

159. Gustavo Arellano, "¡Ask a Mexican!, Special Half-Breed Edición," *OC Weekly*, September 20, 2007.

160. Jennifer Lee and Frank Bean, "America's Changing Color Lines: Immigration, Race/ Ethnicity, and Multiracial Identification," *Annual Review of Sociology* 30 (2004): 221–242.

161. Davis, *Who Is Black?*

162. Mara Loveman and Jeronimo Muniz, "How Puerto Rico Became White: Boundary Dynamics and Inter-Census Racial Reclassification," *American Sociological Review* 72 (2007): 915–939; Brent Staples, "On Race and the Census: Struggles with Categories That No Longer Apply," *New York Times*, February 5, 2007.

Chapter 3: Politics

1. Kay Mills, *This Little Light of Mine: The Life of Fannie Lou Hamer* (New York: Plume, 1994), 119–121.

2. Charles Payne, *I've Got the Light of Freedom: The Organizing Tradition and the Mississippi Freedom Struggle* (Berkeley: University of California Press, 1995), 42.

3. Doug McAdam, *Freedom Summer* (New York: Oxford University Press, 1988); Payne, *I've Got the Light of Freedom*.

4. Payne, *I've Got the Light of Freedom*, 7–11.

5. Ibid.6. Andrew Manis, *A Fire You Can't Put Out: The Civil Rights Life of Birmingham's Reverend Fred Shuttlesworth* (Tuscaloosa: University of Alabama Press, 1999).

7. Martin Luther King, Jr., "Letter from Birmingham Jail," in *Why We Can't Wait* (New York: Signet, 2000, 64–84), 68.

8. Aldon Morris, *The Origins of the Civil Rights Movement: Black Communities Organizing for Change* (New York: Free Press, 1984).

9. Ibid., 30.

10. Ibid.

11. Ibid.

12. Stewart Burns, *Daybreak of Freedom: The Montgomery Bus Boycott* (Chapel Hill: University of North Carolina Press, 1997).

13. Lynne Olson, *Freedom's Daughters: The Unsung Heroines of the Civil Rights Movement from 1830 to 1970* (New York: Scribner, 2002); Jo Ann Robinson, *Montgomery Bus Boycott and the Women Who Started It: The Memoir of Jo Ann Gibson Robinson* (Knoxville: University of Tennessee Press, 1987).

14. Adam Fairclough, *Better Day Coming: Blacks and Equality, 1890–2000* (New York: Penguin, 2001); Taylor Branch, *Parting the Waters: America in the King Years, 1954–1963* (New York: Simon and Schuster, 1989); David Garrow, *Bearing the Cross: Martin Luther King, Jr., and the Southern Christian Leadership Conference* (New York: HarperCollins, 2004 [1986]).

15. Payne, *I've Got the Light of Freedom*, 93.

16. Morris, *Origins of the Civil Rights Movement*; Payne, *I've Got the Light of Freedom*.

17. King, "Letter from Birmingham Jail," 40.

18. John F. Kennedy, "Civil Rights Message," June 11, 1963.

19. Robert Moses, Mieko Kamii, Susan McAllister Swap, and Jeffrey Howard, "The Algebra Project: Organizing in the Spirit of Ella," *Harvard Educational Review* 59 (1989): 423–443.

20. Chandler Davidson and Bernard Grofman, eds., *The Quiet Revolution in the South: The Impact of the Voting Rights Act, 1965–1999* (Princeton, NJ: Princeton University Press, 1994); Payne, *I've Got the Light of Freedom*, 112.

21. McAdam, *Freedom Summer.*

22. David Garrow, "Commentary," in *The Civil Rights Movement in America*, ed. Charles Eagles (Oxford: University of Mississippi Press, 1986), 59–60.

23. McAdam, *Freedom Summer*, 96.

24. Ibid., 97.

25. Payne, *I've Got the Light of Freedom*, 5.

26. King, "Letter from Birmingham Jail," 83.

27. Martin Luther King, Jr., "Address at the Conclusion of the Selma to Montgomery March," in *A Call to Conscience: The Landmark Speeches of Martin Luther King, Jr.*, ed. Clayborn Carson and Kris Shepard (New York: Warner Books, 2001, 111–132), 131.

28. Frank Parker, David Colby, and Minion Morrison, "Mississippi," in *The Quiet Revolution in the South: The Impact of the Voting Rights Act, 1965–1999*, ed. Chandler Davidson and Bernard Grofman (Princeton, NJ: Princeton University Press, 1994), 137–154.

29. Morris, *Origins of the Civil Rights Movement*, 287–288.

30. Thomas Clarkin, *Federal Indian Policy in the Kennedy and Johnson Administrations, 1961–1969* (Albuquerque: University of New Mexico Press, 2001); Joane Nagel, *American Indian Ethnic Renewal: Red Power and the Resurgence of Identity and Culture* (New York: Oxford University Press, 1996).

31. Troy Johnson, Duane Champagne, and Joane Nagel, "American Indian Activism and Transformation: Lessons from Alcatraz," in *American Indian Activism: From Alcatraz to the Longest Walk*, ed. Troy Johnson, Joane Nagel, and Duane Champagne (Urbana: University of Illinois Press, 1997), 9–44.

32. Joane Nagel, *American Indian Ethnic Renewal: Red Power and the Resurgence of Identity and Culture* (New York: Oxford University Press, 1996); Johnson, Champagne, and Nagel, "American Indian Activism and Transformation."

33. Peter Matthiessen, *Sal Si Puedes (Escape If You Can): César Chávez and the New American Revolution* (Berkeley: University of California Press, 2000); Susan Ferriss and Ricardo Sandoval, *The Fight in the Fields: César Chávez and the Farmworkers Movement* (New York: Harvest, 1997).

34. César Chávez, "Eulogy for Rufino Contreras," in *The Words of César Chávez*, ed. Richard Jay Jensen and John Hammerback (College Station: Texas A&M University Press, 2002), 181–182.

35. Ibid.

36. Michael Suleiman, "Introduction: The Arab Immigrant Experience," in *Arabs in America: Building a Future*, ed. Michael Suleiman (Philadelphia: Temple University Press, 1999), 1–21.

37. Edna Bonacich, "A Theory of Middleman Minorities," *American Sociological Review* 38 (1973): 583–594; Suleiman, "Introduction"; Edward Said, *Orientalism*, 287.

38. Michael Suleiman, *Arabs in the Mind of America* (Brattleboro, VT: Amana Books, 1988); Suleiman, "Introduction."

39. William Wei, *The Asian American Movement: A Social History* (Philadelphia: Temple University Press, 1993); Yen Le Espiritu, *Asian American Panethnicity: Bridging Institutions and Identities* (Philadelphia: Temple University Press, 1993), 32–52.

40. Steve Louie and Glenn Omatsu, eds., *Asian Americans: the Movement and the Moment* (Los Angeles: UCLA Asian American Studies Center Press, 2001); Wei, *Asian American Movement.*

41. Nancy MacLean, *Freedom Is Not Enough: The Opening of the American Workplace* (Cambridge, MA: Harvard University Press, 2006).

42. Dan Carter, *From George Wallace to Newt Gingrich: Race in the Conservative Counterrevolution, 1963–1994* (Baton Rouge: Louisiana State University Press, 1996), 6.

43. Steven Rosenstone, Roy Behr, and Edward Lazarus, *Third Parties in America: Citizen Response to Major Political Failure* (Princeton, NJ: Princeton University Press, 1984), 111.

44. Joe R. Feagin, Hernan Vera, and Pinar Batur, *White Racism: The Basics*, Second Edition (New York: Routledge, 2001), 113. See also "Haldeman Diary Shows Nixon Was Wary of Blacks and Jews," *New York Times*, May 18, 1994.

45. Carter, *From George Wallace to Newt Gingrich*, 43.

46. Nick Kotz, *Judgment Days: Lyndon Baines Johnson, Martin Luther King Jr., and the Laws that Changed America* (New York: Houghton Mifflin, 2005), 61.

47. Juan Williams, "Reagan, the South, and Civil Rights," *National Public Radio*, June 10, 2004.

48. Cited in Stephen Steinberg, "The Liberal Retreat from Race during the Post–Civil Rights Era," in *The House That Race Built: Black Americans, U.S. Terrain*, ed. Wahneema Lubiano (New York: Pantheon, 1997), 20–21.

49. Ibid.

50. Daniel Patrick Moynihan, "The Negro Family: The Case for National Action," in *The Moynihan Report and the Politics of Controversy*, ed. Lee Rainwater and William Yancey (Cambridge, MA: MIT Press, 1967), 76.

51. Steinberg, "Liberal Retreat from Race," 23.

52. Stephen Steinberg, *Turning Back: The Retreat from Racial Justice in American Thought and Policy* (Boston: Beacon, 1995).

53. Ian Haney-López, *Dog Whistle Politics: How Coded Racial Appeals Have Reinvented Racism and Wrecked the Middle Class* (Oxford: Oxford University Press, 2013), 1.

54. Nicholas Valentino and David Sears, "Old Times There Are Not Forgotten: Race and Partisan Realignment in the Contemporary South," *American Journal of Political Science* 49 (2005): 672–688; Paul Abramson, John Aldrich, and David Rohde, *Change and Continuity in the 2000 and 2002 Elections* (Washington, DC: CQ Press, 2003); Jeremy Mayer, *Running on Race: Racial Politics in Presidential Campaigns, 1960–2000* (New York: Random House, 2002).

55. Andrew Hacker, *Two Nations: Black and White, Separate, Hostile, Unequal* (New York: Scribner, 2003), 231.

56. Pew Research Center, "A Closer Look at the Parties in 2012: GOP Makes Big Gains among White Working-Class Voters," released August 23, 2012, http://www.people-press.org/ 2012/08/23/a-closer-look-at-the-parties-in-2012.

57. Abramson, Aldrich, and Rohde, *Change and Continuity*; Yvette Alex-Assensoh and Lawrence Hanks, eds., *Black and Multiracial Politics in America* (New York: New York University Press, 2000).

58. Louis DeSipio and Rodolfo de la Garza, "Forever Seen as New: Latino Participation in American Elections," in *Latinos: Remaking America*, ed. Marcelo Suárez-Orozco and Mariela Páez (Berkeley: University of California Press, 2002), 398–409. Rodolfo de la Garza and Louis DeSipio, *Ethnic Ironies: Latino Politics in the 1992 Elections* (Boulder, CO: Westview, 1996).

59. Timothy Noah, "What We Didn't Overcome," *Slate*, November 10, 2008.

60. John Harwood, "Level of White Support for Obama a Surprise," *New York Times*, November 2, 2008.

61. Megan Thee, "Multiple Signs of a Changing Electorate," *New York Times*, November 6, 2008.

62. Julia Preston, "In Big Shift, Latino Vote Was Heavily for Obama," *New York Times*, November 7, 2008.

63. Jackie Calmes and Megan Thee, "Polls Find Obama Built Broader Base Than Past Nominees," *New York Times*, November 5, 2008.

64. *New York Times,* Election 2012: President Exit Polls, available at http://elections.nytimes.com/2012/results/president/exit-polls

65. Seth Stephens-Davidowitz, "How Racist Are We? Ask Google," *New York Times*, June 9, 2012.

66. Ibid.

67. Mark Hugo Lopez and Paul Taylor, *Dissecting the 2008 Electorate: Most Diverse in U.S. History* (Washington, DC: Pew Research Center, 2009).

68. Chris Cillizza, "The Republican Problem with Hispanic Voters—in 7 Charts," *The Fix* (blog), *Washington Post*, March 18, 2013, http://www.washingtonpost.com/blogs/the-fix/wp/2013/03/18/the-republican-problem-with-hispanic-voters-in-7-charts/

69. Albert Camarillo, "Reflections on a Century of Immigration from Mexico to the United States," Workshop on 69, Multidisciplinary Frameworks for the Study of Ethnicity, Migration, and Human Rights, Harvard University, October 4, 2013.

70. Ibid.

71. Micah Cohen, "Can Democrats Turn Texas and Arizona Blue by 2016?" *New York Times*, March 1, 2013.

72. Jonathan Martin, "Beyond Black and White, New Force Reshapes South," *New York Times*, June 25, 2013.

73. Helene Cooper, "Obama to Vie for Arizona as Latino Numbers Rise," *New York Times*, December 1, 2011.

74. Haney-López, *Dog Whistle Politics*, 217—218.

75. U.S. Senate, "Ethnic Diversity in the Senate" (Washington, DC: U.S. Senate, 2007); David Canon, *Race, Redistricting, and Representation: The Unintended Consequences of Majority Black Districts* (Chicago: University of Chicago Press, 1999); Hanes Walton, Jr., and Robert Smith, *American Politics and the African American Quest for Universal Freedom*, 3rd ed. (New York: Addison Wesley Longman, 2000).

76. Kenny Whitby, *The Color of Representation: Congressional Behavior and Black Constituents* (Ann Arbor: University of Michigan Press, 1997); Kenny Whitby and George Krause, "Race, Issue Heterogeneity and Public Policy: The Republican Revolution in the 104th U.S. Congress and the Representation of African-American Policy Interests," *British Journal of Political Science* 31 (2001): 555—572; Katherine Tate, *Black Faces in the Mirror: African Americans and Their Representatives in the U.S. Congress* (Princeton, NJ: Princeton University Press, 2003).

77. Canon, *Race, Redistricting, and Representation.*

78. Michael Dawson, *Black Visions: The Roots of Contemporary African-American Political Ideologies* (Chicago: University of Chicago Press, 2001).

79. Carol Swain, *Black Faces, Black Interests: The Representation of African Americans in Congress* (Cambridge, MA: Harvard University Press, 1993).

80. George Billias, *Elbridge Gerry: Founding Father and Republican Statesman* (New York: McGraw-Hill, 1976).

81. David Lublin and Steve Voss, "Racial Redistricting and Realignment in Southern State Legislatures," *American Journal of Political Science* 44 (2000): 792—810; David Lublin and Steve Voss, "The Missing Middle: Why Median-Voter Theory Can't Save Democrats from Singing the Boll-Weevil Blues," *Journal of Politics* 65 (2003): 227—237; Kevin Hill, "Does the Creation of Majority Black Districts Aid Republicans? An Analysis of the 1992 Congressional Elections in Eight Southern States," *Journal of Politics* 57 (1995): 384—401.

82. Shaw v. Reno, 509 U.S. 630 (1993).

83. Brown et. al, *White-Washing Race*, 198.

84. Ari Berman, "Texas Redistricting Fight Shows Why Voting Rights Act Still Needed," *The Nation*, June 5, 2013.

85. Haney-López, *Dog Whistle Politics*, 161.

86. Alexis de Tocqueville, *Democracy in America* (New York: Perennial Classics 2000 [1835 and 1840]), 251—252.

87. V. O. Key, Jr., *Southern Politics in State and Nation* (Knoxville: University of Tennessee Press, 1984).

88. James Glaser and Martin Gilens, "Interregional Migration and Political Resocialization," *Public Opinion Quarterly* 61 (1997): 72—86; Marylee Taylor, "The Significance of Racial Context," in *Racialized Politics: The Debate about Racism in America*, ed. David Sears, Jim Sidanius, and Lawrence Bobo (Chicago: University of Chicago Press, 2000), 118—136.

89. Lynn Hempel, Julie Dowling, Jason Boardman, and Christopher Ellison, "Racial Threat and White Opposition to Bilingual Education in Texas," *Hispanic Journal of Behavioral Sciences* 35 (2012): 85-102.

90. Robert Huckfeldt and Carol Weitzel Kohfeld, *Race and the Decline of Class in American Politics* (Urbana: University of Illinois Press, 1989).

91. Donald Kinder and Lynn Sanders, *Divided by Color: Racial Politics and Democratic Ideals* (Chicago: University of Chicago Press, 1996), 17.

92. David Sears, Colette Van Laar, Mary Carrillo, and Rick Kosterman, "Is It Really Racism? The Origins of White Americans' Opposition to Race-Targeted Policies," *Public Opinion Quarterly* 61 (1997): 16—53.

93. Martin Gilens, "'Race Coding' and White Opposition to Welfare," *American Political Science Review* 90 (1996): 593—604.

94. Arian Campo-Flores, "Are Tea Partiers Racist?," *Newsweek*, April 25, 2010, http://mag.newsweek.com/2010/04/25/are-tea-partiers-racist.html; Christopher S. Parker, "2010 Multi-State Survey of Race and Politics," University of Washington Institute for the Study of Ethnicity, Race and Sexuality, http://depts.washington.edu/uwiser/racepolitics.html; Kate Zernike and Megan Thee-Brenan, "Poll Finds Tea Party Backers Wealthier and More Educated," *New York Times*, April 14, 2010, http://www.nytimes.com/2010/04/15/us/politics/15poll.html

95. Robb Willer, "The Decline of Whiteness and the Rise of the Tea Party: Movement Mobilization as Reassertion of Group Position," working paper, Stanford University, 2013.

96. Howard Schuman, Charlotte Steeh, Lawrence Bobo, and Maria Krysan, *Racial Attitudes in America: Trends and Interpretations*, Revised Edition (Cambridge, MA: Harvard University Press, 1997), 126.

97. Steven Tuch and Michael Hughes, "Whites' Racial Policy Attitudes," *Social Science Quarterly* 77 (1996): 723—745; Schuman et al., *Racial Attitudes in America*.

98. Schuman et al., *Racial Attitudes in America*, 157, 169—670.

99. Lee Sigelman and Susan Welch, *Black Americans' Views of Racial Inequality: The Dream Deferred* (Cambridge: Cambridge University Press, 1991); Paul Sniderman and Philip Tetlock, "Reflections on American Racism," *Journal of Social Issues* 42 (1986): 173—187.

100. The Editorial Board, "Voter Intimidation, Circa 2012," *New York Times*, September 21, 2012.

101. "Voter Intimidation Efforts In Philadelphia," *National Public Radio*, October 8, 2008; Cindy Chang, "The 2007 Campaign: County G.O.P Asks Candidate to Withdraw over Letter Threat," *New York Times*, October 20, 2006, A19; People for the American Way Foundation, *The Long Shadow of Jim Crow: Voter Intimidation and Suppression in America Today* (Washington, DC: People for the American Way, 2004).

102. National Conference of State Legislatures, *Voter Identification Requirements*, 2013, available at http://www.ncsl.org.

103. Natasha Khan and Corbin Carson, "Election Day Impersonation, an Impetus for Voter ID Laws, a Rarity, Data Show," *The Washington Post*, August 11, 2012; see also Justin Levitt, *The Truth about Voter Fraud* (New York: Brennan Center for Justice, 2007).

104. Life's Little Mysteries Staff, "UFO Sightings are 3,615 Times More Common than Voter Fraud," *Live Science*, June 26, 2012.

105. Brennan Center for Justice, *Citizens without Proof: A Survey of Americans' Possession of Documentary Proof of Citizenship and Photo Identification* (New York: Brennan Center for Justice, 2006).

106. Ari Berman, "Texas Redistricting Fight Shows Why Voting Rights Act Still Needed," *The Nation*, June 5, 2013.

107. "The Fight for Voting Rights, 50 Years Later," editorial, *New York Times*, August 27, 2013, http://www.nytimes.com/2013/08/28/opinion/the-fight-for-voting-rights-50-years-later.html; Adam Liptak, "Supreme Court Invalidates Key Part of Voting Rights Act," *New York Times*, June 25, 2013, http://www.nytimes.com/2013/06/26/us/supreme-court-ruling.html?pagewanted=all

108. Jeff Manza and Christopher Uggen, *Locked Out: Felon Disenfranchisement and American Democracy* (New York: Oxford University Press, 2006).

109. Marc Mauer and Jamie Fellner, *Losing the Vote: The Impact of Felony Disenfranchisement Laws in the United States* (Washington, DC: Human Rights Watch, 1998); Manza and Uggen, *Locked Out*, 79—80.

110. Manza and Uggen, *Locked Out*.

111. Carter, *From George Wallace to Newt Gingrich*, 68—72.

112. Ibid., 77.

113. Kathleen Hall Jamieson, *Dirty Politics* (Oxford: Oxford University Press, 1992), 15–17.

114. Tali Mendelberg, *The Race Card: Campaign Strategies, Implicit Messages, and the Norm of Equality* (Princeton, NJ: Princeton University Press, 2001); Carter, *From George Wallace to Newt Gingrich*.

115. Herbert Parment, *George Bush: The Life of a Lone Star Yankee* (New York: Scribner, 1997), 336.

116. Jamieson, *Dirty Politics*.

117. Ibid.; Mendelberg, *Race Card*, 142.

118. Rick Perlstein, "Exclusive: Lee Atwater's Infamous 1981 Interview on the Southern Strategy," *The Nation,* November 13, 2012, http://www.thenation.com/article/170841/exclusive-lee-atwaters-infamous-1981-interview-southern-strategy

119. Carter, *From George Wallace to Newt Gingrich*, 48.

120. Jonathan Alter and Michael Isikoff, "The Beltway Populist," *Newsweek*, March 4, 1996, 26.

121. Haney-López, *Dog Whistle Politics*, 3.

122. Mendelberg, *Race Card*, 6–7.

123. Ibid.

124. Haney-López, *Dog Whistle Politics*, 111.

125. Ibid., 4–5.

126. Ibid., 131.

127. Ibid., 133.

128. Eduardo Bonilla-Silva, *Racism without Racists: Color-Blind Racism and the Persistence of Racial Inequality in the United States*, 2nd ed. (Oxford: Rowman and Littlefield, 2006), 57.

129. Howard Winant, *The World Is a Ghetto: Race and Democracy since World War II* (New York: Basic Books, 2001), xiv.

Chapter 4: Economics

1. Nation Master, "Gross National Income by Country," 2007, http://www.nationmaster.com/country-info/stats/Economy/Gross-National-Income.

2. Linda Levine, *The Distribution of Household Income and the Middle Class* (Washington, DC: Congressional Research Service, 2012).

3. Donald Barlett and James Steele, *America: What Went Wrong?* (Kansas City, MO: Andrews McMeel, 1992), ix; Melvin Oliver and Thomas Shapiro, *Black Wealth/White Wealth* (New York: Routledge, 1997), 6, 29, 69–69; Jackson Dykman, "America by the Numbers," *Time*, October 30, 2006, 41–54.

4. York Bradshaw and Michael Wallace, *Global Inequalities* (Thousand Oaks, CA: Pine Forge, 1996); Harold Kerbo, *Social Stratification and Inequality: Class Conflict in Historical and Comparative Perspective*, 3rd ed. (New York: McGraw-Hill, 1996).

5. Gerald Jaynes and Robin Williams, Jr., eds., *A Common Destiny: Blacks and American Society* (Washington, DC: National Academy Press, 1989).

6. Ira Katznelson, *When Affirmative Action Was White: The Untold History of Racial Inequality in Twentieth-Century America* (New York: Norton, 2005).

7. Gwendolyn Mink, *The Lady and the Tramp: Race, Gender, and the Origins of the American Welfare State* (Madison: University of Wisconsin Press, 1990); Michael Brown, *Race, Money, and the American Welfare State* (Ithaca, NY: Cornell University Press, 1999); Robert Lieberman, *Shifting the Color Line: Race and the American Welfare State* (Cambridge, MA: Harvard University Press, 1998); Katznelson, *When Affirmative Action Was White*.

8. Cited in Katznelson, *When Affirmative Action Was White*, 48.

9. Cited in Katznelson, *When Affirmative Action Was White*, 60.

10. Frank Dobbin, "The Origins of Private Social Insurance: Public Policy and Fringe Benefits in America, 1920–1950," *American Journal of Sociology* 97 (1992): 1416–1450; Katznelson, *When Affirmative Action Was White*, 53–79.

11. Eric Goldstein, *The Price of Whiteness: Jews, Race, and American Identity* (Princeton, NJ: Princeton University Press, 2006); Leonard Dinnerstein, *Anti-Semitism in America* (New York: Oxford University Press, 1994).

12. Katznelson, *When Affirmative Action Was White*, 116.

13. Michael Bennett, *When Dreams Came True: The GI Bill and the Making of Modern America* (McLean, VA: Brassey's Publishing, 1996).

14. David Onkst, "'First a Negro . . . Incidentally a Veteran': Black World War Two Veterans and the G.I. Bill of Rights in the Deep South, 1944–1948," *Journal of Southern History* 31 (1998): 517–543; Kathleen Frydl, "The GI Bill" (unpublished diss., University of Chicago, 2000); Oliver and Shapiro, *Black Wealth/White Wealth*.

15. Katznelson, *When Affirmative Action Was White*, 23.

16. William Julius Wilson, *The Truly Disadvantaged: The Inner City, the Underclass, and Public Policy* (Chicago: University of Chicago Press, 1987); Walter Powell and Kaisa Snellman, "The Knowledge Economy," *Annual Review of Sociology* 30 (2004): 199–220.

17. Richard Hill and Cynthia Negry, "Deindustrialization and Racial Minorities in the Great Lakes Region, USA," in *The Reshaping of America: Social Consequences of the Changing Economy*, ed. Stanley Eitzen and Maxine Baca Zinn (Englewood Cliffs, NJ: Prentice Hall, 1989), 168–178; Sheldon Danziger and Peter Gottschalk, eds., *Uneven Tides: Rising Inequality in America* (New York: Russell Sage Foundation, 1993).

18. Jerome Culp and Bruce Dunson, "Brothers of a Different Color: A Preliminary Look at Employer Treatment of White and Black Youth," in *The Black Youth Unemployment Crisis*, ed. Richard Freeman and Harry Holzer (Chicago: University of Chicago Press, 1986).

19. Paul Pierson, *Dismantling the Welfare State? Reagan, Thatcher, and the Politics of Retrenchment* (Cambridge: Cambridge University Press, 1994); Margaret Somers and Fred Block, "From Poverty to Perversity: Ideas, Markets, and Institutions over 200 Years of Welfare Debate," *American Sociological Review* 70 (2005): 260–287.

20. Jude Wanniski, *The Way the World Works: How Economies Fail—and Succeed* (New York: Basic, 1978).

21. Frank Levy, *Dollars and Dreams: The Changing American Income Distribution* (New York: Russell Sage Foundation, 1987); Thomas Edsall and Mary Edsall, *Chain Reaction: The Impact of Race, Rights, and Taxes on American Politics* (New York: Norton, 1992); Dan Carter, *From George Wallace to Newt Gingrich: Race in the Conservative Counterrevolution, 1963–1994* (Baton Rouge: Louisiana State University Press, 1996), 60–63.

22. Leslie McCall, *Complex Inequality: Gender, Class, and Race in the New Economy* (New York: Routledge, 2001).

23. Oliver and Shapiro, *Black Wealth/White Wealth*, 2, 30.

24. U.S. Census Bureau, "Table 690, Money Income of Households—Percent Distribution by Income Level, Race, and Hispanic Origin, in Constant (2009) Dollars: 1990 to 2009" (Washington, DC: Government Printing Office, 2009).

25. U.S. Census Bureau, Current Population Survey, *Annual Demographic Survey* (Washington, DC: U.S. Government Printing Office, 2007); Leslie McCall, "Sources of Racial Wage Inequality in Metropolitan Labor Markets: Racial, Ethnic, and Gender Differences," *American Sociological Review* 66 (2001): 520–541; Oliver and Shapiro, *Black Wealth/White Wealth*, 24.

26. Edna Bonacich, "A Theory of Ethnic Antagonism: The Split Labor Market," *Annual Review of Sociology* 37 (1972): 547–559; Lawrence Bobo and Vincent Hutchings, "Perceptions of Racial Group Competition: Extending Blumer's Theory of Group Position to a Multiracial Social Context," *American Sociological Review* 61 (1996): 951–972.

27. Devah Pager, Bruce Western, and Bart Bonikowski, "Discrimination in a Low-Wage Labor Market: A Field Experiment," *American Sociological Review* 74 (2009): 777–799; Robert Adelman, Cameron Lippard, Charles Jaret, and Lesley Williams Reid, "Jobs, Poverty, and Earnings in American Metropolises: Do Immigrants Really Hurt the Economic Outcomes of Blacks?" *Sociological Focus* 38 (2005): 261–285.

28. Quoted in Cord Jefferson, "How Illegal Immigration Hurts Black America," *The Root*, February 10, 2010, http://www.theroot.com/articles/politics/2010/02/how_illegal_immigration_hurts_black_america.html. See also Carol Swain, ed., *Debating Immigration* (New York: Cambridge University Press, 2007).

29. Jefferson, "How Illegal Immigration Hurts Black America."

30. George Borjas and Marta Tienda, "The Economic Consequences of Immigration," *Science* 235 (1987): 645–652; George Borjas, *Friends or Strangers: The Impact of Immigrants on the U.S. Economy* (New York: Basic, 1990).

31. Kirk Semple, "A Somali Influx Unsettles Latino Meatpackers," *New York Times*, October 16, 2008.

32. Susan Gonzalez Baker, "Mexican-Origin Women in Southwestern Labor Markets," in *Latinas and African American Women at Work: Race, Gender, and Economic Inequality*, ed. Irene Browne (New York: Russell Sage Foundation, 1999), 244–269; McCall, "Sources of Racial Wage Inequality."

33. William Barnett, James Baron, and Toby Stuart, "Avenues of Attainment: Occupational Demography and Organizational Careers in the California Civil Service," *American Journal of Sociology* 106 (2000): 88–144.

34. CNN, "Racist Party at Campus," May 15, 2007.

35. Thomas Shapiro, Tatjana Meschede, and Sam Osoro, *The Roots of the Widening Racial Wealth Gap: Explaining the Black-White Economic Divide* (Waltham, MA: Institute for Assets and Social Policy, 2013).

36. Drew Desilver, *Black Incomes Are Up but Their Wealth Isn't* (Washington, DC: Pew Research Center, 2013).

37. Signe-Mary McKernan, Caroline Ratcliffe, Eugene Steuerle, and Sisi Zhang, *Less than Equal: Racial Disparities in Wealth Accumulation* (Washington, DC: Urban Institute, 2013).

38. Brown et al., *White-Washing Race*; Oliver and Shapiro, *Black Wealth/White Wealth*.

39. Thomas Dye, *Who's Running America? The Bush Restoration*, 7th ed. (New York: Prentice Hall, 2001); C. Wright Mills, *The Power Elite* (New York: Oxford University Press, 1959).

40. Matthew Hunt, "Race/Ethnicity and Beliefs about Wealth and Poverty," *Social Science Quarterly* 85 (2004): 827–853.

41. Mills, *Power Elite*, 152.

42. Bill Dedman, "The Color of Money," *Atlanta Journal and Constitution*, May 15–19, 1988; Alicia Munnell, Lynn Browne, James McEneaney, and Geoffrey Tootel, *Mortgage Lending in Boston: Interpreting HMDA Data* (Boston: Federal Reserve Bank of Boston, 1993); Federal Reserve Bulletin, "Expanded HMDA on Residential Lending: One Year Later," *Federal Reserve Bulletin* 78 (1993): 11.

43. Oliver and Shapiro, *Black Wealth/White Wealth*, 142–150.

44. Dana Ford, "Minorities Hit Hardest by Housing Crisis," *Reuters*, November 26, 2007.

45. Jacob S. Rugh and Douglas S. Massey, "Racial Segregation and the American Foreclosure Crisis," *American Sociological Review* 75 (2010): 629–651, 630.

46. McKernan et al., *Less than Equal*, 5.

47. Oliver and Shapiro, *Black Wealth/White Wealth*.

48. Jim Dwyer, "In a Sea of Foreclosures, an Island of Calm," *New York Times*, September 26, 2008;49. Jennifer Liberto, "Poverty Level Doesn't Budge: 50 Million and Counting," *CNNMoney*, November 6, 2013, http://money.cnn.com/2013/11/06/news/economy/poverty-census/; Mark Robert Rank, *One Nation, Underprivileged: Why American Poverty Affects Us All* (New York: Oxford University Press, 2004), 33–34.

50. U.S. Department of Health and Human Services, *Information on Poverty and Income Statistics: A Summary of 2013 Current Population Survey Data* (Washington, DC: ASPE Human Services Policy Staff, 2013).

51. Ibid.

52. Steve Hargraeves, "15% of Americans Living in Poverty," *CNNMoney*, September 17, 2013, http://money.cnn.com/2013/09/17/news/economy/poverty-income/.

53. Sharon Lee, "Poverty and the U.S. Asian Population," *Social Science Quarterly* 75 (1994): 541–559.

54. Martin Gilens, *Why Americans Hate Welfare: Race, Media, and the Politics of Antipoverty Policy* (Chicago: University of Chicago Press, 1999).

55. Herbert Gans, *The War against the Poor: The Underclass and Antipoverty Policy* (New York: Basic Books, 1995), 14, 74.

56. John Hartigan, Jr., *Odd Tribes: Toward a Cultural Analysis of White People* (Durham, NC: Duke University Press, 2005), 61.

57. Gunnar Myrdal, *Challenge to Affluence* (New York: Pantheon, 1962), 53. See also Gans, *War against the Poor*, 27–33; Steinberg, *Turning Back*, ch. 6.

58. John Hartigan, Jr., "Unpopular Culture: The Case of 'White Trash,'" *Cultural Studies* 11 (1997): 316–343; Gans, *War against the Poor*.

59. Robin Kelly, *Yo' Mama's Disfunktional: Fighting the Culture Wars in Urban America* (Boston: Beacon Press, 1997), 18.

60. Martin Luther King, Jr., *Where Do We Go from Here: Chaos or Community?* (New York: Harper and Row, 1967),188.

61. Bureau of Labor Statistics, *The Employment Situation—November 2013* (Washington, DC: U.S. Department of Labor, 2013).

62. Bradley Schiller, *The Economics of Poverty and Discrimination* (Upper Saddle River, NJ: Prentice Hall, 2004); Rank, *One Nation, Underprivileged*.

63. Alejandro Portes and Min Zhou, "The New Second Generation: Segmented Assimilation and Its Variants," *Annals of the American Academy of Political and Social Sciences* 530 (1993): 74–96.

64. David Shipler, *The Working Poor: Invisible in America* (New York: Vintage, 2005); Rank, *One Nation, Underprivileged*, 59.

65. Gilens, *Why Americans Hate Welfare*.

66. Hargraeves, "15% of Americans Living in Poverty."

67. Wilson, *Truly Disadvantaged*, 58–59.

68. Mario Luis Small and Monica McDermott, "The Presence of Organizational Resources in Poor Urban Neighborhoods: An Analysis of Average and Contextual Effects," *Social Forces* 84 (2006): 1698–1724.

69. W. E. B. Du Bois, *Souls of Black Folk* (New York: Dover, 1903 [1994]), 5.

70. James Elliot, "Social Isolation and Labor Market Insulation: Network and Neighborhood Effects on Less-Educated Urban Workers," *Sociological Quarterly* 40 (1999): 199–216; William Julius Wilson, *When Work Disappears: The World of the New Urban Poor* (New York: Knopf, 1996).

71. Paul Jargowsky, *Poverty and Place: Ghettos, Barrios, and the American City* (New York: Russell Sage Foundation, 1997); Wilson, *Truly Disadvantaged*.

72. Mario Luis Small and Katherine Newman, "Urban Poverty after The Truly Disadvantaged: The Rediscovery of the Family, Neighborhood, and Culture," *Annual Review of Sociology* 27 (2001): 23–45; Lincoln Quillian, "Migration Patterns and the Growth of High-Poverty Neighborhoods," *American Journal of Sociology* 105 (1999): 1–37.

73. John Kain, "The Spatial Mismatch Hypothesis: Three Decades Later," *Housing Policy Debate* 3 (1992): 371–460; Wilson, *Truly Disadvantaged*, 40–42; 100–103.

74. St. Clair Drake and Horace Cayton, *Black Metropolis: A Study of Negro Life in a Northern City*, rev. and enlarged ed. (New York: Harbinger, 1962 [1945]), 206.

75. Cited in Oliver and Shapiro, *Black Wealth/White Wealth*, 18.

76. Jargowsky, *Poverty and Place*; Wilson, *Truly Disadvantaged*, 56–57.

77. Wilson, *When Work Disappears*, 54.

78. Mary Pattillo-McCoy, *Black Picket Fences: Privilege and Peril among the Black Middle Class* (Chicago: University of Chicago Press, 1999), 208.

79. Jessie Carney Smith and Carrell Horton, eds., *Statistical Record of Black America*, 4th ed. (Detroit: Gale Research Press, 1997); Frank Wilson, "Rising Tide or Ebb Tide? Recent Changes in the Black Middle Class in the U.S., 1980–1990," *Research in Race and Ethnic Relations* 8 (1995): 21–55; Pattillo-McCoy, *Black Picket Fences*.

80. U.S. Census Bureau, *Census Bureau Reports the Number of Black-Owned Businesses Increased at Triple the National Rate* (Washington, DC: Government Printing Office, 2011).

81. Evelyn Ititani, "Finding Capital Can Be a Tall Order for Black-Owned Firms," *Los Angeles Times*, May 16, 2007; Tammerlin Drummond, "The Million-Dollar Dash," *Time*, December 4, 2000.

82. David Grant, Melvin Oliver, and Angela James, "African Americans: Social and Economic Bifurcation," in *Ethnic Los Angeles*, ed. Roger Waldinger and Mehdi Bozorgmehr (New York: Russell Sage Foundation, 1996), 379–409; Pattillo-McCoy, *Black Picket Fences*.

83. Oliver and Shapiro, *White Wealth/Black Wealth*, 96–97.

84. E. Franklin Frazier, *Black Bourgeoisie* (New York: The Free Press, 1957), 146.

85. Cited ibid., 156.

86. Harvard Project on American Indian Economic Development, *The State of the Native Nations: Conditions under U.S. Policies of Self-Determination* (New York: Oxford, 2007); Stephen Cornell and Joseph Kalt, "Where's the Glue? Institutional and Cultural Foundations of American Indian Economic Development," *Journal of Socioeconomics* 29 (2000): 443–470; Stephen Cornell and Joseph Kalt, "Sovereignty and Nation-Building: The Development Challenge in Indian Country Today," *American Indian Culture and Research Journal* 22 (1998): 187–214.

87. Cornell and Kalt, "Where's the Glue?"; Cornell and Kalt, "Sovereignty and Nation-Building."

88. David Vinje, "Native American Economic Development on Selected Reservations: A Comparative Analysis," *American Journal of Economics and Sociology* 55 (1996): 427–442; Harvard Project on American Indian Economic Development, *State of the Native Nations*.

89. David Wilkens, *American Indian Politics and the American Political System* (Lanham, MD: Rowman and Littlefield, 2002), 41.

90. Miriam Jorgensen and Jonathan Taylor, *What Determines Indian Economic Success? Evidence from Tribal and Individual Indian Enterprises* (Cambridge, MA: Harvard Project on American Indian Economic Development, 2000); Cornell and Kalt, "Where's the Glue?"; Cornell and Kalt, "Sovereignty and Nation-Building."

91. Cornell and Kalt, "Where's the Glue?," 455–456.

92. Cornell and Kalt, "Sovereignty and Nation-Building," 210.

93. Donald J. Hernandez and Jeffrey S. Napierala, "Children in Immigrant Families: Essential to America's Future" (New York: Foundation for Child Development, 2012).

94. Yoshimi Chitose, "Transitions into and out of Poverty: A Comparison between Immigrant and Native Children," *Journal of Poverty* 9 (2005): 63–88; Jennifer Van Hook, Susan Brown, and Maxwell Ndigume Kwenda, "A Decomposition of Trends in Poverty among Children of Immigrants," *Demography* 41 (2004): 649–670; Leif Jensen, "The Demographic Diversity of Immigrants and Their Children," in *Ethnicities: Children of Immigrants in America*, ed. Rubén Rumbaut and Alejandro Portes (New York: Russell Sage Foundation, 2001), 21–56.

95. Center for Immigration Studies, "Immigrants in the United States: A Profile of America's Foreign-Born Population" 2012, http://cis.org/node/3876.

96. Martha Crowley, Daniel Lichter, and Zhenchao Qian, "Beyond Gateway Cities: Economic Restructuring and Poverty among Mexican Immigrant Families and Children," *Family Relations* 55 (2006): 345–360; Eric Tang, "Collateral Damage: Southeast Asian Poverty in the United States," *Social Text* 62 (2000): 55–79; Chitose, "Transitions into and out of Poverty."

97. Alejandro Portes and Min Zhou, "The New Second Generation: Segmented Assimilation and Its Variants among Post-1965 Immigrant Youth," *Annals of the American Academy of Political and Social Science* 530 (1993): 74–98, 82.

98. Roger Waldinger, "Did Manufacturing Matter? The Experience of Yesterday's Second Generation: A Reassessment," *International Migration Review* 41 (2007): 3–39; Alejandro Portes and Rubén Rumbaut, *Immigrant America: A Portrait* (Berkeley: University of California Press, 2006); Roger Waldinger, "Ethnicity and Opportunity in the Plural City," in *Ethnic Los Angeles*, ed. Roger Waldinger and Mehdi Bozorgmehr (New York: Russell Sage Foundation, 1996); Min Zhou, "Segmented Assimilation: Issues, Controversies, and Recent Research on the New Second Generation," *International Migration Review* 31 (1997): 975–1008; Portes and Zhou, "New Second Generation."

99. Alejandro Portes, "Paths of Assimilation in the Second Generation," *Sociological Forum* 21 (2006): 499–504; Richard Alba and Victor Nee, "Rethinking Assimilation Theory for a New Era of Immigration," *International Migration Review* 31 (1997): 826–874; Wilawan Kanjanapan, "The Immigration of Asian Professionals to the United States, 1988–1990," *International Migration Review* 29 (1994): 7–32; Portes and Rumbaut, *Immigrant America*; Waldinger, "Did Manufacturing Matter?"

100. Zhen Zeng and Yu Xie, "Asian-Americans' Earnings Disadvantage Reexamined: The Role of Place of Education," *American Journal of Sociology* 109 (2004): 1075–1108.

101. Alejandro Portes, William Haller, and Luis Eduardo Guarnizo, "Transnational Entrepreneurs: An Alternative Form of Immigrant Economic Adaptation," *American Sociological Review* 67 (2002): 278–298; Patricia Landolt, Lilian Autler, and Sonia Baires, "From Hermano Lejano to Hermano Mayor: The Dialectics of Salvadorian Transnationalism," *Ethnic and Racial Studies* 22 (1999): 290–315; Alejandro Portes and Julia Sensenbrenner, "Embeddedness and Immigration: Notes on the Social Determinants of Economic Action, *American Journal of Sociology* 98 (1993): 1320–1350.

102. Min Zhou and Regina Nordquist, "Work and Its Place in the Lives of Immigrant Women: Garment Workers in New York City's Chinatown," in *Contemporary Asian America: A Multidisciplinary Reader*, ed. Min Zhou and James Gatewood (New York: New York University Press, 2000), 254–277.

103. Alejandro Portes and Min Zhou, "Self-Employment and the Earnings of Immigrants," *American Sociological Review* 61 (1996): 219–230.

104. Alejandro Portes and Leif Jensen, "The Enclave and the Entrants: Patterns of Ethnic Enterprise in Miami before and after Mariel," *American Sociological Review* 54 (1989): 929–949, 945.

105. Alejandro Portes, "Migration, Development, and Segmented Assimilation: A Conceptual Review of the Evidence," *Annals of the American Academy of Arts and Sciences* 610 (2007): 73–97; Mary Waters and Karl Eschbach, "Immigration and Ethnic and Racial Inequality in the United States," *Annual Review of Sociology* 21 (1995): 419–446; Jimy Sanders and Victor Nee, "Limits of Ethnic Solidarity in the Ethnic Enclave," *American Sociological Review* 52 (1987): 745–767; Jimy Sanders and Victor Nee, "Comment on Portes and Jensen: Problems in Resolving the Enclave Economy Debate," *American Sociological Review* 57 (1992): 415–418; Victor Nee and Brett de Barry Nee, *Longtime California: A Documentary Study of an American Chinatown* (New York: Pantheon, 1973); Portes and Jensen, "Enclave and Entrants."

106. Zhou, "Segmented Assimilation"; Waters and Eschbach, "Immigration and Ethnic and Racial Inequality"; Waters, *Black Identities*; Portes, "Migration, Development, and Segmented Assimilation."

107. R. Salvador Oropesa and Nancy Landale, "Immigrant Legacies: Ethnicity, Generation and Children's Familial and Economic Lives," *Social Science Quarterly* 78 (1997): 399–416.

108. Waters, *Black Identities*, 332.

109. Ibid.

110. Office of Family Assistance, *Characteristics and Financial Circumstances of TANF Recipients, Fiscal Year 2009* (Washington, DC: U.S. Department of Health and Human Services, 2009).

111. Philip Moss and Chris Tilly, *Stories Employers Tell: Race, Skill, and Hiring in America* (New York: Russell Sage Foundation, 2001).

112. Marc Bendick, Jr., Charles Jackson, and Victor Reinoso, "Measuring Employment Discrimination through Controlled Experiments," *Review of Black Political Economy* 23 (1994): 25–48; Moss and Tilly, *Stories Employers Tell*.

113. Joleen Kirschenman and Kathryn Neckerman, "'We'd Love to Hire Them, but . . .': The Meaning of Race for Employers," in *The Urban Underclass*, ed. Christopher Jencks and Paul Peterson (Washington, DC: Brookings Institution, 1991), 203–232.

114. Kirschenman and Neckerman, "'We'd Love to Hire Them, but . . .'," 210.

115. Michael Fix and Raymond Struyk, *Clear and Convincing Evidence: Measurement of Discrimination in America* (Washington, DC: Urban Institute Press, 1993); Bendick, Jackson, and Reinoso, "Measuring Employment Discrimination."

116. Marianne Bertrand and Sendhil Mullainathan, "Are Emily and Greg More Employable than Lakisha and Jamal? A Field Experiment on Labor Market Discrimination," NBER Working Paper No. 9873, 2004.

117. Devah Pager, "The Mark of a Criminal Record," *American Journal of Sociology* 108 (2003): 937–975.

118. Moss and Tilly, *Stories Employers Tell.*

119. Pierre Bourdieu, *Distinction: A Social Critique of the Judgment of Taste* (Cambridge, MA: Harvard University Press, 1984 [1979]); Annette Lareau, *Unequal Childhoods: Class, Race, and Family Life* (Berkeley: University of California Press, 2003).

120. Roberto Fernandez and Isabel Fernandez-Mateo, "Networks, Race, and Hiring," *American Sociological Review* 71 (2006): 42–71; James Elliot, "Class, Race, and Job Matching in Contemporary Urban Labor Markets," *Social Science Quarterly* 81 (2000): 1036–1051; Gary Green, Leann Tigges, and Daniel Diaz, "Racial and Ethnic Differences in Job-Search Strategies in Atlanta, Boston, and Los Angeles," *Social Science Quarterly* 80 (1999): 263–278.

121. Edna Bonacich, "Advanced Capitalism and Black/White Race Relations in the United States: A Split Labor Market Interpretation," *American Sociological Review* 41 (1976): 34–51.

122. Horace Cayton and George Mitchell, *Black Workers and the New Unions* (Westport, CT: Negro Universities Press, 1970), x.

123. Bonacich, "Advanced Capitalism and Black/White Race Relations," 50.

124. Edna Bonacich, "A Theory of Ethnic Antagonism: The Split Labor Market," *American Sociological Review* 37 (1972): 547–559, 549.

125. Miriam Jordan, "Carpenters' Union Seeks Immigrants to Spur Clout," *Wall Street Journal*, December 15, 2005.

126. Moon-Kie Jung, "Interracialism: The Ideological Transformation of Hawaii's Working Class," *American Sociological Review* 68 (2003): 373–400.

127. Blumer, "Race Prejudice as a Sense of Group Position": 3.

128. Bobo and Hutchings, "Perceptions of Racial Group Competition."

129. George Wilson and Debra Branch McBrier, "Race and Loss of Privilege: African America/ White Differences in the Determinants of Job Layoffs from Upper-Tier Occupations," *Sociological Forum* 20 (2005): 301–321.

130. James Elliott and Ryan Smith, "Race, Gender, and Workplace Power," *American Sociological Review* 69 (2004): 365–386; Ryan Smith and James Elliott, "Does Ethnic Niching Influence Access to Authority? An Examination of Race and Gender in Three Metro Areas," *Social Forces* 81 (2002): 255–279; Gail McGuire and Barbara Reskin, "Authority Hierarchies at Work: The Impacts of Race and Sex," *Gender and Society* 7 (1993): 487–506; Edward Irons and Gilbert Moore, *Black Managers: The Case of the Banking Industry* (New York: Praeger, 1985).

131. Ryan Smith, "Race, Gender, and Authority in the Workplace: Theory and Research," *Annual Review of Sociology* 28 (2002): 509–542; Gail McGuire, "Gender, Race, and the Shadow Structure: A Study of Informal Networks and Inequality in a Work Organization," *Gender and Society* 16 (2002): 303–322; Joel Podolny and James Baron, "Resources and Relationships: Social Networks and Mobility in the Workplace," *American Sociological Review* 62 (1997): 673–693.

132. Ella Edmondson Bell and Stella Nkomo, *Our Separate Ways: Black and White Women and the Struggle for Professional Identity* (Boston: Harvard Business School Press, 2001); Pamela Braboy Jackson, Peggy Thoits, and Howard Taylor, "Composition of the Workplace and Psychological Well-Being: The Effects of Tokenism on America's Black Elite," *Social Forces* 74 (1995): 543–557; Reskin et al., "The Determinants and Consequences of Workplace Sex and Race Composition."

133. McGuire and Reskin, "Authority Hierarchies at Work," 499.

134. Irene Brown, ed., *Latinas and African American Women at Work: Race, Gender and Economic Inequality* (New York: Russell Sage Foundation, 1999); Melvin Thomas, "Race, Class, and Occupation: An Analysis of Black and White Earnings for Professional and Non- Professional Males, 1940–1990," *Research in Race and Ethnic Relations* 8 (1995): 139–156.

135. Janeen Baxter and Erik Olin Wright, "The Glass Ceiling Hypothesis: A Comparative Study of United States, Sweden and Australia," *Gender and Society* 14 (2000): 275–294; Elliott and Smith, "Race, Gender, and Workplace Power."

136. Ryan Smith, "Racial Differences in Access to Hierarchical Authority: An Analysis of Change over Time, 1972–1994," *Sociological Quarterly* 40 (1999): 367–396; George Wilson, "Pathways to Power: Racial Differences in the Determinants of Job Authority," *Social Problems* 44 (1997): 38–54.

137. James Kluegel, "The Causes and Cost of Racial Exclusion from Job Authority," *American Sociological Review* 43 (1978): 285–301; Erik Olin Wright, Janeen Baxter, and Gunn Elisabeth Birkelund, "The Gender Gap in Workplace Authority: A Cross-National Study, *American Sociological Review* 60 (1995): 407–435.

138. Rosabeth Moss Kanter, *Men and Women of the Corporation* (New York: Basic Books, 1977).

139. Elliott and Smith, "Race, Gender, and Workplace Power," 381.

140. Martin Luther King, Jr., "Showdown for Non-Violence," *Look*, April 16, 1968, 24.

141. Jill Quadagno, *The Color of Welfare: How Racism Undermined the War on Poverty* (New York: Oxford University Press, 1994), 14.

142. Daniel Lichter and Rukamalie Jayakody, "Welfare Reform: How Do We Measure Success?" *Annual Review of Sociology* 28 (2002): 117–141; Alice O'Connor, "Poverty Research and Policy for the Post-Welfare Era," *Annual Review of Sociology* 26 (2000): 547–562; Rank, *One Nation, Underprivileged.*

143. H. Luke Shaefer and Kathryn Edin, "Rising Extreme Poverty in the United States and the Response of Federal Means-Tested Transfer Programs," *Social Service Review* 87 (2013): 250–68.

144. Lichter and Jayakody, "Welfare Reform."

145. Kathryn Edin and Laura Lein, *Making Ends Meet: How Single Mothers Survive Welfare and Low-Wage Work* (New York: Russell Sage Foundation, 1997).

146. Rank, *One Nation, Underprivileged,* 102–104.

147. U.S. Department of Health and Human Services, *Information on Poverty and Income Statistics: A Summary of 2013 Current Population Survey Data* (Washington, DC: ASPE Human Services Policy Staff, 2013).

148. Administration for Children and Families, *Temporary Assistance to Needy Families Fifth Annual Report to Congress* (Washington, DC: Administration for Children and Families, 2003); Jo Anne Schneider, "Pathways to Opportunity: The Role of Race, Social Networks, Institutions, and Neighborhood in Career and Educational Paths for People on Welfare," *Human Organization* 59 (2000): 72–85; U.S. House of Representatives, Committee on Ways and Means, *Green Book* (Washington, DC: Government Printing Office, 1998).

149. Kristen Harknett, "Working and Leaving Welfare: Does Race or Ethnicity Matter?" *Social Science Review* 75 (2001): 359–385; Kathryn Edin and Kathleen Mullan Harris, "Getting Off and Staying Off: Racial Differences in the Work Route of Welfare," in *Latinas and African American Women at Work*, ed. Irene Browne (New York: Russell Sage Foundation, 1999), 270–301.

150. Harknett, "Working and Leaving Welfare."

151. Edin and Harris, "Getting Off and Staying Off."

152. Brown, *Race, Money, and the American Welfare State,* 337–340.

153. Jackson, "Facts Favor Affirmative Action."

154. Joya Misra, Stephanie Moller, Marina Karides, "Envisioning Dependency: Changing Media Depictions of Welfare in the 20th Century," *Social Problems* 50 (2003): 482–504.

155. Edin and Lein, *Making Ends Meet.*

156. Sandra Morgen and Jeff Maskovsky, "The Anthropology of Welfare 'Reform': New Perspectives on U.S. Urban Poverty in the Post-Welfare Era," *Annual Review of Anthropology* 32 (2003): 315–338; Madonna Harrington Meyer, *Care Work: Gender, Labor, and the Welfare State* (New York: Routledge, 2000).

157. Wilson, *Truly Disadvantaged,* 9–10.

158. U.S. House of Representatives, Committee on Ways and Means, *Green Book* (Washington, DC: Government Printing Office, 1993); Rank, *One Nation, Underprivileged,* 104–105; Edin and Lein, *Making Ends Meet.*

159.   Congressional Record, *Debate on the Floor of the House of Representatives about the Personal Responsibility Act of 1995* (Washington, DC: Government Printing Office, March 24, 1995); Edsall and Edsall, *Chain Reaction*, 148.

160.   Rosalee Clawson and Rakuya Trice, "Poverty as We Know It: Media Portrayals of the Poor," *Public Opinion Quarterly* 64 (2000); 53–64; Lucy Williams, "Race, Rat Bites and Unfit Mothers: How Media Discourse Informs Welfare Legislation Debate," *Fordham Urban Law Journal* 22 (1995): 1159–1196; Gilens, *Why Americans Hate Welfare*.

161.   Cybelle Fox, "The Changing Color of Welfare? How Whites' Attitudes toward Latinos Influence Support for Welfare," *American Journal of Sociology* 110 (2004): 580–625; Lawrence Bobo and James Kluegel, "Status, Ideology, and Dimensions of Whites' Racial Beliefs and Attitudes: Progress and Stagnation," in *Racial Attitudes in the 1990s: Continuity and Change*, ed. Steven Tuch and Jack Martin (Westport, CT: Praeger, 1997).

162.   Charlotte Steeh and Maria Krysan, "The Polls—Trends: Affirmative Action and the Public, 1970–1995," *Public Opinion Quarterly* 60 (1996): 128–158.

163.   Brown et al., *White-Washing Race*, 25.

164.   Shannon Harper and Barbara Reskin, "Affirmative Action at School and On the Job," *Annual Review of Sociology* 31 (2005): 357–379; Samuel Leiter and William Leiter, *Affirmative Action in Antidiscrimination Law and Policy: An Overview and Synthesis* (Albany: State University of New York Press, 2002).

165.   David Oppenheimer, "Distinguishing Five Models of Affirmative Action," *Berkeley Women's Law Journal* 4 (1989): 42–61; Harper and Reskin, "Affirmative Action at School and on the Job."

166.   Barbara Reskin, *The Realities of Affirmative Action* (Washington, DC: American Sociological Association, 1998).

167.   Cited in Reskin, *Realities of Affirmative Action*, 10–11.

168.   John Ryan, James Hawdon, and Allison Branick, "The Political Economy of Diversity: Diversity Programs in Fortune 500 Companies," *Social Science Research Online* 7 (2002): www. socresonline.org. uk/7/1/ryan.html; Harry Holzer and David Neumark, "Are Affirmative Action Hires Less Qualified? Evidence from Employer-Employee Data on New Hires," *Journal of Labor Economics* 17 (1999): 534–569; Lauren Edelman, "Legal Ambiguity and Symbolic Structures: Organizational Mediation of Civil Rights Law," *American Journal of Sociology* 97 (1992): 1531–1576; Reskin, *Realities of Affirmative Action*.

169.   James Button and Barbara Rienzo, "The Impact of Affirmative Action: Black Employment in Six Southern Cities," *Social Science Quarterly* 84 (2003): 1–14; Harry Holzer and David Neumark, "What Does Affirmative Action Do?" *Industrial and Labor Relations Review* 53 (2000): 240–271; Charles Moskos and John Sibley Butler, *All That We Can Be: Black Leadership and Racial Integration the Army Way* (New York: Basic Books, 1996); Kevin Merida, "Study Finds Little Evidence of Reverse Discrimination," *Washington Post*, March 31, 1995; Holzer and Neumark, "Are Affirmative Action Hires Less Qualified?"; Reskin, *Realities of Affirmative Action*.

170.   Miriam Komaromy, Kevin Grumbach, Michael Drake, Karen Vranizan, Nicole Lurie, Dennis Keane, and Andrew Bindman, "The Role of Black and Hispanic Physicians in Providing Health Care for Underserved Populations," *New England Journal of Medicine* 334 (1996): 1305–1310; Nolan Penn, Percy Russell, and Harold Simon, "Affirmative Action at Work: A Survey of Graduates of the University of California at San Diego Medical School," *American Journal of Public Health* 76 (1986): 1144–1146.

171.   Faye Crosby, Aarti Iyer, and Sirinda Sincharoen, "Understanding Affirmative Action," *Annual Review of Psychology* 57 (2006): 585–611; Faye Crosby, Aarti Iyer, Susan Clayton, and Roberta Downing, "Affirmative Action: Psychological Data and the Policy Debates," *American Psychologist* 58 (2003): 93–115; Sam Howe Verhovek, "In Poll, Americans Reject Means but Not Ends of Racial Diversity," *New York Times*, December 14, 1997; Barbara Reskin and Patricia Roos, *Job Queues, Gender Queues: Explaining Women's Inroads into Male Occupations* (Philadelphia: Temple University Press, 1990); Jennifer Hochschild, *Facing Up to the American Dream* (Princeton, NJ: Princeton University Press, 1995); Thomas Pettigrew and Joanne Martin, "Shaping the Organizational Context for Black American Inclusion," *Journal of Social Issues* 43 (1987): 41–78.

172.   Faye Crosby and Sharon Herzberger, "For Affirmative Action," in *Affirmative Action: Pros and Cons of Policy and Practice*, ed. R. J. Simon (Washington, DC: American University Press, 1996); Marylee Taylor, "White Backlash to Workplace Affirmative Action: Peril or Myth?" *Social Forces* 73 (1995): 1385–1414.

173. Richard Morin, "Unconventional Wisdom," *Washington Post*, January 12, 1997; Liz McMillen, "Policies Said to Help Companies Hire Qualified Workers at No Extra Cost," *Chronicle of Higher Education*, November 17, 1995; Reskin, *Realities of Affirmative Action*; Crosby and Herzberger, "For Affirmative Action."

174. Wilson, *Truly Disadvantaged*, 113–114.

175. Richard Kahlenberg, *The Remedy: Class, Race, and Affirmative Action* (New York: Basic Books, 1996); Jonathan Leonard, "The Impact of Affirmative Action Regulations and Equal Employment Law on Black Employment," *Journal of Economic Perspectives* 4 (1990): 47; 63; Wilson, *Truly Disadvantaged*.

176. David Williams, James Jackson, Tony Brown, Myriam Torres, Tyrone Forman, and Kendrick Brown, "Traditional and Contemporary Prejudice and Urban Whites' Support for Affirmative Action and Government Help," *Social Problems* 46 (1999): 503–527; Verhovek, "In Poll, Americans Reject Means"; Steeh and Krysan, "Polls."

177. Cited in Reskin, *Realities of Affirmative Action*, 72.

178. Eleanor Holmes Norton, "Affirmative Action in the Workplace," in *The Affirmative Action Debate*, ed. G. Curry (Reading, MA: Addison-Wesley, 1996); Derrick Jackson, "Facts Favor Affirmative Action," *Boston Globe*, October 30, 1996; Morin, "Unconventional Wisdom"; Reskin, *Realities of Affirmative Action*, 73.

179. Cited in *St. Louis Dispatch*, "Affirmative Action Programs Also Help White Men, Report Says," August 23, 1998.

180. Katznelson, *When Affirmative Action Was White*, 153.

181. Reskin, *Realities of Affirmative Action*, 63, 93.

182. Richard Morin, "Misperceptions Cloud Whites' View of Blacks," *Washington Post*, July 11, 2001, A1.

Chapter 5: Housing

1. John Logan and Brian Stults, *The Persistence of Segregation in the Metropolis: New Findings from the 2010 Census* (Washington, DC: US2010 Project, 2011).

2. Stanley Lieberson, *A Piece of the Pie: Blacks and White Immigrants Since 1880* (Berkeley: University of California Press, 1980); Massey and Denton, *American Apartheid*, 22–23, 46–48.

3. Harvey Zorbaugh, *The Gold Coast and the Slum: A Sociological Study of Chicago's Near North Side* (Chicago: University of Chicago Press, 1929), 34.

4. Robert E. Park, "Human Migration and the Marginal Man," *American Journal of Sociology* 33 (1928): 881–893.

5. Oliver Zunz, *The Changing Face of Inequality* (Chicago: University of Chicago Press, 2000).

6. Eileen Diaz McConnell, "Latinos in the Rural Midwest: The Twentieth-Century Historical Context Leading to Contemporary Challenges," in *Apple Pie and Enchiladas: Latino Newcomers in the Rural Midwest*, ed. Ann Millard and Jorge Chapa (Austin: University of Texas Press, 2004), 26–40; Francisco Balderrama and Raymond Rodríguez, *Decade of Betrayal: Mexican Repatriation in the 1930s* (Albuquerque: University of New Mexico Press, 1995); Zaragosa Vargas, *Proletarians of the North: A History of Mexican Industrial Workers in Detroit and the Midwest, 1917–1933* (Berkeley: University of California Press, 1993).

7. Peter Hecht, "Mass Eviction to Mexico in 1930s Spurs Apology," *Sacramento Bee*, December 28, 2005.

8. Donald Fixico, "Federal and State Policies and American Indians," in *A Companion to American Indian History*, ed. Philip Deloria and Neal Salisbury (Malden, MA: Blackwell, 2002), 379–396; Donald Fixico, *Termination and Relocation: Federal Indian Policy, 1945–1960* (Albuquerque: University of New Mexico Press, 1986).

9. Kenneth Philip, *Termination Revisited: American Indians on the Trail to Self-Determination, 1933–1953* (Lincoln: University of Nebraska Press, 1999); Fixico, *Termination and Relocation*.

10. Langston Hughes, "The South," in Sondra Kathryn Wilson, *The Crisis Reader: Stories, Poetry, and Essays from the N.A.A.C.P.'s Crisis Magazine* (New York: Modern Library, 1999 [1922]), 24–25.

11. Nicholas Lemann, *The Promised Land: The Great Black Migration and How It Changed America* (New York: Knopf, 1991); James Grossman, *Land of Hope: Chicago, Black Southerners, and the Great Migration* (Chicago: University of Chicago Press, 1991); Drake and Cayton, *Black Metropolis*, 58.

12. James Loewen, *Sundown Towns: A Hidden Dimension of American Racism* (New York: Touchstone, 2006).

13. Loïc Wacquant, "From Slavery to Mass Incarceration: Rethinking the 'Race Question' in the US," *New Left Review* 13 (2002): 41–60; Allan Spear, *Black Chicago: The Making of a Negro Ghetto, 1890–1920* (Chicago: University of Chicago Press, 1967).

14. Cited in Philip Johnson, *Call Me Neighbor, Call Me Friend: The Case History of the Integration of a Neighborhood on Chicago's South Side* (Garden City, NY: Doubleday, 1965), 17.

15. Thomas Sugrue, *The Origins of the Urban Crisis: Race and Inequality in Postwar Detroit*, Princeton Classic ed. (Princeton, NJ: Princeton University Press, 2005); Spear, *Black Chicago*; Drake and Cayton, *Black Metropolis*.

16. Sugrue, *Origins of the Urban Housing Crisis*, 43.

17. Oliver and Shapiro, *Black Wealth/White Wealth*; Massey and Denton, *American Apartheid*.

18. Lipsitz, *Possessive Investment in Whiteness*, 6.

19. Dominic Capeci, Jr., *Race Relations in Wartime Detroit: The Sojourner Truth Housing Controversy of 1942* (Philadelphia: Temple University Press, 1985); Sugrue, *Origins of the Urban Housing Crisis*, 45.

20. Kenneth Jackson, "Race, Ethnicity, and Real Estate Appraisal: The Home Owners Loan Corporation and the Federal Housing Association," *Journal of Urban History* 6 (1980): 419–452; Sugrue, *Origins of the Urban Housing Crisis*; Oliver and Shapiro, *Black Wealth/White Wealth*.

21. Sugrue, *Origins of the Urban Housing Crisis*, 54.

22. Ibid., 34–36.

23. Robert Mowitz and Deil Wright, *Profile of a Metropolis: A Case Book* (Detroit: Wayne State University Press, 1962), 405, 412.

24. Robert Caro, *The Power Broker: Robert Moses and the Fall of New York* (New York: Vintage, 1975), 12.

25. Michael White, *Urban Renewal and the Residential Structure of the City* (Chicago: Community and Family Studies Center, 1980); Arnold Hirsch, *Making the Second Ghetto: Race and Housing in Chicago 1940–1960* (Chicago: University of Chicago Press, 1998).

26. Caro, *Power Broker*, 7.

27. Jon Teaford, *Rough Road to Resistance: Urban Revitalization in America* (Baltimore, MD: Johns Hopkins University Press, 1990); George Squires, ed., *Unequal Partnerships: The Political Economy of Urban Development in Postwar America* (New Brunswick, NJ: Rutgers University Press, 1989); Sugrue, *Origins of the Urban Housing Crisis*, 47–51.

28. Patrick Jones, *The Selma of the North: Civil Rights Insurgency in Milwaukee* (Cambridge, MA: Harvard University Press, 2009), 208.

29. Ibid., 246.

30. Cited in Sugrue, *Origins of the Urban Housing Crisis*, 210.

31. Sugrue, *Origins of the Urban Housing Crisis*, 195.

32. Kenneth Jackson, *Crabgrass Frontier: The Suburbanization of the United States* (New York: Oxford University Press, 1987); Massey and Denton, *American Apartheid*, 53.

33. Kevin Kruse, *White Flight: Atlanta and the Making of Modern Conservatism* (Princeton, NJ: Princeton University Press, 2005).

34. Massey and Denton, *American Apartheid*, 44.

35. Cited in Sugrue, *Origins of the Urban Housing Crisis*, 247.

36. Drake and Cayton, *Black Metropolis*; Spear, *Black Chicago*; Sugrue, *Origins of the Urban Housing Crisis*, 254–255.

37. Hirsch, *Making the Second Ghetto*; Gilbert Osofsky, *Harlem: The Making of a Ghetto* (New York: Harper and Row, 1968).

38. Stephen Grant Meyer, *As Long as They Don't Move Next Door: Segregation and Racial Conflict in American Neighborhoods* (Oxford: Rowman and Littlefield, 2000), 71.

39. Patrick Jones, "'Not a Color but an Attitude': Fr. James Groppi and Black Power Politics in Milwaukee," in *Groundwork: Local Black Freedom Movements*, ed. Komozi Woodard (New York: New York University Press, 2005).

40. Cheryl Harris, "Whiteness as Property," *Harvard Law Review* 106 (1993): 1707–1791.

41. Albert Mayer and Thomas Hoult, *Race and Residence in Detroit* (Detroit: Urban Research Laboratory, Institute for Urban Studies, Wayne State University, 1962), 2.

42. Baldwin, *Notes of a Native Son* (Boston: Beacon Press, 1955), 93.

43. Anthony Perez, Kimberly Berg, and Daniel Myers, "Police and Riots," *Journal of Black Studies* 34 (2003): 153–183; Joe Feagin and Harlan Hahn, *Ghetto Revolts: The Politics of Violence in American Cities* (New York: Macmillan, 1973).

44. Urban America, Inc. and the Urban Coalition, *One Year Later: An Assessment of the Nation's Response to the Crisis Described by the National Advisory Commission on Civil Disorders* (New York: Praeger, 1969).

45. Valerie Reitman and Mitchell Landsberg, "Watts Riots, 40 Years Later," *Los Angeles Times*, August 11, 2005.

46. Herbert Haines, "Black Radicalization and the Funding of Civil Rights: 1957–1970," *Social Problems* 32 (1983): 31–43; James Button, *Black Violence: Political Impact of the 1960s Riots* (Princeton, NJ: Princeton University Press, 1978); Feagin and Hahn, *Ghetto Revolts*.

47. Kruse, *White Flight*; Sugrue, *Origins of the Urban Crisis*.

48. Cf. Drake and Cayton, *Black Metropolis*, 97.

49. Massey and Denton, *American Apartheid*, 20.

50. Ingrid Gould Ellen, Keren Horn, and Katherine O'Regan, "Pathways to Integration: Examining Changes in the Prevalence of Racially Integrated Neighborhoods," *Cityscape* (2012): 33–53.

51. Ingrid Gould Ellen, *Sharing America's Neighborhoods: The Prospects for Stable Racial Integration* (Cambridge, MA: Harvard University Press, 2000); Camille Zubrinsky Charles, "The Dynamics of Racial Residential Segregation."

52. Sean F. Reardon, Stephen A. Matthews, David O'Sullivan, Barrett A. Lee, Glenn Firebaugh, Chad R. Farrell, and Kendra Bischoff, "The Geographic Scale of Metropolitan Racial Segregation," *Demography* 45 (2008): 489–514;, "The Dynamics of Racial Residential Segregation; Reynolds Farley and William Frey, "Changes in the Segregation of Whites from Blacks during the 1980s: Small Steps toward a More Integrated Society," *American Sociological Review* 59 (1994): 23–45; Massey and Denton, *American Apartheid*.

53. Logan and Stults, *Persistence of Segregation in the Metropolis*, 2–3.

54. John Logan and Richard Alba, "Locational Returns to Human Capital: Minority Access to Suburban Community Resources," *Demography* 30 (1993): 243–268.

55. Marta Tienda and Norma Fuentes, "Hispanics in Metropolitan America: New Realities and Old Debates," *Annual Review of Sociology* 40 (2014): 24.1–24.22; John Iceland, Daniel H. Weinberg, and Lauren Hughes, "The Residential Segregation of Hispanic Subgroups: 1980–2010" (working paper, Pennsylvania State University, March 4, 2013).; Massey and Denton, *American Apartheid*, 112–114.

56. Richard Alba and John Logan, "Minority Proximity to Whites in Suburbs: An Individual- Level Analysis of Segregation," *American Journal of Sociology* 98 (1993): 1388–1427.

57. Nancy Denton, "Are African Americans Still Hypersegregated?," in *Residential Apartheid: The American Legacy*, ed. Robert Bullard, J. Eugene Grigsby, III, and Charles Lee (Los Angeles: UCLA Center for African American Studies, 1994), 49–79.

58. Massey and Denton, *American Apartheid*, 77.

59. Richard Alba, John Logan, and Brian Stults, "How Segregated Are Middle-Class African Americans?" *Social Problems* 47 (2000): 543–558; John Logan, Richard Alba, and Shu-Yin Leung, "Minority Access to White Suburbs: A Multi-Region Comparison," *Social Forces* 74 (1996): 851–882; Massey and Denton, *American Apartheid*, 85–87.

60. Public Policy Forum, "Housing Diversity and Choices: A Metro Milwaukee Opinion Survey," *Public Policy Forum Regional Report* 1 (2004): 1–12.

61. Reynolds Farley, Charlotte Steeh, Maira Krysan, Tara Jackson, and Keith Reeves, "Stereotypes and Segregation: Neighborhoods in the Detroit Area," *American Journal of Sociology* 100 (1994): 750–780; Reynolds Farley, Howard Schuman, S. Bianchi, Diane Colasanto, and S. Hatchett, "Chocolate City, Vanilla Suburbs: Will the Trend toward Racially Separate Communities Continue?" *Social Science Research* 7 (1978): 319–344.

62. Farley et al., "Chocolate City, Vanilla Suburbs"; Massey and Denton, *American Apartheid*.

63. Elizabeth Bruch and Robert Mare, "Neighborhood Choice and Neighborhood Change," *American Journal of Sociology* 112 (2006): 667–709; Robert Sampson and Patrick Sharkey, "Neighborhood Selection and the Social Reproduction of Concentrated Racial Inequality," *Demography* 45 (208): 1–29.

64. David Cutler, Edward Glaeser, and Jacob Vigdor, "The Rise and Decline of the American Ghetto," *Journal of Political Economy* 107 (1999): 455–506; Chicago Commission on Human Relations, *1990 Hate Crime Report* (Chicago: City of Chicago Commission on Human Relations, 1991).

65. Massey and Denton, *American Apartheid*, 15.

66. Matthew Desmond, "Eviction and the Reproduction of Urban Poverty: Fieldnotes," October 2008.

67. Elizabeth Bruch and Robert Mare, "Neighborhood Choice and Neighborhood Change," *American Journal of Sociology* 112 (2006): 667–709.

68. U.S. Department of Housing and Urban Development, *Housing Discrimination Study, 2000* (Washington, DC: Department of Housing and Urban Development, 2000); George Galster, "Research on Discrimination in Housing and Mortgage Markets: Assessment and Future Directions," *Housing Policy Debate* 3 (1992): 639–683.

69. Susan Bertram, *An Audit of Real Estate Sales and Rental Markets of Selected Southern Suburbs* (Homewood, IL: South Suburban Housing Center, 1988).

70. John Yinger, "The Racial Dimension of Urban Housing Markets in the 1980s," in *Divided Neighborhoods: Changing Patterns of Racial Segregation*, ed. Gary Tobin (Newbury Park, CA: Sage, 1987), 43–67.

71. Massey and Denton, *American Apartheid*, 104.

72. U.S. Department of Housing and Urban Development, *Housing Discrimination Study*, 2000.

73. John Yinger, *Closed Doors, Opportunities Lost: The Continuing Costs of Housing Discrimination* (New York: Russell Sage Foundation, 1995).

74. Margery Turner, John Edwards, and Maris Mikelsons, *Housing Discrimination Study: Analyzing Racial and Ethnic Steering* (Washington, DC: U.S. Department of Housing and Urban Development, 1991).

75. Vincent Roscigno and Griff Tester, "Sex Discrimination in Housing," in *The Face of Discrimination: How Race and Gender Impact Work and Home Lives*, ed. Vincent Roscigno (New York: Rowman and Littlefield, 2007), 187–202.

76. Matthew Desmond, Weihua An, Richelle Winkler, and Thomas Ferriss, "Evicting Children," *Social Forces* 92 (2013): 303–327; Matthew Desmond, "Eviction and the Reproduction of Urban Poverty," *American Journal of Sociology* 118 (2012): 88–133; Matthew Desmond and Nicol Valdez, "Unpolicing the Urban Poor: Consequences of Third-Party Policing on Inner-City Women," *American Sociological Review* 78 (2013): 117–141.; Oliver Zunz, *The Changing Face of Inequality* (Chicago: University of Chicago Press, 2000).; Eileen Diaz McConnell, "Latinos in the Rural Midwest: The Twentieth-Century Historical Context Leading to Contemporary Challenges," in Ann Millard and Jorge Chapa, eds., *Apple Pie and Enchiladas: Latino Newcomers in the Rural Midwest* (Austin: University of Texas Press, 2004), 26–40; Francisco Balderrama and Raymond Rodríguez, *Decade of Betrayal: Mexican Repatriation in the 1930s* (Albuquerque: University of New Mexico Press, 1995); Zaragosa Vargas, *Proletarians of the North: A History of Mexican Industrial Workers in Detroit and the Midwest, 1917–1933* (Berkeley and Los Angeles: University of California Press, 1993).

77. James H. Carr and Isaac F. Megbolugbe, "The Federal Reserve Bank of Boston Study on Mortgage Lending Revisited," *Journal of Housing Research* 4 (1993): 277–313, 277. See also Gary A. Dymski, "Discrimination in the Credit and Housing Markets: Findings and Challenges," in *Handbook on the Economics of Discrimination*, ed. William Rodgers, III (Northampton, MA: Edward Elgar, 2006), 215–259.

78. Karen Orren, *Corporate Power and Social Change: The Politics of the Life Insurance Industry* (Baltimore, MD: Johns Hopkins University Press, 1982).

79. Gregory Squires and William Valez, "Neighborhood Racial Composition and Mortgage Lending: City and Suburban Differences," *Journal of Urban Affairs* 9 (1987): 217–232; Massey and Denton, *American Apartheid*, 107.

80. Alba, Logan, and Stults, "How Segregated Are Middle-Class African Americans?"; Logan, Alba, and Leung, "Minority Access to White Suburbs."

81. Yinger, *Closed Doors, Opportunities Lost*.

82. William Julius Wilson, *When Work Disappears: The World of the New Urban Poor* (New York: Vintage, 1996); Kirschenman and Neckerman, "'We'd Love to Hire Them, but . . .'."

83. Douglas Massey and Mary Fischer, "Does Rising Income Bring Integration? New Results for Blacks, Hispanics, and Asians," *Social Science Research* 20 (1999): 316–326; Pattillo-McCoy, *Black Picket Fences*.

84. Massey and Denton, *American Apartheid*, 14.

85. Daphne Kenyon, *The Property Tax-School Funding Dilemma* (Cambridge, MA: Lincoln Institute of Land Policy, 2007).

86. Charles, "Dynamics of Racial Residential Segregation."

87. Sugrue, *Origins of the Urban Housing Crisis*, 229.

88. James Baldwin, "Fifth Avenue, Uptown," in *The Price of the Ticket: Collected Nonfiction 1948–1985* (New York: St. Martin's, 1985 [1960], 205–213), 210.

89. Kenneth Clark, *Dark Ghetto: Dilemmas of Social Power*, 2nd ed. (Hanover, NH: Wesleyan University Press, 1989 [1965]), 32–33. Also see John Dixon, Colin Tredoux, and Beverley Clack, "On the Micro-Ecology of Racial Division: A Neglected Dimension of Segregation," *South African Journal of Psychology* 35 (2005): 395–411.

90. Mark Cordon, "Public Housing, Crime and the Urban Labor Market: A Study of Black Youths in Chicago" (working paper, Malcolm Wiener Center for Social Policy, Harvard University, 1991), 4. See also Sugrue, *Origins of the Urban Housing Crisis*, 81, 86–87.

91. Caro, *Power Broker*, 20.

92. Peter Marcuse and W. Dennis Keating, "The Permanent Housing Crisis: The Failures of Conservatism and the Limitations of Liberalism," in *A Right to Housing: Foundation for a New Social Agenda*, ed. Rachel Bratt, Michael Stone, and Chester Hartman (Philadelphia: Temple University Press, 2006, 139–162); Rachel Bratt, Michael Stone, and Chester Hartman, "Why a Right to Housing Is Needed and Makes Sense: Editor's Introduction," in Bratt, Stone, and Hartman, *Right to Housing*, 1–19; Alex Schwartz, *Housing Policy in the United States*, 2nd ed. (New York: Routledge, 2010).

93. Schwartz, *Housing Policy in the United States*.

94. Anthony Downs, "Introduction: Why Rental Housing Is the Neglected Child of American Shelter," in *Revisiting Rental Housing: Policies, Programs, and Priorities*, ed. Nicolas Retsinas and Eric Belsky (Washington, DC: Brookings Institution, 2008), 1–13.

95. Matthew Desmond, "Unaffordable America: Poverty, Housing, and Eviction," *Fast Focus: Institute for Research on Poverty* 22, 2015; Matthew Desmond and Tracey Shollenberger, "Poverty, Housing, and the Mechanisms of Neighborhood Selection" (paper presented at the American Sociological Association Annual Meeting, New York: August 9–13, 2013). See also Rob Collinson, "Rental Housing Affordability Dynamics, 1990–2009," *Cityscape: A Journal of Policy Development and Research* 13 (2011): 71–103; Barry Steffen, *Worst Case Housing Needs 2009: Report to Congress* (Washington, DC: U.S. Department of Housing and Urban Development, Office of Policy Development and Research, 2011).

96. Matthew Desmond, "Eviction and the Reproduction of Urban Poverty," *American Journal of Sociology* 118 (2012): 88–133; Matthew Desmond and Tracey Shollenberger, "After Eviction: Involuntary Displacement from Housing as a Mechanism of Neighborhood Inequality," *Demography*, forthcoming.

97. Matthew Desmond and Rachel Tolbert Kimbro, "Eviction's Fallout," *Social Forces*, forthcoming (2015); Matthew Desmond, Carl Gershenson, and Barbara Kiviat, "Forced Relocation and Residential Instability among Urban Renters" *Social Service Review*, forthcoming (2015); Matthew Desmond and Carl Gershenson, "Housing and Employment Insecurity among the Working Poor," *Social Problems*, forthcoming (2015); Desmond and Shollenberger, "After Eviction"; Desmond, "Eviction and the Reproduction of Urban Poverty."

98. Massey and Denton, *American Apartheid*, 19.

99. Loïc Wacquant, *Urban Outcasts: A Comparative Sociology of Advanced Marginality* (Cambridge: Polity Press, 2008).

100. Louis Wirth, "The Ghetto," in *Louis Wirth: On Cities and Social Life*, ed. Albert Reiss (Chicago: University of Chicago Press, 1964 [1927]), 84–98.

101. Wacquant, *Urban Outcasts*.

102. Mehdi Bozorgmehr, Claudia Der-Martirosian, and Geroges Sabagh, "Middle Easterners: A New Kind of Immigrant," in *Ethnic Los Angeles*, ed. Roger Waldinger and Mehdi Bozorgmehr (New York: Russell Sage Foundation, 1996), 345–378; Roger Waldinger, "Immigration and Urban Change," *Annual Review of Sociology* 15 (1989): 211–232; Alba and Nee, "Rethinking Assimilation Theory for a New Era of Immigration."

103. Douglas Massey, "Ethnic Residential Segregation: A Theoretical Synthesis and Empirical Review," *Sociology and Social Research* 69 (1985): 315–350.

104. U.S. Department of Housing and Urban Development, *Housing Discrimination Study*, 2000.

105. Peter Marcuse, "The Enclave, the Citadel, and the Ghetto: What Has Changed in the Post-Fordist U.S. City," *Urban Affairs Review* 33 (1997): 228–264; Min Zhou, *Chinatown: The Socioeconomic Potential of an Urban Enclave* (Philadelphia: Temple University Press, 1992).

106. John Logan, Wenquan Zhang, and Richard Alba, "Immigrant Enclaves and Ethnic Communities in New York and Los Angeles," *American Sociological Review* 67 (2002): 299–322.

107. Logan, Zhang, and Alba, "Immigrant Enclaves and Ethnic Communities," 320.

108. Jennifer Lee, *Civility in the City: Blacks, Jews, and Koreans in Urban America* (Cambridge, MA: Harvard University Press, 2002); Roger Waldinger, *Still a Promised City? African Americans and New Immigrants in Postindustrial New York* (Cambridge, MA: Harvard University Press, 1996).

109. Dave Chappelle on Def Poetry Jam, Episode 4, http://www.youtube.com/watch?v=PHbVu3ienHk

110. Lee, *Civility in the City*.

111. Edward Blakely and Gail Snyder, *Fortress America: Gated Communities in the United States* (Washington, DC: Brookings Institution, 1997).

112. David Bauder, "Group Points Out O'Reilly Race Comments," *Washington Post*, September 25, 2007.

113. Brad Plumer, "Poverty Is Growing Twice as Fast in the Suburbs as in Cities," *Washington Post*, May 23, 2013; Paul Jargowsky, *Concentration of Poverty in the New Millennium: Changes in the Prevalence, Composition, and Location of High-Poverty Neighborhoods* (Washington, DC: Century Foundation, 2014).

114. Allan Berube and William Frey, "A Decade of Mixed Blessings: Urban and Suburban Poverty in Census 2000," in *Redefining Urban and Suburban America: Evidence from the 2000 Census*, ed. Allan Berube, Bruce Katz, and Robert Lang (Washington, DC: Brookings Institution, 2005), 111–136.

115. William H. Frey, "Metropolitan Policy Program, Brookings Institution, Melting Pot Cities and Suburbs: Racial and Ethnic Change in Metro America in the 2000s" (Washington, DC: Brookings Institution, 2011).

116. Pattillo-McCoy, *Black Picket Fences*; Charles, "Dynamics of Racial Residential Segregation."

117. Allen Liska, John Logan, and Paul Bellair, "Race and Violent Crime in the Suburbs," *American Sociological Review* 63 (1998): 27–38; Pattillo, "Black Middle-Class Neighborhoods," *Annual Review of Sociology* 31 (2005): 305–329, 322; Pattillo-McCoy, *Black Picket Fences*.

118. Karyn Lacy, "Black Spaces, Black Places: Strategic Assimilation and Identity Construction in Middle-Class Suburbia," *Ethnic and Racial Studies* 27 (2004): 908–930.

119. France Winddance Twine, "Brown-Skinned White Girls: Class, Culture, and the Construction of White Identity in Suburban Communities," in *Displacing Whiteness: Essays in Social and Cultural Criticism*, ed. Ruth Frankenberg (Durham, NC: Duke University Press, 1997), 214–224, 233.

120. Richard Alba and Victor Nee, *Remaking the American Mainstream: Assimilation and Contemporary Immigration* (Cambridge, MA: Harvard University Press, 2003); Richard Alba, John Logan, Brian Stults, Gilbert Marzan, and Wenquan Zhang, "Immigrant Groups and Suburbs: A Reexamination of Suburbanization and Spatial Assimilation," *American Sociological Review* 64 (1999): 446–460; John Horton, *The Politics of Diversity: Immigration, Resistance, and Change in Monterey Park, California* (Philadelphia: Temple University Press, 1992).

121. Susie Ling, "History of Asians in the San Gabriel Valley," IMDiversity.com, downloaded October 20, 2008. See also John Horton and Jose Calderon, *The Politics of Diversity: Immigration, Resistance, and Change in Monterey Park, California* (Philadelphia: Temple University Press, 1995).

122. U.S. Census Bureau, "Estimates of U.S. Urban Population," 2003, https://www.census.gov/popest /data/.

123. C. Matthew Snipp, "Understanding Race and Ethnicity in Rural America," *Rural Sociology* 61 (1989): 125–142, 127.

124. Maggie Rivas-Rodriguez, *Mexican Americans and World War II* (College Station: University of Texas Press, 2005); Jeffrey Harris Cohen, *The Culture of Migration in Southern Mexico* (College Station: University of Texas Press, 2004).

125. American Immigration Law Foundation, *Mexican Immigrant Workers and the U.S. Economy: An Increasingly Vital Role* (Washington, DC: Immigration Policy Focus, 2002).

126. Doris Slesinger and Max Pfeffer, "Migrant Farm Workers," in *Rural Poverty in America*, ed. Cynthia Duncan (Westport, CT: Auburn House, 1992), 125–154; Snipp, "Understanding Race and Ethnicity."

127. U.S. Census Bureau, Small Area Income and Poverty Estimates, *State and County Estimates for 2012* (Washington, DC: Government Printing Office, 2012).

128. Martha Crowley, Daniel Lichter, and Zhenchao Qian, "Beyond Gateway Cities: Economic Restructuring and Poverty among Mexican Immigrant Families and Children," *Family Relations* 55 (2006): 345–360; Joan Anderson, "The U.S.-Mexico Border: A Half Century of Change," *Social Science Journal* 40 (2003): 535–554.

129. Snipp, "Understanding Race and Ethnicity."

130. Russell Thornton, *The Cherokees: A Population History* (Lincoln: University of Nebraska Press, 1990), 174–75.

131. Eva Marie Garroutte, *Real Indians: Identity and the Survival of Native America* (Berkeley: University of California Press, 2003), 67.

132. Robert Bullard, *Dumping on Dixie: Race, Class, and Environmental Quality* (Boulder, CO: Westview, 2000), 98.

133. Robert Bullard, *Environment and Morality: Confronting Environmental Racism in the United States* (Geneva: United Nations Research Institute for Social Development, 2004); Winona LaDuke, *All Our Relations: Native Struggles for Land Rights and Life* (Boston: South End Press, 1999).

134. Margot Roosevelt, "Utah's Toxic Opportunity," *Time*, March 8, 2006.

135. Judy Fahys, "Utah N-Waste Site Backers Call It Quits." *Salt Lake Tribune* (Salt Lake City), December 21, 2012, http://www.sltrib.com/sltrib/politics/55513674-90/waste-utah- license-site.html.

136. U.S. Department of Health and Human Services, Indian Health Service, *Indian Health Disparities* (2014).

137. U.S. Department of Health and Human Services, Indian Health Service, *Trends in Indian Health* (2009).

138. Deborah Robinson, *Environmental Racism: Old Wine in a New Bottle* (Geneva: World Council of Churches, 2000); *Dallas Morning News*, "Study: Public Housing Is Too Often Located Near Toxic Sites," October 3, 2000.

139. Bullard, *Environment and Morality*, iii.

140. U.S. Department of Health and Human Services, Agency for Toxic Substances and Disease Registry, *Health Consultation (Exposure Investigation): Calcasieu Estuary (aka Mossville)* (Lake Charles, Calcasieu Parish, LA: CERLIS No. LA002368173, November 19, 1999); Robinson, *Environmental Racism*.

141. Environmental Sustainability Committee, *Nationwide Waste Statistics* (Houghton: Environmental Sustainability Committee, 2007).

142. Loïc Wacquant, "Territorial Stigmatization in the Age of Advanced Marginality," *Thesis Eleven* 91 (2007): 66–77, 67.

143. Cash, *The Mind of the South*, vii.

144. Hartigan, *Odd Tribes*.

145. Andrea Voyer, "Living Difference and Talking Diversity: Interactions, Identifications, and Institutions" (unpublished working paper, University of Wisconsin—Madison, Department of Sociology), 2013; Jerry Harkavy, "Somalis Find New Lives, Adjustments to Lewiston," *Lewiston Sun Journal*, 2007.

146. Southern Poverty Law Center, "Maine Town's Diversity Rally Outdraws Hate-Group Gathering," March 2004.

147. Alex Kotlowitz, "Our Town," *New York Times Magazine*, August 5, 2007.

148. Ibid., 37.

149. Ibid., 33.

150. Baldwin, "Fifth Avenue, Uptown," 213.

Chapter 6: Crime and Punishment

1. Sister Helen Prejean, *The Death of Innocents: An Eyewitness Account of Wrongful Executions* (New York: Knopf, 2006).

2. Deborah Cray White, *Too Heavy a Load: Black Women in Defense of Themselves, 1894—1994* (New York: Norton, 1999), 25.

3. Quoted in Adam Fairclough, *Better Day Coming: Blacks and Equality, 1890—2000* (New York: Penguin, 2001), 25.

4. Cash, *The Mind of the South*, 119.

5. Patricia Schechter, *Ida B. Wells-Barnett and American Reform, 1880—1930* (Chapel Hill: University of North Carolina Press, 2001), 85—87; Mary Frances Berry, *The Pig Farmer's Daughter and Other Tales of American Justice: Episodes of Racism and Sexism in the Courts from 1865 to the Present* (New York: Vintage, 1999).

6. Glenda Gilmore, *Gender and Jim Crow: Women and the Politics of White Supremacy in North Carolina, 1896—1920* (Chapel Hill: University of North Carolina Press, 1996).

7. Amy Dru Stanley, *From Bondage to Contract: Wage Labor, Marriage, and the Market in the Age of Slave Emancipation* (Cambridge: Cambridge University Press, 1998), 108—110.; Christopher Muller, "Northward Migration and the Rise of Racial Disparity in American Incarceration, 1880—1950," *American Journal of Sociology* 118 (2013): 281—326.

8. Wacquant, "From Slavery to Mass Incarceration," 53.

9. David Oshinsky, *Worse than Slavery: Parchman Farm and the Ordeal of Jim Crow Justice* (New York: Free Press, 1996), 45. Also see David Garland, *Punishment and Modern Society: A Study in Social Theory* (Chicago: University of Chicago Press, 1990), 104—105; Martha Myers, *Race, Labor, and Punishment in the New South* (Columbus: Ohio State University Press, 1998).

10. Roger Daniels, *Prisoners without Trial: Japanese Americans in World War II* (New York: Hill and Wang, 2004); Peter Irons, *Justice at War: The Story of the Japanese American Internment Cases* (Seattle: University of Washington Press, 1993); Roger Daniels, Sandra Taylor, Harry Kitano, and Leonard Arrington, *Japanese Americans, from Relocation to Redress* (Seattle: University of Washington Press, 1991).

11. David Garland, "Introduction: The Meaning of Mass Imprisonment," in *Mass Imprisonment: Social Causes and Consequences*, ed. David Garland (London: Sage, 2001).

12. Bruce Western, *Punishment and Inequality in America* (New York: Russell Sage Foundation, 2006).

13. Eric Schlosser, "The Prison-Industrial Complex," *Atlantic Monthly*, December 1998.

14. Roy Walmsley, *World Prison Population List*, 9th ed. (London: International Centre for Prison Studies, 2011).

15. The Economist, *Pocket World in Figures, 2007 Edition* (London: The Economist Newspaper, 2007); Katherine Beckett and Theodore Sasson, *The Politics of Injustice: Crime and Punishment in America*, 2nd ed. (Thousand Oaks, CA: Sage, 2004); Western, *Punishment and Inequality in America*.

16. The Sentencing Project, *Incarcerated Women* (Washington, DC: The Sentencing Project, 2013).

17. U.S. Department of Justice, *Prisoners in 2010* (Washington, DC: Bureau of Justice Statistics, 2012).

18. *National Association for the Advancement of Colored People*, Criminal Justice Fact Sheet (Washington, DC: NAACP, 2013).

19. Western, *Punishment and Inequality in America*, 16.

20. Ibid., 15–25.

21. Bruce Western and Becky Pettit, "Incarceration and Social Inequality," *Daedalus* 139 (2010): 8–19.

22. Becky Pettit, *Invisible Men: Mass Incarceration and the Myth of Black Progress* (New York: Russell Sage Foundation, 2012).

23. Ibid., 27.

24. Western, *Punishment and Inequality in America*, 48; Beckett and Sasson, *Politics of Injustice*, 14, 18.

25. Western, *Punishment and Inequality in America*, 41.

26. Alfred Blumstein and Allen Beck, "Population Growth in U.S. Prisons, 1980–1996," in *Prisons: Crime and Justice—A Review of the Research*, ed. Michael Tonry (Chicago: University of Chicago Press: 1999), 17–61.

27. Michael Tonry, *Malign Neglect: Race, Crime, and Punishment in America* (New York: Oxford University Press, 1995); Western, *Punishment and Inequality in America*, 42–43, 47.

28. Joan Petersilia, *When Prisoners Come Home: Parole and Prisoner Reentry* (New York: Oxford University Press, 2003); Sasha Abramsky, *Hard Time Blues: How Politics Built a Prison Nation* (New York: Dunne Books, 2002); Western, *Punishment and Inequality in America*, 62–64.

29. Beckett and Sasson, *Politics of Injustice*, 49.

30. Joseph Davey, *The Politics of Prison Expansion: Winning Elections by Waging War on Crime* (Westport, CT: Praeger, 1998); Western, *Punishment and Inequality in America*, 60–61.

31. Quoted in Nancy Marion, *A History of Federal Crime Control Initiatives, 1960–1993* (Westport, CT: Praeger, 1994), 70.

32. Lord Windelsham, *Politics, Punishment and Populism* (New York: Oxford University Press, 1998); Beckett and Sasson, *Politics of Injustice*, 52–65.

33. Angela Y. Davis, *Abolition Democracy: Beyond Prisons, Torture, and Empire* (New York: Seven Stories Press, 2005); Angela Y. Davis, *Are Prisons Obsolete?* (New York: Seven Stories Press, 2003); Nils Christie, *Crime Control as Industry: Towards Gulags, Western Style* (New York: Routledge, 2000).

34. Suevon Lee, "By the Numbers: The U.S.'s Growing For-Profit Detention Industry," *ProPublica*, June 20, 2012.

35. Tonry, *Malign Neglect*, 94.

36. Beckett and Sasson, *Politics of Injustice*, 48.

37. Urban American and Urban Coalition, *One Year Later: An Assessment of the Nation's Response to the Crisis Described by the National Advisory Commission on Civil Disorders* (New York: Praeger, 1968).

38. Leo Carroll and Pamela Irving Jackson, "Minority Composition, Inequality and the Growth of Municipal Police Forces, 1960–71," *Sociological Focus* 15 (1982): 327–346; Susan Welch, "The Impact of Urban Riots on Urban Expenditures," *American Journal of Political Science* 19 (1975): 741–760.

39. Pamela Oliver, "Repression and Crime Control: Why Social Movement Scholars Should Pay Attention to Mass Incarceration as a Form of Repression," *Mobilization* 13 (2008): 1–24.

40. Western, *Punishment and Inequality in America*.

41. Steven Barkan and Steven Cohn, "Why Whites Favor Spending More Money to Fight Crime," *Social Problems* 52 (2005): 300–314; Barry Glassner, *Culture of Fear: Why Americans Are Afraid of the Wrong Things* (New York: Basic Books, 1999).

42. Lydia Saad, "Nearly 4 in 10 Americans Still Fear Walking Alone at Night," *Gallup*, November 5, 2010.

43. Eric Lambert, "Worlds Apart: The Views on Crime and Punishment among White and Minority College Students," *Criminal Justice Studies* 18 (2005): 99–121.

44. Ted Chiricos, Michael Hogan, and Marc Gertz, "Racial Composition of Neighborhood and Fear of Crime," *Criminology* 35 (1997): 107–129; Wesley Skogan, "Crime and the Racial Fears of White Americans," *The Annals of the American Academy of Political and Social* Science (1995) 539: 59–71; Ralph Taylor and Jeanette Covington, "Community Structural Change and Fear of Crime," *Social Problems* 40 (1993): 374–397.

45. Lincoln Quillian and Devah Pager, "Black Neighbors, Higher Crime? The Role of Racial Stereotypes in Evaluations of Neighborhood Crime," *American Journal of Sociology* 107 (2001): 717–767.

46. Ted Chiricos, Ranee McEntire, and Marc Gertz, "Perceived Racial and Ethnic Composition of Neighborhood and Perceived Risk of Crime," *Social Problems* 48 (2001): 322–340. See also Gertrude Moeller, "Fear of Criminal Victimization: The Effect of Neighborhood Racial Composition," *Sociological Inquiry* 59 (1989): 208–221.

47. Glassner, *Culture of Fear*, xxi.

48. Helen Benedict, *Virgin or Vamp: How the Press Covers Sex Crimes* (New York: Oxford University Press, 1992).

49. Glassner, *Culture of Fear*, xxiii.

50. Jeffrey Kluger, "How Americans Are Living Dangerously," *Time*, November 26, 2006.

51. Mary Douglas and Aaron Wildavsky, *Risk and Culture: An Essay on the Selection of Technical and Environmental Danger* (Berkeley: University of California Press, 1982).

52. Tom Smith, *What Americans Say about Jews* (New York: American Jewish Committee, 1991); Paul Sniderman, *The Scar of Race* (Cambridge, MA: Harvard University Press, 1995).

53. Loïc Wacquant, "Race as Civic Felony," *International Social Science Journal* 181 (2005): 127–142; Émile Durkheim, *The Division of Labor in Society* (New York: Free Press, 1997 [1893]).

54. Richard Wright, *Native Son* (New York: HarperCollins, 1998 [1939]), 400.

55. Lambert, "Worlds Apart," 110.

56. Joe Soss, Laura Langbein, and Alan Metelko, "Why Do White Americans Support the Death Penalty?" *Journal of Politics* 65 (2003): 397–421; Devon Johnson, "Punitive Attitudes on Crime: Economic Insecurity, Race Prejudice, or Both?" *Sociological Focus* 12 (2001): 33–54; Mark Peffley and Jon Hurwitz, "Whites' Stereotypes of Blacks: Sources and Politics Consequences," in *Perception and Prejudice: Race and Politics in the United States*, ed. Jon Hurwitz and Mark Peffley (New Haven, CT: Yale University Press, 1998), 58–99; Barkan and Cohn, "Why Whites Favor Spending More Money to Fight Crime."

57. Christine Hauser and Anahad O'Connor, "Virginia Tech Shooting Leaves 33 Dead," *New York Times*, April 16, 2007.

58. Tracy Jan and Michael Kranish, "Fallout from Bombings Threatens Immigrations Measure," *Boston Globe*, April 22, 2013.

59. Patrick Buchanan, "The Dark Side of Diversity," www.townhall.com, May 1, 2007.

60. Eyal Press, "Do Immigrants Make Us Safer?" *New York Times Magazine*, December 3, 2006.

61. Ibid.

62. Tanya Golash-Boza, *Immigration Nation: Raids, Detentions, and Deportations in Post-9/11 America* (Boulder, CO: Paradigm, 2011).

63. Tanya Golash-Boza, "Has President Obama Deported Two Million People? The Real Deal on the Numbers," *Stop Deportations Now*, December 17, 2013.

64. "A War on Janitors," *New York Times*, October 20, 2008.

65. Susan Bibler Coutin, "Contesting Criminality: Illegal Immigration and the Spatialization of Legality," *Theoretical Criminology* 9 (2005): 5–33; Mae Ngai, *Impossible Subjects: Illegal Aliens and the Making of Modern America* (Princeton, NJ: Princeton University Press, 2003); Michael Welch, *Detained: Immigration Laws and the Expanding INS Jail Complex* (Philadelphia: Temple University Press, 2002).

66. Andrew Karmen, *New York Murder Mystery: The True Story behind the Crime Crash of the 1990s* (New York: New York University Press, 2006); Amie Nielsen, Matthew Lee, and Ramiro Martinez, Jr., "Integrating Race, Place and Motive in Social Disorganization Theory: Lessons from a Comparison of Black and Latino Homicide Types in Two Immigrant Destination Cities," *Criminology* 43 (2005):

837–872; Ramiro Martinez, Jr., *Latino Homicide: Immigration, Violence, and Community* (New York: Routledge, 2002); Matthew Lee, Ramiro Martinez, Jr., and Richard Rosenfeld, "Does Immigration Increase Homicide? Negative Evidence from Three Border Cities," *Sociological Quarterly* 42 (2001): 559–580.

67. Tim Wadsworth, "Is Immigration Responsible for Crime Drop? An Assessment of the Influence of Immigration on Changes in Violence Crime between 1990 and 2000," *Social Science Quarterly* 91: 531–553; Garth Davies and Jeffrey Fagan, "Crime and Enforcement in Immigrant Neighborhoods: Evidence from New York City," *Annals of the American Academy of Political and Social Science* 641: 99–124.

68. Robert Sampson, Jeffrey Morenoff, and Stephen Raudenbush, "Social Anatomy of Racial and Ethnic Disparities in Violence," *American Journal of Public Health* 95 (2005): 224–232; Lesley Williams Reid, Harald Weiss, Robert Adelman, and Charles Jaret, "The Immigration-Crime Relationship: Evidence across U.S. Metropolitan Areas," *Social Science Research* 34 (2005): 757–780.

69. Robert Sampson, "Open Doors Don't Invite Criminals," *New York Times*, March 11, 2006.

70. Robert Sampson, Doug McAdam, Heather MacIndoe, and Simon Weffer, "Civil Society Reconsidered: The Durable Nature and Community Structure of Collective Civic Action," *American Journal of Sociology* 111 (2005): 673–714; Robert Sampson and Steve Raudenbush, "Systematic Social Observation of Public Spaces: A New Look at Disorder in Urban Neighborhoods," *American Journal of Sociology* 105 (1999): 603–651; Sampson, Morenoff, and Raudenbusch, "Social Anatomy of Racial and Ethnic Disparities."

71. Jane Jacobs, *The Death and Life of Great American Cities* (New York: Random House, 1961), 32.; Philip Kasinitz, John H. Mollenkopf, and Mary C. Waters, *Inheriting the City: The Children of Immigrants Come of Age* (New York: Russell Sage Foundation, 2008).

72. Elliott Barkan, "Return of the Nativists? California Public Opinion and Immigration in the 1980s and 1990s," *Social Science History* 27 (2002): 229–283; Yueh-Ting Lee, Victor Ottati, and Imtiaz Hussain, "Attitudes toward 'Illegal' Immigration into the United States: California Proposition 187," *Hispanic Journal of Behavioral Sciences* 23 (2001): 430–443.

73. Irene Jung Fiala, "Anything New? The Racial Profiling of Terrorists," *Criminal Justice Studies* 16 (2003): 53–58.

74. Jeffrey Alexander, "From the Depths of Despair: Performance, Counterperformance, and 'September 11,'" *Sociological Theory* 22 (2004): 88–105.

75. Diane Lauderdale, "Birth Outcomes for Arabic-Named Women in California before and after September 11," *Demography* 43 (2006): 185–201; Costas Panagopoulos, "Arab and Muslim Americans and Islam in the Aftermath of 9/11," *Public Opinion Quarterly* 70 (2006): 608–624; American-Arab Anti-Discrimination Committee Research Institute, *Report on Hate Crimes and Discrimination against Arab Americans: September 11, 2001 to October 11, 2002* (Boston: American-Arab Anti-Discrimination Committee Research Institute, 2003).

76. Panagopoulos, "Arab and Muslim Americans and Islam."

77. Arab American Institute, *The American Divide: How We View Arabs and Muslims* (Washington, DC: Arab American Institute, 2012).

78. Nadine Naber, "Ambiguous Insiders: An Investigation of Arab American Invisibility," *Ethnic and Racial Studies* 23 (2000): 37–61.

79. Jack Shaheen, *Real Bad Arabs: How Hollywood Vilifies a People* (Northampton, MA: Olive Branch Press, 2001), 1.

80. Debra Merskin, "The Construction of Arabs as Enemies: Post–September 11 Discourse of George W. Bush," *Mass Communication and Society* 7 (2004): 157–175; Leti Volpp, "The Citizen and the Terrorist," in *September 11 in History: A Watershed Moment?*, ed. Mary Dudziak (Durham, NC: Duke University Press, 2003), 147–162.

81. Alexander, "From the Depths of Despair," 94.

82. Detroit Free Press, *100 Questions and Answers about Arab Americans: A Journalist's Guide* (Detroit: Free Press, 2007); Naber, "Ambiguous Insiders."

83. Leti Volpp, "Disappearing Acts: On Gendered Violence, Pathological Cultures, and Civil Society," *PMLA* 121 (2006): 1632–1638.

84. Strobe Talbot and Nayan Chanda, *The Age of Terror: America and the World After September 11* (New York: Basic Books, 2002); Anne McClintock, *Imperial Leather: Race, Gender, and Sexuality in the Colonial Conquest* (New York: Routledge, 1995), 12; Said, *Orientalism*, xxi.

85. Quoted in Lanita Jacobs-Huey, "'The Arab Is the New Nigger': African American Comics Confront the Irony and Tragedy of September 11," *Transforming Anthropology* 12 (2006): 60–64.

86. Sudhir Venkatesh, *Off the Books: The Underground Economy of the Urban Poor* (Cambridge, MA: Harvard University Press, 2006), 12.

87. United Nations Office on Drugs and Crime, *World Drug Report 2007* (New York: United Nations, 2007); "Class A Capitalists," *Guardian* (London), April 21, 2002.

88. Substance Abuse and Mental Health Services Administration, *National Survey on Drug Use and Health* (Washington, DC: U.S. Department of Health and Human Services, 2012).

89. Andrew Papachristos and David Kirk, "Neighborhood Effects on Street Gang Behavior," in *Studying Youth Gangs*, ed. James F. Short, Jr., and Lorine A. Hughes (Lanham, MD: AltaMira Press, 2006), 63–84; Robert Bursik and Harold Grasmick, *Neighborhoods and Crime: The Dimensions of Effective Community Control* (New York: Lexington Books, 1993).

90. Theo Emery, "In Nashville, a Street Gang Emerges in a Kurdish Enclave," *New York Times*, July 15, 2007; Brenda Coughlin and Sudhir Venkatesh, "The Urban Street Gang after 1970," *Annual Review of Sociology* 29 (2003): 41–64; Eric Schneider, *Vampires, Dragons, and Egyptian Kings: Youth Gangs in Postwar New York* (Princeton, NJ: Princeton University Press, 1999); Irving Spergel, *The Youth Gang Problem: A Community Approach* (New York: Oxford University Press, 1995).

91. C. Ronald Huff, *Gangs in America*, 2nd ed. (Thousand Oaks, CA: Sage, 1996); Martín Sánchez Jankowski, *Islands in the Street: Gangs and American Urban Society* (Berkeley: University of California Press, 1991); Felix Padilla, *The Gang as an American Enterprise* (New Brunswick: Rutgers University Press, 1992); Coughlin and Venkatesh, "Urban Street Gang after 1970."

92. Steven Levitt and Sudhir Venkatesh, "An Economic Analysis of a Drug-Selling Gang's Finances," *Quarterly Journal of Economics* 115 (2000): 755–789.

93. Avelardo Valdez, "Drug Markets in Minority Communities: Consequences for Mexican American Youth Gangs," in *The Many Colors of Crime: Inequalities of Race, Ethnicity, and Crime in America*, ed. Ruth Peterson, Lauren Krivo, and John Hagan (New York: New York University Press, 2006), 221–236.

94. Philippe Bourgois, *In Search of Respect: Selling Crack in El Barrio* (New York: Cambridge University Press, 1995), 4.; Katherine Newman, *No Shame in My Game: The Working Poor in the Inner City* (New York: Vintage and Russell Sage Foundation, 1999).

95. Venkatesh, *Off the Books*, 4, 7.

96. Edwin Sutherland, *White Collar Crime: The Uncut Version* (New Haven, CT: Yale University Press, 1983 [1949]), 7.

97. Kent Kerley and Heith Copes, "The Effects of Criminal Justice Contact on Employment Stability for White-Collar and Street-Level Offenders," *International Journal of Offender Therapy and Comparative Criminology* 48 (2004): 65–84.

98. U.S. Department of Justice, *National Criminal Justice Reference Services* (Washington, DC: U.S. Department of Justice, 2007); Federal Bureau of Investigation, *Financial Crimes Report to the Public* (Washington, DC: U.S. Department of Justice, 2005).

99. David Friedrichs, *Trusted Criminals: White Collar Crime in Contemporary Society* (New York: Wadsworth, 2009), 50.

100. Randall Gordon, Thomas Bindrim, Michael McNicholas, and Teresa Walden, "Perceptions of Blue-Collar and White-Collar Crime: The Effect of Defendant Race on Simulated Juror Decisions," *Journal of Social Psychology* 128 (1987): 191–197.

101. Jeffrey Reiman, *The Rich Get Richer and the Poor Get Prison: Ideology, Class, and Criminal Justice*, 6th ed. (Boston: Allyn and Bacon, 2001).

102. David Harvey, *A Brief History of Neoliberalism* (New York: Oxford University Press, 2005).

103. Michele Black et al., *The National Intimate Partner and Sexual Violence Survey: 2010 Summary Report* (Atlanta: Centers for Disease Control and Prevention, 2010).

104. Ibid.

105. National Coalition against Domestic Violence, *Sexual Assault* (Washington, DC: NCADV Public Policy Office, 2007); U.S. Department of Justice, *National Crime Victimization Survey* (Washington, DC: Bureau of Justice Statistics, 2006); Barbara Nagel, Hisaka Matsuo, Kevin McIntyre, and Nancy Morrison, "Attitudes toward Victims of Rape: Effects of Gender, Race, Religion, and Social Class," *Journal of Interpersonal Violence* 20 (2005): 725–737.

106. Callie Rennison and Mike Planty, "Nonlethal Intimate Partner Violence: Examining Race, Gender, and Income Patterns," *Violence and Victims* 18 (2003): 433–443.

107. Diane Purvin, "At the Crossroads and in the Crosshairs: Social Welfare Policy and Low-Income Women's Vulnerability to Domestic Violence," *Social Problems* 54 (2007): 188–210; National Coalition against Domestic Violence, *Immigrant Victims of Domestic Violence* (Washington, DC: NCADV Public Policy Office, 2007); U.S. Department of Justice, Bureau of Justice Statistics, *Intimate Partner Violence in the U.S.* (Washington, DC: Department of Justice, 2007); Carolyn West, "Black Women and Intimate Partner Violence: New Directions for Research," *Journal of Interpersonal Violence* 19 (2004): 1487–1493; Carolyn West, *Violence in the Lives of Black Women Battered, Black, and Blue* (New York: Haworth, 2002); Richard Tolman and Jody Raphael, "A Review of Research on Welfare and Domestic Violence," *Journal of Social Issues* 56 (2000): 655–682; Sonia Frias and Ronald Angel, "The Risk of Partner Violence Among Low-Income Hispanic Subgroups," *Journal of Marriage and Family* 67 (2005): 552–64.

108. Margaret Abraham, *Speaking the Unspeakable: Marital Violence among South Asian Immigrants in the United States* (New Brunswick, NJ: Rutgers University Press, 2000).

109. Kimberle Crenshaw, "Mapping the Margins: Intersectionality, Identity Politics, and Violence against Women of Color," *Stanford Law Review* 43 (1991): 1241–1299; National Coalition against Domestic Violence, *Immigrant Victims of Domestic Violence*; Abraham, *Speaking the Unspeakable*.

110. Crenshaw, "Mapping the Margins," 1249, 1264.

111. Gary Lafree, *Rape and Criminal Justice: The Social Construction of Assault* (Boulder, CO: Wadsworth, 1980); Crenshaw, "Mapping the Margins," 1269.

112. Jonathan Markovitz, "Anatomy of a Spectacle: Race, Gender, and Memory in the Kobe Bryant Rape Case," *Sociology of Sport Journal* 23 (2006): 396–418; Crenshaw, "Mapping the Margins," 1268.

113. Janet Lauritsen, *How Families and Communities Influence Youth Victimization* (Washington, DC: U.S. Department of Justice, Office of Juvenile Justice and Delinquency Prevention, 2003).

114. Cited in Crenshaw, "Mapping the Margins," 1255.

115. Nellie McKay, "Remembering Anita Hill and Clarence Thomas: What Really Happened When One Black Woman Spoke Out," in *Race-ing Justice, En-gendering Power*, ed. Toni Morrison (New York: Pantheon, 1992, 269–289), 277–278.

116. Katheryn Russell-Brown, *Protecting Our Own: Race, Crime, and African Americans* (Oxford: Rowman and Littlefield, 2006).

117. Crenshaw, "Mapping the Margins," 1273.

118. Cornel West, *Race Matters*, 2nd ed. (New York: Vintage, 2001), 37.

119. Joel Jacobsen, *For the Sake of Argument: A Life in the Law* (New York: Kaplan, 2009), 213.

120. Max Fisher, "Chart: The U.S. Has Far More Gun-Related Killings than Any Other Developed Country," *Washington Post*, December 14, 2012.

121. Alexia Cooper and Erica Smith, *Homicide Trends in the United States, 1980–2008: Annual Rates for 2009 and 2010* (Washington, DC: U.S. Department of Justice, Bureau of Justice Statistics, 2010).

122. Centers for Disease Control and Prevention, *Youth Violence: National Statistics* (Atlanta: Centers for Disease Control and Prevention, 2013).

123. Robert Sampson and Lydia Bean, "Cultural Mechanisms and Killing Fields: A Revised Theory of Community-Level Racial Inequality," in *The Many Colors of Crime: Inequalities of Race, Ethnicity, and Crime in America*, ed. Ruth Peterson, Lauren Krivo, and John Hagan (New York: New York

University Press, 2006), 8–36; Alfred Blumstein and Joel Wallman, "The Crime Drop and Beyond," *Annual Review of Law and Social Science* 2 (2006): 125–46.

124. Glassner, *Culture of Fear*, 111.

125. Karen Sternheimer, "Do Video Games Kill?" *Contexts* 6 (2007): 13–17; David Courtwright, *Violent Land: Single Men and Social Disorder from the Frontier to the Inner City* (Cambridge, MA: Harvard University Press, 1996); Patrick Cooke, "TV Causes Violence?" *New York Times*, August 14, 1993.

126. Glassner, *Culture of Fear*, xix.

127. Josh Sugarman and Michael Rand, *More Gun Dealers than Gas Stations: A Study of Federally Licensed Firearms Dealers in America* (Washington, DC: Violence Policy Center, 1992); Blumstein and Wallman, "Crime Drop and Beyond," 132–133.

128. Franklin Zimring and Gordon Hawkins, *Crime Is Not the Problem: Lethal Violence in America* (New York: Oxford University Press, 1997); Beckett and Sasson, *Politics of Injustice*, 28–29.

129. Robert Sampson and William Julius Wilson, "Toward a Theory of Race, Crime, and Urban Inequality," in *Crime and Inequality*, ed. John Hagan and Ruth Peterson (Stanford, CA: Stanford University Press, 1995), 37–54.

130. María Vélez, "Toward an Understanding of the Lower Rates of Homicide in Latino versus Black Neighborhoods," in *The Many Colors of Crime: Inequalities of Race, Ethnicity, and Crime in America*, ed. Ruth Peterson, Lauren Krivo, and John Hagan (New York: New York University Press, 2006), 91–107.

131. Ruth Person and Lauren Krivo, "Macrostructural Analyses of Race, Ethnicity, and Violent Crime: Recent Lessons and New Directions for Research," *Annual Review of Sociology* 31 (2005): 331–356; Ruth Person and Lauren Krivo, "Racial Segregation and Black Urban Homicide," *Social Forces* 71 (1993): 1001–1026.

132. Scott South and Steven Messner, "Crime and Demography: Multiple Linkages, Reciprocal Relations," *Annual Review of Sociology* 26 (2000): 83–106; Sampson and Bean, "Cultural Mechanisms and Killing Fields."

133. Sampson and Bean, "Cultural Mechanisms and Killing Fields," 12–13.

134. Bruce Rankin and James Quane, "Neighborhood Poverty and the Social Isolation of Inner-City African American Families," *Social Forces* 79 (2000): 139–164; Frank Furstenberg, "How Families Manage Risk and Opportunity in Dangerous Neighborhoods," in *Sociology and the Public Agenda*, ed. William Julius Wilson (Thousand Oaks, CA: Sage, 1993), 231–254; Carol Stack, *All Our Kin: Strategies for Survival in a Black Community* (New York: Basic Books, 1974).

135. Elijah Anderson, *Code of the Street: Decency, Violence, and the Moral Life of the Inner City* (New York: Norton, 1999).

136. Eric Stewart, Christopher Schreck, and Ronald Simons, "'I Ain't Gonna Let No One Disrespect Me': Does the Code of the Street Reduce or Increase Violent Victimization among African American Adolescents?," *Journal of Research in Crime and Delinquency* 43 (2006): 427–458.

137. Orlando Patterson, "A Poverty of the Mind," *New York Times*, March 26, 2006.

138. Robert Sampson and John Laub, "Urban Poverty and the Family Context of Delinquency," *Child Delinquency* 65 (1994): 538–545.

139. Howard Snyder, *Arrest in the United States, 1990–2010* (Washington, DC: U.S. Department of Justice, 2012).

140. Oliver, "Repression and Crime Control."

141. Ian Urbina, "Blacks are Singled Out for Marijuana Arrests, Federal Data Suggests," *New York Times*, June 3, 2013.

142. Stewart D'Alessio and Lisa Stolzenberg, "Race and the Probability of Arrest," *Social Forces* 81 (2003): 1381–1397.

143. Brian Stults and Eric Baumer, "Racial Context and Police Force Size: Evaluating the Empirical Validity of the Minority Threat Hypothesis," *American Journal of Sociology* 113 (2007): 507–546; Stephanie Kent and David Jacobs, "Minority Threat and Police Strength from 1980 to 2000: A Fixed-Effects Analysis of Nonlinear and Interactive Effects in Large U.S. Cities," *Criminology* 43 (2005): 731–760.

144. Alice Goffman, *On the Run: Fugitive Life in an American City* (Chicago: University of Chicago Press, 2014), 4.

145. New York Civil Liberties Union, *Stop-and-Frisk 2011* (New York City: New York Civil Liberties Union, 2012).

146. David Harris, "'Driving While Black' and All Other Traffic Offenses: The Supreme Court and Pretextual Traffic Stops," *Journal of Criminal Law and Criminology* 87 (1999): 544–582; Timothy Flanagan and Michael Vaughn, "Public Opinion about Police Abuse and Force," in *Police Violence: Understanding and Controlling Police Abuse of Force*, ed. William Geller and Hans Toch (New Haven, CT: Yale University Press, 1996), 113–128.

147. Patrick Langan, Lawrence Greenfield, Steven Smith, Matthew Durose, and David Levine, *Contacts between Police and the Public: Findings from the 1999 National Survey* (Washington, DC: U.S. Department of Justice, 2001); State of New Jersey, Office of the Attorney General, *Selected Highlights of the Interim Report of the State Police Review Team Regarding Allegations of Racial Profiling* (Trenton, NJ: Office of the Attorney General, 1999).

148. Quoted in Russell-Brown, *Protecting Our Own*, 67.

149. Lawrence Bobo, and Victor Thompson, "Unfair by Design: The War on Drugs, Race, and the Legitimacy of the Criminal Justice System," *Social Research* 2 (2006): 445–472.

150. Langan et al., *Contacts between Police and the Public*, 7.

151. Russ Buettner and Ray Rivera, "For Owners of Strip Club in Police Shooting, a Decade of Raids and Suits," *New York Times*, December 3, 2006; CNN, "Mayor: Police Barrage at Groom 'Unacceptable,'" November 27, 2006.

152. "Times Topics: Trayvon Martin Case (George Zimmerman)," *New York Times*, 2014. http://topics.nytimes.com/top/reference/timestopics/people/m/trayvon_martin/index.html

153. Lawrence Bobo, "Why the Zimmerman Jury Failed Us," *The Root*, July 14, 2013.

154. Quoted in Reiman, *The Rich Get Richer and the Poor Get Prison*, 109.

155. Reiman, *The Rich Get Richer and the Poor Get Prison*, 127. See also Wendy Leo Moore, *Reproducing Racism: White Space, Elite Law Schools, and Racial Inequality* (Oxford: Rowman and Littlefield, 2007).

156. Richard Lacayo, "You Don't Always Get Perry Mason," *Time*, June 1, 1992.

157. Clarence Page, "Injustice Is Bigger than Jena 6," *Chicago Tribune*, September 24, 2007; Darrell Steffensmier, Jeffrey Ulmer, and John Kramer, "The Interaction of Race, Gender, and Age in Criminal Sentencing: The Punishment Cost of Being Young, Black, and Male," *Criminology* 36 (1998): 763–798; James Nelson, *Disparities in Processing Felony Arrests in New York State, 1990–1992* (Albany: New York State Division of Criminal Justice Services, 1995); Michael Brown, Martin Carnoy, Elliott Currie, Troy Duster, David Oppenheimer, Marjorie Shultz, and David Wellman, *White-Washing Race: The Myth of a Color Blind Society* (Berkeley: University of California Press, 2003), 142–143.

158. Donald F. Tibbs and Tryon P. Woods, "The Jena 6 and Black Punishment: Law and Raw Life in the Domain of Non-Existence," *Seattle Journal for Social Justice* 7 (2008): 235-83.

159. Richard Jones, "In Louisiana, a Tree, a Fight and a Question of Justice," *New York Times*, September 19, 2007; Richard Jones, "Louisiana Protest Echoes the Civil Rights Era," *New York Times*, September 21, 2007; Page, "Injustice Is Bigger Than Jena 6."

160. Mary Frances Berry, *Black Resistance/White Law: A History of Constitutional Racism in America* (New York: Penguin, 1995); Tibbs and Woods, "Jena 6 and Black Punishment."

161. Richard Dieter, *The Death Penalty in Black and White: Who Lives, Who Dies, Who Decides* (Washington, DC: Death Penalty Information Center, 1998); David Baldus, Charles Pulaski, and George Woodworth, "Comparative Review of Death Sentences," *Journal of Criminal Law and Criminology* 4 (1983): 661–753.

162. Innocence Project, *Fact Sheet* (New York: Innocence Project, 2008); Death Penalty Information Center, *Innocence and the Death Penalty* (Washington, DC: Death Penalty Information Center, 2008).

163. Susan Howell, Huey Perry, and Matthew Vile, "Black Cities/White Cities: Evaluating the Police," *Political Behavior* 26 (2004): 45–68; U.S. Department of Justice, *Sourcebook of Criminal Justice Statistics 1999* (Washington, DC: Bureau of Justice Statistics, 2000).

164. Jean Casella and James Ridgeway, "How Many Prisoners Are in Solitary Confinement in the United States?," *Solitary Watch*, February 1, 2012, http://solitarywatch.com/2012/02/01/how-many -prisoners-are-in-solitary-confinement-in-the-united-states/.

165. Jeffrey Kluger, "The Paradox of Supermax," *Time*, February 5, 2007.

166. Devah Pager, "The Mark of a Criminal Record," *American Journal of Sociology* 108 (2003): 937–975.

167. Bruce Western and Becky Pettit, "Incarceration and Racial Inequality in Men's Employment," *Industrial and Labor Relations Review* 54 (2000): 3–16; Harry Holzer, *What Employers Want: Job Prospects for Less Educated Workers* (New York: Russell Sage Foundation, 1996); Wacquant, "From Slavery to Mass Incarceration"; Pager, "Mark of a Criminal Record"; Western, *Punishment and Inequality in America*, 111–115.

168. Western, *Punishment and Inequality in America*, 108–120.

169. Katherine Edin, Timothy Nelson, Rechelle Paranal, "Fatherhood and Incarceration as Potential Turning Points in the Criminal Careers of Unskilled Men," in *Imprisoning America: The Social Effects of Mass Incarceration*, ed. Mary Patillo, David Weiman, and Bruce Western (New York: Russell Sage Foundation, 2004); Sara McLanahan and Gary Sandefur, *Growing Up with a Single Parent: What Hurts, What Helps* (Cambridge, MA: Harvard University Press, 1994); Western, *Punishment and Inequality in America*, chap. 6.

170. Lauren Glaze, *Correctional Populations in the United States, 2010* (Washington, DC: U.S. Department of Justice, Bureau of Justice Statistics, 2010).

171. National Association of State Budget Officers, *State Expenditure Report* (Washington, DC: National Association of State Budget Officers, 2013).

172. Western, *Punishment and Inequality in America*, 172.

173. U.S. Dept. of Justice, Bureau of Justice Statistics, *Census of State Adult Correctional Facilities, 1979*. Conducted by U.S. Dept. of Commerce, Bureau of the Census. 2nd ICPSR ed. (Ann Arbor, MI: Inter-university Consortium for Political and Social Research, 1997); Western, *Punishment and Inequality in America*, 174–185.

174. Kathleen Kingsbury, "The Next Crime Wave," *Time*, December 11, 2006, 74.

175. Western, *Punishment and Inequality in America*, 187.

176. Anne Morrison Piehl and John DiIulio, "Does Prison Pay? Revisited," *Brookings Review* 13 (1995): 21–25; Western, *Punishment and Inequality in America*, 177.

177. David Anderson, "The Deterrence Hypothesis and Picking Pockets at the Pickpocket's Hanging," *American Law and Economics Review* 4 (2002): 295–313; Bureau of Justice Statistics, *Drug and Crime Facts, 1994* (Washington, DC: Department of Justice, 1995); Western, *Punishment and Inequality in America*, chap. 7.

178. Western, *Punishment and Inequality in America*, 185.

179. Gaston Bachelard, *The Psychoanalysis of Fire* (Boston: Beacon Press, 1964), 1.

180. Loïc Wacquant, "The Advent of the Penal State Is Not Destiny," *Social Justice* 28 (2001): 81–87.

181. Lisa Spanierman, V. Paul Poteat, Amanda Beer, and Patrick Ian Armstrong, "Psychological Costs of Racism to Whites: Exploring Patterns through Cluster Analysis," *Journal of Counseling Psychology* 53 (2006): 434–441.

Chapter 7: Education

1. Alexis de Tocqueville, *Democracy in America* (New York: HarperCollins, 2000 [1835/1840]), 12, emphasis ours; Sara Rimer and Alan Finder, "Harvard Steps Up Financial Aid," *New York Times*, December 10, 2007.

2. Mills, *The Sociological Imagination*, 166.

3. K. Tsiania Lomawaima, "American Indian Education: *By* Indians versus *For* Indians," in *A Companion to American Indian History*, ed. Philip Deloria and Neal Salisbury (Malden, MA: Blackwell, 2002), 422–440.

4. Zitkala-Sa, *The School Days of an Indian Girl* (New York: Atlantic Monthly, 1900), 187.

5. Interview with Virgil "Smoker" Marchand, conducted by Jennifer Mason-Ferguson, February 28, 1997, courtesy of Eastern Washington University, Art Department.

6. Brenda Child, *Boarding School Seasons: American Indian Families, 1900–1940* (Lincoln: University of Nebraska Press, 1996); K. Tsiania Lomawaima, *They Called It Prairie Light: The Story of Chilocco Indian School* (Lincoln: University of Nebraska Press, 1994).

7. Lewis Meriam, *The Problem of Indian Administration* (Baltimore, MD: Johns Hopkins University Press for the Institute for Government Research, 1928), 11.

8. Bill Curry, "Hunt Begins for Long-Missing Students," *Globe and Mail*, October 27, 2008.

9. Lomawaima, "American Indian Education," 422–423.

10. Ibid.

11. Fairclough, *Better Day Coming*, 48.

12. Gunnar Myrdal, *An American Dilemma: Volume 2, The Negro Social Structure* (New York: McGraw-Hill Publishers 1964 [1944]), 894.

13. Fairclough, *Better Day Coming*, 48.

14. Ibid., 41–42.

15. James Anderson, *The Education of Blacks in the South, 1986–1935* (Chapel Hill: University of North Carolina Press, 1988); Basil Matthews, *Booker T. Washington: Educator and Inter-Racial Interpreter* (London: SCM Press, 1949); Fairclough, *Better Day Coming*, ch. 3.

16. Lawrence Friedman, "Life 'In the Lion's Mouth': Another Look at Booker T. Washington," *Journal of Negro History* 59 (1974): 337–351; Louis Harlen, *Separate and Unequal: Public School Campaigns and Racism in the Southern Seaboard States, 1901–1915* (New York: Atheneum, 1968); Fairclough, *Better Day Coming*, 46.

17. Fairclough, *Better Day Coming*, 54.

18. W. E. B. Du Bois, *Souls of Black Folk* (New York: Dover, 1903 [1994]), 67.

19. Ibid., 31, 34–35.

20. Ibid., 106.

21. Cited in Myrdal, *American Dilemma*, 884. Also see Hortense Powdermaker, *After Freedom: A Cultural Study in the Deep South* (Madison: University of Wisconsin Press, 1993 [1939]).

22. Cited in Myrdal, *American Dilemma*, 881.

23. James Patterson, *Brown v. Board of Education: A Civil Rights Milestone and Its Troubled Legacy* (New York: Oxford University Press, 2001).

24. Frederick Aguirre, "*Mendez v. Westminster School District*: How It Affected *Brown v. Board of Education*," *Journal of Hispanic Higher Education* 4 (2005): 321–332; Craig Allan Kaplowitz, *LULAC, Mexican Americans, and National Policy* (College Station: Texas A&M University Press, 2005).

25. Cited in Fairclough, *Better Day Coming*, 220.

26. Fairclough, *Better Day Coming*, 222–223.

27. Martin Luther King, Jr., *Why We Can't Wait* (New York: Signet, 2000), 4.

28. Elizabeth Jacoway, *Turn Away Thy Son: Little Rock, the Crisis That Shook the Nation* (New York: Free Press, 2007); Tony Allan Freyer, *Little Rock on Trial: Cooper v. Aaron and School Desegregation* (Lawrence: University Press of Kansas, 2007).

29. Melba Patillo Beals, *Warriors Don't Cry: A Searing Memoir of the Battle to Integrate Little Rock's Central High* (New York: Simon and Schuster, 1995).

30. J. Harvie Wilkinson, III, *From Brown to Bakke: The Supreme Court and School Integration, 1954–1978* (New York: Oxford University Press, 1981), 81.

31. Fairclough, *Better Day Coming*, 324.

32. Thomas Adams Upchurch, *Race Relations in the United States, 1960–1980* (Westport, CT: Greenwood Publishing Group, 2007); Wilkinson, *From Brown to Bakke*.

33. J. Anthony Lukas, *Common Ground: A Turbulent Decade in the Lives of Three American Families* (New York: Vintage Books, 1986).

34. Du Bois, *Black Reconstruction in America*, 714, 725, 722.

35. Fairclough, *Better Day Coming*, 175.

36. Takaki, *A Different Mirror*.

37. Joseph Agassi, *Science and History: A Reassessment of the Historiography of Science* (New York: Springer, 2008); Richard Hughes, "A Hint of Whiteness: History Textbooks and Social Cons truction of Race in the Wake of the Sixties," *Social Studies* 98 (2007): 210—208; Tony Sanchez, "The Depiction of Native Americans in Recent (1991—2004) Secondary American History Textbooks: How Far Have We Come?" *Equity and Excellence in Education* 40 (2007): 311—320; Manning Marable, *Living Black History: How Reimagining the African-American Past Can Remake America's Racial Future* (New York: Basic Civitas Books, 2006).

38. Du Bois, *Black Reconstruction*, 722.

39. Rebecca Aanerud, "Fictions of Whiteness: Speaking the Names of Whiteness in U.S. Literature," in *Displacing Whiteness: Essays in Social and Cultural Criticism*, ed. Ruth Frankenberg (Durham, NC: Duke University Press, 1999), 35—59; Frances Maher and Mary Kay Thompson Tetreault, "Learning in the Dark: How Assumptions of Whiteness Shape Classroom Knowledge," *Harvard Educational Review* 67 (1997): 321—349.

40. Mills, *Sociological Imagination*, 166.

41. Morrison, *Playing in the Dark*, 52, 5.

42. Deloria, Jr., *Custer Died for Your Sins*, 92—93.

43. Mohanty, *Feminism without Borders*, 193.

44. Ibid., 200.

45. Vincent Tinto, *Leaving College: Rethinking the Causes and Cures of Student Attrition*, 2nd ed. (Chicago: University of Chicago Press, 1993).

46. Joe R. Feagin, Hernan Vera, and Nikitah Imani, *The Agony of Education: Black Students at White Colleges and Universities* (New York: Routledge, 1996).

47. Ashby Plant and Patricia Devine, "The Antecedents and Implications of Interracial Anxiety," *Personality and Social Psychology Bulletin* 29 (2003): 790—801; Yolanda Suarez- Balcazat et al., "Experiences of Differential Treatment among College Students of Color," *Journal of Higher Education* 74 (2003): 428—444.

48. Susan Rankin and Robert Dean Reason, "Differing Perceptions: How Students of Color and White Students Perceive Campus Climate for Underrepresented Groups," *Journal of College Student Development* 46 (2005): 43—61.

49. David Berg, "Bringing One's Self to Work: A Jew Reflects," *Journal of Applied Behavioral Science* 38 (2002): 397—415.

50. Cf. Mohanty, *Feminism without Borders*, 203.

51. bell hooks, "Representing Whiteness in the Black Imagination," in *Displacing Whiteness: Essays in Social and Cultural Criticism*, ed. Ruth Frankenberg (Durham, NC: Duke University Press, 1999, 165—179), 167.

52. Monica Biernat and Melvin Manis, "Shifting Standards and Stereotype-Based Judgments," *Journal of Personality and Social Psychology* 66 (1991): 5—20.

53. Rhea Steinpreis, Katie Anders, and Dawn Ritzke, "The Impact of Gender on the Review of the Curricula Vitae of Job Applicants and Tenure Candidates: A National Empirical Study," *Sex Roles* 41(1999): 509—528.

54. Jennifer Mueller, Danielle Dirks, and Leslie Houts Picca, "Unmasking Racism: Halloween Costuming and Engagement of the Racial Order," *Qualitative Sociology* 30 (2007): 315—335; Nahal Toosi, "UW Minority Students Alone in a Sea of White," *Milwaukee Journal Sentinel*, May 24, 2007.

55. CNN, "Racist Party at Campus," May 15, 2007.

56. Fernanda Santos, "Arizona Fraternity Party Stirs Concerns of Racism," *New York Times*, January 22, 2014.

57. U.S. Department of Justice, *Hate Crimes on Campus: The Problem and Efforts to Confront It* (Washington, DC: Office of Justice Programs, 2001).

58. "San Jose State Students Charged with Hate Crime against Black Roommate," *NBC Bay Area*, November 21, 2013.

59. Marie Stetser and Robert Stillwell, *Public High School Four-Year On-Time Graduation Rates and Event Dropout Rates: School Years 2010–2011 and 2011–12* (Washington, DC: National Center for Education Statistics, 2013).

60. Grace Kena et al., National Center for Education Statistics, *The Condition of Education* (Washington, D.C.: U.S. Department of Education, 2014), 3.

61. Ibid., 4. See also Institute of Education Sciences, *Digest of Education Statistics* (Washington, DC: National Center for Education Statistics, 2013).

62. Institute of Education Sciences, "Total Fall Enrollment in Degree-Granting Postsecondary Institutions, by Level of Enrollment, Sex, Attendance Status, and Race/ethnicity of Students: Selected Years, 1976 through 2012," *Digest of Education Statistics* (Washington, DC: National Center for Education Statistics, 2014).

63. Dana Wood, Rachel Kaplan, and Vonnie McLoyd, "Gender Differences in the Educational Expectations of Urban, Low-Income African American Youth: The Role of Parents and the School," *Journal of Youth and Adolescence* 36 (2007): 417–427; Stephanie Bohon, Monica Kirkpatrick Johnson, and Bridget Gorman, "College Aspirations and Expectations among Latino Adolescents in the United States," *Social Problems* 53 (2006): 207–225; Robert Crosnoe, "The Diverse Experiences of Hispanic Students in the American Educational System," *Sociological Forum* 20 (2005): 561–588; Linda Datcher Loury, "Siblings and Gender Differences in African-American College Attendance," *Economics of Education Review* 23 (2004): 213–229; National Center for Education Statistics, *Status and Trends in the Education of Hispanics* (Washington, DC: United States Department of Education, 2003); George Vernez and Lee Mizell, *Goal: To Double the Rate of Hispanics Earning a Bachelor's Degree* (Washington, DC: RAND Corporation, Center for Research on Immigration Policy, 2002).

64. Thom File, *Computer and Internet Use in the United States* (Washington, DC: U.S. Census Bureau, 2013).

65. Robert Bradley and Robert Corwyn, "Socioeconomic Status and Child Development," *Annual Review of Psychology* 53 (2002): 341–369; Dalton Conley, *Being Black, Living in the Red* (Berkeley: University of California Press, 1999); Jeanne Brooks-Gunn and Greg Duncan, "The Effects of Poverty on Children," *Future of Children* 7 (1997): 57–71; Grace Kao and Jennifer Thompson, "Racial and Ethnic Stratification in Educational Achievement and Attainment," *Annual Review of Sociology* 29 (2003): 417–442.

66. Michele Lamont and Annette Lareau, "Cultural Capital: Allusions, Gaps, and Glissandos in Recent Theoretical Developments," *Sociological Theory* 6 (1988): 153–168; Pierre Bourdieu, *Distinction: A Social Critique of the Judgment of Taste* (Cambridge, MA: Harvard University Press, 1984 [1979]).

67. Matthijs Kalmijn and Gerbert Kraaykamp, "Race, Cultural Capital, and Schooling: An Analysis of Trends in the United States," *Sociology of Education* 69 (1996): 22–34; Paul DiMaggio, "Cultural Capital and School Success: The Impact of Status Culture Participation on the Grades of U.S. High School Students," *American Sociological Review* 47 (1982): 189–201.

68. Pierre Bourdieu and Jean-Claude Passeron, *The Inheritors: French Students and Their Relation to Culture* (Chicago: University of Chicago Press, 1979 [1964]), 17.

69. Bourdieu, *Distinction*, 6.

70. Betty Hart and Todd Risley, *Meaningful Differences in the Everyday Experience of Young American Children* (Baltimore, MD: Brookes, 1995). See also Jeanne Brooks-Gunn and Lisa Markman, "The Contribution of Parenting to Ethnic and Racial Gaps in School Readiness," *Future of Children* 15 (2005): 139–168.

71. Lareau, *Unequal Childhoods*.

72. Paul Tough, "What It Takes to Make a Student," *New York Times Magazine*, November 26, 2006, 49.

73. Eric Margolis, Michael Soldatenko, Sandra Acker, and Marina Gair, "Peekaboo: Hiding and Outing the Curriculum," in *The Hidden Curriculum in Higher Education*, ed. Eric Margolis (New York: Routledge, 2001, 1–19), 4–5. See also Philip Jackson, *Life in Classrooms* (New York: Holt, Rinehart, and Winston, 1968).

74. Buffy Smith, *Demystifying the Higher Education System: Rethinking Academic Cultural Capital, Social Capital, and the Academic Mentoring Process* (unpublished PhD diss., University of Wisconsin, Madison, 2004).

75. Vincent Roscigno and James Ainsworth-Darnell, "Race, Cultural Capital, and Educational Resources: Persistent Inequalities and Achievement Returns," *Sociology of Education* 72 (1999): 158–179; Kalmijn and Kraaykamp, "Race, Cultural Capital, and Schooling"; DiMaggio, "Cultural Capital and School Success."

76. Paul DiMaggio and Francie Ostrower, "Participation in the Arts by Black and White Americans," *Social Forces* 68 (1990): 753–778.

77. Pierre Bourdieu and Loïc Wacquant, *An Invitation to Reflexive Sociology* (Chicago: University of Chicago Press, 1992), 119.

78. Angel Steidel and Josefina Contreras, "A New Familism Scale for Use with Latino Populations," *Hispanic Journal of Behavioral Sciences* 25 (2003): 312–330; Angela Valenzuela and Sanford Dornbusch, "Familism and Social Capital in the Academic Achievement of Mexican Origin and Anglo Adolescents," *Social Science Quarterly* 75 (1994): 18–36.

79. Andrew Fuligni, Vivian Tseng, and May Lam, "Attitudes toward Family Obligations among American Adolescents with Asian, Latin American, and European Backgrounds," *Child Development* 70 (1999): 1030–1044; Min Zhou and Carl Bankston, *Growing Up American: How Vietnamese Children Adapt to Life in the United States* (New York: Russell Sage Foundation, 1998); Carola Suarez-Orozco and Marcelo Suarez-Orozco, *Transformations: Immigration, Family Life, and Achievement Motivation among Latino Adolescents* (Stanford, CA: Stanford University Press, 1995).

80. Shana Pribesh and Douglas Downey, "Why Are Residential and School Moves Associated with Poor School Performance?" *Demography* 36 (1999): 521–534; Zhenchao Quian and Sampson Lee Blair, "Racial/Ethnic Differences in Educational Aspirations of High School Seniors," *Sociological Perspectives* 42 (1999): 605–625; Renee Smith-Maddox, "The Social Networks and Resources of African American Eighth Graders: Evidence from the National Education Longitudinal Study of 1988," *Adolescence* 34 (1999): 169–183; Wenfan Yan, "Successful African American Students: The Role of Parental Involvement," *Journal of Negro Education* 68 (1999): 5–22.

81. Natalia Sarkisian, Mariana Gerena, and Naomi Gerstel, "Extended Family Ties among Mexicans, Puerto Ricans, and Whites: Superintegration or Disintegration?" *Family Relations* 55 (2006): 331–344; Daphna Oyserman, Heather Coon, and Markus Kemmelmeier, "Rethinking Individualism and Collectivism: Evaluation of Theoretical Assumptions and Meta-Analyses," *Psychological Bulletin* 128 (2002): 3–72; Yolanda Flores Niemann, Andrea Romero, and Consuelo Arbona, "Effects of Cultural Orientation on the Perception of Conflict between Relationship and Educational Goals for Mexican American College Students," *Hispanic Journal of Behavioral Sciences* 22 (2000): 46–63; Lynn Okagaki and Peter Frensch, "Parenting and Children's School Achievement: A Multiethnic Perspective," *American Educational Research Journal* 35 (1998): 125–144; Algea Harrison, Melvin Wilson, Charles Pine, Samuel Chan, and Raymond Buriel, "Family Ecologies of Ethnic Minority Children," *Child Development* 61 (1990): 347–362; Fabio Sabogal, Gerardo Marin, Regina Otero-Sabogal, Barbara Banoss Marin, and Eliseo Perez-Stable, "Hispanic Familism and Acculturation: What Changes and What Doesn't?" *Hispanic Journal of Behavioral Sciences* 9 (1987): 397–412; Valenzuela and Dornbusch, "Familism and Social Capital."

82. Robert Ream, "Counterfeit Social Capital and Mexican American Underachievement," *Educational Evaluation and Policy Analysis* 25 (2003): 237–262; James Valadez, "The Influence of Social Capital on Mathematics Course Selection by Latino High School Students," *Hispanic Journal of Behavioral Sciences* 24 (2002): 319–339; Ricardo Stanton- Salazar and Sanford Dornbusch, "Social Capital and the Reproduction of Inequality: Information Networks among Mexican-Origin High-School-Students," *Sociology of Education* 68 (1995): 116–135.

83. Jeanne Brooks-Gunn and Lisa Markman, "The Contribution of Parenting to Ethnic and Racial Gaps in School Readiness," *The Future of Children* 15 (2005): 139–168.

84. Clifford Geertz, *The Interpretation of Cultures* (New York: Basic Books, 1973), 216–217.

85. Grace Kena et al., National Center for Education Statistics, *The Condition of Education* (Washington, DC: U.S. Department of Education, 2014), 4. See also Institute of Education Sciences, *Digest of Education Statistics* (Washington, DC: National Center for Education Statistics, 2013).

86. Robert Crosnoe and Ruth Lopez-Turley, "The K-12 Educational Outcomes of Immigrant Youth," *Future of Children* 21 (2011): 129–152.

87. Valerie Ooka Pang, Peggy Han, and Jennifer Pang, "Asian American and Pacific Islander Students: Equity and the Achievement Gap," *Educational Researcher* 40 (2011): 378–389; Kimberly Goyette and Yu Xie, "Educational Expectations of Asian American Youths: Determinants and Ethnic Differences," *Sociology of Education* 72 (1999): 22–36.

88. Chauansheng Chen and Harold Stevenson, "Motivation and Mathematics Achievement: A Comparative Study of Asian-American, Caucasian-American, and East Asian High School Students," *Child Development* 66 (1995): 1215–1234; Kathy Seal, "Asian-American Parenting and Academic Success," *Pacific Standard*, December 13, 2010.

89. Seal, "Asian-American Parenting and Academic Success."

90. Richard Zweigenhaft and G. William Domhoff, *Diversity in the Power Elite: Have Women and Minorities Reached the Top?* (New Haven, CT: Yale University Press, 1998); Morrison Wong and Charles Hirschman, "The New Asian Immigrants," in *Culture, Ethnicity, and Identity*, ed. William McCready (New York: Academic Press, 1983), 395–397; Julian Stanley, "Family Background of Young Asian Americans Who Reason Extremely Well Mathematically," *Journal of the Illinois Council of the Gifted* 1 (1988): 11.

91. Sandy Baum and Stella Flores, "Higher Education and Children in Immigrant Families," *The Future of Children* 21 (2011): 171–193.

92. Cited in Frank Wu, *Yellow: Race in America Beyond Black and White* (New York: Basic Books, 2002), 60–61.

93. William Petersen, "Success Story, Japanese-American Style," *New York Times Magazine*, January 9, 1966.

94. Wu, *Yellow*, 41. See also Keith Osajima, "Asian Americans as the Model Minority: An Analysis of the Popular Press Image in the 1960s and 1980s," in *Contemporary Asian America: A Multidisciplinary Reader*, ed. Min Zhou and James Gatewood (New York: New York University Press, 2000), 449–458.

95. Wu, *Yellow*, 68.

96. Eliza Noh, "Asian American Women and Suicide: Problems of Responsibility and Healing," *Women and Therapy* 30 (2007): 87–107; Eliza Noh, *Suicide among Asian American Women: Influences of Racism and Sexism on Suicide Subjectification* (Berkeley: University of California Press, 2002).

97. All quoted in Wu, *Yellow*, 48.

98. John Ogbu, "Collective Identity and the Burden of 'Acting White' in Black History, Community, and Education," *Urban Review* 36 (2004): 1–35.

99. Scott, *Domination and the Arts of Resistance*, epigraph.

100. Ogbu, "Collective Identity," 28–29.

101. Ronald Ferguson, "What Doesn't Meet the Eye: Understanding and Addressing Racial Achievement Gaps in High Achieving Suburban School Systems," (Washington, D.C.: North Central Regional Educational Laboratory Working Paper #ED 474 390, 2002).

102. Karolyn Tyson, "Weighing In: Elementary-Age Students and the Debate on Attitudes towards School among Black Students," *Social Forces* 80 (2002): 1157–1189; James Ainsworth-Darnell and Douglas Downey, "Assessing the Oppositional Culture Explanation for Racial/Ethnic Differences in School Performance," *American Sociological Review* 63 (1998): 536–553.

103. Angel Harris, "Optimism in the Face of Despair: Black-White Differences in Beliefs about School as a Means for Upward Social Mobility," *Social Science Quarterly* 89 (2008): 629–651; Angel Harris, "I (Don't) Hate School: Revisiting 'Oppositional Culture' Theory of Blacks' Resistance to Schooling," *Social Forces* 85 (2006): 797–834; Monica Johnson, Robert Crosnoe, and Glen Elder, Jr., "Students' Attachment and Academic Engagement: The Role of Race and Ethnicity," *Sociology of Education* 74 (2001): 318–334; Karolyn Tyson, William Darity, and Domini Castellino, "Breeding Animosity: The Significance of School Placement Patterns in the Development of a 'Burden of Acting White'" (unpublished manuscript, Duke University, Terry Sanford Institute for Public Policy, 2004).

104. Prudence Carter, *Keepin' It Real: School Success beyond Black and White* (New York: Oxford University Press, 2005), 53.

105. Patricia J. Williams, *The Alchemy of Race and Rights: Diary of a Law Professor* (Cambridge, MA: Harvard University Press, 2001); Moore, *Reproducing Racism.*

106. Carter, *Keepin' It Real*, 65–66.

107. Claude Steele and Joshua Aronson, "Stereotype Threat and the Intellectual Test Performance of African Americans," *Journal of Personality and Social Psychology* 69 (1995): 797–811, 797.

108. Ibid., 808.

109. Ibid.

110. Jim Blascovich, Steven Spencer, Diane Quinn, and Claude Steele, "African Americans' High Blood Pressure: The Role of Stereotype Threat," *Psychological Science* 12 (2001): 225–229.

111. Catherine Good, Joshua Aronson, and Jayne Ann Harder, "Problems in the Pipeline: Stereotype Threat and Women's Achievement in High-Level Math Courses," *Journal of Applied and Developmental Psychology* 28 (2008): 17–28; Toni Schmader and Michael Johns, "Converging Evidence That Stereotype Threat Reduces Working Memory Capacity," *Journal of Personality and Social Psychology* 85 (2003): 440–452; Jean-Claude Croizet and Theresa Claire, "Extending the Concept of Stereotype Threat to Social Class: The Intellectual Underperformance of Students from Low Socioeconomic Backgrounds," *Personality and Social Psychology Bulletin* 24 (1998): 588–594.

112. Joshua Aronson, Michael Lustina, Catherine Good, and Kelli Keough, "When White Men Can't Do Math: Necessary and Sufficient Factors in Stereotype Threat," *Journal of Experimental Social Psychology* 35 (1999): 29–46.

113. Jonathan Kozol, *Savage Inequalities: Children in American's Schools* (New York: HarperCollins, 1991).

114. Ibid., 112.

115. Kathryn Neckerman, *Schools Betrayed: Roots of Failure in Inner-City Education* (Chicago: University of Chicago Press, 2007); Jeannie Oaks, *Keeping Track: How Schools Structure Inequality*, 2nd ed. (New Haven, CT: Yale University Press, 2005).

116. Douglas Harris, *Lost Learning, Forgotten Promises: A National Analysis of School Racial Segregation, Student Achievement, and "Controlled Choice" Plans* (Washington, DC: Center for American Progress, 2006); Susan Easton, "The New Segregation: Forty Years after Brown, Cities and Suburbs Face a Rising Tide of Racial Isolation," *Harvard Education Letter* 10, January 1994; Gary Orfield, *The Growth of Segregation in American Schools: Changing Patterns of Separation and Poverty since 1968* (Washington, DC: National School Boards Association, 1993).

117. Sheryll Cashin, *The Failure of Integration: How Race and Class Are Undermining the American Dream* (New York: Public Affairs, 2004); Richard Valencia, "Inequalities and the Schooling of Minority Students in Texas: Historical and Contemporary Conditions," *Hispanic Journal of Behavioral Sciences* 22 (2000): 445–459; Gary Orfield and John Yun, "Resegregation in American Schools" (working paper, The Civil Rights Project, Harvard University, 1999).; Andrew Grant-Thomas and Gary Orfield, eds., *Twenty-First Century Color Lines: Multiracial Change in Contemporary America* (Philadelphia: Temple University Press, 2009).

118. Ibid.

119. Mark Dixon, *Public Education Finances: 2011*, U.S. Department of Commerce, Washington, DC: U.S. Census Bureau, May 2013, http://www2.census.gov/govs/school/11f33pub.pdf

120. Paulle, *Toxic Schools*, 100.

121. Kozol, *Savage Inequalities*, 18.

122. Shamus Khan, *Privilege: The Making of an Adolescent Elite at St. Paul's School* (Princeton, NJ: Princeton University Press, 2010), 15–16.

123. Quoted in Cashin, *Failure of Integration*, 220.

124. Samuel Lucas and Mark Berends, "Race and Track Location in U.S. Public Schools," *Research in Social Stratification and Mobility* 25 (2007): 169–187; Jeannie Oaks, *Keeping Track: How Schools Structure Inequality*, 2nd ed. (New Haven, CT: Yale University Press, 2005); Samuel Lucas, "Effectively Maintained Inequality: Education Transitions, Track Mobility, and Social Background Effects," *American Journal of Sociology* 106 (2001): 1642–1690; Roslyn Arlin Mickelson, "Subverting

Swann: First- and Second-Generation Segregation in Charlotte-Mecklenberg Schools," *American Educational Research Journal* 38 (2001): 215–252.

125. Annette Lareau and Erin McNamara Horvat, "Moments of Social Inclusion and Exclusion: Race, Class, and Cultural Capital in Family-School Relationships," *Sociology of Education* 72 (1999): 37–53; William Lacy and Ernest Middleton, "Are Educators Racially Prejudiced? A Cross-Occupational Comparison of Attitudes," *Sociological Focus* 14 (1981): 87–95.

126. Lucas and Berends, "Race and Track Location," 172, emphasis ours.

127. Adam Gamoran, "The Stratification of High School Learning Opportunities," *Sociology of Education* 60 (1987): 135–155.

128. Cf. Wu, *Yellow*, 132–133.

129. Eric Grodsky, "Compensatory Sponsorship in Higher Education," *American Journal of Sociology* 112 (2007): 1662–1712; William Bowen and Derek Bok, *The Shape of the River: Long-Term Consequences of Considering Race in College and University Admissions* (Princeton, NJ: Princeton University Press, 1998).

130. Scott Plous, "Ten Myths about Affirmative Action," in *Understanding Prejudice and Discrimination*, ed. Scott Plous (New York: McGraw-Hill, 2003), 206–212; Bowen and Bok, *Shape of the River*.

131. Brown, et al., *White-Washing Race*, 122.

132. Evan Mandery, "End College Legacy Preferences," *New York Times*, April 24, 2014.

133. Peter Schmidt, Color and Money: How Rich White Kids are Winning the War Over College Affirmative Action (New York: Palgrave Macmillan, 2007); Peter Schmidt, "At the Elite Colleges— Dim White Kids," *Boston Globe*, September 28, 2007; Joe Klein, "There's More Than One Way to Diversify," *Time*, December 18, 2006.

134. Bowen and Bok, *Shape of the River*; Brown et al., *White-Washing Race*.

135. Wilson, *The Truly Disadvantaged*, 147.

136. Jonathan Glater and Alan Finder, "Schools Diversity Based on Income Segregates Some," *New York Times*, July 15, 2007; Thomas Kane, "Misconceptions in the Debate over Affirmative Action in College Admissions," in Gary Orfield and Edward Miller (Eds.) *Chilling Admissions: The Affirmative Action Crisis and the Search for Alternatives* (Cambridge, MA: Harvard Education Publishing Group, 1998, 17-31); Klein, "There's More Than One Way to Diversify."

137. Jerome Karabel, The Chosen: The Hidden History of Admission and Exclusion at Harvard, Yale, and Princeton (Boston: Houghton Mifflin, 2005).

138. Sigal Alon and Marta Tienda, "Diversity, Opportunity, and the Shifting Meritocracy in Higher Education," *American Sociological Review* 72 (2007): 487–511.

139. Shelby Steele, *The Content of Our Character: A New Vision of Race in America* (New York: St. Martin's, 1990); Plous, "Ten Myths about Affirmative Action."

Chapter 8: Aesthetics

1. Robyn Autry, "The Cultural Politics of Truth, Memory, and Reconciliation at Museums in the United States and South Africa" (unpublished manuscript, University of Wisconsin–Madison, Department of Sociology, February 2008); Stephen Weil, *Making Museums Matter* (Washington, DC: Smithsonian Institution, 2001); American Association of Museums, *Trust and Education: Americans' Perception of Museums; Key Findings of the Lake, Snell Perry February 2001 Survey* (Washington, DC: American Association of Museums, 2001).

2. Herman Gray, *Watching Race: Television and the Struggle for "Blackness"* (Minneapolis: University of Minnesota Press, 1995).

3. John Dewey, *Art as Experience* (New York: Capricorn Books, 1934), 12.

4. Martin Berger, *Sight Unseen: Whiteness and American Visual Culture* (Berkeley: University of California Press, 2005), 100.

5. Charmaine Nelson, "Edmonia Lewis's *Death of Cleopatra*: White Marble, Black Skin and the Regulation of Race in American Neoclassical Sculpture," in *Local/Global: Women Artists in the Nineteenth Century*, ed. Deborah Cherry and Janice Helland (Burlington, VT: Ashgate, 2006), 223–243.

6. Nicolas Bancel, Pascal Blanchard, and Sandrine Lemaire, "Ces zoos humains de la République coloniale," *Le Monde diplomatique*, August 2000; Paul Greenhalgh, *Ephemeral Vistas: The Expositions Universelles, Great Exhibitions and World's Fairs, 1851–1939* (Manchester, UK: Manchester University Press, 1988); Berger, *Sight Unseen*, 108–109.

7. Karen Sotiropoulos, *Staging Race: Black Performers in Turn of the Century America* (Cambridge, MA: Harvard University Press, 2006); Dale Cockrell, *Demons of Disorder: Early Blackface Minstrels and Their World* (New York: Cambridge University Press, 1997); Eric Lott, *Love and Theft: Blackface Minstrelsy and the American Working Class* (New York: Oxford University Press, 1993).

8. Julia Kristeva, *The Powers of Horror: An Essay on Abjection* (New York: Columbia University Press, 1982 [1980]).

9. Vijay Prashad, *The Karma of Brown Folk* (Minneapolis: University of Minnesota Press, 2000), 28–30.

10. Arthur Jones, *Wade in the Water: The Wisdom of the Spirituals* (Boulder, CO: Leave a Little Room), p. 22.

11. Du Bois, *Souls of Black Folk*, 156.

12. Craig Werner, *A Change Is Gonna Come: Music, Race, and the Soul of America* (New York: Plume, 1998).

13. James Baldwin, *The Fire Next Time* (New York: Vintage 1993 [1962]), 41–42.

14. Cornel West, "On Afro-American Music: From Bebop to Rap," in *The Cornel West Reader*, ed. Cornel West (New York: Basic Books, 1999, 474–484), 475.

15. Cited in bell hooks, *Black Looks: Race and Representation* (Cambridge: South End Press, 1992), 30.

16. Werner, *Change Is Gonna Come*, 89.

17. Cited in Berger, *Sight Unseen*, 108–109.

18. Black Hawk Hancock, "Learning How to Make Life Swing," *Qualitative Sociology* 20 (2007): 113–133, 113.

19. Vicki Mayer, *Producing Dreams, Consuming Youth: Mexican Americans and Mass Media* (New Brunswick, NJ: Rutgers University Press, 2003).

20. Phillip Brian Harper, "Extra-Special Effects: Televisual Representation and the Claims of 'the Black Experience,'" in *Living Color: Race and Television in the United States*, ed. Sasha Torres (Durham, NC: Duke University Press, 1999), 62–81; Zora Neale Hurston, "What White Publishers Won't Print," in *African American Literary Theory: A Reader*, ed. Winston Napier (New York: New York University Press, 2000 [1947]), 54–57.

21. Vincent Brook, *Something Ain't Kosher Here: The Rise of the "Jewish" Sitcom* (New Brunswick, NJ: Rutgers University Press, 2003).

22. Mel Watkins, "Richard Pryor, Iconoclastic Comedian, Dies at 65," *New York Times*, December 11, 2005.

23. Berger, *Sight Unseen*, 1.

24. Kate Dries, "New York Fashion Week Was Chock-Full of White Models. Again," *Jezebel* (blog), September 17, 2013; Julee Wilson, "Another Black Model, Anais Mali, Shares Her Tale of Blatant Racism in Fashion Industry," *Huffington Post*, February 3, 2014.

25. Guy Trebay, "Ignoring Diversity, Runways Fade to White," *New York Times*, October 14, 2007.

26. American Psychological Association, "Segregation Ruled Unequal, and Therefore Unconstitutional," *Psychology Matters* (July 2007); Ann duCille, "Dyes and Dolls: Multicultural Barbie and the Merchandising of Difference," in *The Black Studies Reader*, ed. Jacqueline Bobo, Cynthia Hudley, and Claudine Michel (New York: Routledge, 2004), 265–280; Kenneth Clark and Mamie Clark, "Emotional Factors in Racial Identification and Preference in Negro Children," *Journal of Negro Education* 19 (1950): 341–350; Kenneth Clark and Mamie Clark, "Skin Color as a Factor in Racial Identification of Negro Preschool Children," *Journal of Social Psychology* 11 (1940): 159–169.

27. Carrie Stetler, "Ethnic Plastic Surgery Grows Popular as Attitudes Change," *Seattle Times*, July 22, 2006. See also Bonnie Berry, *Beauty Bias: Discrimination and Social Power* (Westport, CT: Greenwood, 2007); Kathy Davis, *Dubious Equalities and Embodied Differences: Cultural Studies on Cosmetic Surgery* (Lanham, MD: Rowman and Littlefield, 2003).

28. Andrew Lam, "Plastic Surgery as Racial Surgery," *New America Media*, March 29, 2007.

29. Dwight McBride, *Why I Hate Abercrombie and Fitch: Essays on Race and Sexuality* (New York: New York University Press, 2005), 85–86.

30. Quoted in McBride, *Why I Hate Abercrombie and Fitch*, 86.

31. Ibid.

32. Dana Mastro and Susannah Stern, "Representations of Race in Television Commercials: A Content Analysis of Prime-Time Advertising," *Journal of Broadcasting and Electronic Media* 47 (2003): 638–647.

33. Talib Kweli, "I Try," *Beautiful Struggle* (2004), Hi-Tek.

34. Robyn Autry, "The Cultural Politics of Truth, Memory, and Reconciliation at Museums in the United States and South Africa" (unpublished manuscript, University of Wisconsin–Madison, Department of Sociology, February 2008); Stephen Weil, *Making Museums Matter* (Washington, DC: Smithsonian Institution, 2001); American Association of Museums, *Trust and Education: Americans' Perception of Museums: Key Findings of the Lake, Snell Perry February 2001 Survey* (Washington, DC: American Association of Museums, 2001).

35. Cf. Renato Rosaldo's term "imperial nostalgia." See his *Culture and Truth: The Remaking of Social Analysis* (Boston: Beacon, 1988).

36. Bourdieu, Pierre, *Pascalian meditations* (Stanford University Press, 2000), 65.

37. Dodai Stewart, "Racist *Hunger Games* Fans Are Very Disappointed," *Jezebel* (blog), March 26, 2012.

38. Nina Jacinto, "Victoria's Secret Does It Again: When Racism Meets Fashion," *Racialicious* (blog), September 6, 2012.

39. Adrienne L. Childs, "Ancient Practice Sparks a Rapper's Outrage," *The Root*, October 27, 2012.

40. Fidel Martinez, "Are 'Hilarious Black Neighbor' Videos a Modern Day Minstrel Show?" *The Daily Dot*, May 9, 2013.

41. Jacques Steinberg, "Imus Is Back, Chastened but Still Proudly Obnoxious," *New York Times*, December 4, 2007; Jacques Steinberg, "Shock Radio Shrugs at Imus's Fall and Roughs Up the Usual Victims," *New York Times*, May 6, 2007.

42. Ella Shohat and Robert Stam, *Unthinking Ethnocentrism: Multiculturalism and the Media* (New York: Routledge, 1994), 194.

43. Amar Bakshi, "How the World Sees America," *Post Global*, August 30, 2007.

44. Sue Kim, "Beyond Black and White: Race and Postmodernism in *The Lord of the Rings* Films," *Modern Fiction Studies* 50 (2004): 875–907.

45. David Pilgrim, "New Racist Forms: Jim Crow in the 21st Century" (paper written for Jim Crow Museum of Racist Memorabilia, Ferris State University, 2001); Carole Boston Weatherford, "Japan's Bigoted Exports to Kids," *Christian Science Monitor*, May 4, 2000.

46. Shohat and Stam, *Unthinking Ethnocentrism*, 178–179.

47. Wendy Leo Moore and Jennifer Pierce, "Still Killing Mockingbirds: Narratives of Race and Innocence in Hollywood's Depiction of the White Messiah Lawyer," *Qualitative Sociology* 3 (2007): 171–187; Hernán Vera and Andrew M. Gordon, *Screen Saviors: Hollywood Fictions of Whiteness* (Lanham, MD: Rowman and Littlefield, 2003).

48. Jackson, *Harlemworld*, 197. See also Robyn Wiegman, *American Antimonies: Theorizing Race and Gender* (Durham, NC: Duke University Press, 1995).

49. Melba Joyce Boyd, "Collateral Damages Sustain in the Film *Crash*," *Souls* 9 (2007): 253–265.

50. Deloria, *Custer Died for Your Sins*, 149.

51. Gwendolyn Dubois Shaw, *Speaking the Unspeakable: The Art of Kara Walker* (Durham, NC: Duke University Press, 2004).

52. Michi Itami, "The Irony of Being American," in *Voices of Color: Art and Society in the Americas*, ed. Phoebe Farris-Dufrene (Atlantic Highlands, NJ: Humanities Press, 1997), 20–28.

53. Jean Fisher, "In Search of the 'Inauthentic': Disturbing Signs in Contemporary Native-American Art," in *Race-ing Art History: Critical Readings in Race and Art History*, ed. Kymberly Pinder (New York: Routledge, 2002), 331–340.

54. See Maurice Berger, *White: Whiteness and Race in Contemporary Art* (Baltimore: University of Maryland Center for Art and Visual Culture, 2004).

55. Maurice Berger, "Picturing Whiteness: Nikki S. Lee's Yuppie Project—Photography," *Art Journal* 60 (2001): 54–57.

56. http://www.maconami.blogspot.com/2006/01/in-america-suheir-hammad.html

57. Randal Archibald, "Far From Home, Mexicans Sing Age-Old Ballads of a New Life," *New York Times*, July 6 2007; Taki Telonidis, "Immigrant Songs Offer New Twist on Old Sounds," *National Public Radio*, September 16, 2007.

58. Recording Industry Association of America, "2003 Consumer Profile."

59. West, "On Afro-American Music," 482.

60. Trisha Rose, *Black Noise: Rap Music and Black Culture in Contemporary America* (Hanover, NH: Wesleyan University Press, 1994), 18.

61. Michael C. Dawson, "'Dis Beat Disrupts': Rap, Ideology, and Black Political Attitudes," in *The Cultural Territories of Race: Black and White Boundaries*, ed. Michèle Lamont (Chicago: University of Chicago Press, 1999), 318–342.

62. Rose, *Black Noise*.

63. Paul Gilroy, *Against Race: Imagining Political Culture beyond the Color Line* (Cambridge, MA: Harvard University Press, 2000); Adolph Reed, Jr., "The Allure of Malcolm X," in *Malcolm X: In Our Own Image*, ed. Joe Wood (New York: St. Martin's, 1992), 203–232.

64. Blue Scholars, "Back Home" *Bayani*, Massline/Rawkus, 2007

65. Gilbert Rodman, "Race . . . and Other Four-Letter Words: Eminem and the Cultural Politics of Authenticity," *Popular Communication* 4 (2006): 95–121.

66. Dawson, "'Dis Beat Disrupts.'"

67. Harper, "Extra-Special Effects."

68. Edward Armstrong, "The Rhetoric of Violence in Rap and Country Music," *Sociological Inquiry* 63 (1993): 64–83; Glassner, *Culture of Fear*, 121–127.

69. Kimberlè Crenshaw, "Beyond Racism and Misogyny: Black Feminism and 2 Live Crew," in *Words That Wound: Critical Race Theory, Assaultive Speech, and the First Amendment*, ed. Mari Matsuda, Charles Lawrence III, Richard Delgado, and Kimberlè Crenshaw (Boulder, CO: Westview, 1993), 111–136; Amy Binder, "Constructing Racial Rhetoric," *American Sociological Review* 58 (1993): 753–767.

70. Cited in Bourdieu, *Rules of Art*, 1.

71. Alan Smithee, "Diversity and the Directors Guild of America," *American Thinker*, November 7, 2013.

72. Maxine Naawu, "Representation at the Oscars," *By Their Strange Fruit*, March 3, 2014.

73. Norman Denzin, *Reading Race: Hollywood and the Cinema of Racial Violence* (Thousand Oaks, CA: Sage, 2002); Shohat and Stam, *Unthinking Ethnocentrism*, 184–187.

74. Ben Bagdikian, *The New Media Monopoly*, rev. ed. (Boston: Beacon, 2004); Todd Wirth, "Nationwide Format Oligopolies," *Journal of Radio and Audio Media* 8 (2001): 249–270.

75. Institute of Museum and Library Services, *African American History and Culture in Museums: Strategic Crossroads and New Opportunities* (Washington, DC: Institute of Museum and Library Services, 2004); Lewis Mumford, *The Culture of Cities* (Fort Washington, PA: Harvest Books, 1970).

76. Robert W. Witkin, "Why Did Adorno 'Hate' Jazz?" *Sociological Theory* 18 (2000): 145–170.

77. Patricia Leighten, "The White Pearl and *L'Art nègre*: Picasso, Primitivism, and Anticolonialism," in *Race-ing Art History: Critical Readings in Race and Art History*, ed. Kymberly Pinder (New York: Routledge, 2002), 233–260; Anna Chave, "New Encounters with *Les Demoiselles d'Avignon*: Gender, Race, and the Origins of Cubism," in *Race-ing Art History: Critical Readings in Race and Art History*, ed. Kymberly Pinder (New York: Routledge, 2002), 261–287.

78. Peter Marzio, "Foreword" to John Beardsley, William Arnett, Paul Arnett, and Jane Livingston, *The Quilts of Gee's Bend* (Atlanta: Tinwood Books, 2002).

79. Said, *Orientalism*.

80. Melissa Locker, "Grammys 2014: Macklemore Says Kenrick Lamar 'Was Robbed' on Best Rap Album," *Time*, January 27, 2014.

81. Cornel West, "Horace Pippin's Challenge to Art Criticism," in *The Cornel West Reader*, ed. Cornel West (New York: Basic Books, 1999, 447–455), 454–455.

82. hooks, *Black Looks*, chap. 8.

83. West, "Horace Pippin's Challenge to Art Criticism," 452.

84. Robert Stepto, *From behind the Veil: A Study of Afro-American Narrative*, 2nd ed. (Urbana: University of Illinois Press, 1991); hooks, *Black Looks*, chap. 8.

85. Peter Brinson, "Liberation Frequency: The Free Radio Movement and Alternative Strategies of Media Relations," *Sociological Quarterly* 47 (2006): 543–568; Ronald Jacobs, *Race, Media, and the Crisis of Civil Society: From Watts to Rodney King* (Cambridge: Cambridge University Press, 2000); Ronald Jacobs, "Race, Media, and Civil Society," *International Sociology* 14 (1999): 355–372.

86. William Roy, "Aesthetic Identity, Race, and American Folk Music," *Qualitative Sociology* 25 (2002): 459–469, 460.

87. Richard Peterson, *Creating Country Music: Fabricating Authenticity* (Chicago: University of Chicago Press, 1997); Paul Oliver, *Songsters and Saints: Vocal Traditions on Race Records* (Cambridge: Cambridge University Press, 1984).

88. Hamid Naficy, "Narrowcasting in Diaspora: Middle Eastern Television in Los Angeles," in *Living Color: Race and Television in the United States*, ed. Sasha Torres (Durham, NC: Duke University Press, 1999), 82–96.

89. Lott, *Love and Theft*.

90. Hancock, "Learning How to Make Life Swing."

91. Roy, "Aesthetic Identity, Race, and American Folk Music," 467.

92. Georg Simmel, "Fashion," in *Georg Simmel: On Individuality and Social Forms*, ed. Donald Levine (Chicago: University of Chicago Press, 1971 [1908]), 299.

93. Annette Lynch and Mitchell Strauss, *Changing Fashion: A Critical Introduction to Trend Analysis and Meaning* (Oxford: Berg, 2007).

94. Diana Crane, "High Culture versus Popular Culture Revisited: A Reconceptualization of Recorded Cultures," in *Cultivating Differences: Symbolic Boundaries and the Making of Inequality*, ed. Michèle Lamont and Marcel Fournier (Chicago: University of Chicago Press, 1992), 58–74; Bourdieu, *Distinction*.

95. Lawrence Levine, *Highbrow, Lowbrow: The Emergence of Cultural Hierarchy in America* (Cambridge, MA: Harvard University Press, 1988). See also Paul DiMaggio, "Cultural Entrepreneurship in Nineteenth-Century Boston, Pt. 1," *Media, Culture and Society* 4 (1982): 33–50.

96. Jason Kasson, *Rudeness and Civility: Manners in Nineteenth-Century Urban America* (New York: Hill and Wang, 1990).

97. Berger, *Sight Unseen*, 104.

98. *Glamour*, "Your Race, Your Looks," February 2008; E. R. Shipp, "Braided Hair Style at Issue in Protests over Dress Codes," *New York Times*, September 23, 1987.

99. Rachel Slocum, "Whiteness, Space, and Alternative Food Practice," *Geoform* 38 (2007): 520–533.

100. Bourdieu, *Distinction*, ch. 7.

101. Gia Kourlas, "Where Are All the Black Swans?" *New York Times*, May 6, 2007.

102. Omar Lizardo and Sara Skiles, "Cultural Consumption in the Fine and Popular Arts Realms," *Sociology Compass* (2008): 1–18; Omar Lizardo, "How Cultural Tastes Shape Personal Networks," *American Sociological Review* 71 (2006): 778–807; Richard Peterson and N. Anand, "The Production of Cultural Perspective," *Annual Review of Sociology* 30 (2004): 311–334.

103.   Bethany Bryson, "Anything but Heavy Metal: Symbolic Exclusion and Musical Dislikes," *American Sociological Review* 61 (1996): 884–899. See also Shin-Kap Han, "Unraveling the Brow: What and How of Choice in Musical Preference," *Sociological Perspectives* 46 (2003): 435–459.

104.   Michèle Lamont and Sada Aksartova, "Ordinary Cosmopolitanisms: Strategies for Bridging Racial Boundaries among Working-Class Men," *Theory, Culture, and Society* 19 (2002): 1–25; Bryson, "Anything but Heavy Metal."

105.   Cf. Bonilla-Silva, *Racism without Racists.*

106.   Lizardo and Skiles, "Cultural Consumption."

107.   Rodman, "Race . . . and Other Four-Letter Words," 107.

108.   Lucy Lippard, *Mixed Blessings: New Art in a Multicultural America* (New York: Pantheon Books, 1990); Ralph Ellison, "The Art of Romare Bearden," in Ralph Ellison, *Going to the Territory* (New York: Vintage, 1986), 227–238.

109.   Ben Sisario, "Wizards in the Studio, Anonymous on the Street," *New York Times*, May 6, 2007.

110.   Gargi Chatterjee and Augie Tom, "Is There an Asian American Aesthetics?" in *Contemporary Asian America: A Multidisciplinary Reader*, ed. Min Zhou and James Gatewood (New York: New York University Press, 2000), 627–635; Deloria, *Custer Died for Your Sins*, chap. 7.

111.   Chatterjee and Tom, "Is There an Asian American Aesthetics?," 631.

112.   James Young, "Profound Offense and Cultural Appropriation," *Journal of Aesthetics and Art Criticism* 63 (2005): 135–146.

113.   Bill Cunningham, "Look East," *New York Times*, April 29, 2007.

114.   Bakari Kitwana, *Why White Kids Love Hip Hop: Wankstas, Wiggers, Wannabes, and the new Reality of Race in America* (Basic Civitas Books, 2006), 44.

115.   Cf. E. Patrick Johnson, *Appropriating Blackness: Performance and the Politics of Authenticity* (Durham, NC: Duke University Press, 2003), 236–238.

116.   Quoted in Eva Marie Garroutee, *Real Indians: Identity and Survival of Native America* (Berkeley: University of California Press, 2003), 76.

117.   Kitwana, *Why White Kids Love Hip-Hop*, 124.

118.   Alex Ross, *The Rest Is Noise: Listening to the Twentieth Century* (New York: Farrar, Straus and Giroux, 2007), 101.

119.   Greg Tate, "Nigs R Us, or How Blackfolk Become Fetish Objects," in *Everything but the Burden: What White People Are Taking from Black Culture*, ed. Greg Tate (New York: Harlem Moon, 2003), 1–14.

120.   Mos Def "Rock N Roll," Black on Both Sides, Rawkus Records, 1999.

121.   hooks, *Black Looks*, 26.

122.   Ibid.

123.   Tate, *Everything but the Burden.*

124.   Chrystos, "Today Was a Bad Day Like TB," in *Unsettling America: An Anthology of Contemporary Multicultural Poetry*, ed. Maria Mazziotti Gillan and Jennifer Gillan (New York: Penguin, 1994), 61.

125.   Henry Louis Gates, Jr., "'Authenticity,' or the Lesson of Little Tree," *New York Times Book Review*, November 24, 1991, 26.

126.   Young, "Profound Offense and Cultural Appropriation," 145.

127.   Garroutee, *Real Indians*, 78.

128.   Rodman, "Race . . . and Other Four-Letter Words," 110.

129.   Kerry Rockquemore and David L. Brunsma, *Beyond Black: Biracial Identity in America*, with foreword by Joe R. Feagin, (Lanham, MD: Rowman and Littlefield, 2007); Loretta Winters and Herman DeBose, *New Faces in a Changing America: Multiracial Identity in the 21st Century* (Thousand Oaks, CA: Sage, 2003).

130.   Garroutee, *Real Indians*, 78.

131.   Leslie Marmon Silko, *Ceremony* (New York: Penguin, 1977), 126.

132. Fisher, "In Search of the 'Inauthentic.'"

133. Kwame Anthony Appiah, *Cosmopolitanism: Ethnics in a World of Strangers* (New York: Norton, 2006), 130.

Chapter 9: Associations

1. Myrdal, *American Dilemma*, 810.

2. Tocqueville, *Democracy in America*, 511, 512—513.

3. Judith Shklar, *American Citizenship: The Quest for Inclusion* (Cambridge, MA: Harvard University Press, 1991), 14—15. See also Rogers Smith, *Civic Ideals: Conflicting Visions of Citizenship in U.S. History* (New Haven, CT: Yale University Press, 1997).

4. Hale, *Making Whiteness*, 21.

5. Myrdal, *American Dilemma*, 632.

6. Lillian Smith, *Killers of the Dream*, 95.

7. Geoffrey Ward, "Death's Army," *New York Times Book Review*, January 27, 2008.

8. Theda Skocpol, *Diminished Democracy: From Membership to Management in American Civic Life* (Norman: University of Oklahoma Press, 2003), 55.

9. Theda Skocpol, Ariane Liazos, and Marshall Ganz, *What a Mighty Power We Can Be: African American Fraternal Groups and the Struggle for Racial Equality* (Princeton, NJ: Princeton University Press, 2006), 31.

10. Skocpol, *Diminished Democracy*, 54. See also Drew Gilpin Faust, *The Republic of Suffering: Death and the American Civil War* (New York: Knopf, 2008).

11. Cited in Skocpol, *Diminished Democracy*, 180.

12. David Roediger, *Working toward Whiteness: How America's Immigrants Became White* (New York: Basic Books, 2005); John Stanfield, "Ethnic Pluralism and Civic Responsibility in Post—Cold War America," *Journal of Negro Education* 61 (1992): 287—300; Myrdal, *American Dilemma*, 631—639; Skocpol, *Diminished Democracy*, 179—180.

13. Skocpol, Liazos, and Ganz, *What a Mighty Power We Can Be*, 11, 13. See also Anne Firor Scott, "Most Invisible of All: Black Women's Voluntary Associations," *Journal of Southern History* 1 (1990): 3—22.

14. Michael Schudson, *The Good Citizen: A History of American Civic Life* (Cambridge, MA: Harvard University Press, 1998); Debra Minkoff, *Organizing for Equality: The Evolution of Women's and Racial-Ethnic Organizations in America, 1955—1985* (New Brunswick, NJ: Rutgers University Press, 1995); Skocpol, *Diminished Democracy*, 140—141, 180—181; Myrdal, *American Dilemma*, 842—847.

15. Helen Laville, "If the Time Is Not Ripe, Then It Is Your Job to Ripen the Time! The Transformation of the YWCA in the USA from Segregated Association to Interracial Organization, 1930—1965," *Women's History Review* 15 (2006): 359—383; Adrienne Lash Jones, "Struggle among Saints: African American Women and the YWCA, 1870—1920," in *Men and Women Adrift: The YMCA and the YWCA in the City*, ed. Nina Mjagkij and Margaret Spratt (New York: New York University Press, 1997), 160—184; Judith Weisenfeld, *African American Women and Christian Activism: New York's Black YWCA, 1905—1945* (Cambridge, MA: Harvard University Press, 1998).

16. Paul Moreno, *Black Americans and Organized Labor: A New History* (Baton Rouge: Louisiana State University Press, 2007); Eric Anderson, "Passion and Politics: Race and the Writing of Working-Class History," *Journal of the Historical Society* 6 (2006): 323—356; Michelle Brattain, *The Politics of Whiteness: Race, Workers, and Culture in the Modern South* (Princeton, NJ: Princeton University Press, 2001); William A. Sundstrom, "The Color Line: Racial Norms and Discrimination in Urban Labor Markets, 1910—1950," *Journal of Economic History* 54 (1994): 382—396; Roediger, *Working toward Whiteness*, 49; Katznelson, *When Affirmative Action Was White*.

17. Quoted in Roediger, *Working toward Whiteness*, 213.

18. Drake and Cayton, *Black Metropolis*, 326.

19. Skocpol, *Diminished Democracy*, 181.

20. Howard Schuman, Charlotte Steeh, Lawrence Bobo, and Maria Krysan, *Racial Attitudes in America: Trends and Interpretations*, rev. ed. (Cambridge, MA: Harvard University Press, 1997), 142—144; 254—256.

21. José-Antonio Orosco, "Neighborhood Democracy and Chicana/o Cultural Citizenship in Armando Réndon's *Chicano Manifesto*," *Ethics, Place and Environment* 10 (2007): 121–139; Komozi Woodard, *A Nation within a Nation: Amiri Baraka (LeRoi Jones) and Black Power Politics* (Chapel Hill: University of North Carolina Press, 1999); Ignacio Garc'a, *Chicanismo: The Forging of a Militant Ethos among Mexican Americans* (Tucson: University of Arizona Press, 1997); Anthony Smith, *Nationalism in the Twentieth Century* (New York: New York University, 1979).

22. Dexter Gordon, *Black Identity: Rhetoric, Ideology, and Nineteenth-Century Black Nationalism* (Carbondale: Southern Illinois University Press, 2003).

23. Quoted in Fairclough, *Better Day Coming*, 116.

24. Robert Hill, ed., *The Marcus Garvey and UNIA Papers Volume X, Africa for the Africans, 1921–1922* (Berkeley: University of California Press, 2006); Thandeka Chapman, "Foundations of Multicultural Education: Marcus Garvey and the United Negro Improvement Association," *Journal of Negro Education*, 73 (2004), 424–434; Robert Hill, ed., *The Marcus Garvey and UNIA Papers Volume IX, Africa for the Africans, 1921–1922* (Berkeley: University of California Press, 1995).

25. Quoted in Fairclough, *Better Day Coming*, 118.

26. Ibid., 124.

27. Hale, *Making Whiteness*, 26–27.

28. Fairclough, *Better Day Coming*, ch. 6. See also Hill, *Marcus Garvey and UNIA Papers Volume X*.

29. Malcolm X and Alex Huxley, *The Autobiography of Malcolm X* (New York: Ballantine Books, 1964).

30. Jeff Fleischer, "Nation of Islam Women Look Up and Out," *Women's News*, August 2, 2005.

31. Malcolm X, "The Ballot or the Bullet," Washington Heights, NY. March 29, 1964

32. David Reynolds, *John Brown, Abolitionist: The Man Who Killed Slavery, Sparked the Civil War, and Seeded Civil Rights* (New York: Vintage, 2006).

33. Clayborne Carson, "1965: A Decisive Turning Point in the Long Struggle for Voting Rights," *Crisis* 112 (2005): 16–20; Clayborne Carson, "The Unfinished Dialogue of Martin Luther King, Jr., and Malcolm X," *Souls* 7 (2005), 12–19; James Tyner, *The Geography of Malcolm X: Black Radicalism and the Remaking of American Space* (New York: Routledge, 2005); Fairclough, *Better Day Coming*, ch. 14.

34. Algernon Austin, *Achieving Blackness: Race, Black Nationalism, and Afrocentrism in the Twentieth Century* (New York: New York University Press, 2006), 174–177.

35. James Farmer, *Lay Bare the Heart: An Autobiography of the Civil Rights Movement* (Fort Worth: Texas Christian University Press, 1985), 224.

36. Ossie Davis, "On Malcolm X," in *The Autobiography of Malcolm X*, 525–526.

37. Cited in Simon Szreter, "The State of Social Capital: Bringing Back in Power, Politics, and History," *Theory and Society* 31 (2002): 573–621.

38. Gabriel Almond and Sidney Verba, *The Civic Culture: Political Attitudes and Democracy in Five Nations* (Newbury Park, CA: Sage, 1989 [1963]), ch. 10.

39. Michael Stoll and Janelle Wong, "Immigration and Civic Participation in a Multiracial and Multiethnic Context," *International Migration Review* 41 (2007): 880–908, 898. See also Pei-te Lien, Mary Margaret Conway, and Janelle Wong, eds., *The Politics of Asian Americans: Diversity and Community* (New York: Routledge, 2004); Michael Stoll, "Race, Neighborhood Poverty, and Participation in Voluntary Associations," *Sociological Forum* 16 (2001): 529–557; Pei-te Lien, *The Making of Asian America through Political Participation* (Philadelphia: Temple University Press, 2001).

40. April Clark, Cary Funk, and Paul Taylor, *Americans and Social Trust: Who, Where and Why* (Washington, DC: Pew Research Center, 2007).

41. Quoted in Cynthia Duncan, "Social Capital in America's Poor Rural Communities," in *Social Capital and Poor Communities*, ed. Susan Saegert, J. Phillip Thompson, and Mark Warren (New York: Russell Sage Foundation, 2001, 60–86), 71.

42. Sidney Verba, Kay Lehman Schlozman, and Henry E. Brady, *Voice and Equality: Civic Voluntarism in American Politics* (Cambridge, MA: Harvard University Press, 1995).

43. Kay Lehman Schlozman, Sidney Verba, and Henry E. Brady, "Civic Participation and the Equality Problem," in *Civic Engagement in American Democracy*, ed. Theda Skocpol and Morris Fiorina (Washington, DC: Brookings Institution, 1999), 427–460. See also Don Eberly and Ryan Streeter, *The Soul of Civil Society: Voluntary Associations and the Public Value of Moral Habits* (Lanham, MD: Lexington Books, 2002), ch. 5.

44. Mario Luis Small, "Racial Differences in Networks: Do Neighborhood Conditions Matter?" *Social Science Quarterly* 88 (2007): 320–343; Natasha Hritzuk and David Park, "The Question of Latino Participation: From an SES to a Social Structural Explanation," *Social Science Quarterly* 81 (2000): 151–177; Ester Fuchs, Robert Shapiro, and Lorraine Minnite, "Social Capital, Political Participation, and the Urban Community," in *Social Capital and Poor Communities*, ed. Susan Saegert, J. Phillip Thompson, and Mark Warren (New York: Russell Sage Foundation, 2001), 290–324; Stoll, "Race, Neighborhood Poverty, and Participation"; Verba, Schlozman, and Brady, *Voice and Equality*.

45. Myrdal, *American Dilemma*, 952. See also Skocpol, Liazos, and Ganz, *What a Mighty Power We Can Be*, 6–8, 61–69.

46. Stoll and Wong, "Immigration and Civic Participation," 900.

47. Sampson et al. "Civil Society Reconsidered"; Sampson and Raudenbush, "Systematic Social Observation of Public Spaces"; Sampson, Morenoff, and Raudenbush, "Social Anatomy of Racial and Ethnic Disparities in Violence"; Waldinger, *Still a Promised City?*

48. Min Zhou, "Social Capital in Chinatown: The Role of Community-Based Organizations and Families in the Adaptation of the Younger Generation," in *Contemporary Asian America: A Multidisciplinary Reader*, ed. Min Zhou and James Gatewood (New York: New York University Press, 2000), 315–335; Min Zhou, *Chinatown*.

49. Miller McPherson, Lynn Smith-Lovin, and James Cook, "Birds of a Feather: Homophily in Social Networks," *Annual Review of Sociology* 27 (2001): 415–444, 415, emphasis ours. See also Jason Kaufman, *For the Common Good? American Civic Life and the Golden Age of Fraternity* (New York: Oxford University Press, 2002); Amy Davis, Linda Renzulli, and Howard Aldrich, "Mixing or Matching? The Influence of Voluntary Associations on the Occupational Diversity and Density of Small Business Owners' Networks," *Work and Occupations* 33 (2006): 42–72.

50. Jeffrey Smith, Miller McPherson, and Lynn Smith-Lovin, "Social Distance in the United States: Sex, Race, Religion, Age, and Education Homophily among Confidants, 1985 to 2004," *American Sociological Review* 79 (2014): 432–456; McPherson, Smith-Lovin, and Cook, "Birds of a Feather," 415–444; Peter Marsden, "Core Discussion Networks of Americans," *American Sociological Review* 52 (2004): 122–131.

51. Kaufman, *For the Common Good?*

52. Mark Pachucki, Sabrina Pendergrass, and Michèle Lamont, "Boundary Processes: Recent Theoretical Developments and New Contributions," *Poetics* 35 (2007): 331–351; Michèle Lamont and Virág Molnár, "The Study of Boundaries in the Social Sciences," *Annual Review of Sociology* 28 (2002): 167–195; Michèle Lamont and Marcel Fournier, eds., *Cultivating Differences: Symbolic Boundaries and the Making of Inequality* (Chicago: University of Chicago Press, 1992); Kathryn Manzo, *Creating Boundaries: The Politics of Race and Nation* (Boulder, CO: Lynne Rienner, 1996); Fredrik Barth, *Ethnic Groups and Boundaries* (Boston: Little, Brown, 1969).

53. Edward Finegan and John Rickford, eds., *Language in the USA: Themes for the Twenty-First Century* (New York: Cambridge University Press, 2004); Roseann Duenas Gonzalez and Ildiko Melis, eds., *Language Ideologies: Critical Perspectives on the Official English Movement* (Philadelphia: Lawrence Erlbaum, 2001).

54. Linguistic Society of America, "Resolution: English Only," December 28, 1986.

55. Reuben Buford May and Kenneth Sean Chaplin, "Cracking the Code: Race, Class, and Access to Nightclubs in Urban America," *Qualitative Sociology* 31 (2008): 57–72; David Grazian, *On the Make: The Hustle of Urban Nightlife* (Chicago: University of Chicago Press, 2008).

56. Lawrence Otis Graham, *Our Kind of People: Inside America's Black Upper Class* (New York: HarperCollins, 1999).

57. Robert Putnam, *Bowling Alone: The Collapse and Revival of American Community* (New York: Touchstone Books, 2000), 46.

58. Putnam, *Bowling Alone*, 210. See also M. P. Baumgartner, *The Moral Order of a Suburb* (New York: Oxford University Press, 1988); Kenneth Jackson, *Crabgrass Frontier: The Suburbanization of the United States* (New York: Oxford University Press, 1985).

59. Lewis Mumford, *The Culture of Cities* (New York: Harcourt Brace, 1938), 215.

60. Nancy Gibbs, "One Day in America," *Time*, November 13, 2007; National Public Radio, "Study: Americans Commute an Average 25 Minutes," October 12, 2007; U.S. Census Bureau, *Americans Spend More than 100 Hours Commuting to Work Each Year, Census Bureau Reports* (Washington, DC: U.S. Department of Commerce, 2005).

61. James Wong, *Democracy's Promise: Immigrants and American Civic Institutions* (Ann Arbor: University of Michigan Press, 2006); Jennifer Glanville, "Voluntary Associations and Social Network Structure: Why Organizational Location and Type Are Important," *Sociological Forum* 19 (2004): 465–491; Dora Costa and Matthew Khan, "Civic Engagement and Community Heterogeneity: An Economist's Perspective," *Perspectives on Politics* 1 (2003): 103–111; Alberto Alesina, Reza Baqir, and William Easterly, "Public Goods and Ethnic Divisions," *Quarterly Journal of Economics* 11 (1999): 1243–1284; Putnam, *Bowling Alone*, 291–294, 362; Stoll and Wong, "Immigration and Civic Participation."

62. Rodney Hero, "Social Capital and Racial Inequality in America," *Perspectives on Politics* 1 (2003): 113–122, 120.

63. Amy Rehder Harris, William Evans, and Robert Schwab, "Education Spending in an Aging America," *Journal of Public Economics* 81 (2001): 449–472; Claudia Goldin and Lawrence Katz, "Human Capital and Social Capital: The Rise of Secondary Schooling in America, 1910 to 1940," *Journal of Interdisciplinary History* 29 (1999): 683–723; Costa and Khan, "Civic Engagement and Community Heterogeneity"; Ezro F. P. Luttmer, "Group Loyalty and the Taste for Redistribution." *Journal of Political Economy* 109 (2001):3, 500–528.

64. Satya Mohanty, Linda Martin Alcoff, Michael Hames-Garcia, and Paula Moya, eds., *Identity Politics Reconsidered* (New York: Palgrave Macmillan, 2005); Michael Kenny, *The Politics of Identity: Liberal Political Theory and the Dilemmas of Difference* (Cambridge: Polity Press, 2004); Todd Gitlin, *The Twilight of Common Dreams: Why America Is Wracked by Culture Wars* (New York: Owl Books, 1996); Francis Fukuyama, *Trust: The Social Virtues and the Creation of Prosperity* (New York: Free Press, 1995).

65. Robert Wuthnow, "Democratic Liberalism and the Challenge of Diversity in Late-Twentieth-Century America," in *Diversity and Its Discontents: Cultural Conflict and Common Ground in Contemporary American Society*, ed. Neil J. Smelser and Jeffrey C. Alexander (Princeton, NJ: Princeton University Press, 1999) 22, 24.

66. Delia Balassarri and Peter Bearman, "Dynamics of Political Polarization," *American Sociological Review* 72 (2007): 784–811; Morris Fiorina, with Samuel Abrams, and Jeremy Pope, *Culture Wars? The Myth of Polarized America* (New York: Pearson Longman, 2005); John Evans, "Have Americans' Attitudes Become More Polarized? An Update," *Social Science Quarterly* 84 (2003): 71–90.

67. John Hall and Charles Lindholm, *Is America Breaking Apart?* (Princeton, NJ: Princeton University Press, 1999), xi.

68. Li Minghuan, *"We Need Two Worlds": Chinese Immigrant Associations in a Western Society* (Amsterdam: Amsterdam University Press, 1999), 222–224.

69. Tony Horwitz, *Confederates in the Attic: Dispatches from the Unfinished Civil War* (New York: Vintage, 1999).

70. Coretta Phillips, "The Re-Emergence of the 'Black Spectre': Minority Professional Associations in the Post-Macpherson Era," *Ethnic and Racial Studies* 30 (2007): 375–396; Coretta Phillips, "Facing Inwards and Outwards? Institutional Racism, Race Equality and the Role of Black and Asian Professional Associations," *Criminal Justice* 5 (2005): 357–377.

71. John Allen, "Kappa Komeback," *On Wisconsin* 108 (2007): 35–43; Tamara Brown, Gregory Parks, and Clarenda Phillips, eds., *African American Fraternities and Sororities: The Legacy and the Vision* (Lexington: University Press of Kentucky, 2005).

72. Nancy Fraser, "Rethinking the Public Sphere: A Contribution to the Critique of Actually Existing Democracy," in *Habermas and the Public Sphere*, ed. Craig Calhoun (Cambridge, MA: MIT Press, 1992, 109–142), 123. See also Houston Baker, Jr., "Critical Memory and the Black Public Sphere," *Public Culture* 7 (1994): 3–33; Steven Gregory, "Race, Identity and Political Activism: The Shifting Contours

of the African American Public Sphere," *Public Culture* 7 (1994): 147–164; Jacobs, *Race, Media, and the Crisis of Civil Society.*

73. Karyn Lacy, *Blue-Chip Black: Race, Class, and Status in the New Black Middle Class* (Berkeley: University of California Press, 2007).

74. Quoted in Christina Greene, *Our Separate Ways: Women and the Black Freedom Movement in Durham, North Carolina* (Chapel Hill: University of North Carolina Press, 2005), 27.

75. Manning Marable, "Beyond Racial Identity Politics: Towards a Liberation Theory for Multicultural Democracy," in *Critical Race Theory: The Cutting Edge*, 2nd ed., ed. Richard Delgato and Jean Stefancic (Philadelphia: Temple University Press, 2000), 448–454.

76. Walter Benn Michaels, *The Trouble with Diversity: How We Learned to Love Identity and Ignore Inequality* (New York: Holt, 2006); Wuthnow, "Democratic Liberalism and the Challenge of Diversity," 33.

77. Joshua Glenn, "PC Generation, 1964–1973," *Boston Globe*, January 22, 2008.

78. Bill Lind, "The Origins of Political Correctness," Accuracy in Academia Lecture, 2000, http://www.academia.org.

79. Reynolds, *John Brown, Abolitionist.*

80. Joel Olson, *The Abolition of White Democracy* (Minneapolis: University of Minnesota Press, 2004); Alexander, *Civil Sphere*, ch. 14.

81. Bart Landry, *New Black Middle Class* (Berkeley: University of California Press, 1987), 78, 83.

82. Mark Potok, *The Year in Hate and Extremism* (New Orleans: Southern Poverty Law Center, 2014).

83. Rory McVeigh and David Sikkink, "Organized Racism and the Stranger," *Sociological Forum* 20 (2005): 497–522; Josh Adams and Vincent Roscigno, "White Supremacists, Oppositional Culture and the World Wide Web," *Social Forces* 84 (2005): 759–778.

84. Randy Blazak, "White Boys to Terrorist Men: Target Recruitment of Nazi Skinheads," *American Behavioral Scientist* 44 (2001): 982–1000, 994.

85. Kathleen Blee, *Inside Organized Racism: Women in the Hate Movement* (Berkeley: University of California Press, 2002), 75–76.

86. Ibid.

87. Cited in Carol Swain, *The New White Nationalism in America: Its Challenge to Integration* (New York: Cambridge University Press, 2002), 18.

88. Barbara Perry, "Hate Crimes and Identity Politics," *Theoretical Criminology* 6 (2002): 485–491; Michael Kimmel and Abby L. Ferber, "'White Men Are This Nation': Right-Wing Militias and the Restoration of Rural American Masculinity," *Rural Sociology* 65 (2000): 582–604; Blee, *Inside Organized Racism.*

89. Brentin Mock, *Immigration Backlash: Hate Crimes against Latinos Flourish* (Montgomery, AL: Southern Poverty Law Center Intelligence Project, 2007).

90. Meagan Meuchel Wilson, *Hate Crime Victimization, 2004–2012: Statistical Tables* (Washington, DC: U.S. Department of Justice, Bureau of Justice Statistics, 2014).

91. Mock, "Immigration Backlash."

92. Christopher Lyons, "Stigma or Sympathy? Attributions of Fault to Hate Crime Victims and Offenders," *Social Psychology Quarterly* 69 (2006): 39–59; Kathleen Blee, "Racial Violence in the United States," *Ethnic and Racial Studies* 28 (2005): 599–619; Joachim Savelsberg and Ryan King, "Institutionalizing Collective Memories of Hate: Law and Law Enforcement in Germany and the United States," *American Journal of Sociology* 111 (2005): 579–616.

93. Blee, *Inside Organized Racism*, 7, 9, 189–190.

94. Michael Barkun, *Religion and the Racist Right: The Origins of the Christian Identity Movement* (Chapel Hill: University of North Carolina Press, 1994).

95. Seth Stephens-Davidowitz, "The Data of Hate," *New York Times*, July 12, 2014.

96. Cited in Swain, *New White Nationalism in America*, 336.

97. Phyllis Gerstenfeld, Diana Grant, and Chau-Pu Chiang, "Hate Online: A Content Analysis of Extremist Internet Sites," *Analyses of Social Issues and Public Policy* 3 (2003): 29–44; Brian Levin, "History as a Weapon: How Extremists Deny the Holocaust in North America," *American Behavioral Scientist* 44 (2001): 1001–1031; CNN, "Hate Group Web Sites on the Rise," February 23, 1999.

98. Barbara Perry, "'Button-Down Terror': The Metamorphosis of the Hate Movement." *Sociological Focus* 33 (2000): 2, 113–131; Adams and Roscigno, "White Supremacists, Oppositional Culture and the World Wide Web"; Gerstenfeld, Grant, and Chiang, "Hate Online."

99. Cited in Swain, *New White Nationalism in America*, 326.

100. Gerstenfeld, Grant, and Chiang, "Hate Online."

101. Elissa Lee and Laura Leets, "Persuasive Storytelling by Hate Groups Online: Examining Its Effects on Adolescents," *American Behavioral Scientist* 45 (2002): 927–957; Gerstenfeld, Grant, and Chiang, "Hate Online."

102. Cited in Swain, *New White Nationalism in America*, 32.

103. CNN, "Hate Group Web Sites on the Rise."

104. Eli Lehrer, "On the Fringe," *Policy Review* 117 (2003): book reviews.

105. Leslie David Simon, Javier Corrales, and Donald Wolfensberger, *Democracy and the Internet: Allies or Adversaries?* (Washington, DC: Woodrow Wilson Center Press, 2002), 1.

106. U.S. Department of Commerce, *Exploring the Digital Nation: America's Emerging Online Experience* (Washington, DC: U.S. Department of Commerce, 2013).

107. Alondra Nelson, Thuy Linh N. Tu, and Alicia Hines, eds., *TechniColor: Race, Technology, and Everyday Life* (New York: New York University Press, 2001); U.S. Department of Commerce, *Falling through the Net: Toward Digital Inclusion* (Washington, DC: U.S. Department of Commerce, 2000); U.S. Department of Commerce, *Falling through the Net II: New Data on the Digital Divide* (Washington, DC: U.S. Department of Commerce, 1998).

108. Daniel Bell, *The Coming of Post-Industrial Society: A Venture in Social Forecasting* (New York: Basic Books, 1973).

109. Karen Evans, *Maintaining Community in the Information Age: The Importance of Trust, Place and Situated Knowledge* (New York: Palgrave, 2004).

110. Dale Spender, *Nattering on the Net: Women, Power, and Cyberspace* (Melbourne: Spinifex Press, 1995), xvi.

111. BBC, "China Imposes Online Gaming Curbs," August 25, 2005.

112. Urs Gattiker, *The Internet as a Diverse Community: Cultural, Organizational, and Political Issues* (Mahwah, NJ: Lawrence Erlbaum, 2001).

113. Emily Noelle Ignacio, "E-scaping Boundaries: Bridging Cyberspace and Diaspora Studies through Nethnography," in *Critical Cyber-Culture Studies*, ed. David Silver and Adrienne Massanari (New York: New York University Press, 2006), 181–193; Beth Kolko, Lisa Nakamura, and Gilbert Rodman, eds., *Race in Cyberspace* (New York: Routledge, 1999); Lisa Nakamura, *Cybertypes: Race, Ethnicity, and Identity on the Internet* (New York: Routledge, 2002).

114. Brendesha Tynes, Michael T. Giang, David R. Williams, and Geneene N. Thompson, "Online Racial Discrimination and Psychological Adjustment among Adolescents," *Journal of Adolescent Health* 43 (2008): 565–569.

115. Cited in Nakamura, *Cybertypes*, 47.

116. Ibid., 43.

117. Ibid., 56.

118. Michael Dartnell, *Insurgency Online: Web Activism and Global Conflict* (Toronto: University of Toronto Press, 2006); Diana Saco, *Cybering Democracy: Public Space and the Internet* (Minneapolis: University of Minnesota Press, 2002); Evans, *Maintaining Community in the Information Age*; Simon, Corrales, and Wolfensberger, *Democracy and the Internet*.

119. Bharat Mehra, "An Action Research (AR) Manifesto for Cyberculture Power to 'Marginalized' Cultures of Difference," in *Critical Cyber-Culture Studies*, ed. David Silver and Adrienne Massanari (New York: New York University Press, 2006), 205–215.

120. Ignacio, "E-scaping Boundaries," 187. See also Emily Noelle Ignacio, *Building Diaspora: Filipino Community Formation on the Internet* (New Brunswick, NJ: Rutgers University Press, 2005).

121. Mark Warschauer, "Language, Identity, and the Internet," in *Race in Cyberspace*, ed. Beth Kolko, Lisa Nakamura, and Gilbert Rodman (New York: Routledge, 1999), 151–170.

122. The Group of Eight: Australia's Leading Universities, *Languages in Crisis: A Rescue Plan for Australia* (Manuka: Group of Eight, 2007); Stephen May, "Uncommon Languages: The Challenges and Possibilities of Minority Language Rights," *Journal of Multilingual and Multicultural Development* 21 (2000): 366–385.

123. Warschauer, "Language, Identity, and the Internet."

124. The Pluralism Project, *Statistics by Tradition* (Cambridge, MA: Harvard University Press, 2008); Michael Martin, ed., *The Cambridge Companion to Atheism* (New York: Cambridge University Press, 2005); Michael Hout and Claude Fisher, "Americans with 'No Religion': Why Their Numbers Are Growing," *American Sociological Review* 67 (2002): 165–190; U.S. Bureau of the Census, *Self-Described Religious Identification of Adult Population: 1990–2001* (Washington, DC: Government Printing Office, 2002); Ihsan Bagby, Paul Perl, and Bryan Froehle, *The Mosque in America: A National Portrait* (Washington, DC: Council on American-Islamic Relations, 2001); C. Kirk Hadaway and P. L. Marler, "Did You Really Go to Church This Week? Behind the Poll Data," *The Christian Century*, May 6, 1998; Russell Ash, *The Top 10 of Everything* (New York: DK Publishing, 1997); Martin Bauman, "The Dharma Has Come West: A Survey of Recent Studies and Sources," *Journal of Buddhist Ethics* 4 (1997): http://jbe.la.psu.edu; Pew Research, Religion and Public Life Project, *U.S. Religious Landscape Survey* (Washington, DC: Pew Research, 2008).

125. Stephen Prothero, *Religious Literacy: What Every American Needs to Know—And Doesn't* (New York: HarperCollins, 2007).

126. Damien Cave, "For Congress: Telling Sunni and Shiite," *New York Times*, December 17, 2006. See also Resa Aslan, *No God but God: The Origins, Evolution, and Future of Islam* (New York: Random House, 2006).

127. Prothero, *Religious Literacy*.

128. James Wellman, "Is Religious Violence Inevitable?" *Journal for the Scientific Study of Religion* 43 (2004): 291–306; Robert Wuthnow, "The Challenge of Diversity," *Journal for the Scientific Study of Religion* 43 (2004): 159–170.

129. Jeffrey Jones, *Atheists, Muslims See Most Bias as Presidential Candidates* (Princeton, NJ: Gallup, 2012).

130. Nicholas Kristof, "Obama and the Bigots," *New York Times*, March 9, 2008.

131. CNN, "Mosque Plans Trigger Neighbor's Pig Races," December 31, 2006.

132. Gallup, *Islamophobia: Understanding Anti-Muslim Sentiment in the West* (Washington, DC: Gallup, 2014).

133. Lanita Jacobs-Huey, "'The Arab Is the New Nigger': African American Comics Confront the Irony and Tragedy of September 11," *Transforming Anthropology* 14 (2006): 60–64.

134. Michael Kotzin, "Louis Farrakhan's Anti-Semitism: A Look at the Record," *The Christian Century*, March 2, 1994.

135. Yvonne Chireau and Nathaniel Deutsch, eds., *Black Zion: African American Religious Encounters with Judaism* (New York: Oxford University Press, 2000).

136. Martin Forstenzer, "Offering Support for a Menorah, Unofficially," *New York Times*, December 12, 2006.

137. Michael Emerson, "Who's Succeeding at Making Churches More Multiracial?" *Sojourners*, February 2, 2010; Pew Research, Religion and Public Life Project, *U.S. Religious Landscape Survey* (Washington, DC: Pew Research, 2008).

138. George Yancey and Michael Emerson, "Integrated Sundays: An Exploratory Study into the Formation of Multiracial Churches," *Sociological Focus* 36 (2003): 111–126; Michael Emerson and Karen Chai Kim, "Multiracial Congregations: An Analysis of Their Development and a Typology," *Journal for the Scientific Study of Religion* 42 (2003): 217–227; Kevin Dougherty, "How Monochromatic Is Church Membership? Racial- Ethnic Diversity in Religious Community,"

Sociology of Religion 64 (2003): 65–85; Michael Emerson and Christian Smith, *Divided by Faith: Evangelical Religion and the Problem of Race in America* (New York: Oxford University Press, 2001).

139. Michael Battle, *The Black Church in America: African American Christian Spirituality* (Malden, MA: Blackwell, 2006).

140. Barry Kosmin and Egon Mayer, *American Religious Identification Survey* (New York: Graduate Center of the City University of New York, 2001).

141. Omar McRoberts, *Streets of Glory: Church and Community in a Black Urban Neighborhood* (Chicago: University of Chicago Press, 2003), 7.

142. Ibid., 139.

143. *Boston Globe*, "Turning Around Four Corners," November 8, 1999.

144. Pew Research, Religion and Public Life Project, *The Shifting Religious Identity of Latinos in the United States Survey* (Washington, DC: Pew Research, 2014).

145. David Badillo, *Latinos and the New Immigrant Church* (Baltimore, MD: Johns Hopkins University Press, 2006); Gastón Espinosa, Virgilio Elizondo, and Jesse Miranda, *Hispanic Churches in American Public Life: Summary of Findings* (Notre Dame, IN: Institute for Latino Studies, 2003).

146. David Rieff, "Nuevo Catholics," *New York Times Magazine*, December 24, 2006.

147. Samia El-Badry, *Arab American Demographics* (Alexandria: Allied Media Corporation, 2008); Arab American Institute, "Arab American Demographics," www.aaiusa.org.

148. Pew Research, Religion and Public Life Project, *Asian Americans: A Mosaic of Faiths* (Washington, DC: Pew Research, 2012).

149. Russell Jeung, *Faithful Generations: Race and New Asian American Churches* (New Brunswick, NJ: Rutgers University Press, 2005); Pei-te Lien and Tony Carnes, "The Religious Demography of Asian American Boundary Crossing," in *Asian American Religions: The Making and Remaking of Borders and Boundaries*, ed. Tony Carnes and Fenggang Yang (New York: New York University Press, 2004), 38–54; Fenggang Yang and Helen Rose Ebaugh, "Transformations in New Immigrant Religions and Their Global Implications," *American Sociological Review* 66 (2001): 269–288.

150. R. Murray Thomas, *Manitou and God: North-American Indian Religions and Christian Culture* (Westport, CT: Praeger, 2007); Vine Deloria, Jr., *For This Land: Writings on Religion in America* (New York: Routledge, 1999).

151. Deloria, *For This Land*, 125.

152. Michael Hittman, "Native American Church/Peyote Movement," in *American Indian Religious Traditions: An Encyclopedia*, ed. Suzanne Crawford and Dennis Kelley (Santa Barbara, CA: ABC-CLIO, 2005), 2:599–617.

153. Deloria, *For This Land*, 123.

154. Joseph Epes Brown, *Teaching Spirits: Understanding Native American Religious Traditions* (New York: Oxford University Press, 2001); Deloria, *For This Land*.

155. Pew Research, Religion and Public Life Project, *U.S. Religious Landscape Survey* (Washington, DC: Pew Research, 2008).

156. Carl Bankston, III, "Sangha of the South: Laotian Buddhism and Social Adaptation in Rural Louisiana," in *Contemporary Asian America: A Multidisciplinary Reader*, ed. Min Zhou and James Gatewood (New York: New York University Press, 2000), 357–371; Kosmin and Mayer, *American Religious Identification Survey*.

157. Pew Research, Religion and Public Life Project, *Muslim Americans: No Signs of Growth in Alienation or Support for Extremism* (Washington, DC: Pew Research, 2008).

158. Pew Research, Religion and Public Life Project, *U.S. Religious Landscape Survey* (Washington, DC: Pew Research, 2008).

159. Andrea Elliot, "Muslim Immigration Has Bounced Back," *Seattle Times*, September 10, 2006; Edward Curtis, IV, *Islam in Black America: Identity, Liberation, and Difference in African-American Islamic Thought* (Albany: State University of New York Press, 2002); Bagby, Perl, and Froehle, *Mosque in America*.

160. Eric Goldstein, *The Price of Whiteness: Jews, Race, and American Identity* (Princeton, NJ: Princeton University Press, 2006).

161. Kosmin and Mayer, *American Religious Identification Survey*; Chireau and Deutsch, *Black Zion*.

162. Emerson and Kim, "Multiracial Congregations," 217, emphasis ours.

163. Rodney Stark and Roger Finke, *Acts of Faith: Explaining the Human Side of Religion* (Berkeley: University of California Press, 2000); Emerson and Kim, "Multiracial Congregations," 219.

164. Penny Edgell and Eric Tranby, "Religious Influences on Understandings of Racial Inequality in the United States," *Social Problems* 54 (2007): 263–288; Victor Hinojosa and Jerry Park, "Religion and the Paradox of Racial Inequality Attitudes," *Journal for the Scientific Study of Religion* 42 (2004): 229–238.

165. Emerson and Smith, *Divided by Faith*, 170, 116–117.

166. Ibid., 86–87.

167. Elaine Howard Ecklund, "'Us' and 'Them': The Role of Religion in Mediating and Challenging the 'Model Minority' and Other Civic Boundaries," *Ethnic and Racial Studies* 28 (2005): 132–150; McRoberts, *Streets of Glory*.

168. Pyong Gap Min, "The Structure and Social Functions of Korean Immigrant Churches in the United States," in *Contemporary Asian America: A Multidisciplinary Reader*, ed. Min Zhou and James Gatewood (New York: New York University Press, 2000), 372–391; Silvano Tomasi, *Religious Experience of Italian Americans* (New York: American Italian Historical Association, 1973).

169. Min, "Structure and Social Functions of Korean Immigrant Churches"; Emerson and Kim, "Multiracial Congregations"; Badillo, *Latinos and the New Immigrant Church*.

170. Frances Kostarelos, *Feeling the Spirit: Faith and Hope in an Evangelical Black Storefront Church* (Columbia: University of South Carolina Press, 1995); E. Franklin Frazier, *The Negro Church in America* (New York: Schocken Books, 1963); Min, "Structure and Social Functions of Korean Immigrant Churches."

171. Cornel West, *Prophesy Deliverance! An Afro-American Revolutionary Christianity*, Anniversary Edition (Louisville, KY: Westminster John Knox Press, 2002 [1982]); Morris, *Origins of the Civil Rights Movement*; Deloria, *For This Land*.

172. Pierrette Hondagneu Sotelo, *God's Heart Has No Borders: How Religious Activists Are Working for Immigrant Rights* (Berkeley: University of California Press, 2008); Pierrette Hondagneu Sotelo, ed., *Religion and Social Justice for Immigrants* (New Brunswick, NJ: Rutgers University Press, 2007); Hillary Cunningham, *God and Caesar at the Rio Grande: Sanctuary and the Politics of Religion* (Minneapolis: University of Minnesota Press, 1995); Gregory L. Wiltfang and Doug McAdam, "The Costs and Risks of Social Activism: A Study of Sanctuary Movement Activism," *Social Forces* 69 (1991): 987–1010.

173. Espinosa, Elizondo, and Miranda, *Hispanic Churches in American Public Life*, 17.

174. Michael Paulson, "U.S. Religious Leaders Embrace Cause of Immigrant Children," *New York Times*, July 23, 2014.

175. Cited in Rieff, "Nuevo Catholics," 85–86.

176. Gregory Stanczak, "Strategic Ethnicity: The Construction of Multi-Racial/Multi-Ethnic Religious Community," *Ethnic and Racial Studies* 29 (2006): 856–881; Robert Webber, *The Younger Evangelicals* (Grand Rapids, MI: Baker Books, 2002); Scott Thumma, *Megachurches Today, 2000* (Hartford, CT: Hartford Institute for Religious Research, 2001); Penny Edgell Becker, "Making Inclusive Communities: Congregations and the 'Problem of Race,'" *Social Problems* 45 (1998): 451–472; Nancy Tatom Ammerman, *Congregation and Community* (New Brunswick, NJ: Rutgers University Press, 1997); John McGreevy, *Parish Boundaries: The Catholic Encounter with Race in the Twentieth- Century Urban North* (Chicago: University of Chicago Press, 1996); Jeung, *Faithful Generations*, 151–156; Emerson and Kim, "Multiracial Congregations"; Dougherty, "How Monochromatic Is Church Membership?."

177. George Yancey, "An Examination of the Effects of Residential and Church Integration on Racial Attitudes of Whites," *Sociological Perspectives* 42 (1999): 279–304.

178. Troy Blanchard, "Conservative Protestant Congregations and Racial Residential Segregation: Evaluating the Closed Community Thesis in Metropolitan and Nonmetropolitan Counties," *American Sociological Review* 72 (2007): 416–433.

179. Robert Wuthnow, "Can Religion Revitalize Civil Society? An Institutional Perspective," in *Religion as Social Capital: Producing the Common Good*, ed. Corwin Smidt (Waco, TX: Baylor University Press, 2003), 191–209.

Chapter 10: Intimate Life

1. Bourdieu and Wacquant, *Invitation to Reflexive Sociology*, 183.

2. Ibid., 198.

3. Michael Rosenfeld, *The Age of Independence: Interracial Unions, Same-Sex Unions, and the Changing American Family* (Cambridge, MA: Harvard University Press, 2007); Richard Godbeer, *Sexual Revolution in Early America* (Baltimore, MD: Johns Hopkins University Press, 2002); Michael Drake, ed., *Time, Family and Community: Perspectives on Family and Community History* (Oxford: Blackwell, 1994); Edmund Morgan, *The Puritan Family: Religion and Domestic Relations in Seventeenth-Century New England* (New York: Harper, 1966 [1944]).

4. Judith Stacy, *Brave New Families: Stories of Domestic Upheaval in Late Twentieth Century America* (New York: Basic Books, 1991); Lillian Faderman, *Odd Girls and Twilight Lovers: A History of Lesbian Life in Twentieth-Century America* (New York: Penguin, 1991); Rosenfeld, *Age of Independence*.

5. Orlando Patterson, "Broken Bloodlines: Gender Relations and the Crisis of Marriages and Families among Afro-Americans," in Orlando Patterson, *Rituals of Blood: Consequences of Slavery in Two American Centuries* (New York: Basic Books, 1998), 1–168.

6. Willie Lee Rose, *Slavery and Freedom* (New York: Oxford University Press, 1982), 37–48.

7. Jacqueline Jones, *Labor of Love, Labor of Sorrow: Black Women, Work, and the Family from Slavery to the Present* (New York: Basic Books, 1985), 27.

8. William Dunaway, *The African-American Family in Slavery and Emancipation* (New York: Cambridge University Press, 2003); Wilma King, *Stolen Children: Slave Youth in Nineteenth-Century America* (Bloomington: Indiana University Press, 1995), 13.

9. Deborah Gray White, *Ar'n't I a Woman? Female Slaves in the Plantation South* (New York: Norton, 1985).

10. Jones, *Labor of Love, Labor of Sorrow*, 32.

11. Toni Morrison, *Beloved* (New York: Plume, 1988), 162.

12. Tamara Hareven, *Families, History, and Social Change: Life-Course and Cross Cultural Perspectives* (Boulder, CO: Westview, 2000); Donna Franklin, *Ensuring Inequality: The Structural Transformation of the African-American Family* (New York: Oxford University Press, 1997); Stewart Tolnay, "Black Family Formation and Tenancy in the Farm South, 1900," *American Journal of Sociology* 90 (1984): 305–325.

13. Frank Furstenberg, "The Making of the Black Family: Race and Class in Qualitative Studies in the Twentieth Century," *Annual Review of Sociology* 33 (2007): 429–448; John Dollard, *Caste and Class in a Southern Town* (Madison: University of Wisconsin Press, 1989); Hortense Powdermaker, *After Freedom: A Cultural Study of the Deep South* (New York: Viking, 1939); Jones, *Labor of Love, Labor of Sorrow*; Patterson, "Broken Bloodlines."

14. Roberts, *Killing the Black Body*, 56, 90.

15. Aaron Gullickson, "Black/White Interracial Marriage Trends, 1850–2000," *Journal of Family History* 31 (2006): 289–312; Martha Hodes, *White Women, Black Men: Illicit Sex in the Nineteenth-Century South* (New Haven, CT: Yale University Press, 1997); Joel Williamson, *New People: Miscegenation and Mulattoes in the United States* (Baton Rouge: Louisiana State University Press, 1995); Gary Mills, "Miscegenation and the Free Negro in Antebellum 'Angle' Alabama: A Reexamination of Southern Race Relations," *Journal of American History* 68 (1981): 16–34.

16. Dennesh Sohoni, "Creating the Excluded: Anti-Miscegenation Laws and the Construction of Asian Identity" (paper presented at the American Sociological Association Conference, Montreal, August 2006); Kevin Johnson, ed., *Mixed Race America and the Law: A Reader* (New York: New York University Press, 2003).

17. Cited in Timothy Tyson, *Blood Done Sign My Name* (New York: Three Rivers Press, 2004), 39.

18. Gullickson, "Black/White Interracial Marriage Trends, 1850–2000."

19. Cecilia Conrad, "Racial Trends in Labor Market Access and Wages: Women," in *America Becoming: Racial Trends and Their Consequences*, ed. Neil Smelser, William Julius Wilson, and Faith Mitchell (Washington, DC: National Academy Press, 2001), 2:124–151; Rosenfeld, *Age of Independence*; Stacy, *Brave New Families*; Jones, *Labor of Love, Labor of Sorrow*.

20. Allan Bérubé, *Coming Out under Fire: The History of Gay Men and Women in World War Two* (New York: Free Press, 1990), 6.

21. Renee Romano, *Race Mixing: Black-White Marriage in Postwar America* (Cambridge, MA: Harvard University Press, 2003).

22. Stacy, *Brave New Families*, 12.

23. Jennifer Lee and Frank Bean, "America's Changing Color Lines: Immigration, Race/ Ethnicity, and Multiracial Identification," *Annual Review of Sociology* 30 (2004): 221–242.

24. Rachel Moran, *Interracial Intimacy: The Regulation of Race and Romance* (Chicago: University of Chicago Press, 2001); Gary Sandefur, Molly Martin, Jennifer Eggerling- Boeck, Susan Mannon, and Ann Meier, "An Overview of Racial and Ethnic Demographic Trends," in *America Becoming: Racial Trends and Their Consequences*, ed. Neil Smelser, William Julius Wilson, and Faith Mitchell (Washington, DC: National Academy Press, 2001), 1:40–102; Rosenfeld, *Age of Independence*, 4, 68–71, 80–82.

25. U.S. Census, *Households and Families: 2010* (Washington, DC: U.S. Bureau of the Census, 2012).

26. Wendy Wang, *The Rise of Intermarriage* (Washington, DC: Pew Research and Social Demographic Trends, 2012).

27. Gary Gates, *Same-Sex Couples in Census 2010: Race and Ethnicity* (Washington, DC: U.S. Bureau of the Census, 2012).

28. Howard Schuman, Charlotte Steeh, Lawrence Bobo, and Maria Krysan, *Racial Attitudes in America: Trends and Interpretations*, rev. ed. (Cambridge, MA: Harvard University Press, 1997), 106–107, 242–243.

29. Wang, *Rise of Intermarriage*.

30. Arlie Russell Hochschild, *The Second Shift* (New York: Avon Books, 1990); R. W. Connell, *Gender and Power* (Stanford, CA: Stanford University Press, 1987).

31. Deborah King, "Multiple Jeopardy, Multiple Consciousness: The Context of a Black Feminist Ideology," in *Words of Fire: An Anthology of African-American Feminist Thought*, ed. Beverly Guy-Sheftall (New York: The New Press, 1995), 294–317; bell hooks, *Feminist Theory: From Margin to Center* (Boston: South End Press, 1984); Collins, *Black Feminist Thought*; Jones, *Labor of Love, Labor of Sorrow*; Mohanty, *Feminism without Borders*.

32. Economist, *Pocket World in Figures, 2007 Edition*, 88–89.

33. Julissa Cruz, *Marriage: More than a Century of Change* (Bowling Green, OH: NCFMR, 2013).

34. Ibid.; Nancy Landale and R. S. Oropesa, "Hispanic Families: Stability and Change," *Annual Review of Sociology* 33 (2007): 381–405; Jay Teachman, Lucky Tedrow, and Kyle Crowder, "The Changing Demography of America's Families," *Journal of Marriage and the Family* 62 (2000): 1234–1246.

35. Pamela Smock, "Cohabitation in the United States: An Appraisal of Research Themes, Findings, and Implications," *Annual Review of Sociology* 26 (2000): 1–20; Larry Bumpass and Hsien-Hen Wu, "Trends in Cohabitation and Implications for Children's Family Contexts in the U.S.," *Population Studies* 54 (2000): 29–41; Larry Bumpass and Hsien-Hen Wu, "Cohabitation: How Families of U.S. Children Are Changing," *Focus* (2000): 4–7.

36. Brian Duncan, V. Joseph Hotz, and Stephen Trejo, "Hispanics in the U.S. Labor Market," in *Hispanics and the Future of America*, ed. Marta Tienda and Faith Mitchell (Washington, DC: National Academies Press, 2006), 228–290; Valerie Kincade Oppenheimer, "The Continuing Importance of Men's Economic Position in Marriage Formation," in *Ties That Bind: Perspectives on Marriage and Cohabitation*, ed. Linda Waite, Christine Bachrach, Michelle Hindin, Elizabeth Thomson, and Arland Thornton (Hawthorne, NY: Aldine de Gruyter, 2000), 283–301; Valerie Kincade Oppenheimer, "A Theory of Marriage Timing," *American Journal of Sociology* 94 (1988): 563–591.

37. Wilson, *Truly Disadvantaged*, 83. See also Scott South and Glenna Spitze, "Determinants of Divorce over the Marital Life Course," *American Sociological Review* 51 (1986): 583–590; Teachman, Tedrow, and Crowder, "Changing Demography of America's Families," 1237–1238.

38. Adam Liptak, "U.S. Imprisons One in 100 Adults, Report Finds," *New York Times*, February 29, 2008.

39. William Sabol and James Lynch, "Assessing the Longer-Run Consequences of Incarceration: Effects on Families and Employment," in *Crime Control and Social Justice: The Delicate Balance*, ed. Darnell Hakins, Samuel Myers, Jr., and Randolph Stone (Westport, CT: Greenwood Press, 2003), 3–26; Western, *Punishment and Inequality in America*, 139–145.

40. Belinda Robnett and Cynthia Feliciano, "Patterns of Racial-Ethnic Exclusion by Internet Daters," *Social Forces* 89 (2011): 819.

41. Ken-Hou Lin and Jennifer Lundquist, "Mate Selection in Cyberspace: The Intersection of Race, Gender, and Education," *American Journal of Sociology* 118 (2013): 183–215.

42. Mary McCullough, *Black and White Women as Friends: Building Cross-Race Friendships* (Cresskill, NJ: Hampton Press, 1998).

43. Maureen Reddy, *Crossing the Color Line: Race, Parenting, and Culture* (New Brunswick, NJ: Rutgers University Press, 1994), 81.

44. Gloria Wade-Gayles, *Rooted against the Wind* (Boston: Beacon Press, 1996), 110.

45. Wang, *Rise of Intermarriage*.

46. Ibid.; Zhenchao Qian and Daniel Lichter, "Social Boundaries and Marital Assimilation: Interpreting Trends in Racial and Ethnic Intermarriage," *American Sociological Review* 72 (2007): 68–94; Rosalind Berkowitz King and Jenifer Bratter, "A Path toward Interracial Marriage: Women's First Partners and Husbands across Racial Lines," *Sociological Quarterly* 48 (2007): 343–369; Christine Batson, Zhenchao Qian, and Daniel Lichter, "Interracial and Intraracial Patterns of Mate Selections among America's Diverse Black Population," *Journal of Marriage and the Family* 68 (2006): 658–672; Tavia Simmons and Martin O'Connell, *Married-Couple and Unmarried-Partner Households, 2000* (Washington, DC: Bureau of the Census, 2003); Randall Kennedy, *Interracial Intimacies: Sex, Marriage, Identity, and Adoption* (New York: Pantheon, 2003); Lee and Bean, "America's Changing Color Lines."

47. Robnett and Feliciano, "Patterns of Racial-Ethnic Exclusion."

48. Colleen Fong and Judy Yung, "In Search of the Right Spouse: Interracial Marriage among Chinese and Japanese Americas," in *Contemporary Asian America: A Multidisciplinary Reader*, ed. Min Zhou and James Gatewood (New York: New York University Press, 2000), 589–605, 599.

49. Eduardo Bonilla-Silva, Carla Goar, and David Embrick, "When Whites Flock Together: The Social Psychology of White Habitus," *Critical Sociology* 32 (2006): 229–253.

50. Ronne Hartfield, *Another Way Home: The Tangled Roots of Race in One Chicago Family* (Chicago: University of Chicago Press, 2004), xv. See also Barbara Katz Rothman, *Weaving a Family: Untangling Race and Adoption* (Boston: Beacon Press, 2005).

51. Jeana Bracey, Mayra Bámaca, and Adriana Uma-a-Taylor, "Examining Ethnic Identity and Self-Esteem among Biracial and Monoracial Adolescents," *Journal of Youth and Adolescence* 33 (2004): 123–132; Grace Koa, "Racial Identity and Academic Performance: An Examination of Biracial Asian and African American Youth," *Journal of Asian American Studies* 2 (1999): 223–249; Maria Root, ed., *The Multicultural Experience: Racial Borders as the New Frontier* (Thousand Oaks, CA: Sage, 1996); Ana Mari Cauce et al., "Between a Rock and a Hard Place: Social Adjustment of Biracial Youth," in *Racially Mixed People in America*, ed. Maria Root (Thousand Oaks, CA: Sage, 1992), 207–222.

52. Elliott Lewis, *Face: My Journeys in Multiracial America* (New York: Carroll and Graf, 2006); SanSan Kwan and Kenneth Speirs, eds., *Mixing It Up: Multiracial Subjects* (Austin: University of Texas Press, 2004).

53. Cited in Heather Dalmage, *Tripping the Color Line: Black-White Multiracial Families in a Racially Divided World* (New Brunswick, NJ: Rutgers University Press, 2000), 29.

54. Wendy Roth, "The End of the One-Drop Rule? Labeling of Multiracial Children in Black Intermarriages," *Sociological Forum* 20 (2005): 35–67.

55. Lee and Bean, "America's Changing Color Lines."

56. Wang, *Rise of Intermarriage*.

57. David Crary, "Interracial Marriages Surge across U.S.," *USA Today*, April 12, 2007.

58. Richard Cohen, "Christie's Tea-Party Problem," *Washington Post*, November 11, 2013.

59. Kara Joyner and Grace Kao, "Interracial Relationships and the Transition to Adulthood," *American Sociological Review* 70 (2005): 563–581; Maria Root, *Love's Revolution: Interracial Marriage* (Philadelphia: Temple University Press, 2001); Romano, *Race Mixing*.

60. Jenifer Bratter and Karl Eschbach, "'What about the Couple?' Interracial Marriage and Psychological Distress," *Social Science Research* 35 (2006): 1025–1047.

61. Dalmage, *Tripping the Color Line*, 21.

62. Reddy, *Crossing the Color Line*, 80–85. See also Allen Fisher, "Still 'Not Quite as Good as Having Your Own'? Toward a Sociology of Adoption," *Annual Review of Sociology* 29 (2003): 335–361; Jiannbin Lee Shiao and Mia Tuan, "Korean Adoptees and the Social Context of Ethnic Exploration," *American Journal of Sociology* 113 (2008): 1023–1066.

63. Jane Addams, *Democracy and Social Ethics* (Urbana: University of Illinois Press, 2002 [1902]), 7.

64. Economist, *Pocket World in Figures, 2007 Edition*, 88–89.

65. Sucheng Chan, *Hmong Means Free* (Philadelphia: Temple University Press, 1994). See also Nazli Kibria, "Household Structure and Family Ideologies: The Dynamics of Immigrant Economic Adaptation among Vietnamese Refugees," *Social Problems* 41 (1994): 81–96.

66. Mary Waters, "Immigrant Families at Risk: Factors That Undermine Chances for Success," in *Immigration and the Family: Research and Policy on U.S. Immigrants*, ed. Alan Booth, Ann Crouter, and Nancy Landale (Mahwah, NJ: Lawrence Erlbaum, 1997, 79–87), 84. See also Nancy Foner, "The Immigrant Family: Cultural Legacies and Cultural Changes," in *The New Immigration: An Interdisciplinary Reader*, ed. Marcelo Suárez-Orozco, Carola Suárez-Orozco, and Desirée Baolian Qin (New York: Routledge, 2005), 157–166.

67. Carola Suárez-Oroz, Irina Todorova, and Josephine Louie, "Making Up for Lost Time: The Experience of Separation and Reunification among Immigrant Families," in *The New Immigration: An Interdisciplinary Reader*, ed. Marcelo Suárez-Orozco, Carola Suárez-Orozco, and Desirée Baolian Qin (New York: Routledge, 2005), 179–196.

68. Waters, "Immigrant Families at Risk," 81.

69. U.S. Census Bureau, *America's Families and Living Arrangements: March 2000* by Jason Fields and Lynne Casper, (Washington, DC: Government Printing Office, 2001); Teachman, Tedrow, and Crowder, "Changing Demography of America's Families."

70. Western, *Punishment and Inequality in America*, ch. 6.

71. Elliot Liebow, *Tally's Corner: A Study of Negro Streetcorner Men* (Boston: Little, Brown, 1967), 131, 135–136.

72. Andrew Clarkwest, "Spousal Dissimilarity, Race, and Marital Dissolution," *Journal of Marriage and Family* 69 (2007): 639–653.

73. Jennifer Hickes Lundquist, "The Black-White Gap in Marital Dissolution among Young Adults: What Can a Counterfactual Scenario Tell Us?" *Social Problems* 53 (2006): 421–441; Douglas Massey, "Segregation and Stratification: A Biosocial Perspective," *Du Bois Review* 1 (2004): 7–25; Bruce McEwan, "Allostasis and Allostatic Load: Implications for Neuropsychopharmacology," *Neuropsychopharmacology* 22 (2000): 108–124.

74. Kathleen Kiernan, "European Perspectives on Nonmarital Childbearing," in *Out of Wedlock: Causes and Consequences of Nonmarital Fertility*, ed. Lawrence Wu and Barbara Wolfe (New York: Russell Sage Foundation, 2001), 77–108.

75. Kathryn Edin and Maria Kefalas, *Promises I Can Keep: Why Poor Women Put Motherhood before Marriage* (Berkeley: University of California Press, 2005), 2.

76. Joyce Martin et al., *National Vital Statistics Reports* (Washington, DC: U.S. Department of Health and Human Services, 2013).

77. Maria Cancian and Daniel Meyer, "Responding to Changing Family Organization," *Focus* 22 (2002): 87–92; Lawrence Wu and Barbara Wolfe, "Introduction," in *Out of Wedlock: Causes and Consequences of Nonmarital Fertility*, ed. Lawrence Wu and Barbara Wolfe (New York: Russell Sage Foundation, 2001), xiii–xxxii; Lawrence Wu, Larry Bumpass, and Kelly Musick, "Historical and Life Course

Trajectories of Nonmarital Childbearing," in *Out of Wedlock: Causes and Consequences of Nonmarital Fertility*, ed. Lawrence Wu and Barbara Wolfe (New York: Russell Sage Foundation, 2001), 3–48.

78. Federal Interagency Forum on Children and Family Statistics, *America's Children: Key National Indicators of Well-Being, 2013* (Washington, DC: Federal Interagency Forum on Children and Family Statistics, 2013).

79. Cameron Lynne Macdonald, "Life without Father: Single Mothers in the New America," *Qualitative Sociology* 31 (2008): 89–94. See also Rosanna Hertz, *Single by Chance, Mothers by Choice: How Women Are Choosing Parenthood without Marriage and Creating the New American Family* (New York: Oxford University Press, 2006); Margaret Nelson, *The Social Economy of Single Motherhood: Raising Children in Rural America* (New York: Routledge, 2005).

80. Irwin Garfinkel and Sara McLanahan, "Unwed Parents: Myths, Realities, and Policymaking," *Focus* 22 (2002): 93–97.

81. Federal Interagency Forum on Children and Family Statistics, *America's Children*.

82. Office of Adolescent Health, *Trends in Teen Pregnancy and Childbearing* (Washington, DC: U.S. Department of Health and Human Services, 2013).

83. Bill O'Reilly, *Are African Americans Ignoring Collapse of the Family?* (New York: Fox News, July 16, 2012).

84. Coates, Ta-Nehisi. "Understanding Out-of-Wedlock Births in Black America." *The Atlantic*. June 21, 2014. http://www.theatlantic.com/sexes/archive/2013/06/ understanding-out-of-wedlock-births -in-black-america/277084/

85. Western, *Punishment and Inequality in America*, 137–138.

86. Rachel Shattuck and Rose Kreider, *Social and Economic Characteristics of Currently Unmarried Women with a Recent Birth: 2011* (Washington, DC: U.S. Bureau of the Census, 2013).

87. Patterson, "Broken Bloodlines," 25.

88. Karen Benjamin Guzzo and Frank Furstenberg, Jr., "Multipartnered Fertility among American Men," *Demography* 44 (2007): 583–601.

89. Ronald Mincy and Chien-Chung Huang, "The 'M' Word: The Rise and Fall of Interracial Coalitions on Fathers and Welfare Reform" (paper presented at the Welfare Reform and Child Well-being Conference, Bowling Green State University, March 1, 2002).

90. Kenneth Clark, *Dark Ghetto: Dilemmas of Social Power* (New York: Harper and Row, 1965), 72.

91. Edin and Kefalas, *Promises I Can Keep*, 9.

92. Ibid., 9.

93. Ibid., 6.

94. Michelle Ver Ploeg, "Children from Disrupted Families as Adults: Family Structure, College Attendance and College Completion," *Economics of Education Review* 21 (2002): 171–184; Andrew Cherlin, "New Developments in the Study of Nonmarital Childbearing," in *Out of Wedlock: Causes and Consequences of Nonmarital Fertility*, ed. Lawrence Wu and Barbara Wolfe (New York: Russell Sage Foundation, 2001), 390–402; Sara McLanahan and Gary Sandefur, *Growing Up with a Single Parent: What Hurts, What Helps* (Cambridge, MA: Harvard University Press, 1994).

95. Timothy Grall, *Custodial Mothers and Fathers and Their Child Support: 2003* (Washington, DC: Bureau of the Census, 2006); Elaine Sorensen and Chava Zibman, "Getting to Know Poor Fathers Who Do Not Pay Child Support," *Social Service Review* 75 (2001): 420–434.

96. Ruth N. López Turley and Matthew Desmond, "Contributions to College Costs by Married and Divorced Parents," Institute for Research on Poverty, University of Wisconsin–Madison, 2008; Martha Hill, "The Role of Economic Resources and Remarriage in Financial Assistance for Children of Divorce," *Journal of Family Issues* 13 (1992): 158–178; Sara McLanahan and Karen Booth, "Mother-Only Families: Problems, Prospects, and Politics," *Journal of Marriage and the Family* 51 (1989): 557–580.

97. Edin and Lein, *Making Ends Meet*, 2; Karen Christopher, "A 'Pauperization' of Motherhood'? Single Motherhood and Women's Poverty over Time," *Journal of Poverty* 9 (2005): 1–23;. Sara McLanahan and Erin Kelley, "The Feminization of Poverty: Past and Present," in Janet Saltzman Chafetz, ed., *Handbook of the Sociology of Gender*, ed. Janet Saltzman Chafetz (New York: Kluwer Academic Publishing, 1999), 127–146; Cancian and Meyer, "Responding to Changing Family Organization," 87.

98. H. Luke Shaefer and Kathryn Edin, "Rising Extreme Poverty in the United States and the Response of Federal Means-Tested Transfer Programs," *Social Service Review* 87 (2013): 250–226.

99. Edin and Lein, *Making Ends Meet*, 5. See also Joanna Lipper, *Growing Up Fast* (New York: Picador, 2003); Lillian Rubin, *Families on the Fault Line: America's Working Class Speaks about the Family, the Economy, Race, and Ethnicity* (New York: HarperCollins, 1994).

100. Suet-Ling Pong and Dong-Beom Ju, "The Effects of Change in Family Structure and Income on Dropping out of Middle and High School," *Journal of Family Issues* 21 (2000): 147–169; Sara McLanahan, "Family Structure and the Reproduction of Poverty," *American Journal of Sociology* 90 (1985): 873–901; Ver Ploeg, "Children from Disrupted Families as Adults."

101. Erving Goffman, *Interaction Ritual* (Garden City, NY: Anchor Books, 1967), 1.

102. Erving Goffman, "The Interaction Order: American Sociological Association, 1982 Presidential Address," *American Sociological Review* 48 (1983): 1–17; Erving Goffman, *The Presentation of Self in Everyday Life* (Garden City, NY: Anchor Books, 1959).

103. W. E. B. Du Bois, "The Souls of White Folk," in W. E. B. Du Bois, *Darkwater: Voices from within the Veil* (Mineola, NY: Dover, 1999 [1920]), 17.

104. Patricia Williams, "The Pantomime of Race," in *Seeing a Colorblind Future: The Paradox of Race*, ed. Patricia Williams (New York: Noonday Press, 1997, 17–30), 27.

105. Douglas Maynard and Don Zimmerman, "Topical Talk Ritual and the Social Organization of Relationships," *Social Psychology Quarterly* 47 (1984): 301–316; Ann Rawls, "'Race' as an Interaction Order Phenomenon: W. E. B. DuBois's 'Double Consciousness' Thesis Revisited," *Sociological Theory* (2002) 18: 241–274.

106. Rawls, "'Race' as an Interaction Order Phenomenon."

107. Thomas Kochman, *Black and White: Styles in Conflict* (Chicago: Free Press, 1981); William Labov, *Language in the Inner City* (Philadelphia: University of Pennsylvania Press, 1972); Rawls, "'Race' as an Interaction Order Phenomenon."

108. Rawls, "'Race' as an Interaction Order Phenomenon."

109. In Studs Terkel, *Race: How Blacks and Whites Think and Feel about the American Obsession* (New York: New Press, 1992), 289.

110. Frantz Fanon, *Black Skin, White Masks* (New York: Grove Press, 1952), 44.

111. Johnson, *Appropriating Blackness*, 30.

112. Ibid., 239–240.

113. Hartigan, *Odd Tribes*; Hartigan, *Racial Situations*.

114. Jill Denner and Bianca Guzmán, eds., *Latina Girls: Voices of Strength in the United States* (New York: New York University Press, 2006); Ed Morales, *Living in Spanglish: The Search for Latino Identity in America* (New York: St. Martin's, 2002).

115. Mia Tuan, *Forever Foreigners or Honorary Whites? The Asian Ethnic Experience Today* (New Brunswick, NJ: Rutgers University Press, 2003), 147, 149. See also Ellen Alexander Conley, *The Chosen Shore: Stories of Immigrants* (Berkeley: University of California Press, 2004); Abdelmalek Sayad, *The Suffering of the Immigrant* (Malden, MA: Polity Press, 2004)..

116. Bryant Keither Alexander, *Performing Black Masculinity: Race, Culture, and Queer Identity* (Lanham, MD: Altamira, 2006); Matthew Desmond, *On the Fireline: Living and Dying with Wildland Firefighters* (Chicago: University of Chicago Press, 2007); bell hooks, *We Real Cool: Black Men and Masculinity* (New York: Routledge, 2003); Richard Majors, *Cool Pose: The Dilemmas of Black Manhood in America* (New York: Touchstone, 1993).

117. Joanne Rondilla and Paul Spickard, *Is Lighter Better? Skin-Tone Discrimination among Asian Americans* (Lanham, MD: Rowman and Littlefield, 2007), 51.

118. Joane Nagel, "Ethnicity and Sexuality," *Annual Review of Sociology* 26 (2000): 107–133. See also Abdul JanMohamed, "Sexuality on/of the Racial Border: Foucault, Wright, and the Articulation of 'Racialized Sexuality,'" in *Discourses of Sexuality: From Aristotle to AIDS*, ed. Donna Stanton (Ann Arbor: University of Michigan Press, 1992), 117–137.

119. Sharmila Rudrappa, *Ethnic Routes to Becoming American: Indian Immigrants and the Cultures of Citizenship* (New Brunswick, NJ: Rutgers University Press, 2004). See also Yen Le Espiritu, "'We Don't Sleep around Like White Girls Do': Family, Culture, and Gender in Filipina American Lives," *Signs: Journal of Women and Culture in Society* 26 (2001): 415–440; Monisha Das Gupta, "What Is Indian about You?" A Gendered, Transnational Approach to Ethnicity," *Gender and Society* 11 (1997): 573–596.

120. Joshua Gamson and Dawne Moon, "The Sociology of Sexualities: Queer and Beyond," *Annual Review of Sociology* 30 (2004): 47–64; Michael Kimmel and Rebecca Plante, eds., *Sexualities: Identities, Behaviors, and Society* (New York: Oxford University Press, 2004); Henry Yu, "Mixing Bodies and Cultures: The Meaning of America's Fascination with Sex between 'Orientals' and 'Whites,'" in *Sex, Love, Race: Crossing Boundaries in North American History*, ed. Martha Hodes (New York: New York University Press, 1999), 423–463.

121. Beniot Denizet-Lewis, "Double Lives on the Down Low," *New York Times Magazine*, April 3, 2003; Estelle Freedman, "The Prison Lesbian: Race, Class, and the Construction of the Aggressive Female Homosexual, 1915–1965," in *Sex, Love, Race: Crossing Boundaries in North American History*, ed. Martha Hodes (New York: New York University Press, 1999), 423–443; Rafael D'az, *Latino Gay Men and HIV: Culture, Sexuality, and Risk Behavior* (New York: Routledge, 1997); Rosenfeld, *Age of Independence*.

122. Marla Brettschneider, *The Family Flamboyant: Race Politics, Queer Families, Jewish Lives* (New York: State University of New York Press, 2006); Earl Ofari Hutchinson, "My Gay Problem, Your Black Problem," in *Black Men on Race, Gender, and Sexuality: A Critical Reader*, ed. Devon Carbado (New York: New York University Press, 1999), 303–305; David Eng and Alice Hom, eds., *Queer in Asian America* (Philadelphia: Temple University Press, 1998).

123. Eldridge Cleaver, *Soul on Ice* (New York: McGraw-Hill, 1968), 101–102.

124. Niels Teunis and Gilbert Herdt, eds., *Sexual Inequalities and Social Justice* (Berkeley: University of California Press, 2007); Chong-suk Han, "They Don't Want to Cruise Your Type: Gay Men of Color and the Racial Politics of Exclusion," *Social Identities* 13 (2007): 51–67; Martin Manalansan, IV, "Queer Intersections: Sexuality and Gender in Migration Studies," *International Migration Review* 20 (2006): 224–249; Johnson, *Appropriating Blackness*.

125. Quoted in Johnnetta Betsch Cole and Beverly Guy-Sheftall, *Gender Talk: The Struggle for Women's Equality in African American Communities* (New York: Ballantine, 2003), 165.

126. Patricia Hill Collins, *Black Sexual Politics: African Americans, Gender, and the New Racism* (New York: Routledge, 2004).

127. Gloria Hull, Patricia Bell Scott, and Barbara Smith, eds., *All the Women Are White, All the Blacks Are Men, but Some of Us Are Brave* (New York: The Feminist Press, 1982).

128. Jackson, *Harlemworld*, 171, 188.

129. Johnson, *Appropriating Blackness*.

130. See Barbara Summers, *Black and Beautiful: How Women of Color Changed the Fashion Industry* (New York: HarperCollins, 2001); David Thomas and Naomi Campbell, eds., *Soul Style: Black Women Redefining the Color of Fashion* (New York: Universe Publishing, 2000).

131. Hartigan, *Racial Situations*; Patricia Williams, "The Pantomime of Race," in *Seeing a Color-Blind Future: The Paradox of Race*, ed. Patricia Williams (New York: Noonday Press, 1997, 17–30); Jackson, *Harlemworld*, 185.

132. Christian Lander, *Stuff White People Like: The Definitive Guide to the Unique Taste of Millions* (New York: Random House, 2008).

133. Roy, "Aesthetic Identity, Race, and American Folk Music," 461.

134. Mary Douglas, *Natural Symbols: Explorations in Cosmology* (New York: Routledge, 2003 [1970]), 42–43.

135. John Jackson, Jr., *Real Black: Adventures in Racial Sincerity* (Chicago: University of Chicago Press, 2005).

136. Orlando Patterson, "The New Black Nativism," *Time*, February 8, 2007.

137. Jack Forbes, *Black Africans and Native Americans: Color, Race, and Caste in the Evolution of Red-Black Peoples* (Oxford: Blackwell, 1988).

138. James Clifford, "Identity in Mashpee," in *The Predicament of Culture*, ed. James Clifford (Cambridge, MA: Harvard University Press, 1988).

139. Kathleen J. Fitzgerald, *Beyond White Ethnicity: Developing a Sociological Understanding of Native American Identity Reclamation* (Lanham, MD: Lexington Books, 2007); Joane Nagel, *American Indian Ethnic Renewal: Red Power and the Resurgence of Identity and Culture* (New York: Oxford University Press, 1996).

140. Anne Merline McCulloch and David Wilkins, "Constructing Nations within States: The Quest for Federal Recognition by the Catawba and Lumbee Tribes," *American Indian Quarterly* 19 (1995): 361–388, 369.

141. Gershom Gorenberg, "How Do You Prove You're a Jew?" *New York Times Magazine*, March 2, 2008.

142. Garroutte, *Real Indians*, 81.

143. Alastair Bonnett, *White Identities: Historical and International Perspectives* (Essex, UK: Prentice Hall, 2000), 78.

144. Fanon, *Black Skin, White Masks*, 129.

145. Cited in Fitzgerald, *Beyond White Ethnicity*, 2.

146. Fitzgerald, *Beyond White Ethnicity*; Nagel, *American Indian Ethnic Renewal*.

147. Edward Morris, *An Unexpected Minority: White Kids in an Urban School* (New Brunswick, NJ: Rutgers University Press, 2006), 112. See also Dalton Conley, *Honky* (Berkeley: University of California Press, 2000).

148. Amy Wilkins, "Puerto Rican Wannabes: Sexual Spectacle and the Marking of Race, Class, and Gender Boundaries," *Gender and Society* 18 (2004): 103–121, 104. See also Amy Wilkins, *Wannabes, Goths, and Christians: The Boundaries of Sex, Style, and Status* (Chicago: University of Chicago Press, 2008).

149. Wilkins, "Puerto Rican Wannabes," 113.

150. Annegret Staiger, "'Hoes Can Be Hoed Out, Players Can Be Played Out, But Pimp Is for Life'—The Pimp Phenomenon as Strategy of Identity Formation," *Symbolic Interaction* 28 (2005): 407–428.

151. Wilkins, "Puerto Rican Wannabes"; Fitzgerald, *Beyond White Ethnicity*.

152. Cited in Henry Louis Gates, Jr., "The Close Reader; Both Sides Now," *New York Times*, May 4, 2003.

153. Rogers Brubaker and Frederick Cooper, "Beyond 'Identity,'" *Theory and Society* 28 (2000): 1–47.

154. Robert K. Merton, "Insiders and Outsiders: A Chapter in the Sociology of Knowledge," *American Journal of Sociology* 78 (1972): 9–47, 15.

155. Henry Louis Gates, Jr., "'Authenticity,' or the Lesson of Little Tree," *New York Times Book Review*, November 24, 1991, 26.

156. Michaels, *The Trouble with Diversity*, 7, 19–20, 192.

Chapter 11: Toward Racial Democracy

1. Stephen Toulmin, *Cosmopolis: The Hidden Agenda of Modernity* (Chicago: University of Chicago Press, 1992), 75.

2. Elizabeth Anderson, "Dewey's Moral Philosophy," *The Stanford Encyclopedia of Philosophy* (Fall 2012), http://plato.stanford.edu/archives/fall2012/entries/dewey-moral/.

3. King, "I Have a Dream," Washington, DC, August 28, 1963.

4. Brown et al., *White-washing Race*, 7–8.

5. Amy Gutmann, "Responding to Racial Injustice," in Appiah and Gutmann, *Color Conscious*, 108–109.

6. Supreme Court Justice John Harlan, dissenting opinion to *Plessy v. Ferguson* (1896).

7. See, e.g., Tamar Jacoby, *Someone Else's House: America's Unfinished Struggle for Integration* (New York: Basic Books, 1999); Nathan Glazer, *Affirmative Discrimination: Ethnic Inequality and Public Policy* (Cambridge, MA: Harvard University Press, 1975); Dinesh D'Souza, *The End of Racism: Principles for a Multiracial Society* (New York: The Free Press, 1995); Stephen Thernstrom and Abigail Thernstrom, *America in Black and White: One Nation, Indivisible* (New York: Simon and Schuster, 1997).

8. Todd Gitlin, *The Twilight of Common Dreams: Why America is Wracked by Culture Wars* (New York: Metropolitan Books, 1995); see also Jim Sleeper, *Liberal Racism: How Fixating on Race Subverts the American Dream*, 2nd Edition (Lanham, MD: Rowman & Littlefield, 2002).

9. Barack Obama, "Keynote Address," Democratic National Convention, Boston, MA, July 27, 2004.

10. William James, *Pragmatism* (Indianapolis, IN: Hackett, 1981 [1907]), 26.

11. Elizabeth Anderson, *The Imperative of Integration* (Princeton, NJ: Princeton University Press, 2010), 165.

12. Supreme Court Chief Justice John Roberts, majority opinion to *Parents Involved in Community Schools v. Seattle School District No. 1* (2007).

13. Anderson, *Imperative of Integration*, 172.

14. Ibid., 113.

15. Ibid., 172–175.

16. Bonilla-Silva, *Racism without Racists*.

17. Ibid., 28.

18. Ibid., 30.

19. Ibid., ch. 3; quotations are from p. 53.

20. Appiah and Gutmann, *Color Conscious*, 109.

21. Jeffrey C. Alexander, *The Civil Sphere* (Oxford: Oxford University Press, 2006).

22. J. Hector St. John de Crevecoeur, *Letters from an American Farmer* (New York: Penguin, 1981 [1782]), 66.

23. Israel Zangwill, *The Melting Pot* (New York: Arno Press, 1932 [1909]).

24. Alexander, *Civil Sphere*, 8.

25. Horace Kallen, "Democracy versus the Melting Pot: A Study of American Nationality," *The Nation*, February 18, 1915, 192.

26. Robert Ezra Park, "Our Racial Frontier on the Pacific," in *Race and Culture* (New York: Free Press, 1950 [1926]), 150.

27. Robert Ezra Park, "Human Migration and the Marginal Man," in *Race and Culture* (New York: Free Press, 1950 [1926]), 346.

28. Alexander, *Civil Sphere*, 431–435, 450.

29. Horace Kallen, "Democracy versus the Melting Pot: A Study of American Nationality," *The Nation*, February 25, 1915, 220.

30. Alexander, *Civil Sphere*, 450.

31. Ibid.

32. Jeffrey C. Alexander, *The Civil Sphere* (New York: Oxford University Press, 2006), 451.

33. Will Kymlicka, *Multicultural Citizenship: A Liberal Theory of Minority Rights* (New York: Oxford University Press, 1995).

34. Appiah, *Cosmopolitanism*, xv.

35. Elijah Anderson, *The Cosmopolitan Canopy: Race and Civility in Everyday Life* (New York: Norton, 2011), 280–281.

36. Ibid., 271.

37. Ibid., xiv–xv, xvii.

38. Ibid., 3, 38.

39. Ibid., 277.

40. Ibid., 276.

41. Ibid., 177.

42. Ibid. 263, 264, 168.

43. Ibid., ch. 8.

44. Deral Win Sue et al., "Racial Microaggressions in Everyday Life: Implications for Clinical Practice," *American Psychologist* 62 (2007): 271–286.

45. Anderson, *Cosmopolitan Canopy*, 273.

46. Du Bois, *Souls of Black Folk*, 162–163.

47. Nancy Fraser, "Rethinking Recognition," *New Left Review* 3 (May–June 2000), 112; italics in original.

48. Shannon Sullivan, *Revealing Whiteness: The Unconscious Habits of Racial Privilege* (Bloomington, IN: Indiana University Press, 2006), 193.

49. Elizabeth Blackmar, *Manhattan for Rent, 1785–1850* (Ithaca, NY: Cornell University Press, 1989).

50. Lewis Mumford, *The City in History: Its Origins, Its Transformations, and Its Prospects* (New York: MJF Books, 1961), 418.

51. Sugrue, *Origins of the Urban Crisis*, 54.

52. Gary Rivlin, *Broke, USA: How the Working Poor Became Big Business* (New York: Harper, 2010).

53. John Rawls, *A Theory of Justice* (Cambridge, MA: Harvard University Press, 1971), 115.

54. Ibid. We owe this point regarding natural duties, including that of mutual respect, to Tommie Shelby; see his essay "Justice, Deviance, and the Dark Ghetto," *Philosophy and Public Affairs* 35 (2007), 151ff.

55. John Stuart Mill, *On Liberty* (New York: Norton, 1975 [1859]), 54.

56. Herman Melville, *Moby-Dick, or The Whale* (New York: Penguin, 1992 [1851]), 16, 24, 30. We set aside here alternative interpretations of the Ishmael-Queequeg relationship that emphasize not its racial aspects, but its sexual, homoerotic overtones.

57. Ibid., 55.

58. Ibid., 57.

59. Ibid., 57, 58.

60. Ibid., 64.

61. John Dewey, *Creative Democracy: The Task Before Us* (New York: GP Putnam's Sons, 1940), 227.

62. Ibid., 228.

63. Dewey, *Ethics* (rev. ed.), 307.

64. John Dewey, The Quest for Certainty, 1929, vol. 4 of The Later Works, 1925–1953 (Carbondale: Southern Illinois University Press, 1988), 169–70.

65. Charles Horton Cooley, Social Process (Carbondale: Southern Illinois University Press, 1966 [1918]), 351.

66. Jason D. Hill, *Becoming a Cosmopolitan: What It Means to Be a Human Being in the New Millennium* (Lanham, MD: Rowman and Littlefield, 2000), 14. Quoted in Sullivan, *Revealing Whiteness*, 30.

67. Tocqueville, *Democracy in America*.

68. Jeff Weintraub, "Virtue, Community, and the Sociology of Liberty" (PhD diss., University of California at Berkeley, 1979).

69. Dewey, *Human Nature and Conduct*, ch. 2.

70. Bourdieu, *Pascalian Meditations*, 162.

71. George Herbert Mead, *Mind, Self, and Society: From the Standpoint of a Social Behaviorist* (Chicago: University of Chicago Press, 1934).

72. Ban Ki-moon, "The Right War," *Time*, April 28, 2008.

73. Piven, "Can Power from Below Change the World?," 8.

74. Bourdieu, *Firing Back*, 65.

75. Paul Butler, "Racially Based Jury Nullification: Black Power in the Criminal Justice System," in *Critical Race Theory: The Cutting Edge*, 2nd ed., ed. Richard Delgato and Jean Stefancic (Philadelphia: Temple University Press, 2000), 194–203.

76. Todd Gitlin, *Letters to a Young Activist* (New York: Basic Books, 2003), 49–50.

77. Frances Fox Piven, "Can Power from Below Change the World?," *American Sociological Review* 73 (2008): 1–14.

78. Morris, *Origins of the Civil Rights Movement*.

79. Rodney Hero and Robert Preuhs, "Multiculturalism and Welfare Politics in the USA: A State-Level Comparative Analysis," in *Multiculturalism and the Welfare State: Recognition and Redistribution in Contemporary Democracies*, ed. Keith Banting and Will Kymlicka (New York: Oxford University Press, 2006), 121–151; Howard Winant, *New Politics of Race: Globalism, Difference, Justive* (Minneapolis, MN: University of Minnesota, 2004), 57–62.

80. Gitlin, *Letters to a Young Activist*, 143.

81. Shelby, "Justice, Deviance, and the Dark Ghetto," 154.

82. Walter Benn Michaels, *The Trouble with Diversity: How We Learned to Love Identity and Ignore Inequality* (New York: Holt, 2006); Wuthnow, "Democratic Liberalism and the Challenge of Diversity," 33.

83. See Noel Ignatiev and John Garvey, eds., *Race Traitor* (New York: Routledge, 1996).

84. Frances Fox Piven and Richard Cloward, *Poor People's Movements: Why They Succeed, How They Fail* (New York: Pantheon Books, 1977), ###.

85. Derrick Bell, *And We Are Not Saved: The Elusive Quest for Racial Justice* (New York: Basic Books, 1987), 228–229.

86. Sullivan, *Revealing Whiteness*, 165.

87. Erin Kelly and Frank Dobbin, "How Affirmative Action Became Diversity Management: Employer Response to Antidiscrimination Law, 1961 to 1996," *American Behavioral Scientist* 41 (1988): 960–984.

88. Elizabeth Lasch-Quinn, *Race Experts: How Racial Etiquette, Sensitivity Training, and New Age Therapy Hijacked the Civil Rights Revolution* (New York: Norton, 2001).

89. Alexandra Kalev, Frank Dobbin, and Erin Kelly, "Best Practices or Best Guesses? Assessing the Efficacy of Corporate Affirmative Action and Diversity Policies," *American Sociological Review* 71 (2006): 589–617.

90. Stella M. Nkomo, "Much To Do about Diversity: The Muting of Race, Gender, and Class in Managing Diversity Practice" (conference paper, *International Cross-Cultural Perspectives on Workforce Diversity: The Inclusive Workplace*, Bellagio, Italy, July 2001, 9). Cited in John Wrench, "Diversity Management Can Be Bad for You," *Race and Class* 46 (2003): 80.

91. M. Bendick, Jr., M. L. Egan, and S. Lofhjelm, *The Documentation and Evaluation of Anti-Discrimination Training in the United States* (Geneva: International Labour Office, 1998). Cited in Wrench, "Diversity Management Can Be Bad for You," 77.

92. Lisa Takeuchi Cullen, "Employee Diversity Training Doesn't Work," *Time*, April 26, 2007; Jacqueline Hood, Helen Muller, and Patricia Seitz, "Attitudes of Hispanics and Anglos Surrounding a Workforce Diversity Intervention," *Hispanic Journal of Behavioral Sciences* 23 (2001): 444–458.

93. See Joyce Bell and Douglass Hartmann, "Diversity in Everyday Discourse: The Cultural Ambiguities and Consequences of 'Happy Talk,'" *American Sociological Review* 72 (2007): 895–914. For an ethnographic account, see Andrea M. Voyer, *Strangers and Neighbors: Multiculturalism, Conflict, and Community in America* (New York: Cambridge University Press, 2013), ch. 4.

94. U.S. Department of Justice, *Fair Housing Testing Program* (Washington, DC: U.S. Department of Justice, Civil Rights Division, 2013).

95. John Yinger, "Sustaining the Fair Housing Act," *Cityscape* 4 (1999): 93–106.

96. National Fair Housing Alliance, *Dr. King's Dream Denied: Forty Years of Failed Federal Enforcement* (Washington, DC: NFHA, 2008).

97. Anderson, *Imperative of Integration*, 154.

98. Ibid., 150.

99. Ibid., 151.

100. Ibid., 151.

101. Wilson, *Truly Disadvantaged*, 147.

102. Ibid., 155.

103. César Chávez, "Address to the Commonwealth Club of California, 1984," in *Freedom in America*, ed. Kenneth Bridges (Upper Saddle River, NJ: Pearson, Prentice Hall, 2008 [1979]), 426.

104. Shelby, "Justice, Deviance, and the Dark Ghetto," 156.

105. Classics of the genre include Charles S. Johnson, *The Negro in Chicago: A Study of Race Relations and a Race Riot* (Chicago: University of Chicago Press, 1922); E. Franklin Frazier, *The Negro in Harlem: A Report on Social and Economic Conditions Responsible for the Outbreak of March 19, 1935* (New York: Arno Press, 1968); and *The Kerner Report: Report of the National Advisory Commission on Civil Disorders* (New York: Bantam, 1968). See also Anthony Platt, ed., *The Politics of Riot Commissions, 1917–1970* (New York: Macmillan, 1971).

106. Tommie Shelby, *We Who Are Dark: The Philosophical Foundations of Black Solidarity* (Cambridge, MA: Harvard University Press, 2007), 244.

107. Ibid., 248.

108. Ibid., 249.

109. John Brueggemann and Terry Boswell, "Realizing Solidarity: Sources of Interracial Unionism During the Great Depression," *Work and Occupations* 25 (1998): 436–482; Rich Halpern and Roger Horowitz, *Meatpackers: An Oral History of Black Packinghouse Workers and Their Struggle for Racial and Economic Equality* (New York: Twayne, 1996); James Barrett, *Work and Community in the Jungle: Chicago's Packinghouse Workers, 1894–1922* (Bloomington: University of Illinois Press, 1987); Moon-Kie Jung, "Interracialism: The Ideological Transformation of Hawaii's Working Class," *American Sociological Review* 68 (2003): 373–400.

110. Piven, "Can Power from Below Change the World?," 11.

111. Morris, *Origins of the Civil Rights Movement*.

112. Rodney Hero and Robert Preuhs, "Multiculturalism and Welfare Politics in the USA: A State-Level Comparative Analysis," in Keith Banting and Will Kymlicka, eds., *Multiculturalism and the Welfare State: Recognition and Redistribution in Contemporary Democracies*, ed. Keith Banting and Will Kymlicka (New York: Oxford University Press, 2006), 121–151; Winant, *New Politics of Race*, 57–62.

113. Wu, *Yellow*, 325.

114. Brown et al., *White-Washing Race*, 244.

115. Gitlin, *Twilight of Common Dreams*.

116. Brown et al., *White-Washing Race*, 230.

Credits

Photos

Chapter 1: **2** © Justin Nether **4** Bill Pugliano/Getty Images **8** Comedy Central/ Courtesy Everett Collection **11** Courtesy of Jeff Wall **13** Courtesy of Stephen Wilson **14** THE BOONDOCKS © 2000 Aaron McGruder. Dist. By UNIVERSAL UCLICK. Reprinted with permission. All rights reserved **15** The Granger Collection, NY **16** Everett Collection Inc / Alamy **20** Courtesy of Sikkema Jenkins & Co., New York **22** Laemmle/Zeller Films/ Courtesy Everett Collection **27** William O'Brian The New Yorker Collection/ The Cartoon Bank **29** © Off the Wahl Productions, 2015 **32** The Baltimore Sun **39** The Granger Collection, NY

Chapter 2: **46** SSPL/Getty Images **50** Bibliotheque Nationale, Paris, France / Bridgeman Images **51** The Granger Collection, NYC **52** © 2015 Banco de México Diego Rivera Frida Kahlo Museums Trust, Mexico, D.F./Artists Rights Society (ARS) New York. Photo: De Gostini Picture Library / M. Seemuller / Bridgeman Images. **56** Private Collection/Bridgeman Images **60** The Granger Collection, NYC **61** Bettmann/CORBIS **63** Bettmann/ CORBIS **64** Fox Searchlight/Courtesy Everett Collection **68** Photo12/UIG/ Getty Images **70** Fotosearch/Getty Images **76** University of Washington Libraries, Special Collections, #1678 **77** Michael Ochs Archives/Paramount/Getty Images **79** Klau Library, Cincinnati, Hebrew Union College-Jewish Institute of Religion **81** © Carrie Mae Weems. Courtesy of the artist and Jack Shainman Gallery, New York. **84** BORS © 2012 Matt Bors. Dist. By UNIVERSAL UCLICK. Reprinted with permission. All rights reserved.

Chapter 3: **88** © 2015 The Andy Warhol Foundation for the Visual Arts, Inc./Artists Rights Society (ARS), New York **89** AP Photo **92** Courtesy of the Chicago Defender **94** AP Photo/Gene Herrick **96** Reprinted with permission of the DC Public Library, Star Collection, © Washington Post **97** Bettmann/CORBIS **98** Charles Moore/Black Star **99** Robert W. Kelley/The LIFE Picture Collection/ Getty Images **100** AP Photo **102** VINCE MAGGIORA/San Francisco Chronicle/ Corbis **103** Rick Tejada-Flores **106** AP Photo **118** Chrystal Redekopp, Laboratory for Social Research, Stanford University

Chapter 4: **128** Jim West / The Image Works **130** Bettmann/CORBIS **132** National Archives and Records Administration, NWDNS-44-PA-2260 **134** © Mark Heayn **136** Bob Adelman/Corbis **139** AP Photo/Eric Gay **141** © Wasserman, 1995 Boston Globe **146** The LIFE Images Collection/Getty **149** Gregory Wrona / Alamy **151** Andrew Lichtenstein/Corbis **152** David Butow/ Redux **154** AP Photo/Morry Gash **156** Barry Deutsch, patreon.com/barry

Chapter 5: **168** REUTERS/Larry Downing/ Newscom **171** AP Photo **172** The Phillips Collection, Washington, D.C., USA / Acquired 1942 / Bridgeman Images **173** Courtesy of the Tubman Museum of African American Art, History and Culture, Macon, Georgia **174** Seattle Civil Rights & Labor History Project, University of Washington **175** The Granger Collection, NY **177** Library of Congress **179** Bettmann/CORBIS **189** John Moore/Getty Images **190** David Grossman / Alamy **191** AP Photo/David Longstreath **192** Rich Legg/Getty Images **195** Peter Turnley/Corbis **196** © Robert Durell **198** Mario Tama/Getty Images

Chicago Press. Image by David Sacks/Getty Images.

Chapter 11: **392** Bonnie Jo Mount/ The Washington Post via Getty Images **394** Ellen B. Senisi / The Image Works **395** Robert Sciarrino/Star Ledger/ Corbis **397** Molly Riley/Reuters /Landov **398** BORS © 2013 Matt Bors. Dist. By UNIVERSAL UCLICK. Reprinted with permission. All rights reserved. **399** Library of Congress **401** Private Collection / Bridgeman Images **403** David Bacon/ The Image Works **404** © Sally Ryan **406** © Cory Weaver **417** AP Photo/ Jason Redmond **421** Anne Rand Library, International Longshore and Warehouse Union **422** Photo by Declan Haun/Chicago History Museum/Getty Images

Text

Chrystos: "Today Was a Bad Day Like TB," from *Not Vanishing*. Used by permission of the author, Chrystos, © 1993.

Langston Hughes: "Notes on Commercial Theatre" from *The Collected Poems of Langston Hughes* by Langston Hughes, edited by Arnold Rampersad with David Roessel, Associate Editor, copyright © 1994 by The Estate of Langston Hughes. Used by permission of Alfred A. Knopf, an imprint of the Knopf Doubleday Publishing Group, a division of Random House, Inc. and by permission of Harold Ober Associates Incorporated. All rights reserved. Any third party use of this material, outside of this publication, is prohibited. Interested parties must apply directly to Penguin Random House LLC for permission.

Figures

Figure 3.3: From "U.S. Whites More Solidly Republican in Recent Years," Jeffrey M. Jones, March 24, 2014. Copyright © 2014 Gallup, Inc. All rights reserved. The content is used with permission; however, Gallup retains all rights of republication.

Figure 4.2: From "The racial wealth gap was wide in 1963 and it remains large today," Caroline Ratcliffe and Signe-Mary McKernan, August 6, 2013. Reproduced with permission of Urban Institute in the format Book via Copyright Clearance Center.

Figure 5.1: From "Measures of Spatial Segregation," Sean F. Reardon and David O'Sullivan, *Sociological Methodology*, Vol. 34, No. 1, 2004. Reprinted by permission of the American Sociological Association.

Figure 10.4: From "Mate Selection in Cyberspace: The Intersection of Race, Gender, and Education," Ken-Hou Lin and Jennifer Lundquist, *American Journal of Sociology*, Vol. 119, No. 1, July 2013. © 2013 by The University of Chicago. Reprinted with permission.

Index

American Revolution, 55–56, 419
Americans, 80
American Society of Plastic Surgeons, 288
American Steel, "Loaded Gun," 180
the Americas, 48
    colonization of, 50–54
    "discovery" of, 49
Amherst, Jeffrey, 54
Amos 'n' Andy, 283–84
ancestry, 34
Anderson, Elijah, 230
    The Cosmopolitan Canopy, 401–2
Anderson, Elizabeth, 397, 417
The Andy Griffith Show, 290
Anglo-American culture, 245, 279
Anglo-Saxons, 77–78, 79
Anime, 294
Another Way Home (Hartfield), 366–67
anthropology, 256
anti-Asian sentiment, 76, 131
anti-Chinese movement, 76
antidiscrimination laws, 416–18
anti-immigrant sentiment, 218, 328, 337
    comedy and, 297
    Mexicans and, 220
Antilles, 49
anti-miscegenation laws, *361*
antimiscegenation laws, 358–59, 360–61
anti-Muslim prejudice, *4*, 344–45, *345*
antipoverty programs, 158
antiracism movements, 158
antiracist aesthetic, 286, 295–97, *297*
antiracist appropriation, 281, 312–14, 315
antiracist art, 286, 295–97
antiracist poetry, 296–97
antiracists, white, 30–32
anti-Semitism, 79, 131–32, 336–37,
    345, *345*
Anti-Terrorism and Effective Death
    Penalty Act of 1996, 218
Appiah, Kwame Anthony, 314, 401
appropriation
    antiracist, 281, 312–14, 315
    in art, 301
    cultural, 281, 308–14, *311*, 315
    racist, 281, 310–12, 315
    white aesthetic and, 302–3
Aptheker, Herbert, 65

Arab Americans, 104
    as actors, 294
    Christian, 347
    comedy and, 297
    crimes against, 221
    discrimination against, 345
    fear of terrorism and, 220–22
    hate crimes against, 337
    law enforcement practices and, 11
    racism toward, 221–22
Arabization of terrorism, 220–23, *221*
Arabs
    caricatures of, 293, *293*
    representations of, 294
Arizona, 71, 114, 120, 145, 218
Arizona State University, 258–59
Arkansas Citizens' Council, 252
Armenians, 77
Armstrong, Louis, 285
Aronson, Joshua, 270–71
arrest rates, 210–12, 231
art, 281, 315. *See also* aesthetics; *specific*
    artists
    African American, 286, 295, 296, 303,
      308, 309
    Africanism in, 301, 302
    alternative viewpoints in, 303
    antiracist, 286, 295–96
    appropriation in, 301
    artistic divisions, 281, 315
    Asian American, 286, 295–96
    colonialism and, 314
    Eurocentrism in, 301
    highbrow vs. lowbrow, 305–8
    Japanese American, 295
    Korean American, 296
    modern, 307
    Native American, 296, 308, 309
    nineteenth-century, 282
    Orientalism in, 302
    racial domination and, 281,
      300–301, 315
    racialization of art worlds, 300–307
    racial justice and, 281, 315
    racial nostalgia in, 290, *290*
    racial representation in, 281, 286, 315
    racial structures of the aesthetic
      sphere, 303–5

Bachelard, Gaston, 241
"Back Home" (Blue Scholars), 299
Bacon's Rebellion, 55
the Bahamas, 49
Baker, Craig, 344–45
Baker, Ella, 95, 97–98
Baldwin, James, 14, 32, 37, 187, 284, 359,
    382, 389
banks, housing discrimination and, 185–86
Banton, Michael, 20
barber shops, 334
Bar Mitzvahs, 329
Barnes, Cliff, 122
Barnett, Ross, 31–32
Basie, Count, 310
basketball, 21–22. *See also* National
    Basketball Association
Beals, Melba Patillo, *Warriors Don't
    Cry*, 253
Bean, Lydia, 230
Bearden, Romare, 308
Beatles, "Run for Your Life," 300
beauty, 15, 281, 287–91, *288*, 296,
    301–2, 315
beauty parlors, 334
bebop, 285
Bedford, Henry, 92
"Bed Intruder Song," 292
"Beer for my Horses" (Keith and Nelson),
    289–90
Bell, Daniel, 341
Bell, Mychal, 237
Bell, Sean, 233–34
The Bell Curve (Herrnstein and Murray),
    24–25
Beloit, Wisconsin, 154, *154*
Beloved (Morrison), 357
Bentley, "The Man," 299
Berends, Mark, 275
Berger, Martin, 287
Bernier, François, 80
Berry, Chuck, 310
Bertrand, Marianne, 153
Bhagat Singh Thind, 40
Bigelow, Kathryn, 300
bilingualism, 247
Binet, Alfred, 24
biological determinism, 24–25
biology, 3, 18

Birmingham, Alabama, 97
birth defects, 197
births, out-of-wedlock, 355, 366, 371–75,
    372, 373, 375, 391
Black, Don, 337
black affluence, 142–45
black authenticity, 384–85
Black Belt, 143
Black Bourgeoisie (Frazier), 145
black churches, 346–47, 350
"black codes," 68
Black Entertainment Television, 304
Black Eyed Peas, 301
black face, 320
blackface, 283, *283,* 292, 294
black families, under slavery, 356–58, *356*
"Black Is Beautiful" movement, 15
"black matriarch," 358
Black Metropolis (Cayton and Drake), 143
black Muslims, 324
black nationalism, 322–25, *322*
blackness, 47, 380
    authenticity and, 384–85
    criminalization of, 232
    criminal justice system and, 236–39
    definition of, 63
    fear of, 216
    invention of, 55–57, 86, 87
    literature and, 255–56
    minstrelsy and, 283–84, *283*
    performance of, 383
    racist aesthetic and, 294
    social death and, 64–65
    as totalizing racial category, 85
*Black Noise: Rap Music and Black Culture in
    Contemporary America* (Rose), 298
black-owned businesses, 144
black poverty, 142–45
black power, 323
Black Power (Carmichael and Hamilton), 13
Black Power Movement, 25, 180, 419
"black protectionism," 228
blacks. *See also* African Americans; African
    slave trade; slavery
    citizenship and, 41
    interracial conflict and, 191–92
    naturalization and, 41
    state propaganda caricaturing, 9
"black speak," 292

Cherokee Nation, 73, 103, 195, 347

Chesapeake Colony, 54

Chicago, Illinois, 188, 224
    hate crimes in, 184
    racial uprisings in, 173
    Robert Taylor Homes in, 188

Chicano movement, 89, 127, 322

Chickasaw Nation, 73, 347

children
    biracial, 366–68, 367
    of immigrants, 150–51
    of incarcerated fathers, 374
    of single mothers, 373–77

child support, 375–76

China
    incarceration in, 207
    racial categories in, 35

Chinese-American Planning Council, 327

Chinese Americans
    standardized tests and, 260
    in suburbs, 193–94

Chinese Consolidated Benevolent
    Association, 327

Chinese Exclusion Act of 1882, 77

Chinese immigrants, 75–76, 77, 151
    segregation and, 76
    in suburbs, 193–94
    violence against, 76, 76

Cho, Margaret, 297

Choctaw Nation, 73, 145, 347

Christian Coalition of America, 333

Christianity, 344, 345–46
    evangelical, 349, 352

Christians, nonwhite, 349–50

Chrystos, "Today Was a Bad Day Like TB,"
    312

churches, 328–29, 330. See also religious
    associations
    black, 346–47, 350
    ethnic, 346–47
    segregation and, 320

citizenship, 227
    blacks and, 41
    immigration and, 39–41
    loss of, 47, 87
    Mexican Americans and, 71–72
    restrictions on, 161
    Treaty of Guadalupe Hidalgo and, 71

the city, 188–92
    ethnic enclaves in, 190–91, 190
    ghettoes in, 189–90
    interracial conflict in, 191
    unaffordability of, 188–89

civic engagement
    class and, 326
    immigrants and, 327
    income and, 326
    racial discrepancies in, 317, 353
    racial variation in, 325–27
    social capital and, 331

The Civil Culture (Almond and Verba), 325

civil rights, 89, 127. See also specific
    movements

Civil Rights Act of 1964, 97, 107–8, 162,
    175, 416

Civil Rights Act of 1968, 176, 416

Civil Rights Movement, 3, 86, 89–105, 98,
    99, 123, 125–27, 143, 335, 419, 422
    backlash against, 89, 105–8, 118, 127,
        176, 213–14
    church-driven direct action,
        93–95
    color-blindness and, 395
    education and, 250
    lunch counter sit-ins, 96
    "open housing" marches, 175
    other ethnic movements, 102–5
    prison boom and, 213–14
    repressing the, 213–14
    War on Poverty and, 158
    whites and, 89, 127
    youth-driven direct action, 95–97

civil society, 325–27
    decline of, 330–32, 331
    fragmentation of, 332–34
    homophily and, 331–32
    identity politics and, 332–34

Civil War, 67
    reenactments of, 333, 333

Clapton, Eric, 310

Clark, Kenneth, 187, 374–75

Clarke, Edward, 323

class, 382, 390
    affirmative action and, 277–78
    civic engagement and, 326
    class privileges and, 148–49, 150

culture and, 305–8
education and, 262–63
intersectionality and, 17, 355, 391
social division and, 3
classical ballet, 304–5
classical music, 301, 304, 305–6
classification systems, 47, 87
classroom discussions, whiteness and,
257–58
Clayton, Horace, *Black Metropolis*, 143
Clear Channel Communications, 301
Cleaver, Eldridge, *Soul on Ice*, 382
Cleopatra, 282
Clifford, James, 385
Clinton, Bill, 158–60, 213, 376
Clinton, George, 192
Clinton, Hillary, 124
Coates, Delman, 299
Coates, Ta-Nehisi, 373
"Cocaine Blues" (Cash), 299–300
coded language, 306, 329
code switching, 268
coding, 106–7
Cohen, Richard, 368
collective action, 393, 418–21
college campuses
hate crimes on, 259
whiteness on, 257–59
Collier, John, 247
Collins, Suzanne, *The Hunger Games*, 291
colonialism, 9, 47, 50–54, 87
art and, 314
cultural authenticity and, 314
education and, 246–48
feminism and, 256
indigenous peoples and, 246–47
justice and, 204
resistance to, 74, 102, 350–51
colonias, 194–95, *195*
colonization
racist appropriation as, 311
slavery and, 69
Colorado, 111
*Color and Money: How Rich White Kids Are
Winning the War over College Affirmative
Action* (Schmidt), 277
color-blindness, 30–31, 33–34, 393,
395–98, *395*, *398*, 403, 405, 406, 423
affirmative action and, 396–97
Civil Rights Movement and, 395

"color-blind racism," 397–98
longing for color-blind politics,
125–26
the color line, 3
The Color of Welfare (Quadagno), 158
Columbus, Christopher, 49, 50
comedy, 286
antiracist aesthetic in, 297
Arab Americans and, 297
racist aesthetic in, 293, *293*
comic strips, *14*, 289
commercials, 289
Commission on Interracial Coalition, 321
Committees for Wallace, 123
communities, segregated, 319–20
community activities, participation in,
317, 353
community associations, 422
compassion, 141
the Confederacy, 67, 92
Confederate Army, 67
Confederate flags, 100
Congress of Racial Equality (CORE),
96–97
Connor, Eugene "Bull," 99
conquistadores, 50–51
Contreras, Rufino, 104
conversos, 48
convictions, unjust, 237
Cook, James, 75
cooking, 304
Cooley, Charles, 407
Cooper, David, 56
Copernicus, 49
Cornell, Stephen, 147
corridos, 297, *297*
Cortés, Hernán, 50–51
Corzo, Pedro, 337
Cosby, Bill, 8
The Cosmopolitan Canopy (Anderson),
401–2
cosmopolitanism, 393, 398–403, *399*, *401*,
406–7, 423. *See also* multiculturalism
cotton, 61, *61*
cotton gin, invention of, 61
country music, 289–90, 299–300, 303
Crash, 295
Creek Nation, 73, 347
Crenshaw, Kimberlé, 17–18
Crevecoeur, J. Hector St. John de, 399

immigration laws, 39–40, 39. *See also specific laws*
  domestic violence and, 227
  punishments for violating, 218
immigration policies, 39–40, 39
immigration quotas, 39–40, 39
immigration reform, 111
impersonal market forces, 152, 153
Impossible Subjects: Illegal Aliens and the Making of Modern America (Ngai), 40
Imus, Don, 293
"In America" (Hammad), 296–97
incarceration, 4–5, 122, 203, 209–10, 209, 243
  African Americans and, 213
  costs of, 237–39
  as deterrent, 240–41
  disproportionate incarceration of black men, 237
  education and, 209–10
  families and, 239
  gender and, 209
  lifetime likelihood of, 209
  marriage and, 370–71
  of nonviolent offenders, 210–12
  out-of-wedlock births and, 374
  poverty and, 210
  public safety and, 239–40
  racial disparities in, 203, 243
  rates of, 207–8, 208–9
  recidivism and, 240
  rehabilitation and, 240
Incidents in the Life of a Slave Girl (Jacobs), 64
inclusion, 306
income
  Asian Americans and, 272
  civic participation and, 326
  education and, 272
  flat incomes, 169, 201
  immigration and, 135–36
  income inequality, 134–36, 169, 201
  median household by race, 135
inconvenient facts, value of, 166
indentured servitude, 55–57, 75
Independent Order of Odd Fellows, 319, 319
India, caste system in, 20
Indian Allotment Act, 73–74
Indian Americans, 40
  poverty and, 140
  standardized tests and, 260

Indian Intercourse Act of 1834, 73
"The Indian Problem," 72–73
Indian Removal Act of 1830, 73, 74
"Indian Termination" policies, 102
Indian Territory, 73
Indian Wars, 54–55, 74
indigenous peoples, 50–55. *See also* Native Americans
  Anglicization of, 246, 246
  colonialism and, 246–47
  colonialization and, 222–23
  diseases and, 53–54, 54
  eradication of, 53–55, 54
  oppression of, 51–52
  violence against, 54
  whiteness and, 246
indigenous spirituality, 74
individualism, 118
individualistic fallacy, 3, 7, 253
individual transformation, goals of, 405–7
industrialization, end of, 133–34 (*see also* deindustrialization)
inequality, 3, 6, 118, 393, 423. *See also* discrimination; racism
  in education, 259–78, 260
  responses to, 393, 423 (*see also* racial justice)
informal associations, 328–29
institutional racism, 3, 10–12, 13, 129, 404
  criminal justice system and, 231–32, 237
  death penalty and, 237
  hiring and, 152–54
  interpersonal racism and, 155
  sentencing practices and, 237
  wealth disparities and, 137–38
integration, 178, 183–84, 200, 251–53, 318, 405
  associations and, 321
  backlash against, 178
  ethnic nationalist groups and, 322–33
  fear of, 176–77, 192
  housing discrimination and, 185–86
  social clubs and, 321–22
  unions and, 320, 321
intellectual ability, 21, 23–25
interaction troubles, 377–79
interest rates, 186. *See also* loans; mortgages
"internalized oppression," 14–16
"internalized racism," 14–16

political representation of, 112–13

promotions and, 156

racial identity development and, 411–12

stereotypes of deviant drug use and, 213

in suburbs, 192–93

in supervisory roles, 156

underrepresentation in entertainment industry, 300–301

in the workplace, 130, 156–57

North America

Eurocentric view of, 72

Native American view of, 72

North Carolina, 135–36

gerrymandering and, 115

Voting Rights Act of 1965 and, 120

North Carolina Agricultural and Technical College, 95–96

Northern States, 61–62. *See also* Great Migration

Nuclear Regulatory Commission, 197

Obama, Barack, *4, 8,* 117–18, 124, 125, 218

as biracial, 85

at Democratic National Convention, 396

election of, 109–11, 112, 113

photographic representation of, *118*

O'Connor, Sandra Day, 115

Odd Fellows Lodges. *See* Independent Order of Odd Fellows

Office for Federal Contract Compliance Programs (OFCCP), 162

Office of Federal Acknowledgement, 385–86

Off the Books (Venkatesh), 224

Ogbu, John, 268

Oklahoma City, Oklahoma, 221

"one-drop rule," 63

101st Airborne, 252

online dating. *See* dating

online videos, 292, 341–44. *See also* YouTube

On Loan from the Museum of the American Indian (Durham), 296

open housing laws, 175–76

"open housing" marches, 175

opera, 305, 306

opinions, 355, 391

opium dens, 213

oppression, intersectionality and, 17–18

Orange County Republican party, 119

Orange Is the New Black, 297

O'Reilly, Bill, 192

The O'Reilly Factor, 371–72

organic food movement, 304, 306–7

organizational rules, 157

organizations. *See also specific organizations*

on college campuses, 333

identity politics and, 332–33

multiculturalism and, 333

Orientalism, 302

Orren, Karen, 185–86

Oscar winners, by race, 300, *300*

Oshinsky, David, 206

Otherness, 311, 379

out-of-wedlock births, 355, 366, 371–75, *373, 375,* 391

consequences of, 375–76

incarceration and, 374

poverty and, 374, 376–77, *376*

welfare system and, 376–77

outsider art, 302

outsourcing, 141

Ovechkin, Alexander, 23

overachievement, 267

Ozawa, Seiji, 286

Pacific Islanders, standardized tests and, 260

Page Law, 76–77

Pager, Devah, *144,* 153, 215

painting

abstract, 305

Asian American, 286

Paiute, 74

Palestinian nationalism, *311*

Parchman Prison Farm, 206

Parents Involved in Community Schools v. Seattle School District No. 1, 396, 397

Parent-Teacher Association (PTA), 321

Park, Robert, 399–400

Parker, Charlie, 285

Parks, Rosa, 94

parole, limiting of, 212

partisanship, 123. *See also* politics; *specific parties*

democratic advantage in party affiliation, white vs. nonwhite, *109*

electoral shifts in 2011, *110*

gerrymandering, 113–14, *114*

political representation, 112—13
  racial polarization and, 108—12
  representation and, 108—16
party affiliation, 108—10, *109. See also specific parties*
patriarchy, 358, 359, 362
PATRIOT Act of 2001, 218
patriotism, 25
Patterson, Orlando, 231, 374[HLD1]
Pattillo-McCoy, Mary, 144
Paulle, Bowen, 273
pay disparities, 156
Payne, Charles, 98, 99
Pearl Harbor, 130, 206—7
Penner, Andrew, 36—37
Pentecostal Revival Church, 346
people of color. *See* nonwhites; *specific groups*
performance, 377—78
  of blackness, 383
  of ethnicity, 39, 383—84
  of race, 268—69, 377—78, 383—84, 387—89
  of whiteness, 383
performing arts, 305—6
Personal Responsibility and Work Opportunity Reconciliation Act, 158, 160
Peterson, William, 266
phenotype, 34
Philadelphia, Mississippi, 98, 107
Philadelphia, Pennsylvania, 119
Phillips, Kevin, *The Emerging Republican Majority,* 107
philosophers, 47
Phipps, Susie Guillory, 34
physical differences, 19—21
Picasso, Pablo, 301
Pine Ridge Indian Reservation, 145
Pippin, Horace, 303
Pittsburgh Courier, 94
plantations, 55, 56, 62, 91
plastic surgery, 288, *288*
Playing in the Dark: Whiteness and the Literary Imagination (Morrison), 255—56
playwrights, African American, 286
Plessy, Homer, 63
Plessy v. Ferguson, 63, 69, 396
poetry
  antiracist, 296—97
  racial divisions in, 304

Pokémon, 294
polarization, 53
Poles, 77
policing techniques, 11, 203, *216,* 231—35, *232,* 237, 243
political campaigns, shift from class-based to race-based appeals, 89, 127
political contention, multiracial, 420
"political correctness," 334—35, *335*
political power, 10
political representation, 108—16
  gerrymandering and, 113—15
  substantial, 113
  superficial, 113
political societies, 321
politicians, "law and order," 212—13
politics, 88—127
  color-blind, 125—26
  electoral shifts in 2011, *110*
  implicit racial appeals and, 122—24
  racial polarization of, 89, 127
  racism and, 106—7
polka, 303
pollution, 196
popular culture, 305—8
Portes, Alejandro, 148, 264
Portugal, slave trade and, 57
Portuguese explorers, 49
"postracial," 3—5, 109
Potok, Mark, 339
pottery, Native American, 302
poverty, 4, 47, 87, 129, 139, *141,* 169, 201, 390
  on American Indian reservations, 145—47, *146*
  black, 142—45
  capitalism and, 141
  causes of, 140—42
  deindustrialization and, 142
  domestic violence and, 226
  education and, 261
  families in, *376*
  feminization of, 376, *376*
  homicide and, 230
  incarceration and, 210
  inner-city, 142—43
  marriage and, 370—71
  out-of-wedlock births and, 374, 376, *376*
  poverty rate by race/ethnicity, *140*

racial taxonomies. *See* racial classification

racial terminology, 42–43. *See also* racial categories; *specific terminology*

racial typologies, 80–81

racial uprisings, 173, 176, 178–80, *179*, 214, 232, 419

racism, 3, 5–6

    American, 6

    among nonwhites, 11–13, 14–16

    as a cancer, 3–6

    color-blind, 397–98, *398*

    environmental, 196–98, *196*

    institutional, 3, 10–12, 13, 129, 137–38, 152–55, 231–32, 237, 404

    internalized, 14–16

    on the Internet, 317, 353

    interpersonal, 3, 11–13, 155, 295

    justified in racial discourses of modernity, 80

    organized, 336–37

    other forms of social division and, 3

    politics and, 106–7

    psychological strain of, 371

    refusal to confront head on, 107

    rural white America and, 198

    social psychology of, 13

    southern vs. northern, 172–73

    virtual, 317, 341–43, 353

racist aesthetic

    blackness and, 294

    in comedy, 293, *293*

    in fashion, 291–92, *292*

    in film, 293–95

    people of color and, 293–94

    racial domination and, 294–95

    racist aesthetic and, 293–94

    in radio, 293

    in television, 293–94

racist appropriation, 281, 310–12, 315

    African American culture and, 311

    as colonization, 311

    exoticization and, 311

    minstrelsy and, 311

    music and, 310

    Otherness and, 311

racist propaganda, 9

radio

    corporate domination of, 301

    racist aesthetic in, 293

Spanish-language, 285–86

    talk radio, 293

Rainey, Joseph, 8

Ramsey, Charles, 292

rape, 204, 205, 226, 227

rap music, 299, 302, 307

"Rapper's Delight" (Sugarhill Gang), 298

Ravel, Maurice, 301

Rawls, Anne, 379

Rawls, John, 406, 419

Reagan, Ronald, 107, 122, 123, 133, 160, 415

Reaganomics, 133–34

recidivism, 240

Reconstruction, 68, 69, 93, 248

Redding, Otis, 285

redlining, 174, 185–86

"rednecks," 198, *198*

Red Summer, 173

Refugee Act of 1980, 147

refugees, 147

reggae, 307, 308

reggaetón, 303, 308

rehabilitation, 240

religion, 355, 391. *See also* religious life; religious sphere; *specific religions and groups*

    ethnicity and, 350–52, *351*

    intersectionality and, 355, 391

    racial identity and, 350–51

    racialization of, 317, 345–49, 353

    racialization of the religious sphere, 345–46

    religious illiteracy, 344–45

    religious intolerance, 344–45

    segregation and, 345–46

    social division and, 3

religious associations, 317, 344, 353

    immigrant rights and, 351

    multiracial, 351–52

    social change and, 350–51

religious life

    homophily in, 349–50

    minority communities and, 350

representation. *See also specific groups*

    political (*see* political representation)

    substantial, 113

    superficial, 113

    whiteness and, 287–89, *287*

repression, 48–49

Republican National Committee, 111, 124

segregation, 8–9, 89, 95–96, 96, 127,
169, 172–73, 175, 178, 201. *See also*
desegregation; Jim Crow segregation
associations and, 317, 319–21, 330, 353
backlash against desegregation,
105–6, *106*
in California, 251
Chinese immigrants and, 76
churches and, 320
consequences of, 186–87, *186*
decline of, 181
Detroit, Michigan, housing study
and, *184*
dimensions of, *181*
dismantling of, 176
economic consequences of, 186
economic factors and, 183
education and, 8, 187, 245, *252*, 279
emotional costs of, 187
end of legally enforced, 3
in housing, 181–87
housing discrimination and, 185–86
levels of, 182–83, *182*
living conditions and, 186
material consequences of, 186–87
Mexican Americans and, 251
as organizing principle, 318
persistence of, 181–82, 253–54
personal choice and, 183–84
political consequences of, 186
religion and, 345–46
reproduction of poverty and, 186
resegregation, 272–73
residential, 143
role of personal choice in, 183–84
"separate but equal," 69
symbolic consequences of, 187
Seinfeld, 289
Selective Service Readjustment Act, 132
self, 377–89
self-determination, 322
self-questioning, 409–10
Selma, Alabama, 99–100, *100*
Selma-to-Montgomery March, 99–102,
100
Seminole Nation, 73, 347
sentencing practices, 210–12, 236
institutional racism and, 237
severe, 203, 210–12, 243
unjust, 235–37

"separate but equal" doctrine, 251–52
separatism, 322
September 11, 2001, terrorist attacks of,
221, 222, 344
service economy, 133
Seung-Hui Cho, 217
sexism, 16–17, 382
sexual division of labor, 362
sexuality, 381–82
intersectionality and, 17, 355, 391
social division and, 3
Shakur, Tupac, 299
sharecropping, 91
Shaw v. Reno, 114–15
Shelby, Tommie, 413, 419–20
Sherman, William, 67–68
Shklar, Judith, 317–18
"shock jocks," 293
Shoshone Bannock Pow Wow, *385*
Shuttlesworth, Fred, 93, 94
Silko, Leslie Marmon, *Ceremony*, 313
Silnov, Andrew, 23
Simmel, Georg, 305
Simone, Nina, "Mississippi
Goddamn," 284
Singapore, incarceration in, 207
single motherhood, *366*, 371–75, *373*, *375*.
See also teenage mothers
consequences of, 375–77, *376*
welfare system and, 158, 159
sitcoms, 286
sit-ins, 95–96, *96*
Six-Day War of 1967, 104
Sixteenth Street Baptist Church, 99
skinheads, 336, 337
skin tone, 19
Skocpol, Theda, 321
What a Mighty Power Can Be, 320
Skull Valley Band of Goshutes, 196
slave codes, 62–63, 64
slavery, 9, 55
of Africans, 52, 55–57
capitalism and, 69
children born into, 63
colonization and, 69
Congressional representation and,
61–62
emancipation from, 67–68
families and, 356–58, *356*
flight from, 65